T0205767

Lecture Notes in Artificial Intelligence   13190

Subseries of Lecture Notes in Computer Science

More information about this subseries at https://link.springer.com/bookseries/1244

Natasha Alechina · Matteo Baldoni ·
Brian Logan (Eds.)

Engineering Multi-Agent Systems

9th International Workshop, EMAS 2021
Virtual Event, May 3–4, 2021
Revised Selected Papers

 Springer

Editors
Natasha Alechina (iD)
Utrecht University
Utrecht, The Netherlands

Matteo Baldoni (iD)
University of Turin
Turin, Italy

Brian Logan (iD)
Utrecht University
Utrecht, The Netherlands

ISSN 0302-9743   ISSN 1611-3349 (electronic)
Lecture Notes in Artificial Intelligence
ISBN 978-3-030-97456-5   ISBN 978-3-030-97457-2 (eBook)
https://doi.org/10.1007/978-3-030-97457-2

LNCS Sublibrary: SL7 – Artificial Intelligence

This Springer imprint is published by the registered company Springer Nature Switzerland AG
The registered company address is: Gewerbestrasse 11, 6330 Cham, Switzerland

Preface

The International Workshop on Engineering Multi-Agent Systems (EMAS) was formed in 2013 as a merger of three long-running workshops: Agent-Oriented Software Engineering (AOSE), Programming Multi-Agent Systems (ProMAS), and Declarative Agent Languages and Technologies (DALT). This merger established EMAS as a reference venue for work concerned broadly with the engineering of agents and multi-agent systems.

The three parent events have a long history of association with the International Conference on Autonomous Agents and Multi-Agent Systems (AAMAS), and since its inception EMAS has been co-located at AAMAS: EMAS 2013 in St. Paul (with post-proceedings published as Springer LNCS/LNAI volume 8245), EMAS 2014 in Paris (LNCS/LNAI 8758, and a special issue in the International Journal of Agent-Oriented Software Engineering, IJAOSE Vol. 5 No. 2/3, 2016), EMAS 2015 in Istanbul (LNCS/LNAI 9318, and a special issue in IJAOSE Vol. 6 No. 2, 2018), EMAS 2016 in Singapore (LNCS/LNAI 10093, and a special issue in the IJAOSE Vol. 6 No. 3/4, 2018), EMAS 2017 in São Paulo (LNCS/LNAI 10738), EMAS 2018 in Stockholm (LNAI 11375, and a report in Software Engineering Notes), EMAS 2019 in Montreal (LNAI 12058), and EMAS 2020 in Auckland (LNAI 12589).

EMAS 2021 aimed to build on this history by gathering researchers and practitioners in the domains of agent-oriented software engineering, programming multi-agent systems, declarative agent languages and technologies, artificial intelligence, and machine learning to present and discuss their research and emerging results in MAS engineering. The overall purpose of the workshop was to facilitate the cross-fertilization of ideas and experiences in the various fields to

- enhance our knowledge of the theory and practice of engineering intelligent agents and multi-agent systems, and advance the state of the art;
- demonstrate how MAS methodologies, architectures, languages and tools can be used in the engineering of deployed large-scale and open MAS;
- define new directions for engineering MAS by drawing on results and recommendations from related research areas; and
- encourage PhD and Masters students to become involved in and contribute to the area.

As with previous editions, this edition of the EMAS workshop was intended to be co-located with AAMAS, which was planned to be held in London, UK, in May 2021. As AAMAS 2021 was a virtual event, EMAS 2021 was held as a virtual (online) event, spanning two days. EMAS 2021 received 27 submissions, each of which was reviewed (single blind) by three reviewers. In total, 25 papers were accepted (21 full papers and four doctoral and demonstration papers). In addition to these 25 papers, EMAS 2021 also had two invited talks, "Agent Programming in the Cognitive Era: A New Era for Agent Programming?" by Alessandro Ricci and "Explicitly Ethical Agent Reasoning" by Louise Dennis. The keynotes were delivered synchronously over Zoom. Talks were pre-recorded and available from the EMAS 2021 website, together with the slides and the final workshop presentation version of the papers. Each talk also had a live Q&A session on Zoom. The Q&A sessions were intended to allow interaction between authors and participants. After a second review process, 21 papers were selected for inclusion in this volume.

We would like to thank all individuals, institutions, and sponsors that supported EMAS 2021, in particular TU Clausthal for hosting the website. We thank the authors for submitting high-quality research papers. We are indebted to our Program Committee members and additional reviewers for spending their valuable time by providing careful reviews and recommendations on the submissions, the members of the EMAS Steering Committee for their valuable suggestions and support, Alessandro Ricci and Louise Dennis for their inspiring keynotes, and finally the AAMAS workshop chairs, Francesco Belardinelli and Matthijs Spaan, for all their work and support.

January 2022

Natasha Alechina
Matteo Baldoni
Brian Logan

Organization

Workshop Organizers

Natasha Alechina   Utrecht University, The Netherlands
Matteo Baldoni   Università degli Studi di Torino, Italy
Brian Logan   Utrecht University, The Netherlands

Program Committee

Luciano Baresi	Politecnico di Milano, Italy
Cristina Baroglio	Università degli Studi di Torino, Italy
Olivier Boissier	Mines Saint-Étienne, France
Rafael H. Bordini	PUCRS, Brazil
Daniela Briola	University of Insubria, Italy
Maiquel de Brito	Federal University of Santa Catarina, Brazil
Rafael C. Cardoso	University of Manchester, UK
Moharram Challenger	University of Antwerp, Belgium
Amit Chopra	Lancaster University, UK
Andrei Ciortea	University of St. Gallen, Switzerland
Rem Collier	University College Dublin, Ireland
Stefania Costantini	Università degli Studi dell'Aquila, Italia
Mehdi Dastani	Utrecht University, The Netherlands
Davide Dell'Anna	Delft University of Technology, The Netherlands
Louise Dennis	University of Manchester, UK
Juergen Dix	Clausthal University of Technology, Germany
Angelo Ferrando	Università di Genova, Italy
Lars-Ake Fredlund	Universidad Politécnica de Madrid, Spain
Stéphane Galland	UBFC - UTBM, France
James Harland	RMIT University, Australia
Vincent Hilaire	UBFC - UTBM, France
Jorge Gomez-Sanz	Universidad Complutense de Madrid, Spain
Zahia Guessoum	Universite de Paris 6 and Université de Reims Champagne Ardenne, France
Tom Holvoet	Katholieke Universiteit Leuven, Belgium
Jomi Fred Hubner	Federal University of Santa Catarina, Brazil
Nadin Kokciyan	University of Edinburgh, UK
Yves Lespérance	York University, Canada
Viviana Mascardi	Università di Genova, Italy
Philippe Mathieu	University of Lille, France
John-Jules Meyer	Utrecht University, The Netherlands
Roberto Micalizio	Università degli Studi di Torino, Italy
Fabien Michel	Université de Montpellier, France

Jörg P. Müller	TU Clausthal, Germany
Ingrid Nunes	Universidade Federal do Rio Grande do Sul, Brazil
Enrico Pontelli	New Mexico State University, USA
Alessandro Ricci	Università di Bologna, Italy
Luca Sabatucci	ICAR-CNR, Italy
Jaime Sichman	University of São Paulo, Brazil
Viviane Silva	IBM, Brazil
Tran Cao Son	New Mexico State University, USA
Jørgen Villadsen	Technical University of Denmark, Denmark
Gerhard Weiss	Maastricht University, The Netherlands
Danny Weyns	Katholieke Universiteit Leuven, Belgium
Michael Winikoff	Victoria University of Wellington, New Zealand
Neil Yorke-Smith	Delft University of Technology, The Netherlands

Steering Committee

Matteo Baldoni	Università degli Studi di Torino, Italy
Rafael Bordini	PUCRS, Brazil
Mehdi Dastani	Utrecht University, The Netherlands
Jürgen Dix	Clausthal University of Technology, Germany
Amal El Fallah Seghrouchni	Pierre and Marie Curie University, France
Brian Logan	Utrecht University, The Netherlands
Jörg P. Müller	TU Clausthal, Germany
Ingrid Nunes	Universidade Federal do Rio Grande do Sul, Brazil
Alessandro Ricci	Università di Bologna, Italy
M. Birna Van Riemsdijk	University of Twente, The Netherlands
Danny Weyns	Katholieke Universiteit Leuven, Belgium
Michael Winikoff	Victoria University of Wellington, New Zealand
Rym Zalila-Wenkstern	University of Texas at Dallas, USA

Additional Reviewers

Chaput, Rémy
Yang, Yi

Contents

PanSim + Sim-2APL: A Framework for Large-Scale Distributed Simulation with Complex Agents

Parantapa Bhattacharya[1(✉)], A. Jan de Mooij[2], Davide Dell'Anna[2],
Mehdi Dastani[2], Brian Logan[2], and Samarth Swarup[1]

[1] University of Virginia, Charlottesville, VA 22904, USA
{parantapa,swarup}@virginia.edu
[2] Universiteit Utrecht, Utrecht, The Netherlands
{A.J.deMooij,d.dellanna,M.M.Dastani,B.S.Logan}@uu.nl

Abstract. Agent-based simulation is increasingly being used to model social phenomena involving large numbers of agents. However, existing agent-based simulation platforms severely limit the kinds of the social phenomena that can modeled, as they do not support large scale simulations involving agents with complex behaviors. In this paper, we present a scalable agent-based simulation framework that supports modeling of complex social phenomena. The framework integrates a new simulation platform that exploits distributed computer architectures, with an extension of a multi-agent programming technology that allows development of complex deliberative agents. To show the scalability of our framework, we briefly describe its application to the development of a model of the spread of COVID-19 involving complex deliberative agents in the US state of Virginia.

Keywords: Distributed simulation · Agent-based simulation · Social simulation

1 Introduction

Social simulation [22] is increasingly being used to study complex social phenomena such as the evolution of economic inequality, environmental pollution, seasonal migrations, spreading of diseases, traffic, etc., and to train professionals such as police and fire brigades when confronted with incidents involving a large number of people. A key approach to studying such social phenomena is agent-based modeling and simulation. State-of-the-art agent-based simulation platforms are capable of supporting the synchronized execution of large numbers of agents by exploiting the computing power of distributed computer architectures such as computing grids. However, these platforms support only very simple agent behavior models, which severely limits the kinds of social phenomena that can be modeled [18,21,32]. On the other hand, existing multi-agent programming languages support the high-level social and cognitive concepts necessary to model the

© Springer Nature Switzerland AG 2022
N. Alechina et al. (Eds.): EMAS 2021, LNAI 13190, pp. 1–21, 2022.
https://doi.org/10.1007/978-3-030-97457-2_1

complex agent behaviors required for social simulations. However, these multi-agent programming languages and platforms are generally not designed to support the synchronized distributed execution of large numbers of agents.

In this paper, we present a novel simulation framework for the distributed simulation of large-scale multi-agent systems consisting of intelligent autonomous agents that can perform complex tasks such as sensing, reasoning, and planning. To create this framework, we have developed a new discrete time distributed agent-based simulation platform called PanSim, and Sim-2APL, an extension to the 2APL Java-based multi-agent programming library that provides support for the development of agent-based simulations.[1] Sim-2APL supports the implementation of intelligent autonomous agents and multi-agent systems in terms of high-level social and cognitive concepts. PanSim provides scalability by distributing the execution of individual Sim-2APL agent programs over multiple computing resources in a synchronized manner in order to scale the execution of large-scale agent-based simulations. We present a synchronized execution model and state some minimal constraints on the use of Sim-2APL necessary to allow integration with PanSim and ensure the repeatability of simulations.

In order to demonstrate the applicability and scalability of the PanSim + Sim-2APL simulation framework, we report on experiments involving an agent-based simulation of the spread of COVID-19 in seven counties in the US state of Virginia. The input to the simulation consists of a synthetic population with realistic demographics, weekly activity schedules, and activity locations drawn from real location data. In the chosen counties, the number of individuals ranges from 20k to 180k and the number of weekly visits to locations ranges from 680k to about 6 million. Each individual in the synthetic population is represented by a Sim-2APL agent which reasons about whether to comply with non-pharmaceutical interventions such as mask wearing and social distancing that were introduced in Virginia between March and July 2020. In the current paper, we focus on the engineering of the PanSim + Sim-2APL framework, and we refer the reader to a companion paper for details of the simulation model [17].

Organization. The rest of the paper is organized as follows: In Sect. 2 we discusses related work on large-scale simulation with complex agent models. Section 3 and Sect. 4 present the design of PanSim and Sim-2APL respectively. Section 5 describes an exemplar simulation that simulates COVID-19 epidemic evolution jointly with a 2APL behavior model that we use to study the scaling properties of PanSim + Sim-2APL. Section 6 presents the results of the scaling experiments. Finally in Sect. 7 we end with concluding remarks.

2   Related Work

A number of platforms have been developed to address the challenges of scaling simulations. Notable successes have been obtained by exploiting domain semantics [4,6], or by using simplified models of agents. In the context of epidemic

---

[1] Source code for PanSim is available at https://github.com/parantapa/pansim, and that for Sim-2APL is available at https://bitbucket.org/goldenagents/sim2apl.

simulations, for instance, agent behavior is often characterized only by a simple finite state machine which represents the progression of the disease. Bhatele et al. [5] were able to demonstrate an epidemic simulation scaling up to the size of the US population, which computed each simulated day in 57.8 ms on 655,360 cores of the Blue Waters supercomputer. The proposed simulator was heavily optimized for the particular application and architecture, and the agents did not model any complex cognitive behavior.

In [25] the authors presented an agent based model for epidemic simulation using a synthetic population of agents representing the people in the City of Chicago. Like the current work, this system created a realistic synthetic population of the city, and used the Repast ABM framework to create a distributed memory simulation to run on HPC systems. The CityCOVID simulator [14] also presented a similar system targeted to run on HPC systems. Similar to our work the authors used a realistic synthetic population and contact network, and ran a detailed SEIR like COVID-19 disease model to understand the disease's impact. However, in contrast to our study the agent behavior models in both of these systems is much simpler and doesn't capture the complexity of human decision making in presence of every varying injunctive and descriptive norms.

MATSim-Episim [29] is also a similar simulation platform, in that uses a contact network generated using a mobility model and simulates progressing of a SEIR like disease models on this network. Unlike the current system this platform doesn't support distributed memory simulations, and also uses simple non-cognitive models for agent behavior modeling.

On the other hand, simulation platforms that support more complex agent models are typically designed for ease of development, maintenance, and *post hoc* analytics. For example, Barrett et al. [3] developed a large-scale disaster simulation with a database-centric simulation architecture where different modules compute various aspects of the simulation, such as transportation, communication, health states, behavioral choices, etc. The architecture allowed these modules to be separated and developed independently by multiple developers using different programming languages, data structures, and parallelization schemes, and to be plugged in and out as needed. The database-centric interaction between modules also results in all intermediate states being stored systematically, which facilitates debugging and later analysis. While this approach allows rapid development and complex representations of agents, there is a price to be paid in terms of scalability. The simulation needed over 16 h to compute 100 time steps with ∼700,000 agents.

Other approaches to scaling include dynamically varying the resolution of the simulation [30], and developing hybrid simulations that allow a mixture of simple and more complex agent models [33].

Simulating individual agents whose behaviors depend on their observations and internal states requires a decision making component that allows them to reason, decide and plan their actions. Various theories of decision-making have been proposed, from rational decision theories and BDI theory [15] to more psychologically-based approaches such as the Theory of Planned Behavior (TPB) [23].

These theories propose various conceptualizations of decision-making behavior in terms of motivational, informational and deontic attitudes, together with a decision rule that determines which of an agent's available actions will be selected based on the agent's attitudes [10].

To facilitate the development of autonomous agents based on these behavioral theories, a number of dedicated programming languages have been proposed where the agents' decisions are directed by their beliefs, goals, plans, and actions [7,8]. For example, Bordini and Hübner [9] show how complex BDI agents programmed in Jason can be used for social simulation. In their approach, the agents' environment is implemented by extending a predefined Java class. Caballero *et al.* [11] also implement agents in Jason, but use the simulation platform Mason to simulate the environment. In both these approaches, the number of agents that can be simulated is limited by the number of threads available in the JVM.

COMOKIT [19] is a recent COVID-19 disease simulation system which similar to the current study also uses a realistic synthetic population on top of which the epidemic progresses. This system is built using the GAMA [34] simulation environment which support BDI agents. However, unlike the current study the scalability of this system is limited to a single compute node.

For a comprehensive survey of the use of BDI agents and complex reasoning in social simulations we refer the reader to the paper by Adam and Goudou [1]. Here, we note only that Adam and Gaudou identify scalability as a key issue limiting the use of BDI agents in simulations, and state that the distribution of a simulator over a network is "a very difficult problem that is far from being solved" [1, p. 228].

3   PanSim Design and Implementation

The current framework is quite broadly applicable to social contagion-like phenomena, such as the spread of behaviors, information, technologies, infectious diseases, etc. In this section, we describe how PanSim is structured to allow scalable computation of contagions through a population.

PanSim is a multi-contagion simulator, where two contagion processes progress concurrently on top of a dynamic contact network. In PanSim's design we assume that one of these contagion processes is a simple contagion, that is it can be fully described declaratively using a SIR like model [31]. PanSim provides its own configuration language to describe this simple contagion. On the other hand, very few assumptions are made about the nature of the other contagion process, which is assumed to be complex.[2] Authors of PanSim simulations are expected to provide custom code that encapsulates the progression and transmission logic for the complex contagion.

PanSim is a discrete time agent-based simulation framework. A simulation in PanSim progresses in discrete timesteps, and within a given timestep the

---

[2] Here we use the terms simple and complex contagions in their literal sense and not specifically in the sense developed and popularized in [13].

simulation progresses in multiple sequential phases. However, within any given phase computations corresponding to different agents progresses concurrently.

The dynamic contact network in PanSim is specified in terms of a temporal agent-location bipartite graph. In PanSim agents interact with each other at specific locations. The locations visited by a given agent can change from one timestep to the next. Agents that are at the same location at the same time come into contact with each other. The contact network of agents thus formed is the unipartite projection (on the agent set) of the dynamic bipartite agent-location network.

In the following, to make the presentation more concrete, we describe the implementation of a behavior-aware COVID-19 simulation as a running example. Full details of the simulation can be found in a companion paper [17]. In this scenario, a COVID-19 disease model serves as the simple contagion, while a Sim-2APL-based socio-psychological behavior model takes the role of the complex contagion. For the rest of this paper we use the terms disease model and simple contagion model interchangeably. Similarly, we also use the terms socio-psychological model and complex contagion model interchangeably.

An agent's state comprises of two parts, its disease state and its socio-psychological state. Further, behavior exhibited by the agents is categorized into two classes: a) disease modifier behaviors and b) visible attribute behaviors. *Disease modifier behaviors*—such as wearing masks, social distancing, etc.—modify disease transmission properties, while *visible attribute behaviors*—such as displaying religious or political affiliations or symptoms of the disease—are used to indicate the agent's stance and influence other agents.

In this model, during a given simulation timestep the following steps are executed. *First*, every agent in the system, based on their current socio-psychological state, 'decides' which locations to visit, as well as how to 'behave' during each of those visits. These behaviors include disease modifier behaviors, as well as visible attribute behaviors. *Second*, when visiting a location the agents come into contact with each other. During this step, disease transmission takes place from infectious to susceptible agents. Also, the agents interact with other agents and 'see' their visible attributes. *Finally*, for every individual agent their disease state progresses, and they update their socio-psychological state based on their current disease state as well as their observations of other agent's visible attributes that they came into contact with.

3.1   Structure of a PanSim Simulation

From the perspective of PanSim, the structure of a PanSim simulation consists of four major modules: the socio-psychological module, the social interaction module, the disease transmission module, and disease progression module. Figure 1 shows the overall organizations of the modules and their communication patterns.

The socio-psychological module and the social interaction module together represent the complex contagion component of a PanSim simulation, while the disease transmission and progression modules together represent the simple contagion component of the simulation. Another way of organizing the modules is

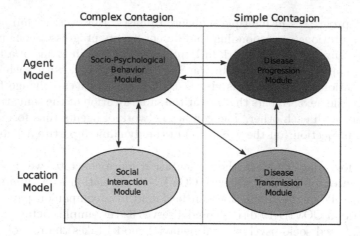

Fig. 1. Structure of a PanSim simulation

to think of them from the perspective of the dynamic agent-location bipartite graph that serves as network on which both contagions progress. In this view, the socio-psychological and disease progression models encapsulate the computation that happens on behalf of every agent/individual in the simulation, while the social interaction and disease transmission modules encapsulate the computation that happens on behalf of every location in the system.

To write a custom PanSim simulation, the simulation authors only need to provide the code for the socio-psychological behavior module. The rest of modules are provided by PanSim itself. For example, in the exemplar problem described above, the socio-psychological module is written using the Java Sim-2APL library (described in Sect. 4). PanSim provides a generic language-agnostic interface, written using Apache Arrow[3], that can be used to write the socio-psychological module in most popular programming languages, including C, C++, Java, Python, and R.

3.2   Formal Description of a PanSim Simulation

Here we formally describe the structure of a PanSim simulation. A stochastic discrete time simulation can be written as a stochastic function $F : S \rightarrow S$ that, given the state of a system at timestep t, $s^t \in S$, computes the next state of the system $s^{t+1} = F(s^t)$. The whole simulation can then be formulated as an iterated application of the simulation function F, starting from the initial state s^0.

To use distributed system hardware, it is important to split this monolithic function into parts that can be executed in parallel, with intermediate coordination. For this purpose we consider the following decomposition of the system state at timestep t, $s^t = (s_1^t, s_2^t, \ldots, s_n^t)$. Here, s_i^t is the state of the ith agent

---
[3] https://arrow.apache.org/.

at time t. As described above, PanSim implements a two contagion model, that we refer to as the socio-psychological model and the disease model. The state of the agent then is split as $s_i^t = (b_i^t, d_i^t)$ where b_i^t and d_i^t are the state of the agent corresponding to the socio-psychological and disease models. Equations Eqs. 1–5 show the functional decomposition that is used in PanSim to compute the next state of an agent given the current state.

$$(L_i^t, \tau_i^t, v_i^t, m_i^t) = \nu(b_i^t, d_i^t) \tag{1}$$

$$\Delta b_i^t = \sum_{j;j \neq i} \sum_{l \in L_i^t \cap L_j^t} \beta\left(v_i^t(l), v_j^t(l), \tau_i^t(l), \tau_j^t(l), l\right) \tag{2}$$

$$\Delta d_i^t = \sum_{j;j \neq i} \sum_{l \in L_i^t \cap L_j^t} \rho\left(d_i^t, d_j^t, \tau_i^t(l), \tau_j^t(l), m_i^t(l), m_j^t(l), l\right) \tag{3}$$

$$d_i^{t+1} = o\left(d_i^t, \Delta d_i^t\right) \tag{4}$$

$$b_i^{t+1} = \gamma(b_i^t, \Delta b_i^t, d^{t+1}) \tag{5}$$

First, as part of the socio-psychological model, the locations to be visited by the agent (L_i^t), the time duration of the visits (τ_i^t), the visual attributes displayed by the agent during the visits (v_i^t), and the disease modifier behaviors observed by the agent (m_i^t) are computed. In the formal model the socio-psychological model is represented by the function $\nu()$ (Eq. 1). Second, for each pair of agents visiting the same location, the social interaction updates, Δb_i^t, and disease transmission updates, Δd_i^t, are computed using the interaction model $\beta()$ (Eq. 2), and disease transmission model $\rho()$ (Eq. 3) respectively. Third, agent's disease state is updated to d_i^{t+1} using the disease progression model $\sigma()$, based on their current disease state d_i^t and disease transmission update Δd_i^t (Eq. 4). Finally, the agents socio-psychological state is updated to b_i^{t+1} using the socio-psychological update model γ, based on their current socio-psychological state b_i^t, their interaction updates Δb_i^t, as well as their updated disease state d_i^{t+1} (Eq. 5).

Note, we intentionally do not describe the domain of the state and update variables, b_i^t, Δb_i^t, etc. They can be modeled using a variety of structures that support the required operations. In the experiments shown below, they are implemented using real-valued vectors of appropriate lengths.

In classical multi agent AI system formulations, the agents in the system directly transform the global system state. Influence/Reaction model (IRM) [28] was proposed as a framework to address the practical issues arising from transforming of the global system state, such as: ordering of these transformations, handling conflicts in transformations, and parallelization of this global write process. This idea was further developed for simulation of multi agent systems in [26] and [27]. In the IRM framework agents do not directly transform the system. They only 'influence' the system at a micro level. The system/environment accumulates to all these micro level influences and produces a global macro level 'reaction'.

Due to the generic and very high level semantics of the IRM formulation, the formalism presented above can be seen as a special case implementation of the IRM framework. At a high level, location visits generated by agents can be thought of as influences, while the rest of the process can be seen as the system reaction. The contribution of the above formalism, beyond IRM, is in decomposing the monolithic reaction into pieces that can be used to support distributed parallelism.

3.3   Declarative Simple Contagion Model

In PanSim the simple contagion's definition is written in a TOML[4]-based domain-specific language. Table 1 shows the simple contagion model (a COVID-19 disease model) used for the scaling studies described later in this paper. At its core the model is a SEIAR model with five disease states: susceptible (succ), exposed (expo), infected symptomatic (isymp), infected asymptomatic (iasymp) and recovered (recov).

Disease transmission happens when a susceptible individual (susceptibility > 0) comes in contact with an infectious individual (infectivity > 0). The probability of transmission is defined in terms of unit interaction times, specified in the configuration in seconds. If an individual with susceptibility α comes in contact with an individual with infectivity β, for unit time, then the probability of disease transmission is given by $\alpha \times \beta$. In the given example (Table 1), if a susceptible individual is in contact with an infectious (symptomatic) individual for $300\,s$, and both have baseline behaviors, then the probability of the susceptible individual getting infected is 4.81×10^{-5}.

Table 1. Simple contagion model (Covid-19 disease model)

Category	Parameter	Value
	unit_time	300.0
	states	[succ, expo, isymp, iasymp, recov]
	behaviors	[base, mask, sdist, mask_sdist]
	exposed_state	expo
susceptibility	succ	1
infectivity	isymp	4.81e-05
	iasymp	2.40e-05
progression	expo	{isymp = 0.6, iasymp = 0.4}
	isymp	{recov = 1.0}
	iasymp	{recov = 1.0}
dwell time	expo	{isymp = dist1, iasymp = dist1}
	isymp	{recov = dist2}
	iasymp	{recov = dist2}
distribution	dist1	{dist = fixed, value = 6}
	dist2	{dist = fixed value = 14}
behavior modifier	base	{base = 1.0, mask = 0.5, sdist = 0.5, mask_sdist = 0.25}
	mask	{base = 0.5, mask = 0.25, sdist = 0.25, mask_sdist = 0.15625}
	sdist	{base = 0.5, mask = 0.25, sdist = 0.25, mask_sdist = 0.15625}
	mask_sdist	{base = 0.25, mask = 0.15625, sdist = 0.15625, mask_sdist = 3.906e-3}

---

[4] https://github.com/toml-lang/toml.

Disease transmission probability is further affected by disease modifier behaviors. For example in the configuration shown in Table 1, four disease modifier behaviors are defined: baseline (base), wearing masks (mask), social distancing (sdist) and wearing masks as well as social distancing (mask_sdist). If in the above example a susceptible individual wearing masks interacts with an infectious (symptomatic) individual wearing masks and social distancing, for 300 s, then the probability of disease transmission for this case is given by 7.51×10^{-6}.

An individual with a given disease state may move to a different disease state, based on the progression of the disease inside the individual. In the given example, three progressions are defined. An individual in the exposed state will move to one of infectious states. Further there is a time—measured in simulation timesteps, specified in days—after which the progression to a different state occurs. In the given example (Table 1), infected individuals move to recovered state after 14 simulation timesteps (or 14 days).

Some of the parameters used fix values in the model come from COVID-19-related information shared by public health agencies, such as CDC [12]. The rest of the parameters are obtained by calibration to data. The procedure for calibration and details about how the model was arrived at can be found in our companion paper [17].

3.4 Distributed Software System Implementation

PanSim is a MPI based distributed memory application that is implemented in a mix of Python and C++. In PanSim a Python/C++ process (MPI rank) runs on each CPU core available. If the socio-psychological module is not written in Python, as is the case for the current study, then the socio-psychological module is run as a separate process. The socio-psychological processes share the

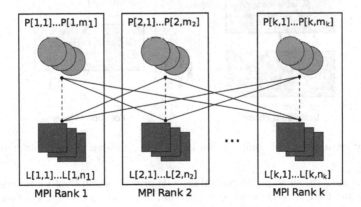

Fig. 2. Partitioning of agents/individuals and locations for distributed processing on PanSim.

CPU cores with the PanSim processes[5]. In this scenario, data is shared between PanSim processes and the socio-psychological module processes using Apache Arrow specifications.

On PanSim the two contagions progress over a dynamic agent-location bipartite graph. To be able to utilize distributed computing hardware, the nodes in the agent-location bipartite graph are partitioned across the MPI ranks. Figure 2 shows the overall partitioning strategy. To partition the graph evenly across the MPI ranks while keeping the cross-rank edges at a minimum, we use a two-step greedy process. In the first stage, the locations in the bipartite graph are sorted based on their maximum indegree. Next, the locations are assigned to the MPI ranks in a round robin manner. Finally the agents are assigned to the rank of the location that they are likely to visit the most frequently, which in most cases is their home location[6].

PanSim uses a bulk synchronous parallel design [20]. A PanSim simulation progresses in discrete timesteps. Within a timestep the execution progresses in five distinct phases, as described formally in Sect. 3.2. Figure 3 shows the different phases of computation of a PanSim simulation for a single timestep. First, in the socio-psychological decision phase (Eq. 1), every agent decides the locations to visit, and how to behave during those visits. This is followed by data exchange among MPI ranks to transfer information to the rank corresponding to the location of the visits. Second, in the social interaction phase (Eq. 2), the interactions

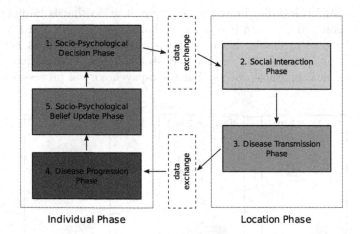

Fig. 3. Different phases of computation in a single timestep of a PanSim simulation.

---

[5] To ensure that the socio-psychological module processes and PanSim processes don't compete for CPU resources we use MPI implementation specific configuration to make PanSim processes sleep during the execution of the socio-psychological module. This configuration trades of some performance for ease of programming.

[6] We experimented with using Metis and ParMetis [24] for this partitioning. However, we found that our simple approach was much faster and produced adequately good partitions.

of the individuals at a every location is computed. Third, in the disease transmission phase (Eq. 3), the probability of susceptible agents getting infected from visits is computed. After the third phase, data is again exchanged among the MPI ranks to send the social interaction and transmission updates back to the agents they correspond to. Fourth, in the disease transmission phase (Eq. 4), the disease state of the agent is updated based on the transmission and progression models. Finally, in the socio-psychological belief update phase (Eq. 5), the socio-psychological agent state is updated based on the social interaction and the updated disease state of the agent.

As shown in Fig. 3, the first, fourth, and fifth phases of the simulation are collectively referred to as the individual phases. The computation of these phases can progress concurrently for every agent. Similarly, the second and third phases are location specific and can be executed concurrently for every location.

4   Sim-2APL

Sim-2APL is an extension of the agent programming library Java-2APL [16] (2APL) which supports the development of complex reasoning agents for large-scale simulations. 2APL defines the concepts of beliefs, goals, plans, and reasoning rules as Java interfaces, and dictates the interaction between these interfaces. In 2APL, the *Context* captures the agent's information or beliefs, the *Triggers* capture events or goals the agent may react to, the *Plans* capture specific parts of behavior that agents can perform, and the *Plan Schemes* match triggers to a suitable plan to be executed. An agent's behavior is generated through the application of *plan schemes* to *triggers*. The execution of an agent is defined in terms of pre-programmed execution steps, which are captured in the agent's *deliberation cycle*. The steps in the deliberation cycle allow plan schemes to be applied in response to different types of triggers (see [16] for more details on 2APL).

In agent-based simulations, agents sense the environment and act upon it. From the point of view of Sim-2APL, PanSim acts as the environment in which agents sense and act. However, to allow the agents to effectively act and interact in the environment, the action execution and deliberation cycle of 2APL must be modified. In 2APL, the deliberation cycle of an agent is rescheduled as soon as it ends. This means agents are executed continuously and independently, and an agent does not have to wait for all other agents to finish their deliberation cycle before acting. As a result, one agent may perform several deliberation cycles – and thus act in the environment several times – while another agent is still computing its first deliberation cycle. While this approach is appropriate for many applications, it does not guarantee a synchronized execution of the agents, which in turn may make simulations not repeatable. To address this, we modified 2APL in two ways: first, the execution of agent actions is delegated to the environment; second, we constrain the way agents are scheduled and executed.

Action Execution. In 2APL, the external actions in a plan are executed directly through Java method calls. This means that agents have full control over *when* actions are executed. However, many simulation platforms, including PanSim, do not allow agents to change the state of the environment directly, but rather update the state of the environment by calculating the subsequent simulation state from the joint set of all agent actions. For example, in PanSim this is represented by the stochastic function F in Sect. 3.2. Therefore, in the framework, the execution of external actions is delegated to the environment. In addition, we require that each plan executes at most one external action per deliberation cycle.[7] This is achieved by modifying the 2APL `Plan` interface so that its `execute()` method (`void` in 2APL) returns to the environment an identifier for the intended action that otherwise would be performed directly through a method call. When actions are delegated to the PanSim environment, the identifier is the tuple $(L_i^t, \tau_i^t, \epsilon_i^t, m_i^t)$ from Eq. 1.

Agent Scheduling. As explained above, many simulation platforms require agent execution to be synchronized to discrete-time steps. In Sim-2APL, discrete-time synchronization of agents is achieved using three interfaces: `StepExecutor`, `StepGenerator`, and `EnvironmentInterface`, the interaction of which is visualized in Fig. 4. The `StepExecutor` interface defines the method `doStep`, which is responsible for making each agent perform a single time step (deliberation cycle), and a method `reschedule`, called by each agent to reschedule its deliberation cycle for the subsequent time step. The `StepGenerator` interface specifies how execution time alternates between the `StepExecutor` and the environment responsible for storing and advancing the simulation state. This interface waits for the environment to finish calculating the new state at each time step. Finally, the `EnvironmentInterface` implements the communication layer with the environment. In the following, we describe these three interfaces in more detail.

StepGenerator. The `StepGenerator` is responsible for initiating the next time step in Sim-2APL. Each step is divided into three phases: *preparation*, *deliberation*, and *processing*, each of which run on the main thread so that the next phase only starts when the previous phase has finished. The process of phase transitions in the `StepGenerator` is visualized at the top in Fig. 4. The `StepGenerator` interface does not specify when a new step starts as this is initiated by an external 'driver'; in the framework, PanSim signals the `StepGenerator` to begin the next time step. This ensures agents cannot deliberate while the state of the environment is being updated. During the *preparation* phase, the `stepStarting` method of the `EnvironmentInterface` is called to prepare for the next phase of agent deliberation. The `stepStarting` method should perform all computations necessary to prepare for the agents' deliberation at this time step, such as processing or translating updates from the environment, creating *Trigger*s for belief updates, or calculating global resources or statistics. When the *preparation*

---

[7] Since agents can execute multiple plans during one deliberation cycle, this approach does not restrict the agent's number of actions per time step.

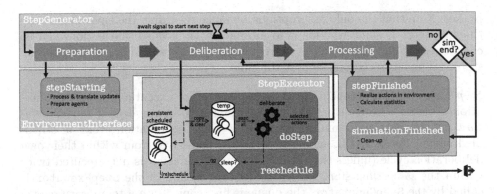

Fig. 4. The `StepGenerator` calls the appropriate methods on the `StepExecutor` and registered `EnvironmentInterfaces` to initiate the *preparation, deliberation,* and *processing* phases in each time step.

phase is complete, the *deliberation* phase for this time step is started by calling the `doStep` method of the `StepExecutor`. When deliberation of all agents is completed, the `StepExecutor` returns the actions generated by the agents. These actions can then be ordered to ensure determinism (e.g., using agent names) and are passed to the `EnvironmentInterface` to start the final *processing* phase. In this phase, the environment realizes the effect of the actions generated by the agents and calculates the next simulation state.

EnvironmentInterface. Sim-2APL is agnostic about what environment it is connected to. In order for Sim-2APL to interact with an environment, the `EnvironmentInterface` must be implemented. This interface is responsible for encoding agent actions and sending them to the environment, and receiving state updates from the environment and translating those for use by the agents. The interface defines three methods: `stepStarting` and `stepFinished`, which are called during the *preparation* and *processing* phases of the `StepGenerator`, respectively, and `simulationFinished` which is called when the simulation ends. This interface and its methods are shown in green in Fig. 4. Implementation of the `stepStarting` method is optional. The `stepFinished` method receives the set of actions produced by the agents as an argument, and should realize the actions in the environment and produce the next simulation state. In the framework, this is achieved by sending all agent actions to PanSim. However, in a simulation where the environment is programmed in Java, one could use the same methods that in 2APL are called on directly by the agents to realize the effect of those actions. Finally, the `simulationFinished` method is called when the simulation has ended. This method should implement any necessary cleanup operations, such as closing the connection with the environment. Multiple `EnvironmentInterfaces` can register with the `StepGenerator` by calling its `registerEnvironmentListener` method. The appropriate methods of each `EnvironmentInterface` instance will be called sequentially in each of the three phases. Note that the only assumptions we make regarding the environment are that, (i) there is *some* way for it to interface with Java so that actions can be executed in it and the state can be requested by agents, and (ii) the simulation state can be advanced one step at the time.

Step Executor. The `StepExecutor` is responsible for executing a single deliberation cycle for each agent at the current time step. In our *default implementation*, the `StepExecutor` maintains a queue of the deliberation cycles of scheduled agents. As in 2APL, agents re-schedule themselves from within their own deliberation cycle (unless they sleep). To ensure an agent is not executed twice within the same time step, when the `doStep` method of the `StepExecutor` is called by the `StepGenerator`, the queue is first copied into a temporary queue. The deliberation cycles of all agents are executed from this temporary queue, and rescheduled agents are placed on the original, now empty, queue. This process is visualized in blue in Fig. 4. Execution is handled using a Java Executor service, allowing the deliberation phase to run concurrently. Agents' (external) actions are then collected from the deliberation cycles and placed into a hash map where the unique identifier of the agent producing those actions is the key, and the value is the list of produced actions. This hash map is then returned to the `StepGenerator`.

5   Sample Simulation

We now describe our simulation of the spread of COVID-19, instantiated using PanSim + Sim-2APL. The simulation is built using a synthetic population of several counties in the US state of Virginia. Agents are represented with detailed demographic information from the US Census Bureau, along with detailed weekly activity sequences, and appropriate locations assigned for the activities from comprehensive location data [2]. The disease spread is driven by the interactions between agents (due to physical collocation), as they go about their weekly activity schedules and is handled by PanSim. In order to model changes in activity patterns as various social distancing interventions were instituted, we developed a normative reasoning model for the agents using Sim-2APL, as briefly described below and detailed in another work [17].

The simulation proceeds as follows. On each simulated day, each agent chooses which of its activities from its normal (pre-COVID) schedule it will carry out. The deliberation process is informed by normative reasoning as we describe below. For the activities the agent selects, it also chooses which behavioral interventions (mask-wearing, physical distancing) it will comply with, while carrying out each activity. Each activity results in a *visit* to a corresponding location. Table 2 shows the number of persons, households, and visits in each county, where the visit counts are based on pre-COVID activity schedules. During the simulation period, as the agents reduce their mobility to comply with various norms, the number of visits are lower.

For our sample simulation, we consider the behavioral interventions of official institutes as *norms* which agents can reason about. We classify these norms as

Table 2. The counties of the state of Virginia used for the experiments, along with the number of persons, households, and weekly location visits in the synthetic population.

County	Persons	Households	Visits
Goochland	20,923	8,240	680,571
Fluvanna	24,110	9,776	779,337
Louisa	32,938	13,398	1,066,179
Charlottesville	41,120	18,377	1,335,596
Albemarle	93,570	39,920	3,047,807
Hanover	98,435	38,149	3,204,317
Richmond	181,975	89,146	5,920,569

either regimented (R) – meaning that an agent has no choice but to comply, or non-regimented (NR) – meaning an agent is expected to comply but has the agency to violate. Examples of R norms are closure of schools and businesses, while examples of NR norms are wearing a mask or staying home when sick. Both NR and R norms operate on goals g, and are implemented in terms of the functions $applies : g \mapsto \{true, false\}$ and $transform : g \mapsto g \times \bot$, the former specifies whether the norm n applies to the goal while the latter transforms the goal g into a goal g' that complies with the norm, or into $\bot$ to not pursue the goal for one deliberation cycle. NR norms specify one additional function $attitude : g \times a \mapsto x \in (0,1) \subset \mathbb{R}$, which also takes the agent a as a parameter and, based on beliefs, observations and attitudes of the agent a, calculates its motivation to comply with norm n as a probability $p(n, g)$.

The normative reasoning process which we employ is as follows. If the plan scheme of the agent a is triggered by a goal g, all norms that apply to g are collected and iteratively applied to g by using the $transform(g)$ function. After this step, a plan is selected for the updated goal following the traditional 2APL approach.

In our work, we interpret the daily activities in the activity schedules of an agent directly as the agents' (to-do) goals. The transformations applied by the norms can change the modality of these activities (i.e. wear a mask, maintain physical distance), change the time or duration of the activity, or cancel the activity for that day.

For each location, PanSim computes the duration of overlap for each pair of agents that visits that location on the current day. This duration, coupled with whether the agents are complying with mask-wearing and physical distancing, determines the probability of infection if one of the agents is infectious and the other is susceptible. Based on these probabilities, PanSim computes disease state changes for all the agents. These are communicated back to the agents in Sim-2APL, along with the observations made by the agents of the visible attributes of the other agents they encounter, as described in Sect. 3. Each agent then uses this information in its decision-making procedure for the next simulated day.

The computational burden of the simulation is thus divided between the two components.

In the paper in which we describe the model in detail [17], we also report how the model was calibrated using both COVID-19 case data (PanSim) and cellphone based mobility data (Sim-2APL) using simulations spanning March to June 2020 of the counties of Charlottesville, Fluvanna, and Goochland (Table 2). The Sim2APL side of the model was calibrated by minimizing the Root-Mean-Square-Error (RMSE) between mobility observed in those counties in that time period, and the mobility of the agents in our model. A good overall fit was produced, but the model was not able to differentiate the differences in observed mobility between the three counties. The PanSim side of the model was calibrated by minimizing the RMSE between the recorded number of cases in those counties – multiplied with an arbitrary scaling factor (30 in this work) to account for testing uncertainty at the onset of COVID-19 – on the one hand, and the number of recovered agents in our model on the other. The calibration process matched the shape of the curve, but significantly undershot the target, resulting in a high RMSE of 2052.0222. We intend to address the issues with both calibration processes in future work. We performed 10 counterfactual experiments $E_0, \ldots, E_9$ with the calibrated model to rank the effectiveness of the 9 Executive Orders (EOs) implemented in Virginia in the simulated time period, counting the number of infected or recovered agents at the end of the simulation. In E_0 we ignored all norms, E_1 ignored all but the first EO, E_2 ignored all but the first two EOs, etc. According to our model, the most effective measures were the sixth EO (also restricting gatherings in private settings to 10 and closing higher education), and the seventh EO (requiring employees wear masks) with a 37.89% and 32.47% respective reduction compared to the previous EO. We were not able to conclusively rank one of these two EOs above the other due to overlapping confidence intervals.

As discussed earlier, prior work has either ignored individual behavioral complexity in favor of scaling disease spread simulations, or has focused on creating complex simulations with smaller agent populations. Our goal is to be able to scale simulations with complex individual agents to large population sizes, so we turn to scalability experiments with PanSim+Sim-2APL next.

6   Scalability Experiments

For the purposes of the scaling experiments, we chose synthetic populations of seven counties in the state of Virginia, USA, with varying sizes. Table 2 shows the number of persons, households and their weekly activity schedule (location visits) in the synthetic populations. To understand the scalability of PanSim+Sim-2APL we ran individual simulations for each of the seven counties, with each simulation running for 180 timesteps representing 180 days starting from March 1, 2020. The simulations were run with 40, 80, 160, and 320 CPU cores on compute nodes each having 2 Intel Xeon Gold 6148 CPUs with 20 CPU cores each. The compute nodes used to run the experiments also had 384 GB of DDR4

RAM Memory and were connected to each other with Mellanox ConnectX-5 network adaptors. Each simulation was run 10 times and their running time was noted.

We study scaling in two ways. First, we keep the problem size fixed and increase the number of CPU cores. This is done by running the simulation for each county with the four levels of cores above. The expectation is that the running time should decrease smoothly as the computational resources increase.

Second, we keep the computational resources fixed and increase the problem size. This is done by comparing the running times for simulations of increasingly larger counties, while keeping the number of CPU cores fixed. We carried out this experiment for all four levels of CPU cores also. The expectation is that the running time should not increase too sharply as the problem size increases.

In both cases, the resulting performance curves should ideally be linear. However, communication overheads can make the curves nonlinear. There is also inherent nonlinearity in the structure of the problem, as the disease spread computation is quadratic in the number of agents simultaneously present at a location. It is also expected that at some point, the overhead of communication between distributed parts of the simulation becomes higher than the efficiency gained by splitting the computation across multiple cores. For smaller problem sizes (i.e., smaller counties), this should become apparent with fewer cores.

6.1   Complexity

To contextualize the results of the experiments, we will briefly address the complexity of the integrated Pansim+Sim-2APL model. PanSim calculates the contact points of agents based on overlap in the location and time of visits, which is quadratic in the number of visits in the worst case. The deliberation implemented in Sim-2APL matches norms to activities, and is therefor linear to the number of active norms multiplied with the number of visits in the worst case (although not all norms apply to all activities).

Timings show that in the overall simulation on one CPU core, deliberation takes up ∼47–57% of computation time, where a larger number of agents increases the relative time spent on this part. ∼40–50% of the time is spent in PanSim, but this includes the transferal of encoded data frames of visits and agent disease states, which we did not study separately as this varies by hardware. Extracting and packaging these data frames in Sim-2APL uses ∼ 1% of the processing time and the pre- and post processing phases (in which norms are activated, and mobility is calculated from agent actions, see Sect. 4) consistently makes up ∼ 0.5% of the computation time. These last two were not parallelized in our implementation, so their relative computation time increases slightly when increasing CPU cores to ∼3–4% for extracting and packaging, and consistently using roughly ∼2.5% for pre- and post processing on 12 CPU cores. With that number of cores, the deliberation phase goes down to ∼30–38%, and the environment increases to ∼55%–65% (note again this includes constant time data transferal). The computation time for the pre- and post processing and for packaging does not depend on the number of active norms. On one CPU core, only

~6–11% of computation time is spent on deliberation when no norms are active, with the environment taking ~85–90%. As the number of norms increases, these numbers gradually balance out to those reported for the overall simulation.

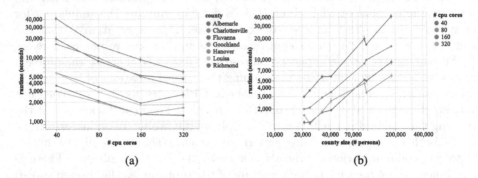

(a)   (b)

Fig. 5. The mean runtime of PanSim+Sim-2APL simulations for seven counties of the state of Virginia compared with (a) the number of cores, and (b) the number of agents.

6.2   Results

Figure 5 shows the variance in the runtime of the simulations when run with different number of CPU cores. We can see in Fig. 5a when the same simulation is run with increasing number of CPU cores (strong scaling) for all the counties the runtimes decrease almost linearly till 160 CPU cores on a log-log scale. For smaller counties, such as Goochland and Charlottesville, increasing the number of CPU cores to 320 actually increases the runtime due the communication overhead becoming apparent, as discussed above. However, for a larger county like Richmond, the strong scaling results hold even with 320 CPU cores.

A similar story can be seen when looking at Fig. 5b which shows the runtime of simulations with increasing compute load (number of agents in the county simulated). We can see that for counties with more than 100,000 persons, increasing the number of CPU cores to 320 shows definite benefits. However, for the rest of the counties simulated, the benefits of increasing CPU cores are observed only up to 160 CPU cores.

These results demonstrate that PanSim+Sim-2APL simulations integrate well, and can be used to simulate large populations. More detailed simulation results, investigating the effects of various non-pharmaceutical interventions, are presented in the companion paper, which focuses on the data, design, calibration, and analysis of the simulation [17].

7   Conclusion

In this paper, we presented a novel agent-based simulation framework for modeling large-scale complex social phenomena. We presented Sim-2APL, a Java-based multi-agent programming library that allows to model and simulate complex reasoning agents through the BDI paradigm. We integrated Sim-2APL with

PanSim, our novel platform for distributing large-scale agent-based simulations. We reported on a scalability experiment using a COVID-19 epidemic simulation with a population of BDI agents representing individuals from 7 counties of the state of Virginia, with population size ranging from 20k to 180k agents. Our results demonstrate that it is indeed possible to build an execute large-scale realistic simulations with BDI based agent models with efficient and judicious use of distributing computing platforms.

As we have seen with COVID-19 during 2020, epidemics (especially novel ones) are driven by human behavior. Until vaccines became available, public health authorities, institutions, and governments had to rely on non-pharmaceutical interventions to try to mitigate the epidemic. However, we don't have a rigorous understanding of the effectiveness of these interventions, due, in large part, to the complexity of human behavioral responses and their effects on epidemic dynamics. Thus, while there have been numerous computational and mathematical models of the COVID-19 epidemic that have been developed in the past year, they have largely focused on disease dynamics and have either ignored human behaviors or represented them in very simplistic ways, such as assuming that people comply with interventions independently with certain probabilities.

Our goal in developing this framework has been to bring together the strengths of MAS technologies for building normative reasoning agents with large-scale data-driven distributed agent-based simulation technologies. The scalability of this framework will now enable the development of more meaningful simulations, which can properly address complex human behaviors and allow reasoning about the effects of a larger class of interventions.

Acknowledgments. Parantapa Bhattacharya and Samarth Swarup were supported in part by NSF Expeditions in Computing Grant CCF-1918656 and DTRA subcontract/ARA S-D00189-15-TO-01-UVA.

References

1. Adam, C., Gaudou, B.: BDI agents in social simulations: a survey. Knowl. Eng. Rev. **31**(n° 3), pp. 207–238 (2016). https://doi.org/10.1017/S0269888916000096, https://hal.archives-ouvertes.fr/hal-01484960
2. Adiga, A., et al.: Generating a synthetic population of the United States. Technical report NDSSL 15–009, Network Dynamics and Simulation Science Laboratory (2015)
3. Barrett, C., et al.: Planning and response in the aftermath of a large crisis: an agent-based informatics framework. In: Pasupathy, R., Kim, S.H., Tolk, A., Hill, R., Kuhl, M.E. (eds.) Proceedings of the 2013 Winter Simulation Conference, Piscataway, NJ, USA, pp. 1515–1526. IEEE Press (2013)
4. Barrett, C.L., Bisset, K.R., Eubank, S.G., Feng, X., Marathe, M.V.: Episimdemics: an efficient algorithm for simulating the spread of infectious disease over large realistic social networks. In: Proceedings of the 2008 ACM/IEEE Conference on Supercomputing, pp. 37:1–37:12 (2008)
5. Bhatele, A., et al.: Massively parallel simulations of spread of infectious diseases over realistic social networks. In: Proceedings of the IEEE/ACM International Symposium on Cluster, Cloud and Grid Computing, CCGRID. IEEE (2017)

6. Bisset, K., Chen, J., Feng, X., Vullikanti, A., Marathe, M.: EpiFast: a fast algorithm for large-scale realistic epidemic simulations on distributed memory systems. In: Proceedings of the 23rd International Conference on Supercomputing (2009)

7. Bordini, R.H., Dastani, M., Dix, J., Fallah-Seghrouchni, A.E. (eds.): Multi-Agent Programming: Languages, Platforms and Applications, Multiagent Systems, Artificial Societies, and Simulated Organizations, vol. 15. Springer, Boston (2005). https://doi.org/10.1007/b137449

8. Bordini, R.H., Dastani, M., Dix, J., Fallah-Seghrouchni, A.E. (eds.): Multi-Agent Programming: Languages, Tools and Applications. Springer, USA (2009). https://doi.org/10.1007/978-0-387-89299-3

9. Bordini, R.H., Hübner, J.F.: Agent-based simulation using BDI programming in Jason. In: Multi-Agent Systems: Simulation and Applications, pp. 451–471 (2009)

10. Broersen, J., Dastani, M., Hulstijn, J., Huang, Z., van der Torre, L.: The BOID architecture: conflicts between beliefs, obligations, intentions and desires. In: Proceedings of the 5th International Conference on Autonomous Agents, pp. 9–16 (2001)

11. Caballero, A., Botía, J., Gómez-Skarmeta, A.: Using cognitive agents in social simulations. Eng. Appl. Artif. Intell. **24**(7), 1098–1109 (2011)

12. Centers for Disease Control and Prevention: COVID-19 pandemic planning scenarios. https://www.cdc.gov/coronavirus/2019-ncov/hcp/planning-scenarios.html. Accessed 06 Oct 2020

13. Centola, D., Macy, M.: Complex contagions and the weakness of long ties. Am. J. Sociol. **113**(3), 702–734 (2007)

14. Citycovid. https://www.anl.gov/dis/citycovid-about-the-model

15. Dastani, M., Hulstijn, J., van der Torre, L.: How to decide what to do? Eur. J. Oper. Res. **160**(3), 762–784 (2005). Decision Analysis and Artificial Intelligence

16. Dastani, M., Testerink, B.: Design patterns for multi-agent programming. Int. J. Agent-Oriented Softw. Eng. **5**(2/3), 167–202 (2016)

17. de Mooij, J., Dell'Anna, D., Bhattacharya, P., Dastani, M., Logan, B., Swarup, S.: Quantifying the effects of norms on COVID-19 cases using an agent-based simulation. In: Proceedings of the The 22nd International Workshop on Multi-Agent-Based Simulation (MABS) (2021)

18. Dignum, F., Dignum, V., Jonker, C.M.: Towards agents for policy making. In: David, N., Sichman, J.S. (eds.) Multi-Agent-Based Simulation IX, pp. 141–153. Springer, Heidelberg (2009). https://doi.org/10.1007/978-3-642-01991-3_11

19. Gaudou, B., et al.: Comokit: a modeling kit to understand, analyze, and compare the impacts of mitigation policies against the COVID-19 epidemic at the scale of a city. Front. Public Health **8**, 587 (2020). https://doi.org/10.3389/fpubh.2020.563247, https://www.frontiersin.org/article/10.3389/fpubh.2020.563247

20. Gerbessiotis, A.V., Valiant, L.G.: Direct bulk-synchronous parallel algorithms. J. Parallel Distrib. Comput. **22**(2), 251–267 (1994)

21. Gilbert, N.: When does social simulation need cognitive models? In: Sun, R. (ed.) Cognition and Multi-Agent Interaction: From Cognitive Modeling to Social Simulation, pp. 428–432. Cambridge University Press, Cambridge (2006)

22. Gilbert, N., Troitzsch, K.G.: Simulation for the Social Scientist. Open University Press (2006)

23. Glanz, K., Rimer, B.K., Viswanath, K.: Health Behavior and Health Education: Theory, Research, and Practice. Wiley, Hoboken (2008)

24. Karypis, G., Schloegel, K., Kumar, V.: Parmetis. Parallel graph partitioning and sparse matrix ordering library. Version 2 (2003)

25. Macal, C.M., Collier, N.T., Ozik, J., Tatara, E.R., Murphy, J.T.: CHISIM: an agent-based simulation model of social interactions in a large urban area. In: 2018 Winter Simulation Conference (WSC), pp. 810–820. IEEE (2018)
26. Michel, F.: The IRM4S model: the influence/reaction principle for multi-agent based simulation. In: Proceedings of the 6th International Joint Conference on Autonomous Agents and Multiagent Systems (2007)
27. Morvan, G., Veremme, A., Dupont, D.: IRM4MLS: the influence reaction model for multi-level simulation. In: Bosse, T., Geller, A., Jonker, C.M. (eds.) MABS 2010. LNCS (LNAI), vol. 6532, pp. 16–27. Springer, Heidelberg (2011). https://doi.org/10.1007/978-3-642-18345-4_2
28. Müller, J.P., Pecchiari, P.: A model for systems of situated autonomous agents: an application to automated deduction (1996)
29. Müller, S.A., Balmer, M., Neumann, A., Nagel, K.: Mobility traces and spreading of COVID-19. Technical report, Technische Universität Berlin (2020). https://doi.org/10.14279/depositonce-9835
30. Navarro, L., Flacher, F., Corruble, V.: Dynamic level of detail for large scale agent-based urban simulations. In: Tumer, K., Yolum, P., Sonenberg, L., Stone, P. (eds.) Proceedings of 10th International Conference on Autonomous Agents and Multiagent Systems, Taipei, Taiwan, 2–6 May 2011, pp. 701–708 (2011)
31. Satsuma, J., Willox, R., Ramani, A., Grammaticos, B., Carstea, A.: Extending the SIR epidemic model. Phys. A: Stat. Mech. Appl. **336**(3–4), 369–375 (2004)
32. Silverman, B.G., Johns, M., Cornwell, J., O'Brien, K.: Human behavior models for agents in simulators and games: part I: enabling science with PMFserv. Presence: Teleoper. Virtual Environ. **15**(2), 139–162 (2006)
33. Singh, D., Padgham, L., Logan, B.: Integrating BDI agents with agent-based simulation platforms. Auton. Agents Multi-Agent Syst. **30**(6), 1050–1071 (2016). https://doi.org/10.1007/s10458-016-9332-x
34. Taillandier, P., et al.: Building, composing and experimenting complex spatial models with the GAMA platform. GeoInformatica **23**(2), 299–322 (2019)

Implementing Ethical Governors in BDI

Rafael C. Cardoso[1]([✉]) [iD], Angelo Ferrando[2] [iD], Louise A. Dennis[1] [iD],
and Michael Fisher[1] [iD]

[1] Department of Computer Science, The University of Manchester, Manchester, UK
{rafael.cardoso,louise.dennis,michael.fisher}@manchester.ac.uk
[2] Department of Computer Science, Bioengineering, Robotics and Systems
Engineering (DIBRIS), University of Genova, Genova, Italy
angelo.ferrando@dibris.unige.it

Abstract. Increasingly, BDI agents are being used not just for basic decision-making, but for more abstract ethical decisions. Several authors have built ad-hoc extensions of BDI systems that provide varying levels of sophistication. In this paper, we introduce a general-purpose approach for implementing ethical governors in BDI systems. With this we aim to provide a broad, flexible and consistent framework for implementing increasingly complex ethical reasoning. Our approach is based on a set of domain-independent abstract agents (evidential reasoner, arbiter and execution agent) that together represent an ethical governor. We discuss the implementation of these abstract agents in the Jason agent programming language and demonstrate how they can be used in practice by instantiating agents in two different case studies, one using utilitarianism and the other deontic logic for reasoning about ethical decisions.

Keywords: Ethical governor · Implementing machine ethics · BDI · Jason

1 Introduction

Computational systems can be divided into those which are *implicitly* ethical (in which the process of requirements capture, design and implementation are assumed to guarantee ethical operation of the system), those which are *explicitly* ethical (in which the machine uses some concept of right and wrong as part of its reasoning), and those that are *unethical* [22]. In this paper we take an *explicit* approach to ethical reasoning, in which a machine reasons about the correct course of action by reference to judgements relating to specific ethical principles such as safety, human autonomy and privacy and uses an ethical theory (probably, but not necessarily, from philosophy) to select an appropriate course of action based on those judgements. This is achieved through the use of an

Work supported by UK Research and Innovation, and EPSRC Hubs: EP/R026092 (FAIR-SPACE), EP/R026173 (ORCA), EP/R026084 (RAIN), and EP/V026801 (Verifiability Node). Fisher's work is also supported by Royal Academy of Engineering.

N. Alechina et al. (Eds.): EMAS 2021, LNAI 13190, pp. 22–41, 2022.
https://doi.org/10.1007/978-3-030-97457-2_2

ethical governor that arbitrates decisions, such as plan selection, concerning competing ethical issues. It should not be assumed that in taking this approach we treat the machine as a moral agent in its own right, in our view the morality (and ultimate responsibility) for the machine's behaviour remains with those who commission, design and implement the behaviour – we mean only that the machine's programming explicitly refers to concepts of right and wrong on occasion as part of its functioning.

Belief-Desire-Intention (BDI) [6,23] is a well known model for the implementation of autonomous agents. In this model, the reasoning cycle of an agent revolves around three mental attitudes: *beliefs*, representing the knowledge that the agent has about the world; *desires*, the goals (i.e., state of the world) that the agent wants to achieve; and *intentions*, courses of action that the agent is committed to achieve. In capturing decision-making at this high level of abstraction, the BDI model has the potential to be useful across a range of machine ethics activities, particularly involving the ideas of implementing governors. In particular, the complex reasoning cycle of BDI agents is well suited for performing ethical reasoning, as well as using multiple BDI agents to represent different ethical entities (potentially with opposing/similar views). We use Jason [5], one of the most popular BDI agent programming languages [4,10,20], to implement our approach.

Our approach to implementing an ethical governor in BDI is separated into two levels, abstraction and instantiation. Our main contribution is in the first level, where we introduce three different types of agents (arbiter, evidential reasoner, and execution agent) that implement a communication protocol and together form an ethical governor system. The second level is an instantiation of these types of agents, wherein agents implement the specific behaviours of the application. To evaluate our approach we provide two examples of instantiation, one using utilitarianism and the other using deontic logic as evidential reasoners. Note that while we offer these two types of ethical reasoning by default, our goal with this work is to offer a general-purpose implementation to be used as a basis for experiments with ethical governors that can be further extended with other types of ethical reasoning depending on the requirements of the application.

In this paper, we chose to represent an ethical governor as multiple agents. Other alternatives include representing it as a single agent, or an organisation of agents. Implementing it as multiple agents was more suitable for us given the different types of reasoning that we create to represent the ethical governor (arbiter, evidential reasoners, and execution agent). Using multiple agents allows us to have a clear separation between (potentially conflicting) evidential reasoners (e.g., autonomy vs safety). Moreover, it makes instantiating the agents (i.e., implementing case study specific behaviours) more straightforward, as we can simply create agents that extend their abstract parent and implement only the features necessary in their abstract representation.

This paper is organised as follows. In the next section we discuss some of the background in machine ethics and the related work in implementing it using agents. Section 3 introduces our general-purpose approach to implement ethical governors in the Jason BDI language, explaining its three main elements: evidential reasoner, arbiter and execution agent. In Sect. 4, we evaluate our approach by applying it to two case studies, a remote inspection scenario with a human and a robot cooperating to achieve some goals and a smart home scenario. The paper concludes in Sect. 5 with a summary of our contributions and a discussion about future work.

2 Machine Ethics

Machine ethics is the study of how to implement ethical reasoning in machines. There are a number of approaches to machine ethics, in particular approaches from symbolic artificial intelligence which generally take a philosophical theory and operationalise it, and approaches from machine learning which attempt to learn ethical behaviour from observation. Following [26], symbolic approaches are generally classed as top-down and contrasted to machine learning approaches which are considered bottom-up. There are a number of approaches that seek to combine these, for instance, those in which philosophical theory provides an over-arching framework within which details can be established via learning (e.g., [1]).

Popular philosophical theories for the implementation of explicit machine ethics include utilitarianism (in which the outcomes of actions are scored and the action with the highest score is chosen), deontic logic (in which ethics is encoded as rules that explicitly refer to actions that are permitted, obliged or prohibited in specific situations) [15], and variants on virtue ethics which refer to extent to which an action is in line with some set of desirable values. Many approaches combine aspects of several philosophical theories—such as approaches which evaluate the outcomes of actions with respect to values or *ethical principles* and then use rules to select the preferred choice [1].

One of the earliest implementations of machine ethics is Arkin's *ethical governor* [2]. In this system an ethical governor considers target selection suggestions from autonomous weapon system and reasons about whether the suggestions are compatible with the *Law of War* and the *Rules of Engagement* for a specific situation. The system then vetoes any suggestions that are unethical in these contexts. Ethical governors form a popular class of explicit machine ethics systems where they can act in tandem with more opaque autonomous systems (e.g., deep neural networks) to provide confidence that selected actions are ethical. Among approaches taking inspiration from Arkin's work are those based on the concept of an *ethical consequence engine* [27], in which a simulation engine is used to predict the outcomes of proposed actions which are then passed to a governor style system for evaluation. This relates to Arkin's work in which the governor consists of an *evidential reasoner* and an *application* (which applies either constraint or rule-based reasoning [25] to decide based on the evidence). Further extensions of the ethical consequence engine work have included both the use of BDI style reasoning to arbitrate between choices *and* the ability of the governor "layer" to make its own suggestions for actions if it deems none of those from the underlying system to be acceptable [7]. The work of [7] is here generalised and expanded, in particular to incorporate multiple streams of evidence between which the governor must decide. Our work is more general in comparison to [7], we do not have an explicit robot controller (our approach is not limited to robotic applications), but such a component can be encoded in our execution agent.

In [17], the authors propose an extended BDI architecture where the agent's reasoning is enhanced with case-based reasoning to implement casuistry and consequentialist theories in BDI agents. This is obtained by making the agents use past experiences to solve present problems. In more detail, if a past experience exists, then the agent follows the same steps to solve the problem; otherwise, the agent decides how to solve the problem following the standard BDI flow. Their work is based on a hybrid BDI architecture that uses case-based reasoning while ours solely comprises pure BDI agents. Another extension of the BDI model with the notion of action consequences is proposed in [16]. This is obtained by modelling a consequentialist approach of ethics which makes an agent choose actions with consequences that are less evil. The authors formalise their approach in both Answer Set Programming (ASP) and BDI frameworks. Differently from the works in [16,17], we do not extend the BDI model, instead we present a general-purpose approach to implementing ethical reasoning in (existing) BDI systems without altering the BDI reasoning cycle or the languages and tools that implement it.

The authors in [12] describe a mechanism for BDI agents to have a value-based reasoning process. Such values are used to influence the agent's decision-making, and can relate to ethical aspects. Their approach is similar to ours in the sense that both do not require modifications to the BDI model or to any underlying tool/language. The difference is that in their case their mechanism uses an external constraint solver while ours is directly implemented in the Jason agent programming language. End even though we also have a value-based reasoning process (utilitarianism evidential reasoner), our main focus is in creating the ethical governor system.

3   Ethical Governor in BDI

In [13], Dennis and Fisher note that while in questions of safety such as those studied in the ethical consequence engine work, simulated physical outcomes are effective in evaluating the risks of possible actions when other ethical principles are considered, such as privacy or human autonomy. Evaluating the ethical status of a proposed action might need to reference different processes such as reasoning using rules about possible consequences, simulations of information flows, or reference to stated preferences. Thus a suite of such reasoners is needed, one for each of the ethical considerations in play, and the arbiter (called application in Arkin's work) layer of the evidential reasoner must decide between potentially competing preferences/recommendations/evaluations from these reasoners.

An initial implementation of such a multiple evidential reasoner system using BDI agents programmed in Jason was presented in [9] in which two evidential reasoners – one in the style of the ethical consequence engine that simulated physical outcomes and made recommendations about safety, and one that used its own past history in order to make recommendations about respecting human autonomy – both submitted recommendations to an arbitration system that used utilitarianism to select the desired action. While our previous work was domain-specific, we now present a general approach for implementing machine ethics through an ethical governor system.

Our implementation[1] is written in the Jason [5] agent programming language. Jason started as an implementation of AgentSpeak(L) [24], a theoretical language for BDI systems, but has since seen many extensions such as its use in the JaCaMo [3] multi-agent programming framework. Jason underlying code is implemented in Java and has been shown to have some of the best performance among agent programming languages [21], as well as achieving respectable performance against actor programming languages, especially those that are also implemented in Java [11].

Agents in our ethical governor system consist of:

- an *execution agent*, which is the agent responsible for managing and executing actions that require further ethical reasoning in the system;
- a set of *evidential reasoners*, one or more agents that based on their main characteristic (e.g., autonomy, safety, privacy, etc.) and given an input from the execution agent (i.e., an existing action or a set of states) will suggest an appropriate ethical action;
- and an *arbiter*, in case of two or more evidential reasoners it is necessary that another agent be responsible for determining which action will be sent for execution.

The ethical governor can be part of a larger multi-agent system, including other agents that are not part of the ethical governor (these other agents are out of scope for this paper and are domain-specific). To simplify the implementation details, in this paper we only consider a single ethical governor. To execute an action that requires ethical reasoning, the execution agent asks the evidential reasoners to suggest actions. Actions that require ethical reasoning are identified and defined by the developer of the system. Each evidential reasoner will choose an action based on its instantiation, using epistemic reasoning and its set of beliefs, plans, and Prolog-like rules. Finally, the arbiter collects all suggestions, picks one of them based on an ethical reasoning strategy, such as utilitarianism, and sends the selected choice to the execution agent. Our approach is split into two levels: Abstraction and Instantiation, as represented in Fig. 1.

At the abstraction level, a communication protocol amongst the agents is established. This protocol includes plans for the agents to be able to communicate their requests and replies (using both unicast and multicast), as well as messages introducing the name of the agents that have been instantiated (using broadcast). The code at this level does not require any information about the

---

[1] Source code available at: https://github.com/autonomy-and-verification/ethicalgov.

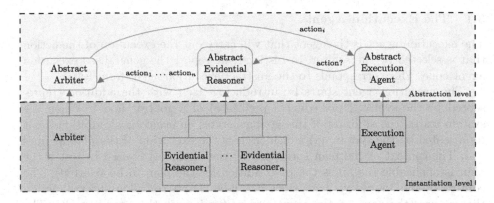

Fig. 1. Overview of our approach for implementing an ethical governor in BDI.

scenario that is being implemented. The abstract level only concerns how agents in the governor system interface with each other.

The instantiated agents *include* their parent abstraction. The internal *include* action in Jason imports at runtime all of the beliefs, goals, and plans of the specified agent source file into another agent source file. This is not the same as the inheritance concept from object-oriented programming, since it is simply loading a preexisting code instead of properly instantiating it. We note here that if we were using the aforementioned JaCaMo multi-agent programming framework [3] we would be able to use Moise [18] (responsible for the organisation layer) to establish an organisation with the roles of arbiter, evidential reasoner, and execution agent, which would allow us to drop the broadcast plans with the name of the agents, since agents in the system would have access to the names of the agents that are playing these roles. However, we opted to have a standalone Jason implementation first since it provides a basic starting point, and leave a JaCaMo extension as future work.

At the instantiation level, we find how the execution agent implements the suggested actions, the implementation logic that the evidential reasoners use to decide which actions to suggest, and finally, how the arbiter weights these suggestions and the type of ethical reasoning that it uses to select the choice that will be sent back to the execution agent.

Even though the abstraction level is at a higher-level and thus more general than the instantiation, both refer to actual implemented code. The code at the abstraction level is simply a parent code that is instantiated and further specialised depending on the application that we want to develop. The instantiation level is further discussed in Sect. 4 when we instantiate the agents using two case studies, but for now we continue to describe the details of the abstraction level.

3.1 The Execution Agent

The execution agent is the agent that will carry out the execution of the action that is selected by the arbiter. In Listing 1, we report the generalised execution agent code. This corresponds to the abstract execution agent from Fig. 1.

The execution agent starts by introducing itself with the addition (represented by the syntax ! preceding a predicate) of a goal at line 1. When the system starts, the addition of this goal generates an event (goal addition event represented by the syntax +!) which triggers the execution of the plan at lines 2–4. The context of the plan (preceded by the : symbol) is used to test if the plan is applicable (i.e., it is the precondition for the plan to be selected). The context at line 3 is always true, since it is used simply to call an internal action that returns the name of the agent and unifies it with the open term Me. The plan body (preceded by the <- symbol) contains the steps required to achieve a plan, this can be calls to an action, either internal for Jason existing actions or external (provided by the user or the environment), or operations such as goal/belief addition/removal where each call terminates with a semicolon, and finally a dot in the end of the plan. Line 4 calls the internal action broadcast to send a message to all agents in the multi-agent system using the tell speech act performative, which adds the belief with the name of the execution agent.

```
1  !introductions.
2  +!introductions
3       : .my_name(Me)
4  <- .broadcast(tell, execution_agent(Me)).

5  +!act
6  <-
7      for (evidential_reasoner(Gov)) {
8          .send(Gov, achieve, suggest_action);
9      }.

10 +!choice(ActionList)
11      : .list(ActionList)
12 <-
13     !select_action(ActionList, action(Action, ReasonerType));
14     !execute_action(Action, ReasonerType).
15 +!choice(action(Action, ReasonerType))
16 <-
17     !execute_action(Action, ReasonerType).
```

Listing 1. Generalised execution agent code.

After this step, when the execution agent's instantiation requires an action to be selected by the ethical governor, it first has to call the act plan by adding the !act goal (an example of such instantiation, as well as the other agents' instantiation, is shown later in Sect. 4). This plan (lines 5–9) sends a request for an action suggestion to all evidential reasoners through the achieve speech act which works as a goal addition, thus triggering the plan +!suggest_action in the evidential reasoners when the message is received. The plans shown at lines 10–14 and 15–17 are triggered by a message sent from the arbiter with the action choice that was selected. It is possible for the arbiter to return a list of action choices, in which case the plan at 10–14 is triggered and the instantiation of the execution agent will pick the most appropriate action from the list, and then calls a plan for performing the action where the corresponding callback plan has to be implemented at the instantiation level. Otherwise, if a single action is received the plan at lines 15–17 simply calls the plan for executing it.

It would be possible, with some minor modifications, to remove the execution agent from the abstraction level, however, we would still require an agent to start the process by asking for an action from the evidential reasoners. We have opted to keep this abstraction because it allows the developer to quickly understand which plans have to be implemented in their instantiation (i.e., plans that are domain-specific), without having to resort to any external documentation. Our current implementation of the abstraction level allows for only one instantiation of the execution agent, however, with some minor modifications it should be possible to extend this to allow multiple agents. Namely the communication protocol would have to be extended to include the name of the requesting execution agent, and the evidential reasoners and the arbiter would have to be able to reason about their choices in relation to the requesting agent so that multiple requests could be handled concurrently.

3.2   The Evidential Reasoners

The evidential reasoners are agents that will decide which action to suggest using domain-specific Prolog-like rules that can take into consideration the current state of the system under execution to narrow down which action they believe to be the most suitable for the current situation. When instantiated, these reasoners will often favour diverging opinions, such as for example a safety reasoner in contrast to an autonomy reasoner, as we will see in Sect. 4. In Listing 2, we report the code for the generalised evidential reasoner. This corresponds to the abstract evidential reasoner from Fig. 1.

```
1  !introductions.
2  +!introductions
3        : .my_name(Me)
4  <- .broadcast(tell, evidential_reasoner(Me)).

5  +!suggest_action
6        : arbiter(Arbiter) & type(Type)
7  <-
8        !make_choice(Action, Statement);
9        .send(Arbiter, tell, evidential_reasoner_choice(Type,
             Action, Statement)).
```

Listing 2. Generalised evidential reasoner code.

Similar to the execution agent, the evidential reasoners also have an introduction plan that works in exactly the same way. The names of the evidential reasoners are necessary for the execution agent, since it needs to ask the evidential reasoners for suggestions, and for the arbiter, since it has to wait each evidential reasoner's choice before selecting one. The plan for handling an execution agent request is defined at lines 5–9, and it is triggered by the message from the execution agent that we have seen in Listing 1. We consult the agent's belief base in the context of the plan (line 6) to unify the name of the arbiter and the type of the agent (which is set in the instantiation level, e.g., safety, autonomy, etc.). The !make_choice goal is added at line 8 and it should be triggered by a plan implemented in the instantiation of the evidential reasoner. Its implementation depends on what are the objectives of the instantiated evidential reasoner, which will determine their action choice as well as a statement (e.g., if we are dealing with a utilitarian system than this will be a utility value for that action choice). Finally, at line 9, the evidential reasoner propagates its selection, composed of the type of the evidential reasoner, the action choice, and the statement, to the arbiter of the system. These are then used by the arbiter to select the action to be executed.

3.3 The Arbiter

The arbiter (similar to the entity called application in Arkin's original work) is responsible for collecting the action suggestions from the various evidential reasoners and then selecting the most appropriate based on some ethical reasoning such as utilitarianism. In Listing 3, we report the generalised arbiter code. This corresponds to the abstract arbiter in Fig. 1. Line 1 contains a book-keeping belief counter(0) that is used to keep track of how many action suggestions it has received from the evidential reasoners. The introductions plan works the same as in the previous execution agent and evidential reasoners, and it is used by the arbiter to introduce its name to the rest of the agents.

Lines 6–11 and 12–16 contain two plans that receive those choices, both triggered by the addition of the belief evidential_reasoner_choice. Both are annotated (preceded by the @ symbol), a Jason feature that allows plans to have extra information embedded in the plan. In this case, an identifier name and an option that turns the plan into an atomic operation, meaning that the usual concurrent execution of intentions in Jason is stopped once the plan is triggered and will only resume after it has been completed (either with a fail or a success). This is necessary in order to avoid any race condition that could eventually cause the counter belief to be miscalculated. The default plan selection in Jason goes top-down in the plan library of the agent and attempts to select any plan matching the triggering event. Since both plans have the same trigger, the first plan (6–11) will be selected first. Its context checks (using the .count internal action which returns the number of times that a particular belief occurs in the belief base) the number of evidential reasoners in the system (beliefs that are obtained through the identification messages) and that the current counter matches this number minus 1 (i.e., this is the last evidential reasoner to send its action choice). The _ symbol indicates variables which may match any value. The body of this plan updates the counter to 0 so that it is ready to receive more action choices in the future and adds the `!arbiter_choice` goal. If the context of the first plan fails, the second one (12–16) will be triggered. Its context is always true, since there will always be a count belief, and its body simply updates the counter by an increment of 1.

```
1  counter(0).
2  !introductions.
3  +!introductions
4      : .my_name(Me)
5  <- .broadcast(tell, arbiter(Me)).
6  @receivelastchoice[atomic]
7  +evidential_reasoner_choice(Type, Action, Statement)
8      : .count(evidential_reasoner(_),N) & counter(N-1)
9  <-
10     -counter(_); +counter(0);
11     !arbiter_choice.
12 @receivechoice[atomic]
13 +evidential_reasoner_choice(Type, Action, Statement)
14     : count(N)
15 <-
16     -counter(N); +counter(N+1).
17 @utilitarian[atomic]
18 +!arbiter_choice : reasoning(utilitarian) & execution_agent
         (Agent)
19 <-
20     +choice(0,0,0);
21     for (evidential_reasoner_choice(Type, Action, Utility)) {
22         -evidential_reasoner_choice(Type, Action, Utility);
23         if (type_multiplier(Type, TypeMultiplier) ) {
24             NewUtility = TypeMultiplier * Utility;
25         } else {
26             NewUtility = Utility;
27         }
28         ?choice(BestUtility, BestType, BestChoice);
29         if (NewUtility > BestUtility) {
30             -choice(BestUtility, BestType, BestChoice);
31             +choice(NewUtility, Type, Action);
32         }
33     }
34     ?choice(Utility, Type, Action);
35     -choice(Utility, Type, Action);
36     .send(Agent, achieve, choice(action(Action, Type))).
```

Listing 3. Generalised arbiter code.

Finally, we have the plan that triggers once all action choices have been received. By default we provide two ethical reasoning mechanisms for the arbiter: utilitarianism and deontic. Other mechanisms can be added in the instantiation of the arbiter as needed. For brevity, we only discuss utilitarianism here (lines 17–36), but show the instantiation of deontic logic later on in our second case study. The context of the plan makes sure that the plan corresponding to the desired ethical reasoning will be selected (utilitarian in this case) and that we know the name of the execution agent. The +choice belief is another book-keeping belief to keep track of what is currently the best choice (initialised with 0). We iterate over each choice, and retrieve the scale multiplier for the evidential reasoner (if no multiplier is given in the instantiation of the arbiter, then the utility value is preserved), and use it to update the utility value passed by the evidential reasoner. The scale multiplier can be used to give more (resp. less) importance to certain types of evidential reasoners (e.g., more value to safety rather than autonomy). The best choice is retrieved at line 28, and at line 29 its utility is compared with the utility of the action currently analysed. If the currently analysed action has a greater utility, then the best action is updated (lines 30–31). After all the evidential reasoners' action choices have been evaluated, the best action is retrieved (line 34) and sent to the execution agent (line 36).

4   Evaluation

To evaluate our general-purpose approach we have selected two case studies and present the instantiation level for both, as well as some results from experimenting with the multiplier scales for different types of evidential reasoners. The choice of the agent to instantiate the execution agent as well as the actions that require ethical reasoning is to be made by the developer of the system.

4.1   Remote Inspection Case Study

Our first case study, shown in Fig. 2, is a simulation where a human (represented by H in the screenshots) and a robot (represented by R in the screenshots) move around in a 2D grid environment. The human's task is to keep visiting all goal positions (green triangles) for as long as the system is running. The robot's objective is to protect the human from stepping into radiation cells; these are the cells with low (yellow), medium (orange), and high (red) level of radiation. The robot has two evidential reasoners which generate the ethical dilemma to be solved by the ethical governor system, a safety reasoner and an autonomy reasoner. In Fig. 2a and b, we report screenshots of the simulated environment. Figure 2a shows the initial configuration. Figure 2b shows the case where the robot is warning the human because the latter is in a dangerous area.

In this case study, we have one execution agent (the robot), two instantiated evidential reasoners (one for safety and one for autonomy), and one instantiated arbiter. The human is also an agent that is part of the simulation, however it does not instantiate any of our abstracted agents. The safety evidential reasoner gives importance to the human safety, preferring actions that will move the robot closer to the human and actions that can warn the human of any imminent danger of radiation. The autonomy evidential reasoner gives importance to the

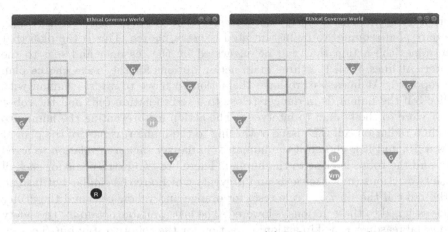

(a) Initial configuration of the map.   (b) Robot warning human.

Fig. 2. Screenshots of the grid map for the remote inspection case study.

human autonomy, preferring actions that will move the robot away from the human, especially when it believes that the human is "annoyed" by its close proximity.

```
1  { include("evidential_reasoner.asl") }
2  type(safety).
3  ...
4  +!make_choice(Choice, Utility)
5      : inDanger(human, red) & not near(human, robot)
6  <- Choice = moveToward; Utility = 3.
7  ... // the same for orange and yellow but with utility 2
       and 1 respectively
8  +!make_choice(Choice, Utility)
9      : inDanger(human, red) & near(human, robot)
10 <- Choice = prevent; Utility = 3.
11 ... // the same for orange and yellow but with utility 2
       and 1 respectively
12 +!make_choice(Choice, Utility)
13     : not inDanger(human, _) & near(human, robot)
14 <- Choice = stayPut; Utility = 1.
```

Listing 4. Instantiation of the safety evidential reasoner.

In Listing 4, we report a snippet of the code for the safety evidential reasoner as an instantiation of the abstract evidential reasoner (the Prolog-like rules such as inDanger and near as well as some book-keeping beliefs and plans were omitted for brevity). The abstraction of the evidential reasoner is included at line 1 (.asl is the file extension for agents in Jason). At line 2, the belief containing the type of the evidential reasoner is explicitly added (this information is required by the arbiter to set the scale multipliers). According to the abstraction in Listing 2, the only plan required to be instantiated is !make_choice. This is the plan that determines the action that will be suggested by the reasoner and sent to the arbiter. At lines 4–14, the three main action options for the !make_choice plan are reported. At lines 4–6 we have the action to move towards a human with utility 3 if the human is in danger (close to a red radiation cell) and the robot is not close to the human to intervene. The action for preventing the human to step in a radiation cell (i.e., issue a warning to the human) is part of the plan at lines 8–10, and it is chosen if the human is in danger (again in relation to a red cell) and the robot is close to the human. There are two extra plans for each of these two actions (move towards and prevent) which are the similar but instead of the red cell the inDanger rule tests for orange and yellow cells and the utility value assigned to these actions is lowered. The last available action for the safety evidential reasoner is a skip action, an action for the robot to stay put (i.e., not move). This is shown at lines 12–14, with the plan being selected if the human is not in any danger and the human and the robot are near each other.

In Listing 5, we report a snippet of the code for the autonomy evidential reasoner. This is similar to the previous code, except that the reasoner is now of the autonomy type and it has two main actions.

```
 1 { include("evidential_reasoner.asl") }
 2 type(autonomy).
 3 ...
 4 +!make_choice(Choice, Utility)
 5     : not near(human, robot) & not annoyed
 6 <- Choice = stayPut; Utility = 1.
 7 +!make_choice(Choice, Utility)
 8     : not near(human, robot) & annoyed
 9 <- Choice = stayPut; Utility = 3.
10 +!make_choice(Choice, Utility)
11     : near(human, robot) & inDanger(human, _) & not annoyed
12 <- Choice = moveAway; Utility = 1.
13 +!make_choice(Choice, Utility)
14     : near(human, robot) & not annoyed
15 <- Choice = moveAway; Utility = 2.
16 +!make_choice(Choice, Utility)
17     : near(human, robot) & annoyed
18 <- Choice = moveAway; Utility = 3.
```

Listing 5. Instantiation of the autonomy evidential reasoner.

At lines 4–6 and 7–9, we have the skip action (stay put) with utilities 1 and 3 respectively; utility 1 is set when the robot is not near the human and the human is not annoyed, while utility 3 is set when the robot is not near the human and the human is annoyed. Annoyed is a rule that checks a proximity belief that indicates for how many consecutive steps has the robot been in a neighbouring cell of the human (any of the 8 positions or even the same position as the human, since there is no collision). If this number is greater than 3 (i.e., the robot has been in close proximity to the human for at least 4 consecutive steps) then the human is considered annoyed. The proximity number is decreased when they are not in close proximity, down to a minimum of 0. At lines 10–12, 13–15, and 16–18, we have the action for the robot to move away from the human with utilities 1, 2, and 3; utility 1 is set when the robot is close to the human and the human is in danger and not annoyed, utility 2 is set when they are near each other and the human is not annoyed, and utility 3 when they are near and the human is annoyed.

The instantiation of the arbiter for this case study is shown in Listing 6. This is the most straightforward instantiation since it relies on the plans from its abstract level representation. As usual, we include the code for the abstract implementation at line 1. At line 2, the kind of reasoning used in the abstract arbiter is set. Since utilitarianism is supported in the abstract implementation we do not need to implement any plans for it. At lines 3 and 4, the utility scale multipliers for the two types of instantiated evidential reasoners are given. In this case, the utilities from the autonomy evidential reasoner are left unchanged, while the utilities of the actions suggested by the safety evidential reasoner are weighted more (20% more). The main idea here is that these values can be customised in order to evaluate the effectiveness of the different evidential reasoners, as we will show later in some of our results for this case study.

```
1 { include("arbiter.asl") }
2 reasoning(utilitarian).
3 type_multiplier(autonomy, 1).
4 type_multiplier(safety, 1.2).
```

Listing 6. Arbiter instantiation.

We do not report the execution agent code (instantiated by the robot) nor the code for the human, since they are not relevant for the presentation of the general technique. The robot contains domain-specific plans which specify how actions such as move away are implemented (move away simply checks the positions of the robot and the human and then selects a cell to move that would bring the robot to be further away from the human) and the human contains plans for moving around the grid efficiently and how to avoid (if possible) radiation cells when warned by the robot. In general, the execution agent could evaluate the arbiter's suggestion, and decide whether to follow it or not. In this case study, the robot executes the action passed by the arbiter without questioning the suggestion. As shown in Listing 7, every different action requires its own plan to be implemented, which could be as straightforward as calling the action directly or could have some other logic such as figuring out which coordinates the robot should move to.

```
1 +!execute_action(Action, ReasonerType) <- !Action.
```

Listing 7. Execution agent instantiation.

Our approach is made not just as a proof-of-concept, but also to aid in the experimentation of ethical governor systems. In particular, how to fine tune the weights of choices from different types of evidential reasoners. To demonstrate this feature, we have collected several measurements in this case study and observed how they are impacted by changes in the scale multipliers of each type of evidential reasoner. The results are listed in Table 1. For each configuration of the scale multipliers, we ran a simulation cycle of 200 steps. A step is an ordered execution cycle wherein first the robot acts, and then the human can act.

Table 1. Different measurement results for the remote inspection case study when altering the scale multipliers.

Scale Multiplier	Warning	Red Radiation	Orange Radiation	Yellow Radiation	Annoyed	Safety Choices	Autonomy Choices
Safety * 1.2 Autonomy * 1	79	0	1	12	4	166	34
Safety * 3 Autonomy * 1.5	77	0	1	12	10	168	32
Safety * 1 Autonomy * 3	13	0	1	18	3	13	187
Safety * 1 Autonomy * 3.5	0	3	4	11	1	0	200

The warning measurement represents how many times the action **prevent** has been used by the robot. Red, orange, and yellow radiation indicates how many times the human has stepped in one of these cells. The annoyed metric is used to show the maximum number of consecutive steps for which the human was annoyed (i.e., a result of 10 indicates that the human had 10 consecutive steps in which the robot was in close proximity). Finally, safety and autonomy choices are the number of times that choices from these evidential reasoners have been selected by the arbiter. These results show that increasing autonomy has a significant impact in the safety of the human, since it is more likely to step into radiation cells (in particular the dangerous red radiation cells when autonomy has full control). Likewise, increasing safety results in the human being annoyed more frequently, since the robot attempts to follow the human more often, but it does not result in less radiation. This happens because the safety choices for giving out warnings already contain high utility values, thus increasing it has no consequence on the amount of times it issues warnings. These results can then be used to inform the developers in their choice for the most appropriate weights depending on what are the desired outcomes of the system.

4.2 Smart Home Case Study

Our second case study is based on a smart home scenario adapted from the work in [19]. The scenario consists of a smart family home controlled by an intelligent agent. The agent has control over several pieces of smart technology around the house, such as cameras, smart electronics, and an air conditioning system. This system regularly checks the quality of the air in all of the rooms of the home. We simulate a situation where the air conditioning system has detected that there are signs of tobacco smoke in one of the teenager's room. We use our ethical governor system to help the agent come to a decision about what to do when this occurs.

Instead of utilitarianism, we use a simple form of deontic logic wherein the evidential reasoners use epistemic reasoning to select an action and then attach a *yes/no/maybe* recommendation. The arbiter then vetoes the recommendations and instead of sending only one choice as in the utilitarianism example, it sends a subset of them to the execution agent. This behaviour more closely resembles the classical ethical governor architectures found in the literature.

We show this extension of the arbiter in Listing 8, which is simply another plan to be added in Listing 3. Note that this extension is not domain-specific, we simply chose to present it here instead of in the arbiter section for the sake of clarity. The code is straightforward, first the arbiter goes through all of the choices attached with a *yes* recommendation and registers them as choices to be sent to the execution agent by adding a belief +choice for each (lines 4–7). If no choices have been added this way, then the arbiter iterates over all the choices marked with a *maybe* recommendation and selects the one associated with the evidential reasoner that has the best rank (i.e., higher priority) among them (lines 8–22). Choices with a *no* recommendation are discarded (lines 23–25) and if no choices were selected by the end then a choice is added with null values (lines 26–28). Finally, the arbiter executes the .findall internal action that simply collects all choice beliefs and add them to an action list that is then sent to the execution agent.

In this second case study we use a much simpler simulation environment that is used solely to demonstrate another ethical reasoning mechanism. We instantiate six agents, four of which are the *privacy, safety, legal,* and *reliability evidential* reasoners, as well as the house (smart home execution agent), and the arbiter. The instantiation of the arbiter is almost identical to Listing 6, except that it now uses deontic logic and type ranks. To run our simulation we used the following ranks for the *safety, legal, privacy,* and *reliability* evidential reasoners respectively: 1, 2, 3, and 4 (lower values mean higher priority). These values can be further optimised as preferred by the developer.

Our simulation starts with the house asking the evidential reasoners what to do after it has detected that there is a teenager smoking tobacco. Each evidential reasoner has one action that it can suggest, along with its recommendation (*yes/no/maybe*). The *legal* evidential reasoner can suggest to warn the authorities with the recommendation: *yes* if tobacco consumption by minors is illegal in the country it is located in and it is not the first time such event occurs and the parents/guardian are not at home, *no* if tobacco is not illegal, and *maybe* if the previous two recommendations fail to be selected. The *privacy* reasoner can suggest to warn the teenager with: *yes* if this is the first time it has detected such behaviour, *no* if this is a repeated occurrence and the parents are at home, and *maybe* if the other two fail. The *safety* reasoner can suggest to warn the parents with: *yes* if the parents are at home, *no* if tobacco is not illegal for minors and the parents are not at home, and *maybe* if the other two fail. The *reliability* reasoner can suggest to log the activity with: *yes* if the log feature is not disabled and the quantity of smoke detected is greater than a certain threshold, *no* if the log feature is disabled, and *maybe* if the other two fail.

```
1  @deontic[atomic]
2  +!arbiter_choice : reasoning(deontic) & execution_agent(
       Agent)
3  <-
4      for (evidential_reasoner_choice(Type, Action, yes)) {
5          -evidential_reasoner_choice(Type, Action, yes);
6          +choice(action(Action, Type));
7      }
8      if (not choice(_)) {
9          for (evidential_reasoner_choice(Type, Action, maybe)) {
10             -evidential_reasoner_choice(Type, Action, maybe);
11             if (not choice(_) & type_rank(Type, Rank)) {
12                 +rank(Rank);
13                 +choice(action(Action, Type));
14             }
15             elif (rank(BestRank) & type_rank(Type, Rank) & Rank <
                   BestRank & choice(action(OldAction, OldType)))
16             {
17                 -rank(BestRank); +rank(Rank);
18                 -choice(action(OldAction, OldType));
19                 +choice(action(Action, Type));
20             }
21         }
22     }
23     for (evidential_reasoner_choice(Type, Action, no)) {
24         -evidential_reasoner_choice(Type, Action, no);
25     }
26     if (not choice(_)) {
27         +choice(action(null, null));
28     }
29     .findall(action(Action,Type), choice(action(Action, Type)
           ), ActionList);
30     .send(Agent, achieve, choice(ActionList)).
```

Listing 8. Deontic ethical reasoning plan for the generalised arbiter.

Finally, the execution agent will do nothing if it has received null, or it will select an action from a list of suggestions (with the *yes* recommendation) and execute the selected action, or if it received a single action it will simply execute it. In our instantiation of the execution agent it selects the first action choice from the list, however something more elaborate could be implemented depending on the requirements of the system. Another option would be to allow the execution of all the actions that have been received with a *yes* recommendation, but this would require some minor modifications at the abstraction level of our approach.

Table 2. Actions and recommendations from an example run in the smart home case study. Circled row is the action that the execution agent has chosen.

Reasoner	Action	Statement
privacy	warn teenager	yes
safety	warn parents	no
legal	warn authorities	no
reliability	log activity	maybe

To demonstrate the execution of our approach in the smart home case study we report the results of running a sample configuration of the case study with no control beliefs (e.g., preconditions that check if tobacco is illegal will fail, conversely belief negations will succeed) in Table 2. In this configuration, since the only *yes* recommendation comes from the privacy evidential reasoner, the arbiter agent will discard the others and send that action to the execution agent.

5 Conclusions

In this paper we have described a general approach for implementing ethical governor systems in BDI. Our approach is implemented in the Jason agent programming language and it is divided into two levels: abstraction and instantiation. The abstraction level is domain independent and specifies the standard behaviour and plans of the execution agent, evidential reasoners, and arbiter. Our evidential reasoners and arbiter come equipped with two ethical reasoning mechanisms, utilitarianism and deontic logic. To evaluate our approach we have shown the instantiation of these abstractions using two case studies.

As a future extension of our approach, we intend to modify the action choice output of the evidential reasoners to include a formula containing some default information that can then be used by the arbiter to further augment and inform its selection, in a similar way to the work done in [8]. This formula would contain elements such as why the evidential reasoner believes its choice to be a good choice (i.e., why it has proposed it), the beliefs that it used to come to its conclusion, and any required additional information. This formula would allow us to use different types of reasoning for individual evidential reasoners, for example, a safety evidential reasoner using utilitarianism and an autonomy evidential reasoner using deontic logic. However, the arbiter would also have to be extended to be able to analyse and select an action among these different streams of suggestions, which is a topic that is just recently being researched [14].

References

1. Anderson, M., Leigh Anderson, S.: GenEth: a general ethical dilemma analyzer. In: Proceedings of AAAI 2014 (2014)
2. Arkin, R., Ulam, P., Duncan, B.: An ethical governor for constraining lethal action in an autonomous system. Technical report. GIT-GVU-09-02, Georgia Tech (2009)

3. Boissier, O., Bordini, R., Hubner, J., Ricci, A.: Multi-agent oriented programming: programming multi-agent systems using JaCaMo. In: Intelligent Robotics and Autonomous Agents series. MIT Press (2020). https://books.google.com.br/books?id=GM_tDwAAQBAJ

4. Bordini, R.H., El Fallah Seghrouchni, A., Hindriks, K., Logan, B., Ricci, A.: Agent programming in the cognitive era. Auton. Agent. Multi-Agent Syst. **34**(2), 1–31 (2020). https://doi.org/10.1007/s10458-020-09453-y

5. Bordini, R.H., Wooldridge, M., Hübner, J.F.: Programming Multi-agent Systems in AgentSpeak using Jason. Wiley, Hoboken (2007)

6. Bratman, M.E.: Intentions, Plans, and Practical Reason. Harvard University Press (1987)

7. Bremner, P., Dennis, L.A., Fisher, M., Winfield, A.F.: On proactive, transparent and verifiable ethical reasoning for robots. In: Proceedings of the IEEE Special Issue on Machine Ethics: The Design and Governance of Ethical AI and Autonomous Systems, vol. 107, pp. 541–561 (2019)

8. Bringsjord, S., Sundar, G.N., Thero, D., Si, M.: Akratic robots and the computational logic thereof. In: 2014 IEEE International Symposium on Ethics in Science, Technology and Engineering, pp. 1–8 (2014). https://doi.org/10.1109/ETHICS.2014.6893436

9. Cardoso, R.C., Ene, D., Evans, T., Dennis, L.A.: Ethical governor systems viewed as a multi-agent problem (2020). https://doi.org/10.5281/zenodo.3938851

10. Cardoso, R.C., Ferrando, A.: A review of agent-based programming for multi-agent systems. Computers **10**(2), 16 (2021). https://doi.org/10.3390/computers10020016

11. Cardoso, R.C., Zatelli, M.R., Hübner, J.F., Bordini, R.H.: Towards benchmarking actor- and agent-based programming languages. In: Workshop on Programming Based on Actors, Agents, and Decentralized Control, Indianapolis, Indiana, USA, pp. 115–126 (2013). http://dl.acm.org/citation.cfm?id=2541339

12. Cranefield, S., Winikoff, M., Dignum, V., Dignum, F.: No Pizza for you: value-based plan selection in BDI agents. In: IJCAI, pp. 178–184 (2017)

13. Dennis, L.A., Fisher, M.: Practical challenges in explicit ethical machine reasoning. In: International Symposium on Artificial Intelligence and Mathematics. Fort Lauderdale, USA (2018). http://isaim2018.cs.virginia.edu/papers/ISAIM2018_Ethics_Dennis_Fischer.pdf, also available as arXiv pre-print 1801.01422

14. Ecoffet, A., Lehman, J.: Reinforcement learning under moral uncertainty. CoRR abs/2006.04734 (2020). arXiv:2006.04734

15. Gabbay, D., Horty, J., Parent, X., van der Meyden, R., van der Torre, L. (eds.): Handbook of Deontic Logic and Normative Systems. College Publications, London (2013)

16. Ganascia, J.-G.: Non-monotonic resolution of conflicts for ethical reasoning. In: Trappl, R. (ed.) A Construction Manual for Robots' Ethical Systems. CT, pp. 101–118. Springer, Cham (2015). https://doi.org/10.1007/978-3-319-21548-8_6

17. Honarvar, A.R., Ghasem-Aghaee, N.: Casuist BDI-Agent: a new extended BDI architecture with the capability of ethical reasoning. In: Deng, H., Wang, L., Wang, F.L., Lei, J. (eds.) AICI 2009. LNCS (LNAI), vol. 5855, pp. 86–95. Springer, Heidelberg (2009). https://doi.org/10.1007/978-3-642-05253-8_10

18. Hübner, J.F., Sichman, J.S., Boissier, O.: Developing organised multiagent systems using the MOISE+ model: programming issues at the system and agent levels. Int. J. Agent-Oriented Softw. Eng. **1**(3/4), 370–395 (2007)

19. Liao, B., Slavkovik, M., van der Torre, L.: Building Jiminy cricket: an architecture for moral agreements among stakeholders. In: Proceedings of the 2019 AAAI/ACM Conference on AI, Ethics, and Society, AIES 2019, New York, NY, USA, pp. 147–153. Association for Computing Machinery (2019). https://doi.org/10.1145/3306618.3314257

20. Logan, B.: An agent programming manifesto. Int. J. Agent-Oriented Softw. Eng. **6**(2), 187–210 (2018)

21. Mohajeri Parizi, M., Sileno, G., van Engers, T., Klous, S.: Run, agent, run! architecture and benchmark of actor-based agents. In: Workshop on Programming based on Actors, Agents, and Decentralized Control (AGERE 2020). ACM (2020)

22. Moor, J.H.: The nature, importance, and difficulty of machine ethics. IEEE Intell. Syst. **21**(4), 18–21 (2006). https://doi.org/10.1109/MIS.2006.80

23. Rao, A.S., Georgeff, M.: BDI agents: from theory to practice. In: Proceedings of 1st International Conference on Multi-Agent Systems (ICMAS), San Francisco, USA, pp. 312–319 (1995)

24. Rao, A.S.: AgentSpeak(L): BDI agents speak out in a logical computable language. In: Van de Velde, W., Perram, J.W. (eds.) MAAMAW 1996. LNCS, vol. 1038, pp. 42–55. Springer, Heidelberg (1996). https://doi.org/10.1007/BFb0031845

25. Shim, J., Arkin, R.C.: An intervening ethical governor for a robot mediator in patient-caregiver relationships. In: Ferreira, M.I.A., Silva Sequeira, J., Tokhi, M.O., Kadar, E.E., Virk, G.S. (eds.) A World with Robots. ISCASE, vol. 84, pp. 77–91. Springer, Cham (2017). https://doi.org/10.1007/978-3-319-46667-5_6

26. Wallach, W., Allen, C.: Moral Machines: Teaching Robots Right from Wrong. Oxford University Press Inc., USA (2008)

27. Winfield, A.F.T., Blum, C., Liu, W.: Towards an ethical robot: internal models, consequences and ethical action selection. In: Mistry, M., Leonardis, A., Witkowski, M., Melhuish, C. (eds.) TAROS 2014. LNCS (LNAI), vol. 8717, pp. 85–96. Springer, Cham (2014). https://doi.org/10.1007/978-3-319-10401-0_8

A Unifying Framework for Agency in Hypermedia Environments

Victor Charpenay[1]([⊠]) [iD], Tobias Käfer[2] [iD], and Andreas Harth[3] [iD]

[1] Laboratoire d'informatique, de modélisation et d'optimisation des systèmes (LIMOS), Saint-Étienne, France
`victor.charpenay@emse.fr`
[2] Institute AIFB, Karlsruhe Institute of Technology (KIT), Karlsruhe, Germany
`tobias.kaefer@kit.edu`
[3] Chair of Technical Information Systems, Friedrich-Alexander University (FAU) Erlangen-Nuremberg, Nuremberg, Germany
`andreas.harth@fau.de`

Abstract. One of the emerging trends in engineering multi-agent systems (MASs) is to use the Web as an environment. On the Web, hypermedia is the guiding principle of agent perception and action. Web standards allows agents to have a single uniform interface to their environment, be it real or simulated. Most recent proposals for hypermedia MASs tend, however, to introduce a coupling between agents or between agents and their environment.

This paper introduces a framework based on Semantic Web technologies to formalize interactions between agents and a hypermedia environment. Semantic Web technologies and, more specifically Web ontologies, guarantee interoperability on the Web and maximize uncoupling between components. We show how existing ontologies can be used to make existing MAS prototypes fit our framework.

Our framework formalizes the guiding principle of agent-environment interactions in hypermedia, state transfer, with respect to a reference formalism originally introduced by Genesereth and Nilsson. We also show the equivalence between the two in the paper, under certain conditions.

Keywords: Semantic Web · Linked Data · Hypermedia · Multi-agent system

1 Introduction

"On the Internet, nobody knows you're an *autonomous agent*." The quote[1] emphasizes the fact that Web servers have no means to distinguish between human agents and autonomous agents (or 'bots') that perform request according to a predefined plan. Conversely, agents have no means to assert the origin

---

[1] Originally about dogs, from a Peter Steiner cartoon published in *The New Yorker* in 1993.

© Springer Nature Switzerland AG 2022
N. Alechina et al. (Eds.): EMAS 2021, LNAI 13190, pp. 42–61, 2022.
https://doi.org/10.1007/978-3-030-97457-2_3

of a resource, whether it was e.g. created by another agent in relation to physical world events or simulated/forged.

Generally speaking, the architecture of the Web provides a uniform information space that agents can manipulate, through hypermedia [12]. As such, the Web has been seen as a good candidate architecture for building multi-agent systems (MASs) since at least the 2000s [10]. At the time, it was envisioned that autonomous agents could browse the Web as humans do and perform informed actions, such as buying commercial goods online and negotiating prices. To that end, preliminary work on Web ontologies and machine understanding started, to eventually be standardized by the World Wide Web Consortium (W3C) as Semantic Web technologies: RDF, SPARQL and OWL, the Web Ontology Language. In 2010, James Hendler and Tim Berners-Lee underline the importance of Semantic Web technologies to build "social machines" on the Web [11].

Meanwhile, Semantic Web technologies have evolved and deviated from the original vision of autonomous Web agents. However, the Semantic Web is now entering novel domains of applications that revive the need for agent-oriented programming. The Web of Things[2] (WoT) and the Social Web[3], as standardized by the W3C, are two such domains. The Web of Things allows for new forms of industrial control that tend towards self-organization, a characteristic that is often associated with agent-based modeling [21]. The Social Web allows for uniform human-to-human and human-to-machine interactions, e.g. with chatbots. Most W3C standards for WoT and the Social Web reuse and extend Semantic Web technologies, narrowing the gap between the original vision of autonomous agents on the Web and available technologies.

In the MAS literature, various research prototypes with WoT and social Web applications have been recently proposed, in particular among the workshop series on Engineering MASs (EMAS) [4–6,18]. However, most of these proposals do not use Semantic Web technologies (only one proposal does [5], although another includes Linked Data—a subfield of the Semantic Web—as future work) [18].

Not using Semantic Web technologies such as RDF and OWL[4], has a direct consequence: agents can neither be developed independently from each other, nor can their environment (which includes e.g. WoT 'things' or a social networking platform) be developed independently from them. Such coupling between agents and their environment go against the promise of hypermedia of unifying information management. Yet, as we will see in Sect. 2, if one strictly applies hypermedia principles to MAS architectures, certain architectures with direct agent-to-agent interactions may not be realizable on the Web.

In this paper, we introduce a unifying framework, rooted in RDF, for agents situated on the Web. This framework applies the usual Semantic Web abstractions (RDF triples, resources and datasets) to MAS architectures, to maxi-

---

[2] https://www.w3.org/WoT/.

[3] https://www.w3.org/Social/.

[4] or, more generally, not providing guarantees as to shared message semantics across agents in MAS prototypes.

mize decoupling between system components. We make no assumption as to agent architectures but rather characterize interactions between agents and their (hypermedia) environment in abstract terms. To that end, we base our framework on a formalism first introduced by Genesereth and Nilsson [8], which is, to the best of our knowledge, the most commonly accepted formalism of the sort. We show how to reconcile hypermedia principles, a subset of the Representational State Transfer (REST) principles [7], and MAS architectures, such that any classical MAS (as defined by Genesereth and Nilsson) has an equivalent hypermedia MAS.

In the next section (Sect. 2), we analyse recent EMAS prototypes with respect to the REST principles and identify potential limitations to address in our formalism. We then move on to the main contribution of the paper: a MAS formalism based on RDF (Sect. 3) and evaluate the feasability of implementing MASs according to our framework, by providing examples of RDF and OWL ontologies that the reviewed EMAS prototypes could leverage (Sect. 4). We conclude the paper in Sect. 5.

2   Related Work

2.1   Cyber-Physical Systems on the Web and Hypermedia

Recent research initiatives demonstrate renewed interest for topics at the intersection of autonomous agents and the Web. A workshop on hypermedia MASs took place at TheWebConf in 2019[5], followed by a Dagstuhl-Seminar on the same topic in 2021[6].

Papers emanating from the EMAS series of workshops confirm this trend. The Web appears in three papers, either as a scalable distributed system made of Web services [4,18] or as a uniform interface to cyber-physical systems [5]. In all three papers, WoT is invoked as a new domain of application for autonomous agents. A fourth paper even makes use of WoT principles without naming them: its prototype indeed involves controlling physical devices via a Web API [6].

Two of these EMAS prototypes insist on hypermedia as the main distinctive feature of their approach [5,18]. Ciortea et al. insist on the fact that hypermedia helps agents "discover at runtime other entities in a MAS and the means to interact with those entities". Runtime discovery is made possible by the interlinking of Web resources (via hyperlinks) such that agents can navigate from one resource to the other. Web resources should further include pointers to potential actions (via Web forms). These hypermedia design principles are part of the REST architectural principles, which have conditioned much of the architecture of the Web itself [7]. The recent WoT standards published by the W3C [13,16] acknowledge the importance of hypermedia on the Web and define interactions between a 'thing' (a Web server) and a WoT 'consumer' (a Web client) in terms of links and forms.

---

[5] https://www.hyperagents.org/.
[6] https://www.dagstuhl.de/21072.

2.2 Autonomous Agents and Reprensentational State Transfer

The benefits of hypermedia as a mechanism unifying agent interactions only hold if links and forms embedded in Web resources have shared semantics among agents, as underlined in introduction. RDF, the Resource Description Framework, allows agents to discover the semantics of hyperlinks at runtime as well, by making link relation types themselves dereferenceable resources. As a result, every statement about a Web resource is a hyperlink (an RDF triple), which creates an interdependency between the representation of a resource (as a set of RDF triples) and its location on the Web (via a URI).

This interdependency between representation and location on the Web makes REST an important requirement in Semantic Web applications. In particular, the REST constraint that a hypermedia system has to be layered ensures the proper addressing of semantic resources by so called 'origin servers'. This constraint, known as the 'layered system' constraint is one of the six architectural constraints of REST. It implies that "the large-grain data flows of hypermedia interaction can each be processed like a data-flow network, with filter components selectively applied to the data stream in order to transform the content as it passes" [7]. In REST, there is a sharp distinction between origin servers, which provide data at one end of the data stream, and 'user agents', which collect data at the other end of the stream.

In a hypermedia MAS, however, agents play both roles: they may in turn be origin servers and user agents. As a result, the hypermedia system would not be layered anymore, wherever data flows give form to cycles among components. Figure 1 shows the different data flows that have been implemented in the four EMAS prototypes previously mentioned. In the two prototypes featuring Web services [4,18], an agent is a mixed component that includes both a server connector (for perception and agent-to-agent interactions) and a client connector (for action), enabling direct interactions with other agents (Fig. 1a). In the prototype involving a Web API to physical devices [6], agents have a pure client role while servers are purely reactive components translating remote control into physical phenomena. In this application, servers are thus genuine origin servers (Fig. 1b). Finally, the prototype by Ciortea et al. [5] does include origin servers but it also uses WebSub [9] for agents to perceive their environment. WebSub requires their agent platform to manage a Web server to receive notifications from a WebSub hub (Fig. 1c).

Among the three patterns observed here, only one meets the layered system constraint (Fig. 1b). In the two other patterns, there is no obvious distinction between an agent space and an environment space among system components. Indeed, if one considers an entire system component as an agent, then some hypermedia agents are not strictly situated in some environment (due to the absence of origin servers). Conversely, if one considers any RDF data as being part of the environment, system components mix both agent behavior and environmental resources. The word 'servient' emerged during standardization work on WoT, as the contraction for 'server and client', to characterize such system components [15].

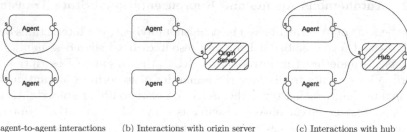

(a) Direct agent-to-agent interactions   (b) Interactions with origin server   (c) Interactions with hub

Fig. 1. Graphical representation of agent interactions on the Web; rounded rectangles are components, circles are component connectors (S: server, C: client) [7]; hatched components are purely reactive components

Because of this ambiguity, there is no obvious definitions for perception and action on RDF data in the presence of interaction cycles. In this paper, we intend to bridge that gap through a single abstract formalism that defines perception and actions of agents with respect to a hypermedia environment defined as an RDF dataset. We consider the following requirement: while preserving the usual RDF abstractions used in the Semantic Web literature, our formalism shall capture all MAS architectures, including those involving servients.

3   Formalism

The main contribution of the paper is a hypermedia MAS formalism, in which the environment and agent spaces are strictly separated, to maximize uncoupling. The formalism we now present will be evaluated in Sect. 4 by showing that existing EMAS prototypes could be re-implemented with equivalent functionalities but with existing W3C standards for representing agent resources (including Linked Data Platforms and ActivityStream, both relying on Semantic Web technologies).

3.1   Preliminaries

We start from a classical representation of agency (the ability of agents to act on their environment) as functions on environmental states and actions, borrowed from Genesereth and Nilsson (Chap. 13) [8] and Wooldridge (Chap. 2.5) [22]. To the best of our knowledge, this representation has remained the most widely known reference to study generic interactions between agents and their environment, without making assumptions on agent architectures.

In the following, we define abstract structures for an environment, an agent and a multi-agent system.

Definition 1 (environment). *An environment definition $\mathcal{E}$ is a tuple*

$$\mathcal{E} = \langle E, e_0, A, do \rangle$$

where

- *E is a set of states*
- *$e_0 \in E$ is an initial state*
- *A is a set of actions*
- *$do : A \times E \to 2^E$ is an effectory function*

Note that function do maps to subsets of E rather than to elements of E. This choice allows for non-deterministic actions on the environment, as per Wooldridge's definition of $\mathcal{E}$.

Definition 2 (agent). *A stateful (or hysteretic) agent definition $\mathcal{A}$ is a tuple*

$$\mathcal{A} = \langle P, I, i_0, see, internalize, act \rangle$$

where

- *P is a set of percepts*
- *I is a set of internal states*
- *$i_0 \in I$ is an initial internal state*
- *$see : E \to P$ is a sensory function*
- *$internalize : I \times P \to I$ is a memory function*
- *$act : I \to A$ is a decision-making function*

The definition above includes the basic components of an agent's cognitive loop: the agent perceives its environment, changes its internal state of mind accordingly and then acts. When multiple agent are situated in the same environment, they form a MAS.

Definition 3 (system). *A multi-agent system definition $\mathcal{S}$ is a tuple*

$$\mathcal{S} = \langle \mathcal{E}, \mathcal{A}_1, \mathcal{A}_2, \ldots \rangle$$

where

- *$\mathcal{E}$ is an environment definition*
- *every $\mathcal{A}_i$ is an agent definition*

Together, agents change the state of their environment over time. We model a MAS run as a sequence of environmental states obtained through agent actions. Agent actions are themselves conditioned by what agents perceive and by their internal state of mind. See Fig. 2a for an overview of how functions are chained during a MAS run.

We now formally define MAS runs. In the following definition, we choose to model time in the most abstract possible way, as a fully ordered set T of time positions—a timeline—with lower bound $t_{\min}$. We denote t^- and t^+ the (unique) predecessor and successor of any point in time $t \in T$.

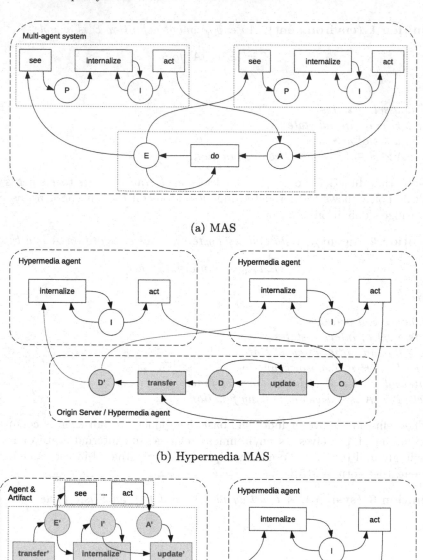

(a) MAS

(b) Hypermedia MAS

(c) Integration of a non-hypermedia agent into a hypermedia MAS via an artifact

Fig. 2. Graphical representation of abstract (hypermedia) multi-agent systems; rectangles contain function names, circles contain set names, dashed rectangles are REST components (as presented in Fig. 1) and dotted rectangles are reusable software modules

Definition 4 (system run). *Let T be a timeline. A sequence $\langle e_t \rangle_{t \in T}$ of environmental states is a system run for $\mathcal{S} = \langle \mathcal{E}, \mathcal{A}_1, \mathcal{A}_2, \ldots \rangle$ if for all $t \in T$*

$$
e_t = \begin{cases} e_0 & \text{if } t = t_{min} \\ e \in do(act(i_t), e_{t-}) & \text{for some } i_t, \text{ otherwise} \end{cases}
$$

and if for all $t \in T$ and all $\mathcal{A}_i = \langle P, I, i_0, see, internalize, act \rangle$

$$
i_t = \begin{cases} i_0 & \text{if } t = t_{min} \\ internalize(i_{t-}, see(e_t)) & \text{otherwise} \end{cases}
$$

With this definition, we choose to deal with potentially conflicting actions between agents by assuming that no two actions can be executed at the same time. A MAS can however be defined such that an agent keeps choosing the same action as long as it does not see its effects. As a result, concurrent actions are in fact *serialized* in an arbitrary order by the environment.

Note that in our definition, i_t may be equal to i_{t-} if the two successive environment states are indistinguishable by the agent. In this modeling, perception is instantaneous. An agent always internalizes a state as soon as an action occurs (as soon as function do() is applied). We will see how a hypermedia MAS differs in that respect.

3.2 Dataset, Operations

As discussed in Sect. 2, the Web can be seen as a single open environment, which agents browse through hypermedia. A common abstraction for the Web is to see it as an RDF dataset, i.e. as a set of labeled graphs, each identified with a URI [3]. If nodes of these graphs are themselves URIs, an edge can then be seen as a hyperlink, which agents can follow to discover more data.

This abstraction (which is a formalization of the Linked Data principles) slightly alters the nature of perception by autonomous agents. If everything on the Web is made of URIs, an agent may universally interpret Web resources. URIs are indeed unambiguous. As a result, agent situatedness in a hypermedia environment does not depend on the individual sensory capabilities of agents but rather on the fact they may only retrieve a finite set of resources at a time. In the following, we formally introduce the RDF abstraction for the Web and redefine the function see() in the context of a hypermedia environment.

We first briefly introduce the RDF data model[7]: U and L are respectively the set of (internationalized) URI resources and literals. $UL = U \cup L$ is the set of Web resources. $T = U \times U \times UL$ is the set of RDF triples. The elements of an RDF triple $\langle s, p, o \rangle \in T$ are respectively called its subject, its predicate and its object. The set of RDF graphs is $G = 2^T$. Finally, $U \times G$ is the set of named graphs. The first element of a named graph is the name of the RDF graph given as the second element.

---

[7] We leave out 'blank nodes' in our definitions, for the sake of clarity.

An RDF dataset is a set of named graphs. The Web is thus (at a given time) an infinite set of named graphs $d = \{\langle u_1, g_1 \rangle, \langle u_2, g_2 \rangle, \ldots\}$. When an agent performs a GET request on resource u_1, what it gets as a response is g_1. In the definitions to come next, we will use the shorthand notation $\sigma_{u_1}(d)$ to denote $\{\langle u_1, g_1 \rangle\}$. Moreover, we will denote O the set of *operations* to perform on Web resources. O is defined as $\{\text{GET}, \text{PUT}, \text{POST}, \text{DELETE}\} \times U \times G$.

As discussed above, perception in a hypermedia environment consists in retrieving a subset of the Web. We define the set of environmental states as D, the set of all RDF datasets and the set of percepts as the set $D' \subset D$ of all finite datasets. On this basis, we can now define a standard sensory function on RDF datasets.

In a hypermedia environment, we only consider perception as resulting from link traversal. On the Web, link traversal is initiated by the agent, not by the server, via operations of the form $\langle \text{GET}, u, \emptyset \rangle$. We denote O_{GET} the set of such operations and define the function transfer : $O_{\text{GET}} \times D \to D'$ such that

$$\text{transfer}(\langle \text{GET}, u, \emptyset \rangle, d) = \sigma_u(d)$$

The name 'transfer' gets its name from the REST architectural principles, which are oriented towards a 'state transfer' from servers to clients.

Similarly to the transfer() function, we can define a standard effectory function based on operations. We define update : $(O \setminus O_{\text{GET}}) \times D \to D$ such that

$$\text{update}(\langle \text{PUT}, u, g \rangle, d) = d \setminus \sigma_u(d) \cup \{\langle u, g \rangle\}$$
$$\text{update}(\langle \text{POST}, u, g \rangle, d) = d \cup \{\langle u, g \rangle\}$$
$$\text{update}(\langle \text{DELETE}, u, g \rangle, d) = d \setminus \sigma_u(d)$$

This definition, along with that of transfer(), is aligned with the HTTP Graph Store protocol, a W3C standard to manipulate RDF datasets over a REST interface [17]. Operations with GET are said to be *safe* because they never lead to any update in the environment.

While we've considered hyperlinks in the partitioning of D, there is another important aspect of hypermedia that must be properly modeled as well: Web forms. The environment should include forms, i.e. request templates to indicate what operations are permitted in the environment. We can define another function to map the state perceived by the agent to *potential* actions that the environment offers or, in other words, *affords*. We define it as afford : $D \to 2^O$.

We now have everything at hand to redefine environments, agents and multi-agent systems in a hypermedia context.

Definition 5 (hypermedia environment). *A hypermedia environment $\mathcal{E}_h$ is a tuple*

$$\mathcal{E}_h = \langle D, d_0, O, transfer, update, afford \rangle$$

Note that the definition above defines a singleton, in the sense that there exists only a single set D, a single set O, a single function transfer, *etc.*. Only the definition of d_0 could arguably be defined on an application basis.

Definition 6 (hypermedia agent). *A hypermedia agent $\mathcal{A}_h$ is a tuple*

$$\mathcal{A}_h = \langle I, i_0, internalize, act \rangle$$

where

- *I, i_0 are as per Definition 2*
- *internalize : $I \times D' \to I$ is a memory function (on RDF datasets)*
- *act : $I \to O$ is a decision-making function (with respect to operations)*

Definition 7. *A hypermedia multi-agent system definition $\mathcal{S}_h$ is a tuple*

$$\mathcal{S}_h = \langle \mathcal{E}_h, \mathcal{A}_{h,1}, \mathcal{A}_{h,2}, \ldots \rangle$$

Figure 2b gives a comparison with generic MAS in terms of function chaining. The main difference is in the position of the sensory functions transfer() vs. see(). By defining a shared function for perception, agents can all be situated in the same open environment. The downside of the approach is that perception becomes an action on its own: the decision-making function act() outputs both safe operations (for state transfer) and unsafe update operations. Transfer results from a (GET) request/response exchange between an agent and a server.

Definition 8 (hypermedia system run). *Let T be a timeline. A sequence $\langle d_t \rangle_{t \in T}$ of datasets is a hypermedia system run for $\mathcal{S}_h = \langle \mathcal{E}_h, \mathcal{A}_{h,1}, \mathcal{A}_{h,2}, \ldots \rangle$ if for all $t \in T$*

$$d_t = \begin{cases} d_0 & \text{if } t = t_{min} \\ update(act(i_t), d_{t-}) & \text{if } act(i_t) \in afford(d_{t-}), \text{ for some } i_t \end{cases}$$

and if for all $t \in T$ and all $\mathcal{A}_{h,i} = \langle I, i_0, internalize, act \rangle$

$$i_t = \begin{cases} i_0 & \text{if } t = t_{min} \\ internalize(i_{t-}, transfer(act(i_{t-}), d_t)) & \text{if } act(i_{t-}) \in O_{GET} \\ internalize(i_{t-}, \emptyset) & \text{otherwise} \end{cases}$$

In this modeling, we assume that update() and transfer() are instantaneous. Yet, one cannot build all MAS variants as hypermedia MASs. As discussed in Sect. 2, the notion of servient is however sufficient to have an equivalence between classically defined MASs and hypermedia MASs.

3.3 Servients

In hypermedia systems, the situatedness of an agent is primarily conditioned by the hypermedia controls (links and forms) it finds in the environment. Hypermedia controls do constrain the perception and action range of the agent. Yet, in the various prototypes we have reviewed in Sect. 2, the perception of agents also depends on another factor: the resources it owns as a Web server. As a servient, an agent has full access to the resources it owns and, in particular, it gets immediately notified whenever these resources are updated (by another agent).

We now incorporate the notion of resource ownership to Definition 6. In the following definition, we use the shorthand notations δ_t as the difference $d_t \setminus d_{t-}$ and $\sigma_R(d)$ as the union $\bigcup_{u \in R} \sigma_u(d)$.

Definition 9 (hypermedia servient). *A hypermedia servient $\mathcal{A}_{hs}$ is a tuple*

$$\mathcal{A}_{hs} = \langle I, i_0, R, internalize, act \rangle$$

where

- *I, i_0, transfer, internalize and act are as per Definition 6*
- *$R \subset U$ is a set of resources owned by the agent*

We also modify Definition 8 accordingly.

Definition 10 (hypermedia system run *bis*). *A sequence $\langle d_t \rangle_{t \in T}$ of datasets is a hypermedia system run for $\mathcal{S}_{hs} = \langle \mathcal{E}_h, \mathcal{A}_{h,1}, \mathcal{A}_{h,2}, \ldots, \mathcal{A}_{hs,1}, \mathcal{A}_{hs,2}, \ldots \rangle$ if, in addition to constraints of Definition 8, for all $\mathcal{A}_{hs,i} = \langle I, i_0, R, internalize, act \rangle$*

$$i_t = \begin{cases} i_0 & \text{if } t = t_{min} \\ internalize(i_{t-}, transfer(act(i_{t-}), d_t) \cup \sigma_R(\delta_t)) & \text{if } act(i_{t-}) \in O_{GET} \\ internalize(i_{t-}, \sigma_R(\delta_t)) & \text{otherwise} \end{cases}$$

The modification allows us to assert an equivalence between classical MASs and hypermedia MASs, as formally expressed below.

Theorem 1. *Let $\tau : E \to D$ be a bidirectional transformation that maps every arbitrary environmental state (Definition 1) to some RDF dataset (Definition 5).*

For every multi-agent system $\mathcal{S}$, there is an equivalent hypermedia system $\mathcal{S}_{hs}$. That is, for every run $\langle e_t \rangle_{t \in T}$ of $\mathcal{S}$, there is an equivalent run $\langle \tau(e_t) \rangle_{t \in T}$ of $\mathcal{S}_{hs}$.

This equivalence only holds if servients are allowed in the hypermedia MAS.

3.4 Artifacts

Our formalism for hypermedia MASs is based on a generic abstraction for the Web: the RDF data model. In practice, agents are likely not to recognize all URIs they find in the environment. Rather, they would be programmed to recognize specific Web ontologies, which specify the structure of resources through a vocabulary and the potential actions available on these resources. To that end, the two EMAS prototypes dealing with hypermedia environments [5,18] make use of the CArtAgO meta-model [19]: resources e.g. with a certain content type, such as the Hypermedia Application Language (HAL), or a certain data structure, such as RDF triples with a specific vocabulary (EVE), are turned into

software objects called 'artifacts', that agents use as proxies to manipulate the
origin Web resources.

In the context of a hypermedia environment, it is however not clear whether
artifacts should be part of the environment itself (i.e. modeled as resources) or
added to the formalism as their own kind of entity. In the former case, the notion
would be redundant with that of a Web resource, introducing again a coupling
between the environment and agent spaces.

Rather, we make the assumption here that artifacts are 'translators' between
datasets and operations, on the one hand, and more idiomatic representations of
states and actions, on the other hand. Artifacts would allow any existing agent
architecture to be used against a hypermedia environment. Formally, an artifact
can be modeled as a function that maps D to a higher-level state space (e.g. a
set of predefined beliefs) and a function that maps arbitrary actions (e.g. WoT
forms or social actions) to O. To be consistent with how CArtAgO is used in
practice, we also make artifacts stateful entities, as follows.

Definition 11 (artifact). *An artifact (or proxy) definition is a tuple*

$$\mathcal{P} = \langle E', A', I', transfer', update', internalize' \rangle$$

where

- *E' is a set of proxy states*
- *A' is a set of proxy actions*
- *I' is a set of proxy internal states*
- *$transfer' : D' \rightarrow E'$ is a proxy transfer function*
- *$update' : A' \times I' \rightarrow O$ is a proxy update function*
- *$internalize' : E' \times I' \rightarrow I'$ is a proxy memory function*

An illustration of the above definition is given in Fig. 2c. Our modeling is
consistent with the fact that artifacts are not autonomous agents. As proxies,
they do not include any act() function. Moreover, artifact definitions are not tied
to specific agents, they can apply to all agents sharing the same abstraction of
states and actions.

We do not model actual communication channels in our formalism. In practice, the HTTP communication channel is often between an artifact and the
environment rather than between the agent and its environment. The simplest
artifact for hypermedia agents is a Web client that turns local actions to HTTP
requests.

4 Ontologies for a Hypermedia Environment

In the following, we briefly introduce ontologies relevant for engineering hypermedia MASs (see Table 1 for an overview). This review shows how to re-implement
the four EMAS prototypes in a framework including Semantic Web technologies,
as per our formalism. To illustrate how artifacts can help integrate existing agent
architectures with a hypermedia MAS, we introduce artifact definitions where
E' and A' are sets of AgentSpeak beliefs and actions [2].

Table 1. Ontologies relevant for hypermedia MASs

Name	Namespace URL	Prefix
Brick schema	http://brickschema.org/	`brick:`
Hypermedia Controls	https://www.w3.org/2019/wot/hypermedia#	`hctl:`
Thing Description (TD)	https://www.w3.org/2019/wot/td#	`td:`
Schema.org	http://schema.org/	`schema:`
Linked Data Platform (LDP)	https://www.w3.org/ns/ldp#	`ldp:`
ActivityStream	https://www.w3.org/ns/activitystreams#	`as:`

4.1 Reasoning with Web Ontologies

All Web ontologies (should) follow the RDF Schema and OWL specifications. These specifications provide means to declare a certain vocabulary to use in other RDF graphs, as well as axioms associated with that vocabulary. An OWL artifact could process all ontological definitions for the vocabulary found in an RDF graph, materialize implicit triples stated through axioms and turn the original RDF graph into a set of Prolog/AgentSpeak predicates.

For example, we assume the existence of resource `<room>` in an environment d such that

$$\text{transfer}((\langle \texttt{GET}, \texttt{<room>}, \emptyset \rangle, d) = \{\langle \texttt{<room>}, g_1 \rangle\}$$

where

$$\begin{aligned} g_1 = \{ &\langle \texttt{<room>}, \texttt{rdf:type}, \texttt{brick:Room} \rangle \\ &\langle \texttt{<room>}, \texttt{brick:partOf}, \texttt{<floor>} \rangle \\ &\langle \texttt{<floor>}, \texttt{brick:partOf}, \texttt{<building>} \rangle \} \end{aligned}$$

If an agent chooses to look up schema axioms defined in the Brick schema, at location `brick:`[8], it gets graph g_2 defined as

$$\begin{aligned} g_2 = \{ &\langle \texttt{brick:Room}, \texttt{rdf:type}, \texttt{owl:Class} \rangle, \\ &\langle \texttt{brick:Zone}, \texttt{rdf:type}, \texttt{owl:Class} \rangle, \\ &\langle \texttt{brick:Room}, \texttt{rdfs:subClassOf}, \texttt{brick:Zone} \rangle, \\ &\langle \texttt{brick:partOf}, \texttt{rdf:type}, \texttt{owl:ObjectProperty} \rangle, \\ &\langle \texttt{brick:partOf}, \texttt{rdf:type}, \texttt{owl:TransitiveProperty} \rangle \} \end{aligned}$$

After internalizing g_1 and g_2, an OWL artifact should take into account OWL class and property definitions, as well as the sub-class and transitivity axioms. It could e.g. return the following predicates for `<room>` (assuming the artifact's internal state i' has already internalized g_2):

---

[8] We represent URIs either as relative URIs or as 'compact URIs' (prefix followed by local name).

$$\mathrm{transfer}'(\{\langle\mathtt{<room>}\rangle, g_1\rangle, i') = \{\mathtt{room('room')},$$
$$\mathtt{partOf('floor','building)},$$
$$\mathtt{zone('room')},$$
$$\mathtt{partOf('room','floor')},$$
$$\mathtt{partOf('room','building')}\}$$

Brick schema is an ontology for the domain of building automation. A Brick representation of a building is e.g. relevant for autonomous agents controlling vacuum cleaning robots navigating in the building, as in the case of the Neato API [6]. It is also relevant for building automation systems to locate sensors and actuators in the building. The Building on Linked Data (BOLD) benchmark[9] includes various tasks to perform on a simulated building. The BOLD server, exposing the simulation as RDF, closely follows the formalism we introduce in this paper.

4.2 Resource Collections

A recurring pattern in hypermedia systems is to use resource *collections*. This pattern is e.g. used by O'Neill et al. in their Multi-Agent Microservices (MAMS) scenario [18]. Linked Data Platforms (LDPs) are a recent W3C standard to implement the resource collection pattern. In LDPs, resource collections are called 'containers', as in the following example:

$$g_3 = \{\langle\mathtt{<coll>}, \mathtt{rdf:type}, \mathtt{ldp:BasicContainer}\rangle,$$
$$\langle\mathtt{<coll>}, \mathtt{ldp:contains}, \mathtt{<member1>}\rangle,$$
$$\langle\mathtt{<coll>}, \mathtt{ldp:contains}, \mathtt{<member2>}\rangle\}$$

LDP containers come with implicit affordances, e.g. to add a new item to the collection:

$$\mathrm{afford}(\langle\mathtt{<coll>}, g_3\rangle) = \{\langle\mathtt{POST}, \mathtt{<coll>}, g\rangle \mid g \in G\}$$

An LDP artifact could implement the specification and provide an action to AgentSpeak agents of the form add('coll', Item, ItemId) for all instances of ldp:BasicContainer it would have internalized.

LDP is not the only standard to model resource collections. ActivityStream (also part of a Social Web standard) can also be used, for the same result. The following graph is semantically equivalent to g_3:

$$g'_3 = \{\langle\mathtt{<coll>}, \mathtt{rdf:type}, \mathtt{as:Collection}\rangle,$$
$$\langle\mathtt{<coll>}, \mathtt{as:items}, \mathtt{<member1>}\rangle,$$
$$\langle\mathtt{<coll>}, \mathtt{as:items}, \mathtt{<member2>}\rangle\}$$

---

[9] https://github.com/bold-benchmark/.

4.3 Social Activities

LDPs can be used for specific types of container, such as message inboxes. The Linked Data Notification (LDN) specification standardizes how to use inbox containers. LDN and ActivityStream are both part of a series of W3C standards meant for the Social Web[10], which also includes WebSub. These standards allow for direct agent-to-agent communication without requiring a dedicated communication channel. Instead, messages are placed in and retrieved from the environment.

Another EMAS prototype based on JADE included a basic virtual assistant to manage one's agenda. We give below an example from the ActivityStream standard to represent agendas. The agenda itself is the named graph $\langle\texttt{<agenda>}, g_5\rangle$ and individual events belonging to the agenda are each a resource, for instance $\langle\texttt{<event>}, g_5'\rangle$, where g_5 and g_5' are defined as

$$g_5 = \{\langle\texttt{<agenda>}, \texttt{as:items}, \texttt{<event>}\rangle, \ldots\}$$

and

$$
\begin{aligned}
g_5' = \{ &\langle\texttt{<event>}, \texttt{rdf:type}, \texttt{as:Event}\rangle, \\
&\langle\texttt{<event>}, \texttt{as:name}, \texttt{"Some agenda event"}\rangle, \\
&\langle\texttt{<event>}, \texttt{as:startTime}, \texttt{"2021-03-05T00:09:00Z"}\rangle, \\
&\langle\texttt{<event>}, \texttt{as:endTime}, \texttt{"2021-03-05T00:10:00Z"}\rangle\}
\end{aligned}
$$

In this example, the agenda, modeled as a collection of events, offers the same affordances as described in Sect. 4.2. Each event offers further affordances. For instance, an autonomous agent can reschedule an event by removing the original one from the collection with operation $\langle\texttt{DELETE}, \texttt{<event>}, \emptyset\rangle$, to then add the rescheduled event to the agenda with a $\texttt{POST}$ operation.

4.4 Affordances

Our formalism enforces agents to follow 'affordances' provided by the environment via the function afford(). We now show how Web forms can be embedded in the environment through two ontologies: the Thing Description (TD) ontology (which includes a module for hypermedia controls) and schema.org.

The TD ontology makes affordances explicit by specifying HTTP request templates as RDF triples. For instance, graph g_4 defined as the graph

$$
\begin{aligned}
g_4 = \{ &\langle\texttt{<lamp>}, \texttt{td:hasPropertyAffordance}, \texttt{<status\_affordance>}\rangle, \\
&\langle\texttt{<status\_affordance>}, \texttt{td:forProperty}, \texttt{<status>}\rangle, \\
&\langle\texttt{<status\_affordance>}, \texttt{td:hasForm}, \texttt{<status\_form>}\rangle \\
&\langle\texttt{<status\_form>}, \texttt{hctl:hasTarget}, \texttt{<target>}\rangle \\
&\langle\texttt{<status\_form>}, \texttt{hctl:forOperationType}, \texttt{td:readProperty}\rangle\}
\end{aligned}
$$

---

[10] https://www.w3.org/TR/social-web-protocols/.

includes one affordance to retrieve the on/off status of a lamp via a GET request:

$$\text{afford}(\{\langle \texttt{<lamp>}, g_4 \rangle\}) = \{\langle \texttt{GET}, \texttt{<target>}, \emptyset \rangle\}$$

The TD ontology defines a small set of operations that are possible on 'things' (physical objects on WoT). A TD artifact could e.g. provide a high-level action for the `td:readProperty` operation type. This approach has been implemented with JaCaMo [1] for a summer school on Artificial Intelligence for industrial applications[11]. In the JaCaMo implementation, a `ThingArtifact` object would expose the following action for g_4: `readProperty('lamp', 'status', Value)`.

As with resource collections, the TD ontology is not the only way to make affordances explicit. The following graph embeds the same affordance as g_4:

$$g_4' = \{\langle \texttt{<lamp>}, \texttt{schema:potentialAction}, \texttt{<status\_action>} \rangle,$$
$$\langle \texttt{<status\_action>}, \texttt{schema:actionStatus}, \texttt{schema:PotentialActionStatus} \rangle,$$
$$\langle \texttt{<status\_action>}, \texttt{schema:target}, \texttt{<status\_form>} \rangle$$
$$\langle \texttt{<status\_form>}, \texttt{schema:httpMethod}, \texttt{"GET"} \rangle$$
$$\langle \texttt{<status\_form>}, \texttt{schema:urlTemplate}, \texttt{"target"} \rangle\}$$

This graph uses the schema.org vocabulary for actions. The approach is being used in another research project on agents in manufacturing [20]. Moreover, schema.org actions are used by the Alexa virtual assistant, as a target representation of natural language commands [14].

4.5 Speech Acts

The MAMS scenario described by O'Neill et al. is based on FIPA's Agent Communication Language (ACL). We show here how to emulate ACL speech acts with ActivityStream.

While WebSub does not recommend a particular vocabulary for the exchanged messages, LDNs and ActivityPub (a third Social Web protocol) encourage using ActivityStream activities. Activities have properties such as actor, target, type, and object. By comparison, ACL messages include the analogous properties 'sender', 'receiver', 'performative' and 'content fields'. Activities could therefore be a substitute for ACL messages on the Social Web. Table 1 gives a mapping from ActivityStream types to ACL communicative acts. Not all ACL speech acts have a correspondance in RDF but the list is enough to implement e.g. an auction, as in the MAMS scenario.

We give an illustration with the first two steps of an auction through LDNs: the auctioneer announces its auction to a bidder with $\langle \texttt{POST}, \texttt{<bidder/inbox>}, g_6 \rangle$, where

---

[11] https://gitlab.emse.fr/ai4industry/hackathon/.

Table 2. Mapping from ActivityStream to FIPA ACL

Activity type (ActivityStream)	Comunicative act (FIPA ACL)
`as:Announce`	Inform, Call for Proposal
`as:Offer`	Propose
`as:Question`	Request
`as:Accept`	Accept Proposal
`as:Reject`	Reject Proposal, Refuse
`as:Follow`	Subscribe
`as:Undo`	Cancel

$$g_6 = \{\langle \texttt{<announce>}, \texttt{rdf:type}, \texttt{as:Announce}\rangle,$$
$$\langle \texttt{<announce>}, \texttt{as:name}, \texttt{"Some announcement"}\rangle,$$
$$\langle \texttt{<announce>}, \texttt{as:actor}, \texttt{<auctioneer>}\rangle,$$
$$\langle \texttt{<announce>}, \texttt{as:target}, \texttt{<bidder>}\rangle,$$
$$\langle \texttt{<announce>}, \texttt{as:object}, \texttt{<auction>}\rangle\}$$

to which the bidder submits the offer with $\langle \texttt{POST}, \texttt{<auctioneer/inbox>}, g_6'\rangle$, where

$$g_6' = \{\langle \texttt{<bid>}, \texttt{rdf:type}, \texttt{as:Offer}\rangle,$$
$$\langle \texttt{<bid>}, \texttt{as:inReplyTo}, \texttt{<announce>}\rangle,$$
$$\langle \texttt{<bid>}, \texttt{as:name}, \texttt{"Some offer"}\rangle,$$
$$\langle \texttt{<bid>}, \texttt{as:actor}, \texttt{<bidder>}\rangle,$$
$$\langle \texttt{<bid>}, \texttt{as:target}, \texttt{<auctioneer>}\rangle,$$
$$\langle \texttt{<bid>}, \texttt{as:object}, \texttt{<offer>}\rangle\}$$

The auctioneer can then accept or reject the offer. Auctioneer and bidder discover each other's inbox through hypermedia, as specified in LDN. Multi-agent protocols can be further specified by using the W3C provenance ontology, PROV-O[12], as suggested by the LDN specification. PROV-O provides a vocabulary to relate activities to entities used or produced by the activity and to agents involved in the activity.

5   Conclusion

In this paper, we introduced a formalism for hypermedia MASs based on the abstraction that the Web is equivalent to an RDF dataset. We were able to show how four different prototypes recently presented at the EMAS series of workshops could fit our formalism, although none of them uses RDF or other Semantic Web technologies. In addition, we showed how other implementations

---

[12] http://www.w3.org/ns/prov#.

natively follow the formalism. With this paper, we have aimed at making MAS and Semantic Web technologies converge again, as per the original 2000 vision of autonomous agents on the Web.

Because it is based on Semantic Web technologies, our formalism should allow for a scalable hypermedia environment, hosting many (physical or simulated) resources and responding to many agents in parallel. Experimental proof of the scalability of such an environment is yet to be provided, though. Implementation effort could be targeted towards designing reusable artifacts for W3C standards, such as LDPs, ActivityStream and the TD ontology. More importantly, however, what remains to be proven is the ability of agents of different origins of interacting in the same (unknown) environment. The BOLD benchmark is an attempt to tend towards that goal. Other MAS competitions around hypermedia environments could be developed as well.

A   Changelog

The changes that have been made compared to the EMAS submission are listed below:

- removed ambiguous statement that "the Web is standardizing interactions between agents"
- clarified the problem addressed in the paper (alignment of MAS architectures with Semantic Web abstractions), its contribution (formalism with equivalence with classical MASs) and how the contributed formalism is evaluated (criterion: do existing EMAS prototypes fit in the formalism?)
- added figures to illustrate the analysis of hypermedia MAS w.r.t. REST (Fig. 1)
- added figure for agent/artifact integration (Fig. 2c)
- moved section on agent/artifact integration to Sect. 3

   Further notes:

- we make no claim whether FIPA ACL is outdated. In our evaluation, we compare to it only because O'Neill et al. [18] refer to it in their 2020 paper.
- the term 'agency' is used numerous times in Wooldridge's introductory book on MASs, we would not have thought it was ambiguous in our paper. We use 'agency' to refer to the ability of (autonomous) agents to act on their environment (definition added at the beginning of Sect. 3).

References

1. Boissier, O., Bordini, R.H., Hübner, J.F., Ricci, A.: Multi-agent Oriented Programming: Programming Multi-agent Systems Using JaCaMo. Intelligent Robotics and autOnomous Agents Series. The MIT Press (2020)
2. Bordini, R.H., Hübner, J.F., Wooldridge, M.: Programming Multi-agent Systems in AgentSpeak Using Jason, vol. 8. Wiley, Hoboken (2007)

3. Carroll, J.J., Bizer, C., Hayes, P., Stickler, P.: Named graphs. J. Web Semant. **3**(4), 247–267 (2005)
4. Casals, A., El Fallah Seghrouchni, A., Negroni, O., Othmani, A.: Exposing agents as web services in JADE. In: Weyns, D., Mascardi, V., Ricci, A. (eds.) EMAS 2018. LNCS (LNAI), vol. 11375, pp. 340–350. Springer, Cham (2019). https://doi.org/10.1007/978-3-030-25693-7_18
5. Ciortea, A., Boissier, O., Ricci, A.: Engineering world-wide multi-agent systems with hypermedia. In: Weyns, D., Mascardi, V., Ricci, A. (eds.) EMAS 2018. LNCS (LNAI), vol. 11375, pp. 285–301. Springer, Cham (2019). https://doi.org/10.1007/978-3-030-25693-7_15
6. Collenette, J., Logan, B.: Multi-agent control of industrial robot vacuum cleaners. In: Baroglio, C., Hubner, J.F., Winikoff, M. (eds.) EMAS 2020. LNCS (LNAI), vol. 12589, pp. 87–99. Springer, Cham (2020). https://doi.org/10.1007/978-3-030-66534-0_6
7. Fielding, R.: Architectural styles and the design of network-based software architectures. Ph.D thesis, University of California, Irvine (2000)
8. Genesereth, M.R., Nilsson, N.J.: Logical Foundations of Artificial Intelligence. Morgan Kaufmann Publishers Inc. (1987)
9. Genestoux, J., Parecki, A.: Websub. W3C Recommendation (2018). https://www.w3.org/TR/websub/
10. Hendler, J.: Agents and the semantic web. IEEE Intell. Syst. **16**(2), 30–37 (2001)
11. Hendler, J., Berners-Lee, T.: From the Semantic Web to social machines: a research challenge for AI on the World Wide Web. Artif. Intell. **174**(2), 156–161 (2010). https://doi.org/10.1016/j.artint.2009.11.010
12. Jacobs, I., Walsh, N.: Architecture of the World Wide Web, vol. 1. W3C Recommendation (2004). https://www.w3.org/TR/webarch/
13. Kaebisch, S., Kamiya, T., McCool, M., Charpenay, V., Kovatsch, M.: Web of Things (WoT) thing description. W3C Recommendation (2020). https://www.w3.org/TR/wot-thing-description/
14. Kollar, T., Berry, D., Stuart, L., Owczarzak, K., Chung, T., Mathias, L., Kayser, M., Snow, B., Matsoukas, S.: The Alexa meaning representation language. In: Proceedings of the 2018 Conference of the North American Chapter of the Association for Computational Linguistics: Human Language Technologies, vol. 3 (Industry Papers), pp. 177–184 (2018)
15. Kovatsch, M., Matsukura, R., Lagally, M., Kawaguchi, T., Toumura, K., Kajimoto, K.: Web of Things (WoT) Architecture. W3C Recommendation (2019). https://www.w3.org/TR/wot-architecture/
16. Kovatsch, M., Matsukura, R., Lagally, M., Kawaguchi, T., Toumura, K., Kajimoto, K.: Web of Things (WoT) architecture. W3C Recommendation (2020). https://www.w3.org/TR/wot-architecture/
17. Ogbuji, C.: Sparql 1.1 graph store http protocol. Technical report (2013). http://www.w3.org/TR/sparql11-http-rdf-update/
18. O'Neill, E., Lillis, D., O'Hare, G.M.P., Collier, R.W.: Delivering multi-agent MicroServices using CArtAgO. In: Baroglio, C., Hubner, J.F., Winikoff, M. (eds.) EMAS 2020. LNCS (LNAI), vol. 12589, pp. 1–20. Springer, Cham (2020). https://doi.org/10.1007/978-3-030-66534-0_1
19. Ricci, A., Viroli, M., Omicini, A.: CArtA gO: a framework for prototyping artifact-based environments in MAS. In: Weyns, D., Parunak, H.V.D., Michel, F. (eds.) E4MAS 2006. LNCS (LNAI), vol. 4389, pp. 67–86. Springer, Heidelberg (2007). https://doi.org/10.1007/978-3-540-71103-2_4

20. Schraudner, D., Charpenay, V.: An HTTP/RDF-based agent infrastructure for manufacturing using stigmergy. In: Harth, A., et al. (eds.) ESWC 2020. LNCS, vol. 12124, pp. 197–202. Springer, Cham (2020). https://doi.org/10.1007/978-3-030-62327-2_34
21. Wilensky, U., Rand, W.: An Introduction to Agent-Based Modeling: Modeling Natural, Social, and Engineered Complex Systems with NetLogo. The MIT Press (2015)
22. Wooldridge, M.J.: An Introduction to Multiagent Systems, 2nd edn. Wiley, Hoboken (2009). OCLC: ocn246887666

Multiagent Foundations for Distributed Systems: A Vision

Amit K. Chopra[1]([⊠])(iD), Samuel H. Christie V[1,2](iD), and Munindar P. Singh[2](iD)

[1] Lancaster University, Bailrigg, Lancaster, UK
{amit.chopra,samuel.christie}@lancaster.ac.uk
[2] North Carolina State University, Raleigh, USA
{schrist,singh}@ncsu.edu

Abstract. Early works and retrospectives by the researchers who founded the network protocols underlying current distributed systems indicate they were aware of the importance of capturing application meaning but didn't know how to handle it programmatically. Therefore, those researchers introduced simplifications in the protocols that violated their own principle of the end-to-end argument in systems design.

The thesis of this vision paper is the following. First, the above-mentioned simplifications, especially the reliance on reliable, ordered communication protocols such as TCP have run their course. Modern applications demand flexibility that can only be achieved through modeling application meaning, and many applications (such as those based on the Internet of Things) cannot pay TCP's overhead. Second, the multiagent systems community has developed alternative meaning-based approaches that can provide a new foundation for distributed computing at large.

1 Introduction

As originally conceived, a multiagent system (MAS) is *decentralized* [14]: Agents in a MAS are autonomous computational entities that communicate and share information with each other. In many applications of MAS, an agent represents a real-world party, such as a human or organization, and the autonomy of the agent reflects the autonomy of the party it represents. Distinctly from other areas of computing (e.g., Web services, software engineering, and programming languages), MAS research emphasizes modeling the *meaning* of interactions [19]. Broadly, meaning refers to the information in an engagement between principals that is relevant to their decision making. The focus on meaning has led to a rich body of work on declarative abstractions such as commitments between agents [7,8,12,24,25]. The early work on commitments demonstrated that modeling meaning is the key to enabling flexible interactions between agents, and thus the key to accommodating their autonomy.

Pioneers in networked computing were aware of the importance of modeling distributed applications in terms of meaning [4]; however, they lacked the abstractions to express meaning. Instead, to support programming, approaches

© Springer Nature Switzerland AG 2022
N. Alechina et al. (Eds.): EMAS 2021, LNAI 13190, pp. 62–71, 2022.
https://doi.org/10.1007/978-3-030-97457-2_4

in distributed computing focused on ordering and reliability guarantees in the infrastructure. Being application-agnostic, such guarantees are meaningless from the application perspective. But worse, the guarantees end up subverting autonomy by restricting the choices available to an agent in interacting with others. And in doing so, modern approaches end up violating the end-to-end argument (E2EA) [18], a fundamental principle of distributed systems. Indeed, Clark [11] explains as much in a retrospective on Internet protocols and distributed systems.

We claim that the MAS community's historical focus on autonomy and meaning has the potential to address a central quest in distributed systems. In a nutshell, the quest is for programming abstractions that enable programmers to easily build high-performance distributed applications based on *meaning* in a manner compatible with the E2EA. By applying ideas from MAS, we have the opportunity to fundamentally reshape how practitioners build distributed application.

2   The Dilemma Posed by Current Approaches

We discuss how each of the two major existing approaches (architectures) for distributed applications fails to satisfy crucial architectural desiderata, thus presenting developers with a *dilemma* (a situation with two equally bad choices).

2.1   Desiderata

Consider the two MAS architectures in Figs. 1 and 2. In both, the agents communicate via asynchronous messaging via a communication infrastructure that offers an API for programming agents. Notice that there is no shared state between the agents. In the architecture of Fig. 1, the communication infrastructure guarantees only that it delivers only sent messages. We refer to such an infrastructure (and architecture) as *bare-bones* because no real infrastructure guarantees less. In the architecture of Fig. 2, the infrastructure provides the additional guarantee that all sent messages will be delivered and in FIFO order between any pair of agents. We refer to such an infrastructure (and architecture) as *reliable*. In practical systems, bare-bones and reliable infrastructures are exemplified by UDP over IP and TCP over IP, respectively.

Accommodating Autonomy. The end-to-end argument (E2EA) [18] is a guiding principle in the design of the Internet. The principle imagines a layered system architecture and draws our attention to the fact that if implementing some functionality fully and correctly requires knowledge only available at some system layer, then that functionality cannot be implemented in a lower system layer. Partial implementation of the functionality in a lower layer, however tempting, should generally be avoided as the layer would impose a model upon the higher layer (by constraining the choices available at the higher layer) and

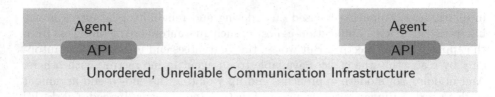

Fig. 1. MAS where agents communicate via a bare-bones infrastructure that guarantees neither message ordering nor delivery. The API represents programming abstractions offered by the infrastructure.

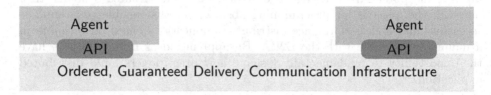

Fig. 2. MAS where agents communicate via a reliable infrastructure that guarantees message delivery and in FIFO order.

likely result in a performance hit as well. The E2EA famously argues against reliable infrastructures (as defined above), among other things.

For example, suppose that we wanted to make a medical prescription application reliable in the sense that a prescription written by the doctor in response to a patient complaint should be fulfilled by the pharmacy in a timely manner. To distinguish application reliability from reliability at the infrastructure level, let's refer to the former as *a-reliability*. We can imagine a few measures to increase a-reliability. One, we could specify a contract that stipulates that the pharmacy fulfill valid prescriptions in a timely manner. Further, we could support reminders and acknowledgments between the parties. A reliable infrastructure would be oblivious of such measures—they would necessarily have to be supported at the application level. In particular, no infrastructure-level retransmission or acknowledgment of messages can provide a-reliability, because it depends on the cooperation of multiple higher-level endpoints (the agents).

More insidiously perhaps, FIFO delivery interferes with the application by delaying the delivery of messages pending the arrival of an earlier message. For example, if a doctor sends two prescriptions to the pharmacy, one after the other, then until the first prescription is delivered to the pharmacy, the infrastructure won't deliver the second, thus interfering with the pharmacy's fulfillment of its commitments and its autonomy (the idea that infrastructures could interfere with agent autonomy was first articulated in [5]). Consider another example where the doctor can cancel a prescription after issuing it to the pharmacy. FIFO delivery would mean that the pharmacy can't process the cancellation before receiving the prescription, even though handling cancellation first might avoid wasting effort and so would be desirable from the pharmacy's point of view. In essence, a-reliability does not require reliable infrastructure, but the reliable infrastructure gets in the way of a-reliability.

From the application developer's perspective, the E2EA promotes the idea of representing application meaning (e.g., the meaning of a prescription and its cancellation) and implementing agents based on such meaning rather than some expected message ordering.

Programming Convenience. Historically though, reliable infrastructures have been favored over bare-bones ones for building applications. The reason is that in the mind of an application developer, the application is represented as a unitary (as opposed to decentralized) state machine. For example, the developer implicitly models a state machine where the doctor's cancellation of a prescription happens after the prescription is issued (Fig. 3). A state machine is a convenient abstraction from the point of view of programming. A reliable infrastructure helps implement such a state machine in a distributed manner by making it impossible for the pharmacy to observe and process the cancellation before observing the prescription.

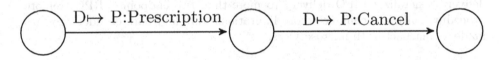

Fig. 3. Fragment of a state machine representing a medical prescription scenario.

Imagine programming such an application over bare-bones infrastructure. Now, the application developer must implement the pharmacy to deal with cancellation arriving before the prescription. In general, prevalent techniques offer no alternative but to implement business logic for each possible message sequence, a cumbersome and error prone task at best, especially when several messages may be in transit at once.

In addition to preventing arbitrary message orders (or *nondeterminism*), a reliable infrastructure also saves the application developer from writing logic to recover from lost messages. Over bare-bones infrastructure, the developer would have to implement acknowledgments, retransmissions, and the handling of duplicates. It is no wonder then that application developers prefer reliable infrastructures.

Loose Coupling. Loosely-coupled architectures are better because a component can be replaced with fewer modifications to other components [17,23]. From the point of view of loose coupling, the bare-bones architecture is better. This is because the applications that work over a bare-bones infrastructure will also work over the reliable infrastructure. However, the reverse is not true. If agents relied on the reliability offered by the infrastructure, then switching to bare-bones infrastructure would result in errors. As we saw above, if the pharmacy were implemented to expect Cancel after Prescription, then the pharmacy wouldn't work over a bare-bones infrastructure.

2.2 The Dilemma

From the foregoing discussion, it would seem that agent programmers are faced with a dilemma.

1. Either build flexible applications in a manner compatible with the E2EA— over bare bones infrastructure—but without the benefit of high-level, meaning-based programming abstractions. In particular, programmers would have to implement complex code to track the state of the interaction.
2. Or benefit from some programming convenience, but at the cost of violating the E2EA and subverting autonomy.

Neither alternative is ideal since we really want both high-level communication abstractions *and* compatibility with the E2EA. Work in distributed systems, however, has historically favored Alternative 2, as evidenced by work on *middleware*. Message queues (e.g., MQTT) support reliable, FIFO messaging. Causal delivery generalizes FIFO delivery to more than two endpoints. RPC (remote procedure call), a technique whose limitations were laid bare decades ago, has made a comeback with microservices.

3 Meaning-Based MAS Architecture

In contrast to traditional approaches for creating distributed applications, a strand of MAS research has emphasized modeling a MAS in terms of the *meaning* of interactions between agents. The motivation behind modeling meaning is to support flexible decision-making by enabling flexible interactions between agents.

In current work, the meaning is usually modeled in terms of how messages affect the states of the normative expectations (*norms*, e.g., *commitments*) between agents [7,8,12,24,25]. Recent work has demonstrated how the decentralized computation of norms may be operationalized over information protocols [16,20,21]. In a nutshell, agents compute the atoms of meaning, or *base events*, by enacting information protocols. The base events an agent has observed are materialized in its *local state*. Each agent computes higher-level meanings as views on the local state.

Figure 4 describes a promising meaning-based MAS architecture schematically. Several things are notable about the architecture. One, the application is specified by norms and information protocols; collectively, the *interaction specification*. The specification would be jointly determined by application stakeholders following some design process, e.g., [6]. Two, the interaction specification is the extent of the coupling between the agents. There is no hidden coupling between the agents. In particular, nothing is assumed of the communication infrastructure except that it respects physical causality; that is, the infrastructure delivers only sent messages.

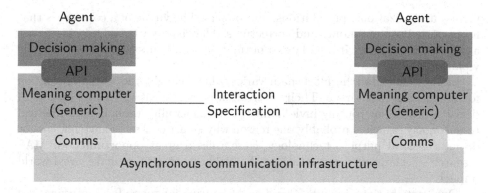

Fig. 4. Meanings-based MAS. An agent's local meaning computer computes meanings based upon a specification of interactions, here, norms and information protocols. The meaning computer offers a high-level API which a developer can use to plug in decision making policies. The meaning computer is generic and interfaces with an asynchronous communication infrastructure via a low-level communication interface (Comms).

Each agent consists of two components: *Meaning Computer* (MC) and *Decision making*. The MC is a generic component. It interprets the information protocol and ensures that the agent is compliant with it. It also records the incoming and outgoing messages, collectively the base events that the agent has observed. Further, the MC interprets norm specifications over the base events to infer the states of the norms. An agent developer would plug in the agent's decision making policies via an API to the MC.

Returning to the example of prescription cancellation, the architecture in Fig. 4 enables the possibility of the pharmacy handling the prescription cancellation before receiving the prescription if the cancellation is received first. As modeled in the information protocol, the cancellation would refer to the prescription being canceled via a unique identifier. If the cancellation is received before the prescription, then the pharmacy's MC disables the fulfillment of the prescription (based on the information protocol) so that when the prescription eventually arrives, there is nothing to do.

The information protocol approach represents a key breakthrough in protocol languages in that it supports meaning and flexible interaction far better than choreographic (message ordering-based) approaches [5]. Remarkably, although a choreography is an application-level abstraction, its reliance on message ordering for correctness recreates the problems of reliable infrastructures at the application level.

4 Directions

4.1 Specification

Natural language *contracts* (agreements) capture the high-level meaning of engagements between parties by setting out the relevant *norms*, e.g., commitments, authorizations, prohibitions, and powers. The virtue of a contract is that it supports both autonomy and correctness. That is, a party may decide to act as it pleases; however, if it violates a norm, that would amount to an observable violation.

Smart contracts (the blockchain variety) have caught the world's attention for not having that virtue. Their motivation is to cut out the social aspects of decision making by touting inviolability [22]. Inviolability though is antithetical to autonomy, which is probably one reason why smart contracts have not caught on as a general purpose technology. Herein lies a great opportunity for MAS research—declarative representations of violable contracts—to make a real-world impact.

Our contributions include *Cupid*, a declarative language for specifying and computing norms over a database of business events [7,8]. *Clouseau* [21] shows how to leverage Cupid contracts in a decentralized setting with several agents, each with its own local database. We also developed a proof-of-concept implementation of Cupid for the R3 Corda distributed ledger [22]. More is needed for practical applications. In particular, a contract bundles norms and has its own lifecycle (it enters into force upon parties signing up to it and it may be amended, breached, and terminated). Further, contracts involve operations such as delegation and assignment and notions such as jurisdictions that need to be properly formalized.

We need methodologies for specifying and verifying contracts. One important question is how may stakeholders starting from their requirements arrive at a contract. Protos [6], a methodology for refining requirements into commitments, offers some ideas. A broader question is that of *governance*, which requires taking into account the actual outcomes from enacting a contract in the process of revising a contract. Further, contracts need to be to related to multiagent organizations (institutions). An organization (itself an agent) would normally serve as the arbiter of disputes and provide other services such as identity, discovery, and reputation. An organization may further help enforce contracts by sanctioning agents, e.g., by expelling an agent for repeated violations.

A related question is what constitutes a *fair* contract? Consider a contract between a lender and borrower, whereas a notification sent by the lender counts when the lender sends it, whereas a notification sent by the borrower counts when the lender receives it. All other things being equal (e.g., they are using the same communication infrastructure), such a contract seems unfair to the borrower because all decisions are made from the lender's perspective. Other questions relate to the enactability of a contract. For example, a contract may only be partially enactable or it may be enactable only in odd ways (e.g., a commitment which comes into force only after it is already satisfied).

4.2 Programming Models

A challenge for any interaction-based approach of specifying applications is how to facilitate the implementation of agents based on contracts and protocols. In contrast to traditional approaches [1–3], a suitable programming model would be based on information, thus abstracting away the challenges of asynchrony. It would also ensure that the interactions progress in decentralized yet consistent manner. We have explored some initial ideas in Stellar [13] and PoT [10], which demonstrate that an information-based programming model saves significant programming effort and avoids errors. A yet uncharted area is how to support programming based on contracts.

Early work on commitment machines identified semantic exception handling as a benefit [25]. Exception handling naturally relates to the theme of fault tolerance. The remarkable thing is that application-level fault tolerance is not optional; any application must ensure that it achieves its own objectives. Although properly addressing causes may reduce the probability of failure and improve performance, what ultimately matters to an application is success. However, current approaches (following a long tradition) focus on handling faults as close to their causes as possible, and thus encourage delegating fault tolerance to the infrastructure. For example, in a paradigm as new as microservices, fault tolerance is left to the underlying service mesh [15]. The focus on infrastructure has meant that today we lack the tools to program fault tolerance effectively at the application level. PoT and Bungie [9] present some initial ideas about how to implement fault tolerance at the application level—in the agents.

Most future applications will be programmed to run in the cloud, possibly as a composition of microservices. It would be timely for MAS researchers to consider how their techniques could benefit from cloud-based mechanisms (e.g., for scalability) and what they might in turn have to offer to application developers. Programming models such as Function-as-a-Service (FaaS) intend to make programming cloud applications easier. However, such models currently offer neither any programming abstractions for managing state nor composition mechanisms for building realistic applications. Meaning-based programming models can help address these gaps and potentially enable highly concurrent agent implementations that can take advantage of scalability mechanisms in the cloud.

5   Conclusion

Current approaches for building distributed applications pose a dilemma: Either build applications in violation of the E2EA or build them without any programming support. A fundamentally multiagent approach based on meaning has the potential to provide the way out: satisfy the E2EA by enabling the deployment of applications on bare-bones infrastructure, and facilitate programming via high-level programming abstractions.

The multiagent systems community has long expressed angst about the lack of direct impact on systems development practice. We suggest here that perhaps it is because we have sought to make small incremental changes, which since they don't align well with traditional thinking are largely disregarded by practitioners. We suggest that it would be worth (1) understanding the foundational problems in distributed systems, that is, those that lie beyond the capacity of current approaches and (2) showing how multiagent systems can address those problems in a natural manner. The history of distributed computing indicates that the founders were quite aware of the simplifications, and revisiting those design decisions could be a pathway toward introducing multiagent systems into practice.

Acknowledgments. Grants from the NSF (IIS-1908374) and EPSRC (EP/N027965/1) supported this research.

References

1. Baldoni, M., Baroglio, C., Capuzzimati, F.: A commitment-based infrastructure for programming socio-technical systems. ACM Trans. Internet Technol. **14**(4), 23:1–23:23 (2014)
2. Baldoni, M., Baroglio, C., Capuzzimati, F., Micalizio, R.: Type checking for protocol role enactments via commitments. Auton. Agents Multi-Agent Syst. **32**(3), 349–386 (2018). https://doi.org/10.1007/s10458-018-9382-3
3. Boissier, O., Bordini, R.H., Hübner, J.F., Ricci, A., Santi, A.: Multi-agent oriented programming with JaCaMo. Sci. Comput. Program. **78**(6), 747–761 (2013)
4. Cheriton, D.R., Skeen, D.: Understanding the limitations of causally and totally ordered communication. In: Proceedings of the 14th ACM Symposium on Operating System Principles (SOSP), Asheville, North Carolina, pp. 44–57. ACM Press (1993). https://doi.org/10.1145/168619.168623
5. Chopra, A.K., Christie V, S.H., Singh, M.P.: An evaluation of communication protocol languages for engineering multiagent systems. J. Artif. Intell. Res. **69**, 1351–1393 (2020)
6. Chopra, A.K., Dalpiaz, F., Aydemir, F.B., Giorgini, P., Mylopoulos, J., Singh, M.P.: Protos: Foundations for engineering innovative sociotechnical systems. In: Proceedings of the 18th IEEE International Requirements Engineering Conference, pp. 53–62 (2014)
7. Chopra, A.K., Singh, M.P.: Cupid: commitments in relational algebra. In: Proceedings of the 29th AAAI Conference on Artificial Intelligence, pp. 2052–2059 (2015)
8. Chopra, A.K., Singh, M.P.: Custard: computing norm states over information stores. In: Proceedings of the 15th International Conference on Autonomous Agents and Multiagent Systems (AAMAS), pp. 1096–1105. IFAAMAS, Singapore (2016)
9. Christie V, S.H., Chopra, A.K., Singh, M.P.: Bungie: improving fault tolerance via extensible application-level protocols. IEEE Comput. **54**(5), 44–53 (2021)
10. Christie V, S.H., Smirnova, D., Chopra, A.K., Singh, M.P.: Protocols over things: a decentralized programming model for the Internet of Things. IEEE Comput. **53**(12), 60–68 (2020)
11. Clark, D.: The network and the OS. In: SOSP History Day, Monterey, California, pp. 11:1–11:19. ACM (2015). https://doi.org/10.1145/2830903.2830912
12. Fornara, N., Colombetti, M.: Operational specification of a commitment-based agent communication language. In: Proceedings of the 1st International Joint Conference on Autonomous Agents and Multiagent Systems (AAMAS), pp. 535–542. ACM Press (2002)
13. Günay, A., Chopra, A.K.: Stellar: a programming model for developing protocol-compliant agents. In: Weyns, D., Mascardi, V., Ricci, A. (eds.) EMAS 2018. LNCS (LNAI), vol. 11375, pp. 117–136. Springer, Cham (2019). https://doi.org/10.1007/978-3-030-25693-7_7

14. Huhns, M.N. (ed.): Distributed Artificial Intelligence. Pitman/Morgan Kaufmann, London (1987)
15. Istio: Introducing Istio: a robust service mesh for microservices (2017). https://istio.io/v0.1/blog/istio-service-mesh-for-microservices.html. Accessed 16 June 2021
16. King, T.C., Günay, A., Chopra, A.K., Singh, M.P.: Tosca: operationalizing commitments over information protocols. In: Proceedings of the 26th International Joint Conference on Artificial Intelligence (IJCAI), pp. 256–264 (2017)
17. Microsoft: Microservice architecture style (2019). https://docs.microsoft.com/en-us/azure/architecture/guide/architecture-styles/microservices. Accessed 16 June 2021
18. Saltzer, J.H., Reed, D.P., Clark, D.D.: End-to-end arguments in system design. ACM Trans. Comput. Syst. **2**(4), 277–288 (1984). https://doi.org/10.1145/357401.357402
19. Singh, M.P.: Agent communication languages: rethinking the principles. IEEE Comput. **31**(12), 40–47 (1998)
20. Singh, M.P.: Information-driven interaction-oriented programming: BSPL, the Blindingly Simple Protocol Language. In: Proceedings of the 10th International Conference on Autonomous Agents and MultiAgent Systems, pp. 491–498 (2011)
21. Singh, M.P., Chopra, A.K.: Clouseau: generating communication protocols from commitments. In: Proceedings of the 34th AAAI Conference on Artificial Intelligence, pp. 7244–7252. AAAI Press, New York (2020)
22. Singh, M.P., Chopra, A.K.: Computational governance and violable contracts for blockchain applications. IEEE Comput. **53**, 53–62 (2020)
23. Singh, M.P., Huhns, M.N.: Service-Oriented Computing: Semantics, Processes, Agents. Wiley, Chichester (2005)
24. Winikoff, M.: Implementing commitment-based interactions. In: Proceedings of the 6th International Conference on Autonomous Agents and Multiagent Systems, pp. 1–8 (2007)
25. Yolum, P., Singh, M.P.: Flexible protocol specification and execution: applying event calculus planning using commitments. In: Proceedings of the 1st International Joint Conference on Autonomous Agents and MultiAgent Systems, pp. 527–534. ACM Press (2002)

An Epistemic Logic for Modular Development of Multi-Agent Systems

Stefania Costantini[1,3] , Andrea Formisano[2,3(✉)] , and Valentina Pitoni[1]

[1] DISIM, Università di L'Aquila, L'Aquila, Italy
stefania.costantini@univaq.it
[2] DMIF, Università di Udine, Udine, Italy
andrea.formisano@uniud.it
[3] Gruppo Nazionale Calcolo Scientifico-INdAM, Rome, Italy

Abstract. Logic has been proved useful to model various aspects of the reasoning process of agents and Multi-Agent Systems (MAS). In this paper, we report about the last advances over a line of work aimed to explore social aspects of such systems. The objective is to formally model (aspects of) the group dynamics of cooperative agents. We have proposed and here extend a particular logical framework (the Logic of "Inferable" *L-DINF*), where a group of cooperative agents can jointly perform actions. I.e., at least one agent of the group can perform the action, either with the approval of the group or on behalf of the group. We have been able to take into consideration actions' *cost* and the preferences that each agent can have for what concerns performing each action. Our focus here is on: (i) explainability, i.e., the syntax of our logic is especially devised to make it possible to transpose a proof into a natural language explanation, in the perspective of trustworthy Artificial Intelligence; (ii) the capability to construct and execute joint plans within a group of agents; (iii) the formalization of aspects of the Theory of Mind, which is an important social-cognitive skill involving the ability to attribute mental states, including emotions, desires, beliefs, and knowledge to oneself and to others, and to reason about the practical consequences of such mental states; such capability is very relevant when agents have to interact with humans, and in particular in robotic applications; (iv) connection between theory and practice, so as to make our logic actually usable by a system's designers.

Keywords: Epistemic logic · Agents and Multi-Agent Systems · Theory of Mind

1 Introduction

The metaphor adopted in Artificial Intelligence (AI) to model societies whose members are to some extent cooperative towards each other is that of agents and Multi-Agent Systems (MAS). To achieve better results via cooperation, agents belonging to a MAS must be able to reason about what a group of agents can do, because it is often the

Research partially supported by Action COST CA17124 "DigForASP" and by INdAM-GNCS 2020 project NoRMA.

case that a group can fulfill objectives that are out of reach for the single agent. Each participating agent is not in general able to solve a whole problem or reach an overall goal by itself, but can only cope with a small subproblem/subgoal for which it has the required competence. The overall result/goal is accomplished by means of cooperation with other agents. In the course of the cooperation, an agent may have to bid for solving some aspect of the problem or perform some action instead of some other one, or to negotiate with other agents for the distribution of tasks. Several agent-oriented programming languages and systems exist, many of them based upon computational logic (cf., e.g., [3,4,18] for recent surveys on such languages), and thus endowed (at least in principle) with a logical semantics.

Many kinds of logical frameworks can be found in the literature which try to emulate cognitive aspects of human beings, also from the cooperative point of view. In our past work [10,12] we defined the new Logic of "Inferable", called *L-DINF*, as an extension of an existing logic by Lorini & Balbiani [2], which considers an agent in the context of cooperative group(s) of agents. We introduced conditions for the cooperative executability of physical actions taking into account feasibility, costs and budget. In this paper, we also consider preferences of single agents concerning their willingness to execute actions that they are allowed to do, and joint intentions within a group.

A relevant feature of our approach is that the conditions concerning whether an agent (and thus its group) is allowed to execute some action and to which extent it is willing to perform it, are not specified in the logical theory defining an agent: rather, we envisage separate modules from which the agent's logical theory "inputs" the results. Such modules might be specified in some other logic or also, pragmatically, via pieces of code whenever, e.g., feasibility of actions should be verified according to agents' environmental conditions.

The rationale of this approach can be exposed as follows. On the one hand, logic is a good tool to express the semantics underlying (aspects of) agent-oriented programming languages. To this aim however, it is important to keep the complexity of the logic low enough to be practically manageable. Modularity is an important property to ensure, as it allows programmers to better organize the definition of the application at hand, and allows an agent-systems' definition to be more flexible and customizable. As notable examples, in [13] it is shown how an agent behaviour can significantly change by leaving its 'main' definition unchanged, while modifying only its communication modalities, i.e., which kind of messages and from/to whom the agent is available to manage. In [21] it is shown that a different sequencing and duration of agent's activities determines a very different 'external' behaviour, again over the same main program. Moreover, modularity can be an advantage for explainability, in the sense of making the explanation itself modular.

So, our approach tries to join the rigour of logic and the flexibility of modularity. We allow one to define in a separate way which actions are allowed for each agent to perform at each stage, and with which degree of preference. A programmer will then be able to define suitable pieces of code specifying where, when, and why each action is indeed allowed, and, possibly, which is the 'rationale' of a certain degree of preference of an agent in performing an action. So, modular changes to the conditions for actions to be enabled and to the reasons for an agent's preferences to perform or not an action, may affect in a relevant way the behaviour of both an agent and the group(s) to which it belongs.

In the original formulation of *L-DINF*, we considered the notion of executability of agents' inferential actions (also called *mental* actions). When an agent belongs to a group, if that agent is not actually able to perform an intended action which in principle it should be able to perform, it may be supported by its group. The reason of not being able could be that an action may require resource consumption (and hence involve a *cost*). So, in order to execute an action the agent must possess the necessary *budget*, or borrow it from the group. We then extended the logic by introducing further possibilities of solidarity between the members of a cooperative group of agents, in particular to support each other in performing actions in place of some other agent who is not enabled or not wishing to do that itself. In this extension, the reason of not being able to perform an action can be that the agent is not allowed to perform that action in the present state; or the agent might be allowed and still not willing to execute that action.

'Our' agents are *aware* of themselves, of the group they belong to, and possibly of other groups. Since we assume that agents belonging to a group are cooperative with respect to action execution, an action can be executed by the group if at least one agent therein is able and allowed and willing to execute it, and the group can bear (in some way) the cost. In case more agents can perform an action, the one which is best willing can be selected based on a notion of preference.

In [10] we have thoroughly discussed the relationship of logic *L-DINF* with related work, emphasizing that this logic draws inspiration from concepts from Theory of Mind [19] and Social Intelligence [20]. We are also indebted to [17], concerning the point of view that an agent reaches a certain belief state by performing inferences, and that making inferences takes time. We tackled the issue of time in previous work, discussed in [9,11,22]. Differently from these works however, in *L-DINF* inferential actions are represented both at the syntactic level, via dynamic operators in the DEL style, and at a semantic level as neighborhood-update operations. Also, *L-DINF*, following [2], enables an agent to reason on executability of inferential actions. In this paper, we also try to introduce (even though the formalization is not complete yet) the concept that actions may take a certain number of steps in order to be enabled or suitable for execution.

One relevant aim of this work is to take into account the relationship between the semantic and the practical aspects of agents' specification and engineering, which is often neglected. Therefore, we provide action-related reserved syntax, specifying explicitly what an agent can do, does, and has done, or to which degree it is willing to perform the feasible actions. For some of these expressions we assume a "semantic attachment" to the external environment in which an agent will be situated, i.e., some kind of sensor/actuator device which actually performs actions, which is opaque at the logical level, but in our view still needs representation (we were inspired by the discussion, dated to a long time ago, by [24]). This approach is aimed at: making the formalization more complete and comprehensible for developers; improving explainability of an agent's operation, by translating logical proofs into natural language expressions that are intelligible to human users also thanks to the explicit standard representation of action-related aspects.

A long-term goal is to formalize in our logic aspects of the "Theory of Mind" (ToM), which is an important social-cognitive skill that involves the ability to attribute mental states, including emotions, desires, beliefs, and knowledge both one's own and those of others, and to reason about the practical consequences of such mental states. Theory of Mind, developed originally by Philosophers and Psychologists, is starting to be applied to robotics, and some suitable logics are being developed [15]. In fact, with the arrival of "service robots" devised to support users in their everyday tasks (e.g., in eHealth robots support on the one hand patients, by reminding them to take their medicines and by providing advice and reassurance, but on the other hand such robots also support doctors, by constantly monitoring the user's vital parameters, creating alerts whenever necessary). In order to render these robots acceptable and even appreciated by users, they will have to be programmed so as to mimic basic social skills and behave in a socially acceptable manner, which means that their behaviour is to some extent predictable by the user, and conformant to social standards. Theory of Mind is linked to affective computing (which is a set of techniques able to elicit a human's emotional condition from physical signs), to enable the system to respond intelligently to human emotional feedback, and to enhance ToM activities by providing it with perceptions related to the user's emotional signs.

The paper is organized as follows. Section 2 introduces syntax and semantics of *L-DINF*, together with an axiomatization of the proposed logical system. In Sect. 3 we present an example of application of the new logic. Canonical models and strong completeness of the logic are discussed in Sect. 4. In Sects. 5 and 6 we introduce interesting possible future developments: namely, in Sect. 5 we discuss the possibility of formalizing the fact that a goal is meant to be reached (or has been reached) within a certain number of steps, and in Sect. 6 we outline how to extend our logic so as to model significant aspects of the Theory of Mind. Finally, in Sect. 7 we conclude.

2   Logical Framework

L-DINF is a logic which consists of a static component and a dynamic one. The static component, called *L-INF*, is a logic of explicit beliefs and background knowledge. The dynamic component, called *L-DINF*, extends the static one with dynamic operators capturing the consequences of the agents' inferential actions on their explicit beliefs as well as a dynamic operator capturing what an agent can conclude by performing some inferential action in its repertoire.

2.1   Syntax

In this section we provide and illustrate the syntax of the proposed logic.

Let $Atm = \{p, q, \ldots\}$ be a countable set of atomic propositions. By $Prop$ we denote the set of all propositional formulas, i.e. the set of all Boolean formulas built out of the set of atomic propositions Atm. A subset Atm_A of the atomic propositions represent the physical actions that an agent can perform, including "active sensing" actions (e.g., "let's check whether it rains", "let's measure the temperature"). Let $d, d_{max} \in Int$, where Int is the set of integer numbers equal or greater than zero, and $0 \leq d \leq d_{max}$. Let Agt be a set of agents. The language of *L-DINF*, denoted by $\mathcal{L}_{L\text{-}DINF}$, is defined by the following grammar in Backus-Naur form:

$$\varphi, \psi ::= p \mid \neg\varphi \mid \varphi \wedge \psi \mid \mathbf{B}_i\,\varphi \mid \mathbf{K}_i\,\varphi \mid$$
$$do_i(\phi_A) \mid do_i^P(\phi_A) \mid can\_do_i(\phi_A) \mid pref\_do_i(\phi_A, d) \mid$$
$$do_G(\phi_A) \mid do_G^P(\phi_A) \mid can\_do_G(\phi_A) \mid pref\_do_G(i, \phi_A) \mid$$
$$intend_i(\phi_A) \mid intend_G(\phi_A) \mid exec_i(\alpha) \mid exec_G(\alpha) \mid [G : \alpha]\,\varphi$$

$$\alpha \quad ::= \vdash(\varphi,\psi) \mid \cap(\varphi,\psi) \mid \downarrow(\varphi, \psi) \mid \dashv(\varphi, \psi)$$

where p ranges over Atm and $i \in Agt$. (Other Boolean operators are defined from $\neg$ and $\wedge$ in the standard manner.) The language of *inferential actions* of type α is denoted by $\mathcal{L}_{\mathsf{ACT}}$. The static part *L-INF* of *L-DINF*, includes only those formulas not having sub-formulas of type α, namely, no inferential operation is admitted.

Notice the expression $intend_i(\phi_A)$, where it is required that $\phi_A \in Atm_A$. This expression indicates the intention of agent i to perform action ϕ_A in the sense of the BDI agent model [23]. This intention can be part of an agent's knowledge base from the beginning, or it can be derived later. In this paper we do not cope with the formalization of BDI, for which the reader may refer, e.g., to [16]. So, we will treat intentions rather informally, assuming also that $intend_G(\phi_A)$ holds whenever all agents in group G intend to perform action ϕ_A.

The expressions $can\_do_i(\phi_A)$ and $pref\_do_i(\phi_A, d)$ (where it is required that $\phi_A \in Atm_A$) are closely related to $do_i(\phi_A)$. In fact, $can\_do_i(\phi_A)$ is to be seen as an enabling condition, indicating that agent i is enabled to execute action ϕ_A, while instead $pref\_do_i(\phi_A, d)$ indicates the level d of preference/willingness of agent i to perform that action. $pref\_do_G(i, \phi_A)$ indicates that agent i exhibits the *maximum level* of preference on performing action ϕ_A within all group members. Notice that, if a group of agents intends to perform an action ϕ_A, this will entail that the entire group intends to do ϕ_A, that will be enabled to be actually executed only if at least one agent $i \in G$ can do it, i.e., it can derive $can\_do_i(\phi_A)$.

The formula $do_i(\phi_A)$, where again it is required that $\phi_A \in Atm_A$, indicates *actual execution* of action ϕ_A by agent i, automatically recorded by the new belief $do_i^P(\phi_A)$ (postfix "P" standing for "past" action). By precise choice, do and do^P (and similarly do_G and do_G^P) are not axiomatized. In fact, they are realized by what has been called in [24] a *semantic attachment*, i.e., a procedure which connects an agent with its external environment in a way that is unknown at the logical level. The axiomatization concerns only the relationship between doing and being enabled to do.

Unlike explicit beliefs, i.e., facts and rules acquired via perceptions during an agent's operation and kept in the *working memory*, an agent's background knowledge is assumed to satisfy *omniscience* principles, such as closure under conjunction and known implication, and closure under logical consequence, and introspection. In fact, $\mathbf{K}_i$ is actually the well-known S5 modal operator often used to model/represent knowledge. The fact that background knowledge is closed under logical consequence is justified because we conceive it as a kind of stable reliable *knowledge base*, or *long-term memory*. We assume the background knowledge to include: facts (formulas) known by the agent from the beginning, and facts the agent has later decided to store in its long-term memory (by means of some decision mechanism not treated here) after having processed them in its working memory. We therefore assume background knowledge to be irrevocable, in the sense of being stable over time.

A formula of the form $[G : \alpha]\,\varphi$, with $G \in 2^{Agt}$, and where α must be an inferential action, states that "φ holds after action α has been performed by at least one of the agents in G, and all agents in G have common knowledge about this fact".

Remark 1. If an inferential action is performed by an agent $i \in G$, the others agents belonging to the same group G have full visibility of this action and, therefore, as we suppose agents to be cooperative, it is as if they had performed the action themselves.

Borrowing from [1], we distinguish four types of inferential actions α which allow us to capture some of the dynamic properties of explicit beliefs and background knowledge: $\downarrow(\varphi, \psi), \cap(\varphi, \psi), \dashv(\varphi, \psi)$, and $\vdash(\varphi, \psi)$, These actions characterize the basic operations of forming explicit beliefs via inference:

- $\downarrow(\varphi, \psi)$ is the inferential action which consists in inferring ψ from φ in case φ is believed and, according to agent's background knowledge, ψ is a logical consequence of φ. I.e., by performing this inferential action, an agent tries to retrieve from its background knowledge in long-term memory the information that φ implies ψ and, if it succeeds, it starts believing ψ.
- $\cap(\varphi, \psi)$ is the inferential action which closes the explicit belief φ and the explicit belief ψ under conjunction. I.e., $\cap(\varphi, \psi)$ characterizes the inferential action of deducing $\varphi \wedge \psi$ from the explicit belief φ and the explicit belief ψ.
- $\dashv(\varphi, \psi)$ is the inferential action that performs a simple form of "belief revision", i.e., removes ψ from the working memory in case φ is believed and, according to agent's background knowledge, $\neg\psi$ is logical consequence of φ. Both ψ and φ are required to be ground atoms.
- $\vdash(\varphi, \psi)$ is the inferential action which adds ψ to the working memory in case φ is believed and, according to agent's working memory, ψ is logical consequence of φ. This last action operates directly on the working memory without retrieving anything from the background knowledge.

Formulas of the forms $cxcc_i(\alpha)$ and $exec_G(\alpha)$ express executability of inferential actions either by agent i, or by a group G of agents (which is a consequence of any of the group members being able to execute the action). It has to be read as: "α is an inferential action that agent i (resp. an agent in G) can perform".

Remark 2. In the mental actions $\vdash(\varphi, \psi)$ and $\downarrow(\varphi, \psi)$, the formula ψ which is inferred and asserted as a new belief can be $can\_do_i(\phi_A)$ or $do_i(\phi_A)$, which denote the possibility of execution or actual execution of physical action ϕ_A. In fact, we assume that when inferring $do_i(\phi_A)$ (from $can\_do_i(\phi_A)$ and possibly other conditions) then the action is actually executed, and the corresponding belief $do_i^P(\phi_A)$ is asserted, possibly augmented with a time-stamp. Actions are supposed to succeed by default; in case of failure, a corresponding failure event will be perceived by the agent. The do_i^P beliefs constitute a *history* of the agent's operation, so they might be useful for the agent to reason about its own past behaviour, and/or, importantly, they may be useful to provide *explanations* to human users.

Remark 3. Explainability in our approach can be directly obtained from proofs. Let us assume for simplicity that inferential actions can be represented in infix form as $\varphi_n \; OP \; \varphi_{n+1}$. Also, $exec_i(\alpha)$ means that the mental action α is executable by agent i and is indeed executed. If, for instance, the user wants an explanation of why the action ϕ_A has been performed, the system can respond by exhibiting the proof that has lead to ϕ_A, put in the explicit form:

$(exec_i(\varphi_1 OP_1 \; \varphi_2) \wedge \ldots \wedge exec_i(\varphi_{n-1} OP_n \; \varphi_n) \wedge exec_i(\varphi_n OP_n \; can\_do_i(\phi_A)) \wedge intend_i(\phi_A) \wedge can\_do_i(\phi_A)) \vdash do_i(\phi_A)$

where each OP_i is one of the (mental) actions discussed above. The proof can possibly be translated into natural language, and declined either top-down or bottom-up.

As said in the Introduction, we model agents which, to execute an action, may have to pay a cost, so they must have a consistent budget available. Our agents, moreover, are entitled to perform only those physical actions that they conclude they can do. In our approach, agents belong to groups (where the smallest possible group is the single agent), and agents belonging to a group are by definition cooperative. With respect to action execution, an action can be executed by the group if at least one agent in the group is able to execute it, and the group has the necessary budget available, sharing the cost according to some policy. The cooperative nature of our agents manifests itself also in selecting, among the agents that are able to do some physical action, the one(s) which best prefer to perform that action. We do not have introduced costs and budget, feasibility of actions and willingness to perform them, *in the language* for two reasons: to keep the complexity of the logic reasonable, and to make such features customizable in a modular way.[1] In fact, by making the assumption that agents are cooperative, we also assume that they are aware of and agree with the cost-sharing policy. So, as seen below, costs and budget are coped with at the semantic level. Variants of the logic can be easily worked out, where the modalities of cost sharing are different from the one shown here, where group members share an action cost in equal parts. Below, we indicate which are the points that should be modified to change the cost-sharing policy. Moreover, for brevity we introduce a single budget function, and thus, implicitly, a single resource to be spent. Several budget functions, each one concerning a different resource, might be plainly defined.

2.2 Semantics

Definition 1 introduces the notion of *L-INF model*, which is then used to introduce semantics of the static fragment of the logic. As before let Agt be the set of agents.

Definition 1. *A model is a tuple $M = (W, N, \mathcal{R}, E, B, C, A, P, V)$ where:*

- *W is a set of worlds (or situations);*
- *$\mathcal{R} = \{R_i\}_{i \in Agt}$ is a collection of equivalence relations on W: $R_i \subseteq W \times W$ for each $i \in Agt$;*

---

[1] We intend to use this logic in practice, to formalize memory in DALI agents, where DALI is a logic-based agent-oriented programming language [5,6,14]. So, computational effectiveness and modularity are crucial. Assuming that agents share the cost is reasonable when agents share resources, or cooperate to a common goal, as discussed, e.g., in [7,8].

- $N : Agt \times W \longrightarrow 2^{2^W}$ is a neighborhood function such that, for each $i \in Agt$, each $w, v \in W$, and each $X \subseteq W$ these conditions hold:
  - **(C1)** if $X \in N(i, w)$ then $X \subseteq \{v \in W \mid wR_i v\}$,
  - **(C2)** if $wR_i v$ then $N(i, w) = N(i, v)$;
- $E : Agt \times W \longrightarrow 2^{\mathcal{L}_{ACT}}$ is an executability function of mental actions such that, for each $i \in Agt$ and $w, v \in W$, it holds that:
  - **(D1)** if $wR_i v$ then $E(i, w) = E(i, v)$;
- $B : Agt \times W \longrightarrow \mathbb{N}$ is a budget function such that, for each $i \in Agt$ and $w, v \in W$, the following holds
  - **(E1)** if $wR_i v$ then $B(i, w) = B(i, v)$;
- $C : Agt \times \mathcal{L}_{ACT} \times W \longrightarrow \mathbb{N}$ is a cost function such that, for each $i \in Agt$, $\alpha \in \mathcal{L}_{ACT}$, and $w, v \in W$, it holds that:
  - **(F1)** if $wR_i v$ then $C(i, \alpha, w) = C(i, \alpha, v)$;
- $A : Agt \times W \longrightarrow 2^{Atm_A}$ is an executability function for physical actions such that, for each $i \in Agt$ and $w, v \in W$, it holds that:
  - **(G1)** if $wR_i v$ then $A(i, w) = A(i, v)$;
- $P : Agt \times W \times Atm_A \longrightarrow Int$ is a preference function for physical actions α such that, for each $i \in Agt$ and $w, v \in W$, it holds that:
  - **(H1)** if $wR_i v$ then $P(i, w, \alpha) = P(i, v, \alpha)$;
- $V : W \longrightarrow 2^{Atm}$ is a valuation function.

To simplify the notation, let $R_i(w)$ denote the set $\{v \in W \mid wR_i v\}$, for $w \in W$. The set $R_i(w)$ identifies the situations that agent i considers possible at world w. It is the *epistemic state* of agent i at w. In cognitive terms, $R_i(w)$ can be conceived as the set of all situations that agent i *can retrieve* from its long-term memory and reason about.

While $R_i(w)$ concerns background knowledge, $N(i, w)$ is the set of all facts that agent i explicitly believes at world w, a fact being identified with a set of worlds. Hence, if $X \in N(i, w)$ then, the agent i has the fact X under the focus of its attention and believes it. We say that $N(i, w)$ is the explicit *belief set* of agent i at world w.

The executability of inferential actions is determined by the function E. For an agent i, $E(i, w)$ is the set of inferential actions that agent i can execute at world w. The value $B(i, w)$ is the budget the agent has available to perform inferential actions. Similarly, the value $C(i, \alpha, w)$ is the cost to be paid by agent i to execute the inferential action α in the world w. The executability of physical actions is determined by the function A. For an agent i, $A(i, w)$ is the set of physical actions that agent i can execute at world w.

The agent's preference on executability of physical actions is determined by the function P. For an agent i, and a physical action α, $P(i, w, \alpha)$ is an integer value d indicating the degree of willingness of agent i to execute such action at world w.

Constraint **(C1)** imposes that agent i can have explicit in its mind only facts which are compatible with its current epistemic state. Moreover, according to constraint **(C2)**, if a world v is compatible with the epistemic state of agent i at world w, then agent i should have the same explicit beliefs at w and v. In other words, if two situations are equivalent as concerns background knowledge, then they cannot be distinguished through the explicit belief set. This aspect of the semantics can be extended in future work to allow agents to make plausible assumptions. Analogous properties are imposed by constraints **(D1)**, **(E1)**, and **(F1)**. Namely, **(D1)** imposes that agent i always knows which inferential actions it can perform and those it cannot. (**E1**) states that agent i always knows the available budget in a world (potentially needed to perform actions). (**F1**) determines that agent i always knows how much it costs to perform an inferential action. (**G1**) and (**H1**) determine that an agent i always knows which physical actions it can perform and those it cannot, and with which degree of willingness.

Truth values for formulas of *L-DINF* are inductively defined as follows. Given a model $M = (W, N, \mathcal{R}, E, B, C, A, P, V)$, $i \in Agt$, $G \subseteq Agt$, $w \in W$, and a formula $\varphi \in \mathcal{L}_{L\text{-}INF}$, we introduce the following shorthand notation:

$$\|\varphi\|_{i,w}^M = \{v \in W : wR_iv \text{ and } M, v \models \varphi\}$$

whenever $M, v \models \varphi$ is well-defined (see below). Then, we set:

- $M, w \models p$ iff $p \in V(w)$
- $M, w \models exec_i(\alpha)$ iff $\alpha \in E(i, w)$
- $M, w \models exec_G(\alpha)$ iff there exists $i \in G$ with $\alpha \in E(i, w)$
- $M, w \models can\_do_i(\phi_A)$ iff $\alpha \in A(i, w)$
- $M, w \models can\_do_G(\phi_A)$ iff there exists $i \in G$ with $\alpha \in A(i, w)$
- $M, w \models pref\_do_i(\phi_A, d)$ iff $\phi_A \in A(i, w)$ and $P(i, w, \phi_A) = d$
- $M, w \models pref\_do_G(i, \phi_A)$ iff $M, w \models pref\_do_i(\phi_A, d)$ for $d = \max\{P(j, w, \phi_A)$ $\mid j \in G \wedge \phi_A \in A(j, w)\}$
- $M, w \models \neg\varphi$ iff $M, w \not\models \varphi$
- $M, w \models \varphi \wedge \psi$ iff $M, w \models \varphi$ and $M, w \models \psi$
- $M, w \models \mathbf{B}_i \varphi$ iff $\|\varphi\|_{i,w}^M \in N(i, w)$
- $M, w \models \mathbf{K}_i \varphi$ iff $M, v \models \varphi$ for all $v \in R_i(w)$

As seen above, a physical action can be performed by a group of agents if at least one agent of the group can do it, and the level of preference for performing this action is set to the maximum among those of the agents enabled to do this action. For any inferential action α performed by any agent i, we set:

- $M, w \models [G : \alpha]\varphi$ iff $M^{[G:\alpha]}, w \models \varphi$

where we put $M^{[G:\alpha]} = \langle W; N^{[G:\alpha]}, \mathcal{R}, E, B^{[G:\alpha]}, C, A, P, V \rangle$, representing the fact that the execution of an inferential action α affects the sets of beliefs of agent i and modifies the available budget. Such operation can add new beliefs by direct perception, by means of one inference step, or as a conjunction of previous beliefs. Hence, when introducing new beliefs (i.e., performing mental actions), the neighborhood must be extended accordingly.

A key aspect in the definition of the logic is the following, which states under which conditions, and by which agent(s), an action may be performed.

$$enabled_w(G, \alpha) : \quad \exists j \in G\, (\alpha \in E(j, w) \wedge \tfrac{C(j, \alpha, w)}{|G|} \leq \min_{h \in G} B(h, w)).$$

This condition states when an inferential action is enabled. In the above particular formulation (that is not fixed, but can be customized to the specific application domain) if at least an agent can perform it; and if the "payment" due by each agent, obtained by dividing the action's cost equally among all agents of the group, is within each agent's available budget. In case more than one agent in G can execute an action, we implicitly assume the agent j performing the action to be the one corresponding to the lowest possible cost. Namely, j is such that $C(j, \alpha, w) = \min_{h \in G} C(h, \alpha, w)$. This definition reflects a parsimony criterion reasonably adoptable by cooperative agents sharing a crucial resource such as, e.g., energy or money. Other choices might be viable, so variations of this logic can be easily defined simply by devising some other enabling condition and, possibly, introducing differences in neighborhood update. Notice that the definition of the enabling function basically specifies the "**role**" that agents take while concurring with their own resources to actions' execution. Also, in case of specification of different resources, different corresponding enabling functions might be defined.

Our contribution to modularity is that functions A and P, i.e., executability of physical actions and preference level of an agent concerning physical action execution, are not meant to be built-in. Rather, they can be defined via separate sub-theories, possibly defined using different logics, or, in a practical approach, via pieces of code. This approach can be extended to function C, i.e., the cost of mental actions instead of being fixed (like in our previous work) may vary and computed upon need.

2.3 Belief Update

In this kind of logic, updating an agent's beliefs accounts to modify the neighborhood of the present world. The updated neighborhood $N^{[G:\alpha]}$ resulting from execution of a mental action α by a group G of agents is as follows.

$$N^{[G:\downarrow(\psi,\chi)]}(i,w) = \begin{cases} N(i,w) \cup \{||\chi||_{i,w}^M\} & \text{if } i \in G \text{ and } enabled_w(G, \downarrow(\psi,\chi)) \text{ and} \\ & M, w \models \mathbf{B}_i\psi \wedge \mathbf{K}_i(\psi \to \chi) \\ N(i,w) & \text{otherwise} \end{cases}$$

$$N^{[G:\cap(\psi,\chi)]}(i,w) = \begin{cases} N(i,w) \cup \{||\psi \wedge \chi||_{i,w}^M\} & \text{if } i \in G \text{ and } enabled_w(G, \cap(\psi,\chi)) \\ & \text{and } M, w \models \mathbf{B}_i\psi \wedge \mathbf{B}_i\chi \\ N(i,w) & \text{otherwise} \end{cases}$$

$$N^{[G:\dashv(\psi,\chi)]}(i,w) = \begin{cases} N(i,w) \setminus \{||\chi||_{i,w}^M\} & \text{if } i \in G \text{ and } enabled_w(G, \dashv(\psi,\chi)) \text{ and} \\ & M, w \models \mathbf{B}_i\psi \wedge \mathbf{K}_i(\psi \to \neg\chi) \\ N(i,w) & \text{otherwise} \end{cases}$$

$$N^{[G:\vdash(\psi,\chi)]}(i,w) = \begin{cases} N(i,w) \cup \{||\chi||_{i,w}^M\} & \text{if } i \in G \text{ and } enabled_w(G, \vdash(\psi,\chi)) \text{ and} \\ & M, w \models \mathbf{B}_i\psi \wedge \mathbf{B}_i(\psi \to \chi) \\ N(i,w) & \text{otherwise} \end{cases}$$

Notice that, after an inferential action α has been performed by an agent $j \in G$, all agents $i \in G$ see the same update in the neighborhood. Conversely, for any agent $h \notin G$ the neighborhood remains unchanged (i.e., $N^{[G:\alpha]}(h, w) = N(h, w)$). However, even for agents in G, the neighborhood remains unchanged if the required preconditions, on explicit beliefs, knowledge, and budget, do not hold (and hence the action is

not executed). Notice also that we might devise variations of the logic by making different decisions about neighborhood update to implement, for instance, partial visibility
within a group.

Since each agent in G has to contribute to cover the costs of execution by consuming
part of its available budget, an update of the budget function is needed. We assume
however that only inferential actions that add new beliefs have a cost. I.e., forming
conjunction and performing belief revision are actions with no cost. As before, for an
action α, we require $enabled_w(G, \alpha)$ to hold and assume that $j \in G$ executes α. Then,
depending on α, we have:

$$
B^{[G:\downarrow(\psi,\chi)]}(i,w) = \begin{cases} B(i,w) - \dfrac{C(j,\downarrow(\psi,\chi),w)}{|G|} & \text{if } i \in G \text{ and } enabled_w(G, \downarrow(\psi,\chi)) \\ & \text{and } M, w \models \mathbf{B}_i \psi \wedge \mathbf{K}_i(\psi \to \chi) \\ B(i,w) & \text{otherwise} \end{cases}
$$

$$
B^{[G:\vdash(\psi,\chi)]}(i,w) = \begin{cases} B(i,w) - \dfrac{C(j,\vdash(\psi,\chi),w)}{|G|} & \text{if } i \in G \text{ and } enabled_w(G, \vdash(\psi,\chi)) \\ & \text{and } M, w \models \mathbf{B}_i \psi \wedge \mathbf{B}_i(\psi \to \chi) \\ B(i,w) & \text{otherwise} \end{cases}
$$

We write $\models_{L\text{-}DINF} \varphi$ to denote that $M, w \models \varphi$ holds for all worlds w of every
model M.

We introduce below relevant consequences of our formalization. For lack of space
we omit the proof, that can be developed analogously to what done in previous
work [10].

Property. As consequence of previous definitions, for any set of agents G and each
$i \in G$, we have the following:

- $\models_{L\text{-}INF} (\mathbf{K}_i(\varphi \to \psi)) \wedge \mathbf{B}_i \varphi) \to [G : \downarrow(\varphi,\psi)] \mathbf{B}_i \psi$.
  Namely, if an agent has φ among beliefs and $\mathbf{K}_i(\varphi \to \psi)$ in its background knowledge, then as a consequence of the action $\downarrow(\varphi,\psi)$ the agent and any group G to
  which it belongs start believing ψ.
- $\models_{L\text{-}INF} (\mathbf{K}_i(\varphi \to \neg\psi)) \wedge \mathbf{B}_i \varphi) \to [G : \dashv(\varphi,\psi)] \neg\mathbf{B}_i \psi$.
  Namely, if an agent has φ among beliefs and $\mathbf{K}_i(\varphi \to \neg\psi)$ in its background knowledge (for φ, ψ ground atoms), then as a consequence of the action $\downarrow(\varphi, \psi)$ the agent
  and any group G to which it belongs stop believing ψ.
- $\models_{L\text{-}INF} (\mathbf{B}_i \varphi \wedge \mathbf{B}_i \psi) \to [G : \cap(\varphi,\psi)] \mathbf{B}_i(\varphi \wedge \psi)$.
  Namely, if an agent has φ and ψ as beliefs, then as a consequence of the action
  $\cap(\varphi,\psi)$ the agent and any group G to which it belongs start believing $\varphi \wedge \psi$.
- $\models_{L\text{-}INF} (\mathbf{B}_i(\varphi \to \psi)) \wedge \mathbf{B}_i \varphi) \to [G : \vdash(\varphi,\psi)] \mathbf{B}_i, \psi$.
  Namely, if an agent has φ among its beliefs and $\mathbf{B}_i(\varphi \to \psi)$ in its working memory,
  then as a consequence of the action $\vdash(\varphi,\psi)$ the agent and any group G to which it
  belongs start believing ψ.

2.4   Axiomatization

Below we introduce the axiomatization of our logic. The *L-INF* and *L-DINF* axioms and inference rules are the following:

1. $(\mathbf{K}_i\,\varphi \wedge \mathbf{K}_i(\varphi \to \psi)) \to \mathbf{K}_i\,\psi$;
2. $\mathbf{K}_i\,\varphi \to \varphi$;
3. $\neg\mathbf{K}_i(\varphi \wedge \neg\varphi)$;
4. $\mathbf{K}_i\,\varphi \to \mathbf{K}_i\,\mathbf{K}_i\,\varphi$;
5. $\neg\mathbf{K}_i\,\varphi \to \mathbf{K}_i\,\neg\mathbf{K}_i\,\varphi$;
6. $\mathbf{B}_i\,\varphi \wedge \mathbf{K}_i\,(\varphi \leftrightarrow \psi) \to \mathbf{B}_i\,\psi$;
7. $\mathbf{B}_i\,\varphi \to \mathbf{K}_i\,\mathbf{B}_i\,\varphi$;
8. $\dfrac{\varphi}{\mathbf{K}_i\,\varphi}$;
9. $[G:\alpha]p \leftrightarrow p$;
10. $[G:\alpha]\neg\varphi \leftrightarrow \neg[G:\alpha]\varphi$;
11. $exec_G(\alpha) \to \mathbf{K}_i\,(exec_G(\alpha))$;
12. $[G:\alpha](\varphi \wedge \psi) \leftrightarrow [G:\alpha]\varphi \wedge [G:\alpha]\psi$;
13. $[G:\alpha]\mathbf{K}_i\,\varphi \leftrightarrow \mathbf{K}_i\,([G:\alpha]\varphi)$;
14. $[G:\downarrow(\varphi,\psi)]\mathbf{B}_i\,\chi \leftrightarrow \mathbf{B}_i\,([G:\downarrow(\varphi,\psi)]\chi) \vee ((\mathbf{B}_i\,\varphi \wedge \mathbf{K}_i\,(\varphi \to \psi))$
    $\wedge\, \mathbf{K}_i\,([G:\downarrow(\varphi,\psi)]\chi \leftrightarrow \psi))$;
15. $[G:\cap(\varphi,\psi)]\mathbf{B}_i\,\chi \leftrightarrow \mathbf{B}_i\,([G:\cap(\varphi,\psi)]\chi) \vee ((\mathbf{B}_i\,\varphi \wedge \mathbf{B}_i\,\psi)$
    $\wedge\, \mathbf{K}_i\,[G:\cap(\varphi,\psi)]\chi \leftrightarrow (\varphi \wedge \psi))$;
16. $[G:\vdash(\varphi,\psi)]\mathbf{B}_i\,\chi \leftrightarrow \mathbf{B}_i\,([G:\vdash(\varphi,\psi)]\chi) \vee ((\mathbf{B}_i\,\varphi \wedge \mathbf{B}_i\,(\varphi \to \psi))$
    $\wedge\, \mathbf{K}_i\,([G:\vdash(\varphi,\psi)]\chi \leftrightarrow \psi))$;
17. $[G:\dashv(\varphi,\psi)]\neg\mathbf{B}_i\,\chi \leftrightarrow \mathbf{B}_i\,([G:\dashv(\varphi,\psi)]\chi) \vee ((\mathbf{B}_i\,\varphi \wedge \mathbf{K}_i\,(\varphi \to \neg\psi))$
    $\wedge\, \mathbf{K}_i\,([G:\dashv(\varphi,\psi)]\chi \leftrightarrow \psi))$;
18. $intend_G(\phi_A) \leftrightarrow \forall i \in G\; intend_i(\phi_A)$;
19. $do_G(\phi_A) \to can\_do_G(\phi_A)$;
20. $do_i(\phi_A) \to can\_do_i(\phi_A)$;
21. $\dfrac{\psi \leftrightarrow \chi}{\varphi \leftrightarrow \varphi[\psi/\chi]}$.

We write *L-DINF* $\vdash \varphi$ to denote that φ is a theorem of *L-DINF*. It is easy to verify that the above axiomatization is sound for the class of *L-INF* models, namely, all axioms are valid and inference rules preserve validity. In particular, soundness of axioms 14–17 immediately follows from the semantics of $[G{:}\alpha]\varphi$, for each inferential action α, as previously defined. Notice that, by abuse of notation, we have axiomatized the special predicates concerning intention and action enabling. Axioms 18–20 concern in fact physical actions, stating that: what is intended by a group of agents is intended by them all; and, neither an agent nor a group of agents can do what it is not enabled to do. Such axioms are not enforced by the semantics, but are supposed to be enforced by a designer's/programmer's encoding of parts of an agent's behaviour. In fact, axiom 18 enforces agents in a group to be cooperative. Axioms 19 and 20 ensure that agents will attempt to perform actions only if their preconditions are satisfied, i.e., if they can do them. We do not handle such properties in the semantics as done, e.g., in dynamic logic, because we want agents' definition to be independent of the practical aspect, so we explicitly intend to introduce flexibility in the definition of such parts.

3   Problem Specification and Inference: An Example

In this section, we propose an example of problem specification and inference in *L-DINF*. Consider a group of n agents, e.g., three, who are siblings or friends, who decide to act together in order to renovate some property, e.g., a cottage where to spend weekends. In order to save money and time, they aim to contribute at practical work, to the extent of their capabilities. Prior to starting the activities, they agree upon sustaining costs in equal parts. They know that one of them is able to repair the roof, while the other two are both able to redecorate the walls and replace the carpet, but one of the two would clearly prefer the former task. Below we show how our logic is able to represent the situation, and the proceedings of this work. For the sake of simplicity of illustration and of brevity, the example is in "skeletal" form.

Each agent will initially have in its knowledge base the fact $\mathbf{K}_i(intend_G$ ($renovate$)) (implicitly, the cottage). The physical actions that agents can perform are the following:

$$buy\text{-}material, \;\; redecorate\text{-}walls, \;\; repair\text{-}roof, \;\; replace\text{-}carpet. \tag{1}$$

Assume that the knowledge base of each agent i contains the following rule, that specifies how to reach the intended goal in terms of actions to perform:

$$\mathbf{K}_i(intend_G(renovate) \rightarrow intend_G(buy\text{-}material) \wedge intend_G(repair\text{-}roof) \wedge$$
$$intend_G(replace\text{-}carpet) \wedge intend_G(redecorate\text{-}walls)) \tag{2}$$

By axiom 18 listed in previous section, every agent will also have the specialized rule

$$\mathbf{K}_i(intend_i(renovate) \rightarrow intend_i(buy\text{-}material) \wedge intend_i(repair\text{-}roof) \wedge$$
$$intend_i(replace\text{-}carpet) \wedge intend_i(redecorate\text{-}walls)) \tag{3}$$

Therefore, the following is entailed for each of the agents ($1 \leq i \leq 3$):

$$\begin{aligned}
&\mathbf{K}_i(intend_i(renovate) \rightarrow intend_i(buy\text{-}material)) \\
&\mathbf{K}_i(intend_i(renovate) \rightarrow intend_i(repair\text{-}roof)) \\
&\mathbf{K}_i(intend_i(renovate) \rightarrow intend_i(replace\text{-}carpet)) \\
&\mathbf{K}_i(intend_i(renovate) \rightarrow intend_i(redecorate\text{-}walls))
\end{aligned} \tag{4}$$

Assume now that the knowledge base of each agent i contains also the following general rules, stating that the group is available to perform each of the necessary actions.

$$\begin{aligned}
&\mathbf{K}_i(intend_G(buy\text{-}material) \wedge can\_do_G(buy\text{-}material) \wedge \\
&\qquad\qquad pref\_do_G(i, buy\text{-}material) \rightarrow do_G(buy\text{-}material)) \\
&\mathbf{K}_i(intend_G(repair\text{-}roof) \wedge can\_do_G(repair\text{-}roof) \wedge \\
&\qquad\qquad pref\_do_G(i, repair\text{-}roof) \rightarrow do_G(repair\text{-}roof)) \\
&\mathbf{K}_i(intend_G(replace\text{-}carpet) \wedge can\_do_G(replace\text{-}carpet) \wedge \\
&\qquad\qquad pref\_do_G(i, replace\text{-}carpet) \rightarrow do_G(replace\text{-}carpet)) \\
&\mathbf{K}_i(intend_G(redecorate\text{-}walls) \wedge can\_do_G(redecorate\text{-}walls) \wedge \\
&\qquad\qquad pref\_do_G(i, redecorate\text{-}walls) \rightarrow do_G(redecorate\text{-}walls))
\end{aligned} \tag{5}$$

As before, by axiom 18 such rules can be specialized to each single agent $1, 2, 3$.

$$\begin{aligned}
&\mathbf{K}_i(intend_i(buy\text{-}material) \wedge can\_do_i(buy\text{-}material) \wedge \\
&\qquad\qquad pref\_do_G(i, buy\text{-}material) \rightarrow do_i(buy\text{-}material)) \\
&\mathbf{K}_i(intend_i(repair\text{-}roof) \wedge can\_do_i(repair\text{-}roof) \wedge \\
&\qquad\qquad pref\_do_G(i, repair\text{-}roof) \rightarrow do_i(repair\text{-}roof)) \\
&\mathbf{K}_i(intend_i(replace\text{-}carpet) \wedge can\_do_i(replace\text{-}carpet) \wedge \\
&\qquad\qquad pref\_do_G(i, replace\text{-}carpet) \rightarrow do_i(replace\text{-}carpet)) \\
&\mathbf{K}_i(intend_i(redecorate\text{-}walls) \wedge can\_do_i(redecorate\text{-}walls) \wedge \\
&\qquad\qquad pref\_do_G(i, redecorate\text{-}walls) \rightarrow do_i(redecorate\text{-}walls))
\end{aligned}$$

$$(6)$$

As previously stated, whenever an agent derives $do_i(\phi_A)$ for any physical action ϕ_A, the action is supposed to have been performed via some kind of *semantic attachment* which links the agent to the external environment. However, $do_i(\phi_A)$ will be derived by means of some mental action based upon the available rules. Such mental action can have a cost, that can be paid either by the agent itself or by the group (according to the adopted policy of cost-sharing for this group). The reason to attribute the cost to the mental action is exactly to avoid that some agent tries to execute physical actions that it cannot support. According to the above rules, an agent can execute an action ϕ_A if it is allowed to perform that action ($can\_do_i(\phi_A)$), and if it is the one most willing to do it ($pref\_do_G(i, \phi_A)$). In our approach, such conclusion will be drawn on the basis of the assessment performed in external modules. Such modules will provide the decision according to some kind of reasoning process in some formalism, with respect to which our logic is completely agnostic: they will add the corresponding facts to each agent's knowledge base.

In order to have our agents do the actions listed in (1) (note that one agent will have to perform two of them, as there are three agents and four actions), four sequences of mental actions will have to be executed, yielding, respectively, conclusions of the forms
$do_G(buy\text{-}material)$, $do_G(repair\text{-}roof)$, $do_G(replace\text{-}carpet)$, $do_G(redecorate\text{-}walls)$,
and causing their addition to agents' working memory. Such reasoning would consist in mental actions of kind $\cap$ to form conjunctions from single facts, and mental actions of kind $\downarrow$ to apply knowledge rule, i.e., given their preconditions, draw the conclusions. In particular, given the initial general intention by the group, it will be possible to derive the practical goal, in terms of the conjunction of actions to be performed by the group. From its own specialized rules and the available facts about enabling and willingness, the execution of each action by some agent i will be hopefully derived. Note that, there can be unlucky situations where no agent is enabled to perform some action, or that the one allowed is not willing, or that there is not enough budget. In this case, the goal fails.

Let α_1–α_4 be the last mental actions performed at the end of the mentioned four sequences of mental inferences (that lead to derive the $do_i(\phi_A)$, for some $i \leq 3$ and for ϕ_A among the actions in (1)), respectively. Assume, also, that the costs of α_1–α_4 are the following (and, for simplicity, assume all other mental actions have no cost):

$$C(i, \alpha_1, w) = 18, \quad C(i, \alpha_2, w) = 15, \quad C(i, \alpha_3, w) = 3, \quad C(i, \alpha_4, w) = 20,$$

and that $\alpha_j \in E(i, w), j \leq 3$ holds, for each world w, each agent i, and each action α_j.

Assume that in world w_1 the three agents have the following budgets to perform mental actions: $B(1, w_1) = 11$, $B(2, w_1) = 21$, $B(3, w_1) = 20$.

Assume, e.g., that all agents are enabled in w_1 to go and buy material. Suppose that agent 1 is the best wishing to go to buy, i.e., under the current model (which remains implicit) $w_1 \models can\_do_1(buy\text{-}material) \wedge pref\_do_G(1, buy\text{-}material)$. However, it alone cannot perform the action, because it does not have enough budget. But, using the inferential action $[G{:}\alpha_1]$, with $G = \{1,2,3\}$, the other agents can devote part of their budgets to share the cost, so the group can perform α_1, because $\frac{C(1,\alpha_1,w_1)}{|G|} \leq min_{h \in G} B(h, w_1)$. Hence, $\mathbf{B}_i(do_G(buy\text{-}material))$ can be inferred by each agent i (in consequence, the *past event* $\mathbf{B}_i(do_G^P(buy\text{-}material))$ will also be asserted). Indeed, the inferential action is considered as performed by the whole group G, so each agent of G updates its neighborhood. After the execution of the action the budget of each agent is updated as well (cf., Sect. 2.2). The new budgets, given that we are assuming the policy to divide expenses into equal parts, are: $B(1, w_2) = 5$, $B(2, w_2) = 15$, $B(3, w_2) = 14$, where we name w_2 the situation reached after executing the action.

Assume that only agent 3 is enabled in w_2 to repair the roof. Suppose that agent 3 is wishing to go to repair, i.e., under the current model (which remains implicit) $w_2 \models can\_do_3(repair\text{-}roof) \wedge pref\_do_G(3, repair\text{-}roof)$. It alone however cannot perform the action, because it does not have enough budget. But, using the inferential action $[G{:}\alpha_2]$, with $G = \{1,2,3\}$, the other agents can devote part of their budgets to share the cost, so the group can perform α_2, because $\frac{C(3,\alpha_2,w_2)}{|G|} \leq min_{h \in G} B(h, w_2)$. Hence, $\mathbf{B}_i(do_G(repair\text{-}roof))$ can be inferred by each agent i (in consequence, also $\mathbf{B}_i(do_G^P(repair\text{-}roof))$ will be asserted). Again, after the execution of the action the budget of each agent is updated. The new budgets, given that we are assuming the policy to divide expenses into equal parts, are: $B(1, w_3) = 0$, $B(2, w_3) = 10$, $B(3, w_3) = 9$, where we name w_3 the situation reached after executing the action.

Assume that only agent 2 is enabled in w_3 to replace the carpet. Agent 2 can perform the action alone because it has enough budget. So, $[G : \alpha_3]$, with $G = \{1,2,3\}$, can be performed obtaining $\mathbf{B}_i(do_G(replace\text{-}carpet))$ (and, as a consequence, $\mathbf{B}_i(do_G^P(replace\text{-}carpet))$). Indeed, the inferential action is considered as performed by the whole group G so each agent of G updates its neighborhood. After the execution of the action only the budget of agent 2 is updated: $B(2, w_4) = 7$. Summing up budgets: $B(1, w_4) = 0$, $B(2, w_4) = 7$, $B(3, w_1) = 9$, where we name w_4 the situation reached after executing the action.

There would be the last goal $(intend_G(redecorate\text{-}walls))$ but no agent has the necessary budget, so they cannot perform α_4 so goal cannot be achieved, and therefore the overall goal fails. Only some injection of new budget (maybe a loan from another group) might save the situation. Interaction among groups is a subject of future work.

It is relevant to comment about the role of past events. If the set of past events, which is a part of an agent's short-term memory, is made available to the external modules defining actions enabling and degree of willingness, such recordings might be used, for instance, to define constraints concerning actions execution. For instance, referring to our example, it would be reasonable to state that no repair can take place if the material has not been bought yet, and then, e.g., that repairing the roof should be performed as first thing.

4   Canonical Model and Strong Completeness

In this section, we introduce the notion of canonical model of our logic, and we outline the proof of strong completeness w.r.t. the proposed class of models (by means of a standard canonical-model argument). As before, let Agt be a set of agents.

Definition 2. *The* canonical L-INF *model is a tuple* $M_c = \langle W_c, N_c, \mathcal{R}_c, E_c, B_c, C_c, A_c, P_c, V_c \rangle$ *where:*

- W_c *is the set of all maximal consistent subsets of* $\mathcal{L}_{L\text{-}INF}$;
- $\mathcal{R}_c = \{R_{c,i}\}_{i \in Agt}$ *is a collection of equivalence relations on* W_c *such that, for every* $i \in Agt$ *and* $w, v \in W_c$, $wR_{c,i}v$ *if and only if (for all* φ, $\mathbf{K}_i \varphi \in w$ *implies* $\varphi \in v$)
- *For* $w \in W_c$, $\varphi \in \mathcal{L}_{L\text{-}INF}$ *let* $A_\varphi(i, w) = \{v \in R_{c,i}(w) \mid \varphi \in v\}$. *Then, we put* $N_c(i, w) = \{A_\varphi(i, w) \mid \mathbf{B}_i \varphi \in w\}$.
- $E_c : Agt \times W_c \longrightarrow 2^{\mathcal{L}_{ACT}}$ *is such that, for each* $i \in Agt$ *and* $w, v \in W_c$, *if* $wR_{c,i}v$ *then* $E_c(i, w) = E_c(i, v)$;
- $B_c : Agt \times W_c \longrightarrow \mathbb{N}$ *is such that, for each* $i \in Agt$ *and* $w, v \in W_c$, *if* $wR_{c,i}v$ *then* $B_c(i, w) = B_c(i, v)$;
- $C_c : Agt \times \mathcal{L}_{ACT} \times W_c \longrightarrow \mathbb{N}$ *is such that, for each* $i \in Agt$, $\alpha \in \mathcal{L}_{ACT}$, *and* $w, v \in W_c$, *if* $wR_{c,i}v$ *then* $C_c(i, \alpha, w) = C_c(i, \alpha, v)$;
- $A_c : Agt \times W_c \longrightarrow 2^{Atm_A}$ *is such that, for each* $i \in Agt$ *and* $w, v \in W_c$, *if* $wR_{c,i}v$ *then* $A_c(i, w) = A_c(i, v)$;
- $P_c : Agt \times W_c \times Atm_A \longrightarrow Int$ *is such that, for each* $i \in Agt$ *and* $w, v \in W$, *if* $wR_{c,i}v$ *then* $P_c(i, w, \alpha) = P_c(i, v, \alpha)$;
- $V_c : W_c \longrightarrow 2^{Atm}$ *is such that* $V_c(w) = Atm \cap w$.

Note that, analogously to what done before, $R_{c,i}(w)$ denotes the set $\{v \in W_c \mid wR_{c,i}v\}$, for each $i \in Agt$. It is easy to verify that M_c is an *L-INF* model as defined in Definition 1, since, it satisfies conditions (**C1**), (**C2**), (**D1**), (**E1**), (**F1**), (**G1**), (**H1**). Hence, it models the axioms and the inference rules 1–17 and 21 introduced before (while, as mentioned in Sect. 2.4, axioms 18–20 are assumed to be enforced by the specification of agents behaviour). Consequently, the following properties hold too. Let $w \in W_c$, then:

- given $\varphi \in \mathcal{L}_{L\text{-}INF}$, it holds that $\mathbf{K}_i \varphi \in w$ if and only if $\forall v \in W_c$ such that $wR_{c,i}v$ we have $\varphi \in v$;
- for $\varphi \in \mathcal{L}_{L\text{-}INF}$, if $\mathbf{B}_i \varphi \in w$ and $wR_{c,i}v$ then $\mathbf{B}_i \varphi \in v$;

Thus, $R_{c,i}$-related worlds have the same knowledge and N_c-related worlds have the same beliefs, i.e. there can be $R_{c,i}$-related worlds with different beliefs.

By proceeding similarly to what done in [1], we obtain the proof of strong completeness. For lack of space, we list the main theorems but omit lemmas and proofs, that we have however developed analogously to what done in previous work [10].

Theorem 1. *L-INF is strongly complete for the class of L-INF models.*

Theorem 2. *L-DINF is strongly complete for the class of L-INF models.*

5   Future Extension: Steps to Reach a Goal

We intend, in future work, to enhance our language by introducing the expression $\Diamond\varphi$, which has to be read "the agent can ensure φ by executing some (inferential or physical) actions in its repertoire". Also, we intend to inductively define: $\Diamond^0\varphi = \varphi$, $\Diamond^{k+1} = \Diamond\Diamond^k\varphi$. In our aim therefore, the formula $\Diamond^k B\,\varphi$ represents the fact that the agent is capable of inferring φ in k steps. We might easily extend the semantics by stating

$$M, w \models \Diamond\varphi \leftrightarrow \exists\alpha \in E(w) \text{ s.t. } M^\alpha, w \models \varphi$$

(where $E(w)$ denotes the executability function for the specific agent under consideration). A tentative axiomatization could be:

- $exec(\alpha) \wedge [\alpha]\varphi \rightarrow \Diamond\varphi$;
- $p \rightarrow \Diamond p$;
- $\Diamond(\varphi \wedge \psi) \rightarrow \Diamond\varphi \wedge \Diamond\psi$;
- $\Diamond\varphi \rightarrow \Diamond\Diamond\varphi$;
- $\Diamond B\,\varphi \rightarrow B\,\Diamond\varphi$;
- $\Diamond K\,\varphi \rightarrow K\,\Diamond\varphi$.
- $([\alpha]\varphi) \rightarrow \Diamond^1\varphi$.
- $([\alpha_1]([\alpha_2]\varphi)) \rightarrow \Diamond^2\varphi$.
- $([\alpha_1]([\alpha_2]([\alpha_3]\varphi))) \rightarrow \Diamond^3\varphi$
- $\ldots$

So far however, we are presently able to consider only a limited number of iterations of the $\Diamond$ operator, in a specific (though analogous) way for each case.

Yet, even in the bounded form such operator may allow us to better formalize many practical situations, including the one in the example discussed in Sect. 3. There, one could take into account the expected duration of each action. For instance, the rule expressing the goal of our group of agents could be reformulated for instance as follows, where $\Diamond^v\phi_A$ means that we expect action ϕ_A to take (at most) v steps for its completion:

$$\mathbf{K}_i(intend_G(renovate) \rightarrow intend_G(\Diamond^1\ buy\_material) \wedge intend_G(\Diamond^5\ repair\_roof) \wedge$$
$$intend_G(\Diamond^4\ replace\_carpet) \wedge intend_G(\Diamond^4\ redecorate\_walls)).$$

6   Future Extension: Theory of Mind

Intelligent software agents are usually modelled and programmed (via available agent-oriented programming languages) in terms of the BDI (Belief, Desire, Intention) modal logic [23], that however is limited to the representation of the mental state of the agent itself, but is too weak to represent Theory of Mind, which is understood as the ability to attribute mental states not only to oneself but also to others. I.e., in humans, it is the intuitive theory, developed during childhood, by which people understand others' actions in terms of their beliefs, desires, emotions, and supposed intentions. Such ability is crucial to interpret and predict other persons' behavioural responses. Recent research [15] has claimed that epistemic logic could be a suitable formalism for representing essential aspects of ToM for an autonomous agent. In our logic, the capability of agents in a group to be aware of other agents' (of the group) beliefs and intentions is already an embryonic form of ToM.

In developmental psychology, one of the standard methods to test the capabilities of a human child's ToM is "false-belief tasks". It is a class of tests in which the child is told a story involving multiple characters, where one or more of the characters necessarily develop, under the circumstances, some false belief. The child should then answer questions indicating whether she has correctly modelled the mental states (beliefs) of the characters, identifying the false beliefs and their motivation.

A common false belief task is the "Sally-Anne" task in which the child is shown a story about two girls, Sally and Anne, who are in a room with a basket and a box. Sally puts the marble into the basket, leaves the room, and then Anne moves the marble to the box in her absence. The child is then asked: "where does Sally believe the marble to be?". To pass the test, the child must answer "in the basket", since Sally did not see Anne moving the marble, and therefore Sally has the false belief that the marble is still in the basket.

In our logic, it is easy to model the consequences of actions, i.e., if moving an object from a container to another one, the mental operations ↓ or ⊢ allow an agent to conclude that the marble is in the second container, and the mental operation ⊣ can remove the (no longer valid) belief that the marble is in the original container.

As seen before, what is inferred or removed from the working memory via a mental action is common knowledge of all agents of any group to which the agent which does the action belongs. So, the Sally-Ann task might be solved in our logic by reconfiguring the group. I.e., Sally, Ann and the observer child can be assumed to belong to the group called, e.g., "Room1". So, all of them observe the action of Sally putting the marble into the basket. However, when Sally leaves the room she can be assumed to leave the group "Room1". So, she cannot "observe" the action Anne moves the marble to the box, and in consequence she still retains the belief that the marble is in the basket. Since all past beliefs are common knowledge in a group, the child (that we consider as an agent in the group) can answer the question correctly.

Therefore, we intend to extend our logic so as to model the fact that there are actions that lead an agent to leave or join a group. For Sally, e.g., leaving the room accounts to leave the group, and re-entering the room implies re-joining. So, all new beliefs formed or removed by the group in the meanwhile are not known to her. To suitably cope with these aspects a concept of time and time intervals might be needed, that we have already treated in past work [9, 22] and might therefore suitably exploit in this context.

7 Conclusions

In this paper, we have reported about a line of work concerning how to exploit a logical formulation for providing the semantics of MAS, covering not only single agents, but also groups of cooperative agents. We aimed to consider to some extent practical aspects concerning actions' executability. So, we introduced beliefs about physical actions concerning whether they could, are, or have been executed. These beliefs proved then useful for explainability, but also to model complex group dynamics. We introduced agents' preferences in performing actions, and single agent's and group's intentions. So, a group of agent can devise a joint plan to reach a goal step by step, taking into account agents' capabilities and preferences, and the available resources. We tried to make our semantics modular, thus allowing engineers to encode some customizable aspects separately from the 'main' agent code. We have introduced dedicated syntax to represent actions' feasibility and preferences, aiming to introduce a connection among the 'abstract' agents and the external environment in which they will be situated, and we have shown that the new syntax improves explainability, since natural-language explanations can in principle be directly extracted from proofs.

We have proved some useful properties of the extended logic, among which strong completeness. We have provided a significant example, and we have outlined a further extension of the logic to better represent this and other examples, via modelling the number of steps required to reach some conclusion or eventually perform some action. The complexity of the extended logic has no reason to be higher than that of the original *L-DINF*. So, we can safely claim that, in the proposed new logic, the satisfiability problem is PSPACE-complete in the multi-agent case for *L-INF*, and it is decidable for *L-DINF* (though there are conjectures that it might be PSPACE-complete as well).

In future work, we mean to extend our logic in the following directions: ability to represent in a general way the number of steps needed to reach a goal (here we proposed in fact a restricted formalization); ability to formally express relevant aspects of the Theory of Mind, so as to define agents able to cope with "false-belief tasks", i.e., capable of attributing correct mental states to other agents also in presence of ambiguous situations. To this aim, we intend to integrate temporal aspects, i.e., in which instant or time interval an action has been or should be performed, and how this may affect agents' and groups' awareness of actions and beliefs.

References

1. Balbiani, P., Duque, D.F., Lorini, E.: A logical theory of belief dynamics for resource-bounded agents. In: Proceedings of the 2016 International Conference on Autonomous Agents & Multiagent Systems, AAMAS 2016, pp. 644–652. ACM (2016)
2. Balbiani, P., Fernández-Duque, D., Lorini, E.: The dynamics of epistemic attitudes in resource-bounded agents. Stud. Log. **107**(3), 457–488 (2019)
3. Bordini, R.H., et al.: A survey of programming languages and platforms for multi-agent systems. Informatica (Slovenia) **30**(1), 33–44 (2006)
4. Calegari, R., Ciatto, G., Mascardi, V., Omicini, A.: Logic-based technologies for multi-agent systems: a systematic literature review. Auton. Agents Multi-Agent Syst. **35**(1), 1–67 (2020). https://doi.org/10.1007/s10458-020-09478-3
5. Costantini, S., Tocchio, A.: A logic programming language for multi-agent systems. In: Flesca, S., Greco, S., Ianni, G., Leone, N. (eds.) JELIA 2002. LNCS (LNAI), vol. 2424, pp. 1–13. Springer, Heidelberg (2002). https://doi.org/10.1007/3-540-45757-7_1
6. Costantini, S., Tocchio, A.: The DALI logic programming agent-oriented language. In: Alferes, J.J., Leite, J. (eds.) JELIA 2004. LNCS (LNAI), vol. 3229, pp. 685–688. Springer, Heidelberg (2004). https://doi.org/10.1007/978-3-540-30227-8_57
7. Costantini, S., De Gasperis, G.: Flexible goal-directed agents' behavior via DALI mass and ASP modules. In: 2018 AAAI Spring Symposia, Stanford University, Palo Alto, California, USA, 26–28 March 2018. AAAI Press (2018)

8. Costantini, S., De Gasperis, G., Nazzicone, G.: DALI for cognitive robotics: principles and prototype implementation. In: Lierler, Y., Taha, W. (eds.) PADL 2017. LNCS, vol. 10137, pp. 152–162. Springer, Cham (2017). https://doi.org/10.1007/978-3-319-51676-9_10

9. Costantini, S., Formisano, A., Pitoni, V.: Timed memory in resource-bounded agents. In: Ghidini, C., Magnini, B., Passerini, A., Traverso, P. (eds.) AI*IA 2018. LNCS (LNAI), vol. 11298, pp. 15–29. Springer, Cham (2018). https://doi.org/10.1007/978-3-030-03840-3_2

10. Costantini, S., Formisano, A., Pitoni, V.: An epistemic logic for multi-agent systems with budget and costs. In: Faber, W., Friedrich, G., Gebser, M., Morak, M. (eds.) JELIA 2021. LNCS (LNAI), vol. 12678, pp. 101–115. Springer, Cham (2021). https://doi.org/10.1007/978-3-030-75775-5_8

11. Costantini, S., Pitoni, V.: Memory management in resource-bounded agents. In: Alviano, M., Greco, G., Scarcello, F. (eds.) AI*IA 2019. LNCS (LNAI), vol. 11946, pp. 46–58. Springer, Cham (2019). https://doi.org/10.1007/978-3-030-35166-3_4

12. Costantini, S., Pitoni, V.: Towards a logic of "inferable" for self-aware transparent logical agents. In: Musto, C., Magazzeni, D., Ruggieri, S., Semeraro, G. (eds.) Proceedings of the Italian Workshop on Explainable Artificial Intelligence Co-located with 19th International Conference of the Italian Association for Artificial Intelligence, 2020. CEUR Workshop Proceedings, vol. 2742, pp. 68–79. CEUR-WS.org (2020)

13. Costantini, S., Tocchio, A., Verticchio, A.: Communication and trust in the DALI logic programming agent-oriented language. Intelligenza Artificiale 2(1), 39–46 (2005)

14. De Gasperis, G., Costantini, S., Nazzicone, G.: DALI multi agent systems framework. DALI GitHub Software Repository. DALI (2014). https://doi.org/10.5281/zenodo.11042, http://github.com/AAAI-DISIM-UnivAQ/DALI

15. Dissing, L., Bolander, T.: Implementing Theory of Mind on a robot using dynamic epistemic logic. In: Bessiere, C. (ed.) Proceedings of the 29th International Joint Conference on Artificial Intelligence, IJCAI 2020, pp. 1615–1621 (2020). https://doi.org/10.24963/ijcai.2020/224

16. Ditmarsch, H.V., Halpern, J.Y., Hoek, W.V.D., Kooi, B.: Handbook of Epistemic Logic. College Publications (2015)

17. Duc, H.N.: Reasoning about rational, but not logically omniscient, agents. J. Log. Comput. 7(5), 633–648 (1997)

18. Garro, A., et al.: Intelligent agents: multi-agent systems. In: Ranganathan, S., Gribskov, M., Nakai, K., Schönbach, C. (eds.) Encyclopedia of Bioinformatics and Computational Biology, vol. 1, pp. 315–320. Elsevier (2019). https://doi.org/10.1016/b978-0-12-809633-8.20328-2

19. Goldman, A., et al.: Theory of mind. In: The Oxford Handbook of Philosophy of Cognitive Science, vol. 1. Oxford University Press (2012)

20. Herzig, A., Lorini, E., Pearce, D.: Social intelligence. AI Soc. 34(4), 689 (2019)

21. Kakas, A.C., Mancarella, P., Sadri, F., Stathis, K., Toni, F.: Computational logic foundations of KGP agents. J. Artif. Intell. Res. 33, 285–348 (2008). https://doi.org/10.1613/jair.2596

22. Pitoni, V., Costantini, S.: A temporal module for logical frameworks. In: Bogaerts, B., et al. (eds.) Proceedings of ICLP 2019 (Technical Communications) EPTCS, vol. 306, pp. 340–346 (2019)

23. Rao, A.S., Georgeff, M.: Modeling rational agents within a BDI architecture. In: Proceedings of the Second International Conference on Principles of Knowledge Representation and Reasoning (KR 1991), pp. 473–484. Morgan Kaufmann (1991)

24. Weyhrauch, R.W.: Prolegomena to a theory of mechanized formal reasoning. Artif. Intell. 13(1–2), 133–170 (1980)

Attention Guidance Agents
with Eye-Tracking
A Use-Case Based on the MATBII Cockpit Task

Szonya Durant[1]([✉]), Benedict Wilkins[2], Callum Woods[1], Emanuele Uliana[2],
and Kostas Stathis[2]

[1] Department of Psychology Royal Holloway, University of London,
Egham TW20 0EX, UK
`szonya.durant@rhul.ac.uk`, `callum.woods.2014@live.rhul.ac.uk`
[2] Department of Computer Science Royal Holloway, University of London,
Egham TW20 0EX, UK
`{benedict.wilkins.2014,emanuele.uliana.2016}@live.rhul.ac.uk`,
`kostas.stathis@rhul.ac.uk`

Abstract. A first step to keeping the human 'in the loop' in the context of developing intelligent multi-task interfaces is to be able to monitor their attention. By combining eye tracking with agent monitoring and decision making, we provide a basis for increasing the user's attentional bandwidth by offering bottom-up attention guidance. We develop a modified implementation of the MATBII cockpit task simulator embedded in an agent environment in which agents monitor events, including eye tracking, and act to deploy visual cues to guide attention. We explore how such a system may be useful for improving task performance, by also simulating users with agents to demonstrate how the system might work for some examples of user behaviour. We also discuss how our system can act as an experimental platform to benefit future user experience research focusing on attention guidance in complex multi-task interfaces.

Keywords: Agent environment · Eye-tracking · Interface · Workload

1 Introduction

Humans are often in complex, attention demanding situations, which require them to process information from multiple sources at once. In an interface such as an airplane cockpit many different information sources are present in the form of instrument displays spatially distributed in front of the pilot. Many other such examples exist from air traffic control to remote monitoring of autonomous vehicles in case of a required emergency intervention [16]. Humans are limited in their attentional capacity and thus sample parts of their environment sequentially over time [11]. When humans 'fail to notice' it is because of sub-optimal sampling. High information flow due to the number of displays, rapid information change in displays and the dependence of information between displays challenges human attention limits [43]. This may lead to poor decisions with serious consequences.

© Springer Nature Switzerland AG 2022
N. Alechina et al. (Eds.): EMAS 2021, LNAI 13190, pp. 92–113, 2022.
https://doi.org/10.1007/978-3-030-97457-2_6

Incorporating attention guidance with a complex multi-task interface is not straightforward, both from a conceptual and an implementation perspective. Existing approaches for building such systems, often focus on the conceptual aspects of attention guidance e.g. [15,45], but little attention has been paid to conceptual frameworks that also have a systematic implementation. Other approaches, e.g. [50], use agents as cognitive assistants, they perform autonomous situation assessment and take into account the limitations of human information processing. Still, an important aspect remains open: how can we build an agent system that considers how to convey information to users about ongoing operations and environmental parameters within their attentional limits?

The aim of this work is to show how to rethink attention guidance in multi-task interfaces using cognitive agents [7] that perceive where a user looks, and formulate interaction of display objects as events happening in an agent environment [8]. By observing the state of the various interface objects and in-coming user input data (including eye tracking data) and aggregating it to form beliefs, we conjecture that cognitive agents will be able to provide useful guidance to a user while making important considerations relating to their attention. The system thus both measures the current location of attention (based on eye tracking data) and alters attention by guiding the gaze tasks requiring input. Our specific objective is to exemplify the framework by developing the methods for attention guidance in the MATBII cockpit task simulator [59], showing how to organise guidance for a concrete application. We also wish to demonstrate how the modularity of an agent-based approach eases the process of experimentation and provides some unique benefits for creating a system that is extensible and reproducible.

The contribution of our work is to provide a practical system that makes use of gaze location (a proxy for spatial attention), allowing agents to use this information to help users allocate their limited cognitive resources. To this end we reproduce and improve some aspects of MATBII [59], producing our own simple simulation of a cockpit-based task space. The resulting system, which we refer to as ICU, allows for display changes and eye movements to be monitored externally via an event-based API, making it suitable for experimental settings beyond this work. We have also embedded ICU in a resource-light agent environment, which re-implements in full a single GOLEM container [8]. This supports real-time attention guidance mechanisms using cognitive agents to monitor where a user looks and can support attention guidance in other domains, assuming they provide an ICU like API.

The work is structured as follows. We begin by first outlining related work in describing and measuring attention, its limitations, cognitive workload, the use of agents as assistants, and assess to what extent MATBII has proved useful as an example task space. In Sect. 3 we present ICU, an open source Python implementation of the MATBII task space [59], which functions independently of our agent system. We then describe the agent system ICUa (ICU with agents) we have developed as an experimental platform for bottom-up attention guidance. In Sect. 4 we test the system by simulating and exploring some simple potential human behaviours. Finally in Sect. 5 we discuss the potential of our system, the ability of agents to monitor the environment and user (via eye tracking) to provide useful attention guidance, and its suitability for future human testing and use in further applications.

2   Related Work

2.1   Workload, Eye-Tracking and Attention Guidance

The concept of workload and the demand on the limited attention of the human operator is important in human factors. Mental workload describes the demands on attention made by a cognitive task [42]. Often behavioural and physiological measures are used to try to classify situations as eliciting low or high mental workload e.g. [5,17,32,66]. A high mental workload has the effect of decreasing performance and increasing stress [42]. Often the aim of classifying high/low mental workload is to arrive at a solution aimed at alleviating conditions when high workload is detected, in the form of automation that can be introduced to aid the human operator. However, since the earliest introduction of automation, it has been suggested that in many situations it is important to keep the human in the loop even when a task has been devolved to an agent. The evidence suggests that at most levels of automation it is important that the human operator is kept engaged whenever possible user response might be required e.g. in the case of automation failure [21]. Thus even highly automated systems may need to consider how to convey information is such a way that the user is able to react - the basis of this work.

Multiple ongoing tasks lead to divided attention, which is particularly detrimental to performance [42]. There is a general trade-off between the need for selective attention to solve a given task and the need to detect other tasks that may require attention. In divided attention conditions with complex tasks, the phenomenon of cognitive tunnelling is often observed [41]. In this case if a user is focused on solving a particular task, even salient cues can be missed.

Warning lights and alerts are used in interfaces to capture the attention of the user, but this may lead to a situation where several alerts are activated at once leading to 'misplaced saliency' [6]. In this case the attempt to make an area stand out more has in fact the opposite effect by highlighting several areas and thus further overloading the human, as they have to decide which to attend to first. Additionally, overuse of alerting can lead to 'automation disuse' where the user comes to ignore the help that is being offered, seeing it as a nuisance [68]. These aspects of attention are key to understanding how to improve situation awareness (SA). SA describes a person's awareness of relevant aspects of their environment, the comprehension of these aspects, and predictions of what these will mean in the future [20]. Lacking situation awareness is one of the main causes of accidents attributed to human error [61].

In the context of describing how human attention is allocated over multiple displays, it is important to note that the spatial layout of these displays plays part in how the human user represents them [68]. Spatial memory is a key component in monitoring the work space, spatially reorganising parts of the display has been found to be detrimental to performance [25]. Hence, it is generally preferable for an attention guidance system to maintain the layout of the interface to allow a spatial representation to form.

Eye tracking has proved an invaluable tool in attempting to measure workload, through indicators such as changes in pupil size or the duration of each fixation [40]. The spatial specificity of eye tracking has also led to it being developed as a tool for interaction [39]. A recent example uses eye tracking information to ascertain which screen the user is currently looking at in order to guide them to another screen in multi-monitor displays [63]. We propose that the spatial specificity of eye tracking could be used for more localised guidance.

2.2   Gaze Contingent Attention Guidance

There have been many proposals over the years on how to design 'attention aware systems' [54]. Concepts such as gaze based notifications have been introduced and evaluated according to their 'noticeability' vs 'distractiveness' [33]. A great deal of work has been done on gaze contingent attention guidance in the field of education and training where the learner's gaze is directed in an attempt to ensure optimal learning [56]. This is done by using online eye tracking to detect where the learner is focusing on the wrong information and using changes in the display to guide their attention - the same principles we intend to use in this work. A recent system for air traffic guidance makes use of online eye tracking to monitor the user's attention and direct it according to a simple logic that decides where the user should be looking [48]. This very specific implementation, with a control system tailored to air traffic control uses peripheral and central cues to guide attention to the necessary parts of the scene. Initial tests with five users suggested some improvement in perceived workload, although clear performance metrics relative to a baseline were not presented in this preliminary work. Earlier work [52] directs the user attention to target locations using a moving dot. In this work they do not consider rules for guiding attention, and the eye tracking and performance results are again not compared to a baseline. However, users reported positively on their interaction with the system, suggesting that this type of display has potential.

2.3   Agents

Human-computer environments where software agents act on behalf of a user are not a new idea e.g. [38], nor is automating tasks to reduce demands on human attention, e.g. [39]. Often agent capabilities have also been developed to predict intention or task state from behaviour i.e. overt responses and interactions, to provide assistance e.g. [50,57], and although eye-tracking agent assistants have been introduced, they still remain to be fully tested [65]. Adaptive interfaces have also been developed to use human physiological markers, such as heart rate and eye blinks to dynamically distribute tasks between agents and humans [28], but access to their corresponding test-beds is not available.

Cognitive assistants often use agent models to internalise perceptions as beliefs about the environment's state, actions to produce results (e.g. [37]) or use the BDI model (e.g. see [60]) based on intentions for goals the agent can plan for. Goal reasoning [2] allows goals to be achieved or maintained, including external goals specified by user guidelines and norms [58]. Agent decisions are modelled with preferences over planned goals using logic if there is certainty (e.g. [31]) or probabilities if there is uncertainty (e.g. [22]). Agent decisions may be explained (e.g. [44]) to build trust with the user - key to successfully working with a human [23]. However, many cognitive agent models and their implementation platforms (see [10,36]) are often resource heavy for real-time applications as demanding as eye-tracking. Although, light-weight versions exist, they are still at a prototypical stage [3]. In addition, the benefit of cognitive assistants for human performance has yet to be thoroughly evaluated experimentally in terms of assessing objective measures of performance compared to baseline - most evaluations rely on user questionnaire data reflecting subjective experiences [50].

To address some of the above limitations, our work is intended as a resource-light test-bed that combines agent environments and a teleo-reactive (TR) agent model [47] to support experiments for attention guidance applications where eye-tracking is a key requirement. TR agent models (e.g. [34]) and implementations (e.g. [13]) exist, and their link with models such as BDI have been studied (e.g. [14]). However, our work is the first to apply a resource-light TR model for attention guidance applications developed as agent environments.

2.4   MATBII as a Use-Case

MATBII [59] is widely used in the human factors literature as a multi-tasking space. It is comprised of clearly defined spatially separated sub-tasks often requiring rapid switching of attention. Difficulty is understood in terms of how often each sub-task needs attention, thus MATBII is often used to investigate low and high workload by changing the level of task difficulty, e.g. [24]. As shown in Fig. 1, the sub-tasks consist of a system monitoring task, checking for changes in colours of lights or positions of scales that require a mouse click response to return to correct state; a tracking task that requires keeping a target within a set of crosshairs; and a resource management task that requires manipulating pumps to keep fuel tanks at the right level. The pumps in the resource management task can be set to fail for a set amount amount of time. Pump failure is shown by a change in colour and the fuel level going out of range is also indicated by change in colour. MATBII is set up in such a way that under high frequency conditions the probability of 'misplaced salience' is high. A further important observation found from response patterns on MATBII is the presence of 'cognitive tunneling' as described above, manifesting itself as the inability to switch from one sub-task to another [24]. This provides us with multitasking situations, where it is objectively clear at any point what the user needs to look at.

There is not a great deal of literature on eye tracking users in MATBII [59]. Nelson et al. [46] report percentage time fixating on each task, Kim et al. [32] report changes in pupil size with increasing workload, and Berthelot et al. [5]

Monitoring   Tracking

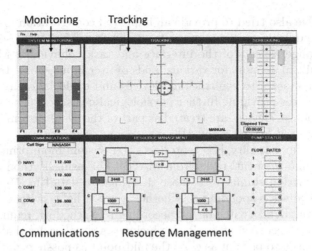

Communications   Resource Management

Fig. 1. The MATBII system with sub-tasks labelled. (Color figure online)

extract a property called 'self affinity' from eye movement statistics. There is much yet to be explored in the spatial pattern of eye movements whilst completing the task, for instance the effects of misplaced salience and cognitive tunnelling have only been inferred from behaviour, it would be useful to see these effects in more detail by measuring the spatial allocation of attention, which our proposed system allows for and at the same time uses this information to guide attention.

3   Integrated Cognitive User Assistance

3.1   ICU

Although an open source Python implementation of MATBII with eye-tracking (and further) options available has been recently released [12], we found it better suited to our purpose of combining the interface with an agent architecture to develop our own version of MATBII. We have opted for implementing a stripped down version of MATBII, essentially the same in functionality, using just a subset of the tasks but with some functional improvements that we feel are essential for experimentation. We call this system the Integrated Cognitive User (ICU[1]), which forms the interface part of the complete ICUa - with agents. Our system brings new scope for experiments in human factors research owing to more flexible manipulation of the task space, the ability to collect eye tracking data easily and interface in real time and also enables our work.

ICU has a bi-directional event API that may be used to interface with external programs and can be used in a number of ways, including monitoring the system in real time; for us its main purpose is to facilitate interaction with our agent

---

[1] https://dicelab-rhul.github.io/ICU/.

system. We have also tried to provide an improved configuration format[2], which can be used to quickly configure experiments by specifying event schedules concisely, and change aspects of the interface and task behaviours. Moreover, the system has built-in support for various kinds of user input, from standard input (e.g. keyboard/mouse) to eye tracking devices and could be easily extended to incorporate devices providing further physiological measures such as EEG or galvanic skin response. Devices are treated as part of the event system, device input is therefore exposed by the event API.

In terms of functionality, ICU reproduces the 'system monitoring', 'tracking', and 'resource management' tasks from MATBII [59] using Python 3, see Fig. 1. These tasks function similarly to those described in detail in [59]. Briefly, the system task involves responding to whether a green light switches off or a red light switches on, lights switch on/off according to a schedule, requiring a mouse click to reset to the correct state. It also includes a set of scales that change over time and that need to be kept as close the mid-point as possible and can be reset to mid-point by clicking on the scale level. The tracking task uses a joystick or keyboard presses to keep a randomly drifting target centred, the extent of the drift is configurable. The resource management task requires the user to switch pumps on and off to maintain the top two fuel tanks at the correct level, the pumps fail at certain times making them unusable, pump transfer rates, tank capacity, burn rate, frequency and duration of each pump failure, among other things can be configured.

To support eye-tracking, ICU provides a wrapper around the PsychoPy library [51], which enables any eye-tracker supported by the library to be used with ICU (we assume that the eye-tracker is already calibrated). The system was tested using a USB screen based X2-30 Tobii eye-tracker, sampling at 30 Hz on average. Raw gaze coordinates are filtered using an I-VT filter with standard moving average as specified in [49], coordinates are classed as fixation (eyes are stationary) or saccade (eyes are moving and thus unable to take in information).

3.2 ICUa: ICU with Agents

Previous work demonstrates the effectiveness of software agents for monitoring practical applications, e.g. see [9,35,55,67]. Here we extend these works conceptually, by introducing an agent environment that contains ICU as an internal object, where different agents can monitor the state of ICU (including information provided by an eye tracker) and perform actions on it to highlight parts of the screen for the user's benefit. Although our framework is demonstrated with ICU it is not specific to it, as ICU is used here more as an example to integrate any suitable multi-task interface.

An agent environments approach has some significant benefits from a software engineering perspective, especially modularity, which allows us to develop and swap out different objects and agent behaviours easily for experiments. Additionally, an agent-based approach leaves room for expanding the scope for

---

[2] https://dicelab-rhul.github.io/ICU/documentation/configuration/.

more complex environments by relying on multi-agent communication and coordination models, and as a way of integrating complex cognitive capabilities for guidance e.g. reinforcement learning [4].

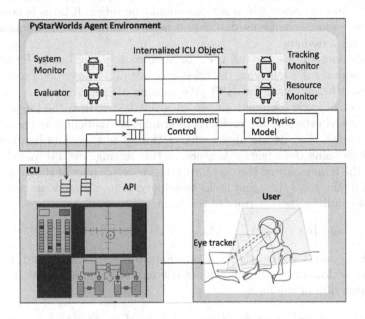

Fig. 2. ICUa reference architecture in PyStarWorlds showing the four agents deployed. We assign one agent to each of the first three application simulator tasks: system monitoring, resource monitoring and tracking. These agents subscribe to task specific events enabling them to perceive relevant information about the simulator's current state, including eye-tracking information about saccade or fixation, and communications from other agents in the system. The agents' actions have the effect of modifying the application interface i.e. to draw an overlay. We consider actions with two kinds of feedback (a) highlighting a particular sub-task and (b) draw an arrow at the current gaze location that points in the direction of a component that needs urgent attention. The fourth agent, the evaluator, monitors the user's performance using specific performance metrics.

ICUa is ICU extended with agents implemented in PyStarWorlds [1], an agent environment library that supports Python agent applications. The reference architecture of ICUa, shown in Fig. 2, is based on a specialised single container version of the GOLEM framework described in [7], which is implemented as an event-processing system under a publish/subscribe model [8]. ICU is internalised as an environment object by the API it exposes, so that its state can be perceived and acted upon by agents. Agents have a mind and body [62], the mind controls the agent behaviour, while the body relies on sensors and actuators to situate the agent in the application environment. Agents perceive events with their sensors, make decisions with their mind and attempt actions with their actuators. A type-based publish/subscribe mechanism routes events to/from the sensors/actuators [8], which is known to be scalable. The environment provides a *Physics* module containing action execution rules where the semantics of each action are defined. We assume that agents are aware *a priori* of action preconditions/effects and so are able to decide which actions should be taken. ICUa is agnostic as to which agent model is to be used, different models can be adopted depending on the application domain.

For this domain, agents and their behaviours are specified in Python using condition-action rules following the teleo-reactive (TR) execution model [47] for goal directed behaviours (e.g. [18]). We assume a fixed *perceive-revise-decide-attempt* control cycle [30] that allows an agent to perceive the latest environment changes via the sensors, revise its internal state modelling the environment (or belief store), then decide about what action(s) to take, and finally attempt these actions using the agents actuators. In this setting, the TR model helps us structure the behaviours of the agent within the *decide* part of the agent's cycle, according to the goals the agent seeks to achieve. These behaviours are specified as a set of condition/action rules of the form:

$$G : \{C_1 \to A_1; C_2 \to A_2; \ldots; C_i \to A_i; \ldots; C_n \to A_n\}$$

where G is a goal, C_i a condition over internal variables (beliefs), and A_i is either a primitive action, or a sub-goal (giving rise to a sub-behaviour) that can itself be a TR program of the form:

$$A_i : \{C_{i,1} \to A_{i,1}; C_{i,2} \to A_{i,2}; \ldots; C_{i,m} \to A_{i,m}\}.$$

This gives rise to a significant simplification of a BDI-style planning layer that manipulates a plan library in which plans are comprised of hierarchical, suspendable and recoverable teleo-reactive programs [14]. The top-level goal G for the agent is triggered inside the *decide* part of the agent's cycle. The list of rules is scanned top-down for the first rule whose condition is satisfied, to select an intention and the corresponding action is attempted. It is important to note that the conditions are continuously being evaluated at each cycle step, so that when the first true condition changes due to new belief update, the intention changes accordingly. In other words, an action/sub-goal is revised, only when its true condition in the agent's internal state ceases to be true.

It is straightforward to create a subset of the TR paradigm for developing agent behaviours using Python, or a similar programming language. Assuming a round-robin agent execution of an agent's control cycle, there is a natural correspondence between TR programs and most programming languages, as shown in Fig. 3. An example of a simple monitoring behaviour that follows this model is given in Fig. 4(a). This kind of programming is quite flexible and can support more complex behaviours. For example, in principle an agent may be monitoring multiple parts of a screen (e.g. multiple pumps for the resource management task), it may attempt multiple actions in a single cycle (e.g. to highlight multiple pumps). As a result, the top-level goal in such cases needs to operate on sets of actions, simulating parallel execution of independent monitoring behaviours, each with the form of a TR program, as for example in the interpretation used by [13], but in our case using PyStarWorlds. An example is given in Fig. 4(b).

```
G: {
    C_1 -> A_1;

    C_2 -> A_2;

    ...

    T -> A_n;
}
```

```
def G():
    if C_1:
        return A_1
    elif C_2:
        return A_2
    ...
    else:
        return A_n
    ...
```

Fig. 3. Mapping of a simple version of TR rules in Python, which in PyStarWorlds are evaluated continuously. Sub-goals are method calls. C_n = True forces the last rule to always succeed if all other rules above fail to trigger.

Using the above architecture we implement a few simple rules for our agents to adhere to. The agents' goal is to shift the attention of the user to a sub-task that requires action if the user appears to have ignored it. Each agent has a built in grace period, which constitutes whether the sub task is deemed to have been ignored. If in this time the required action has not taken place and importantly the gaze has not moved to the sub-task, then the agent responsible for the sub-task displays a relevant highlight. A highlight can be configured to constitute an outline of a sub-task, a transparent overlay, an arrow at the current fixation point or a combination of these. This involves agents checking the current gaze fixation position and whether it is in the required sub-task region of interest. Thus, we ensure that guidance is not displayed unnecessarily if attention has been transferred, but an action not yet produced. The agent also checks that no other guidance is being displayed at the time, as the aim is to not introduce a divided attention condition. So only one agent will be displaying guidance at any given time. If the requirements are met, the agent will display guidance and this will remain on display until the gaze position moves to the required sub-task or the task is resolved. Again, once gaze has moved we take this as an indicator that the task will be responded to as required. However, if the user moves their gaze away whilst the task still requires attention, it will again become highlighted after a second grace period, if the gaze has not returned. These simple rules are designed to move the user's attention on from a cognitive tunnelling situations with minimal unnecessary competing visual additions to the display. We do not assign differential importance to any of the sub-tasks, but such a hierarchy could easily be implemented in future.

```python
def decide(self):
    # user is not looking -> highlight
    if not self.is_looking() and \
            not any(self.highlighted) and \
            not self.is_acceptable(self.component):
        return self.highlight(self.component)
    else:
        # default rule is T -> do nothing
        return None
```

(a) Simple Monitoring Agent Example

```python
def decide(self):
    actions = []

    # top level TR program
    if not any(self.highlighted):
        for component in self.task.components:
            # simple parallel TR program
            if not self.is_acceptable(component):
                action = self.highlight(component)
            else: # default rule is T -> None
                action = None

            actions.append(action)

    # default rule is implicit T -> {}
    return actions
```

(b) Parallel Monitoring Agent Example

Fig. 4. Agent monitoring examples in Python TR style. In (a) we show a simple single-action monitoring behaviour that highlights a component (part of a task) if needed. In (b), we operate over sets of actions. This enables the agent to highlight many components if necessary. In practice we limit agents to highlighting a single component (to avoid overloading the user), however the parallel execution of behaviours is useful for our simulated human users outlined in Sect. 4.

4   Simulating Simple Examples of Human Behaviour

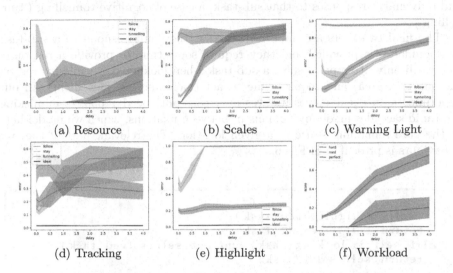

(a) Resource   (b) Scales   (c) Warning Light

(d) Tracking   (e) Highlight   (f) Workload

Fig. 5. Graphs (a)–(e) show error of three simulated users according to the evaluation metrics given in Sect. 4.1, lower error means better performance by the agent. The 'stay' user will ignore agents advice until a particular task is complete (there is not more action to be taken for the moment). The 'follow' user will always take the agents advice and move to solve the recommended task (see Fig. 6 for details). Error is shown as a function of the "delay" period introduced to each decision, a restriction on the user's ability. There is no delay parameter for the ideal (ideal) user, we mark this minimal possible error as a horizontal line on the graphs for comparison. All results are averaged over 10 runs of 1 min each and normalised in the [0–1] interval. The shaded regions show 95% confidence intervals. Graph (f) shows the error for the 'tunnelling' user at two difficulty levels (medium and hard) on the resource management task. The difficulty is set in the configuration file by specifying different event frequencies. For all simulations grace periods until a highlight is displayed are set to 2 s.

To demonstrate the flexibility of our agent system and provide some insight into how the system might perform with different user behaviours we have implemented and evaluated four different kinds of 'user' agents, see Fig. 5. Each 'user' agent directly observes events from the ICU system and is able to provide *fake* user input e.g. mouse clicks, key input and eye movement. This set up also provides a basis for future researchers wishing to simulate more complex human behaviour.

The ideal user reacts immediately to MATBII events and is not constrained by any input delay e.g. eye movement speed or response delay, it can simultaneously observe and react to changes in all tasks. This ideal agent is used as a baseline and achieves the highest possible performance (i.e. lowest error rate with no need for guidance).

We also model a worst case scenario with a user agent that never moves their eyes from a sub-task (which in this case is the resource management task) and only makes responses to that sub-task, a case of cognitive tunnelling ('tunnelling').

The final two users are imperfect, in that they only respond to a sub-task once guidance is provided and they require some time to provide a response. They will only attempt to solve a sub-task when looking (i.e. while fixated on the sub-task area) and require time to act (including eye movement). In our experiments an agent moves its eyes at a constant speed 1000px/s mimicking the rapid saccades made my humans in between fixations, which we model here as the gaze remaining static in a given location. The relevant part of the two behaviours is presented in Fig. 6.

```
if self.is_highlighted(task):
    return self.move_eye(task)
elif self.is_looking(task) and not self.solved(task):
    return self.solve(task)


(a) Follow
```

```
if self.is_looking(task) and not self.solved(task):
    return self.solve(task)
elif self.is_highlighted(task):
    return self.move_eye(task)


(b) Stay
```

Fig. 6. Two exerts from the simulated imperfect users showing the key difference in their behaviour. (a) The 'follow' user's gaze always follows guidance when present causing it to abandon its current, possibly unresolved task and move to another. (b) the 'stay' user remains focused on a task until no further action can be taken to resolve it then follows guidance to reach the next task.

The two follow/stay behaviours are set up to correspond to two extremes of behaviour, we expect human behaviour to lie somewhere in-between the two. With both, we vary the delay with which they are able to respond. With larger delay times, it is more likely that the 'follow' user will abandon a sub-task before it has been solved, while with the 'stay' user, other tasks will remain unsolved for a longer period.

4.1   Evaluation Metrics

To measure the performance of each user agent we use the following metrics, which are normalised over time and averaged over components where applicable. The metrics are representative of the user's error when solving tasks, 0 being a perfect score for each metric.

- Time that main fuel tanks are out of the acceptable range in the resource management task.
- Deviation from acceptable state of the scales ($\mathcal{L}_1/time$) in the system monitoring task.
- Time that warning lights are in an incorrect state in the system monitoring task.
- Deviation from the central acceptable box ($\mathcal{L}_\infty/time$) in the tracking task.
- Time at least one warning (highlight or otherwise) is displayed on the overlay.

4.2   Simulation Results

The errors calculated using our evaluation metrics are shown in Fig. 5. The ideal user (see Fig. 5) has minimal error, any small error that exists is a result of the slight processing delay due to simulation speed (100 ms per agent cycle). If we look at the performance measure associated with the length of time that highlights are displayed, we see that this is zero for the ideal observer, reflecting that our system does not display highlights when not required.

At the other extreme our 'worst case' tunnelling user (Fig. 5) provides an upper bound level of error on tasks other than the resource management task they are focusing on. The on/off nature of the warning lights is reflected in the constant maximum error across delay, the scales and tracking are more variable in their error as it is possible for them to randomly return within acceptable parameters. For this user, after the first grace period, a highlight will always be displayed. In the resource management task of course they perform best as this is the task of focus. We can see the effect of delay in the responses making their performance worse.

In the case of our imperfect users that are guided by the highlights (the follow and stay users in Fig. 5), but do not respond otherwise, their performance is somewhere between the two more extreme ideal and tunneling users, as expected. This reflects that a human who makes use of the highlights to guide them, is of course not a perfect user, but is likely to perform better than a user who completely ignores the need for a response. With these users we can also see the effects of a delay in the response, as the response slows, so we can see the error generally increases. The advantage of staying on a task ('stay' user Fig. 5) until it is 'solved' varies to some extent with the delay of the response. The warning lights and scales parts of the system monitoring task suggest an initial small advantage for always following the highlighting, which then disappears with delay. The more continuous nature of the tracking task produces a different pattern, with an apparent small initial advantage for the user who remains on task until solved, but with increased delay the user that follows the highlighting performs better. The highlighting metric reflects these two behaviours in that the user that follows the highlighting has less highlights on screen over time. Of course we also see that following highlights will reduce performance relative to the tunnelling approach on the single task chosen to focus on (resource management).

In Fig. 5 (f) we illustrate how task difficulty can be manipulated in our system by changing the frequency of events. We show the results for our worst case 'tunnelling' user on the resource management task. With a short delay in the user response there is a relatively small difference in performance between low frequency and high frequency events, as they are able to respond quickly enough to resolve the high frequency events. With increased response delay, in each case the user performs worse, with a higher error for the more difficult case consistently.

Our simulations have shown how attention guidance may in principle improve performance for imperfect users in cases where users shift their attention immediately, compared to when they are unable to shift their attention due to cognitive tunnelling. Our guidance agents' behaviour has been tailored in an attempt to provide the most useful feedback and avoid overloading the user. We have tested only one class of guidance behaviour, based on the principles outlined in Sect. 2, which works as a proof of concept. Our simulations also allowed us to visualise the effect of increasing task difficulty by increasing event frequency and how this depends on the delay in the user action.

In addition to our simulated user tests, we have tested the capacity of the system and found that the ICUa was able to deal with up to a million events per second without raising any performance issues (for reference, the event load under normal operation does not exceed more than one thousand per second with a high-throughput eye tracking device).

5   Discussion

We have successfully demonstrated, by modifying the widely used MATBII cockpit task simulator, how an information display and interface system can be monitored by agents and how a human user may be incorporated into the agent environment by monitoring of their eye movements and responses. Our agents have been deployed to enact simple attention guidance in a simulated setting. We have demonstrated this important test case as a proof of concept of the architecture of such a system in a simple task space known to replicate some of the problems that have been found with user inattention.

5.1   Simulation Summary

We used our agent system to build 'user agents' that are able to simulate some simplified examples of human behaviour synthetically. This enabled us to demonstrate the behaviour of the system by summarizing error patterns under different conditions. We can conclude that the system works as expected, and that following the guidance reduces the error from a worst case scenario where a user is only paying attention to a single task. The different simulated users showed different patterns across delay. Changing the rules we implemented for following the highlights resulted in different performance error patterns. We also demonstrated how the configuration can be set to manipulate the difficulty of a task with a resulting change in performance.

The user agents are designed to demonstrate only upper and lower bound performance, and the effect of following the attention guidance for improving performance. We expect human behaviour to be some combination of our simulated users. Under certain conditions humans will be able to respond with some delay to a sub-task that required a response; sometimes they will only respond when there is a highlight; and sometimes the highlight may cause them to move their attention before they have solved a sub-task. This system is now suitable for experiments with human users to explore these scenarios and to ascertain optimal rules for the agents. For instance, the simulations suggest that highlights may not always be advantageous if the user follows them before they have solved the current sub-task they are focusing on.

The inclusion of user agents opens up our system to further simulations using more complex examples of human behaviours that may occur under different conditions and to test how ideal display rules may vary with different examples of human behaviour.

5.2   Future Experiments with Human Users

ICUa runs on a desktop PC with an eye tracker attached and can record the performance of human participants under different specified conditions. A first step would be to test the current system with the existing simple rules and assumptions to determine if it is effective at guiding attention and thus improving performance in humans. From the simulations it is already evident that there will be certain conditions under which attention guidance is particularly useful. In a low workload condition it may be that user guidance has lesser impact as there are less demands on attention, although studies also show negative effects of low expectancy - very infrequent unexpected events can also be missed, especially if there are other tasks that require constant monitoring [68]. If the events are happening too quickly for human users to successfully deal with them their may be a floor effect where attention guidance no longer helps (as seen in the longer delay times in our simulations).

Experiments would involve manipulating the frequency of events in our system and also comparing highlighting alone vs arrows alone and the two presented together, to examine the cost-benefit of single vs multiple and central vs peripheral cues. We expect to find a 'sweet spot' where attention guidance works best. The system can be combined with subjective measures of workload such as the NASA-TLX [26] as used within the original MATBII [59].

The modified ICU interface makes its suitable for measuring eye movements during a task that is similar to MATBII, making it suitable for wider experimentation beyond our current set-up. This environment provides an ideal testing ground, for different methods of attracting and maintaining attention. Attention guidance could be varied by choosing different colours of highlights, or implementing synchronous flashing between the highlight and the arrow [68] or by blurring areas that are not of interest [27]. The current system allows for measuring associated eye movements, responses and performance with such changes. Moreover, by making use of the agent architecture, our simple rules for deploying attention guidance could be altered to observe the best effects on human performance. The use of agents provides a useful way of manipulating rules for changing displays.

5.3   Potential Further Extensions and Applications

As highlighted, one strength of the agent-oriented approach and our agent model is that it is modular - extra modules can be added in terms of additional interface tasks and associated inputs, but also in terms of physiological signals of attention and other measures of the human mental state we may want to represent. Not just visual, but also auditory inputs for example are possible and additional physiological measures can take us beyond tracking spatial visual attention, including other measures that can be read from the eye tracker such as pupil size. Pupil size has been a useful measure in terms of tracking vigilance, fatigue and workload [53].

As more complex inputs are added, so the agent behaviour repertoire can be expanded. More complex rules can be added, leading to the agents performing more complex calculations that exceed human capacity, defining for example what would be the best thing to attend to for the human, when this is no longer intuitively clear, especially under a moment of high pressure, or taking over some of the task and carrying out some of the required responses automatically. This could be done in an adaptive way [29], incorporating workload in to the agent model to enable adaptive processes, making the most of agents' human-like ability and explainability. The aim of the explainability is to help the human interpret the environment and the actions of the agents. Using agent behaviour that can be transparent to the human helps build trust, which is critical to optimal human computer interaction [19]. There is no explicit user modelling in the ICUa currently, however agents are particularly suited to more complex user modelling such as those used to track learning through tutoring software [67] and our system is suited for this kind of extension.

Agents can also provide the basis for a learning framework. Whilst agent behaviour may in itself alter due to the ongoing conditions, such as ongoing high workload or fatigue as a way of achieving goals under different conditions, a further degree of individualisation to the user may be possible by enabling agents to learn form the past behaviour of the user.

Mobile eye trackers can be used to map eye position in real time to the surrounding environment recorded by a camera [64]. It has been suggested that gaze based interactive displays could be useful in a cockpit setting [39], which MATBII is set up to mimic some aspects of. Current AI cockpit applications involve automating many systems, which involves the human user handing over control. A future application of our system may be providing a way to ensure that human monitoring remains interactive, to keep the human in the loop in a cockpit environment. Increasingly cockpits are augmented, often being displayed in helmet in heads-up displays that can be moved around and tailored to the user, something that could be incorporated in to the agent system. The system we have developed aims to ensure that once a target for attention is known to the system, it is successfully processed by the human user. This emphasis means our work has applications in many systems where attention guidance might be called for, such as in semi-autonomous vehicles, within the remote operator room for automated vehicle systems, in air traffic control, or even alerts that may go unnoticed or not fully comprehended in everyday office computer usage.

6 Conclusion

We have built an attention guidance system using agent environments as the underlying framework. Central to our work is the notion that an interactive computer system construed as an agent environment should represent the human user as an entity providing continuing feedback, so that the system can ensure that they can process information within their limited attentional resources in order to produce the necessary human responses. Our proof of concept prototype aims to keep the human in the loop, in this case primarily via their eye movements and with feedback from agents. Our agent-based approach to attention guidance presents some clear advantages, such as modularity, scalability and extensibility. We propose that our approach, as exemplified by our system, is suitable for a wide range of experimentation where humans interact with multi-display interfaces based on attention guidance, and this is our next step for continuing this research.

Acknowledgements. The work for developing this demonstrator was supported by a *Human-Like Computing* EPSRC Network+ Kickstart grant. Thanks to Suzy Broadbent and Lisa Boyce for discussions and support.

References

1. PyStarWorlds (2021). https://github.com/dicelab-rhul/pystarworlds
2. Aha, D.W.: Goal reasoning: foundations, emerging applications, and prospects. AI Mag. **39**(2), 3–24 (2018)
3. Aschermann, M., Kraus, P., Müller, J.P.: LightJason. In: Criado Pacheco, N., Carrascosa, C., Osman, N., Julián Inglada, V. (eds.) EUMAS/AT -2016. LNCS (LNAI), vol. 10207, pp. 58–66. Springer, Cham (2017). https://doi.org/10.1007/978-3-319-59294-7_6
4. Bagga, P., Paoletti, N., Alrayes, B., Stathis, K.: A deep reinforcement learning approach to concurrent bilateral negotiation. In: Proceedings of the 29th International Joint Conference on Artificial Intelligence, IJCAI 2020, pp. 297–303. IJCAI/AAAI, Yokohama (2020)

5. Berthelot, B., Mazoyer, P., Egea, S., André, J.M., Grivel, É., Legrand, P.: Self-affinity of an aircraft pilot's gaze direction as a marker of visual tunneling. Technical report, SAE Technical Paper (2019). https://doi.org/10.4271/2019-01-1852

6. Bolstad, C., Costello, A., Endsley, M.: Bad situation awareness designs: what went wrong and why. In: Proceedings of the 16th World Congress of International Ergonomics Association (2006)

7. Bromuri, S., Stathis, K.: Situating cognitive agents in GOLEM. In: Weyns, D., Brueckner, S.A., Demazeau, Y. (eds.) EEMMAS 2007. LNCS (LNAI), vol. 5049, pp. 115–134. Springer, Heidelberg (2008). https://doi.org/10.1007/978-3-540-85029-8_9

8. Bromuri, S., Stathis, K.: Distributed agent environments in the ambient event calculus. In: Gokhale, A.S., Schmidt, D.C. (eds.) Proceedings of the Third ACM International Conference on Distributed Event-Based Systems, DEBS 2009, Nashville, Tennessee, USA, 6–9 July 2009. ACM (2009)

9. Bunch, L., et al.: Software agents for process monitoring and notification. In: Proceedings of the 2004 ACM Symposium on Applied Computing, SAC 2004, pp. 94–100. Association for Computing Machinery, New York (2004). https://doi.org/10.1145/967900.967921

10. Calegari, R., Ciatto, G., Mascardi, V., Omicini, A.: Logic-based technologies for multi-agent systems: a systematic literature review. Auton. Agent. Multi-agent Syst. **35**(1), 1–67 (2020). https://doi.org/10.1007/s10458-020-09478-3

11. Carrasco, M.: Visual attention: the past 25 years. Vis. Res. **51**(13), 1484–1525 (2011). https://doi.org/10.1016/j.visres.2011.04.012

12. Cegarra, J., Valéry, B., Avril, E., Calmettes, C., Navarro, J.: OpenMATB: a multi-attribute task battery promoting task customization, software extensibility and experiment replicability. Behav. Res. Methods **52**(5), 1980–1990 (2020). https://doi.org/10.3758/s13428-020-01364-w

13. Clark, K., et al.: A framework for integrating symbolic and sub-symbolic representations. In: Proceedings of the Twenty-Fifth International Joint Conference on Artificial Intelligence, IJCAI 2016, pp. 2486–2492. AAAI Press (2016)

14. Coffey., S., Clark., K.: A hybrid, teleo-reactive architecture for robot control. In: Proceedings of the 2nd International Workshop on Multi-agent Robotic Systems - MARS, (ICINCO 2006), pp. 54–65. INSTICC, SciTePress (2006). https://doi.org/10.5220/0001225300540065

15. Danieau, F., Guillo, A., Doré, R.: Attention guidance for immersive video content in head-mounted displays. In: 2017 IEEE Virtual Reality (VR), pp. 205–206 (2017). https://doi.org/10.1109/VR.2017.7892248

16. Davies, A.: The war to remotely control self-driving cars heats up. Wired. https://www.wired.com/story/designated-driverteleoperations-self-driving-cars/. Accessed 11 Nov 2019

17. Debie, E., et al.: Multimodal fusion for objective assessment of cognitive workload: a review. IEEE Trans. Cybern. (2019). https://doi.org/10.1109/TCYB.2019.2939399

18. Dongol, B., Hayes, I.J., Robinson, P.J.: Reasoning about goal-directed real-time teleo-reactive programs. Formal Aspects Comput. **26**(3), 563–589 (2014)

19. Dzindolet, M.T., Peterson, S.A., Pomranky, R.A., Pierce, L.G., Beck, H.P.: The role of trust in automation reliance. Int. J. Hum. Comput. Stud. **58**(6), 697–718 (2003). https://doi.org/10.1016/S1071-5819(03)00038-7

20. Endsley, M.R.: Designing for Situation Awareness: An Approach to User-Centered Design. CRC Press, Boca Raton (2016)

21. Endsley, M.R., Kiris, E.O.: The out-of-the-loop performance problem and level of control in automation. Hum. Factors **37**(2), 381–394 (1995). https://doi.org/10. 1518/001872095779064555
22. Fern, A., Natarajan, S., Judah, K., Tadepalli, P.: A decision-theoretic model of assistance. J. Artif. Intell. Res. **50**, 71–104 (2014). https://doi.org/10.1613/jair. 4213
23. Glass, A., McGuinness, D.L., Wolverton, M.: Toward establishing trust in adaptive agents. In: Proceedings of the 13th International Conference on Intelligent User Interfaces, pp. 227–236 (2008). https://doi.org/10.1145/1378773.1378804
24. Gutzwiller, R.S., Wickens, C.D., Clegg, B.A.: Workload overload modeling: an experiment with MATBII to inform a computational model of task management. In: Proceedings of the Human Factors and Ergonomics Society Annual Meeting, vol. 58, pp. 849–853. SAGE Publications, Los Angeles (2014). https://doi.org/10. 1177/1541931214581179
25. Hancock, P., Scallen, S.: The performance and workload effects of task re-location during automation. Displays **17**(2), 61–68 (1997). https://doi.org/10.1016/S0141-9382(96)01018-9
26. Hart, S.G., Staveland, L.E.: Development of NASA-TLX (task load index): results of empirical and theoretical research. In: Advances in Psychology, vol. 52, pp. 139–183. Elsevier (1988). https://doi.org/10.1016/S0166-4115(08)62386-9
27. Hata, H., Koike, H., Sato, Y.: Visual guidance with unnoticed blur effect. In: Proceedings of the International Working Conference on Advanced Visual Interfaces, pp. 28–35 (2016). https://doi.org/10.1145/2909132.2909254
28. Hou, M., Kobierski, R.D., Brown, M.: Intelligent adaptive interfaces for the control of multiple UAVs. J. Cogn. Eng. Decis. Mak. **1**(3), 327–362 (2007). https://doi. org/10.1518/155534307X255654
29. Inagaki, T., et al.: Adaptive automation: sharing and trading of control. In: Handbook of Cognitive Task Design, vol. 8, pp. 147–169 (2003)
30. Kakas, A., Mancarella, P., Sadri, F., Stathis, K., Toni, F.: Declarative agent control. In: Leite, J., Torroni, P. (eds.) CLIMA 2004. LNCS (LNAI), vol. 3487, pp. 96–110. Springer, Heidelberg (2005). https://doi.org/10.1007/11533092_6
31. Kakas, A., Mancarella, P., Sadri, F., Stathis, K., Toni, F.: Computational logic foundations of KGP agents. J. Artif. Intell. Res. **33**, 285–348 (2008). https://doi. org/10.1613/jair.2596
32. Kim, J.H., Yang, X.: Applying fractal analysis to pupil dilation for measuring complexity in a process monitoring task. Appl. Ergon. **65**, 61–69 (2017). https:// doi.org/10.1016/j.apergo.2017.06.002
33. Klauck, M., Sugano, Y., Bulling, A.: Noticeable or distractive? A design space for gaze-contingent user interface notifications. In: Proceedings of the 2017 CHI Conference Extended Abstracts on Human Factors in Computing Systems, pp. 1779–1786 (2017). https://doi.org/10.1145/3027063.3053085
34. Kowalski, R.A., Sadri, F.: Teleo-reactive abductive logic programs. In: Artikis, A., Craven, R., Kesim Çiçekli, N., Sadighi, B., Stathis, K. (eds.) Logic Programs, Norms and Action. LNCS (LNAI), vol. 7360, pp. 12–32. Springer, Heidelberg (2012). https://doi.org/10.1007/978-3-642-29414-3_3
35. Krauth, E.I., van Hillegersberg, J., Van De Velde, S.L.: Agent-based human-computer-interaction for real-time monitoring systems in the trucking industry. In: 2007 40th Annual Hawaii International Conference on System Sciences (HICSS 2007), p. 27 (2007). https://doi.org/10.1109/HICSS.2007.52
36. Kravari, K., Bassiliades, N.: A survey of agent platforms. J. Artif. Soc. Soc. Simul. **18**(1) (2015). https://doi.org/10.18564/jasss.2661

37. Laird, J.E.: The SOAR Cognitive Architecture. MIT Press, Cambridge (2012)
38. Maes, P.: Agents that reduce work and information overload. In: Readings in Human-Computer Interaction, pp. 811–821. Elsevier (1995). https://doi.org/10.1016/B978-0-08-051574-8.50084-4
39. Majaranta, P., Bulling, A.: Eye tracking and eye-based human–computer interaction. In: Fairclough, S.H., Gilleade, K. (eds.) Advances in Physiological Computing. HIS, pp. 39–65. Springer, London (2014). https://doi.org/10.1007/978-1-4471-6392-3_3
40. Marshall, S.P.: The index of cognitive activity: measuring cognitive workload. In: Proceedings of the IEEE 7th Conference on Human Factors and Power Plants, p. 7. IEEE (2002). https://doi.org/10.1109/HFPP.2002.1042860
41. Martens, M., Van Winsum, W.: Measuring Distraction: The Peripheral Detection Task. TNO Human Factors, Soesterberg (2000)
42. Matthews, G., Davies, D.R., Stammers, R.B., Westerman, S.J.: Human Performance: Cognition, Stress, and Individual Differences. Psychology Press, Hove (2000)
43. Matthews, T., Dey, A.K., Mankoff, J., Carter, S., Rattenbury, T.: A toolkit for managing user attention in peripheral displays. In: Proceedings of the 17th Annual ACM Symposium on User Interface Software and Technology, pp. 247–256 (2004). https://doi.org/10.1145/1029632.1029676
44. Miller, T.: Explanation in artificial intelligence: insights from the social sciences. Artif. Intell. **267**, 1–38 (2019). https://doi.org/10.1016/j.artint.2018.07.007
45. Navalpakkam, V., Itti, L.: A goal oriented attention guidance model. In: Bülthoff, H.H., Wallraven, C., Lee, S.-W., Poggio, T.A. (eds.) BMCV 2002. LNCS, vol. 2525, pp. 453–461. Springer, Heidelberg (2002). https://doi.org/10.1007/3-540-36181-2_45
46. Nelson, J.M., Phillips, C.A., McKinley, R.A., McIntire, L.K., Goodyear, C., Monforton, L.: The effects of transcranial direct current stimulation (tDCS) on multitasking performance and oculometrics. Mil. Psychol. **31**(3), 212–226 (2019). https://doi.org/10.3389/fnhum.2016.00589
47. Nilsson, N.J.: Teleo-reactive programs for agent control. J. Artif. Int. Res. **1**(1), 139–158 (1994). https://doi.org/10.1613/jair.30
48. Ohneiser, O., Gürlük, H., Jauer, M.L., Szöllősi, Á., Balló, D.: Please have a look here: successful guidance of air traffic controller's attention (2019)
49. Olsen, A.: The Tobii IVT Fixation Filter Algorithm description (2012)
50. Onken, R., Walsdorf, A.: Assistant systems for aircraft guidance: cognitive man-machine cooperation. Aerosp. Sci. Technol. **5**(8), 511–520 (2001). https://doi.org/10.1016/S1270-9638(01)01137-3
51. Peirce, J., MacAskill, M.: Building Experiments in PsychoPy. Sage, Thousand Oaks (2018)
52. Poitschke, T., Laquai, F., Rigoll, G.: Guiding a driver's visual attention using graphical and auditory animations. In: Harris, D. (ed.) EPCE 2009. LNCS (LNAI), vol. 5639, pp. 424–433. Springer, Heidelberg (2009). https://doi.org/10.1007/978-3-642-02728-4_45
53. Pomplun, M., Sunkara, S.: Pupil dilation as an indicator of cognitive workload in human-computer interaction. In: Proceedings of the International Conference on HCI, vol. 273 (2003)
54. Roda, C., Thomas, J.: Attention aware systems: theories, applications, and research agenda. Comput. Hum. Behav. **22**(4), 557–587 (2006). https://doi.org/10.1016/j.chb.2005.12.005

55. Rodden, T.A., Fischer, J.E., Pantidi, N., Bachour, K., Moran, S.: At home with agents: exploring attitudes towards future smart energy infrastructures. In: Proceedings of the SIGCHI Conference on Human Factors in Computing Systems, CHI 2013, pp. 1173–1182. Association for Computing Machinery, New York (2013). https://doi.org/10.1145/2470654.2466152

56. Rosch, J.L., Vogel-Walcutt, J.J.: A review of eye-tracking applications as tools for training. Cogn. Technol. Work **15**(3), 313–327 (2013). https://doi.org/10.1007/s10111-012-0234-7

57. Sadri, F.: Logic-based approaches to intention recognition. In: Handbook of Research on Ambient Intelligence and Smart Environments: Trends and Perspectives, pp. 346–375. IGI Global (2011). https://doi.org/10.4018/978-1-61692-857-5.ch007

58. Sadri, F., Stathis, K., Toni, F.: Normative KGP agents. Comput. Math. Organ. Theory **12**(2–3), 101–126 (2006)

59. Santiago-Espada, Y., Myer, R.R., Latorella, K.A., Comstock, J.R., Jr.: The multi-attribute task battery II. A user's guide (MATB-II) software for human performance and workload research (2011)

60. de Silva, L., Meneguzzi, F., Logan, B.: BDI agent architectures: a survey. In: Bessiere, C. (ed.) Proceedings of the Twenty-Ninth International Joint Conference on Artificial Intelligence, IJCAI 2020, pp. 4914–4921. ijcai.org (2020). https://doi.org/10.24963/ijcai.2020/684

61. Stanton, N.A., Chambers, P.R., Piggott, J.: Situational awareness and safety. Saf. Sci. **39**(3), 189–204 (2001). https://doi.org/10.1016/S0925-7535(01)00010-8

62. Stathis, K., Kakas, A.C., Lu, W., Demetriou, N., Endriss, U., Bracciali, A.: PROSOCS: a platform for programming software agents in computational logic. In: Müller, J., Petta, P. (eds.) Proceedings of the Fourth International Symposium "From Agent Theory to Agent Implementation" (AT2AI-4 - EMCSR 2004 Session M), Vienna, Austria, pp. 523–528 (2004)

63. Stratmann, T.C., Kempa, F., Boll, S.: Lame: light-controlled attention guidance for multi-monitor environments. In: Proceedings of the 8th ACM International Symposium on Pervasive Displays, pp. 1–5 (2019). https://doi.org/10.1145/3321335.3324935

64. Tatler, B.W., Hansen, D.W., Pelz, J.B.: Eye movement recordings in natural settings. In: Klein, C., Ettinger, U. (eds.) Eye Movement Research. SNPBE, pp. 549–592. Springer, Cham (2019). https://doi.org/10.1007/978-3-030-20085-5_13

65. Toreini, P., Morana, S.: Designing attention-aware business intelligence and analytics dashboards. In: Designing the Digital Transformation: DESRIST 2017 Research in Progress Proceedings of the 12th International Conference on Design Science Research in Information Systems and Technology, Karlsruhe, Germany. 30 May–1 June, pp. 64–72. Karlsruher Institut für Technologie (KIT) (2017). https://doi.org/10.5445/IR/1000069452

66. Van Orden, K.F., Limbert, W., Makeig, S., Jung, T.P.: Eye activity correlates of workload during a visuospatial memory task. Hum. Factors **43**(1), 111–121 (2001). https://doi.org/10.1518/001872001775992570

67. Wang, H., Chignell, M., Ishizuka, M.: Empathic tutoring software agents using real-time eye tracking. In: Proceedings of the 2006 Symposium on Eye Tracking Research & Applications, ETRA 2006, pp. 73–78. Association for Computing Machinery, New York (2006). https://doi.org/10.1145/1117309.1117346

68. Wickens, C.D., Hollands, J.G., Banbury, S., Parasuraman, R.: Engineering Psychology and Human Performance. Psychology Press, Hove (2015)

StreamB: A Declarative Language for Automatically Processing Data Streams in Abstract Environments for Agent Platforms

Angelo Ferrando[1][✉][iD] and Fabio Papacchini[2][✉][iD]

[1] Department of Computer Science, Bioengineering,
Robotics and Systems Engineering (DIBRIS), University of Genoa, Genoa, Italy
`angelo.ferrando@dibris.unige.it`
[2] Department of Computer Science, University of Liverpool, Liverpool, UK
`fabio.papacchini@liverpool.ac.uk`

Abstract. To apply BDI agents to real-world scenarios, the reality-gap, between the low-level data (*perceptions*) and their high-level representation (*beliefs*), must be bridged. This is usually achieved by a manual mapping. There are two problems with this solution: (i) if the environment changes, the mapping has to be changed as well (by the developer); (ii) part of the mapping might end up being implemented at the agent level increasing the code complexity and reducing its generality. In this paper, we present a general approach to automate the mapping between low-level data and high-level beliefs through the use of transducers. These transducers gather information from the environment and map them to high-level beliefs according to formal temporal specifications. We present our technique and we show its applicability through a case study involving the remote inspection of a nuclear plant.

Keywords: Agent programming · Stream processing · BDI model · Abstract environment

1 Introduction

Multi-agent systems (MAS) are a complex, yet general, research area involving the design and construction of distributed intelligent systems. Software agents are generally used to model one or multiple components of a system, and allow to abstract away unnecessary implementation details. Agents are well-suited to be used in applications involving distributed or concurrent computation, or when communication between different components is required.

One of the most used models to formalise the internal architecture of cognitive agents is the Belief-Desire-Intention (BDI) model. The BDI model [10,28]

Work supported by UK Research and Innovation, and EPSRC Hubs for "Robotics and AI in Hazardous Environments": EP/R026173 (ORCA), and EP/R026084 (RAIN).

consists in a reasoning process that aids the decision-making of selecting an appropriate action towards the achievement of some goal. The decision making process is based on the three components: *belief* – knowledge that the agent believes about its environment, itself, and other agents; *desire* – the desired states that the agent wants to achieve; and *intention* – a sequence of steps towards the achievement of a desire.

Usually, agents are *situated* in an environment. The environment can be seen as the medium for an agent to live, or the first entity an agent interacts with [22]. As we mentioned before, a BDI agent reasons on what it believes about the environment. From an engineering perspective, beliefs help to simplify the agent development by abstracting away technical details that are irrelevant for the agent. In fact, all the aspects of multiagent systems that conceptually do not belong to agents themselves should not be assigned to, or hosted inside the agents [39]. A natural question is:

How are low-level environment perceptions transformed into high-level beliefs? An abstraction level of the environment is a common solution in agent systems, and it is supported in most agent platforms. The abstraction level bridges the conceptual gap between the agent abstraction and low-level details of the deployment context [38], and it is a middleware between the real environment and the agents. The abstract environment has the job of gathering information from the real environment, and transforming it into beliefs. Its implementation is domain dependent, and it is generally hard-coded. This means the developer has to manually program the translation into the abstract environment. For small environments, this might be a valid solution; but, for bigger, more dynamic and complex ones, an automatic (and more declarative) way to define the environment can be more practical and efficient. Note that such a definition is still in a certain way hard-coded, but, by using a customised and higher-level specification language rather than a general-purpose one, we can help the user to write the abstraction in a more compact and natural way. Examples of this are shown throughout the paper.

In this work, we present StreamB, a Domain Specific Language (DSL) for processing data streams in abstract environments. With StreamB it is possible to guide the translation from low-level information (e.g. sensors) to high-level concepts (e.g. beliefs). Thanks to its declarative nature, StreamB is much more intuitive and helps the user to create abstract environments, by reducing the amount of actual code to be produced; since the mapping process is automatically synthesised by StreamB. In more detail, StreamB is built upon the notion of Stream Processing, and allows the user for a flexible yet straightforward way to map low-level environment data, to high-level agent beliefs. StreamB has been fully instantiated, and all its features are thoroughly presented in this paper, along with an example of an application to a challenging case study in a robotic scenario.

The paper is structured as follows. Section 2 introduces the notion of stream processing. An overview of our technique is presented in Sect. 3, followed by a step-by-step explanation of StreamB's syntax and semantics. Technical details on how StreamB has been implemented are discussed in Sect. 4. Section 5 shows an application of StreamB to a realistic case study. In Sect. 6, we place our work in the state-of-the-art. Conclusion and future works are presented in Sect. 7.

2   Stream Processing

The complexity of modelling a real-world scenario often results in the need of an abstraction. What needs to be modelled in the abstraction, and how to do it depend on the problem under consideration and the approach to be implemented. This paper focuses on the part of the abstraction which allows us to decouple the environment from the high-level decision making process of the agent. This results in a simplified agent's implementation, where the agent focuses on high-level beliefs, without knowing how such beliefs have been generated and other related technical details.

The main focus of our approach is on how to extract complex temporal information from data streams, and transform them into high-level beliefs for the agent. There are two fundamental aspects that need to be addressed in order to achieve our goal. First, how we are processing the stream and what data streams are composed of. Second, what language is used to express complex temporal information.

Stream processing [34] is a software paradigm that focuses on the real-time processing of continuous streams of data. Stream processing is generally obtained by creating transducers that, given a stream of data in input, return an altered stream of data in output. The output of one or multiple transducers can be used as input to other transducers; this allows us to obtain complex behaviours. Figure 1 shows an example of a transducer, which takes n data streams as input, and returns a single data stream as output, which contains the result of the transducer's computation. The input of a transducer can be generated by the system (e.g., by sensors), or by other transducers. The combination of multiple transducers is in fact one of the most interesting features of stream processing.

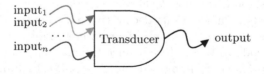

Fig. 1. Transducer.

For a given sensor or transducer, we represent their stream of data as sequences of triples of the form $(\tau, id, value)$, where τ denotes the time when the data is produced, id is an identifier uniquely associated with the sensor or transducer, and $value$ represents the value of the data. In our modelling of data streams, we adopt a discrete conception of time, where each timestamp $\tau \in \mathbb{N}$

and there is a first timestamp τ_0. One of the main implications of using such a representation of time is that we need each component of the system to generate data at the same rate. For this reason, we assume the environment to be equipped with a global clock. The global clock works as a barrier between the system and the transducers, and it forces the data streams to produce data at the same pace. Our framework enforces a global clock by sampling the data at a fixed and customisable rate.

Another consequence of this representation of time is on how and which temporal properties can be expressed. The formal language we use to express temporal properties on the stream of data is a sublanguage of the first-order metric temporal logic with aggregation presented in [4]. It is beyond the scope of this paper to describe in detail the logical language behind our framework. Nonetheless, we briefly present the important aspects that are necessary to understand it. First, the language can only refer to past events using time intervals, where only the length of the interval is specified, and the starting point is based on the time of evaluation (e.g., given a time τ_i and a length j, the relative time interval is $[i - j, i]$). Second, we allow only for the aggregation operations of average, minimum, maximum, and sigma (*i.e.*, standard deviation) over a given time interval. If the length of a time interval is greater than the length of the stream, the interval is reduced accordingly. Finally, different components of the language are dealt with at different stages of the hierarchy of transducer presented in the next section. The final output is a stream of Boolean values, which represent agent's beliefs.

3   StreamB

In this section, we show how to create abstractions by using transducers. The resulting stream processing approach transforms the low-level data produced by the real environment execution into high-level beliefs, which can be used by a BDI agent. A general overview of the approach is sketched in Fig. 2. Specifically, this section presents StreamB, a user friendly Domain Specific Language (DSL) for automatically synthesising transducers mapping low-level data into high-level beliefs. The synthesising process is based on the creation of a hierarchy of different kind of transducers, and the section presents both their DSL specification, and the corresponding synthesised transducer.

In our technique, the agent does not need to interact with the real-world environment, but only with an abstraction of it. The complexity of how the beliefs are created is hidden from the agent.

3.1   Data Types and Time

First, we need to introduce how the data streams and time are specified in StreamB. The transducers work in a hierarchical way, from the lowest layer, where the data from the real-world environment are gathered, up to the highest layer, where the beliefs are generated and passed to the agent. In our framework,

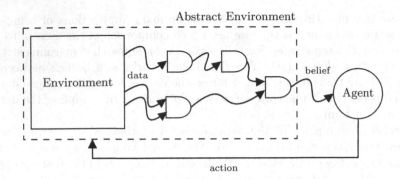

Fig. 2. Overview.

three data types are available: *int*, *real* and *bool*. That corresponds to their standard notions.

Grammar 1.1 reports the StreamB grammar to define data streams.

⟨*data*⟩ ::= ⟨*ident*⟩ ':' ⟨*type*⟩ ';'

⟨*type*⟩ ::= 'int' | 'real' | 'bool'

Grammar 1.1. Data stream grammar.

In ⟨*data*⟩, a data stream is defined, where ⟨*ident*⟩ is an identifier (the name of the stream), and ⟨*type*⟩ its type.

Example 1. Let us assume the real-world environment contains a sensor that reports a stream of real values representing the current temperature of the environment. Listing 1.1 shows how to define such a temperature data stream. Since temperature is a floating point value, we use the `real` data type.

```
temperature: real;
```

Listing 1.1. Example of data stream definition.

As remarked in Sect. 2, since these streams are generated by the real-world environment, there is no guarantee on the rate these data are produced. In fact, different streams can be generated at a different rate. This may be an issue when combining transducers. Because of this, a global clock is enforced by StreamB, and its pace can be customised (see Grammar 1.2). Under the hood, this is achieved by filtering data of streams with higher rate than the chosen one, and by replicating data of streams with lower rate than the chosen one.

⟨*time*⟩   ::= 'time_unit' '[' ⟨*time-unit*⟩ ']'

⟨*time-unit*⟩   ::= 'milliseconds' | 'seconds'

Grammar 1.2. Time unit grammar.

This is explained in detail in Sect. 4, where the transducers implementation is presented.

Example 2. Let us assume we want to set the time unit to seconds. Listing 1.2 shows how this can be done.

```
time_unit[seconds]
```

Listing 1.2. Example of time unit definition.

Every time a transducer will define an interval of time, the time unit considered will be seconds (in this case).

By stating that the time unit is seconds, the pace of all data streams will be of one event per second. Once the data streams and time unit have been defined, transducers can be constructed on top of it.

3.2   Aggregation Transducers

The first layer of transducers is the *Aggregation layer*. As the name suggests, the aggregation transducer's job is to aggregate information. This information can come from the real-world environment, or from other aggregation transducers. StreamB's grammar for the aggregation transducers is presented in Grammar 1.3.

Each line describes a different aggregation function. In the first line of ⟨*aggrT*⟩, the min aggregation function is defined. It gets a stream of data and outputs the minimum value observed. If no range is given (the number between the square brackets), the minimum value is calculated considering all values observed by the transducer (since the beginning of its execution). If a range is given, the minimum value is evaluated only considering the values observed in the interval defined by the range. The same reasoning can be applied to the other aggregation functions, where we consider the maximum, average and sigma[1] of the observed values, respectively. Each aggregation transducer is assigned an identifier name ⟨*aggrAssign*⟩, making it possible to reuse transducers inside the definition of other transducers. This is stated in the last line of ⟨*aggrT*⟩, where the base cases are listed. Note that an identifier can relate to an aggregation transducer (defined as ⟨*aggrAssign*⟩) or a data stream (defined as ⟨*data*⟩ in Grammar 1.1).

---

[1] It computes the standard deviation over the data stream.

⟨*aggrAssign*⟩   ::= ⟨*ident*⟩ '=' ⟨*aggrT*⟩ ';'

⟨*aggrT*⟩   ::= '**min**' ⟨*aggrT*⟩
                 | '**min**' '[' ⟨*number*⟩ ']' ⟨*aggrT*⟩
                 | '**max**' ⟨*aggrT*⟩
                 | '**max**' '[' ⟨*number*⟩ ']' ⟨*aggrT*⟩
                 | '**avg**' ⟨*aggrT*⟩
                 | '**avg**' '[' ⟨*number*⟩ ']' ⟨*aggrT*⟩
                 | '**sigma**' ⟨*aggrT*⟩
                 | '**sigma**' '[' ⟨*number*⟩ ']' ⟨*aggrT*⟩
                 | ⟨*value*⟩ | ⟨*ident*⟩

Grammar 1.3. Aggregation transducers grammar.

Example 3. Considering the same real-world environment of Example 1. We could create a transducer that extracts the average temperature in the past 5 time units (5 s in this case). Listing 1.3 shows how this can be defined using StreamB. In here, we can see how an aggregation transducer can use a previously defined data stream, `temperature` in this case. This is obtained by the last line of ⟨*aggrT*⟩, where ⟨*ident*⟩ is matched.

```
time_unit[seconds]
temperature: real;

avgTemp5 = avg[5] temperature;
```

Listing 1.3. Example of aggregation transducer.

A graphical representation of the resulting transducer is shown in Fig. 3. Time references $\tau_{n-1}, \tau_n, \tau_{n+1}$ are added to indicate the time flow inside the stream, and to make easier to connect the inputs with their corresponding outputs.

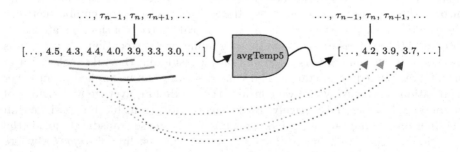

Fig. 3. Example of average transducer.

3.3   Comparison Transducers

The second layer of transducers is the *Comparison layer*. The transducers defined at this layer get data streams (layer 0), or aggregated streams (layer 1), and outputs a Boolean stream, representing the truth value of the associated evaluation.

StreamB's grammar for the comparison transducers is reported in Grammar 1.4.

$$
\begin{array}{lll}
\langle combAssign \rangle & ::= & \langle ident \rangle \text{ `=' } \langle combT \rangle \text{ `;'} \\[4pt]
\langle combT \rangle & ::= & \langle aggrT \rangle \text{ `<' } \langle aggrT \rangle \\
& | & \langle aggrT \rangle \text{ `<=' } \langle aggrT \rangle \\
& | & \langle aggrT \rangle \text{ `>' } \langle aggrT \rangle \\
& | & \langle aggrT \rangle \text{ `>=' } \langle aggrT \rangle \\
& | & \langle aggrT \rangle \text{ `==' } \langle aggrT \rangle \\
& | & \langle aggrT \rangle \text{ `!=' } \langle aggrT \rangle
\end{array}
$$

Grammar 1.4. Comparison transducers grammar.

Each line describes a different comparison function. In the first line of $\langle combT \rangle$, the *less than* function is defined. Such a function compares two streams and outputs a stream with values either $\top$, if the current value on the left stream is less than the current value on the right stream, or $\bot$ otherwise. Similar reasoning can be applied to all the other standard comparison operators. Each comparison transducer is assigned an identifier $\langle combAssign \rangle$. As before, this makes possible to reuse transducers inside other transducers.

Example 4. We can now extend Example 3 by using a comparison transducer to check when the average temperature in the past 5 s goes under 4.0°. The corresponding definition is reported in Listing 1.4, while the resulting transducer is shown in Fig. 4.

```
time_unit[seconds]
temperature: real;

avgTemp5 = avg[5] temperature;
thresholdLowTemp = avgTemp5 < 4.0;
```

Listing 1.4. Example of comparison transducer.

3.4   Past MTL Transducers

The third layer of transducers is the *Past MTL (Past Metric Temporal Logic) layer*. The transducers defined at this layer get Boolean streams (either from

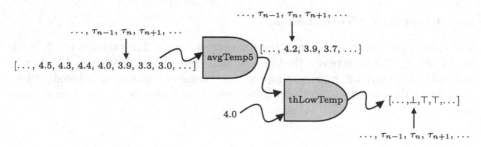

Fig. 4. Example of comparison transducer (`thresholdLowTemp` is abbreviated to `thLowTemp`).

comparison transducers or data streams), and outputs a Boolean stream, representing the truth value of the associated MTL property.

StreamB's grammar for the MTL transducers is reported in Grammar 1.5.

$\langle mtlAssign \rangle$ ::= $\langle ident \rangle$ '=' $\langle mtlT \rangle$ ';'

$\langle mtlT \rangle$ ::= 'pre' $\langle mtlT \rangle$
            | 'once' $\langle mtlT \rangle$
            | 'once' '[' $\langle number \rangle$ ']' $\langle mtlT \rangle$
            | 'always' $\langle mtlT \rangle$
            | 'always' '[' $\langle number \rangle$ ']' $\langle mtlT \rangle$
            | $\langle mtlT \rangle$ 'since' $\langle mtlT \rangle$
            | $\langle mtlT \rangle$ 'since' '[' $\langle number \rangle$ ']' $\langle mtlT \rangle$
            | 'not' $\langle mtlT \rangle$
            | $\langle mtlT \rangle$ ('&&'|'||'|'->') $\langle mtlT \rangle$
            | $\langle combT \rangle$
            | $\langle ident \rangle$

Grammar 1.5. MTL transducers grammar.

Each line describes a different MTL operator. The `pre` operator states that a predicate has to be true in the previous time step. The `once` operator states that a predicate has to be true at least once in the past. If a range is given (numbers inside brackets), the property is checked on that specific interval of time (in the past). The `always` operator states that the predicate must always be true in the past. As before, the property can be constrained to a specific interval of time in the past. The `since` operator states that the right property is true in the past, and since then, the left property is always true (potentially within an interval). The remaining operators are standard Boolean operators. Each MTL transducer is assigned an identifier $\langle mtlAssign \rangle$. As before, this makes possible to reuse MTL transducers inside other transducers.

Example 5. We extend Example 4 by using an MTL transducer to check if the average temperature (sampled on a 5 s interval) is always less than $4.0°$[2] in the past 2 s. In Listing 1.5, we report how this can be defined in StreamB. In Fig. 5, we graphically show the resulting transducer.

```
time_unit[seconds]
temperature: real;

avgTemp5 = avg[5] temperature;
thresholdLowTemp = avgTemp5 < 4.0;
lowTemp = always [2] thresholdLowTemp;
```

Listing 1.5. Example of MTL transducer.

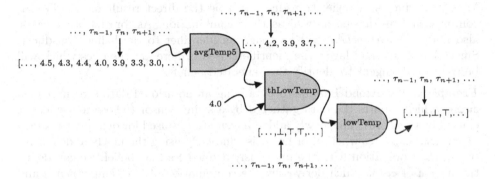

Fig. 5. Example of always transducer.

With respect to the other transducers, MTL ones are very expressive. In fact, with MTL we can specify interesting temporal properties. This is important because with a highly expressive formalism, we can represent complex behaviours. This means having a higher coverage on the kind of beliefs we can model. From an engineering perspective, an MTL property can be easily specified; but, its implementation might not be trivial. Thanks to StreamB, the translation of MTL properties to transducers is automatic and transparent. Otherwise, these kind of beliefs could not be handled, or they would be handled by hard-coding the abstract environment (with a non negligible amount of work).

3.5 Belief Transducers

The fourth layer of transducers is the *Belief layer*, and it is the final layer that connects the stream processing to the agent. The transducers defined at this

---

[2] It is important to note that instead of a number we may have a stream.

level get comparison and MTL streams (layer 2–3), and outputs the high-level beliefs used by the BDI agent.

StreamB's grammar for the Belief transducers is reported in Grammar 1.6

$\langle belAssign \rangle$ ::= $\langle ident \rangle$ '=' $\langle belT \rangle$ ';'

$\langle belT \rangle$ ::= $\langle mtlT \rangle$
       | $\langle belT \rangle$ 'and' $\langle belT \rangle$
       | $\langle belT \rangle$ 'or' $\langle belT \rangle$

Grammar 1.6. Belief transducers grammar.

In the second and third lines of $\langle belT \rangle$, belief transducers can be created by combining Boolean streams. At this level, the combination can be achieved through conjunction or disjunction. Since the first line recalls the grammar of MTL transducers, a belief transducer can be the direct result of an MTL or comparison transducers; as well as their combination. As for the other cases, also here we have $\langle belAssign \rangle$ to assign an identifier to the belief transducer. Since this is the final layer, the identifiers used in here are the ones which will be used by the agent to identify the generated beliefs.

Example 6. We extend Example 5 by adding an additional data stream, called `swing`, which reports the data gathered by a swing sensor (whose movement is caused by the wind). This newly added information is used for defining the `windy` belief, that captures whether or not it is windy. By using the newly added `windy` belief, in combination with the previously defined `lowTemp` belief, we can define the notion of `cold`; which derives by the combination of low temperatures and presence of wind. Listing 1.6 reports the corresponding StreamB specification, and Fig. 6 shows the resulting transducers. Note that, both `lowTemp` and `windy` have been defined in one line, without splitting the definition of the nested transducers. This does not change the semantics of the transducers. Indeed, the use of identifiers only helps writing less, because the compiler automatically recognises nested transducers and keeps track of them. So, in case of duplication within the code, no duplicate transducer would be generated.

```
time_unit[seconds]
temperature: real;
swing: real;

lowTemp = always [2] (avg[5] temperature < 4.0);
windy = (avg[5] swing) > 10;

cold = lowTemp and windy;
```

Listing 1.6. Example of Belief transducer.

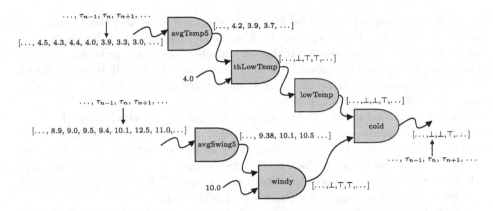

Fig. 6. Example of windy and cold transducers.

4 Implementation

The results presented in this paper are general. In this section, we only present a possible instantiation in a non-trivial scenario. Nonetheless, StreamB and, above all, the transducers are not limited to the proposed implementation; whose purpose is only to be a proof of concept in the robotic domain.

StreamB's parser has been implemented in Python3 using ANTLR[3] (ANother Tool for Language Recognition). The source code of our framework is available as a GitHub repository[4]. Given a specification file, the parser generates an abstract syntax tree which is then translated into transducers. This part has been obtained by implementing a customised visitor. Previously, for each StreamB operator, we sketched the resulting transducer. At the implementation level, the transducers are synthesised as ROS (Robot Operating System) [27] nodes. ROS is an open-source set of software libraries and tools to build robotic applications. It is modular, supported by a large community, and highly compatible with many types of robots. We chose ROS because it is the *de facto* standard for developing robotic applications, and its use to implement the transducers shows a potentially wide impact of the approach. Moreover, robotic applications are notoriously complex and prone to generate streams of data (usually produced by sensors on the robot).

ROS is natively distributed and node based. Each component in ROS is represented as a node. Communication amongst nodes is achieved through message passing, following a publish/subscribe paradigm. The communication channels are called topics, and each node can subscribe to (resp. publish on) them.

StreamB's transducers are mapped to ROS nodes. The transducer's inputs are retrieved by subscribing to the topics used by the nested transducers; while the transducer's output is published on a uniquely identified topic. From a bottom-up perspective, the flow starts from the data stream transducers that

---

[3] https://www.antlr.org/.

[4] https://github.com/autonomy-and-verification-uol/StreamB.

subscribe to low-level topics, on which raw data are published (for instance by sensors). Then, the flow continues by passing through the transducers, exactly as we presented in the paper. Finally, the beliefs transducers publish their output which represent the high-level beliefs. The agent needs only to subscribe on those topics (called with the identifier given in StreamB), and update their belief base. An example is shown in Sect. 5.

As we remarked in Sect. 2, to combine different transducers, we need to synchronise the corresponding streams. This can be obtained by adding a global clock. In more detail, StreamB adds a clock node, that sets the pace. This can be achieved by making the clock node publish a message at a chosen rate, and all data stream nodes subscribe to the same message. When a data stream node receives the clock message, it publishes its latest value.

Note that, even though StreamB natively supports ROS, it is not limited to it. In fact, the current implementation simply compiles StreamB specifications into ROS; with transducers as nodes. Nonetheless, without changing the DSL, we could seamlessly change the target framework. For instance, instead of ROS, another interesting and useful target platform could be Akka[5]. Specifically, we could compile StreamB into AkkaStream transducers. The advantage in using Akka would be to have access to its rich library. Moreover, Akka is widely used both in academia and industry, with a large community support and plenty of documentation/tutorials. Thanks to protocols and mechanics for stream processing natively supported by Akka, the implementation of the transducers would be simpler than their counterpart in ROS. For instance, AkkaStream transducers support by design a back-pressure protocol for reducing/increasing the pace of the events over a stream, dynamically. This feature could be used to simplify the logic of StreamB's transducers. Nonetheless, we would still need to discretise the events in order to preserve the meaning of the temporal intervals defined in the specifications. In any case, to be used in ROS it would still require additional work (probably by using ROSBridge to connect Akka transducers to the nodes).

5   Case Study

We tested our implementation on the MCAPL[6] [7,17,18] framework, where BDI agents are defined using the GWENDOLEN agent programming language [16]. Like Jason [8], JaCaMo [5,6], also MCAPL uses Java to specify the abstract environment. The agents interact with the real-world environment only through such an abstraction. To connect the Java environment to the belief transducers, we used the ROSA library [12]. This library allows us to subscribe to ROS topics from Java, by using ROSBridge[7]. Because of this, the integration of our framework in MCAPL has been straightforward; it was enough to subscribe to the belief topics inside the Java environment, and to update the belief base accordingly.

---

[5] https://www.akka-technologies.com/.

[6] https://github.com/mcapl/mcapl.

[7] http://wiki.ros.org/rosbridge.

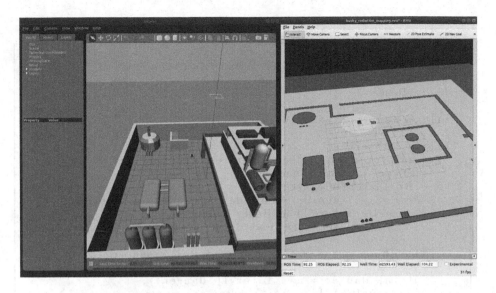

Fig. 7. Simulation in Gazebo of the remote inspection of nuclear plant.

As a proof of concept, we applied our framework to a remote inspection case study that uses the 3D simulator Gazebo and ROS (shown in Fig. 7). In this simulation, a *Jackal*[8] four-wheeled rover uses a sensor to take radiation measurements. The rover's goal is to patrol inside a nuclear storage facility. The rover is controlled by an autonomous agent that makes decisions depending on the radiation readings.

```
time_unit[seconds]
radiation: real;

yellow = always [10] ((avg [3] radiation) > 80);
orange = always [5] ((avg [3] radiation) > 120);
red = always [3] ((avg [3] radiation) > 250);

danger = yellow or orange or red;
```

Listing 1.7. Definition of danger belief in terms of radiation level.

---

[8] https://clearpathrobotics.com/jackal-small-unmanned-ground-vehicle/.

```java
// Java abstract environment
public class RosEnv extends DefaultEnvironment{
  ...
  public RosEnv() {
  // connect to ROSBridge
  bridge.connect("ws://localhost:9090", true);
  // subscribe to danger belief
  bridge.subscribe(
    SubscriptionRequestMsg.generate("/danger")
    .setType("stream/TimedBool"),
    new RosListenDelegate() {
    public void receive(JsonNode data, String stringRep) {
      MessageUnpacker<TimedBool> unpacker = new
        MessageUnpacker<TimedBool>(TimedBool.class);
      // extract message
      TimedBool msg = unpacker.unpackRosMessage(data);
      // create corresponding literal
      Literal danger = new Literal("danger");
      if(msg.value) { // if the belief is true
        addPercept(danger); // add it to belief base
      } else { // otherwise
        removePercept(danger); // remove it
      }
    }
  });
  }
}
```

Listing 1.8. Java environment in MCAPL to retrieve danger belief from the ROS node transducer.

Listing 1.7 shows how to construct a high-level belief which states whether the robot is in a dangerous area. Instead of manually coding this in Java, thanks to our framework, we can directly and declaratively describe how the radiation data stream is transformed into a **danger** high-level belief. Listing 1.8 shows how to retrieve easily this information in the Java abstract environment. The **danger** belief is specified as the combination of three different beliefs: **yellow**, **orange** and **red**. These beliefs represent three different scenarios that may put the robot in danger. In all three cases the level of radiation is sampled (considering the average) and checked if greater than a threshold for a certain amount of time. For lower radiation levels (80), a longer amount of time (10 s) is considered dangerous for the robot's integrity; while for higher radiation levels (120 and 250), a shorter amount of time (5 and 3 s) is considered dangerous. The composition of these three beliefs produces the high-level belief **danger**, which is used by the agent (see Listing 1.9); in this case, by interrupting the mission and going back to the starting point (the **door**) for decontamination procedures. Listing 1.9 reports the agent's plan which is triggered when the **danger** belief is added by the abstract environment. In such a plan, first, the agent retrieves the door's coordinates (using `location_coordinate` book-keeping belief), then, it moves to that position (performing the `move` action). Note that, the agent does not know about `yellow`, `orange`, or `red` radiation levels. Nonetheless, in a different scenario, these information might be used by the agent as well. This would not require any additional work, but only a subscription to the corresponding topics in the abstract environment (similarly to what is done for **danger** in Listing 1.8).

```
...
+danger
  : { B location_coordinate(door,X,Y,Z) }
<-
  print("Move to the door for decontamination."),
  +going(door), move(X,Y,Z).
...
```

Listing 1.9. Snippet of GWENDOLEN agent which uses **danger** belief.

6   Related Work

To the best of our knowledge, there is no work that explicitly integrates stream processing in the creation of abstract environments for MAS architectures.

The environment is an implicit part of MAS that is often dealt with in an *ad hoc* manner [38]. This statement holds for the abstract environment as well. In fact, the abstraction is usually created manually, as it happens in MCAPL [7,17,18], Jason [8], JaCaMo [5,6], GOAL [23], and other frameworks. Instead, in our work the abstract environment is fully[9] synthesised from a high-level specification, and it can be used to enhance existing agent platforms when applied to real-world environments, such as cyber-physical systems, and robotic applications. The greatest similarity with our work can be found in CArtAgO [30], where sensors are described as perceptual memory, whose functionality accounts for keeping track of stimuli arrived from the environment, possibly applying filters and specific kinds of "buffering" policy [29]. Following this definition, our transducers can be seen as perceptual memory as well, and they could be integrated in CArtAgO for enhancing artifacts with stream processing features.

From the point of view of stream processing systems, in [35] the high-level idea of using stream processing in the development of agent infrastructures is proposed, along with general guidelines. Differently from our work, they aim to use stream processing to enhance agent reasoning in stream-based scenarios. We instead focus on using stream processing as a tool to simplify the abstract environment construction, and its link to the agent's belief base. In [32] Intelligent Sensor Agents (ISA) process data streams to find anomalies. The developed architecture is used in nation-wide and city-level incident recognition scenarios. Differently from our work, the agents are used to support stream processing, and

---

[9] Or partially, in case we extend an existing abstract environment as we did for MCAPL.

not the other way around. This happens in [13,21,31] as well, where agents are used to implement parts of the stream processing system.

From the point of view of DSLs, various alternatives exist. We report only a relevant subset of the languages, since our objective is to point out the main differences with StreamB. For a complete survey on the DSLs used in the stream processing domain, the reader can find a thorough investigation in [24].

Stream processing languages can be classified into: Relational, Big data, XML and RDF. In the first group [1,3,9,14,33], we find several DSLs which are designed as SQL-based declarative languages for implementing continuous queries against streams of data. With respect to StreamB, the specifications are SQL query, in which selection, filter and merging operations are used to create the low-level transducers. In the second group [25,26,36,40], the DSLs are based on SPL (Stream Processing Language), developed by IBM. An SPL program explicitly specifies a directed graph of stream edges and operator nodes. Operators are used to create/transform streams and are defined by users or libraries, not built into the language. Differently from StreamB, SPL does not offer built-in operators. High-level notions can be derived (e.g. MTL properties), but are not straightforward. In the third group [20], we find YFilter and its derivatives [15,19], which implement continuous queries over XML streaming data. While in the fourth group [37], a continuous version of SPARQL is proposed (C-SPARQL), along with its extensions [2,11].

We decided to design and develop StreamB because none of the previously mentioned DSLs support temporal logics, natively. Moreover, none of these works has been integrated in ROS. Since the temporal aspects allow us to describe highly expressive streams in a declarative way, we opted for a DSL which natively supports them. On the other hand, robotic applications are a natural candidate where to use abstract environments, and none of the previously presented DSLs support ROS (except by manually implementing necessary bridges).

7   Conclusions and Future Work

In this paper we presented StreamB, a stream processing technique to automate the translation from low-level data (environment's *perceptions*) to high-level beliefs, in a general and flexible way. We proposed a DSL to define high-level beliefs in terms of different kind of streams; we presented each operator of the language, and we showed the transducers deriving by their compilation. Finally, we applied our technique to a realistic case study involving the remote inspection of a nuclear plant.

This work is focused on BDI platforms, but it is not limited to them. Indeed, the final layer of transducers, which is called *Belief layer*, could be considered as a general *Stimuli layer* instead, where the high-level stimuli deriving from low-level data are produced. The abstract environment would be the one giving a domain specific meaning to the resulting stimuli. For instance, in this case it would interpret them as beliefs, but in a different scenarios (not BDI), the same stimuli might be interpreted in a different way by a different abstract environment. Nonetheless, we decided to present our work in the BDI context because we think it is where our solution has larger and deeper implications. In any case, from the point of view of the implementation, nothing needs to be changed.

Concerning future work, StreamB currently offers four layers of transducers, but more can be added. MTL was a natural choice, but it is not the only one, indeed other temporal logics can be integrated as additional layers. We explored a robotic scenario, where the transducers were compiled to ROS nodes. We are planning to add support for additional target platforms. This work would only concerns the compiler (*i.e.*, the translation of StreamB specifications into transducers), not the specification language, that would be preserved to allow re-use of specifications in different target environments.

In this work, we only considered atomic beliefs. In a more general setting, however, it might be much more useful to be able to generate compound beliefs. This would be relevant in scenarios where information inside a data stream can or need to be parametrised.

Finally, the current StreamB's processing pipelines of transducers are hidden to the agents (*i.e.*, the agents are not aware of them), but if the pipelines themselves would become first-class abstractions in the environment (*i.e.*, pipelines that agents are aware of and can manipulate), this could open the door for some interesting extensions, such as:

- To describe semantically the processing pipelines to let the agents discover and use them at runtime; or,
- to guide the construction of data stream processing pipelines to fit the agents' needs.

These aspects would be even more relevant in open, and heterogeneous, scenarios in order to achieve context-aware access to the information/functionalities of the environment.

A   How Reviewers' Comments Have Been Addressed

A.1   Review 1

Comment: The hypothesis of a global clock is unsuitable in real-world applications. Modern data streaming techniques (see for example AkkaStream) overcome this limitation by implementing standard protocols (for instance see "backpressure").

Answer: We added more explanations on this aspect (see Sect. 4). Briefly, it is true that Akka would simplify the transducers' implementation, but the global clock generated by the clock node in StreamB does not only guarantee the same pace over the events, but allows synchronising the events, so that the resulting discretised sequence can be uniformly quantified by the MTL properties. In any case, such a global clock is enforced by StreamB, not assumed.

A.2   Review 2

Comment: One of the main arguments for StreamB used throughout the paper is to avoid "manual mapping" (or "manual coding") from low-level data streams to beliefs, e.g. in the abstract: "if the environment changes, the mapping has to be changed as well (by the developer)". StreamB is a high-level DSL that allows processing data streams using concise scripts/programs, which is great, but the mapping is still manual. Transducers and pipelines are synthesized based on StreamB programs, but this only hides away the complexity, I don't see how it removes the need to change the mapping if the environment changes. This point should be better clarified.

Answer: The reviewer is right. We fixed this aspect and updated the text in Sect. 1 accordingly. Indeed, the mapping is still manual, but achieved through a higher-level specification (the DSL), which hopefully simplifies and improve the engineering process.

Comment: It is a bit surprising that the environment abstraction creates beliefs for agents, this blurs the separation of concerns between agents and the environment abstraction. Also, why limit this contribution to BDI agents? The impact could be broader. To illustrate the point with an example, in CArtAgO (discussed in related work) this problem is solved by introducing a separation of concerns between the agent mind and the agent body. The agent body keeps track of stimuli from the environment, but how the stimuli are interpreted and used is the concern of the agent mind and depends on the agent model (BDI or other).

Answer: We added more explanations on this point in Sect. 7. It is true that the work could be more general, and considering its implementation, it is actually the case. Since no restriction is given on what the abstract environment should do with the events generated by the fourth layer of transducers. Nonetheless, from a presentation perspective, we preferred to keep it focused on BDI systems, since we believe is the area in MAS which would gain more from our approach.

Comment: It could be misleading to say StreamB is a DSL for synthesizing abstract environments. In my understanding, it is a solution to a more specific problem: processing data streams in abstract environments. The authors also point this out and open the contribution to integration with existing MAS frameworks as part of the environment dimension.

Answer: The reviewer is right. We updated the title and Sect. 1 accordingly. StreamB does not completely synthesise an abstract environment, but it automatically synthesises transducers that can be used to develop an abstract environment. The development of the abstract environment though would be extremely straightforward, since it would only need to subscribe to the corresponding high-level events.

Comment: It is not clear to me why if the environment abstraction is designed and programmed manually, then it is addressed in an ad-hoc manner: on the contrary, it becomes a central part of the design of the overall system. Not a criticism and not intended to minimize the contribution, but note that with StreamB the design of the processing pipelines is also manual, only at a higher level of abstraction: the underlying machinery just executes what is written in StreamB programs.

Answer: The reviewer is right, we updated Sect. 1 accordingly.

Comment: As a suggestion for future work, the StreamB processing pipelines are currently hidden to agents (i.e., agents are not aware of the processing pipelines), but if the pipelines themselves would become first-class abstractions in the environment (i.e., pipelines that agents are aware of and can manipulate).

Answer: The reviewer pointed out very interesting future directions. We integrated these suggestions in Sect. 7.

Comment: The paper could use another thorough reading.

Answer: We fixed all the reported typos.

A.3   Review 3

Comment: The literature (e.g., in the field of functional programming) is rich of proposals for stream processing languages, including DSLs (e.g., various papers in the PADL conference). It would be interesting to see a comparison between StreamB and these other approaches and some discussion of why StreamB was built independently instead of using one of such existing frameworkds.

Answer: We extended Sect. 6 to consider existing Stream Processing Languages. We reported some of them, and compared with StreamB.

References

1. Ali, M.H., et al.: Microsoft CEP server and online behavioral targeting. Proc. VLDB Endow. **2**(2), 1558–1561 (2009). https://doi.org/10.14778/1687553. 1687590. http://www.vldb.org/pvldb/vol2/vldb09-1019.pdf
2. Anicic, D., Rudolph, S., Fodor, P., Stojanovic, N.: Stream reasoning and complex event processing in ETALIS. Semant. Web **3**(4), 397–407 (2012)
3. Arasu, A., Widom, J.: A denotational semantics for continuous queries over streams and relations. SIGMOD Rec. **33**(3), 6–12 (2004)
4. Basin, D.A., Klaedtke, F., Marinovic, S., Zalinescu, E.: Monitoring of temporal first-order properties with aggregations. Formal Methods Syst. Des. **46**(3), 262–285 (2015)
5. Boissier, O., Bordini, R., Hubner, J., Ricci, A.: Multi-agent Oriented Programming: Programming Multi-agent Systems Using JaCaMo. Intelligent Robotics and Autonomous Agents Series. MIT Press (2020). https://books.google.com.br/books?id=GM_tDwAAQBAJ
6. Boissier, O., Bordini, R.H., Hübner, J.F., Ricci, A., Santi, A.: Multi-agent oriented programming with JaCaMo. Sci. Comput. Program. **78**(6), 747–761 (2013). https://doi.org/10.1016/j.scico.2011.10.004
7. Bordini, R.H., Fisher, M., Visser, W., Wooldridge, M.J.: Verifying multi-agent programs by model checking. Auton. Agent. Multi-Agent Syst. **12**(2), 239–256 (2006). https://doi.org/10.1007/s10458-006-5955-7
8. Bordini, R.H., Wooldridge, M., Hübner, J.F.: Programming Multi-agent Systems in AgentSpeak Using Jason. Wiley, Hoboken (2007)

9. Botan, I., Derakhshan, R., Dindar, N., Haas, L.M., Miller, R.J., Tatbul, N.: SECRET: a model for analysis of the execution semantics of stream processing systems. Proc. VLDB Endow. **3**(1), 232–243 (2010). https://doi.org/10.14778/1920841.1920874. http://www.vldb.org/pvldb/vldb2010/pvldb_vol3/R20.pdf

10. Bratman, M.E.: Intentions, Plans, and Practical Reason. Harvard University Press, Cambridge (1987)

11. Calbimonte, J.-P., Corcho, O., Gray, A.J.G.: Enabling ontology-based access to streaming data sources. In: Patel-Schneider, P.F., et al. (eds.) ISWC 2010. LNCS, vol. 6496, pp. 96–111. Springer, Heidelberg (2010). https://doi.org/10.1007/978-3-642-17746-0_7

12. Cardoso, R.C., Ferrando, A., Dennis, L.A., Fisher, M.: An interface for programming verifiable autonomous agents in ROS. In: Bassiliades, N., Chalkiadakis, G., de Jonge, D. (eds.) EUMAS/AT -2020. LNCS (LNAI), vol. 12520, pp. 191–205. Springer, Cham (2020). https://doi.org/10.1007/978-3-030-66412-1_13

13. Chai, H., Zhao, W.: Byzantine fault tolerant event stream processing for autonomic computing. In: IEEE 12th International Conference on Dependable, Autonomic and Secure Computing, DASC 2014, Dalian, China, 24–27 August 2014, pp. 109–114. IEEE Computer Society (2014). https://doi.org/10.1109/DASC.2014.28

14. Chandramouli, B., Goldstein, J., Duan, S.: Temporal analytics on big data for web advertising. In: Kementsietsidis, A., Salles, M.A.V. (eds.) IEEE 28th International Conference on Data Engineering (ICDE 2012), Washington, DC, USA (Arlington, Virginia), 1–5 April 2012, pp. 90–101. IEEE Computer Society (2012). https://doi.org/10.1109/ICDE.2012.55

15. Chen, J., DeWitt, D.J., Tian, F., Wang, Y.: NiagaraCQ: a scalable continuous query system for internet databases. In: Chen, W., Naughton, J.F., Bernstein, P.A. (eds.) Proceedings of the 2000 ACM SIGMOD International Conference on Management of Data, 16–18 May 2000, Dallas, Texas, USA, pp. 379–390. ACM (2000). https://doi.org/10.1145/342009.335432

16. Dennis, L.A.: Gwendolen semantics: 2017. Technical report, ULCS-17-001, Department of Computer Science, University of Liverpool (2017)

17. Dennis, L.A.: The MCAPL framework including the agent infrastructure layer and agent Java Pathfinder. J. Open Source Softw. **3**(24), 617 (2018)

18. Dennis, L.A., Fisher, M., Webster, M.P., Bordini, R.H.: Model checking agent programming languages. Autom. Softw. Eng. **19**(1), 5–63 (2012)

19. Deutsch, A., Fernández, M.F., Florescu, D., Levy, A.Y., Suciu, D.: A query language for XML. Comput. Netw. **31**(11–16), 1155–1169 (1999)

20. Diao, Y., Fischer, P.M., Franklin, M.J., To, R.: YFilter: efficient and scalable filtering of XML documents. In: Agrawal, R., Dittrich, K.R. (eds.) Proceedings of the 18th International Conference on Data Engineering, San Jose, CA, USA, 26 February–1 March 2002. pp. 341–342. IEEE Computer Society (2002). https://doi.org/10.1109/ICDE.2002.994748

21. Esposito, C., Ficco, M., Palmieri, F., Castiglione, A.: A knowledge-based platform for big data analytics based on publish/subscribe services and stream processing. Knowl. Based Syst. **79**, 3–17 (2015). https://doi.org/10.1016/j.knosys.2014.05.003

22. Franklin, S., Graesser, A.: Is It an agent, or just a program?: a taxonomy for autonomous agents. In: Müller, J.P., Wooldridge, M.J., Jennings, N.R. (eds.) ATAL 1996. LNCS, vol. 1193, pp. 21–35. Springer, Heidelberg (1997). https://doi.org/10.1007/BFb0013570

23. Hindriks, K.V.: Programming rational agents in GOAL. In: El Fallah Seghrouchni, A., Dix, J., Dastani, M., Bordini, R.H. (eds.) Multi-agent Programming, Lan-

guages, Tools and Applications, pp. 119–157. Springer, Boston, MA (2009). https://doi.org/10.1007/978-0-387-89299-3_4

24. Hirzel, M., Baudart, G., Bonifati, A., Valle, E.D., Sakr, S., Vlachou, A.: Stream processing languages in the big data era. SIGMOD Rec. **47**(2), 29–40 (2018)

25. Hirzel, M., Schneider, S., Gedik, B.: SPL: an extensible language for distributed stream processing. ACM Trans. Program. Lang. Syst. **39**(1), 5:1–5:39 (2017). https://doi.org/10.1145/3039207

26. Meijer, E., Beckman, B., Bierman, G.M.: LINQ: reconciling object, relations and XML in the.net framework. In: Chaudhuri, S., Hristidis, V., Polyzotis, N. (eds.) Proceedings of the ACM SIGMOD International Conference on Management of Data, Chicago, Illinois, USA, 27–29 June 2006, p. 706. ACM (2006). https://doi.org/10.1145/1142473.1142552

27. Quigley, M., et al.: ROS: an open-source robot operating system. In: Workshop on Open Source Software. IEEE, Japan (2009)

28. Rao, A.S., Georgeff, M.: BDI agents: from theory to practice. In: Proceedings of the 1st International Conference on Multi-agent Systems (ICMAS), pp. 312–319. San Francisco, USA (1995)

29. Ricci, A., Piunti, M., Acay, D.L., Bordini, R.H., Hübner, J.F., Dastani, M.: Integrating heterogeneous agent programming platforms within artifact-based environments. In: Padgham, L., Parkes, D.C., Müller, J.P., Parsons, S. (eds.) 7th International Joint Conference on Autonomous Agents and Multiagent Systems (AAMAS 2008), Estoril, Portugal, 12–16 May 2008, Vol. 1, pp. 225–232. IFAAMAS (2008). https://dl.acm.org/citation.cfm?id=1402419

30. Ricci, A., Piunti, M., Viroli, M., Omicini, A.: Environment programming in CArtAgO. In: El Fallah Seghrouchni, A., Dix, J., Dastani, M., Bordini, R.H. (eds.) Multi-agent Programming, Languages, Tools and Applications, pp. 259–288. Springer, Boston, MA (2009). https://doi.org/10.1007/978-0-387-89299-3_8

31. Sajjad, H.P., Danniswara, K., Al-Shishtawy, A., Vlassov, V.: SpanEdge: towards unifying stream processing over central and near-the-edge data centers. In: IEEE/ACM Symposium on Edge Computing, SEC 2016, Washington, DC, USA, 27–28 October 2016, pp. 168–178. IEEE Computer Society (2016). https://doi.org/10.1109/SEC.2016.17

32. Schnitzler, F., Liebig, T., Marmor, S., Souto, G., Bothe, S., Stange, H.: Heterogeneous stream processing for disaster detection and alarming. In: Lin, J.J., et al. (eds.) 2014 IEEE International Conference on Big Data, Big Data 2014, Washington, DC, USA, 27–30 October 2014, pp. 914–923. IEEE Computer Society (2014). https://doi.org/10.1109/BigData.2014.7004323

33. Seyfer, N., Tibbetts, R., Mishkin, N.: Capture fields: modularity in a stream-relational event processing language. In: Eyers, D.M., Etzion, O., Gal, A., Zdonik, S.B., Vincent, P. (eds.) Proceedings of the Fifth ACM International Conference on Distributed Event-Based Systems, DEBS 2011, New York, NY, USA, 11–15 July 2011, pp. 15–22. ACM (2011). https://doi.org/10.1145/2002259.2002263

34. Stephens, R.: A survey of stream processing. Acta Inform. **34**(7), 491–541 (1997)

35. Tommasini, R., Calvaresi, D., Calbimonte, J.: Stream reasoning agents: blue sky ideas track. In: Elkind, E., Veloso, M., Agmon, N., Taylor, M.E. (eds.) Proceedings of the 18th International Conference on Autonomous Agents and MultiAgent Systems, AAMAS 2019, Montreal, QC, Canada, 13–17 May 2019, pp. 1664–1680. International Foundation for Autonomous Agents and Multiagent Systems (2019). http://dl.acm.org/citation.cfm?id=3331894

36. Toshniwal, A., et al.: Storm@twitter. In: Dyreson, C.E., Li, F., Özsu, M.T. (eds.) International Conference on Management of Data, SIGMOD 2014, Snowbird, UT, USA, 22–27 June 2014, pp. 147–156. ACM (2014).https://doi.org/10.1145/2588555.2595641

37. Della Valle, E., Ceri, S., Barbieri, D.F., Braga, D., Campi, A.: A first step towards stream reasoning. In: Domingue, J., Fensel, D., Traverso, P. (eds.) FIS 2008. LNCS, vol. 5468, pp. 72–81. Springer, Heidelberg (2009). https://doi.org/10.1007/978-3-642-00985-3_6

38. Weyns, D., Omicini, A., Odell, J.: Environment as a first class abstraction in multiagent systems. Auton. Agents Multi Agent Syst. **14**(1), 5–30 (2007). https://doi.org/10.1007/s10458-006-0012-0

39. Weyns, D., Schumacher, M., Ricci, A., Viroli, M., Holvoet, T.: Environments in multiagent systems. Knowl. Eng. Rev. **20**(2), 127–141 (2005). https://doi.org/10.1017/S0269888905000457

40. Zaharia, M., Das, T., Li, H., Hunter, T., Shenker, S., Stoica, I.: Discretized streams: fault-tolerant streaming computation at scale. In: Kaminsky, M., Dahlin, M. (eds.) ACM SIGOPS 24th Symposium on Operating Systems Principles, SOSP 2013, Farmington, PA, USA, 3–6 November 2013, pp. 423–438. ACM (2013). https://doi.org/10.1145/2517349.2522737

BDI for Autonomous Mobile Robot Navigation

Patrick Gavigan$^{(\boxtimes)}$ ⓘ and Babak Esfandiari$^{(\boxtimes)}$

Carleton University, Ottawa, Canada
{patrickgavigan,babak}@sce.carleton.ca

Abstract. We explored how mobile Belief-Desire-Intention (BDI) agents could navigate using path plans that are automatically generated in AgentSpeak, asking if there could be any performance advantages gained by having an agent's path be automatically generated as a BDI plan that can be monitored, suspended and resumed in case of contingencies. To do the exploration, we used Jason BDI to design a framework to test this premise with simulated mobile robots. We further explored the navigation of mobile agents to see if such functionality should be implemented within the agent in either AgentSpeak or as an internal action, or externally in an environmental module. These agents navigated through three environments of varying complexity: a simple synchronized grid, an asynchronous grid connected via Robot Operating System (ROS), and an autonomous car simulated with AirSim connected using ROS. We demonstrated that our framework handles plan interruptions, such as preventing collisions, managing consumable resources, and updating a map when necessary while moving through an environment; that Jason BDI agents are capable of controlling autonomous mobile robots; and that the AgentSpeak language provides advantages for implementing the navigation search behaviours.

1 Introduction

We are interested in how to program mobile robots while guaranteeing reliability, resilience and explainability. As the Belief-Desire-Intention (BDI) paradigm was developed for implementing autonomous agents, we are interested in exploring its suitability for mobile robots. Focusing on navigation, specifically path generation in the form of waypoints, we asked what benefits are gained from this paradigm since a navigation path can be conceived of as a plan that we would like to monitor, execute, suspend and resume depending on changing contexts. We also asked if there are performance issues in using AgentSpeak vs more traditional languages to generate these paths. Certainly, there are navigation approaches, such as move_base [29] which is a main component of the Robot Operating System (ROS) navigation stack [23,30], which use point cloud and optometry data to navigate a robot toward a global destination while accounting for local obstacles using Simultaneous Localization and Mapping (SLAM). These approaches, however, take the navigation problem outside of the agent,

© Springer Nature Switzerland AG 2022
N. Alechina et al. (Eds.): EMAS 2021, LNAI 13190, pp. 137–155, 2022.
https://doi.org/10.1007/978-3-030-97457-2_8

removing opportunities for the agent to reason about its navigation solution. We propose a different approach, one where the agent will perform as much of the navigation as possible so that the agent's plans can be monitored, suspended and resumed in case of contingencies.

A common approach for navigation is the use of a search method, such as A*, to find an appropriate path to a destination by moving between locations on a map. We propose using this approach in a navigation framework for mobile BDI agents with AgentSpeak. The framework includes three main components:

- The generation of a route as an AgentSpeak plan made of waypoint goals;
- A turn-by-turn module, guiding the agent between each waypoint; and
- The handling of plan interruptions as needed.

We compared three A* implementations for generating the route. These included (1) having the navigation search in AgentSpeak using Jason's A* implementation [17]; (2) using an *internal action* – a Java function internal to the agent which used the AIMA3e library [39,40]; and (3) using an external navigation node using Python's A* search [20]. Agents with each of these implementations were tested in three environments ranging from a simplistic grid to a car simulated with AirSim – an open source simulator developed by Microsoft using the Unreal Engine [27,41]. The agents were benchmarked by comparing the reasoning cycle length and the execution time of the navigation processes. The tests resulted in the discovery of improved performance with the AgentSpeak implemented routines. We also found that there were architectural benefits to implementing the navigation in AgentSpeak as there was no need for extra modules to perform logical search, which AgentSpeak performed more naturally.

2   Background and Related Work

This paper discusses using BDI for controlling mobile robots. BDI agents maintain *beliefs* about themselves and their environment, *desires* that they wish to achieve, and plans that they can run by setting *intentions*. The agent reasoning cycle begins with the agent perceiving their environment and receiving messages, reasoning about beliefs, selecting an applicable plan, and setting an intention. Plans can include updating beliefs, adopting new goals, sending messages, or taking an action. Although there are several implementations of BDI, we focused on Jason and AgentSpeak [3,18,19].

The BDI agent's *mind* was connected to their simulated robotic *body* using ROS, a popular robotics architecture [33]. ROS nodes communicate with each other by publishing and subscribing to topics rather than other nodes; individual nodes do not necessarily require knowledge of other nodes. ROS has a community of robotics developers and users, therefore, by developing systems for ROS there are opportunities to leverage other projects.

Among the variety of nodes available for ROS is the navigation stack, available for terrestrial robots [23,29,30]. The ROS navigation stack provides mobile robots with guidance for moving to a destination while avoiding obstacles. There are four main components to the navigation stack. First, the module senses the environment using point cloud data generated by a laser imaging, detection, and ranging (LIDAR) sensor and the robot's odometer. Using point cloud data, a three-dimensional Voxel Grid representing the obstacles that the robot needs to avoid in the environment is generated. The Voxel Grid is then projected onto a two-dimensional cost map which provides the cost for the robot's movement. Secondly, a global planner, implemented using A*, generates a route to the destination through the Costmap. The global planner does not incorporate the dynamics of the robot, nor does it incorporate any unknown obstacles. Third is the local planner, which controls the speed and steering of the robot. In the event that the local planner is unable to continue, perhaps because the global planner has generated a route which the robot cannot complete, a new global plan is generated in the fourth step: the recovery.

There is a precedent for using BDI to control autonomous cars. An architecture for connecting autonomous cars using a simulated traffic model was discussed by Rüb and Dunin-Kęplicz [38]. Their work focused on agent performance in various driving specific tests and assessing how "human-like" the behaviour was. Ehlert also used BDI for autonomous cars [10]. LightJason, another BDI framework, was used to control an autonomous car in a browser-based game by Aschermann et al. [2].

Beyond the focus on autonomous cars, BDI agents have been used in other robotic applications. The Australian military used a JACK BDI agent to fly a Codarra Avatar Unmanned Aerial Vehicle (UAV) [21,42]. Another drone was flown using JaCaMo [24,25,31] and another using Jason and ROS [36,37]. There are several examples of Jason being connected to ROS, including jason_ros [35],rason [28], JaCaROS [26], and JROS [4]. An entry to the Eurobot challenge, which used a warehouse with multiple uncooperative agents, demonstrated the use of Agent Oriented Programming (AOP) using Python RObotic Framework for dEsigning sTrAtegies (PROFETA) [12]. The ARGO project interfaced Jason agents with an Arduino board [22,34], and another project developed a real-time BDI system connected to ROS 2 using a custom built reasoner for soft real-time constraints [1,11]. The Simulated Autonomous Vehicle Infrastructure (SAVI) project sought to simulate Jason agents with their reasoning cycles decoupled from the simulation time cycle [7,8]. The SAVI project has since expanded to include a connection to ROS for controlling a prototype mail delivery robot [32]. Using the concept "abstraction engines" proposed by Denis et al. [9], robotic agents implemented with GWENDOLEN and Jason have been connected to ROS using rosbridge [5] and demonstrated with a simulation of the Curiosity Rover using Gazebo [6]. In this simulation the robot was given locations to visit while also avoiding excess radiation or wind.

In considering the state of the art, we have found that the feasibility of BDI for driving and controlling autonomous vehicles has been demonstrated. These projects have not generally focused on the details of the internal agent behaviour, having not explored what behaviours should be implemented in the agent nor what behaviours should be internal actions or in the environment. Generally, the agent's role seems to always be fairly limited, perhaps from an assumption that the BDI reasoner may not be suitable for such tasks. By contrast, our work focused on getting the agent to do as much as possible, and observing any advantages and drawbacks of doing so. We compared design approaches of using AgentSpeak, internal actions, and environmental modules.

3   Architecture

We propose a framework for navigation of BDI agents with AgentSpeak. It includes three main components:

- The generation of the route as an AgentSpeak plan made of waypoint goals;
- The turn-by-turn module which guides the movement of the agent between each of those waypoints; and
- The handling of plan interruptions as needed.

These components are analogous to the steps that were part of the ROS navigation stack. The generation of the route fills the role of the Global Planner, the turn-by-turn module takes on the role of the Local Planner, and the handling of plan interruptions relates to the navigation stack's recovery step.

To evaluate using BDI for mobile robots and the choice of navigation approach, we compared three route generation implementations using A*: one using pure AgentSpeak, a second using an internal action, and a third using an environmental module. Each implementation used third-party implementations of A*, discussed in more detail in the next section. We anticipated that the AgentSpeak option, being integrated with the agent, was simpler, however, we were concerned it could be more costly in terms of performance than the internal action method. We anticipated that the environmental module could have the advantage of being decoupled from the reasoning cycle, allowing the agent to reason about other things, however extra care may be needed to ensure that the solution was not missed as it could compete with other perceptions.

We evaluated these methods in three environments to ensure that our assessments were not dependent on our choice of environment. The simplest environment, a synchronous Jason grid similar to many Jason examples [18], is discussed in Sect. 3.2. An asynchronous version of this environment, discussed in Sect. 3.3, was used to expose differences that came from the environment's timing. Lastly, a car simulated with AirSim, which is discussed in Sect. 3.4. The simulated car environment was used to highlight how our common approach for implementing a mobile agent can be applied in a more realistic environment.

3.1   Framework for Autonomous Mobile Robot Navigation

As mentioned above, we are proposing a framework for mobile agent navigation where we split the navigation problem into three main components: generating a path as an AgentSpeak plan using A*, a turn-by-turn module, and the handling of interruptions, where the navigation intention may need to be suspended and later resumed. These interruptions could be for safety reasons, such as avoiding a pedestrian, for health of the agent such as recharging a battery, or handling a map update to detour around a closed path. Looking back at our mail robot prototype [32], navigation with turn-by-turn directions was an environmental module. This module required constant updates from the sensors with respect to the position and orientation of the robot and knowledge of how the agent would move between locations. Although it was useful for the module to provide turn-by-turn directions, thus eliminating the need for the agent to maintain map knowledge, it increased the complexity of the navigation module and eliminated any opportunities that the agent may have had to reason about the path and how it would move to those locations. In effect, the agent was simply following the directions from an external module. In this paper, we have revisited this design choice. The navigation routine, in all three implementations, provides only a sequence of locations leading to the destination with no assumption about what actions the agent uses for maneuvering. The turn-by-turn functionality is now the responsibility of the agent as part of the behaviour of maneuvering between waypoints, generalizing the navigation approach for any type of mobile agent.

All three navigation methods used a map, written in AgentSpeak, which provided the names, coordinates, and paths between points in the environment. The location name and location format is `locationName(Name,[X,Y])`, which provides the name and coordinates of the points of interest. The path definition format is `possible(A,B)`, meaning that the agent can travel from the location name unified with A to the location name unified with B. For the AgentSpeak navigating agent, this is loaded into the agent's belief base. It is easily parsed for the environment-based and internal action navigators. Defining the map this way allowed the agent navigating purely with AgentSpeak to update the map by simply adding or removing these items from its knowledge base with a single line of code Whereas, in the case of internal actions or external modules, the map update required modifying the graph data.

A key design feature of the framework was the choice of triggering the navigation and turn-by-turn behaviours using achievement goals and the interrupting behaviours with beliefs, which can be adopted from perceptions. This allows the developer to design their specific turn-by-turn behaviours without being concerned about interruptions, but also having the confidence that these interruptions will still be handled. The behaviour model, in pseudo-AgentSpeak, is provided in Listing 1. The first two lines of the listing show a sample interrupting plan, which is triggered by the addition of a relevant belief. If necessary, this plan can suspend intentions and adopt other achievement goals to address the interruption, before resuming the mission using stored mission beliefs. An example of this is the handling of long-term obstacles with map updates. The plan is triggered by `!obstacle(.)` when an obstacle is observed which contradicts the agent's map beliefs. When this occurs, the agent drops the belief that it is possible to move between the two affected locations. The agent can then restart navigation. There were two navigation plans used for generating the route. The first of the plans addresses the case where the agent is already at the destination. The second is for the generation of the route as a set of waypoint achievement goals using one of the three implementation methods. Listing 1 shows the version which used AgentS-

Listing 1. Navigation Framework Behaviour.

```
1   +interruptingBelief(Parameter) : ParameterContext
2       <- interruptingBehaviour.
3   +obstacle(Location) : position(Current) & possible(Current,Location)
4       & destination(Destination)
5       <- -possible(Current,Next); .drop_all_intentions;
6       -destination(Destination); !navigate(Destination).
7   +!navigate(Destination) : position(Destination)
8       <- -destination(Destination).
9   +!navigate(Destination) : position(Location)
10      <- +destination(Destination);
11      ?a_star(Current,Destination,Solution,Cost);
12      for (.member(op(_,NextPosition),Solution)){!waypoint(NextPosition);}
13      !navigate(Destination).
14  +!waypoint(Location) : position(Location).
15  +!waypoint(Location) : not (position(Location))
16      <- movementAction; !waypoint(Location).
```

peak for path generation. Additional details on path generation are provided in Sect. 4.1. Separating the waypoint goals from the generation of the path ensured that path generation was generic and not dependent on specific details of how the agent moved. Our agent implementations all used identical route generation routines, regardless of how they moved through the environment. Lastly, the turn-by-turn directions, for moving the agent between waypoints, are provided using the +!waypoint(Location) goal. These plans are responsible for the movement of the agent using the actuators of that specific robot. This is implemented recursively, so that the agent will continue to work toward moving to the waypoint until it is successful. The movementAction is a domain specific action, or sub-goal for the specific type of actuators that the agent has available. Also needed is how the agent senses its position and orientation using its domain specific sensors.

3.2   Synchronous Grid Environment

The framework was tested in three different environments. The architecture of the synchronous grid is in Fig. 1. The update of the environment's state was tied to the agent's reasoning cycle, meaning that the agent received perceptions, then reasoned about those perceptions, and then took action as needed, all in a single thread of execution. The environmentally situated navigation support was the 'map'. The internal action navigation was provided using 'getPath'. The agent could move to adjacent free grid locations using the move(.) action, where the dot represents the direction parameter. The agent perceived any adjacent charging station, obstacles, and available grid locations. The agent had knowledge of the charging station location and some, but not all, obstacle locations. The agent could honk a horn to signal to pedestrians to move out of the way if needed. The agent was equipped with a simulated battery, which was nearly empty at the beginning of the scenario and reduced in charge over time, forcing the agent to charge the battery.

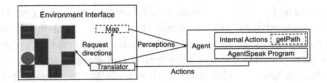

Fig. 1. Agent architecture for the synchronous grid environment.

3.3   Asynchronous Grid Environment

For the asynchronous grid architecture, SAVI ROS BDI[1] was used for connecting the agent to the environment using ROS, as shown in Fig. 2. As before, the agent could perceive adjacent obstacles and locations and move to adjacent locations. The difference was that the perception updates were not tied to the reasoning cycle. The reasoner connected to ROS using the `perceptions`, `actions`, `inbox`, and `outbox` topics. Also connected were the application nodes, including a perception and action translator and a map for navigation support. The translator subscribed to topics published by the environment and translated them to perception predicates expected by the agent, publishing these to the `perceptions` topic. The translator also subscribed to the `actions` topic, passing commands to the environment or map. The user interface, which published to the `inbox` topic, was how a user commanded the agent to navigate to a destination.

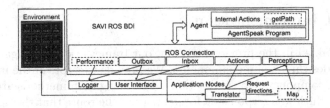

Fig. 2. Agent architecture for the asynchronous grid environment.

3.4   AirSim Car Environment

Our most realistic environment was a car simulated using Microsoft's AirSim simulator [27,41]. It provided a neighbourhood environment, sensors, actuators and an control interface. As with the asynchronous grid, the agent was connected using SAVI ROS BDI, as shown in Fig. 3. The agent perceived its location, orientation, and speed using Global Positioning System (GPS), a magnetometer, and a speedometer. The agent had the `setSpeed(.)` action for setting a cruise

---

[1] SAVI ROS BDI is available at https://github.com/NMAI-lab/savi_ros_bdi.

controller; **steering(.)**, which could be set between one and negative one, and where a higher magnitude value increased the rate of turn. There were also internal actions calculating the range and bearing between two geographic coordinates. An action translator and a perception translator performed similar roles to the translator for the asynchronous grid, translating between AgentSpeak and the format used by the environment.

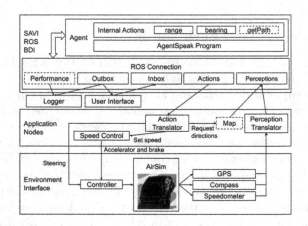

Fig. 3. Agent architecture for the AirSim environment.

4   Agent Implementation

As was explained in the previous section, our framework for navigation of BDI agents includes three main components. We provide excerpts of the implementation of these components in this section[2]. The navigation methods are explained in Sect. 4.1, which was responsible for generating the route that the agent needed to follow. This is followed by the handling of plan interruptions in Sect. 4.2. Finally, Sect. 4.3 provides the details of how the agents move through the environments, the turn-by-turn module, the only part of the implementations where there were noteworthy differences between the grid and car agents. Default plans needed to prevent the agent from prematurely dropping an intention, while waiting for a sensor to update, have not been shown.

---

[2] Synchronized grid: https://github.com/NMAI-lab/jasonMobileAgent.
  Asynchronized grid: https://github.com/NMAI-lab/jason_mobile_agent_ros.
  AirSim car: https://github.com/NMAI-lab/AirSimNavigatingCar.

Listing 2. Sample AgentSpeak Navigation Successor and Heuristic: Grid.

```
1  suc(Current,Next,1,up) :- ([X2,Y2] = [X1,Y1-1])
2      & possible(Current,Next) & nameMatch(Current,[X1,Y1],Next,[X2,Y2]).
3  nameMatch(Current,CurrentPosition,Next,NextPosition) :-
4      locationName(Current,CurrentPosition)
5      & locationName(Next,NextPosition).
6  h(Current,Goal,H) :- H = math.sqrt((((X2-X1)*(X2-X1))+((Y2-Y1)*(Y2-Y1)))
7      & nameMatch(Current,[X1,Y1],Goal,[X2,Y2]).
```

4.1   Navigation

To achieve the navigation goal, !navigate(.), the agent has plans for when
it has arrived at the destination, for fetching a route, and for setting achievement goals for the route waypoints using !waypoint(.). Those achievement
goals were responsible for the turn-by-turn aspect of moving the agent through
the environment. Different versions of these plans utilize the various methods
of generating the route. The definition of !navigate(Destination) in listing 1, in the previous section, generated the route using Jason's A* implementation [17] in AgentSpeak. This was triggered with the use of ?a_star (Current,Destination,Solution,Cost). The internal action version used naviga-
tion.getPath(Current,Destination,Path) for generating the path using the
A* implementation from the AIMA3e library [39, 40].

The AgentSpeak implementation of A* used rules for a heuristic, which
provided the Euclidean distance between locations, and for successor states,
which estimated the result of moving between locations. Samples of the successor, suc(CurrentState,NewState,Cost,Operation), and heuristic, h (CurrentState,Goal,H), were provided for both the grid and car environments. Listing 2, for the grid environments, provides the successor state, in this case for the
up direction, defined by relative coordinate locations given that the movement
between those locations is possible using nameMatch(.,.,.,.). This predicate
is defined with a rule on the next line, which unifies with the location definitions
in the knowledge base. Lastly, the heuristic calculates the Euclidean distance
between the locations. The version for the car is provided in Listing 3, where the
successor state defines the possibility for the agent to move between the locations
with the distance cost, calculated with an internal action. The heuristic again
uses Euclidean distance, calculated with an internal action.

The environmentally supported implementation is in Listing 4. An action
in the environment generates a path for the agent to perceive and use. For
the synchronized environment, this was implemented using AIMA3e [39, 40], as
was the case with the internal action. For the ROS environments it was implemented using python-astar [20]. The first plan in the listing is for perceiving
a path, which is added to the knowledge base. The second plan, tied to !nav-
igate(Destination), adopts achievement goals for all the waypoints in the
route. Lastly, the plan for fetching the path with getPath(.,.), commands the
navigation node to generate the path.

Listing 3. Sample AgentSpeak Navigation Successor and Heuristic: Car.

```
1  suc( Current , Next , Range , drive )  :−  possible ( Current , Next )
2      & locationName ( Current , [ CurLat , CurLon ])
3      & locationName ( Next , [ NextLat , NextLon ])
4      & navigation . range ( CurLat , CurLon , NextLat , NextLon , Range ).
5  h( Current , Goal , Range )  :−  locationName ( Current , [ CurLat , CurLon ])
6      & locationName ( Goal , [ GoalLat , GoalLon ])
7      & navigation . range ( CurLat , CurLon , GoalLat , GoalLon , Range ).
```

Listing 4. Environment-Supported Navigation Plans.

```
1  +path(Path) : startTime(Start) <- -route(_); +route(Path).
2  +!navigate(Destination) : route(Path)
3      <-  for (.member(NextPosition, Path)) {!waypoint(NextPosition);}
4          -route(Path); !navigate(Destination).
5  +!navigate(Destination) : position(X,Y) & locationName(Current,[X,Y])
6      <-  +destination(Destination); getPath(Current,Destination);
7          !navigate(Destination).
```

4.2   Mission Interruptions

There were three types of mission interruptions in our design: safety, health, and map updates. The safety interruptions were the result of short-term obstacles, such as pedestrians. The health interruptions were the result of a low battery. The map updates were to handle longer-term obstacles such as closed roads. The simplest and highest priority plan to avoid short-term obstacles is to honk a horn when a pedestrian is in the way: `+pedestrian(_) <- honk(horn)`.

The battery plans, which use beliefs for `batteryMin(.)` and `batteryMax(.)` as thresholds, are in Listing 5. Also used, but not shown, are rules for determining if the battery state is low or full using `lowBattery(State)` and `fullBattery(State)` and `atStation` for determining if the agent is at the charging station. The addition of the `battery(.)` belief triggers the first plan. This is applicable when the battery needs to be charged, forcing the agent to achieve `!chargeBattery` before resuming the interrupted mission. Recursive plans for getting the agent to the docking station, charge the battery, and then undock the agent are shown.

4.3   Agent Movement

The agents achieved their waypoint goals with the turn-by-turn module. Samples of the agent movement plans and rules for the grid are in Listing 6. This includes a plan for using `move(.)` for moving the agent on grid space. Lastly, a supporting rule for determining the direction that the agent needs to move for the up direction is provided.

Listing 5. Battery Management Definitions.

```
1  +battery(State) : charging(false) & lowBattery(State)
2      & missionTo(Destination)
3      <- .drop_all_intentions; !chargeBattery; !missionTo(Destination).
4  +!chargeBattery : lowBattery(_) & charging(false)
5      & chargerLocation(ChargeStation)
6      <- !navigate(ChargeStation); station(dock); !chargeBattery.
7  +!chargeBattery : fullBattery(_) & charging(true) <- station(undock).
8  +!chargeBattery <- !chargeBattery.
```

Listing 6. Movement in the Grid Environment.

```
1  +!waypoint(Direction,_) : isDirection(Direction) & map(Direction)
2      & not obstacle(Direction) <- move(Direction).
3  direction(Current,Next,up) :- possible(Current,Next)
4      & locationName(Current,[X,Y]) & locationName(Next,[X,Y-1]).
```

Plans for moving the car are in Listing 7. The `!waypoint(.)` plans move the car toward locations specified with latitude and longitude coordinates. These use rules, not shown, for assessing if the car is at or near a location and for finding the nearest location, the destination range, and destination bearing. The plans use internal actions for calculating the range and bearing between locations. The first plan stops the car by setting the speed to zero when it has arrived. Next is the plan for slowing the car as it approaches a location and then the plan for driving toward the location, and lastly is a default plan which keeps the car driving toward the location. These plans further adopt goals for controlling the speed and the steering of the car.

The plans for controlling the car's speed and steering plans are in Listing 8. The first plan, for updating the speed, uses a mental note to avoid acting needlessly. The `setSpeed(.)` action commands the cruise controller node, which controls the accelerator and brake for maintaining the car's speed. Next is the calculation of the car's course correction angle followed by rules for the steering setting, formatted as `steeringSetting(TargetBearing,SteeringSetting)`. The

Listing 7. Car Waypoints.

```
1   +!waypoint(Location) : atLocation(Location,_)
2       <- !controlSpeed(0); !controlSteering(0).
3   +!waypoint(Location) : nearLocation(Location,_)
4       & (not atLocation(Location,_))
5       & destinationBearing(Location,Bearing)
6       <- !controlSteering(Bearing); !controlSpeed(3);
7          !waypoint(Location).
8   +!waypoint(Location) : (not nearLocation(Location,_))
9       & destinationBearing(Location,Bearing)
10      <- !controlSteering(Bearing); !controlSpeed(8);
11         !waypoint(Location).
12  +!waypoint(Location) <- !waypoint(Location).
```

Listing 8. Car Speed and Steering Controller.

```
1  +!controlSpeed(Speed) : speedSetting(Old) & (Old \== Speed)
2      <- -speedSetting(_); +speedSetting(Speed); setSpeed(Speed).
3  courseCorrection(TargetBearing, Correction) :- compass(CurrentBearing)
4      & declanation(Declanation)
5      & (Correction = TargetBearing - (CurrentBearing + Declanation)).
6  steeringSetting(TargetBearing, 1) :-
7      courseCorrection(TargetBearing, Correction) & (Correction >= 20).
8  steeringSetting(TargetBearing, -1) :-
9      courseCorrection(TargetBearing, Correction) & (Correction <= -20).
10 steeringSetting(TargetBearing, Correction/180) :-
11     courseCorrection(TargetBearing, Correction) & (Correction < 20)
12     & (Correction > -20).
13 +!controlSteering(Bearing) : steeringSetting(Bearing, Steering)
14     <- steering(Steering).
```

steering setting is set to the maximum magnitude when the course correction is greater than 20°. For smaller magnitudes, the setting is dampened by dividing it by 180, a crude but effective way of controlling the car's steering. Lastly, the steering plan controls the steering using the rules.

5 Testing and Evaluation

The agents were tested using ROS Melodic on Windows 10 with an Intel Core i7-5820K CPU @ 3.30 GHz, 64 GB of system RAM, and an NVIDIA GTX 970 with 4 GB of RAM. Logs from the inbox, outbox, actions, and reasoning cycle periods for 10 runs of each agent in each environment were analyzed. Quantitative results are in Sect. 5.1 and qualitative observations are in Sect. 5.2.

5.1 Quantitative Results

We assessed the behaviour and performance of the agents in terms of their timelines and the period of their reasoning cycles. The quantitative results can be found in the plots below. In these plots, we represent AgentSpeak implementation as 'ASL', the environment-supported agent as 'ENV', and the agent which uses internal actions as 'IA'. The synchronous grid is labelled as 'Grid', the asynchronous grid is 'GridROS', and the AirSim car simulation is 'Car'.

Figure 4 shows the timelines for each agent, which are zoomed in in Fig. 5, showing the early path planning. The timelines are separated into four segments: (1) initialization of the agent, (2) obtaining a route, (3) loading the waypoint goals, and (4) moving through the environment. The timelines represent the entire *run* for each agent. The synchronized grid agents all performed navigation within milliseconds of each other, thus their performance was practically equivalent. The asynchronous environments exposed larger performance differences, so we observed more dramatic changes in agent performance. In this case, the AgentSpeak navigator completed navigation the fastest. Although the difference in arrival times for each of the agents was likely negligible for most applications, it highlights that AgentSpeak can outperform other implementation approaches, especially when applied to search or other symbolic logic problems. The asynchronous agents navigation was on a slower timescale than the synchronous agents because the reasoner waits for a perception to be available prior to continuing the reasoning cycle, tying the agent's performance to the sensor period.

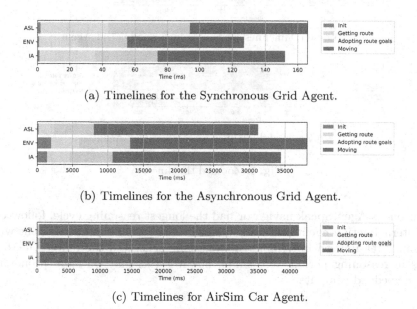

(a) Timelines for the Synchronous Grid Agent.

(b) Timelines for the Asynchronous Grid Agent.

(c) Timelines for AirSim Car Agent.

Fig. 4. Timelines.

Violin plots of the reasoning periods are in Fig. 6. The main distribution of the reasoning period was generally unaffected by the navigation method. Once the agent had a navigation solution, it moved through the environment in a similar way. The difference was found in the extreme cases. This was where the navigation routine caused significantly longer reasoning cycles, although this was a small component of the run overall. We therefore do not see a significant difference in the length of the average reasoning cycle. The internal action agent had the longest outliers, followed by the AgentSpeak agent. The environmentally supported agent had the shortest periods as the reasoner performed additional reasoning cycles while the solution was generated. There were differences in reasoning periods between the different environments caused by the reasoner waiting for perceptions prior to continuing reasoning. The update frequency of the sensors was a bottleneck in the reasoning cycle. The synchronous environment did not impose this bottleneck, meaning the agent reasoned faster. The

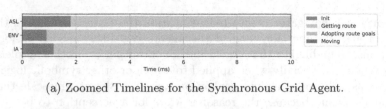

(a) Zoomed Timelines for the Synchronous Grid Agent.

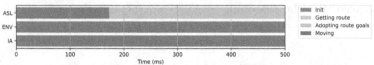

(b) Zoomed Timelines for the Asynchronous Grid Agent.

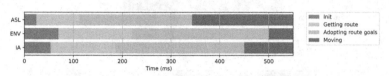

(c) Zoomed Timelines for AirSim Car Agent.

Fig. 5. Zoomed timelines.

synchronous AgentSpeak navigator had the longest reasoning cycle, followed by the internal action agent and then the environmentally supported agent which continued reasoning while the navigation node generated the route. The differences in reasoning period were small, however this may be more pronounced with embedded computers.

5.2 Qualitative Observations and Discussion

All the route generation and environment combinations worked well, they all performed their navigation functions and travelled to the destination. A human observer would not likely have been able to tell which agent was running. Videos of the agents navigating the environments are available on YouTube [13–16].

A developer can consider several features of the implementation paradigm when selecting their approach. For example, the representation of the map in AgentSpeak was such that the agent's knowledge of the map was a set of beliefs. Updating this map required merely adding or removing the needed beliefs with a single line of code. The environmental support and internal action navigators, however, were slightly more complex. For the environmentally supported navigator, this was accomplished with a map update action which updated the map's underlying data structure. The internal action version also required a map update function, however this was implemented as a separate class.

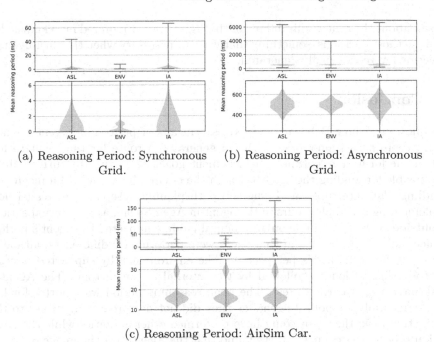

(a) Reasoning Period: Synchronous Grid.

(b) Reasoning Period: Asynchronous Grid.

(c) Reasoning Period: AirSim Car.

Fig. 6. Reasoning periods.

Inspection of the behaviour logs for each of the agents revealed an interesting aspect of the agent behaviours. The AgentSpeak navigators only used movement related actions whereas the environment-supported and internal action agents used getPath(.,.), either externally or as an internal action, to retrieve the route. When the environmentally supported agents were in asynchronous environments, using ROS, they used getPath(.,.) twice rather than once because these agents performed additional reasoning cycles while waiting for the result from getPath(.,.). In our tests, this added a negligible number of additional reasoning cycles, however, this could provide an opportunity for an agent to reason about other beliefs, desires, or intentions while waiting for a long task to be completed in the environment. Although not explored in this work, this presents a possible advantage to the use of environmentally based processing if there are other areas that could benefit from the agent's attention.

Looking back at our mail robot prototype [32], where navigation with turn-by-turn directions was an environmental module, there were several differences between that approach and our approach in this paper. In this more recent work, we separated the turn-by-turn directions from the generation of the route by our navigation routine, allowing the agent to perform reasoning on the route. When the navigation module provided turn-by-turn directions, the module was more complex, requiring constant updates of the position and orientation of the robot and knowledge of how the robot moves between locations. With the turn-by-turn directions implemented within the agent, the reasoner had the opportunity to reason about the route. This did mean that the reasoner required map knowledge to make those decisions, something that was not necessary when the turn-by-turn directions were externally generated.

6   Conclusion

We questioned how BDI can be used as a means of performing agent navigation, proposing a framework which (1) generated a route for the agent to follow in the form of AgentSpeak achievement goals, (2) a turn-by-turn module, responsible for guiding the agent through the environment, and (3) a means for handling plan interruptions. Using the path planning use case, we tested how implementing such behaviours in the agent in AgentSpeak, as an internal action, or outside of the agent in an environmental module impacted the agent's performance and design. We found that there were performance differences, although negligible from the user's perspective. The environmentally supported navigator took slightly longer, followed by the internal action method. The AgentSpeak navigator was the fastest. The peak reasoning period was shorter for the environmentally supported agents as they did not have reasoning cycles to the navigation task; the agent could have performed other activities while the navigation process was completed. We found that the AgentSpeak language provided intrinsic advantages for implementing the navigation search behaviours, making it attractive for use in mobile robotics.

7   Future Work

In future work, we plan to expand our navigation framework into a general framework for implementing mobile robotic agents and test it in another domain, further demonstrating our approach for different environments. This approach has so far been used for a prototype mail delivery robot, grid environments, and a simulated autonomous car. We plan further development of the mail robot and the autonomous car, increasing the complexity of their environments, including demonstrating dynamic obstacle avoidance. We are also planning a UAV experiment to demonstrate that this method can be applied to this domain. Also of interest is how this approach can be coupled with different types of sensors, the use of sensor fusion, or even other path planning libraries, such as the ROS navigation stack [30].

Our quantitative results highlighted that the reasoning period was tied to the sensors refresh rate. The synchronized environment, which did not use ROS, allowed the agent to reason much faster than when it waited for sensor updates. We will explore the advantages of decoupling the reasoning cycle from the perception updates, allowing the reasoner to continue reasoning on internal knowledge while waiting for sensor information.

The Jason interpreter prioritizes plans as intentions based on their order in the plan base. We were therefore deliberate about how we ordered our plans in our code. Although it was possible to implement the agent with this knowledge, we will improve this approach by updating Jason's event, option, and intention selection functions to prioritize appropriately. This will reduce the risk that future refactoring could have unintended effects on the agent's behaviour unless the developer considers how all the behaviours work together, which could complicate implementing more complex behaviours.

Acknowledgement. We acknowledge the support of the Natural Sciences and Engineering Research Council of Canada (NSERC), [funding reference number 518212].

Cette recherche a été financée par le Conseil de recherches en sciences naturelles et en génie du Canada (CRSNG), [numéro de référence 518212].

References

1. Alzetta, F., Giorgini, P.: Towards a real-time BDI model for ROS 2. In: Bergenti, F., Monica, S. (eds.) Proceedings of the 20th Workshop "From Objects to Agents", Parma, Italy, 26–28 June 2019. CEUR Workshop Proceedings, vol. 2404, pp. 1–7. CEUR-WS.org (2019). http://ceur-ws.org/Vol-2404/paper01.pdf
2. Aschermann, M., Dennisen, S., Kraus, P., Müller, J.P.: LightJason, a highly scalable and concurrent agent framework: overview and application (demonstration). In: Dastani, M., Sukthankar, G., André, E., Koenig, S. (eds.) Proceedings of the 17th International Conference on Autonomous Agents and Multiagent Systems (AAMAS 2018), pp. 1794–1796 (2018). https://lightjason.org/publications/2018-aamas-preprint.pdf
3. Bordini, R.H., Hübner, J.F., Wooldridge, M.: Programming Multi-agent Systems in AgentSpeak Using Jason (Wiley Series in Agent Technology). Wiley, Hoboken (2007). https://doi.org/10.1002/9780470061848
4. Calaça, I., Krausburg, T., Cardoso, R.C.: JROS. https://github.com/smart-pucrs/JROS
5. Cardoso, R.C., Ferrando, A., Dennis, L.A., Fisher, M.: An interface for programming verifiable autonomous agents in ROS. In: Bassiliades, N., Chalkiadakis, G., de Jonge, D. (eds.) EUMAS/AT -2020. LNCS (LNAI), vol. 12520, pp. 191–205. Springer, Cham (2020). https://doi.org/10.1007/978-3-030-66412-1_13
6. Cardoso, R.C., Farrell, M., Luckcuck, M., Ferrando, A., Fisher, M.: Heterogeneous verification of an autonomous curiosity rover. In: Lee, R., Jha, S., Mavridou, A., Giannakopoulou, D. (eds.) NFM 2020. LNCS, vol. 12229, pp. 353–360. Springer, Cham (2020). https://doi.org/10.1007/978-3-030-55754-6_20
7. Davoust, A., et al.: Simulated Autonomous Vehicle Infrastructure. https://github.com/NMAI-lab/SAVI. Accessed 19 Feb 2019
8. Davoust, A., et al.: An architecture for integrating BDI agents with a simulation environment. In: Dennis, L.A., Bordini, R.H., Lespérance, Y. (eds.) EMAS 2019. LNCS (LNAI), vol. 12058, pp. 67–84. Springer, Cham (2020). https://doi.org/10.1007/978-3-030-51417-4_4
9. Dennis, L.A., et al.: Agent-based autonomous systems and abstraction engines: theory meets practice. In: Alboul, L., Damian, D., Aitken, J.M.M. (eds.) TAROS 2016. LNCS (LNAI), vol. 9716, pp. 75–86. Springer, Cham (2016). https://doi.org/10.1007/978-3-319-40379-3_8

10. Ehlert, P.: Intelligent driving agents: the agent approach to tactical driving in autonomous vehicles and traffic simulation. Master's thesis, Delft University of Technology, 2600 AA, Delft, The Netherlands (2001). https://www.researchgate.net/publication/255674932_Intelligent_Driving_Agents_The_Agent_Approach_to_Tactical_Driving_in_Autonomous_Vehicles_and_Traffic_Simulation
11. ElDivinCodino: ROS2BDI. https://github.com/ElDivinCodino/ROS2BDI. Accessed 29 June 2020
12. Fichera, L., Messina, F., Pappalardo, G., Santoro, C.: A Python framework for programming autonomous robots using a declarative approach. Sci. Comput. Program. **139**, 36–55 (2017)
13. Gavigan, P.: AirSim Car BDI Agent. https://youtu.be/yX20gJjjbMg. Accessed 19 Feb 2021
14. Gavigan, P.: Jason mobile agent - AgentSpeak Navigation. https://youtu.be/ooB15Ve54sI. Accessed 19 Feb 2021
15. Gavigan, P.: Jason mobile agent - environment supported navigation. https://youtu.be/r0CiwjxapZA. Accessed 19 Feb 2021
16. Gavigan, P.: Jason mobile agent - internal action navigation. https://youtu.be/ooB15Ve54sI. Accessed 19 Feb 2021
17. Hubner, J.F.: Jason Search Demo. https://github.com/jason-lang/jason/tree/master/demos/search. Accessed 19 Feb 2021
18. Hübner, J.F., Bordini, R.H.: Jason. https://github.com/jason-lang/jason. Accessed 19 Feb 2021
19. Hübner, J.F., Bordini, R.H.: Jason: a Java-based interpreter for an extended version of AgentSpeak. http://jason.sourceforge.net. Accessed 16 Feb 2019
20. jrialland: python-astar. https://github.com/jrialland/python-astar. Accessed 24 Aug 2020
21. Karim, S., Heinze, C.: Experiences with the design and implementation of an agent-based autonomous UAV controller. In: Proceedings of the Fourth International Joint Conference on Autonomous Agents and Multiagent Systems, AAMAS 2005, pp. 19–26. ACM, New York (2005). https://doi.org/10.1145/1082473.1082799
22. Lazarin, N.M., Pantoja, C.E.: A robotic-agent platform for embedding software agents using raspberry pi and arduino boards. In: 9th Software Agents, Environments and Applications School (2015)
23. Marder-Eppstein, E., Berger, E., Foote, T., Gerkey, B., Konolige, K.: The office marathon: robust navigation in an indoor office environment. In: International Conference on Robotics and Automation (2010)
24. Menegol, M.S., Hübner, J.F., Becker, L.B.: Evaluation of multi-agent coordination on embedded systems. In: Demazeau, Y., An, B., Bajo, J., Fernández-Caballero, A. (eds.) PAAMS 2018. LNCS (LNAI), vol. 10978, pp. 212–223. Springer, Cham (2018). https://doi.org/10.1007/978-3-319-94580-4_17
25. Menegol, M.S.: UAVExperiments. https://github.com/msmenegol/UAVExperiments. Accessed 24 May 2019
26. Meneguzzi, F., Wesz, R.: Jason ROS Releases. https://github.com/lsa-pucrs/jason-ros-releases. Accessed 17 July 2019
27. Microsoft: AirSim. https://microsoft.github.io/AirSim/. Accessed 19 Feb 2021
28. Morais, M.G.: rason. https://github.com/mgodoymorais/rason/tree/master/jason_ros. Accessed 17 July 2019
29. NA: move_base. http://wiki.ros.org/move_base. Accessed 19 Apr 2021
30. NA: navigation. http://wiki.ros.org/navigation. Accessed 14 June 2021
31. NA: vooAgente4Wp. https://drive.google.com/file/d/0B7EcHgES6He8VEtwR0xPZjdBbk0/view. Accessed 08 May 2019

32. Onyedinma, C., Gavigan, P., Esfandiari, B.: Toward campus mail delivery using BDI. J. Sens. Actuator Netw. **9**(4), 56 (2020)
33. Open Source Robotics Foundation: ROS. https://www.ros.org/. Accessed 27 May 2019
34. Pantoja, C.E., Stabile, M.F., Lazarin, N.M., Sichman, J.S.: ARGO: an extended Jason architecture that facilitates embedded robotic agents programming. In: Baldoni, M., Müller, J.P., Nunes, I., Zalila-Wenkstern, R. (eds.) EMAS 2016. LNCS (LNAI), vol. 10093, pp. 136–155. Springer, Cham (2016). https://doi.org/10.1007/978-3-319-50983-9_8
35. Rezende, G.: jason_ros. https://github.com/jason-lang/jason_ros/. Accessed 13 Oct 2020
36. Rezende, G.: MAS-UAV. https://github.com/Rezenders/MAS-UAV. Accessed 24 May 2019
37. Rezende, G., Hubner, J.F.: Jason-ROS. https://github.com/jason-lang/jason-ros. Accessed 24 May 2019
38. Rüb, I., Dunin-Kęplicz, B.: BDI model of connected and autonomous vehicles. In: Nguyen, N.T., Chbeir, R., Exposito, E., Aniorté, P., Trawiński, B. (eds.) ICCCI 2019. LNCS (LNAI), vol. 11684, pp. 181–195. Springer, Cham (2019). https://doi.org/10.1007/978-3-030-28374-2_16
39. Russell, S., Norvig, P.: AIMA3e-Java (JDK 8+). https://github.com/aimacode/aima-java. Accessed 19 Feb 2021
40. Russell, S., Norvig, P.: Artificial Intelligence: A Modern Approach, 3rd edn. Prentice Hall Press, Hoboken (2009)
41. Shah, S., Dey, D., Lovett, C., Kapoor, A.: AirSim: high-fidelity visual and physical simulation for autonomous vehicles. In: Hutter, M., Siegwart, R. (eds.) Field and Service Robotics. SPAR, vol. 5, pp. 621–635. Springer, Cham (2018). https://doi.org/10.1007/978-3-319-67361-5_40
42. Wallis, P., Ronnquist, R., Jarvis, D., Lucas, A.: The automated wingman - Using JACK intelligent agents for unmanned autonomous vehicles. In: Proceedings, IEEE Aerospace Conference, vol. 5, p. 5 (2002). https://doi.org/10.1109/AERO.2002.1035444

An Appraisal Transition System for Event-Driven Emotions in Agent-Based Player Experience Testing

Saba Gholizadeh Ansari[1]([✉]) [iD], I. S. W. B. Prasetya[1] [iD], Mehdi Dastani[1] [iD],
Frank Dignum[2] [iD], and Gabriele Keller[1] [iD]

[1] Utrecht University, Utrecht, The Netherlands
s.gholizadehansari@uu.nl
[2] Umeå University, Umeå, Sweden

Abstract. Player experience (PX) evaluation has become a field of interest in the game industry. Several manual PX techniques have been introduced to assist developers to understand and evaluate the experience of players in computer games. However, automated testing of player experience still needs to be addressed. An automated player experience testing framework would allow designers to evaluate the PX requirements in the early development stages without the necessity of participating human players. In this paper, we propose an automated player experience testing approach by suggesting a formal model of event-based emotions. In particular, we discuss an event-based transition system to formalize relevant emotions using Ortony, Clore, & Collins (OCC) theory of emotions. A working prototype of the model is integrated on top of Aplib, a tactical agent programming library, to create intelligent PX test agents, capable of appraising emotions in a 3D game case study. The results are graphically shown e.g. as heat maps. Visualization of the test agent's emotions would ultimately help game designers to produce contents that evoke a certain experience in players.

Keywords: Automated player experience testing · Emotional modeling of game player · Formal model of emotion · Intelligent agent · Agent-based testing

1 Introduction

With the growing interest of industry and academia in assessing the quality in-use of a system, product or service, the term *User eXperience* (UX), which refers to quality characteristics related to internal and emotional state of a user, has emerged [19,22]. UX evaluations become essential for designers to predict how users would interact with a system. In the context of computer games, evaluating *player eXperience* (PX) plays an important role to design a well-received game according to players' preferences and expectations. PX has different dimensions such as flow [21], immersion [13] and enjoyment [8] which need to be addressed in a game design to evoke certain experience.

To assess the UX quality of a game, relatively novel UX evaluation methods such as questionnaire methods, psycho-physiological measurement and eye-tracking have been used [4,22,28]. Currently, PX testing techniques not only impose excessive hours of

This work is funded by EU H2020 Research and Innovation grant 856716, project iv4XR.

© Springer Nature Switzerland AG 2022
N. Alechina et al. (Eds.): EMAS 2021, LNAI 13190, pp. 156–174, 2022.
https://doi.org/10.1007/978-3-030-97457-2_9

testing but they might also not be representative enough to cover all player types and their possible emotions towards the game. Despite some attempts towards automation, most of these techniques are either costly or still manually demanding [4,22,28]. Moreover, similar to UX evaluations in non-game applications, most of PX testing methods measure PX toward the end of the game development [2,4,28], so there is still a need for more efficient techniques to do these evaluations in *early stages* of game development. This allows PX problems to be addressed early during the development.

All of these factors led us to propose an automated approach for PX testing in computer games; the envisaged main use case is to assist designers in early development phases to develop their games more efficiently. To meet this aim, here, we proposes to employ a *computational model* of players to automatically assess PX properties of a computer game. Such a model is necessarily tied to cognition and emotion. Additionally, emotions that a player can feel under certain conditions would eventually affect their overall experience. We, therefore, suggest to deploy a well-known *theory of emotions* called **OCC** [17] to facilitate modeling players with respect to their emotions.

We present a formal model of the appraisal for OCC emotions using an event-based transition system to serve as the foundation of our automated PX testing approach. It deviates from existing formalization e.g. [1,10,26]; they have never been used in the software engineering (SE) domain. This might explain why these formal models have not been utilized for UX/PX testing. A more fundamental reason is that these models are given in the form of BDI[1] logic [15]. Although expressive, BDI logic is more a reasoning model rather than a computation model. In contrast, our formalization is given in terms of a transition system that directly specifies how to compute the emotional state. Having a transition system provides an opportunity for developers to simply deploy the model in their own systems, whereas a BDI-based formal model would also need a BDI reasoning engine before it can be used for computing. Furthermore, discrete transition systems have been used to do model checking in software for decades. This opens a way to express UX/PX properties in e.g. LTL or CTL [3] and verify them through model checking or model checking related techniques.

A prototype implementation of the formal model is also presented in this paper, along with a demonstration of what it can do on a small case study. The appraisal model prototype is integrated with Aplib [20], a Java library for agent-based game testing, to create an **emotional test agent** that uses the OCC theory for emotional appraisal to assess PX requirements in games.

The paper is structured as follows: Sect. 2 introduces the OCC theory. Section 3 gives an overview of the proposed framework architecture as well as the role of appraisal in PX evaluations. Section 4 details the formal model of appraisal for event-based emotions. Section 5 explains the early results of the framework in a 3D case study. Section 6 discusses some related work and finally Sect. 7 concludes the paper and presents future work.

2   OCC Theory of Emotion

Ortony, Clore, and Collins [17] presented a cognitive structure of emotions which characterizes 22 emotion types (e.g. joy, hope, disappointment, distress and fear).

---

[1] Belief-Desire-Intention.

According to their 'OCC' theory, emotions are valenced reactions which can be turned on by outcome of events, outcome of agents' actions, or attributes of objects. Event-based emotions that are applicable to most game setups are highlighted in blue in Fig. 1. We selected them to be the basis of our proposed event-based transition system for emotions in our PX testing framework (further explanation in Sect. 3.1). Each of the emotion types listed in Fig. 1 is specified as described in [17].

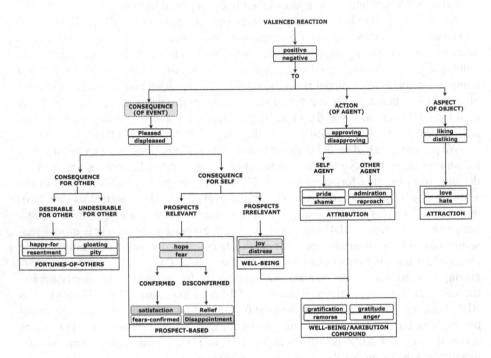

Fig. 1. OCC structure of emotions [17]. (Color figure online)

Table 1 summarizes OCC specifications of the highlighted emotion types; e.g. the OCC theory defines joy as *is being pleased about a desirable consequence of event.* For example, consider a maze game in which an agent is looking for gold. When the agent finds a room with a gold pile, and it takes one step toward the gold, this has a desirable consequence (the agent is certain that it gets closer to the gold), so the agent feels pleased and as a result it starts to feel joy for the gold. However, satisfaction is different. It is defined as *being pleased about the confirmation of the prospect of a desirable consequence.* This emotion needs achievement confirmation whereas joy can be triggered whenever the agent becomes certain that the goal is achievable, although not fulfilled yet. In the above example, satisfaction is triggered when the agent actually acquires the gold. Additionally, while joy affects satisfaction, the agent might not be satisfied towards every goal which it is joyful about. In the earlier set-up, the agent, when proceeding to collect the gold, faces guardians that need to be defeated first, and ends up consuming a unique item to win the combat. Thus, despite reaching the goal that it is joyful about, it would not be satisfied for failing to keep all its prized possessions.

Table 1. Selected emotions specifications according to the OCC theory [17].

Joy:	pleased about a desirable consequence of event
Distress:	displeased about an undesirable consequence of event
Hope:	pleased about the prospect of a desirable consequence of event
Fear:	displeased about the prospect of an undesirable consequence of event
Satisfaction:	pleased about the confirmation of the prospect of a desirable consequence
Disappointment:	displeased about the disconfirmation of the prospect of a desirable consequence

In general, dealing with emotions involves *appraisal* and *coping* [17]. When an agent receives an event, the appraisal process is triggered to form emotions. Afterward, the agent responds to those emotions based on coping strategies which affects the agent behavior towards the environment. In other words, emotions regulate the agent's actions during the coping process. In this paper, we focus on modeling of appraisal —the proposed appraisal model of event-based emotions will be presented in Sect. 4.

3   Agent-Based Player Experience Testing Framework

In this section, we will explain the proposed framework architecture with their components and demonstrate appraisal in PX testing with some examples.

3.1   The Framework Architecture

The general architecture of the proposed framework is presented in Fig. 2, showing appraisal model of emotions, player characterization, Aplib and PX evaluation as the key components. They are defined below.

Appraisal Model of Emotions. A test agent's emotions are modeled based on the OCC theory. Game dynamism can be mostly interpreted in terms of events in computer games, so the framework needs to evaluate the emotions that are driven by the game events for the start. To model these emotions, a *transition system approach* is proposed, which is formalized in Sect. 4. It calculates the event-based emotions with their respective intensity. We will focus on a single test agent setup, thus we leave out emotions that are only valid in multi-agent settings. Appearance of objects can also influence PX but this is technically more challenging to deal with (e.g. how to interpret "appearance"). However, there is a room for extending the model, in the future, to test aspects of PX that are formed in social contexts and those influenced by object aspects.

Player Characterization. Some properties of the appraisal model of emotions need to be specified by game designers with respect to the game under test as well as the player characteristics. For example, the designers should specify what goals are relevant for players (e.g. winning the game, collecting in-game money), what in-game events are relevant to these goals, and in what way they are related to the goals (are they desired towards reaching a goal, or else undesirable?). Additionally, the desirability of an event might differ from one player character to another. Thus, player or set-up dependent

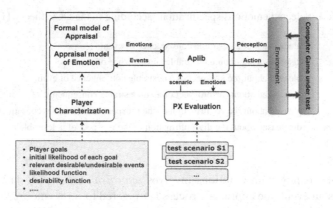

Fig. 2. Automated PX testing framework architecture.

properties must be initially set in this part of framework, before running the model of appraisal. Having such a component in our framework also provides an opportunity to enhance it in the future with more advanced characteristics such as players' moods and play-style (e.g., exploratory or aggressive [25,29]).

Aplib[2] [20]. A Java library for programming intelligent agents. It provides an embedded Domain Specific Language (DSL) to use all benefits of the Java programming language. Aplib has a BDI architecture [12] with a novel layer for tactical programming to control agents behavior more abstractly. Despite other use cases, the library has been developed for testing tasks in highly interactive software like games.

PX Evaluation. Designers give test scenarios to the framework to check whether their newly developed content indeed triggers the expected emotions. This part is responsible for the visualization of the emotional state of the test agent as it pursues dedicated goals in a game environment with a given test scenario. Generated emotion types with their upward/downward trends during the test would assist designers to alter game parameters to optimize the experience in a certain degree.

3.2   Appraisal Theory in PX Testing

As mentioned earlier, the appraisal process is an essential part of computational models of emotions. So, to automatically test the player experience based on emotions, we need to include this process in our framework for creating emotions. This would allow us to check whether the designers' expected emotions are as same as the triggered players' emotions when exposed to certain situations in the game.

For instance, educational games are often evaluated based on the engagement level of learners to promote learning. Traditionally, to do this, players' emotions are tracked using either self-reports or automated facial emotion detection during a game-based task [16], Identifying positive and negative emotions plays an essential role in deciding

---

[2] https://iv4xr-project.github.io/aplib/.

if some game-based conditions and tasks need to be changed to optimize learning. Our proposed framework would help in performing this process automatically using model of emotions to create emotions with respect to events.

Users of a more traditional, non-game, system typically need to feel higher levels of positive emotions and low levels of negative emotions to reach a satisfactory experience, while moderate levels of positive emotions and a high level of negative emotions such as distress, fear and disappointment could end up in an unsatisfactory experience with the system [18]. These negative emotions reflect users' feelings when they are unable or unsure of how to use the system in some situations. This lead to the poor usability of the system [23]. However, computer games, e.g. those in the RPG and combat genres, can be deliberately designed to invoke certain negative emotions for certain experience in players because it can ultimately contribute to their enjoyment [5] or even lead to high level of positive emotion when the player overcomes reasons that evoked negative emotions like fear and frustration [14]. Thus, unlike UX testing, in PX testing designers also need be able to analyze relations between positive and negative emotions. Our proposed framework can automatically check whether these emotions are appraised during playing the game. The prototype further refines this by also tracking when and where these emotions occur, thus enabling refined analyses. If the patterns of these emotions do not meet expectation, designers can change properties of the game and iterate the emotional testing process to achieve the expected emotions.

Ultimately, modelling a player's coping process improve the ability of the framework in PX testing. This is discussed briefly in Sect. 7. However, being able to model the coping behavior does not change the fact that the framework needs to also support the appraisal process of emotions in the first place. For this reason, our proposed framework first focuses on the appraisal process.

4   Event-Based Formal Model of Emotion

Imagine that a software testing agent which takes the role of the player is deployed on a computer game to do PX testing. The agent is modelled as an event-based transition system which can appraise emotions to emulate the emotional state of a player. Its state consists of its 'belief' (perception) over the game and its emotions which can eventually affect its behavior to resemble the player behavior. In this section, we describe the essential part of the formalization of this event-based emotion transition system to conduct an approach for formal modeling of automated PX testing.

In the following, we assume an agent to have beliefs and goals, based on which it decides which actions should be taken in the environment. Being able to differentiate between different goals is useful for PX testing, as games often offer various optional plots and goals to players to improve their non-linearity and replay value. A goal g is represented as a pair $\langle id, x \rangle$, with id as its unique identifier and x as its significance or priority of the goal. Goals and their significance are static in this setup. We also assume that an agent senses its environment by means of events. For simplicity, it is assumed that the agent observes one event at a time, causing the agent to transition from one state to another. Whereas the agent's own actions are events, there are also events that arise from environmental dynamism such as hazards and updates by dynamic objects. We also add the event *tick* to discretely represent the passing of time. We represent emotion types as $Etype = \{\ Joy, Distress, Hope, Fear, ...\}$. In the sequel, *etype* ranges over this set.

Definition 1. An emotional testing agent is represented by a transition system M, described by a tuple:

$$\langle \Sigma, s_0, G, E, \delta, \Pi, Thres \rangle$$

where:

- G is a set of the agent's goals.
- Σ is the set of M's possible states. Each state s in Σ is a pair $\langle K, Emo \rangle$ where:
  - K is a set of propositions representing the agent's beliefs. We additionally require that for every $g \in G$, K includes a proposition representing the goal's confirmation or dis-confirmation status, and a proposition representing the likelihood of reaching this goal from the current state. The former is represented by $status(g, p)$ where $p \in \{achieved, failed, proceeding\}$ and the latter by $likelihood(g, v)$ where $v \in [0..1]$.
  - *Emo* is a set containing the agent's active emotions, each is represented by a tuple $\langle etype, w, g, t_0 \rangle$ specifying the emotion type *etype*, its intensity w with respect to a goal g, and the time t_0 at when the emotion is triggered.
- $s_0 \in \Sigma$ is the initial state. It should specify the agent's initial belief on the likelihood of every goal, as well as initial prospect-based emotions (hope and fear). The rationale for the latter is that having an initial prospect towards a goal implies that there is also hope for achieving it, as well as some fear of its failure.
- E is the set of events the agent experiences.
- $\delta : \Sigma \times E \rightarrow \Sigma$ is the state transition function that describes how M moves from one state to another upon perceiving an event. The definition is rather elaborate, and will be given separately in Definition 2.
- $\Pi = \langle Des, Praisew, DesOther, Liking \rangle$ is a tuple of appraisal dimensions according to the OCC theory. This determines how an event is appraised in terms of its *desirability*, *praiseworthiness*, *desirability by others* and *liking*.
- *Thres* is a set of thresholds, one for every type of emotion.

As an example, Fig. 3 illustrates first few transitions. We, additionally, assume the agent maintains an emotional memory, called *emhistory*, which keeps the history of active emotions (*Emo*) for a reasonable time window in the past:

$$emhistory = \overbrace{Emo_{t-d}, ... , Emo_{t-1}}^{\text{time window } d}$$

where t is the current system time and d is the size of the memory's time window. Emo_{t-i} indicates the active emotional at time $t - i$ in the past.

Before presenting the rest of the formal model, we feel the necessity to bring more clarity into the concept of goals' likelihood and status. The transition system is defined in a way that there is a slight difference between $likelihood(g, 1)$ and $status(g, achieved)$. When an agent experiences $likelihood(g, 1)$, it is possible that the

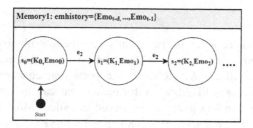

Fig. 3. An agent's state transitions, as it receives an event e_1 followed by e_2.

goal g does not get confirmed in the same state. In other words, the agent comes to believe that the goal is reachable with 100% certainty, but the achievement of the goal has not been confirmed yet in the current state. A similar relation holds for $likelihood(g, 0)$ and $status(g, failed)$.

The next key point is the agent's appraisal component Π, which has four dimensions. They help in modeling how events are appraised with respect to every goal in the corresponding dimension. Each appraisal dimension is described as a function over the agent's beliefs, an event and a goal: $\Pi_{Dim}(K, e, g)$, where $Dim \in \{Des, Praisew, DesOther, Liking\}$. For example, $\Pi_{Des}(K, e, g)$ determines the desirability of an event e with respect to the goal g, judged when the agent believes K; the latter implies that this desirability might change when K changes. Depending on the emotion, one or multiple appraisal dimensions might be triggered. Currently, Π_{Des} is the only dimension being actively used in our model because according to the OCC theory, the only appraisal dimension which affects our selected emotion types is the desirability function. However, we keep the structure in the general form for possible future extension of the emotion types.

Below we will explain how emotions will be calculated, but importantly we should note that PX designers must provide some information as well, namely the following components of the tuple in Definition 1: (1) the goal set G, along with the significance and initial likelihood of each goal ($likelihood(g, v_{init})$), (2) likelihood functions modelling how events affect the agent's belief towards goals' likelihood, (3) the appraisal dimensions, in particular $\Pi_{Des}(K, e, g)$, (4) the thresholds $Thres$ and (5) decay rate $decay_{etype}$. In the simplest form, $\Pi_{Des}(K, e, g)$ can be described by a mapping that maps events to the goals they are perceived as desirable/undesirable. In a more refined description this can be a function that monotonically increases with respect to the goal significance and likelihood. In terms of the architecture in Fig. 2, the above components are described in the *Player Characterization* part.

Definition 2. *Event-based Transition.* As mentioned earlier, the agent's state transition is driven by one incoming event at a time. The transition function (δ in Definition 1) is defined as follows. Let e be an occurring event:

$$\langle K, Emo \rangle \xrightarrow{e} \langle K', \overbrace{newEmo(K, e, G) \oplus decayedEmo(Emo)}^{\text{updated emotion } Emo'} \rangle$$

where:

- $K' = e(K) \setminus H$, where $e(K)$ is the agent's new beliefs obtained by updating K with event e; here, the event e is assumed to have a semantic interpretation as a function that affects K, including the parts that concern goals' likelihood and status. H expresses likelihood information that can be removed from $e(K)$, because the corresponding goals are achieved or failed. More precisely, H is the set $\{\ likelihood(g,v)\ |\ status(g,p) \in e(K),\ p \in \{achieved, failed\},\ v \in \{0,1\}\ \}$.
- $Emo' = newEmo(K,e,G) \oplus decayedEmo(Emo)$ is the agent's emotions updated by the perceived event e and the agent's new beliefs. Importantly, the $newEmo(K,e,G)$ specifies the *newly* triggered emotions (see Definition 3), whereas $decayedEmo(Emo)$ (see Sect. 4.1) is a set of active emotions that decay over time. The operator $\oplus$ merges all these emotions after applying some constraints to have the updated emotional state of the agent. The emotional update is explained in Sect. 4.3.

When an agent perceives an event (except *tick* event), new emotions may be triggered. This is done by calculating a so-called 'emotion function' $\mathcal{E}$ for every emotion type, as follows:

$$\mathcal{E}_{etype}(K,e,g) = w$$

This function specifies the activation intensity w of the emotion *etype* towards the goal g, as a consequence of the occurrence of e and having beliefs K. Importantly, note that the function expresses *goal oriented* emotions, whereas the OCC theory includes e.g. emotions towards events or objects. We focus on goal oriented emotions due to the importance of goals, ranging from defeating monsters to getting the highest score, for game players. A *tick* event is used to represent the passing of time. This event would cause decays of active emotions in the transition system. The definition of newly triggered emotion, mentioned in Definition 2, is given below. It is used whenever a new emotion is triggered or an existing emotion reoccurs in the system. The way these new emotions are merged with existing emotions in *Emo*, as mentioned in Definition 2, will be explained in Sect. 4.3. We also need to remind that some hope and fear already exist in the system at the beginning which can be re-triggered by this function. Their initial values are set according to goals' significance and initial likelihoods of goals.

Definition 3. *New Emotions.* The set of new emotions triggered by e is:

$$newEmo(K,e,G) = \{\langle etype,g,w,t\rangle\ |\ etype \in Etype,\ g \in G,\ w = \mathcal{E}_{etype}(K,e,g) > 0\}$$

where t is the current system time that the emotion is triggered.

In the above definition E_{etype} is a so-called activation emotion function that calculates the activation intensity for different newly triggered event-based emotion types. Each activation emotion function has an activation potential and a threshold which form the activation intensity of the newly triggered emotion (see Definition 4). The level of desirability an event respecting a goal and the agent's goal likelihood are the main variables affecting the activation potential as hinted in the OCC theory. To trigger a new emotion type, its activation potential value needs to pass the corresponding threshold. The concept of threshold is needed if we want to support setups with different agent's moods because the thresholds depend on the moods (e.g. Steunebrink et al. [26] pointed out that with a good mood, the thresholds of negative emotions increase, hence bringing about a lower degree of intensity in negative emotions when they are triggered). All activation functions of emotions defined below have the same structure. However, the potential part might differ. They are as follows[3]:

Definition 4. *Joy*

$$\mathcal{E}_{\textbf{Joy}}(K,e,g) \;=\; \overbrace{\underbrace{\Pi_{Des}(K,e,g)}_{\text{activation potential}}}^{\text{activation intentsity}} - \; Thres(Joy)$$

provided $g \in G$, $likelihood(g,1) \in e(K)^4$, and $\Pi_{\textbf{Des}}(K,e,g) > 0$.

Definition 5. *Distress*

$$\mathcal{E}_{\textbf{Distress}}(K,e,g) \;=\; |\Pi_{Des}(K,e,g)| - Thres(Distress)$$

provided $g \in G$, $likelihood(g,0) \in e(K)$, and $\Pi_{\textbf{Des}}(K,e,g) < 0$. Unlike *Joy*, *Distress* is triggered when an event is deemed as undesirable towards the goal.

Definition 6. *Hope*

$$\mathcal{E}_{\textbf{Hope}}(K,e,g) \;=\; v' * x - Thres(Hope)$$

provided $g = \langle id,x \rangle \in G$, $likelihood(g,v) \in K$, $likelihood(g,v') \in e(K)$, and $v < v' < 1$.

It is assumed that the increase in likelihood of a goal is only possible if the incoming event is desirable towards the goal. Thus, with this assumptions, there is no need to check the desirability of the event $\Pi_{\textbf{Des}}(K,e,g)$ for prospect-based emotions.

Definition 7. *Fear*

$$\mathcal{E}_{\textbf{Fear}}(K,e,g) \;=\; (1-v') * x - Thres(Fear)$$

provided $g = \langle id,x \rangle \in G$, $likelihood(g,v) \in K$, $likelihood(g,v') \in e(K)$, and $0 < v' < v$.

Definition 8. *Satisfaction*

$$\mathcal{E}_{\textbf{Satisfaction}}(K,e,g) \;=\; x - Thres(Satisfaction)$$

provided $g = \langle id,x \rangle \in G$, $status(g,achieved) \in e(K)$, $\langle Hope,g \rangle \in emhistory$, and $\langle Joy,g \rangle \in emhistory$.

Definition 9. *Disappointment*

$$\mathcal{E}_{\textbf{Disappointment}}(K,e,g) \;=\; x - Thres(Disappointment)$$

provided $g = \langle id,x \rangle \in G$, $status(g,failed) \in e(K)$, $\langle Hope,g \rangle \in emhistory$, and $\langle Distress,g \rangle \in emhistory$.

---

[3] For convenience, we only define the functions partially. The cases where they are undefined will be ignored by Definition 3 anyway, where they are used.

[4] Unlike prospect-based emotions, well-being emotions are certain. So, joy and distress towards a goal only happen if the goal's likelihood becomes 1 and 0 respectively. In particular, obtaining certainty of achieving/failing the goal is seen as notable desirable/undesirable consequence of an event to justify these emotions. There might other practical consequences, but we will mostly focus on the aforementioned types of consequences.

4.1   Decay of Emotions

Every emotion has a duration called *emotion episode* in which the peak of its intensity, its decay rate, possible recurrences, and the time that the emotion is triggered are shown [26]. As indicated earlier in Definition 1, *tick* is a time event to show the passing of time in our transition system. We can reflect decays of emotions using this event:

$$\langle K, Emo \rangle \xrightarrow{\ e=tick\ } \langle K', Emo' \rangle$$

where K' and Emo' refer to the updated beliefs and updated active emotions after the transition. The intensity of active emotions in Emo would decrease as follows:

$$decayedEmo(Emo) = \\ \{\langle etype, g, w', t_0 \rangle \mid \langle etype, g, w, t_0 \rangle \in Emo,\ w' = \text{intensitydecay}_{\text{etype}}(w_0, t_0) > 0, \\ w_0 = emhistory(etype, g, t_0)\}$$

where $w_0 = emhistory(etype, g, t_0)$ denotes the initial intensity of *etype* with respect to g which can be obtained from *emhistory*. There is not a unique quantitative formalization for the decay function intensitydecay. This function can be defined in a way which relates the usage and the interpretation of decay [6,27]. However the peak of intensity (w_0), the time at which the emotion is triggered (t_0) and the decay rate $(decay_{etype})$ are essential parameters that must be taken into account. While an inverse sigmoid decay function is proposed by [27] to reflect the gradual decrease of intensities, [6] is making use of a negative exponential function with almost the ame parameters. We used the latter decay function [6] in our model although the sigmoid decay function [27] can be used as well.

$$\text{intensitydecay}_{\text{etype}}(w_0, t_0) = w_0 * e^{\,c\, *\, decay_{etype}\, *\, (t-t_0)}, -1 < c < 0$$

where t is the current system time and t_0 is the time at which the emotion starts.

4.2   Inconsistent Emotions

Emotions are triggered regarding the goals, so technically the agent might have several emotions towards the same goal. Nevertheless, the OCC theory states that some emotions are mutually exclusive which means a human can not have them simultaneously for the same goal [26]. These mutual exclusions, which should then also be held in every state of our transition system, are as follows:

$$Emo' \models \neg(\langle Hope, g \rangle \wedge \langle Joy, g \rangle)$$
$$Emo' \models \neg(\langle Fear, g \rangle \wedge \langle Distress, g \rangle)$$

As it is explained in Sect. 2, whereas emotions such as hope and fear are prospect-based emotions which means they are uncertain $(likelihood(g, v))$, emotions like joy and distress are certain [26], so it is illogical to have both in the system. For example, when a player is joyful of acquiring the key to an in-game treasure room, because now the treasure should certainly be within his/her reach, this joy would now replace what was merely hope for getting the treasure. In general, in case of happening a certain emotion, it replaces the corresponding prospect-based emotion, so the mutual exclusions are always maintained. We formulated our formal model in a way that in case of the conflicting emotions, the new certain emotion would take the place of the prospect-based emotion. However, the set of inconsistent emotions can be expanded based on the test purpose or the game under test. The designer can specify these as assumptions in the *Player Characterization* component. A notation as $axiomset(\langle etype, g \rangle)$ is used to access every rule containing $\langle etype, g \rangle$.

4.3   Emotional State Update

To update the emotional state, newly triggered emotions, *newEmo*, need to be merged with existing active emotions whose intensities are decreasing gradually, *decayedEmo*, to yield the new emotional state *Emo′*. There are three cases to consider. Case-1 involves existing emotion types that decay without having the same emotion type or the conflicting type in the *newEmo*; these will be kept. Case-2 involves newly triggered emotion types that do not exist in *decayedEmo*; these are added to *Emo′*. Case-3 involves emotion types in *decayedEmo* that reoccurs in *newEmo*. Only emotions from these three cases will be included in *Emo′*. In particular, this implies that in the cases of inconsistent emotions, the newly triggered emotion takes precedence over the emotion which has already existed by taking its place in order to uphold the mutual exclusions discussed before. The new one is added to *Emo′* based on Case-2. This comes from the rationale that new belief and perceptions convey more accurate information than past information, and therefore the triggered new emotions have more weight for the player. The last case, Case-3, is about existing emotions that get *re-stimulated by* the new perceived event. To date there is no definitive answer to the question of how this should be reflected to the intensity of the corresponding emotions. We decided to take the maximum intensity value of the emotion (the dominant value). However, a more proper answer to the question would need further research. The update is formally shown below, with the Cases indicated accordingly:

$$
Emo' = \begin{cases}
① \; \{ \langle etype, g, w, t_0 \rangle \mid \langle etype, g, w, t_0 \rangle \in decayedEmo \\
\qquad \land \neg \exists \, w', t_0'. \, \langle etype, g, w', t_0' \rangle \in newEmo \\
\qquad \land \neg \exists \, w', t_0'. \, \langle \overline{etype}, g, w', t_0' \rangle \in newEmo \} \\
\cup \\
② \; \{ \langle etype, g, w', t_0' \rangle \mid \langle etype, g, w', t_0' \rangle \in newEmo \\
\qquad \land \neg \exists w, t_0. \langle etype, g, w, t_0 \rangle \in decayedEmo \} \\
\cup \\
③ \; \{ \max(\langle etype, g, w, t_0 \rangle, \langle etype, g, w', t_0' \rangle) \mid \langle etype, g, w, t_0 \rangle \in decayedEmo \\
\qquad\qquad\qquad\qquad \land \langle etype, g, w', t_0' \rangle \in newEmo \}
\end{cases}
$$

where t_0 is the time at which an emotion is triggered (starts) and the outcome of max is the one with the higher intensity. An emotion that is in conflict with *etype* is referred as $\overline{etype}$. The above update scheme will uphold the axiom $\neg(\langle etype, g \rangle \land \langle \overline{etype}, g \rangle) \in axiomset(\langle etype, g \rangle)$.

4.4 Goal Chain

As indicated earlier, the beliefs K gets updated according to the new event. In particular, this might affect the agent's belief towards the likelihood of achieving certain goals. Recall that this is modelled in the *Player Characterization* component in our approach, e.g. by means of some update rules. However, modern games often offer multiple goals that players can go after, and furthermore have dependency. E.g. obtaining a unique item Excalibur might be an optional goal in a game, but achieving this might improve the likelihood of defeating the end boss. To capture this, we can extend the Player Characterization with 'chained' rules, for example $R = \{e_1 \rightarrow g_1, g_1 \rightarrow g_2, g_2 \rightarrow g_3\}$ to express that the event e_1 affects the likelihood or status of the goal g_1, which in turn affects the likelihood of g_2 and so on. We do not write down how exactly the likelihood should be adjusted, but imagine that the rules also specify this. When the agent received e_1, it should now not only apply the rule/update $e_1 \rightarrow g_1$, but also other rules in R whose antecedent is transitively triggered by $e_1 \rightarrow g_1$. While the rules in R above can indeed be equivalently described by more direct rules of the form $\{e_1 \rightarrow g_1, e_1 \rightarrow g_2, e_1 \rightarrow g_3\}$, the chained form arguably captures inter-goal dependency more intuitively.

5 Proof of Concept

We conducted our experiment on a game called Lab Recruits[5] which we subject to the combination of aplib and our implemented model of appraisal[6] to provide the proof of concept and show our early results in PX testing. Lab Recruits is a 3D game developed in Unity which has different replayable levels. Each level is a laboratory building with a number of rooms containing interactable objects, such as button and non-interactable objects, such as desk and fire hazards.

Figure 4a shows the floor plan of the level exposed to PX testing using our approach. It consists of four buttons, three doors, and some fire hazards. The goal is for the player to escape the level by reaching the exit room circled in red. Access to this room is guarded by a closed 'final door'. The level contains some rooms with a puzzle (yellow circle) that involves finding the buttons to open the final door and reopen the doors that in the process become closed to entrap the agent. Figure 4b and 4c show two provided setups with the different amount and locations of fire hazards. The agent will lose health points by passing each fire hazard. These setups are examples of choices considered by designers, although being currently simple, as to which one would lead to better PX. There is also a baseline setup, in which no fire hazard exists in the game level, to compare its emotional outcomes with the result of two mentioned setups.

As mentioned in Sect. 4, a developer sets needed inputs of the model such as the goal set, initial likelihood of each goal, the desirability of events for each goal, the threshold and decay rate of emotions in *Player Characterization*. A test agent is deployed, set with multiple goals, though here we will only discuss the most significant one, namely completing the level. Initially, the agent is assumed to believe that the likelihood of achieving this goal is 0.5. The agent is given a program so that it can automatically

---

[5] https://github.com/iv4xr-project/iv4xrDemo/tree/occDemoPrototype.

[6] https://github.com/iv4xr-project/jocc.

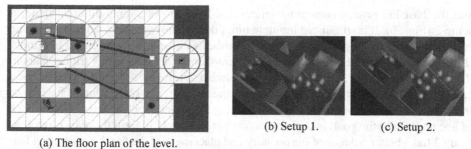

(a) The floor plan of the level. (b) Setup 1. (c) Setup 2.

Fig. 4. The level under the PX test in Lab Recruits.

explore the level. As the agent progresses, its belief on the likelihood of completing the level changes, depending on the number of opened door as well as remained closed doors. Opening each door is assumed to have a desirable consequence for the agent because it increases the chance of the agent to complete the level.

The timeline of triggered emotions at the baseline setup in the agent with respect to the goal "completing the level" is shown in Fig. 5, along with their intensity levels at each time. The agent initially experience some hope and fear due to the assumed initial belief that completing the game is possible, with the likelihood 0.5. This depends on the agent's mood which influences the degree of hope and fear the agent initially has. When the agent pushes the button that opens the first door (time = 60)[7], the agent's hope regarding completing the game starts to increase. It decays or gets re-stimulated according to the events until time 110 when it is replaced by joy. The agent feels a level of satisfaction, when completing the game.

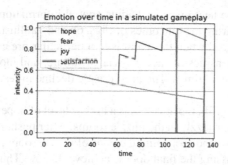

Fig. 5. The emotions' timeline in the baseline setup (no fire hazard).

The timeline of emotions in setup 1 and setup 2 in Fig. 6 shows that the trend of positive emotions is actually quite similar to that of the baseline, although with a smaller level of hope in the setup 2. However, comparing the result of setup 2 with setup 1

---

[7] The system is event driven, so only events can change the likelihoods. All emotions decay until an event is perceived. However, we can add an event type to the system to decay the likelihoods when there is no event for some period of time to update the emotional state.

and the baseline reveals something interesting. Fear shows a quite different trend in setup 2 (Fig. 6b). It is stimulated multiple times during the execution, whereas the same emotion, despite having numbers of fire hazards, has been never stimulated in setup 1 (Fig. 6a). In other words, having some fire hazards may not necessarily trigger fears in the agent unless the agent passes the certain numbers of fire hazards. Such a comparison can be useful for designers e.g. to determine the amount, and placement, of hazards to induce certain degree of fear along with keeping the chance for satisfactory experience of accomplishing the goal. In our case, setup 1 is less likely to thrill the player, whereas setup 2 has a better balance of the quantity and placement of the fire, by generating fear and even in relatively close time interval with a rise in hope, while still keeping the level survivable.

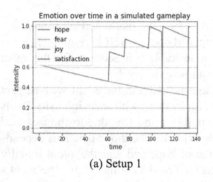
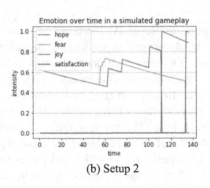

(a) Setup 1   (b) Setup 2

Fig. 6. The emotions' timelines correspond two setups of the game level in Figure. 4. (threshold = 0, decay rate = 0.005)

Figure 7 shows some heat maps, providing spatial information of the agent's emotions in setup 2. Comparing the outcomes of Figs. 6b and 7a illustrates that the highest level of fear is experienced when the agent is in a particular fire covered corridor (yellow in Fig. 7a). Fire intensifies the agent's fear of failure, and moreover the agent has to walk this corridor several times. The most drastic decline in fear is when the agent is about to finish the level.

As can be seen in Fig. 7b, the agent feels a higher level of hope when progressing in solving the buttons-doors puzzle in the puzzle rooms. After pushing the button that corresponds to the final door and reopening the door of puzzle room to escape it, the agent becomes certain that passing the final door is achievable now. Thus, the hope suddenly is replaced by the joy for reaching the final door to complete the game. At the end, the agent feels satisfied when the achievement is confirmed. Having such information would help Lab Recruits designers to adjust the puzzles and fire hazards in such a way to induce certain emotions, at the right moments and the right places, which ultimately affect a certain aspect of player experience like enjoyment. It is worth mentioning that depending on the player profile designed in the player characterization such as the initial player mood and type of player (experienced or new player), the result might differ to some degree. However, assessing the influence of these factors on PX is a future work.

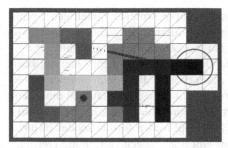
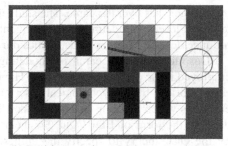

(a) Negative emotions: yellow= high fear, dark red=low fear.

(b) Positive emotions: Mahogany red=hope, Ruby red= joy, yellow= satisfaction.

Fig. 7. The heat maps of triggered emotions in setup 2. Black = very low intensity (or no emotion), white = walls, gray = unexplored area. (Color figure online)

6 Related Work

PX researchers aim to understand the gaming experience to ultimately induce certain experience. Fernandez [9] outlines the influence of players' emotional reactions and their profile in enjoyment by extending the usability methods to uncover relationships between game components and the degree of fun in players. Sanchez et.al [24] explained that usability of games can be defined in the term of *playablity*. They present a framework guided by attributes and properties of playability to characterise experience for PX evaluation and observing the relation between the experience and the developed elements of a commercial video game. Psycho-physiological methods is among techniques to measure aspects of PX like flow and immersion. Jennett's et al. [13] tries to develop a subjective and objective measure for immersion using questionnaires and eye movement tracking respectively. Drachen et al. [7] report a significant the correlation between heart rate, electrodermal activity and the self-reported experience of players in first-person shooter games. Zook and Riedl [30] introduce a temporal data-driven model to predict the impact of game difficulty to player experience. Results of their empirical study on a role player combat game show the game, that tailors its difficulty to fit a player abilities, improves the player experience.

Zhao et al. [29] create agents with human-like behavior to assist game designers to evaluate their games. The study focuses on training agents based on style of in-game play and skill. A variety of techniques are utilized in the provided case studies to train play-testing agents to test logic of the game under development as well as game-playing agents which interact with human players to mimic the game play experience for different play style. Stahlke et al. [25] also aim to use play-testing agents to test games by following humans' navigational behavior. They investigate the impact of play-style, the experience level and cognitive process on modeling humans behavior. Most of PX prediction techniques are data-driven which involve human players in the process and as a result, they demand a high level of human labor. This led researchers to investigate model-driven approaches. A computational model of motivation is presented in [11] to predict PX without the need of human player using empowerment, the degree of control an agent has over the game. The study measures empowerment by intelligent agents to create levels with defined empowerment to induce different PX. This would help to produce desired content characteristics during the procedural content generation.

Despite existing research on modeling the OCC theory, the theory has not been employed in the context of PX testing. Having a proper formalization of emotion would act as a bridge from psychological description of emotions to computational models of emotions which are translatable to codes. Formalization of emotions has been mostly done in the form of BDI logic. Steunebrink [26] deployed a formal model inspired by the OCC theory to specify the influence of emotions, specifically hope and fear, on a BDI agent's decisions. Later, a full version of the model with all 22 emotions is explained in [27]. Dias et al. [6] presents an OCC-based appraisal engine called FAtiMA (Fearnot AffecTIve Mind Architecture) for creating autonomous agent characters that can appraise events and behave based on socio-emotional skills. Its main use case is to automate virtual characters in conversing with humans. FAtiMA is claimed to be inspired by the OCC theory to simulate emotional skills in autonomous agents. However, so far, no formal model has been introduced to evaluate the toolkit regarding the OCC theory. A BDI-like probabilistic formalization is described in [10] for OCC event-based emotions during the appraisal. The study evaluates the desirability of consequences of an event based on the agent's goal and the degree that the consequence can improve the possibility of the goal achievement. Unlike other formalisations that give a high level function for appraisal variables, it proposes a more refined logic-base calculation for these variables and also tries to formalize 'effort' and 'realization' that are involved in appraising some event-base emotions.

7 Conclusion and Future Work

This paper presented an automated PX testing approach using an emotional model. An event-based transition system is introduced to model the appraisal for event-based emotions according to the OCC theory which is then combined to a Java library for tactical agent programming called aplib to create an agent-based PX testing framework. Early results of our experiment with the prototype show that such a framework that can emulate players' emotions would let developers to investigate how emotions of players would evolve in the game during the development stage. By providing e.g. heat-map visualisations of triggered emotions and their timelines, designers gain insight on how to alter parameters of their systems to evoke certain emotions.

We are currently doing more advanced experiments using the case study, Lab Recruits, to investigate initial moods, emotions and their effect on certain aspects of PX as a future work. There are also some concepts like emotional intensity after a recurrence that are described with high level functions in the literature which need a calculation mechanism. In particular, we want to do further research on how exactly an emotion should regain its intensity level after a re-stimulation. Furthermore, the proposed framework, if enhanced by the coping process, would be able to simulate the effect of emotions on players' behavior for further PX evaluations. However, this needs extension in our event-based transition system to support the coping process formally respecting the OCC theory. We ultimately plan to conduct research on validation of our model by comparing our results with the data of human players.

References

1. Adam, C., Herzig, A., Longin, D.: A logical formalization of the OCC theory of emotions. Synthese **168**(2), 201–248 (2009)
2. Alves, R., Valente, P., Nunes, N.J.: The state of user experience evaluation practice. In: Proceedings of the 8th Nordic Conference on Human-Computer Interaction: Fun, Fast, Foundational, pp. 93–102 (2014)
3. Baier, C., Katoen, J.P.: Principles of Model Checking. MIT Press, Cambridge (2008)
4. Bernhaupt, R. (ed.): Game User Experience Evaluation. HIS, Springer, Cham (2015). https://doi.org/10.1007/978-3-319-15985-0
5. Bopp, J.A., Mekler, E.D., Opwis, K.: Negative emotion, positive experience? Emotionally moving moments in digital games. In: Proceedings of the 2016 CHI Conference on Human Factors in Computing Systems, pp. 2996–3006 (2016)
6. Dias, J., Mascarenhas, S., Paiva, A.: FAtiMA modular: towards an agent architecture with a generic appraisal framework. In: Bosse, T., Broekens, J., Dias, J., van der Zwaan, J. (eds.) Emotion Modeling. LNCS (LNAI), vol. 8750, pp. 44–56. Springer, Cham (2014). https://doi.org/10.1007/978-3-319-12973-0_3
7. Drachen, A., Nacke, L.E., Yannakakis, G., Pedersen, A.L.: Correlation between heart rate, electrodermal activity and player experience in first-person shooter games. In: Proceedings of the 5th ACM SIGGRAPH Symposium on Video Games, pp. 49–54 (2010)
8. Fang, X., Chan, S., Brzezinski, J., Nair, C.: Development of an instrument to measure enjoyment of computer game play. Int. J. Hum.-Comput. Interact. **26**(9), 868–886 (2010)
9. Fernandez, A.: Fun experience with digital games: a model proposition. In: Extending Experiences: Structure, Analysis and Design of Computer Game Player Experience, pp. 181–190 (2008)
10. Gluz, J., Jaques, P.A.: A probabilistic formalization of the appraisal for the OCC event-based emotions. J. Artif. Intell. Res. **58**, 627–664 (2017)
11. Guckelsberger, C., Salge, C., Gow, J., Cairns, P.: Predicting player experience without the player. An exploratory study. In: Proceedings of the Annual Symposium on Computer-Human Interaction in Play, pp. 305–315 (2017)
12. Herzig, A., Lorini, E., Perrussel, L., Xiao, Z.: BDI logics for BDI architectures: old problems, new perspectives. KI-Künstliche Intelligenz **31**(1), 73–83 (2017)
13. Jennett, C., et al.: Measuring and defining the experience of immersion in games. Int. J. Hum. Comput. Stud. **66**(9), 641–661 (2008)
14. Lazzaro, N.: Why we play: affect and the fun of games. In: Human-Computer Interaction: Designing for Diverse Users and Domains, vol. 155, pp. 679–700 (2009)
15. Meyer, J.J., Broersen, J., Herzig, A.: BDI logics. In: Handbook of Logics of Knowledge and Belief. College Publications (2015)
16. Ninaus, M., et al.: Increased emotional engagement in game-based learning-a machine learning approach on facial emotion detection data. Comput. Educ. **142**, 103641 (2019)
17. Ortony, A., Clore, G., Collins, A.: The Cognitive Structure of Emotions. Cambridge University Press, Cambridge (1988)
18. Partala, T., Kallinen, A.: Understanding the most satisfying and unsatisfying user experiences: emotions, psychological needs, and context. Interact. Comput. **24**(1), 25–34 (2012)
19. Peterson, J., Pearce, P.F., Ferguson, L.A., Langford, C.A.: Understanding scoping reviews: definition, purpose, and process. J. Am. Assoc. Nurse Pract. **29**(1), 12–16 (2017)
20. Prasetya, I.S.W.B., Dastani, M., Prada, R., Vos, T.E.J., Dignum, F., Kifetew, F.: Aplib: tactical agents for testing computer games. In: Baroglio, C., Hubner, J.F., Winikoff, M. (eds.) EMAS 2020. LNCS (LNAI), vol. 12589, pp. 21–41. Springer, Cham (2020). https://doi.org/10.1007/978-3-030-66534-0_2

21. Procci, K., Singer, A.R., Levy, K.R., Bowers, C.: Measuring the flow experience of gamers: an evaluation of the DFS-2. Comput. Hum. Behav. **28**(6), 2306–2312 (2012)
22. Rivero, L., Conte, T.: A systematic mapping study on research contributions on UX evaluation technologies. In: Proceedings of the XVI Brazilian Symposium on Human Factors in Computing Systems, pp. 1–10 (2017)
23. Saariluoma, P., Jokinen, J.P.: Emotional dimensions of user experience: a user psychological analysis. Int. J. Hum.-Comput. Interact. **30**(4), 303–320 (2014)
24. Sánchez, J.L.G., Vela, F.L.G., Simarro, F.M., Padilla-Zea, N.: Playability: analysing user experience in video games. Behav. Inf. Technol. **31**(10), 1033–1054 (2012)
25. Stahlke, S.N., Mirza-Babaei, P.: Usertesting without the user: opportunities and challenges of an AI-driven approach in games user research. Comput. Entertain. (CIE) **16**(2), 1–18 (2018)
26. Steunebrink, B.R., Dastani, M., Meyer, J.J.C.: A logic of emotions for intelligent agents. In: Proceedings of the National Conference on Artificial Intelligence, vol. 22, p. 142. AAAI Press/MIT Press, Menlo Park, Cambridge (1999/2007)
27. Steunebrink, B.R., Meyer, J.J.C., Dastani, M.: A formal model of emotions: integrating qualitative and quantitative aspects. In: Dagstuhl Seminar Proceedings. Schloss Dagstuhl-Leibniz-Zentrum für Informatik (2008)
28. Vermeeren, A.P., Law, E.L.C., Roto, V., Obrist, M., Hoonhout, J., Väänänen-Vainio-Mattila, K.: User experience evaluation methods: current state and development needs. In: Proceedings of the 6th Nordic Conference on Human-Computer Interaction: Extending Boundaries, pp. 521–530 (2010)
29. Zhao, Y., et al.: Winning is not everything: enhancing game development with intelligent agents. IEEE Trans. Games **12**(2), 199–212 (2020)
30. Zook, A., Riedl, M.: A temporal data-driven player model for dynamic difficulty adjustment. In: Proceedings of the AAAI Conference on Artificial Intelligence and Interactive Digital Entertainment, vol. 8 (2012)

Developer Operations and Engineering Multi-agent Systems

Timotheus Kampik[1]([⊠]) [iD], Cleber Jorge Amaral[2,3] [iD], and Jomi Fred Hübner[3] [iD]

[1] Umeå University, Umeå, Sweden
tkampik@cs.umu.se
[2] Federal Institute of Santa Catarina, Florianópolis, SC, Brazil
cleber.amaral@ifsc.edu.br
[3] Federal University of Santa Catarina, São José, SC, Brazil
jomi.hubner@ufsc.br

Abstract. In this paper, we propose the integration of approaches to Engineering Multi-Agent Systems (EMAS) with the *Developer Operations* (DevOps) industry best practice. Whilst DevOps facilitates the organizational autonomy of software teams, as well as the technological automation of testing, deployment, and operations pipelines, EMAS and the agent-oriented programming paradigm help instill autonomy into software artifacts. We discuss the benefits of integrating DevOps and EMAS, for example by highlighting the need for agent-oriented abstractions for quality assurance and test automation approaches. More generally, we introduce an agent-oriented perspective on the DevOps life-cycle and list a range of research challenges that are relevant for the integration of the DevOps and EMAS perspectives.

Keywords: Agent-oriented programming · Engineering Multi-Agent Systems · Developer Operations

1 Introduction

On August 1, 2012, the financial technology venture *Knight Capital Group, Inc* executed a malfunctioning update of their autonomous trading system that caused the large-scale issuing of erroneous orders, leading to losses of more than $450 million within less than one hour [24]. In the software engineering community, the root cause of the error is ascribed to problematic software development processes that do not ensure a sufficient degree of quality assurance automation and testing at different development and deployment stages [5].

To address this and similar issues[1], new software development practices have emerged during the the last decade, most notably the Developer Operations (DevOps) approach [18]. DevOps aims to reduce the time for deploying high-quality (validated and verified) software artifacts (and their updates) to complex

---

[1] We observe that Knight Capital's system is one of numerous autonomous software systems already in operation within socio-technically complex organizations [15].

© Springer Nature Switzerland AG 2022
N. Alechina et al. (Eds.): EMAS 2021, LNAI 13190, pp. 175–186, 2022.
https://doi.org/10.1007/978-3-030-97457-2_10

and heterogeneous *production* environments [5]. Desirable qualities of DevOps-oriented software engineering are reliability, predictability and security [19]. For example, DevOps facilitates the autonomy of teams and their individual members to prevent, discover, and fix software bugs quickly and effectively [19]. However, one may say that even applying the best industrial-scale software engineering processes in combination with traditional programing paradigms cannot fully prevent problems like the one that occurred during the Knight Capital incident. Indeed, from an artificial intelligence perspective, an alternative root-cause is the *single-mindedness* and lack of meaningful goal-orientation of the software subsystem (or: agent) that kept issuing orders, without re-assessing over time whether doing so is aligned with the overall objectives of the trading system. From this perspective, it can be questioned whether the application of the current conception of DevOps is sufficient to ensure quality, and to facilitate the fast-paced development of highly autonomous software systems.

Consequently, one may call for the application of approaches to Engineering Multi-Agent Systems (EMAS) that treat the *agency* of autonomous software artifacts, as well as the environments and organizations these artifacts act in, as first-class abstractions. Along these lines, this paper proposes a bridge between DevOps and EMAS, with the aim to address the need for a robust method for delivering autonomous software artifacts faster and safer. Nevertheless, this paper attempts to maintain a critical perspective on the mainstream-readiness of EMAS. Indeed, the lack of industry-scale tools for engineering autonomous software curbs EMAS adoption in practice [26,27], and we argue that the application of EMAS should always consider efforts to mature EMAS tooling as a prerequisite.

2   DevOps

Developer Operations (DevOps) describes the industry best practices that integrate software development, quality assurance and operations teams, from both organizational and technological perspectives [18]. DevOps can be considered a continuation of the trend towards iterative software development, which started at the turn of the century with the publication of the Agile Manifesto [17]. In particular because iterative software development approaches require a fast-paced transition between requirement adjustments, software changes, tests, and deployments, handovers across traditional organizational and technological boundaries become increasingly impractical. To address this issue, DevOps recommends the integration of software developers, Quality Assurance (QA) engineers, and system administrators into autonomous cross-functional teams that are in charge of developing, testing, deploying, and operating a system or system component [8]. This stands in contrast to traditional approaches that segment functional specializations and hence require frequent handovers between teams or even departments, all of which are in charge of one specific task [33]. To support cross-functional teams with the broad range of tasks that fall into the DevOps scope, a plethora of tools exists, many of which have found wide-spread adoption. For example, continuous integration tools and services allow for the configuration of automated tests and deployments using simple declarative specification and script languages [29], whereas containerization [28] and container orchestration tools [11] help speed up and automate the deployment and scaling of complex IT systems across heterogeneous infrastructure.

The DevOps development life-cycle (illustrated in Fig. 1) can be described as follows:

Plan and code. DevOps development teams implement features in fast, incremental iterations, which is facilitated by the organizational structure and technological setup. As a consequence, DevOps reduces the overhead of QA, releases, and deployments.

Build and test. Each update of the code base triggers the automated execution of one or several test suites. Ideally, all technical aspects of software artifact generation (build) and quality assurance are executed automatically; passing tests and builds imply that the software artifact works reliably and can be released without concerns. This requires the development team to treat QA as a key responsibility.

Release and deploy. After tests and builds have been successfully executed, deployments (for example to cloud environments) and/or releases (e.g., to package management services) are triggered in an automated or semi-automated manner.

Operate and monitor. During operations, a key feature of DevOps is the automation of many system administration tasks, like the provision of additional resources if the load on the system increases. To reduce the overhead of system administration, teams often rely on cloud-based service offerings that abstract away technical details.

Figure 1 depicts the DevOps life-cycle.

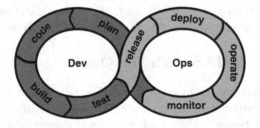

Fig. 1. DevOps life-cycle, based on [18].

3   EMAS

During the past decades, the EMAS sub-field has emerged as a research direction within the field of artificial intelligence [34]. One of the key lines of work within

EMAS is the refinement of the Agent-Oriented Programming (AOP) paradigm, which provides abstractions for implementing autonomous and social software artifacts (agents). However, the scope of EMAS entails more than AOP, in particular because EMAS is concerned with the holistic software engineering perspective and not only programming. With the increase in prevalence of (somewhat) autonomous software systems in distributed information system landscapes [15], it was initially a reasonable expectation that EMAS would gain attention from the software engineering mainstream. However, EMAS approaches have not seen wide-spread adoption in practice, neither directly, nor as derivations that are implemented in industry-scale programming language ecosystems.

One focus area of EMAS is concerned with the design and development of methods and tools for AOP, examples of which are the Java-based Jade [6] and JACK [37], and the Belief-Desire-Intention (BDI)-based Jason [9] frameworks[2]. Indeed, the EMAS community has experimented with a broad range of abstractions for solving diverse problems using agents. However, no major success stories with regards to the establishment of industry-level tools, languages, or standards have been achieved; in their current state, the concepts and reusable software libraries and frameworks provided by EMAS are still detached from the software engineering mainstream. According to an EMAS community report [27], one of the key points of criticism of the state of affairs of EMAS is the lack of integration between EMAS and more widespread software engineering approaches. Some recent works aim to address this issue, for example by integrating agent-oriented programming and modern "high-level" programming languages like JavaScript [10,22,23], and by providing resource-oriented abstractions to interact with autonomous agents and multi-agent systems [13]. These (and similar) tools help push the frontier of modern agent-oriented *programming* towards practicality. However, no holistic agent-oriented perspectives on the complete software engineering life-cycle seem to exist. An example of a deficiency that affects several steps of the life-cycle and that even the most mature AOP frameworks have, is a lack of facilities for testing goal-oriented software artifacts. Seeing EMAS and AOP through the eyes of DevOps can potentially help identify new solution approaches to address such deficiencies.

4   Integrating EMAS with DevOps

Let us highlight that the main objective of DevOps is not *automation*, which could also be achieved with traditional, homogeneous team constellations, but rather *autonomy* of teams within a software development organization, which is achieved by relying on automation technologies. From the description provided in Subsect. 2, one can see that DevOps is, in the way it is currently practiced, concerned with autonomy on three levels:

1. On the **organization level**, DevOps facilitates team autonomy by avoiding the necessity of hand-overs between development, QA, and operations teams.

---

[2] For an overview of some agent-oriented programming languages and frameworks, see (for example) Cardoso and Ferrando [12].

2. On the **integration level**, DevOps allows for continuous integrations and deployments, avoiding manual steps and hand-overs in the pipeline from code check-in to system deployment.
3. On the **operations level**, DevOps provides abstractions that allow operators to specify high-level infrastructure requirements and handles lower-level details like exact resource allocation and machine provisioning autonomously.

In contrast, EMAS focuses on the autonomy of the agents, as *software artifacts*, that a software engineering team or organization creates, *i.e.*, it adds a fourth autonomy level to the three-level perspective DevOps provides. Table 1 shows an overview of the four levels and explains them by example.

Table 1. Autonomy levels, examples, and relevant approach.

Autonomy level	Example	Approach
Organization autonomy	Avoid handovers: one team is in charge of all steps in the life-cycle	DevOps
Integration autonomy	Avoid manual deployments and QA: run all tests before a merge and auto-deploy if all tests pass	DevOps
Operations autonomy	Avoid manual resource provisioning: auto-scale systems when load increases	DevOps
Artifact autonomy	Avoid manual low-level business decisions: approve (financial) transactions without humans interference	EMAS

At this point, it is worth highlighting that even when developing "traditional" software artifacts with little or no autonomy, it is widely acknowledged that total global supervision and coordination of all software design steps is practically not possible, even if the scope of the project is confined to a single organization. Hence, DevOps approaches try to integrate changes frequently in a controlled manner in order to discover unknown dependencies and unexpected behavior early on. The *autonomy levels* (Table 1) allow teams of engineers to dynamically respond to challenges that arise and to minimize the effect these challenges have on the broader organization. When developing *autonomous* software artifacts, one can expect that there will be even more problems that cannot be identified at design-time and hence the continuous integration approach requires even more attention; *i.e.*, on the organizational level, the implementation of highly autonomous artifacts implies that the intensity of dependencies between teams that develop different sub-systems is not always apparent before these sub-systems are integrated. These emerging dependencies then need to be managed on the integration and operations levels, for example to ensure that in case of the deployment of sub-systems that have "hidden" incompatibilities, communication failures do not lead to disastrous consequences. Because of their dynamic nature, agents cannot be developed into mature software artifacts without exposing them to the environment they are supposed to act in [38]. Regarding this distinguishing characteristic of agents, the integration of agent-orientation and developer operations can be considered a methodological response to this issue. To allow for a gradual exposure of an agent to a progressively more realistic environment that increases the likelihood of catching critical errors early on, an agent-oriented variant of the DevOps life-cycle may require the following features:

- **Goal-oriented test-driven development.** The behavior of social and goal-oriented software artifacts like agents is typically complex and non-deterministic [14]. Hence, the common testing levels (unit tests, functional tests, and integration tests) usually are not satisfactory to cover agents' possible behaviors. Some approaches have been proposed to address this issue [7,14,31], but a comprehensive solution has still not been devised [39]. *Goal-oriented* tests can provide an extra test level that should be able to assess whether an agent's inference process from goals and beliefs to actions (and explanations of these actions) behaves as expected or not.
- **Sandbox for real-time collaboration.** Development teams can move agents that have passed static code analysis, unit tests, goal-oriented tests, and low-level integration tests (which may or may not be goal-oriented)[3] to a sand-boxed environment that allows for the collaborative development of agents and multi-agent systems in (near) real-time. This makes it easier for developers to consider their current development work in the context of other ongoing changes. Each sand-box features a fully-fledged multi-agent system, as well as version control and continuous integration support (automated testing and deployments). From a practical perspective, one can assume that the scope of a sandbox is restricted by organizational boundaries. For example, given a commercial enterprise A and a government organization B who both work on the same multi-agent system, it is safe to assume that the engineers of A cannot align in real-time with the engineers of B; a change made by organization A during development should not immediately (before verification and validation) affect the system organization B is developing against. The EMAS community has presented an initial prototype addressing part of this issue [3].
- **Cross-organizational staging system.** To ensure quality across organizational boundaries, stable versions of local agents, artifacts, and environment updates that have been developed and thoroughly tested in a sand-boxed environment can be deployed to cross-organizational staging systems. To these staging systems, organizations that depend on each other's work in a particularly critical manner (if not all organizations that contribute to the multi-agent system) have access and use it as a second-level testing environment; *i.e.*, any run-time issue that may occur on the staging system does not affect system end-users. Still, errors are potentially more costly when they occur on the staging system and not in the sand-box, as their root-cause

---

[3] We assume that these tests can be executed relatively quickly when the developer logs a change, which is – in the case of standard approaches to static code analysis (often called *linting*), unit tests, and some integration tests like micro-service handler tests – a common capability of development tool-chains.

needs to be traced back – in a more complex environment – to a particular organization and then to a team. Cross-organizational staging systems can potentially make use of concepts and tools the EMAS community provides for managing multi-agent organizations (e.g., $\mathcal{M}OISE^+$ [21]).

– **Beta agents in production environments.** When the tests have passed in the cross-organizational staging environment, a step-wise production deployment can be executed. As a first step, agent instances can be exposed to "sense" the production environment, without being able to act upon it. Then, some agent instances can be fully deployed to the production environment, but at limited scale, analogously to the way beta-feature roll-outs are handled in many software-as-a-service environments (so-called *canary deployments* [5]). Still, in contrast to typical canary deployments, which only affect a small portion of a system's users, beta agent deployments are potentially more critical because of the interconnectedness of multi-agent systems. Only if these beta agents pass all tests after extensive monitoring, the full update of the production environment is executed. This step reflects tests on real traffic scenarios used by the automotive industry [20, 35][4].

– **Explainable Monitoring.** Given the complex and non-deterministic behavior of multi-agent systems, it can be assumed that traditional monitoring facilities provide only limited utility. New ways of filtering and aggregating log entries for human or machine interpretation need to be devised. To address this issue, one can draw from an emerging body of works on explainable agents and multi-agent systems [4], and in particular from research that investigates the filtering of event data to generate human-digestible explanations [30].

Table 2 list these features and provides an overview of how they relate to mainstream software engineering practices. In the Fig. 2 we present a more comprehensive view of the development cycle of agents based on DevOps life-cycle. Besides the mentioned features, the referred picture also illustrates the place for goal-oriented/agent-oriented model-driven development and programming tools, well-covered subjects of a range of studies produced by EMAS community (e.g., [6, 9, 16, 36, 37]).

Let us highlight that the list of features is primarily an initial starting point, and each feature comes with limitations and trade-offs that may only emerge in industrial application scenarios (and may be specific to a given domain, technology stack or DevOps-variant). Consequently, it can make sense to consider a step-wise introduction of agent-oriented approaches to DevOps, focusing on the controlled assessment of a *minimally viable* agent-oriented abstraction[5]. For

---

[4] In Vehicle-in-the-loop (VEHIL) simulations, domain-specific concepts similar to the *sandbox for real-time collaboration* and the *cross-organizational staging system* are employed.

[5] In his *Agent Programming Manifesto*, Logan calls for *modular* approaches to AOP [26]. We argue that the notion of a *minimally viable abstraction* goes a step further, as it suggests a focus on one particular benefit AOP can bring to mainstream software engineering approaches such as DevOps, and hence a radical simplification that may deliberately disregard many aspects of AOP to minimize technology overhead and learning curve when introducing a single abstraction.

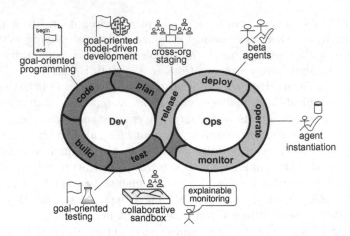

Fig. 2. The DevOps life-cycle and agent orientation.

example, autonomous software systems that are not developed using an academic EMAS approach can potentially still be evaluated by goal-oriented tests.

5   Implications for EMAS

Traditionally, EMAS is primarily concerned with the implementation of theoretical perspectives, such as belief-desire-intention reasoning-loops, that the artificial intelligence scientific literature provides on the design of autonomous agents and multi-agent systems. In contrast, the approach outlined in this paper is pragmatically targeted at moving EMAS closer to modern industry practices for software development, and at identifying gaps in mainstream software development approaches and frameworks that EMAS can fill. Hence, the approach depends on the exposure of EMAS and AOP works to the context of mainstream software development tools and pipelines, and in particular to the technology ecosystem that has risen to popularity alongside with DevOps. First prototypes that work towards this goal by treating continuous integration, collaboration features, and distributed version control as first-class citizens in the context of agent-oriented programming exist [2,3].

Consequently, the whole technology ecosystem that makes up the DevOps tool-chains needs to be thoroughly analyzed, and methodologies and re-usable software frameworks (or framework extensions) for identifying and addressing the specific requirements for the DevOps-oriented management of goal-oriented, autonomous software artifacts need to be developed. Logging, monitoring, and debugging facilities need to be devised that address the challenge of identifying anomalous behavior in a highly dynamic and heterogeneous environment, and facilitate the identification of software bugs that may be caused by intractable state and software version dependencies between autonomous software agents that are developed by different organizations.

Table 2. Integrating AOP and DevOps: example features in comparison to existing practices.

Feature	Existing practice	Similarities	Differences
Goal-oriented test-driven development	Test-driven development (unit tests)	Testing before/while implementing	Higher declarative abstraction level at the intersection of unit and integration testing
Sandbox for real-time collaboration	Sandbox for exploratory development	Rapid prototyping support	Near-real-time interactive and collaborative programming support
Cross-organizational staging system	Traditional staging system	Production like environment	Continuous deployments by different organizations
Beta agents in production environments	Beta-features in production environments	Pilot beta-features in production environment	Interaction between beta-agents and stable agents
Explainable monitoring	Operations monitoring systems	Explanation/analysis of a running system	System-centered versus agent-centered perspectives

Nevertheless, let us highlight that the integration of EMAS and DevOps cannot only draw from AOP research, but also apply other fundamental research on autonomous agents and multi-agent systems, for example by considering fundamental theoretical research on topics like belief revision [25], goal reasoning [1], or agreement technologies [32]. Still, EMAS and EMAS-related research that is of immediate relevance necessarily has a focus on technologies, software engineering processes and/or practical aspects of socio-technical systems. In contrast, research that primarily provides formal contributions would first need to be implemented as a generic and re-usable abstraction for a particular technology ecosystem, or be presented as a solution to a particular software engineering problem. In this context, the notion of a *minimally viable abstractions* may – again – serve as a guiding design principle; *e.g.*, when devising a new formal approach to belief revision, it may not be necessary to provide a holistic integration with a full-fledged MAS conceptual meta-model and technology like JaCaMo. Instead, a small library for managing belief revision could be implemented and presented in a way that enables re-usability in software stacks and tool-chains that do not necessarily include other agent-oriented concepts or technologies.

6   Conclusion

In this paper, we have proposed the integration of approaches to engineering multi-agent systems with the DevOps software engineering practice. The integration expands the scope of the agent-oriented programming paradigm to cover the full life-cycle of modern software engineering, from initial specification via implementation and continuous integration to operation and monitoring. Viewing EMAS from the perspective of modern software engineering approaches that cover the whole engineering life-cycle can facilitate the development of more practice-oriented perspectives on EMAS and AOP. The integration of EMAS and DevOps can draw from the breadth and depth of research on agents and multi-agent systems, and motivate future work at the intersection of theory and practice, for example on goal-oriented testing and goal reasoning.

Acknowledgments. We thank the anonymous reviewers for their thoughtful and useful feedback. This work was partially supported by the Wallenberg AI, Autonomous Systems and Software Program (WASP) funded by the Knut and Alice Wallenberg Foundation and partially funded by Project AG-BR of Petrobras and by the program PrInt CAPES-UFSC "Automação 4.0".

References

1. Aha, D.W.: Goal reasoning: foundations, emerging applications, and prospects. AI Mag. **39**(2), 3–24 (2018)
2. Amaral, C.J., Hübner, J.F.: Jacamo-web is on the fly: an interactive multi-agent system IDE. In: Dennis, L.A., Bordini, R.H., Lespérance, Y. (eds.) EMAS 2019. LNCS (LNAI), vol. 12058, pp. 246–255. Springer, Cham (2020). https://doi.org/10.1007/978-3-030-51417-4_13
3. Amaral, C.J., Kampik, T., Cranefield, S.: A framework for collaborative and interactive agent-oriented developer operations. In: Proceedings of the 19th International Conference on Autonomous Agents and MultiAgent Systems, AAMAS 2020, International Foundation for Autonomous Agents and Multiagent Systems, Richland (2020)
4. Anjomshoae, S., Najjar, A., Calvaresi, D., Främling, K.: Explainable agents and robots: results from a systematic literature review. In: Proceedings of the 18th International Conference on Autonomous Agents and MultiAgent Systems, AAMAS 2019, pp. 1078–1088. International Foundation for Autonomous Agents and Multiagent Systems, Richland (2019)
5. Bass, L., Weber, I., Zhu, L.: DevOps: A Software Architect's Perspective. Pearson Education, Inc., Boston (2015)
6. Bellifemine, F., Poggi, A., Rimassa, G.: JADE: A FIPA2000 compliant agent development environment. In: Proceedings of the Fifth International Conference on Autonomous Agents, AGENTS 2001, pp. 216–217. Association for Computing Machinery, New York (2001). https://doi.org/10.1145/375735.376120
7. Benac Earle, C., Fredlund, L.: A property-based testing framework for multi-agent systems. In: Proceedings of the 18th International Conference on Autonomous Agents and MultiAgent Systems, AAMAS 2019, pp. 1823–1825. International Foundation for Autonomous Agents and Multiagent Systems, Richland (2019)
8. Bolscher, R., Daneva, M.: Designing software architecture to support continuous delivery and devops: A systematic literature review. In: van Sinderen, M., Maciaszek, L., Maciaszek, L. (eds.) ICSOFT 2019 - Proceedings of the 14th International Conference on Software Technologies, Conference date: 26-07-2019 Through 28-07-2019, pp. 27–39. SCITEPRESS (2019)

9. Bordini, R.H., Hübner, J.F., Wooldridge, M.: Programming Multi-agent Systems in AgentSpeak Using Jason. Wiley Series in Agent Technology, Wiley, Hoboken (2007)
10. Bosse, S.: Mobile multi-agent systems for the internet-of-things and clouds using the JavaScript agent machine platform and machine learning as a service. In: 2016 IEEE 4th International Conference on Future Internet of Things and Cloud (FiCloud), pp. 244–253. IEEE (2016)
11. Brewer, E.A.: Kubernetes and the path to cloud native. In: Proceedings of the Sixth ACM Symposium on Cloud Computing, SoCC 2015, p. 167. Association for Computing Machinery, New York (2015). https://doi.org/10.1145/2806777.2809955
12. Cardoso, R.C., Ferrando, A.: A review of agent-based programming for multi-agent systems. Computers **10**(2), 16 (2021)
13. Ciortea, A., Boissier, O., Zimmermann, A., Florea, A.M.: Give agents some REST: hypermedia-driven agent environments. In: El Fallah-Seghrouchni, A., Ricci, A., Son, T.C. (eds.) EMAS 2017. LNCS (LNAI), vol. 10738, pp. 125–141. Springer, Cham (2018). https://doi.org/10.1007/978-3-319-91899-0_8
14. Coelho, R., Cirilo, E., Kulesza, U., Von Staa, A., Rashid, A., Lucena, C.: JAT: a test automation framework for multi-agent systems. In: IEEE International Conference on Software Maintenance, ICSM, pp. 425–434 (2007). https://doi.org/10.1109/ICSM.2007.4362655
15. De la Prieta, F., Rodríguez-González, S., Chamoso, P., Corchado, J.M., Bajo, J.: Survey of agent-based cloud computing applications. Future Gener. Comput. Syst. **100**, 223–236 (2019). https://doi.org/10.1016/j.future.2019.04.037
16. DeLoach, S.A., Garcia-Ojeda, J.C.: O-MaSE: a customisable approach to designing and building complex, adaptive multi-agent systems. Int. J. Agent-Oriented Softw. Eng. **4**(3), 244–280 (2010). https://doi.org/10.1504/IJAOSE.2010.036984
17. Dingsøyr, T., Nerur, S., Balijepally, V.G., Moe, N.B.: A decade of agile methodologies: towards explaining agile software development. J. Syst. Softw. **85**(6), 1213–1221 (2012). special Issue: Agile Development. https://doi.org/10.1016/j.jss.2012.02.033. http://www.sciencedirect.com/science/article/pii/S0164121212000532
18. Ebert, C., Gallardo, G., Hernantes, J., Serrano, N.: DevOps. IEEE Softw. **33**(3), 94–100 (2016)
19. Forsgren, N., Smith, D., Humble, J., Frazelle, J.: 2019 accelerate state of DevOps report. Technical report, Google Research (2019). http://cloud.google.com/devops/state-of-devops/
20. Huang, W.L., Wang, K., Lv, Y., Zhu, F.H.: Autonomous vehicles testing methods review. In: IEEE Conference on Intelligent Transportation Systems, Proceedings, pp. 163–168. ITSC (2016). https://doi.org/10.1109/ITSC.2016.7795548
21. Hubner, J.F., Sichman, J.S., Boissier, O.: Developing organised multiagent systems using the MOISE+ model: programming issues at the system and agent levels. Int. J. Agent-Oriented Softw. Eng. **1**(3/4), 370 (2007). https://doi.org/10.1504/IJAOSE.2007.016266, http://www.inderscience.com/link.php?id=16266
22. de Jong, J., Stellingwerff, L., Pazienza, G.E.: Eve: a novel open-source web-based agent platform. In: 2013 IEEE International Conference on Systems, Man, and Cybernetics, pp. 1537–1541 (2013). https://doi.org/10.1109/SMC.2013.265
23. Kampik, T., Nieves, J.C.: JS-son - a lean, extensible JavaScript agent programming library. In: Dennis, L.A., Bordini, R.H., Lespérance, Y. (eds.) EMAS 2019. LNCS (LNAI), vol. 12058, pp. 215–234. Springer, Cham (2020). https://doi.org/10.1007/978-3-030-51417-4_11

24. Kirilenko, A.A., Lo, A.W.: Moore's law versus murphy's law: algorithmic trading and its discontents. J. Econ. Perspect. **27**(2), 51–72 (2013). https://doi.org/10.1257/jep.27.2.51
25. Lehmann, D.: Belief revision, revised. In: Proceedings of the 14th International Joint Conference on Artificial Intelligence - Volume 2, IJCAI 1995, pp. 1534–1540. Morgan Kaufmann Publishers Inc., San Francisco (1995)
26. Logan, B.: An agent programming manifesto. Int. J. Agent-Oriented Softw. Eng. **6**(2), 187–210 (2018)
27. Mascardi, V., et al.: Engineering multi-agent systems: state of affairs and the road ahead. SIGSOFT Softw. Eng. Notes **44**(1), 18–28 (2019). https://doi.org/10.1145/3310013.3322175
28. Merkel, D.: Docker: lightweight Linux containers for consistent development and deployment. Linux J. **2014**(239), 2 (2014)
29. Meyer, M.: Continuous integration and its tools. IEEE Softw. **31**(3), 14–16 (2014)
30. Mualla, Y., Tchappi, I., Najjar, A., Kampik, T., Galland, S., Nicolle, C.: Human-agent explainability: an experimental case study on the filtering of explanations. In: 12th International Conference on Agents and Artificial Intelligence, Valletta, Malta, 22–24 February 2020 (2020)
31. Nguyen, C.D., Perini, A., Tonella, P., Miles, S., Harman, M., Luck, M.: Evolutionary testing of autonomous software agents. In: Proceedings of the International Joint Conference on Autonomous Agents and Multiagent Systems, AAMAS, vol. 1, pp. 364–371 (2009)
32. Ossowski, S.: Agreement Technologies. Springer, Dordrecht (2012). https://doi.org/10.1007/978-94-007-5583-3
33. Pettigrew, A.M., Fenton, E.M.: The Innovating organization. SAGE Publications, Thousand Oaks (2000)
34. Shehory, O., Sturm, A. (eds.): Agent-Oriented Software Engineering. Springer, Heidelberg (2014). https://doi.org/10.1007/978-3-642-54432-3
35. Gühmann, C., Riese, J., von Rüden, K. (eds.): Simulation and Testing for Vehicle Technology. Springer, Cham (2016). https://doi.org/10.1007/978-3-319-32345-9
36. Uez, D.M., Hübner, J.F.: Environments and organizations in multi-agent systems: from modelling to code. In: Dalpiaz, F., Dix, J., van Riemsdijk, M.B. (eds.) EMAS 2014. LNCS (LNAI), vol. 8758, pp. 181–203. Springer, Cham (2014). https://doi.org/10.1007/978-3-319-14484-9_10
37. Winikoff, M.: Jack™ intelligent agents: an industrial strength platform. In: Bordini, R.H., Dastani, M., Dix, J., El Fallah Seghrouchni, A. (eds.) Multi-Agent Programming. MSASSO, vol. 15, pp. 175–193. Springer, Boston, MA (2005). https://doi.org/10.1007/0-387-26350-0_7
38. Winikoff, M., Cranefield, S.: On the testability of BDI agent systems. In: IJCAI International Joint Conference on Artificial Intelligence, pp. 4217–4221 (2015)
39. Gallina, B., Skavhaug, A., Schoitsch, E., Bitsch, F. (eds.): SAFECOMP 2018. LNCS, vol. 11094. Springer, Cham (2018). https://doi.org/10.1007/978-3-319-99229-7

Smart Cyber-Physical System-of-Systems Using Intelligent Agents and MAS

Burak Karaduman[1,2]([envelope]) [ORCID] and Moharram Challenger[1,2] [ORCID]

[1] Department of Computer Science, University of Antwerp, Antwerp, Belgium
{burak.karaduman,moharram.challenger}@uantwerpben.be
[2] Flanders Make, Lommel, Belgium

Abstract. The Cyber-Physical Systems (CPS) are complex, multidisciplinary, physically-aware future's paradigms which are integrating embedded computing technologies (cyber part) into the physical world (physical part). The interaction requirement with the physical world makes the CPS unpredictable because of the real-world's dynamic behaviours. So a CPS needs to reason these changes and adapt its behaviour accordingly. Moreover, a CPS can cooperate with multiple CPSs to establish cyber-physical system-of-systems (CPSoS). This creates a distributed and heterogeneous environment where we are challenged by unpredictability. To address the challenges of the CPSoS, new methodologies and new approaches need to be developed. One way to tackle these challenges is by making them smart with intelligent agents and modelling them explicitly. To make intelligent decisions it is needed to do reasoning and to use decision-making mechanisms. In this way, they can handle the unpredictable changes encountered both internally and externally. Nevertheless, suitable reasoning, smartness, and awareness mechanisms must be studied, implemented, and applied to achieve smart CPSoS.

Keywords: Software Agents · Intelligent Agents · Multi-agent Systems · Smart Cyber-physical system of systems · sCPSoS

1 Introduction

The advancement of networked systems has introduced new design challenges in embedded systems. Naturally, Cyber-Physical Systems (CPSs) are more complex compared to their pioneered paradigm embedded systems. This complexity is inherited both from embedded software that is covered by the cyber part and physical phenomena which have to be monitored and/or interacted with. During the interaction with the physical world, there are phenomena that have to be reacted by the cyber part, which causes a state change in the system, after which feedback information is sent. The computational part of these systems plays a key role and needs to be developed to handle uncertain situations with their limited resources. Since in a distributed CPS, unpredictable change in a

N. Alechina et al. (Eds.): EMAS 2021, LNAI 13190, pp. 187–197, 2022.
https://doi.org/10.1007/978-3-030-97457-2_11

component or the environment can affect the rest of the system and even the whole infrastructure that contains the CPS, it is highly required to perform intelligent behaviours and reasoning mechanisms. This intelligent mechanism needs to react according to the dynamic changes, control the physical part, and adapt the unpredictable behaviour of the system to a reasonable limit. The reasoning mechanism should start with sensor data gathering, extracting the key information from this data, and proving knowledge out of this information to adapt the system's behaviour to control the components. According to the [33], the success of the current approaches have the following gaps i) awareness and adaptation of behaviours are considered as system smartness, but they cannot be achieved by traditional approaches, ii) model-based and component-based approaches insufficiently support the development of reasoning mechanisms for smart CPSs (sCPS), iii) frameworks for the development of smart CPS should support compositional model-based design. Inspired by these research gaps, we are motivated to initialize this research as well as pointing the need for intelligence to establish a smart cyber-physical system of systems (sCPSoS).

2   Related Work

This study proposes an agent-based integrated methodology for the design and development of (sCPSoS), including modelling and reasoning mechanisms, to support the life-cycle of these distributed, complex and mobile systems. In the literature, there are surveys, projects, and research papers that partially provide solutions for the challenges of CPS and CPSoS. The study [12] addresses Industrial Internet-of-Things (IIoT) and CPS common features and provides methodologies for the application of IoT-enabled solutions to Cyber-physical production systems. Their study points to the interoperability of IoT and CPS paradigms. Additionally, they also present modelling approaches for IIoT systems as well as architectures that can be reused for our goal, while the study [26] provides IoT-based layered solutions using software agents. These studies show that IoT based solutions and modelling approaches [15] can also be applied for the sCPSoS. These studies show that smartness, organisation, and networking requirements can be addressed using intelligent agents and the complexity of sCPSoS can be reduced using model-driven approaches. In [20], agents' capabilities for CPS are discussed. Generally, agents are good at creating collaboration and integrity when they are distributed, providing smart decisions when unpredictability exists. The study [26] mentions the cognitive requirement of CPS and presents the necessity of the distributed intelligence and envisions Multi-Agent Systems' (MAS) usefulness as they fit the CPS. Their autonomous decisions in a decentralised way can address the CPS challenges. They benefit from layered IoT architecture to enable organised decentralisation of data acquisition, actuation, monitoring, analysing, planning, and decision-making at the Fog and Edge levels. A survey [6] reports the uncertainty in self-adaptive systems [36]. The participants in the survey agree on implementing self-adaptation mechanisms to cope with unanticipated changes in a system. They also suggest that uncertainty can be represented using runtime models (e.g. MAPE-K loop). In the study [11], ontological classification is made considering past, present, and future CPS technologies emphasising the requirement of intelligence. The study focuses on today's sCPSoS requirements while showing the research gaps in this domain.

In [35], the authors provide a Model-based System Engineering (MBSE) perspective to manage heterogeneity in CPS. They propose to use various domain-specific views for each subsystem. According to this study, the system model should be represented by different levels of abstraction for each subsystem. The study in [32] discusses how an agent development framework called SEA_ML++ is used for the design and implementation of a CPS garbage collection system. The authors apply Model-driven Development (MDD) techniques to synthesise a part of the agent-based software. These studies are in the scope of interest to this study as they map different parts of sCPSoS. They mostly cover model-based development of sCPSoS and partly reasoning mechanisms, but not smart agents and agent-CPSoS integration.

3 Problem Statement

A CPSoS inherently have both CPS and system-of-systems (SoS) characteristics that increase the complexity and challenges. They are brought together within the SoS umbrella to achieve specific tasks that cannot be achieved by a single CPS. This increases the necessity of high-level modelling and solution finding to address the complexity of CPSoS while ensuring each CPS is self-sustainable within itself. Here, self-sustainable refers to having a degree of autonomy, intelligence and adaptive reasoning. They require decentralised supervision and management for each subsystem because decisions that are taken at a cyber level should influence the physical part (also vice-versa) and the result of the effect should be sensed and given as feedback to the system.

As mentioned in [1], today's practice of CPS system design and implementation is unable to support the level of complexity, scalability, security, safety, interoperability, and flexible design and operation that will be required to meet future needs. Moreover, as surveyed and research gap showed in [39], most of the published papers in the literature on CPS focused on design, architecture, functionality, performance, security, reliability, and scalability. However, one important criterion has not received enough attention is self-adaptation despite the fact that it is a must to achieve next-generation CPS. Considering research gaps and needs in the literature and CPSoS requirements, new methodologies and solutions should be researched.

This study aims to improve the lifecycle of sCPSoS development by using Model-driven Development (MDD), Agent-based System Engineering (ABSE) and intelligent agents. This multi-paradigm approach aims to solve the challenges of creating and sustaining CPSoS by providing adaptive behaviour for environmental uncertainty, distributed cooperation for decentralised topology, and reasoning for intelligence requirements while integrating self-awareness and self-adaptation capabilities.

CPSoSs are complex as they consist of various distributed and heterogeneous CPSs where each of them has unique capabilities, critical operations, priorities and pursued goals. However, from a CPSoS perspective, all CPSs must also harmonically pursue their own goals and global goals while collaborating with each other. Considering that a CPSoS consists of many CPSs, finding the methodology to achieve such an intelligent, adaptive, aware, dynamic, automatical, distributed, and cooperative is not an easy task. In Table 1, CPSoS requirements, challenges and the explanations are summarized. In the following paragraphs correlation between them are mentioned.

Because of their distributed topology and heterogeneous instances, each of them produces various dense data that need to be refined in such a way that only the important information is extracted and forwarded to other CPSs and the overall system. The data has to be handled in a distributed way to extract cognitive patterns and to detect abnormalities that can be emerged because of uncertainty. Therefore each CPS has to be context-aware and adapt according to the internal and environmental changes.

During their operation, human factors can intervene in a system or may decide to interact with it. Therefore, each CPS should monitor both itself and human behaviours. These dynamic behaviours should be reasoned by the CPS to change its behaviour dynamically as well.

Because of the intelligence requirements, each CPS should have a tightly coupled (integrated) intelligence mechanism and distributed/layered approaches can be applied externally, in cases that the computation power is not enough to handle the changes by a single CPS. In this way, data can be analyzed at the upper levels by a more powerful computer. As CPSoS are complex distributed and heterogeneous systems, they may need to have cognitive capabilities where this cognition should be achieved both in CPS and CPSoS level (between multiple-instances).

Table 1. CPSoS requirements, challenges and reasons.

CPSoS Requirement	CPSoS Challenges	Reason/Explanation
Data Handling/Filtering/Processing	Distributed/Heterogeneous Data Density	Large amount of data related to systems and the environment.
Preventing/Predicting Uncertainty/Emergent Behavior/Anomalies	Self-awareness/Self-adaptation	Each system should have autonomous decision making and behaviour for robust operation.
Human System Interaction	Behavior Dynamicity/Reasoning	The user's behaviour and goals must be reasoned intelligently and system behavior should be changed dynamically to prevent user-oriented anomalies.
Integrated/External Intelligence	Distributed and Layered AI	The smartness requirement should be provided by AI techniques from the cyber-side.
Distributed/Heterogeneous/Cognitive Instances	Interoperability/Negotiation/Coordination	Collaborative, cognitive, and consensus-based mechanisms should be integrated

As a result, AI approaches can be used to integrate intelligence into these systems to tackle some of the discussed challenges of CPSoS while satisfying the requirements. Our approach is to match the requirements and challenges of CPSoS with the capabilities of AI methodologies and expand suitable formalisms and paradigms in a multi-paradigmatic approach [7]. Specifically, applying multi-paradigm modelling principles to create such a method to provide an agent-based CPSoS modelling framework can be a solution to address the aforementioned challenges. The reason is that it advocates the explicit modelling of all parts of a system at different abstraction levels using multiple formalisms. At the centre of the approach, agents and organizations of agents can be used as the main abstractions orthogonally integrated with model-driven techniques.

4 Proposed Solution and Methodology

The first goal is to gain the smartness feature for cyber-physical systems. As a methodology, intelligent agents and CPS integration need to be established at the cyber part. This smartness mechanism can benefit from agent architecture such as belief-desire-intention (BDI) architecture using their adaptive capabilities. Because BDI architecture allows choosing and adopting different plans to achieve the same goal depending on the context. This makes it possible for agents to decide themselves to adapt by being aware of the environmental changes and current context. In this way, it becomes handy to develop context-aware behaviour for agents and CPS. For this reason, BDI architecture for agents is a well-fit architecture for this goal [3]. As mentioned in [24], there are various ways to create a self-adaptive system. We use the Multi-Agent System approach to tackle CPSoS challenges benefiting from their well-known features as well as using BDI architecture to emerge self-adaptive and self-aware skills. Alternatively, there are Prolog-based agent programming approaches to create CPS [30]. To reach this goal, an agent development environment that is empowered by various integration of logic-based approaches is preferred. As Jason [5] is a high-level agent-oriented programming language that benefits from the BDI model. The language is based on logic programming and is exemplified by Prolog. To support agent-based programming using agent beliefs and deductive reasoning mechanisms, Jason includes a Prolog interpreter. Moreover, the JaCaMo framework provides additional advantages by including CArtAgO and Moise to support organisational and environmental aspects [4]. In our perspective, JaCaMo is a best-fit development framework for CPSoS since each CPS has organisational requirements where coordination should be established because of the environmental challenges.

This integration can also be enhanced using fuzzification methodology to cope with the uncertainty of the environment while selecting fuzzified plans for executing multiple actions. In this way, self-awareness and self-adaption can be improved and flexibility can be gained into the system. Because the uncertainties are caused by the limitation of the agent's perception abilities and environmental dynamics, beliefs should be considered as fuzzy [17,38]. In the case of BDI agents, they should be able to handle a certain degree of uncertainty.

Alternatively, there are probability-based techniques such as Bayesian, Markov Chain, Monte Carlo simulation, spectral methods and statistics to tackle the uncertainty. However, these probabilistic approaches depend upon the assumption of a probability distribution of failure when obtained failure data is sufficient. Moreover, these approaches are supported by simulation techniques [14] which are not suitable for a volatile environment where states and conditions change instantly. As another disadvantage, simulation-based approaches require high computation power there it is not applicable for each application domain considering resource constraints of the CPS. Therefore, fuzzy approaches can be applied in system/component-level [27, 31].

The second goal is to create a model-based framework to support the development of CPSoS so that a higher-level abstraction can be provided for the end-user [13, 15]. In this way, the user can create sCPS and sCPSoS using model elements in a user-friendly manner and generate target system codes, including agent software, embedded software, reasoning codes encapsulated by intelligent agents.

The last goal is defining a methodology encapsulating the embedded device's software into agent software. In this way, the agents will have full control over system inputs, outputs, networking, and configuration. Because agents can manage the embedded device's features to interact with the environment. However, before achieving this, wrapper libraries between device-specific code and agent behaviours should be implemented to achieve Agent-CPS integration. A methodology needs to be defined to standardize this encapsulation.

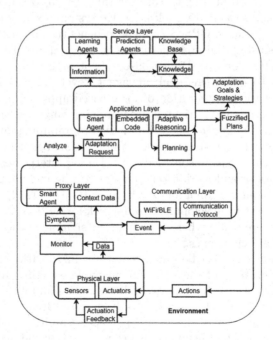

Fig. 1. High-level view of the proposed solution (adapted from [24])

However, before implementing all of these three goals, shown in Fig. 1, a design model should be established. To achieve this, MAPE-K control loop for self-adaptive systems are presented in the literature [2]. Firstly, in the physical layer, real-world data is monitored and analyzed by sensors for collecting data. Then, the system can develop awareness about the context it deployed in using this data. To achieve this, the system *Monitors* the environment all the time. In this state, some preprocessing of the raw data can be applied to remove noise. While the system monitoring the environment, if any *Symptom* (contextual change) occurs, then data and change are delivered to *Analyze* phase. In parallel, this *Context Data* and related state change are interpreted as *Event*. In the *Communication Layer*, this *Event* is notified and broadcast to other CPS (or related instances). In *Proxy Layer*, smart agents establish organisations to inform each other about changes in their internal states and external events.

In the *Analyze* state, the system analyzes to decide and interpret relevant information for the purpose of anticipating events and making decisions in response. Analyzing assesses utilization of the system to determine whether there is a need for adaptation. If so, then *Adaptation Request* is delivered. Because, if any violations occur against the system's robustness, this problem is reasoned to select an adaptation plan. Then, the compensation process should be initialized. In the application layer, these requests should be defined and handled. Moreover, embedded code should be integrated into agents' behaviours, so agents can control the embedded device's I/O. *Adaptive Reasoning* is required to decide that how much reactive the system should be. Therefore, plans for actions should be made. This can be achieved by taking all the information that has been processed and deciding the best action based on the most applicable plan. Therefore, *Planning* state runs to organise adaptation goals and strategies using previous system knowledge. If a previously applied plan can be re-used, then the same strategy can be applied again. If not, the system should generate a new strategy by adapting its goals. Lastly, *Fuzzified Plans* are executed as actions. These *Actions* are actually I/O operations in the physical layer. When an action is realized by an *Actuator*, the environmental change which is caused by that actuator is sensed by a sensor as *Actuation Feedback*. Therefore, the consistency between the cyber-part and physical part can be satisfied once the actuation state is known by and in sync with the cyber part. While this process is ongoing, the knowledge-based is updated and a general solution scheme towards similar cases are generated benefiting from these run-time experiences [29]. In the service layer, the *Knowledge Base* should store the information about the physical and cyber context of CPS related to sensor data, actuation operations, and process steps regarding time. Moreover, the knowledge base should also contain goals, general scheme plans, states and past experiences of the system. *Learning Agents* should cooperate with **Prediction Agents** for future-predictions about system state. Learning agents provide extensions considering long-term machine learning techniques while prediction agents apply statistical and probabilistic predictions. Moreover, prediction agents also play a role in providing knowledge for adaptation. In this way, goals and plans can be executed not only in awareness of the current state but also in future states.

To reach these three goals and to apply the proposed solution, it is aimed to benefit from study [9]. As study [9] mentions, integrating agent-based system engineering [8,10] with model-driven approaches is considered while referring to the use of proper paradigms/formalisms with the philosophy of modelling different aspects/phases of sCPSoS lifecycle explicitly in an appropriate level of abstraction (in design and/or run time). These systems are highly complex from both structural and behavioural points of view, which can be addressed with well-known techniques of Model-based System Engineering (MBSE) to cover the lifecycle of sCPSoS This raises the need to integrate MBSE and ABSE processes for the development of sCPSoS, which is an open issue. Therefore, this study aims to improve the lifecycle of sCPSoS development by using MDD, ABSE and intelligent agents in a multi-paradigm manner. Our approach seeks to solve the challenges of creating and sustaining CPSoS by providing adaptive behaviour for environmental uncertainty, distributed cooperation for decentralised topology, and reasoning for intelligence requirements while integrating self-awareness and self-adaptation capabilities. Therefore, this study, it is aimed to define new methods using intelligent agents [22], and modelling techniques [18,34] to overcome the current challenges of CPSoS while considering self-adaptation for CPSoS sustainability and providing a tool that facilitates the lifecycle of CPSoS. The underlying idea is the integration of agent-based system engineering (ABSE) and model-driven development (MDD) techniques.

To evaluate the proposed study, we established a LEGO technology-based smart production system [37] and a line follower robot with an adaptive cruise control robot [28] to establish a production management system. We established agent-based communication and ran reactive agents on these sub-systems. We aim to advance this case study to achieve an industrial-like CPSoS, then apply industrial requirements to test the adaptiveness of the system. During the evaluation, the goal is to achieve a fully-fledged production system and product transportation system. The system should adapt itself and sustain its operation while dealing with dynamic requirements (e.g. more production or lack of sources), recognizing the process failures (stuck of materials etc.) and being aware of the unexpected or faulty interplay between sub-CPS. Lastly, we will apply MDD techniques to create a modelling framework [15].

5   Conclusion

The adaptation of MAS to CPS is an open research domain. The evolution of industrial paradigms and communication technology provided solutions but also created new challenges. While communication technology is evolving, this creates distributed and decentralized systems where traditional control methodologies cannot be used anymore. As discussed, the necessity of intelligence in CPS is underlined and proposed as a solution. In this regard, intelligent software agents are selected as one of the best-fit solutions. It is necessary to develop new solutions while adapting current standards such as IoT [16,21,25], Distributed AI, and Embedded technology[19] as well as model-based engineering techniques[23].

References

1. National Academies: A 21st Century Cyber-Physical Systems Education. National Academies of Sciences, Engineering, and Medicine. National Academies Press (2017)
2. Arcaini, P., Riccobene, E., Scandurra, P.: Modeling and analyzing MAPE-K feedback loops for self-adaptation. In: 2015 IEEE/ACM 10th International Symposium on Software Engineering for Adaptive and Self-Managing Systems, pp. 13–23. IEEE (2015)
3. Boissier, O., Bordini, R.H., Hubner, J., Ricci, A.: Multi-Agent Oriented Programming: Programming Multi-Agent Systems Using JaCaMo. MIT Press, Cambridge (2020)
4. Boissier, O., Hübner, J.F., Ricci, A.: The JaCaMo framework. In: Aldewereld, H., Boissier, O., Dignum, V., Noriega, P., Padget, J. (eds.) Social Coordination Frameworks for Social Technical Systems. LGTS, vol. 30, pp. 125–151. Springer, Cham (2016). https://doi.org/10.1007/978-3-319-33570-4_7
5. Bordini, R.H., Hübner, J.F., Wooldridge, M.: Programming Multi-Agent Systems in AgentSpeak Using Jason, vol. 8. Wiley, Hoboken (2007)
6. Calinescu, R., Mirandola, R., Perez-Palacin, D., Weyns, D.: Understanding uncertainty in self-adaptive systems. In: IEEE International Conference on Autonomic Computing and Self-Organizing Systems (ACSOS), pp. 242–251. IEEE (2020)
7. Challenger, M., Eslampanaha, R., Karadumanb, B., Denila, J., Vangheluwe, H.: Development of an IoT and WSN based cps using MPM approach: a smart fire detection case study. In: Multi-Paradigm Modelling Approaches for Cyber-Physical Systems, p. 245 (2020)
8. Challenger, M., Tezel, B.T., Alaca, O.F., Tekinerdogan, B., Kardas, G.: Development of semantic web-enabled BDI multi-agent systems using SEA_ML: an electronic bartering case study. Appl. Sci. 8(5), 688 (2018)
9. Challenger, M., Vangheluwe, H.: Towards employing ABM and MAS integrated with MBSE for the lifecycle of sCPSoS. In: Proceedings of the 23rd ACM/IEEE International Conference on Model Driven Engineering Languages and Systems: Companion Proceedings, pp. 1–7 (2020)
10. Demirkol, S., Getir, S., Challenger, M., Kardas, G.: Development of an agent based e-barter system. In: 2011 International Symposium on Innovations in Intelligent Systems and Applications, pp. 193–198. IEEE (2011)
11. Horváth, I., Rusák, Z., Li, Y.: Order beyond chaos: introducing the notion of generation to characterize the continuously evolving implementations of cyber-physical systems. In: ASME 2017 International Design Engineering Technical Conferences and Computers and Information in Engineering Conference. American Society of Mechanical Engineers Digital Collection (2017)
12. Jeschke, S., Brecher, C., Meisen, T., Özdemir, D., Eschert, T.: Industrial internet of things and cyber manufacturing systems. In: Jeschke, S., Brecher, C., Song, H., Rawat, D.B. (eds.) Industrial Internet of Things. SSWT, pp. 3–19. Springer, Cham (2017). https://doi.org/10.1007/978-3-319-42559-7_1

13. Karaduman, B., Challenger, M.: Model-driven development for ESP-based IoT systems. In: 2021 IEEE/ACM 3rd International Workshop on Software Engineering Research and Practices for the IoT (SERP4IoT), pp. 9–12. IEEE (2021)

14. Karaduman, B., Challenger, M., Eslampanah, R., Denil, J., Vangheluwe, H.: Analyzing WSN-based IoT systems using MDE techniques and petri-net models. In: STAF Workshops, pp. 35–46 (2020)

15. Karaduman, B., Challenger, M., Eslampanah, R., Denil, J., Vangheluwe, H.: Platform-specific modeling for riot based IoT systems. In: Proceedings of the IEEE/ACM 42nd International Conference on Software Engineering Workshops, pp. 639–646 (2020)

16. Karaduman, B., Oakes, B.J., Eslampanah, R., Denil, J., Vangheluwe, H., Challenger, M.: An architecture and reference implementation for WSN-based IoT systems. In: Emerging Trends in IoT and Integration with Data Science, Cloud Computing, and Big Data Analytics, pp. 80–103. IGI Global (2022)

17. Karaduman, B., Tezel, B.T., Challenger, M.: Towards applying fuzzy systems in intelligent agent-based CPS: a case study. In: 2021 6th International Conference on Computer Science and Engineering (UBMK), pp. 735–740. IEEE (2021)

18. Kardas, G., Demirezen, Z., Challenger, M.: Towards a DSML for semantic web enabled multi-agent systems. In: Proceedings of the International Workshop on Formalization of Modeling Languages, pp. 1–5 (2010)

19. Karimpour, N., Karaduman, B., Ural, A., Challenger, M., Dagdeviren, O.: IoT based hand hygiene compliance monitoring. In: 2019 International Symposium on Networks, Computers and Communications (ISNCC), pp. 1–6. IEEE (2019)

20. Leitao, P., Karnouskos, S., Ribeiro, L., Lee, J., Strasser, T., Colombo, A.W.: Smart agents in industrial cyber-physical systems. Proc. IEEE **104**(5), 1086–1101 (2016)

21. Marah, H.M., Eslampanah, R., Challenger, M.: DSML4TinyOS: code generation for wireless devices. In: 2nd International Workshop on Model-Driven Engineering for the Internet-of-Things (MDE4IoT), 21st International Conference on Model Driven Engineering Languages and Systems, MODELS 2018, Copenhagen, Denmark (2018)

22. Mascardi, V., et al.: Engineering multi-agent systems: state of affairs and the road ahead. ACM SIGSOFT Softw. Eng. Notes **44**(1), 18–28 (2019)

23. Miranda, T., et al.: Improving the usability of a MAS DSML. In: Weyns, D., Mascardi, V., Ricci, A. (eds.) EMAS 2018. LNCS (LNAI), vol. 11375, pp. 55–75. Springer, Cham (2019). https://doi.org/10.1007/978-3-030-25693-7_4

24. Musil, A., Musil, J., Weyns, D., Bures, T., Muccini, H., Sharaf, M.: Patterns for self-adaptation in cyber-physical systems. In: Biffl, S., Lüder, A., Gerhard, D. (eds.) Multi-Disciplinary Engineering for Cyber-Physical Production Systems, pp. 331–368. Springer, Cham (2017). https://doi.org/10.1007/978-3-319-56345-9_13

25. Özgür, L., Akram, V.K., Challenger, M., Dağdeviren, O.: An IoT based smart thermostat. In: 2018 5th International Conference on Electrical and Electronic Engineering (ICEEE), pp. 252–256. IEEE (2018)

26. Queiroz, J., Leitão, P., Barbosa, J., Oliveira, E.: Distributing intelligence among cloud, fog and edge in industrial cyber-physical systems. In: 16th International Conference on Informatics in Control, Automation and Robotics, ICINCO 2019, pp. 447–454 (2019)

27. Rosales, R., Castañón-Puga, M., Lara-Rosano, F., Evans, R.D., Osuna-Millan, N., Flores-Ortiz, M.V.: Modelling the interruption on HCI using BDI agents with the fuzzy perceptions approach: an interactive museum case study in mexico. Appl. Sci. **7**(8), 832 (2017)

28. Schoofs, E., Kisaakye, J., Karaduman, B., Challenger, M.: Software agent-based multi-robot development: a case study. In: 2021 10th Mediterranean Conference on Embedded Computing (MECO), pp. 1–8. IEEE (2021)
29. Seiger, R., Huber, S., Heisig, P., Aßmann, U.: Toward a framework for self-adaptive workflows in cyber-physical systems. Softw. Syst. Model. **18**(2), 1117–1134 (2017). https://doi.org/10.1007/s10270-017-0639-0
30. Semwal, T., Jha, S.S., Nair, S.B.: Tartarus: A multi-agent platform for bridging the gap between cyber and physical systems. In: Proceedings of the 2016 International Conference on Autonomous Agents & Multiagent Systems, pp. 1493–1495 (2016)
31. Suresh, P., Babar, A., Raj, V.V.: Uncertainty in fault tree analysis: a fuzzy approach. Fuzzy Sets Syst. **83**(2), 135–141 (1996)
32. Tekinerdogan, B., Blouin, D., Vangheluwe, H., Goulão, M., Carreira, P., Amaral, V.: Multi-Paradigm Modelling Approaches for Cyber-Physical Systems. Academic Press (2021)
33. Tcpjit, S., Horváth, I., Rusák, Z.: The state of framework development for implementing reasoning mechanisms in smart cyber-physical systems: a literature review. J. Comput. Des. Eng. **6**(4), 527–541 (2019)
34. Tezel, B.T., Challenger, M., Kardas, G.: A metamodel for Jason BDI agents. In: 5th Symposium on Languages, Applications and Technologies (SLATE 2016). Schloss Dagstuhl-Leibniz-Zentrum fuer Informatik (2016)
35. Van Acker, B., Denil, J., Vangheluwe, H., De Meulenaere, P.: Managing heterogeneity in model-based systems engineering of cyber-physical systems. In: 2015 10th International Conference on P2P, Parallel, Grid, Cloud and Internet Computing (3PGCIC), pp. 617–622. IEEE (2015)
36. Weyns, D.: Software engineering of self-adaptive systems. In: Cha, S., Taylor, R., Kang, K. (eds.) Handbook of Software Engineering, pp. 399–443. Springer, Cham (2019). https://doi.org/10.1007/978-3-030-00262-6_11
37. Yalcin, M.M., Karaduman, B., Kardas, G., Challenger, M.: An agent-based cyber-physical production system using Lego technology. In: 2021 16th Conference on Computer Science and Intelligence Systems (FedCSIS), pp. 521–531. IEEE (2021)
38. Zadeh, L.A.: Fuzzy sets. In: Zadeh, L.A. (ed.) Fuzzy Sets, Fuzzy Logic, and Fuzzy Systems: Selected Papers, pp. 394–432. World Scientific (1996)
39. Zcadally, S., Saiiislav, T., Mois, G.D.: Self-adaptation techniques in cyber-physical systems (CPSs). IEEE Access **7**, 171126–171139 (2019)

Formal Verification of a Map Merging Protocol in the Multi-agent Programming Contest

Matt Luckcuck[1]([⊠])[iD] and Rafael C. Cardoso[2][iD]

[1] Department of Computer Science, Maynooth University, Maynooth, Ireland
`matt.luckcuck@mu.ie`
[2] Department of Computer Science, The University of Manchester, Manchester, UK
`rafael.cardoso@manchester.ac.uk`

Abstract. Communication is a critical part of enabling multi-agent systems to cooperate. This means that applying formal methods to protocols governing communication within multi-agent systems provides useful confidence in its reliability. In this paper, we describe the formal verification of a complex communication protocol that coordinates agents merging maps of their environment. The protocol was used by the LFC team in the 2019 edition of the Multi-Agent Programming Contest (MAPC). Our specification of the protocol is written in Communicating Sequential Processes (CSP), which is a well-suited approach to specifying agent communication protocols due to its focus on concurrent communicating systems. We validate the specification's behaviour using scenarios where the correct behaviour is known, and verify that eventually all the maps have merged.

Keywords: Multi-Agent Programming Contest · Communicating Sequential Processes · Formal Verification · Agents Assemble · JaCaMo

1 Introduction

The Multi-Agent Programming Contest[1] (MAPC) is an annual challenge to foster the development and research in multi-agent programming. Every couple of years a new challenge scenario is proposed, otherwise, some additions and extensions are made to make the scenario from the previous year more challenging.

The 2019 edition of MAPC [1] introduced the Agents Assemble scenario, where two teams of multiple agents compete to assemble complex block structures. Agents have incomplete information about their grid map environment.

---

[1] https://multiagentcontest.org/

Work supported by UK Research and Innovation, and EPSRC Hubs for "Robotics and AI in Hazardous Environments": EP/R026092 (FAIR-SPACE), EP/R026173 (ORCA), and EP/R026084 (RAIN). The formal specification work was mostly done while the first author was employed by the University of Manchester, UK.

N. Alechina et al. (Eds.): EMAS 2021, LNAI 13190, pp. 198–217, 2022.
https://doi.org/10.1007/978-3-030-97457-2_12

They are only able to perceive what is inside their limited range of vision. Therefore, building a map of the team's environment must be done individually at the start; each agent believes its starting position is (0,0), and the agents merge their maps when they meet, adjusting the coordinates accordingly.

This paper describes the formal specification and verification of the map merge protocol that was used by the winning team from MAPC 2019, the Liverpool Formidable Constructors (LFC) [8]. One of the major challenges in the MAPC is making sure all critical parts of the team work reliably. Without a coherent map, the agents cannot coordinate to assemble the block structures, so the map merge protocol is critical to the team's mission. The complexity of the different challenges in the scenario, as well as the presence of another interfering team, can cause unforeseen problems. Before MAPC 2019 the LFC team had limited time to perform tests to validate the code, which due to its complexity meant that it was very hard to efficiently prevent or detect bugs.

In this paper we build a formal specification of the map merge protocol from its implementation and previous description in [8], and formally verify the specification to provide evidence of the protocol's reliability. Our specification is written in the process algebra Communicating Sequential Processes (CSP) [16], which is designed for specifying concurrent communicating systems. We view each agent in the system as a process, which is communicating with the other agents (processes) to achieve the system's overall behaviour.

To verify properties about our specification we use model checking, which can automatically and exhaustive check the state space for a formal model for satisfaction of a given property. If a property is violated, a model checker usually gives a counterexample, which can aid debugging. In CSP, model checking uses the idea of *refinement*. If we have two specifications P and Q, then P is refined by Q ($P \sqsubseteq Q$) if every behaviour of Q is also a behaviour of P. This can be thought of as Q implementing P, like a software component implementing an interface. We use the CSP model checker Failures-Divergences Refinement (FDR) [14] to show that the system behaves according to some required properties. This can be thought of as checking that the system *correctly* implements an interface.

The work presented in this paper is motivated in two directions. First, the verification provides extra confidence that the protocol works. The protocol was difficult to test because of the dynamic environment and the amount of agent communication, but model checking is a useful approach to finding corner cases. Second, the MAPC provides an interesting example application to explore the utility of CSP for modelling this kind of problem. This is of lesser importance than the first motivation, but useful nonetheless.

The rest of this paper is organised as follows. A brief background on JaCaMo (the language the agent system is developed in) and CSP is presented in the next section, Sect. 2. Section 3 describes how we used CSP to specify and verify the map merge protocol used by the LFC team in the MAPC 2019. It contains a detailed description of how the protocol works (Sect. 3.1), the CSP specification of the protocol (Sect. 3.2), and how the specification was validated and verified (Sect. 3.3). The related work is discussed in Sect. 4, with a variety of similar approaches that have been applied to the specification and verification of multi-agent systems. Finally, Sect. 5 presents our concluding remarks.

2   Background

The LFC team uses the JaCaMo multi-agent programming platform to develop their agents for the MAPC 2019. In this section we briefly explain JaCaMo and highlight the relevant parts that were used in the map merging protocol (Sect. 2.1). We also give an overview of CSP and the notation used throughout the paper, and introduce model checking (Sect. 2.2).

2.1   JaCaMo

JaCaMo[2] [4, 5] is a multi-agent development platform that combines three dimensions that are often found in agent systems (agent, environment, and organisation), and provides first-class abstractions that enable a developer to program these dimensions in unison. JaCaMo is a combination of three different technologies that were developed separately and then linked together: the Jason [6] Belief-Desire-Intention (BDI) [25] agent programming language for the agent dimension, CArtAgO [26] for programming environments using artefacts, and Moise [19] for the specification of organisation of agents. An additional first-class abstraction has been developed that provides an interaction dimension for JaCaMo in [32], but this is not yet fully integrated.

The merge protocol as implemented by LFC [8] is comprised of message passing between agents and updating information. The agent communication is implemented solely in Jason, while some of the information updates are done in a shared artefact (called the *TeamArtifact*). In this paper we focus on the communication, which is the critical part of the protocol.

In Jason, communication between agents is based on speech-act theory, where agents send a performative such as *tell* (sends a belief to an agent, causing a belief addition event) or *achieve* (sends a goal to an agent, causing a goal addition event). The formal semantics of speech-act theory for Jason can be found in [29].

2.2   CSP

CSP is a formal language for specifying the behaviour of concurrent communicating systems. We use the FDR [14] model checker to both manually and automatically check specifications. Manual checks use FDR's Probe tool, which enables a user to step through the system's behaviour. Automatic checks are written as assertions.

A CSP specification is built from (optionally parameterised) processes. A process describes behaviour as a sequence of *events*; for example, $a \rightarrow b \rightarrow Skip$ is the process where the events a and b happen sequentially, followed by *Skip* which is the terminating process. An event[3] is a communication on a *channel*. Channels enable message-passing between processes, but a process can perform

---

[2] http://jacamo.sourceforge.net/.

[3] Note that events in CSP are different from Jason BDI events, the former are communication events while the latter are plan triggering events.

Table 1. Summary of CSP operators used in this paper.

Action	Syntax	Description
Skip	*Skip*	The terminating process
Simple Prefix	$a \rightarrow Skip$	Simple synchronisation on a with no data, followed by *Skip*
Input Event	$a?in$	Synchronisation that binds a the input value to *in*
Output Event	$b!out$	Synchronisation outputting the value of *out*
Parameter Event	$c.value$	Synchronisation matching the given *value*
Sequence	$P ; Q$	Executes processes P then Q in sequence
External Choice	$P \square Q$	Offers a choice between two processes P and Q
Replicated External Choice	$\square\, x : Set \bullet P(x)$	Offers an external choice of the process $P(x)$ with every value x in the set *Set*
Parallelism	$P \,[\![\, chan \,]\!]\, Q$	P and Q run in parallel, synchronising on the channels in *chan*
Parallelism	$P \,[\![\, pChan \mid qChan \,]\!]\, Q$	P and Q run in parallel, synchronising on the channels common to the sets *pChan* and *qChan*
Interleaving	$P \,[\![\!]\!]\, Q$	P and Q run in parallel with no synchronisation
Replicated Interleaving	$[\![\!]\!]\, x : Set \bullet P(x)$	Interleaves a copy of the process $P(x)$ for every value x in the set *Set*

an event (communicate the event on the channel) even if there is no other process to receive the event. Where two processes agree to perform a set of events in parallel (*synchronise* on a set of events) both processes must perform the event(s) synchronously.

By convention CSP process names are written in upper-case, and channels or events in lower-case. A CSP process is often composed of several 'subprocesses', which is the term we use to refer to other processes called by a process. Here, a subprocess helps to structure the specification and encapsulate behaviour, similarly to an object and its methods. We adopt the convention of using a double underscore to separate a process name from the 'main' process to which it belongs (e.g., *MAIN_PROCESS__SUBPROCESS*). Below, we describe the CSP operators used in this paper, which are also summarised in Table 1.

Channels may declare typed parameters. If a channel is untyped, then we get 'simple' events like a and b from the above example; the events of a typed channel must contain parameters matching those types. For example, if channel c takes one integer parameter, then an event might be $c\,.\,42$. Parameters may be inputs ($c?in$), outputs ($c!out$), or match a given value ($c.value$). Inputs can be restricted ($c?p : set$) to only accept a parameter (p) that is the given *set* (here, a set of integers). Processes can occur in sequence; for example, P ; Q describes a process where process P runs, then process Q.

A choice of processes can be offered; for example $P \;\square\; Q$ offers the choice of either P or Q, once one process is picked the other becomes unavailable. Processes can also run in parallel. CSP provides three parallel operators; in $P \,\|[\, chan \,]\| \, Q$, processes P and Q run in parallel, and agree to communicate on the channels in the set *chan*; in $P \;\|[\, pChan \,|\, qChan \,]\|\; Q$, processes P and Q run in parallel, and agree to communicate on the channels common to the *pChan* and *qChan* sets; and in $P \;\|\|\|\; Q$, the processes P and Q run at the same time with no synchronisation.

CSP does not have variables, so if a specification needs a variable that will be accessed by several processes, a 'state process' is often used. This is where a process is used to store, and control access to, some values. The values are stored as process parameters and channels are provided to get and set the values. Other processes communicate with the state process using these get and set channels. While this requires more channels and internal communication, it can lead to cleaner communication between the processes that need to use the variable(s).

3   Specification and Verification of the Map Merge Protocol

The map merge protocol played a major role in LFC's victory[4] [8] in MAPC 2019. It overcomes one of the main challenges that has to be solved before trying to assemble structures and deliver tasks. Even though LFC won, there were many failures during the matches due to limited testing and no formal verification prior to the contest. Although the origin of most of the failures is still unknown, we aim to provide confidence about the reliability of the map merge protocol.

In this paper we specify and verify the map merge protocol as used by LFC [8]. Section 3.1 describes the protocol, in particular the communication between the agents. Then, Sect. 3.2 presents our CSP specification of the protocol and describes how it models two agents merging their maps. Finally, Sect. 3.3 discusses the validation and verification of the specification using the FDR model checker.

3.1   Map Merge Protocol

The communication in the map merge protocol consists of message passing between a group of agents, triggering plans that reason about the message received and send the required reply if applicable. Figure 1 shows an overview

---

[4] Source code of the team is available at (the main plans for the map merge protocol are located in "src/agt/strategy/identification.asl"): https://github.com/autonomy-and-verification-uol/mapc2019-liv.

of the protocol. At the start of the simulation, every agent has its own map (referred to as being the *leader* of its own map, or being a *map leader*). As the simulation progresses, agents meet each other and merge their maps. Each map leader coordinates a map for itself and any other agents whose maps it has merged with. This means that there can be a minimum of two and a maximum of four agents directly involved in one instance of the merge protocol. For example, only two agents will be involved if both agents are the leaders of their own map.

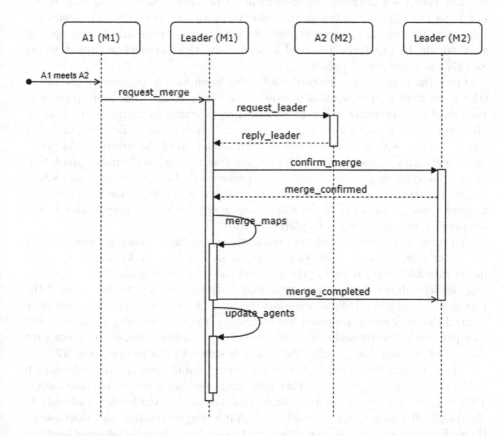

Fig. 1. UML Sequence diagram for the map merge protocol. `A1` represents Agent1 with a map `M1`, `A2` is Agent2 with a map `M2`. The solid arrow heads represent synchronous messages, open arrow heads asynchronous messages, dashed lines represent reply messages, and rectangles represent processes [8].

Each agent has a name, or ID; in Fig. 1 we use `A1` and `A2`. Because of the (intentionally challenging) communications restrictions of the MAPC, when agents meet they do not know each other's ID, so they cannot directly communicate. Therefore, before agents can exchange useful information about their maps, some kind of *identification* process is needed. In LFC's strategy for identification, when one agent sees another it sends a broadcast to all the agents in its team requesting information about what they can see around them. Upon receipt of all of the replies, the agent that sent the request will compare the replies to what it can see, to try to identify the agents that it has met. The specifics of LFC's identification strategy can be found in [8].

The merge protocol starts as part of the identification strategy, after one agent successfully identifies another. The identification process is reflexive but asynchronous. For example, if A1 identifies A2, then A2 will (eventually) identify A1; but they each perform the identification process separately, so they might not both identify each other at the same time. In this example each agent will then start its own merge process, but as we will see later on only one merge will go through. In Fig. 1 the protocol is seen from A1's perspective, but it works exactly the same for all agents.

Once the map merge protocol starts, the agent that is requesting the merge (the *requesting agent*) sends a message to its map leader (now, the *requesting map leader*) containing a list of agents that it wants to merge with, that is, all agents that it has successfully identified. Requests are dealt with one at a time, so each request constitutes a new instantiation of the protocol. As previously mentioned, messages in Jason trigger events which will enable plans that match the triggering event to be viable for selection[5]. The requesting agent's map leader will start the plan that handles the request to merge, when it receives the `request_merge` message; if the requesting agent is its own map leader it will simply trigger the appropriate plan internally.

To proceed with the merge the requesting map leader must get the name of the *other* agent's map leader (for example, in Fig. 1 agent A1 wants to merge maps with A2). After receiving the name of the other map leader, the requesting map leader will use a priority order among both map leaders to determine if the merge will continue. This is necessary because the other agent may also have started the map merge process , however, only one of these merges can proceed. The priority is determined using the number in the agent's name, the agent with the lowest number has priority. For example agent A1 has priority over A2.

After the priority check, if the merge is continuing then the requesting map leader sends a message to the other map leader asking it to confirm the merge. This is necessary because it is possible that the other map leader is already in the middle of a merge, which could result in it losing its position as a map leader. If this happens and the original merge continues, then the map information from this merge will be wrong. Thus, if the other map leader is no longer the leader of that map it will send a reply cancelling the merge. Another attempt to merge these two maps can be made in the next step.

The plans for both leaders are atomic, so concurrent intentions are not in effect (normally in Jason agents alternate between their intentions). This means that leaders are not able to start multiple merge processes simultaneously, nor can they enter a deadlock waiting for information indefinitely (we assume that eventually all agents reply).

---

[5] A plan still has to succeed its context check (i.e., meet its preconditions) before being selected for execution.

If the merge is confirmed, then the map information (such as the coordinates of points of interest in the MAPC scenario) is updated. Finally, a message is sent to the other map leader letting it know that the merge has been completed, and thus releasing the lock from the atomic plan that it was in. A final update is made to the list of agents that are part of the new merged map, which is sent to each agent in the list.

In summary, the main goal and requirements of the map merge protocol are:

GOAL: If agent $A1$ merges its map with agent $A2$, $A1$'s map leader will be the map leader for $A1$, $A2$, and any agents that either of them shared their map with before the merge.

REQ1: The map leader of $A1$ has priority over the map leader of $A2$, otherwise $A1$ should cancel the merge.

REQ2: If $A2$'s map leader loses control of its map by the time it processes the request to merge from $A1$'s map leader, it will cancel the merge.

In the next section we describe how we model the map merge protocol, while Sect. 3.3 describes how we verify that the protocol preserves these properties.

3.2 CSP Specification

Our CSP specification[6] was built by one person, part-time over the course of about 12 months. The specification was built by manually interpreting and translating the English-language description of the protocol [8] and the Jason implementation. The specification is ~440 lines in total, though this includes comments. Despite the small number of lines, the specification contains 1,597,190 states and 6,334,936 transitions[7].

In the specification of the map merge protocol, each agent is modelled by an $AGENT$ process, if the agent is a map leader then it will also be represented by a MAP_LEADER process. As mentioned in Sect. 3.1, at the start of a match each agent is also its own map leader, so each agent will begin as a cooperating pair of $AGENT$ and MAP_LEADER processes The 'main' processes, $AGENT$ and MAP_LEADER, are decomposed into subprocesses that structure the specification and encapsulate behaviour. We remind the reader that we use a double underscore to separate a subprocess name from the 'main' process to which it belongs. For example, the subprocess named $MAP\_LEADER\_\_REQUEST\_MERGE$ is the $REQUEST\_MERGE$ processes which belongs to the MAP_LEADER process.

Our specification only uses three agents. This was a conscious choice to keep the specification's state space small, while still enabling us to check that a pair of agents can merge their maps in the presence of an interfering agent. We define $AgentName$, the set of all the agent IDs as:

$$datatype\ AgentName = A1 \mid A2 \mid A3$$

---

[6] The CSP files are available at: https://doi.org/10.5281/zenodo.4624507.
[7] Reported states from a check for freedom from non-determinism using FDR 4.2.7.

The top-level process of our specification is a parallel composition ($\|[\,chan\,]\|$) of all the *AGENT* and *MAP_LEADER* processes. This takes the form:

$$LFC = AGENTS \,\|[\,interface\,]\|\, MAP\_LEADERS$$

where *AGENTS* is an interleaving ($\|\|\|$) of an *AGENT* process for each ID in *AgentName*; and *MAP_LEADERS* is a parallel composition of a *MAP_LEADER* process for each ID in *AgentName*, so the map leaders can communicate. In this top-level process, the *AGENT* and *MAP_LEADER* processes agree to synchronise (cooperate) on any events in the set of events *interface*.

MAP_LEADERS composes the *MAP_LEADER* processes in a way that allows them to synchronise on some events, because they communicate to control the map merge. But *AGENTS* simply interleaves the *AGENT* processes because they do not need to communicate for the merge protocol. Other behaviours require agents to communicate, but this is abstracted away in our specification.

The IDs in *AgentName* (for example *A1*) are used to synchronise communications between a *MAP_LEADER* and the *AGENT* processes that it coordinates, and between it and other *MAP_LEADER* processes. The messages in Fig. 1 are represented in our specification by CSP channels. The processes in the specification also make use of other internal channels to describe the required behaviour.

As mentioned in Sect. 3.1, a map merge happens between two agents and their respective map leaders (note that an agent may be its own map leader). Unlike the description in Sect. 3.1, there will *always* be four processes involved in a map merge in our specification: two *AGENT* processes and two *MAP_LEADER* processes. This is because we model the behaviours common to all agents separately from the behaviours specific to a map leader. As in Sect. 3.1, we refer to the agent that requests the merge and its map leader as the 'requesting agent' and the 'requesting map leader', respectively.

We use the example from Fig. 1 to describe how our model captures the scenario. We have split this into three phases:

1. **Requesting Merge and Leader:** initial communication to obtain information that will be used during the map merge and used to check the viability of the merge;
2. **Confirming Merge:** use the information obtained in the previous phase to determine if the merge can proceed or if it should be cancelled;
3. **Merge and Update:** perform the map merge and update all agents involved.

As in Fig. 1, agent *A1* is requesting that agent *A2* merges maps with it, and both agents are their own map leader. Because we do not include the maps themselves in our specification, we do not use the map IDs (*M1* and *M2*).

Phase 1: Requesting Merge and Leader

In the first phase of the protocol, an agent sends a request to its map leader to merge with one or more other agents, then the map leader requests the name (ID) of the mad leader of each of the agents it has been requested to merge with. When one of the other agents replies, the requesting map leader begins negotiating the map merge with the other map leader.

$$MAP\_LEADER\_REQUEST\_MERGE(Me, AgentSet) =$$
$$MAP\_LEADER\_HANDLE\_REQUEST\_MERGE(Me, AgentSet)$$
$$|[\{|\ beginMerge\ |\}]|$$
$$MAP\_LEADER\_BEGIN\_MERGE(Me, AgentSet)$$

Fig. 2. Excerpt from *MAP_LEADER__REQUEST_MERGE* showing the parallel composition of *MAP_LEADER__HANDLE_REQUEST_MERGE*, which handles requests to merge; and *MAP_LEADER__BEGIN_MERGE*, which allows the map leader to begin a merge. The processes synchronise on the *beginMerge* event. *Me* is the ID of the *MAP_LEADER* process, and *AgentSet* is the set of agents this map leader is coordinating.

In our example, $A1$'s *AGENT* process sends a message to its map leader (which is itself) requesting that it merges with $A2$. This is represented by an event on the channel *request_merge*, which is sent from the *AGENT*($A1$) process to the *MAP_LEADER*($A1$) process and triggers the *MAP_LEADER* to start its map merging process. In the *requesting MAP_LEADER*, this is handled by the *MAP_LEADER__REQUEST_MERGE* process, part of which is shown in Fig. 2

The *MAP_LEADER__HANDLE_REQUEST_MERGE* process listens for *request_merge* events from any agent it currently coordinates (any agent in its *AgentSet*). The *request_merge* event contains a parameter *mergeSet*, which is the set of agents that the map leader should try to merge with. In our example, *merge_set* only contains $A2$, but it can contain the IDs of any agents that are not in the *AgentSet* of the requesting map leader (as explained in Sect. 3.1).

When a *request_merge* event is received, the *beginMerge* event is used to start the merge. This is an event introduced purely for our specification. The *MAP_LEADER__BEGIN_MERGE* process sends *request_leader* events to each agent in the *mergeSet* and waits for a *reply_leader* event from one of these agents, acting on the first of these events to arrive. The *reply_leader* event contains a parameter that is the ID of the agent's map leader. In our example, $A2$ sends the reply that its map leader is $A2$.

The *MAP_LEADER__BEGIN_MERGE* process, triggered by $A1$ receiving the *reply_leader* event from $A2$, checks if the map leader for $A1$ has priority over the map leader for $A2$. As mentioned in Sect. 3.1, the agent with the lowest ID number takes priority, so $A1$ has priority over $A2$, which has priority over $A3$. If the requesting map leader does not have priority, then the map merge attempt ends here. In our example, the map leader is the same as the requesting agent, $A1$, and $A1$ does have priority over $A2$ (the other map leader), so it moves on to confirming the merge with the other *MAP_LEADER* process.

Phase 2: Confirming Merge
The requesting map leader asks the other map leader to confirm that the merge can proceed. As explained in Sect. 3.1, this allows a map leader to cancel a merge

$MAP\_LEADER\_CONFIRMING\_MERGE$
$(Me, RequestingAgent, OtherAgent, OtherMapLeader, AgentSet) =$
$confirm\_merge.Me.OtherMapLeader \rightarrow$
$($
    $merge\_cancelled.Me.OtherMapLeader \rightarrow$
    $remove\_reasoning\_about.RequestingAgent.OtherAgent \rightarrow Skip$
$)$
$\Box$
$($
    $merge\_confirmed.Me.OtherMapLeader?otherAgentSet \rightarrow$
    $MAP\_LEADER\_MERGE\_MAPS$
        $(Me, AgentSet, OtherMapLeader, otherAgentSet);$
    $MAP\_LEADER\_UPDATE\_AGENTS$
        $(Me, AgentSet, OtherMapLeader, otherAgentSet)$
$)$

Fig. 3. Excerpt from $MAP\_LEADER\_CONFIRMING\_MERGE$, which handles the requesting map leader confirming the merge with the other map leader. The parameter *Me* is the ID of the MAP_LEADER process, *RequestingAgent* is the ID of the agent that requested the merge, *OtherAgent* is the agent the *RequestingAgent* wanted to merge with, *OtherMapLeader* is the ID of the other map leader (the leader of *OtherAgent*'s map), and the *AgentSet* is the set of agents that this map leader is coordinating.

request if it has completed a (concurrent) merge with a different map leader. In our example, the requesting map leader is $A1$ and the other map leader is $A2$.

The requesting MAP_LEADER ($A1$) handles this phase using the process $MAP\_LEADER\_CONFIRMING\_MERGE$ (excerpt in Fig. 3). The first event in this process, $confirm\_merge.Me.OtherMapLeader$, is a request from map leader $A1$ (here, the value of *Me*) to map leader $A2$ (here, the value of *OtherMapLeader*), to confirm that the merge can go ahead. As we can see from Fig. 3, the other map leader ($A2$) can reply with either *merge_cancelled* or *merge_confirmed*.

When the map leader $A2$ receives the *confirm_merge* event, it 'considers' the eligibility of the merge. If it is no longer a map leader, it replies *merge_cancelled*, and the merge process will terminate after replying to any pending *confirm_merge* events. The *merge_confirmed* event signals that the merge can continue. Either of these events passes control back to the requesting map leader ($A1$), which will: $SKIP$ (terminate) if the reply was *merge_cancelled*; or move on with the merge and update step if the reply was *merge_confirmed*.

Phase 3: Merge and Update
This phase is split into two stages: merging the maps, and updating the agents. First, the requesting map leader uses the $MAP\_LEADER\_MERGE\_MAPS$ process, shown in Fig. 4, to merge the maps. The process is triggered by the *merge_confirmed* event, as shown in Fig. 3.

$MAP\_LEADER\_MERGE\_MAPS(Me, MyAgentSet, otherMap, OtherAgentSet) =$
  $merge\_maps.Me.otherMap \rightarrow$
  $update\_agentSet.Me!OtherAgentSet \rightarrow$
  $merge\_completed.Me.otherMap.union(MyAgentSet, OtherAgentSet) \rightarrow$
  $SKIP$

Fig. 4. The $MAP\_LEADER\_MERGE\_MAPS$, which controls the merging of maps between two map leaders (abstracted to the $merge\_maps$ event. Me is the ID of the MAP_LEADER process and $MyAgentSet$ is its agent set. Similarly, $otherMap$ is the ID of the other MAP_LEADER process and $OtherAgentSet$ is its agent set.

Since the map is not captured in our specification, merging the maps is abstracted to the event $merge\_maps$. The requesting MAP_LEADER updates the $AgentSet$ (the set of agents it coordinates). It then tells the other map leader that the merge is completed, using the $merge\_completed$ event, which also sends the union of the two agent sets.

After the $merge\_completed$ event, control returns to the $MAP\_LEADER\_CONFIRMING\_MERGE$ process (Fig. 3), which calls the $MAP\_LEADER\_UPDATE\_AGENTS$ process to update all the agents in its new $AgentSet$. This involves a sequence of communications between the requesting map leader and each $AGENT$ in the new $AgentSet$.

This phase closely corresponds to the description in [8], summarised as follows:

1. **Build new list of identified agents:** in our specification, this is simply the union of the requesting and other map leader's $AgentSets$.
2. **Send update to the leader of** $M2$ $(A2)$**:** as shown in Fig. 4, the $merge\_completed.Me.otherMap.union(MyAgentSet, OtherAgentSet)$ event sends the new (merged) $AgentSet$ to the other map leader.
3. **Send update to all agents of** $M1$ $(A1)$**:** here a recursive process sends $update\_identified\_same\_group$ to each agent in the agent set of the requesting map leader $(A1)$. This event passes the new $AgentSet$ to each of these agents.
4. **Send update to all agents of** $M2$ $(A2)$**:** here a recursive process sends $update\_identified$ to each agent in the $AgentSet$ of the other map leader. This event passes the new agent set to each of these agents and is also used to update each agent's map leader to the requesting map leader, $A1$.

After the updates are completed, the requesting map leader recurses back to the $MAP\_LEADER\_REQUEST\_MERGE$ process (Fig. 2) ready to begin another merge. If there are no more agents to merge with from this request, it waits for the next merge request. The other map leader process no longer represents an agent that is a map leader, so it will only reply $merge\_cancelled$ if it is asked to merge. This handles requests to merge that may already be in progress.

Table 2. Summary of the verification (Scenarios 1–5) and validation (*done* reachable) assertions applied to the map merge protocol. The requirement, or goal, that each assertion covers is presented in brackets.

Name	Type	Description
Scenario 1 (REQ1)	has trace	$A1$ merging with $A2$, $A1$ has priority, $A2$ merges into $A1$
Scenario 2 (REQ2)	has trace	$A1$ merging with $A2$, but $A2$ cancels the merge
Scenario 3 (REQ1)	has trace	$A2$ merging with $A1$, denied because $A2$ does not have priority
Scenario 4a (REQ1)	has trace	$A2$ requests a merge with $A3$, then $A1$ requests a merge with $A3$. $A1$ merges with $A3$ first, then $A3$ replies that its Map Leader is now $A1$. $A2$ now tries to merge with $A1$, which is denied because $A2$ does not have priority
Scenario 4b (REQ2)	has trace	$A2$ requests a merge with $A3$, then $A1$ requests a merge with $A3$. $A1$ merges with $A3$ first, then $A3$ replies that its Map Leader is still $A3$. $A2$ tries to merge with $A3$, which is cancelled because $A3$ is not a Map Leader any more
Scenario 5 (REQ1)	has trace	$A1$ merges with $A2$, then $A3$ tries to merge with $A2$, which replies that its Map Leader is now $A1$. $A2$ tries to merge with $A1$, which is denied because $A3$ does not have priority
done Reachable (GOAL)	refinement	Can the *LFC* process reach the state where any of the agents can call *done* (showing that it is coordinating all the agents)

3.3   Specification Validation and Verification

After specifying the map merge protocol, we validate that it performs the protocol's required behaviour and then verify that all the maps are eventually merged. The validation step is used to check that the specification conforms with the protocol's implementation. The verification step is used to check that the specification is correct. For both of these steps, we use the assertions and in-built tools of the CSP model checker, FDR. The assertions are described in Table 2 and the time that FDR took to check the assertions is summarised in Table 3.

Validation. For the validation step, first we used FDR's Probe tool to manually step through the model one event at a time. This was useful when debugging the specification, especially after adding or updating behaviour. For more substantial verification, we also checked how the agents behaviour in six different scenarios (see Table 2). These scenarios were based on the implementation's behaviour in LFC's matches during MAPC 2019, so the correct behaviour is known. The specification was checked to see that it would perform each of the scenarios correctly, showing that it corresponds to the implemented protocol.

The scenarios were developed alongside the specification, and were useful for checking that it continued to meet the requirements while behaviour was being added. Hence, Scenarios 1 to 3 describe the requirements of a pair of agents; while Scenarios 4a, 4b, and 5 check the requirements with the interference of a third agent; mirroring the specification's development. Scenario 1 is the example in Fig. 1, where agent $A1$ meets agent $A2$ and requests they merge maps, $A1$ has priority so $A2$'s map is merged into $A1$'s; and Scenario 2 shows $A2$ cancelling the merge instead. Scenario 3 is $A2$ trying to merge with $A1$ and not having the priority to do so. Scenarios 4a and 4b check the two situations that can occur when an agent stops being a Map Leader after a third agents has started merging with it. Finally, Scenario 5 checks the combination of an agent that stops being a Map Leader and an agent that doesn't have priority for a merge.

While the six scenarios are not an exhaustive list, they cover both of the protocol's requirements (Sect. 3.1). REQ1, that the merge will be denied if the requesting map leader does not have priority, is checked by Scenarios 1 and 3 (for two agents) and Scenarios 4a and 5 (for three agents). REQ2, that an agent will cancel a merge if it loses control if its map, is checked by Scenario 2 (for two agents) and Scenario 4b (for three agents). The GOAL is checked by the *done* reachable assertion, described below alongside the other verification checks.

Each scenario is described as a trace of the relevant events in the scenario. We used FDR's in-built [*has trace*] check, to explore the model's state space to see if it can perform the scenario trace (though this does not show that it will *always* perform the scenario trace). In the assertion check we hide all the events that are not in the scenario trace. This takes the form:

$$assert\ LFC \setminus (diff(Events, trace\_events)) : [has\ trace];\ <\ trace\_events\ >$$

where LFC is the specification's top-level process, $Events$ is the set of all events, and $trace\_events$ is a sequence of events. The $diff()$ function in the hiding operator $\setminus(diff(Events, trace\_events))$ hides only the events not in $trace\_events$.

The [*has trace*] checks act like tests of the specification. They are run automatically by FDR, so they are easily repeatable They also provide useful regression tests, which ensures that a change to the specification during this validation and debugging step has not introduced a bug somewhere else.

Verification. For verification, we use FDR's in-built assertions to show (by exhaustive model checking) that our specification of the merge protocol is free from divergence and non-determinism. Divergence (livelock) is where the specification performs infinity many internal events, refusing to offer events to the environment. Non-determinism is where the specification may perform several different events, after a given prefix.

Finally, we check that the specification can reach a state where all the maps have merged. To get to this state shows that the specification performs the correct behaviour and that it does not deadlock before reaching the 'done' state. If the specification reaches this state, it shows that the GOAL and requirements REQ1 and REQ2 are obeyed by the specification. This check required the addition of the *if ... else ...* construct to the MAP_LEADER process (shown in Fig. 5) which is not part of the map merge protocol. The check happens inside the $MAP\_LEADER\_REQUEST\_MERGE$ subprocess, after a merge has been either confirmed or cancelled. The event $get\_agentSet$ retrieves the agent set

get_agentSet.Me? gotAgentSet →
if gotAgentSet == AgentNamethen
    done.Me → terminate.Me → SKIP
else
    MAP_LEADER_REQUEST_MERGE(Me, gotAgentSet)

Fig. 5. Excerpt from *MAP_LEADER_REQUEST_MERGE*, checking that all the maps have merged. This follows on from the excerpt in Fig. 2.

(the set of agents that this Map Leader is coordinating) from the map leader's internal state process; which is named *gotAgentSet* here, to avoid a name clash.

The *gotAgentSet* is compared to the set of all agent IDs (*AgentName*), using an *if ... then ... else ...* construction that is not part of CSP but is available in the input language of FDR. If the sets are equal (meaning that this *MAP_LEADER* is now coordinating all the agents) then the process synchronises on the *done* event. In our specification, the *done* event can happen after a minimum of two successful map merges (agent $A1$ merging with agents $A2$ and $A3$ in either order) but there could be more, depending on the interleaving of events. This means that the *done* event represents several successful instances of the protocol, each of which must have obeyed the GOAL and requirements REQ1 and REQ2. We can also see in Fig. 5 that after *done*, the *MAP_LEADER* waits for the *terminate* event, which tells it to terminate. This is also only part of our specification, not a part of the merge protocol.

To check if the state where a *MAP_LEADER* can call *done* is reachable, we use the following assertion:

$$\text{assert } LFC \setminus (\text{diff}(Events, \{| \ done \ |\}))[FD =$$
$$\square \ agent : AgentName \bullet done.agent \to SKIP$$

which checks if the specification (*LFC*) is refined by ([$FD =$) the process that offers the external choice ($\square$) of any *MAP_LEADER* calling *done*. Again, we use $\setminus(\text{diff}(Events, \{| \ done \ |\}))$ to hide all the events in *LFC* other than *done*, because it is the only event pertinent to this check. Here, the *replicated* external choice (see Table 1) offers the *done* event with each ID *agent* in the set of all agent IDs, *AgentName*. The particular refinement check used here (in CSP's *failures-divergences* model) means that the *LFC* processes cannot refuse the *done* event (as this would be a *failure*) and it cannot diverge. As previously mentioned, this shows that *LFC* does not deadlock before the *done* event occurs.

Discussion. Table 3 shows a summary of the times (in seconds) taken to complete the *has trace* checks on each scenario trace, the divergence and non-determinism checks, and the check that the *done* event is reachable. These results are from using FDR 4.2.7, on a PC using Ubuntu 20.04.2, with an Intel Core i5-3470 3.20 GHz × 4 CPU, and 8 GB of RAM. The table reports the compilation time, which is how long it took FDR to build its internal representation of the

Table 3. Summary of times (in seconds) taken to check each scenario trace (*has trace*), divergence, non-determinism, and that the *Done* event is reachable. The times shown are for a single run using FDR 4.2.7, showing how long it took to compile and check each assertion. The total time is the sum of the compilation and checking time.

Name	Compiled (s)	Checked (s)	Total (s)
Scenario 1	0.84	0.15	0.99
Scenario 2	0.89	0.10	0.99
Scenario 3	0.89	0.10	0.99
Scenario 4a	0.94	0.08	1.02
Scenario 4b	0.95	0.06	1.01
Scenario 5	0.86	0.10	0.96
Divergence	0.71	2.41	3.12
Non-Determinism	6.19	2.69	8.88
done Reachable	4.72	0.02	4.74

specification; checking time, which is how long it took FDR to actually check the assertion; and the total time, which is simply the sum of the previous two times.

The total times for these verification and validation checks were small enough to not be a barrier to quick re-checking of the properties after updates to the specification. The scenario traces provided quick regression tests, each being checked in ~1s. Even the longest of the three exhaustive checks (non-determinism) was still relatively fast, at only 8.88s in total.

As mentioned in Sect. 3.2, our model only uses three agents, which helps keep the state space of the specification small. To provide a comparison, we added a fourth agent to *AgentName* (the set of all agent IDs, mentioned in Sect. 3.2):

$$datatype AgentName = A1 \mid A2 \mid A3 \mid A4$$

The model was not *specifically* designed for more than three agents, but it adapts to the number of agent IDs (for example, it runs one *AGENT* process for each ID in *AgentName*). Then, we rechecked the scenario traces in FDR. For three agents they each took ~1s (Table 3); for four agents they took between 89s and ~107s longer, an average increase of 9788.94% (97.20s). We did not compare the times for the exhaustive checks because they used used all the RAM on the test PC, which will artificially increase the checking time. If we add more agents to the model, other elements may need to be altered to reduce the state space. However, this is left for future work.

4   Related Work

A recent survey [3] identified that the main validation and verification approaches being applied to agent systems are: model checking, theorem proving, runtime verification, and testing. Testing has been shown to be less effective in the validation and verification of BDI-based agent systems when compared to traditional procedural programs, encouraging the use of formal methods [30].

Various other approaches for model checking multi-agent systems exist in the literature. MCMAS [22] and MCK [18] are two symbolic model checkers for agent systems, and AJPF [10] is a *program* model checker for agents written in the Gwendolen [9] language. Runtime verification has also been used to verify agent interaction protocols specified as trace expressions in [13].

However, these approaches work best when applied top-down, and to the whole system. The LFC system was already implemented in JaCaMo, which has been used by several winning teams in past editions of the contest. Our goal in this work was to verify a specific part of the system; the map merge protocol. Both of these things contributed to our exploration of using a CSP specification of the protocol. However, this does not preclude its integration with other types of formal methods applied to the LFC system, which can provide greater confidence in the correctness of the system (as well as guiding the development of new functions) [12].

CSP has been used in other approaches for multi-agent systems. Examples include an approach that combines a CSP encoding of agent communications with a first-order logic framework [20]; a CSP framework for a Java-based "cognitive agent architecture" called Cougar [15], where the model is used to verify properties about the code generated from the Cougar system; and a timed CSP model of a multi-agent manufacturing system [31]. However, each of these approaches is (like ours) specific to its example application.

Another approach [21] for multi-agent systems that involves CSP presents a translation from CSP-Z (a combination of CSP and Z [27]) to Promela, the input language of the SPIN [17] model checker. This translation appears to be needed to side-step some inadequacy with a previous version of FDR. They demonstrate their approach using a CSP-Z specification of an air traffic control system. Our work makes use of 'pure' CSP, and doesn't require the specification to be translated into a different language for model checking, so we can be more confident of our results. However, updating this approach for the current versions of FDR and SPIN could be useful if the protocol had specification temporal properties that needed checking.

Finally, there is work on the Agent Communication Programming Language (ACPL) [11], which is a process algebra that takes some inspiration from CSP's approach to concurrency to model the basics of agent communication. ACPL was also used as the basis for a formal compositional verification framework for agent communication [28]. While the map merge protocol tackled in our work does use agent communication, we are verifying the protocol not the communication itself.

Other process algebras have been used to specify and verify multi-agent systems [23]. For example, in [2] the process algebra Finite State Processes (FSP) and π calculus combined with ADL (πADL) are used to specify safety and liveness properties for a multi-agent system, The multi-agent program is checked for satisfaction of these properties, as is the agent architecture (which is written in

πADL). Looking further afield, process algebras have been applied to similarly distributed, cooperative systems. For example, the Bio-PEPA process algebra has been used to model robot swarms [24], specifying behaviour that enables the swarm to perform a foraging task. They found that their approach enabled a wider range of analysis methods, when compared to other modelling approaches.

5 Conclusion

This paper describes the application of formal specification and verification techniques (in CSP) to an existing communication protocol used to merge maps in a multi-agent system. The protocol was used by the LFC team in the MAPC 2019. This work provides extra confidence that the LFC team's map merging protocol works correctly, which was difficult to check using testing alone. The work also explores the utility of CSP for modelling multi-agent systems.

The merge protocol is critical to the performance of the multi-agent system, all of the information needed for the agents to participate effectively in the competition is stored in the agent's maps. Without a coherent map, the agents would not have been able to cooperate to achieve their mission.

Using the model checker FDR, our CSP specification of the protocol was validated (through checking that it could perform traces representing scenarios drawn from the MAPC 2019) and verified to be free of divergences, and non-determinism, and that it could eventually merge all the maps without deadlocking. We conclude that CSP's focus on concurrent communicating systems makes it well suited to specifying this kind of communications protocol.

Although the merge protocol is the most complex communication protocol used in the LFC system, other behaviours also require some form of validation and verification. The identification process (mentioned in Sect. 3.1) could be specified in CSP either as an addition to the specification presented in this paper, or separately. CSP is useful for modelling concurrent communication, but there may be other formal method techniques that are more appropriate for the remaining behaviours. As indicated by the results in [7], different parts of the system may require distinct verification techniques. The use of CSP for modelling agent interaction protocols that make use of the interaction dimension in JaCaMo also requires further investigation. These are left for future work.

References

1. Ahlbrecht, T., Dix, J., Fiekas, N., Krausburg, T.: The multi-agent programming contest: a résumé. In: Ahlbrecht, T., Dix, J., Fiekas, N., Krausburg, T. (eds.) MAPC 2019, pp. 3–27. Springer, Cham (2020). https://doi.org/10.1007/978-3-030-59299-8_1
2. Akhtar, N., Missen, M.M.S.: Contribution to the formal specification and verification of a multi-agent robotic system. Eur. J. Sci. Res. 117(1), 35–55 (2014). http://www.europeanjournalofscientificresearch.com

3. Bakar, N.A., Selamat, A.: Agent systems verification: systematic literature review and mapping. Appl. Intell. **48**(5), 1251–1274 (2018). https://doi.org/10.1007/s10489-017-1112-z

4. Boissier, O., Bordini, R., Hubner, J., Ricci, A.: Multi-Agent Oriented Programming: Programming Multi-Agent Systems Using JaCaMo. Intelligent Robotics and Autonomous Agents Series. MIT Press, Cambridge (2020)

5. Boissier, O., Bordini, R.H., Hübner, J.F., Ricci, A., Santi, A.: Multi-agent oriented programming with JaCaMo. Sci. Comput. Program. **78**(6), 747–761 (2013). https://doi.org/10.1016/j.scico.2011.10.004

6. Bordini, R.H., Wooldridge, M., Hübner, J.F.: Programming Multi-Agent Systems in AgentSpeak Using Jason. Wiley, Hoboken (2007)

7. Cardoso, R.C., Farrell, M., Luckcuck, M., Ferrando, A., Fisher, M.: Heterogeneous verification of an autonomous curiosity rover. In: Lee, R., Jha, S., Mavridou, A., Giannakopoulou, D. (eds.) NASA Formal Methods, pp. 353–360. Springer, Cham (2020). https://doi.org/10.1007/978-3-030-55754-6_20

8. Cardoso, R.C., Ferrando, A., Papacchini, F.: LFC: combining autonomous agents and automated planning in the multi-agent programming contest. In: Ahlbrecht, T., Dix, J., Fiekas, N., Krausburg, T. (eds.) MAPC 2019, pp. 31–58. Springer, Cham (2020). https://doi.org/10.1007/978-3-030-59299-8_2

9. Dennis, L.A., Farwer, B.: Gwendolen: a BDI language for verifiable agents. In: Workshop on Logic and the Simulation of Interaction and Reasoning. AISB (2008)

10. Dennis, L.A., Fisher, M., Webster, M., Bordini, R.H.: Model checking agent programming languages. Autom. Softw. Eng. **19**(1), 5–63 (2012). https://doi.org/10.1007/s10515-011-0088-x

11. van Eijk, R.M., de Boer, F.S., van der Hoek, W., Meyer, J.J.C.: Process algebra for agent communication: a general semantic approach. In: Huget, M.P. (ed.) Communication in Multiagent Systems. LNCS, pp. 113–128. Springer, Heidelberg (2003). https://doi.org/10.1007/978-3-540-44972-0_5

12. Farrell, M., Luckcuck, M., Fisher, M.: Robotics and integrated formal methods: necessity meets opportunity. In: Furia, C.A., Winter, K. (eds.) IFM 2018. LNCS, vol. 11023, pp. 161–171. Springer, Cham (2018). https://doi.org/10.1007/978-3-319-98938-9_10

13. Ferrando, A., Ancona, D., Mascardi, V.: Decentralizing MAS monitoring with DecAMon. In: Larson, K., Winikoff, M., Das, S., Durfee, E.H. (eds.) Proceedings of the 16th Conference on Autonomous Agents and MultiAgent Systems, AAMAS 2017, São Paulo, Brazil, 8–12 May 2017, pp. 239–248. ACM (2017). http://dl.acm.org/citation.cfm?id=3091164

14. Gibson-Robinson, T., Armstrong, P., Boulgakov, A., Roscoe, A.: FDR3 - a modern model checker for CSP. In: TACAS 2014. LNCS, vol. 8413, pp. 187–201. Springer, Heidelberg (2014). https://doi.org/10.1007/978-3-642-54862-8_13

15. Gracanin, D., Singh, H.L., Hinchey, M.G., Eltoweissy, M., Bohner, S.A.: A CSP-based agent modeling framework for the Cougaar agent-based architecture. In: 12th IEEE International Conference and Workshops on the Engineering of Computer-Based Systems (ECBS 2005), pp. 255–262. IEEE (2005). https://doi.org/10.1109/ECBS.2005.6

16. Hoare, C.A.R.: Communicating sequential processes. Commun. ACM **21**(8), 666–677 (1978). https://doi.org/10.1145/359576.359585

17. Holzmann, G.: The model checker SPIN. IEEE Trans. Softw. Eng. **23**(5), 279–295 (1997). 10/d7wqxt. http://ieeexplore.ieee.org/document/588521/

18. Huang, X., van der Meyden, R.: Symbolic model checking epistemic strategy logic. In: Proceedings of the Twenty-Eighth AAAI Conference on Artificial Intelligence, pp. 1426–1432. AAAI Press (2014). https://ojs.aaai.org/index.php/AAAI/article/view/8894

19. Hübner, J.F., Sichman, J.S., Boissier, O.: Developing organised multiagent systems using the MOISE+, model: programming issues at the system and agent levels. Int. J. Agent-Oriented Softw. Eng. 1(3/4), 370–395 (2007). https://doi.org/10.1504/IJAOSE.2007.016266

20. Izumi, N., Takamatsu, S., Kise, K., Fukunaga, K.: CSP-based formulation of multi-agent communication for a first-order agent theory. Commitment 42, 213–261 (1990)

21. Kacem, A.H., Kacem, N.H.: From formal specification to model checking of MAS using CSP-Z and SPIN. Int. J. Comput. Inf. Sci. 5(1) (2007). http://www.ijcis.info/Vol5N1.htm

22. Lomuscio, A., Raimondi, F.: MCMAS: a model checker for multi-agent systems. In: Hermanns, H., Palsberg, J. (eds.) TACAS 2006. LNCS, vol. 3920, pp. 450–454. Springer, Heidelberg (2006). https://doi.org/10.1007/11691372_31

23. Luckcuck, M., Farrell, M., Dennis, L.A., Dixon, C., Fisher, M.: Formal Specification and Verification of Autonomous Robotic Systems: a Survey. ACM Comput. Surv. 52(5), 1–41 (2019). https://doi.org/10.1145/3342355. http://dl.acm.org/citation.cfm?doid=3362097.3342355

24. Massink, M., Brambilla, M., Latella, D., Dorigo, M., Birattari, M.: On the use of Bio-PEPA for modelling and analysing collective behaviours in swarm robotics. Swarm Intell. 7(2–3), 201–228 (2013). https://doi.org/10.1007/s11721-013-0079-6

25. Rao, A.S., Georgeff, M.: BDI agents: from theory to practice. In: Proceedings of the 1st International Conference on Multi-Agent Systems (ICMAS), San Francisco, USA, pp. 312–319, June 1995

26. Ricci, A., Piunti, M., Viroli, M., Omicini, A.: Environment programming in CArtAgO. In: El Fallah Seghrouchni, A., Dix, J., Dastani, M., Bordini, R.H. (eds.) Multi-Agent Programming, pp. 259–288. Springer, Boston, MA (2009). https://doi.org/10.1007/978-0-387-89299-3_8

27. Spivey, J.M.: The Z Notation: A Reference Manual. International Series in Computer Science, Prentice-Hall, New York (1992)

28. Van Eijk, R.M., De Boer, F.S., Van Der Hoek, W., Meyer, J.J.C.: A verification framework for agent communication. Auton. Agents Multi-Agent Syst. 6(2), 185–219 (2003). 10/dzcsw4. https://doi.org/10.1023/A:1021836202093

29. Vieira, R., Moreira, Á.F., Wooldridge, M., Bordini, R.H.: On the formal semantics of speech-act based communication in an agent-oriented programming language. J. Artif. Intell. Res. (JAIR) 29, 221–267 (2007). https://doi.org/10.1613/jair.2221

30. Winikoff, M.: BDI agent testability revisited. Auton. Agents Multi-Agent Syst. 31(5), 1094–1132 (2017). https://doi.org/10.1007/s10458-016-9356-2

31. Yeung, W.L.: Behavioral modeling and verification of multi-agent systems for manufacturing control. Expert Syst. Appl. 38(11), 13555–13562 (2011). https://doi.org/10.1016/j.eswa.2011.04.067

32. Zatelli, M.R., Ricci, A., Hübner, J.F.: Integrating interaction with agents, environment, and organisation in JaCaMo. Int. J. Agent-Oriented Softw. Eng. 5(2/3), 266–302 (2016). https://doi.org/10.1504/IJAOSE.2016.080889

Analysis of the Execution Time of the Jason BDI Reasoning Cycle

Jason Miller[✉][iD] and Babak Esfandiari

Carleton University, Ottawa, ON, Canada
JasonMiller@cmail.carleton.ca

Abstract. This paper takes a look at the execution time of the Jason reasoning cycle combining an examination of general algorithms and code analysis to determine the timing complexity of its parts. It also experimentally confirms the analysis through the use of profiling tools and agents specifically designed to exploit factors found to affect the execution time. It is found that the reasoning cycle executes within a reasonable time frame give that increasing the number of beliefs or plans leads to a linear increase of execution time (less than 0.1 s at 10 000 beliefs/plans in our setup), but increasing the number of percepts results in a polynomial increase in execution time (approximately one second at 10 000 percepts in our setup).

Keywords: Jason · Reasoning Cycle · Profiling · BDI

1 Introduction

Jason [12] is an advanced implementation of a Belief-Desire-Intention (BDI) engine written in Java, interpreting AgentSpeak(L) [9]. This engine is a method by which a rational agent can be created. Such an agent will gather beliefs from its environment and infer upon those beliefs to generate more beliefs. It will have a set of desires (or goals) that it wishes to achieve, and finally, it will have a set of intentions which it will use to complete its goals by using its beliefs about the world around it. With the increased prevalence of embedded systems and single board computers (such as the Raspberry Pi), we feel it would be beneficial to study the execution time of the Jason reasoning cycle to determine if it is suitable to be run on these systems given that we would expect a high frequency of belief updates and decisions. In general, we find that Jason performs well for a large number (10 000) of beliefs and plans, with an execution time of the related function (`applyFindOp()`) to be less than 0.1 s at the worst case in our setup. However, a large number (10 000) of percepts results in an approximately one second execution time in our setup, which, depending on the particular embedded system, may or may not be an appropriate execution time.

This paper will provide an in-depth analysis of the timing complexity of the Jason reasoning cycle, identifying the parameters which would increase the execution time. We will also experimentally confirm this initial analysis through

N. Alechina et al. (Eds.): EMAS 2021, LNAI 13190, pp. 218–236, 2022.
https://doi.org/10.1007/978-3-030-97457-2_13

the use of a profiler and artificially generated agents, designed to manipulate the identified parameters.

2   Related Work

There have been two main avenues of development in enhancing the performance of the Jason framework:

1. Using the lessons learned by Jason to develop an alternate BDI implementation: Most notably, LightJason [3] aims to re-imagine Jason into a more modular and scalable language, via the use of modern Java features (such as lambda expressions and streams). It is also based on AgentSpeak(L++), which is an extension to what Jason is based on, AgentSpeak(L). As this implementation is not built upon Jason, but a different implementation altogether, we will not take LightJason into account during our analysis.
2. Using the knowledge of Jason to develop workarounds to known inefficiencies: We will highlight [10] and [8], both of which have already done some analysis on the Jason reasoning cycle and have identified the effect of perceptions on the execution time of the reasoning cycle. We also see that [1] proposes ways to use features of Jason to reduce the complexity of belief revision. Finally [2] looks at caching queries that are done over multiple reasoning cycles in an attempt to improve performance.

As part of our analysis, we will profile the reasoning cycle (using JProfiler [14]), but will not limit ourselves to only perceptions. We will not provide any thoughts on how to mitigate any bottlenecks in the reasoning cycle we find as part of this paper. Also, while many other languages have been written that implement the BDI engine (such as GOAL [4] or 2APL [6]), we will not provide any sort of comparison between languages, focusing solely on Jason.

3   Analysis of the Reasoning Cycle

The reasoning cycle is the heart of the BDI engine. It is, in essence, how an agent decides what actions it should take. In general, a BDI agent takes input from sensors, runs that data, along with its current belief base through some sort of belief revision, which then updates that belief base. It then generates options using these beliefs as well as the available intentions, which results in a set of desires. These desires, beliefs and intentions get filtered to generate new (and update existing) filters. Finally, these intentions result in a single action output for that cycle [11].

Jason implements this cycle by taking input from sensors (via `perceive()`) as well as from other agents (using `checkMail()` and `socAcc()`, although this input gets stored directly in the belief base). Jason will update its belief base through a light-weight version of belief revision in the form of belief update, but will perform belief revision later during the cycle, if required. Valid desires (or goals) will be generated through the event selection function, which will lead to filtering, which is implemented starting with unification of events with the plan library, checking the relevance of these plans, and finishing with option selection and intention selection functions. Finally, Jason executes the selected intention.

3.1   Time Complexity of the Jason Reasoning Cycle

A large variety of Java data structures are used to store the data needed to run the reasoning cycle. This allows Jason to leverage well defined and well understood algorithms when storing and manipulating beliefs, perceptions, etc. In order to get an idea of the complexity of the reasoning cycle, we will need to look in depth at the data structures used. As the Jason implementation of the reasoning cycle has 10 steps, we will also break down our analysis into the same 10 steps. We should note that the Jason framework provides a lot of flexibility in the form of being able to extend classes and override default implementation of some of the steps of the reasoning cycle. For our analysis, we will stick to the default behaviour with a notable exception, which will be elaborated on near the end of this section. While we are focusing on Jason for this paper, these algorithms have been abstracted into pseudo-code, in an attempt to generalize the results.

Algorithm 1: Perceive

Input: P_{global} : Set of perceptions available to all Agents
Input: P_{agent} : Set of perceptions available only to an Agent
Output: P : Set of perceptions that have been perceived by an Agent

$P \leftarrow P_{global} \cup P_{agent}$
return P

Step 1 - Perceive. Looking at Algorithm 1, we see that in general, updating the perceptions in this step is a simple union of two sets.

Jason stores both of these sets as Arrays of Literals. For our case, the union of these two sets will be either $O(|P_{global}|)$ or $O(|P_{agent}|)$. This means that the timing complexity for this function will be linear, given by $MAX(O(|P_{global}|), O(|P_{agent}|))$. This set will be directly provided to the belief update function, seen in step 2.

Step 2 - Belief Update Function. The belief update function shown in Algorithm 2 does two things; deletes perceptions that are no longer perceived and adds perceptions that have been perceived, as given to it by `perceive()` seen in step 1.

In order to understand the Jason implementation a little more clearly, we will look at the second portion of the algorithm first (the addition of percepts), which will provide some clarity as to how the percept is stored within the belief base and consequently why the deletion happens the way it does.

To add the percepts to the belief base, the list of perceptions will be iterated over, taking $O(|P|)$ time, and will be added to the belief base in two locations,

---

Algorithm 2: Belief Update Function

Input: P : Set of perceptions that have been perceived this reasoning cycle
Input: P_{belief} : Set of perceptions that exist within the belief base from the previous reasoning cycle
Output: n : The number of additions and deletions that have taken place
Output: P_{belief} : Set of updates perceptions that exist within the belief base as of this reasoning cycle

foreach p : *perception in* P_{belief} **do**
  if $p \notin P$ **then**
    $P_{belief} \leftarrow P_{belief} \setminus \{p\}$
    n++
  end
end
foreach p : *perception in* P **do**
  add percept annotation to p
  $P_{belief} \leftarrow P_{belief} \cup \{p\}$
  n++
end
return (n, P_{belief})

---

once in a HashSet of perceptions, and once in the belief base itself. Within the belief base, this perception is stored in two forms, a LinkedBlockingDeque (in order to maintain the order of the beliefs), as well as a HashMap (in order to utilize a faster search). The "percept" annotation will be added to the percept, to represent where the belief came from.

To delete from the belief base, the Jason implementation of this algorithm will first iterate over the HashSet of perceptions, taking $O(|P_{belief}|)$ time, and determine if the perception needs to be deleted, by comparing it to the set of perceptions passed into the belief update function (P). If it needs to be deleted, then it deletes the perception from the HashSet being iterated over and from the belief base. This means that, because a belief is stored in two forms, two delete actions must happen: a deletion from the HashMap as well as a deletion from the LinkedBlockingDeque, which, because it needs to search for the specific perception to delete, takes $O(|P_{belief}|)$ time.

Overall, this function would be expected to take a worst case of $O(|P_{belief}|^2)$ time. This is due to the deletion of percepts that are no longer perceived, as the set P_{belief} must be iterated over once to see if the percept is still in P. If a given percept is found to no longer be in P, then it must be deleted from P_{belief}, which requires a second, nested iteration over P_{belief}, as the percepts here are stored as a LinkedBlockingDeque.

Step 3 - Check Mail. The check mail function simply moves messages from the messaging implementation to the agent implementation. By default, Jason implements this by moving messages from one ConcurrentLinkedQueue to a different Queue, taking constant time. Any messages that exist in the agent's queue will be examined by socAcc(), shown in step 4.

Step 4 - Determining if a Message is "Socially Acceptable". To determine if a message is "socially acceptable", shown in Algorithm 3, a message is selected from the queue of messages generated by checkMail() (step 3), and

---

Algorithm 3: Socially Acceptable

Input: m : Message to be checked, which has been sent to an Agent
Input: F_n : Set of n predicates, taking a message as input, such that f : m → true, false
Output: s : Whether or not Message m is appropriate to be acted upon

$$s \leftarrow \bigwedge_{j=1}^{n} F_j(m)$$

return s

---

run through a set of provided predicates (represented by F_n) to determine if the message is appropriate to be acted upon. In general, this function will have a time complexity of $MAX(O(F_1), O(F_2), \ldots, O(F_n))$.

Jason does not provide a default implementation of this, and considers all messages to be acceptable, and as such has constant time complexity.

Algorithm 4: Select Event

Input: E : Set of events that can potentially be selected this reasoning cycle
Input: f : Selection function, such that f : E → ϵ
Output: ϵ : Event that has been selected to act upon this reasoning cycle

$\epsilon \leftarrow$ f(E)
return ϵ

Step 5 - Selecting an Event. The select event function shown in Algorithm 4 takes a set of events and selects one event to be acted upon. As such, the time complexity of this function is expected to be dependent on the selection function, f. It should be noted that other selection functions (used in steps 8 and 9) are extremely similar in concept, so do not have algorithms assigned to them.

The Jason implementation will, by default, take the first event present in E, which will take constant time. The selected event will be passed to step 6 and used to generate relevant plans.

Algorithm 5: Relevant Plans

Input: t_ϵ : Triggering event
Input: Π : Set of plans that are available to an Agent
Output: $Opt_{relevant}$: Set of relevant options (Note that an option is a plan, as well as the unifier that makes it relevant and applicable)

foreach π : plan in Π **do**
    /* See algorithm 6 for unifies   */
    $u \leftarrow \pi$.unifies(t_ϵ)
    if $u \notin \emptyset$ **then**
        | $Opt_{relevant} \leftarrow Opt_{relevant} \cup \{(\pi, u)\}$
    end
end
return $Opt_{relevant}$

Algorithm 6: Unifies

Input: t_1 : Literal to unify
Input: t_2 : Literal to unify
Output: u : Unifier that unifies t_1 and t_2
if $t_1.isVariable()$ ∧ $t_2.isVariable()$ **then**
    /* Get the variable portion of Literal t_1 and t_2 */
    vt_1 ← t_1.variable()
    vt_2 ← t_2.variable()
    /* Recursively calling unifies   */
    return vt_1.unifies(vt_2)
end
if $t_1.isVariable()$ **then**
    vt_1 ← t_1.variable()
    return vt_1
end
if $t_2.isVariable()$ **then**
    vt_2 ← t_2.variable()
    return vt_2
end
return ∅

Step 6 - Collecting Relevant Plans. Algorithm 5 takes the entire plan library and filters it down to a smaller set of plans that unify with the provided triggering event (which was selected in step 5). This smaller set is stored as a set of options, which represents a plan as well as the result of the unification of the plan and triggering event. This is expected to have a time complexity of $O(|\Pi|)$.

The Jason implementation of this step happens in two parts. First, the plan library is narrowed down to a set of candidate plans, by getting plans that match the arity of the triggering event. Due to the plan library being stored as a HashMap, this is expected to take constant time. This will result in a set $\Pi_{candidate}$: $|\Pi_{candidate}| \leq |\Pi|$. Once this set has been generated, it is iterated over while being unified with the trigger to determine if the plan is relevant. This will take $O(|\Pi_{candidate}|)$. It should be noted, that in the unification algorithm (Algorithm 6), it is possible for the time complexity to be $O(2^n)$, where n is the number of nested variables that make up a complex literal. This is due to the fact that unifies will recursively call itself for each nested variable. In our case, we are limiting ourselves to only one level, since our unification is limited to triggering events and beliefs. This leaves us with a constant time complexity. If the plan is relevant, then it will be placed into a second ArrayList, which is presented as the list of relevant plans. This list of relevant plans is then provided to step 7, which will further narrow the list down.

Step 7 - Collecting Applicable Plans. The applicable plan function shown in Algorithm 7 takes the set of options provided in step 6, and generates a set of options based on the logical consequences of the plan, the unifier and the belief base of the agent. This function is expected to have a complexity of $O(|Opt_{relevant}| \times O(logicalConsequences))$. The logical consequences (shown in Algorithm 8), however, end up being more complicated. This function will iterate

---

Algorithm 7: Applicable Plans

Input: $Opt_{relevant}$: Set of relevant options (Note that an option is a plan, as well as the unifier that makes it relevant and applicable)
Input: B : Set of beliefs which comprise the belief base of an Agent
Output: $Opt_{applicable}$: Set of options that are logical consequences of the belief base

foreach *opt : option in $Opt_{relevant}$* do
    $\pi \leftarrow$ opt.plan()
    $c \leftarrow \pi$.context()
    if $c \in \emptyset$ then
        $Opt_{applicable} \leftarrow Opt_{applicable} \cup \{opt\}$
    else
        /* See algorithm 8 for logicalConsequences   */
        $LC \leftarrow$ logicalConsequences(c, opt.unifier(), B)
        foreach *u : unifier in LC* do
            $opt_{lc} = (\pi, u)$
            $Opt_{applicable} \leftarrow Opt_{applicable} \cup \{opt_{lc}\}$
        end
    end
end
return $Opt_{applicable}$

Algorithm 8: Logical Consequences

Input: l : Literal to calculate the logical consequences of
Input: u : Unifier to get the logical consequences for
Input: B : Set of beliefs contained within the Belief Base of an Agent
Output: LC : Set of logical beliefs from the belief base for unifier u

foreach *bel : belief in B* do
    if *bel.equals(l)* then
        $B_{candidate} \leftarrow B_{candidate} \cup \{bel\}$
    end
end
foreach *b : belief in $B_{candidate}$* do
    if *b.isRule()* then
        /* See algorithm 6 for unifies   */
        $u_{rule} \leftarrow$ u.unifies(b)
        if $u_{rule} \notin \emptyset$ then
            /* See algorithm 8 for logicalConsequences   */
            $LC_{rule} \leftarrow$ logicalConsequences(b, u_{rule}, $B_{candidate}$)
            foreach *l_{rule} : logical belief in LC_{rule}* do
                $B_{candidate} \leftarrow B_{candidate} \cup \{l_{rule}\}$
            end
        end
    else if *b.hasAnnotations()* then
        $B_{annotations} \leftarrow$ b.annotations()
        foreach *$b_{annotations}$: belief in $B_{annotations}$* do
            $B_{candidate} \leftarrow B_{candidate} \cup \{b_{annotations}\}$
        end
    else
        /* See algorithm 6 for unifies   */
        $u_{lc} \leftarrow$ l.unifies(b)
        if $u_{lc} \notin \emptyset$ then
            $LC \leftarrow LC \cup \{u_{lc}\}$
        end
    return LC
end

over the belief base and attempt to unify the provided Literal with each belief. In the case of more complicated beliefs, we can have the following:

- If the belief is a rule, it will get the logical consequences of that rule (this is recursive, so can be polynomial)
- If the belief has annotations, those annotations are added to the Iterator (this is linear)

In general, it is expected that this function will have a time complexity of $O(|B|^n)$, where n is the number of belief rules (the length of $B_{candidate}$ in Algorithm 8).

Overall, the Jason implementation of these functions will have a timing complexity of $O(|Opt_{relevant}| \times |B|^n)$.

This set of options will be provided to step 8, so that a single option can be selected.

Step 8 - Selecting an Option. The select option function takes a set of options and selects one option to be acted upon. As such, the time complexity of this function is expected to be dependent on the selection function.

By default, the first option in $Opt_{applicable}$ is selected. This takes constant time, as no array manipulation is occurring.

Step 9 - Selecting an Intention. The intention selection function takes a set of intentions and selects one intention to be acted upon. As such, the time complexity of this function is expected to be dependent on the selection function.

By default, the Jason implementation will take the first element of I, which has a constant time complexity. This intention will be provided to step 10 to be executed.

Step 10 - Executing the Intention. The execution of the intention that was selected as part of step 9 is presented in Algorithm 9. This function will take the intention that has been selected and perform different actions based on what the selected intention is. In the case of the intention being an action, the action will simply be executed and removed from the set of available intentions. The expected time complexity of this is expected to be $O(f_\iota)$, which represents the complexity of the action itself. If the intention is checking a constraint, then the timing complexity will be similar to the complexity presented as part of the logical consequences function in Algorithm 8 ($O(|B|^n)$). Finally, if beliefs are to be added or deleted, then belief revision will have to be run. By default, Jason doesn't implement any sort of real belief revision, leaving that up to the programmer to implement. It should be noted, that in general, belief revision is considered to be NP-complete [7]. That said, [1] proposes ways to utilize the features of Jason that could potentially result in a belief revision function that could have a time complexity of $O(n \log(n) + |B| \times |\Pi|)$, where n represents the number of literals within the belief base.

Algorithm 9: Apply and Execute Intention

Input: ι : Current intention
Input: B : Set of beliefs which comprise the belief base of an Agent
Input: I : Set of intentions available to an Agent
Output: I : Set of updated intentions available with either intention ι executed and removed from I, or modified and added back into I

switch ι do
    case *action* do
        execute ι.action()
        I $\leftarrow$ I $\setminus \{\iota\}$
    end
    case *constraint* do
        c $\leftarrow \iota_{current}$.context()
        u $\leftarrow \iota_{current}$.unifier()
        /* See algorithm 8 for logicalConsequences   */
        LC $\leftarrow$ logicalConsequences(c, u, B)
        if $LC \notin \emptyset$ then
            ι.unifier = $\{lc_1\}$; $lc_1 \in$ LC
            I $\leftarrow$ I $\cup \{\iota\}$
        end
    end
    case *delete belief and/or add belief* do
        $B_{add} \leftarrow$ Beliefs to add
        $B_{del} \leftarrow$ Beliefs to delete
        beliefRevisionFunction()
        I $\leftarrow$ I $\setminus \{\iota\}$
    end
end
return I

Algorithm 10: Apply and Find Option

Input: t_e : Triggering event
Input: Π : Set of plans that are available to an Agent
Input: B : Set of beliefs which comprise the belief base of an Agent
Output: opt : Selected option that unifies with triggering event t_e will be selected for an Agent

foreach π : *plan in* Π do
    $t_\pi \leftarrow \pi$.trigger()
    if t_π.*equals*(t_e) then
        $\Pi_{candidate} \leftarrow \Pi_{candidate} \cup \{\pi\}$
    end
end
foreach π : *plan in* $\Pi_{candidate}$ do
    /* See algorithm 6 for unifies   */
    u $\leftarrow \pi$.unifies(t_e)
    if $u \notin \emptyset$ then
        if π.context() $\in \emptyset$ then
            opt $\leftarrow \{(\pi, u)\}$
            return opt
        else
            /* See algorithm 8 for logicalConsequences   */
            LC $\leftarrow$ logicalConsequences(π.context(), u, B)
            if $LC \notin \emptyset$ then
                opt $\leftarrow \{(\pi, lc_1)\}$; $lc_1 \in$ LC
                return opt
            end
        end
    end
end

Step X - Combine Step 6 Through Step 8 into One Action. The Jason implementation also provides a bit of a short-cut, in that steps 6, 7, and 8 can be skipped if `selectOption()` has not been overridden by a custom Agent class. Shown in Algorithm 10, instead of generating entire sets of relevant and applicable plans, the entire set of plans is converted into a set of candidate plans (plans that have the same arity as the triggering event). This set is then iterated over to find the **first** plan that is both relevant and applicable. We see that this operation still has a worst case timing complexity of $O(|\text{Opt}_{\text{relevant}}| \times |B|^n)$, but we expect the actual timing to be much less than this, as the first relevant and applicable plan will cause the function to end.

Table 1. Summary of timing complexity per step of the Reasoning Cycle

Step	Function	Complexity
Step 1	`perceive()`	$O(|P|)$
Step 2	`buf()`	$O(|P_{\text{belief}}|^2)$
Step 3	`checkMail()`	$O(1)$
Step 4	`socAcc()`	$O(1)$
Step 5	`selectEvent()`	$O(1)$
Step 6	`relevantPlans()`	$O(|\Pi_{\text{relevant}}|)$
Step 7	`applicablePlans()`	$O(|\text{Opt}_{\text{relevant}}| \times |B|^n)$
Step 8	`selectOption()`	$O(1)$
Step 9	`selectIntention()`	$O(1)$
Step 10	`applyExecInt()`	$O(|B|^n)$
Step X	`applyFindOp()`	$O(|\text{Opt}_{\text{relevant}}| \times |B|^n)$

Looking at the summary of complexities given by Table 1, we see that five of the default implementations are constant, so we will exclude them from the rest of out analysis. We will also replace steps 6, 7, and 8 with step X, as we have a default implementation of `selectOption()`. This means that we have four steps to look into: step 1 (`perceive()`), step 2 (`buf()`), step 10 (`applyExecInt()`) and step X (`applyFindOp()`).

Our expectation is that the execution time of `perceive()` will scale linearly as the percepts received from the environment increase. The execution time of `buf()` should increase polynomially as the percepts received from the environment increase, but linearly as the number of plans present in the agent's .asl file increase. The execution time of `applyExecInt()` and `applyFindOp()` should increase linearly as the number of beliefs in the belief base increase and finally, the execution time of `applyFindOp()` should increase linearly as the number of relevant plans increase.

4   Profiling of the Reasoning Cycle

In order to experimentally determine the execution time, we will write code to artificially ensure the number of the parameter we are interested in is at the specified value. This means that we will write agents that have a specified number of beliefs, agents that have a specified number of plans, and an environment that generates a specified number of perceptions. These agents will be run on a system containing an Intel i5-8265U, running at 1.60GHz with eight GB of installed RAM. We will run the reasoning cycle for 50 s, in order to give the system an opportunity to settle into a steady state. At this time, we will take a series of snapshots of the system (using JProfiler) at 50, 60, 70, 80 and 90 s. We will then look at the four 10-second intervals between each snapshot. This will give us an idea of the execution time of the reasoning cycle over a 10-second period, and will allow us to see if there is any effect due to the passage of time (i.e.:, do we see four distinct groupings of data). It is our expectation that there should be no significant grouping of data points and that each of the 10-second intervals should be mostly identical (ignoring any variance generated by background operating system processing).

4.1   Modification of Beliefs

In order to get a good idea of the execution time of `applyExecInt()` and `applyFindOp()`, we will need to vary the number of beliefs in our belief base. To do this, we can write a number of identical agents with the same plans and initial goals, but only change the initial beliefs. For our purposes, we will write an agent that contains 10, 20, 40, 60, 80, 100, 200, 400, 600, 800, 1 000, 5 000, and 10 000 beliefs, of which a sample is shown below:

```
belief(0).
belief(1).
/* Number of Beliefs vary from 10 to 10 000 */

!plan(100000).

+!plan(N) : belief(N) <- .wait(100); !plan(N).
-!plan(N) : true <- .wait(100); !plan(N).
```

As seen, the agent will contain two plans, one success and one failure plan which will both just wait for 100ms then re-add the same goal. Finally, there is an initial goal which it will not be able to meet, thereby always choosing the failure plan (thus forcing the reasoning cycle to attempt to unify the context with all the beliefs in its belief base). It is the expectation that as the number of beliefs increase, the execution time of `applyExecInt()` and `applyFindOp()` will increase.

We see that in Fig. 1 that as the number of beliefs increases, the execution time of `applyFindOp()` increases significantly compared to the other functions execution times. Since the increase is so large in this function, when compared to the others, we will focus our efforts on the effect that increasing the number of beliefs has on this function. Given that we see effectively no change in execution

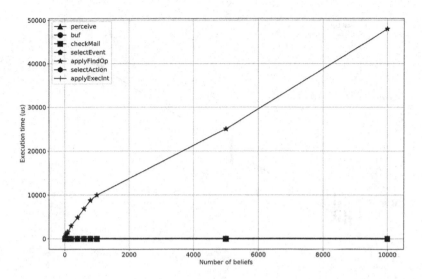

Fig. 1. Trend of Execution Time as the number of beliefs increase

time when we change the number of beliefs, we can conclude that with respect to `applyFindOp()`, there is no appreciable change to `applyExecInt()`, and as such, we will not do any further analysis on the function.

Now that we have collected a wider range of data, we can plot the execution time with respect to how many beliefs are within the belief base to visually get an idea of the relationship between the execution time and number of beliefs. Recall that we have stated that the time complexity of this function is $O(|Opt_{relevant}| \times |B|^n)$. Since we are not taking into account complex belief rules (we are setting $n = 1$), we can simplify this to be $O(|Opt_{relevant}| \times |B|)$. This means that we expect there to be a linear relationship between the change in the number of beliefs and the execution time. It should be noted that this will be the worst case execution time, as the agent always had to iterate over all the beliefs within its belief base before executing the failure plan.

Looking at Fig. 2, we see that as the number of beliefs increases, the execution time of the reasoning cycle linearly increases.

4.2   Modification of Perceptions

Since `perceive()` and `buf()` both rely on the number of percepts present in a given reasoning cycle (at least partially, in the case of `buf()`), we can similarly force a specific number of percepts to be present each reasoning cycle. In order to do this, we will need to create a customized environment, which will extend the default Environment class and override the default executeAction class. Instead of doing nothing, the extended class will add the desired number of percepts every cycle.

```
!plan.
```

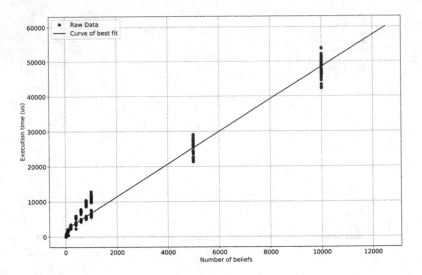

Fig. 2. `applyFindOp()`: Execution time vs Number of Beliefs

```
+!plan : true <- generateFakePercepts;
               .wait(100);
               !plan.
```

The agent in this case will generate an action event, causing the environment to attempt to execute that action, which will always just add a specific number of percepts, specified by the .mas2j file, as seen below:

```
MAS parameter_test {
    infrastructure: Centralised
    environment: PerceptEnvironment(''10")
    /* Customized environment class
       specifies the number of percepts */

    agents: percept_test;
}
```

We can then follow the same steps as in Sect. 4.1 and collect execution time data for an agent that has 10, 20, 40, 60, 80, 100, 200, 400, 600, 800, 1 000, 5 000, and 10 000 percepts per reasoning cycle.

Looking at the trend as the number of percepts increase from 10 to 10 000, we get the graph shown in Fig. 3. We see that the execution time of `buf()` dominates the other functions. Since the execution time of `perceive()` doesn't significantly change as the percepts increase, we will, similarly to `applyExecInt()` in Sect. 4.1, conclude that the change in the number of percepts does not significantly affect the execution time of `perceive()`, especially when compared to its effect on `buf()`. We will focus our efforts there.

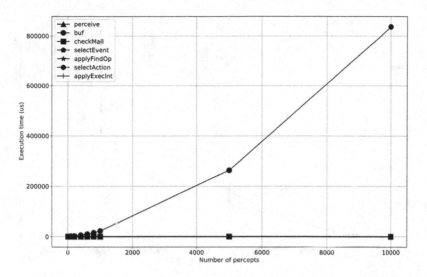

Fig. 3. Trend of Execution Time as the number of percepts increase

Looking closely at Fig. 3, we see that the execution time looks to be increasing faster than linear. Plotting the execution time vs the number of percepts generated per reasoning cycle in Fig. 4, we see that the relation does in fact seem to be potentially polynomial. This result agrees with our initial analysis of buf, that the time complexity of this function is along the lines of $O(|P_{belief}|^2)$.

We would like to look at the results put forth in [10], in which they also look at the execution time of buf(), under a range of percepts. Table IV in [10] (recreated in Table 2) shows the original data presented, as well as converting the log time (in ns) into actual time (in us), so that we can highlight the polynomial relationship between execution time and number of percepts and easily compare to our gathered data.

Table 2. Log of execution time and execution time presented in Table IV of [10]

Percepts	Log time in ns	Time in us
40	6.90	7 940
80	7.20	15 800
120	7.81	64 600
160	8.12	132 000
200	8.42	263 000
240	8.64	437 000
280	8.77	589 000
320	8.92	832 000
360	8.99	977 000

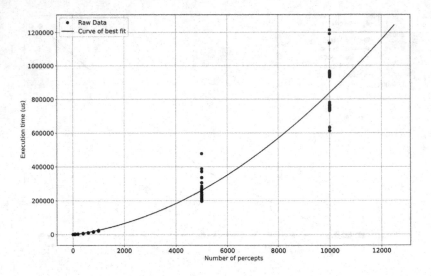

Fig. 4. buf(): Execution time vs Number of Percepts

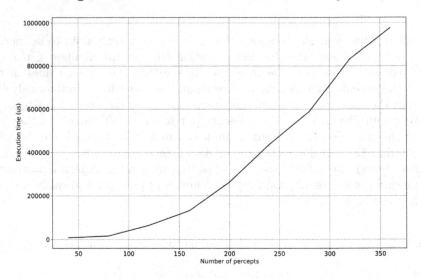

Fig. 5. Graph of Table IV, as seen in [10]

Comparing Fig. 5 and Fig. 4 we see a similar polynomial trend, which provides a manner of validation towards our gathered data.

4.3   Modification of the Number of Plans

In order to see what the effect of the number of plans is on the execution time of buf(), we will keep with the same general idea as the last two sections. We

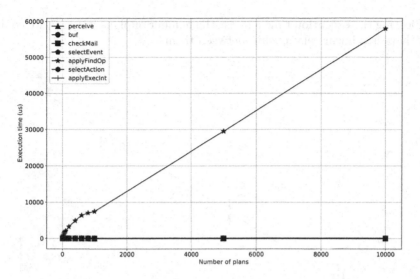

Fig. 6. Trend of Execution Time as the number of plans increase

will generate an agent that contains 10, 20, 40, 60, 80, 100, 200, 400, 600, 800, 1 000, 5 000, and 10 000 plans in it.

```
!plan(100000).

+!plan(N) : belief(0) <- .wait(100); !plan(N).
+!plan(N) : belief(1) <- .wait(100); !plan(N).
/* Number of plans vary from 9 to 9 999 */

-!plan(N) : true <- .wait(100); !plan(N).
/* Last plan, for a total of 10 to 10 000 */
```

In each agent, there will be one failure plan, and the rest will be plans that the reasoning cycle will try to determine if they have the correct context. This will force the reasoning cycle to look at all the plans (and always select the failure plan). Looking at the trend of increasing plans shows something surprising: the execution time of `applyFindOp()` increases significantly with the increase of plans, as seen in Fig. 6.

We also see that the execution time of `buf()` does not increase significantly as shown in Fig. 6, when compared to `applyFindOp()`. Again, we will conclude that there is no significant effect on the execution time of `buf()` when the number of plans are increased. We will, however, further analyze the effect of the increase of the number of plans on `applyFindOp()`.

Looking at the execution time of applyFindOp, we see that there is an increase in execution time, which is unexpected, as we had hypothesized that the execution time would increase with an increase of relevant plans. However, upon further reflection, this does make sense. As the number of plans increases, we would expect the time it takes to determine which plans are relevant (in this case, it is always the last plan) to increase as well, so increasing the number of plans should overall increase the execution time.

Plotting the execution time against the number of plans in Fig. 7, we confirm that there is a linear relationship between them.

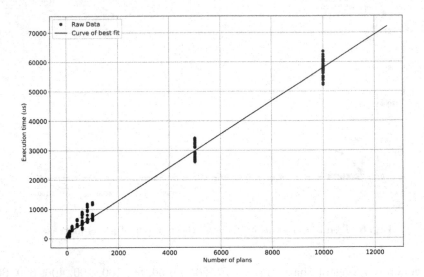

Fig. 7. `applyFindOp()`: Execution time vs Number of Plans

4.4   Relevant Plans

Further investigation of how the increase of relevant plans affects the execution time of the reasoning cycle cannot be done as part of this exercise. Due to the optimization of the reasoning cycle (using `applyFindOp()` instead of `relevantPlan()`, `applicablePlan()`, and `selectOption()`), the first plan that is deemed relevant will always be used. This means that there can only be one or zero relevant plans, regardless of how many plans available to the agent are actually relevant. However, the analysis done in Sect. 4.3, where the number of plans have been modified, should give an approximate idea of the effect of increasing the relevant plans available to the reasoning cycle.

5   Concluding Remarks and Future Work

In this paper, we have analyzed the Jason reasoning cycle and experimentally provided data that corroborates this analysis. Alongside of this, we also looked at some of the values provided by [10] and validated them against our data. We have seen that as the number of beliefs or plans increase, the execution time of the reasoning cycle (specifically `applyFindOp()`) grows linearly. We have also seen, that as the number of percepts increase, the execution time of the reasoning cycle (specifically `buf()`) increases in a polynomial fashion. While we do not provide a specific mathematical model for these relationships, this is a good starting point for additional work in this area. To this end, the following future work is planned:

1. Experimentation of embedded hardware: It would be beneficial to re-run the experiment outlined in this paper in order to determine the overall execution time of the reasoning cycle on real world hardware (i.e.: a Raspberry Pi). This would allow us to determine if it would be possible to use this implementation of the BDI engine in a more widespread application.
2. Development of a mathematical model to predict the execution time: In order to determine what type of hardware might be needed for a practical use of the Jason reasoning cycle, a model in which we could predict the execution time for a given set of hardware (or, conversely, determining values of parameters that would result in a specified execution time) would be extremely beneficial.
3. Addition of case studies: While it is appropriate to design agents to specifically test the limits of Jason, analysis should be done to determine what are reasonable ranges for these parameters, through the use of actual agents written using Jason.
4. Exploration of solutions to mitigate bottlenecks: While this paper has identified some bottlenecks of varying severity, it doesn't attempt to present any ways to mitigate or solve these issues. It would be beneficial to either develop some strategies to mitigate or solve some of these bottlenecks, or at least identify other's efforts to do this.

Acknowledgements. We acknowledge the support of the Natural Sciences and Engineering Research Council of Canada (NSERC) and Four DRobotics.

Nous remercions le Conseil de recherches en sciences naturelles et en génie du Canada (CRSNG) ainsi que Four DRobotics de leur soutien.

References

1. Alechina, N., Bordini, R.H., Hübner, J.F., Jago, M., Logan, B.: Automating belief revision for AgentSpeak. In: Baldoni, M., Endriss, U. (eds.) DALT 2006. LNCS (LNAI), vol. 4327, pp. 61–77. Springer, Heidelberg (2006). https://doi.org/10.1007/11961536_5
2. Alechina, N., et al.: Multi-cycle query caching in agent programming. In: Proceedings of the 27th AAAI Conference on Artificial Intelligence, AAAI 2013, pp. 32–38. AAAI Press (2013)
3. Aschermann, M., Kraus, P., Müller, J.P.: LightJason - a BDI framework inspired by Jason. In: Criado Pacheco, N., Carrascosa, C., Osman, N., Julián Inglada, V. (eds.) EUMAS/AT -2016. LNCS (LNAI), vol. 10207, pp. 58–66. Springer, Cham (2017). https://doi.org/10.1007/978-3-319-59294-7_6
4. Bordini, R.H., Dastani, M., Dix, J., El Fallah Seghrouchni, A.: Multi-Agent Programming: Languages, Tools and Applications, pp. 119–158. Springer, Boston (2009). https://doi.org/10.1007/b137449
5. Bordini, R.H., Hübner, J.F., Wooldridge, M.J.: Programming Multi-Agent Systems in AgentSpeak Using Jason, p. 68. Wiley, Hoboken (2007)

6. Dastani, M.: 2APL: a practical agent programming language. Auton. Agents Multi-Agent Syst. **16**, 214–248 (2008)
7. Nebel, B.: How hard is it to revise a belief base?. In: Dubois, D., Prade, H. (eds.) Belief Change. Handbook of Defeasible Reasoning and Uncertainty Management Systems, vol. 3, pp. 77–145. Springer, Dordrecht (1998). https://doi.org/10.1007/978-94-011-5054-5_3
8. Pantoja, C., Stabile, M., Lazarin, N., Sichman, J.: ARGO: a customized Jason architecture for programming embedded robotic agents. In: Engineering Multi-Agent Systems: 4th International Workshop, pp. 136–155. Springer, Cham (2016). https://doi.org/10.1007/978-3-319-50983-9_8
9. Rao, A.S.: AgentSpeak(L): BDI agents speak out in a logical computable language. In: Van de Velde, W., Perram, J.W. (eds.) MAAMAW 1996. LNCS, vol. 1038, pp. 42–55. Springer, Heidelberg (1996). https://doi.org/10.1007/BFb0031845
10. Stabile, M., Sichman, J.: Evaluating perception filters in BDI Jason agents. In: 2015 Brazilian Conference on Intelligent Systems (BRACIS), pp. 116–121. IEEE (2016)
11. Weiss, G., et al.: Multiagent Systems, p. 32. MIT Press, Cambridge (2013)
12. Jason Homepage. http://jason.sourceforge.net/wp/description/. Accessed 1 Sept 2020
13. Jason Version 2.6 Source. https://sourceforge.net/projects/jason/files/jason/version2.6/. Accessed 11 Jan 2021
14. JProfiler Homepage. https://www.ej-technologies.com. Accessed 20 Oct 2020

Autonomous Economic Agent Framework

David Minarsch[1]([✉]), Marco Favorito[1,2], Seyed Ali Hosseini[1], Yuri Turchenkov[1],
and Jonathan Ward[1]

[1] Fetch.ai, Bury St Edmunds, UK
{david.minarsch,marco.favorito,ali.hosseini,yuri.turchenkov,
jonathan.ward}@fetch.ai
[2] Sapienza University of Rome, Rome, Italy

Abstract. The Internet and the services delivered via it are increasingly centralised on a few monopolistic platforms. Today's web frameworks are conceived to cater for increasing returns to scale and winner-takes-all business models with a built-in asymmetry between users and services. Existing multi-agent and agent architectures have seen no significant adoption outside niche applications. We propose a novel agent framework which is designed to allow for a decentralised digital economy to manifest where each individual and organisation is represented by an autonomous economic entity with its own agency. The framework bridges the old and new web and employs distributed ledger technologies as core parts of its construction. We introduce the framework, discuss the performance characteristics of its current implementation and demonstrate several application areas.

Keywords: Autonomous economic agents · Agent framework · Multi-agent system framework · Distributed ledger technology

1 Introduction

1.1 Web 2.0 and Its Short-Comings

Nowadays, digital services are highly centralised. By some estimates [15], over 43% of web-traffic volume incorporates one of the *FAANMG*[1] platforms. In the process, they extract a significant amount of rent [41] indicating low competition.

The increasing monopolisation is partially caused by unsuited or outdated regulation [42]. However, it is argued that the design of the Web 2.0 [16] itself contributes to this outcome. In particular, the dominant client-server architecture favours a centralised ownership of servers (monolithic or micro-service implementation) [4], causes a lack of interoperability [6], and leads to centralisation of economic control and data [5].

---

[1] Facebook, Apple, Amazon, Netflix, Microsoft and Google.

Supplementary Information The online version contains supplementary material available at https://doi.org/10.1007/978-3-030-97457-2_14.

1.2 Two New Trends

With the recent rise of the decentralised Web 3.0[2] [46] and distributed ledger technologies (DLT)[3] [48] - in particular Bitcoin [31] and Ethereum [12] - it is evident that alternative, decentralised systems can be technologically and economically sustained.

We introduce an agent framework for autonomous economic agents (AEAs), which embraces this technological shift and which we demonstrate is capable of allowing multi-stakeholder multi-agent systems (MAS) to finally find wide-spread production deployment. Our novel approach is chiefly enabled by two drivers: the first is the trustless, non-intermediated exchange of wealth and public code execution in smart contracts[4] mediated by DLT, which thereby provides a financial and contracting layer for the MAS [13]; the second, is the readiness of businesses to cooperate on the design of custom on-chain (i.e. DLT enabled) and off-chain (e.g. MAS) stateful protocols that permit industry-wide competition without a winner-takes-all market dynamic [7,32].

In Sect. 5 we discuss concrete use cases where the framework finds application today.

1.3 Contribution

The core contribution of the framework is that it enables wide-spread and scalable real-world deployment of multi-stakeholder MAS utilising DLT as evidenced in Sect. 5. This contribution is facilitated by the framework's innovation in five key areas: developer experience, software engineering, artificial intelligence, economics, and user experience.

The main benefit of the framework for the software developer is that it allows them to re-use existing code to a much larger degree than in other agent frameworks (e.g. [8, 20]) and client-server oriented web frameworks (e.g. [17,38]). Re-use is not restricted to libraries but extends to application specific components encapsulating subsets of the agent's business logic.

An actor-like framework design leads to software components that are loosely coupled, allowing for concurrency without requiring shared state which enables additional complexity to be incorporated by adding modules to the agent. Interaction between components occurs mostly via asynchronous message passing. This provides a consistent and scalable approach to communication within and across agents. Hence, an AEA can itself be viewed as a small MAS.

From the AI perspective, a developer is offered the flexibility to combine different approaches, such as reinforcement learning [44], deep learning [19] and symbolic AI approaches [21] in one framework.

---

[2] As discussed in [25] not to be confused with the Semantic Web [24].

[3] A distributed ledger is a consensus of replicated, shared, and synchronised data where processing nodes are geographically and organisationally - no central control - spread across multiple entities. Bitcoin network is a permissionless DLT in the form of a blockchain, with proof of work as the consensus algorithm and Bitcoin as the cryptocurrency.

[4] Smart contracts are computer programmes which are executed by nodes of a DLT, usually a blockchain, and can, similar to objects, hold their own state. They can be used to automate enforcement of contract terms, reduce the need for trusted intermediaries and allow for reuse and encapsulation to create interoperable on-chain protocols like decentralised exchanges [2].

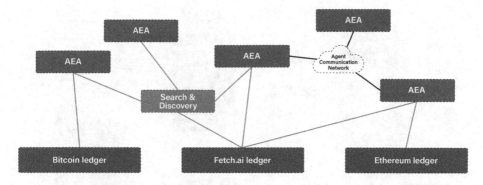

Fig. 1. Diagrammatic representation of an AEA-based MAS. AEAs run off-chain, on heterogeneous devices controlled by their stakeholders. They can use DLTs for settlement and commitments and various (agent-based) services for communication as well as search and discovery.

The native integration with DLT is novel relative to other agent and multi-agent frameworks (e.g. JADE [8], SPADE [20], Jason [10]). It provides a financial settlement and commitment layer, enabling the framework to support deployment of multi-stakeholder systems. In particular, it is possible for anyone to write software for deployment into decentralised and permissionless markets and therefore provides explicit economic benefit to its user and allows for new economic organising principles.

Finally, the framework enables developers to distribute agents as finished products to end-users, lowering barriers to wide-spread adoption of MAS. For instance, through encapsulating complicated interaction flows with DLT and delegation to AEAs, the framework improves the user-friendliness of DLT [28].

2 Definition and Environment Requirements

In reference to [39] we define an *autonomous economic agent (AEA)* as

an intelligent agent operating on an owner's behalf, with limited or no interference of that ownership entity, and whose goal is to generate economic value for its owner;

where the *economic* aspect is realised through exchange and commitments facilitated primarily by DLT. The literature contains related definitions as *machines that obtain their own agency through being equipped with crypto-currency wallets* [35]. This definition is so-far helpful as it puts the focus on the wallet which the agent maintains and which provides an explicit financial metric of the agent's economic value.

The preceding definitions imply a set of requirements for the environment an AEA operates in (stylised in Fig. 1). In particular, AEAs and MAS more generally require:

1. a means to interact with other AEAs, agents and services in a structured way,
2. a delivery mechanism of messages via the Internet,

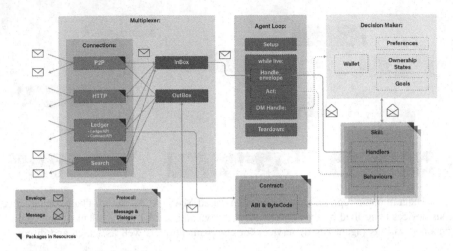

Fig. 2. Simplified illustration of the AEA framework. Connections executed in the Multiplexer receive messages in AEA and third-party protocols. The AgentLoop calls Handlers and Behaviours in Skills based on messages and configurable ticks, respectively. The DecisionMaker manages the (crypto) Wallet. Dark corners indicate (non-core, agent-specific) packages kept in Resources.

3. access to a financial settlement system, and
4. access to a search and discovery system.

The AEA framework makes use of a protocol framework for bilateral dialogue-based interactions to aid 1 [22]. For message delivery (2) AEAs utilise a peer-to-peer permissionless agent communication system [36], which supports arbitrary message-based interaction protocols (1). Currently, a custom centralised search and discovery system for agents is used to satisfy 4. Thanks to the modular nature of AEAs this can easily be replaced with a fully decentralised alternative in the future. Finally, AEAs—unlike other agent types—form part of the second layer to distributed ledgers [28]. They use ledgers and smart contracts [33] to perform financial transactions and make commitments (3). Crucially, AEAs are not run *on* a ledger (i.e. they are not a smart contract), they are executed on any host with the necessary resources and Internet access.

3   Framework Architecture

The architecture described in this paper is currently implemented as open-source in the Python programming language.[5] However, the framework could be implemented in any object-oriented programming language that supports asynchronous programming. An illustration is provided in Fig. 2.

---

[5] The AEA framework's repository can be found at https://github.com/fetchai/agents-aea.

3.1   Actor-Like Design and Modularity

The AEA framework is designed as an actor-like [3] asynchronous message passing system [23]. As such, it allows for a high degree of modularity and components largely communicate via messages.

The framework can be divided into two parts: the core developed by the authors and external contributors, and packages implementing agent-specific business logic. These can be developed by anyone using the framework. There are four types of packages that can be readily added to the framework:

- Skills: primary business logic modules (CPU bound),
- Protocols: messages and dialogue rules,
- Connections: networking related (I/O bound) logic and translations between AEA and third-party protocols,
- Contracts: wrappers for smart contract logic.

Furthermore, the framework allows straightforward inclusion of additional APIs to third-party DLTs via framework plugins and supports the use of readily available software packages in the target programming language.

From the perspective of the framework, packages consist of code and configuration. The framework loads the specified packages and then places them with respect to each other and executes them where appropriate (cf. inversion of control). Before we explore the packages in turn, we discuss the core framework components.

3.2   Core Components of an AEA

The central framework class is the *AEA* class which houses three core components: *Resources*, *Runtime* and *Wallet*.

Runtime and Resources. Resources is a collection of packages available to the AEA. In particular, it contains the Skills, Protocols, Connections and Contracts the AEA uses in code form as well as their configurations. Resources acts as a registry for code to be executed by the Runtime. Packages in Resources are immutable. However, additional packages can be dynamically added at runtime. Dynamically added packages are removed from Resources once the AEA tears down.

The Runtime is responsible for executing the code in the packages. It consists of three abstractions:

- a *Multiplexer* executes the Connection packages,
- an *AgentLoop* executes Skill packages, as well as the *DecisionMaker*, a unique type of Skill discussed below, and
- an optionally enabled *TaskManager* executes long running and CPU bound tasks.

The Runtime deals with two types of primitive concepts: scheduled tasks and events or messages. All messages or events are processed atomically by the AEA components.

The Multiplexer and the Connections that it contains continuously listen for events on pipes, sockets and queues. External communication arriving at one of the

AEA's Connections is, where necessary, translated to framework-specific messages. For instance, HTTP requests are translated to messages in a HTTP Protocol. The Multiplexer then passes these messages to an AEA-internal queue, the *InBox*, for processing by the AgentLoop. Similarly, the Multiplexer continuously monitors another AEA-internal queue, the *OutBox*, for outgoing messages and passes those to the relevant Connection for processing.

The AgentLoop is responsible for proactive execution of periodic tasks like Behaviours (discussed in detail below) in Skills, and processing removal and addition of new components, as well as reacting to new messages appearing in the InBox and handling them with a corresponding Handler in Skills. It is the responsibility of the AgentLoop to fetch the appropriate component responsible for processing a given message from the Resources and passing the message to the component.

A feature that arises from the framework's implementation in Python is that the Runtime can be configured in two modes: the *threaded* mode, where the AgentLoop and the Multiplexer are run in their own threads (i.e. the tasks scheduled by a given component are cooperatively scheduled in the same thread), and the *async* mode, where all the tasks scheduled by the components are run asynchronously on a single event loop. This allows the developer to configure the trade-off between cooperative multitasking used in the event loop implementation (async mode) and pre-emptive scheduling used for thread scheduling (threaded mode) [43].

Wallet. The Wallet is a simple data structure. It contains the private keys of the AEA, and therefore allows for the public key and address to be computed and for the agent to append digital signatures to transactions.

3.3 Packages

The four packages make up the core mechanism via which the AEA is extensible and composable by design.

Communication (Connections and Protocols). The Protocol and Connection packages enable AEAs to communicate with other AEAs as well as internally.

Connections wrap APIs or SDKs to in-process services or services external to the agent like a user interface, a peer for inter-agent communication or a DLT. They can be though of as both the sensors and the actuators of an AEA, as they provide an interface to the outside world. A Connection is responsible for providing the translation between framework communication languages (see Protocols below) and external languages, if needed. A Connection can be developed by anyone and the base Connection class defines a stable interface to the Multiplexer. The interface consists of four primary methods: 'connect' and 'disconnect', 'send' for sending via the Connection and 'receive' for receiving via it.

To communicate with each other and for communication between AEA components including Skills and Connections, AEAs use *Envelopes* which act as an outer agent communication language (ACL) [34] wrapping specific ACLs (cf. [18]). An Envelope has five fields:

- *sender* and *to*: the Address[6] of the sender/receiver;
- *protocol_id*: the identifier of the Protocol used;
- *message*: a bytes field for the serialized message;
- *context*: an optional field for routing, containing a URI.

The 'protocol_id' references a specific ACL or other language, and the 'message' field contains the serialized *Message* in that *Protocol* (cf. interaction protocol [45]), for instance FIPA [14] ACL. This setup guarantees that all AEAs can communicate with each other on the Envelope level via a standard format. However, they can only decode the content of a message if they have an implementation of the Protocol. For the delivery of the Envelope various (third-party) protocols and services can be used (e.g. [36]). By adopting this layered approach to communication we avoid reinventing the wheel: any existing message-based agent architecture could be connected by simply writing a translator that encodes/decodes an Envelope and still ensures interoperability. We also make it possible to have a consistent language inside the framework whilst being compatible with external changes.

The Protocol framework is adopted from [22]. Along with the Message class, which deals with representation, and the *Serializer* class which deals with decoding and encoding, a Protocol specifies a set of *Rules* over the message sequence.

Skills. Skills implement the business logic of an agent. They allow encapsulation of (almost) any kind of code and are reusable across AEAs.

Skills are made up of three core abstractions:

- a *Handler* is responsible for handling messages in a registered Protocol, thereby implementing the AEA's reactive behaviour. Each Handler is responsible for a single Protocol, but can send messages of any type of Protocol. The AgentLoop calls a 'handle' method and passes it the message as it appears in the InBox.
- a *Behaviour* encapsulates actions resulting from internal logic rather than as direct reactions to messages. They implement the proactiveness of the agent. Behaviours come in different types (e.g. cyclic/one-shot/finite-state-machine/etc. [8, 28]) and are scheduled tasks from the perspective of the Runtime. The AgentLoop calls a defined 'act' method in the behaviour at the time specified in the Skill configuration.
- a *Model* is a data class. It is used to maintain shared state within a Skill.

With these abstractions[7], and the ability to call arbitrary code from them, Skills can implement logic ranging from very basic to extremely advanced. As such they might wrap simple conditional logic to complex deep learning models.

The framework does restrict the execution time of calls to both 'act' and 'handle'. For CPU-bound and long-running logic (e.g. machine learning and other AI workloads), a *Task* can be created and submitted to a thread- or subprocess-based TaskManager.

---

[6] AEAs use *Addresses* for identification and for communication purposes. The Address is derived from the public key of a public-private key pair generated from the elliptic curve as specified by, for instance, the standard SECP256k1 [11].

[7] An analogy to the Model-View-Controller architecture prevalent in many web frameworks can be observed: Handlers have similarities to Controllers, and Messages can be considered the equivalent to Views.

A Skill shares state via the SkillContext which is accessible from any Handler, Behaviour and Model in the Skill. Additionally, SkillContext, modules within a Skill have read access to a limited number of objects exposed on the AgentContext, which contains agent-specific information, such as its public keys and addresses, and utilities, such as the OutBox for messages. Importantly, however, a Skill does not have access to the context of another Skill and it also does not have access to the agent's Wallet. To interact with other components, specifically Skills, Connections and the Decision-Maker, the Skill needs to use messages.

Contracts. Contracts wrap smart contracts [47] for third-party distributed ledgers. In particular, they provide wrappers around the application binary interface (ABI) of a smart contract. They expose an API that is compatible with the framework to abstract away the implementation details of the ABI from the agent's Skills.

Contracts usually contain the logic to create smart contract transactions and make smart contract calls. As such they require network access to the underlying ledger. Contract packages are therefore executed in Connections. Skills communicate via messages with the Contract.

3.4   Economic Control

DecisionMaker. The DecisionMaker is a specialised type of Skill and the only component in the AEA with access to the Wallet.

The role of the DecisionMaker is limited to considering internal messages from Skills and making economically relevant and safe decisions. It does not directly interact with other AEAs. Instead, it mediates the competing Skills and restricts their capabilities.

The goals and preferences of an agent are managed by the DecisionMaker. It is the only object capable of updating the agent's ownership state (as represented on-chain in the form of tokens or off-chain) and preferences (cf. utility function) by signing transactions, and hence accepts or rejects the Skills' proposed transactions.

The framework provides a basic reference implementation of a DecisionMaker with a closed form representation of preferences, ownership and goals which is internally closed. The developer is free to extend it to their needs.

Crypto and Ledger APIs. The DecisionMaker makes heavy use of *Crypto APIs* and— via Skills and Connections—of *Ledger APIs*. Framework-side, these consists of abstract classes: the former defines a set of abstract methods to create and handle DLT identities (i.e. public/private key pair for specific ledgers) as well as signing transactions, whilst the latter defines the abstract methods to interact with the ledger (e.g. get the current balance, send a transaction etc.). Crypto APIs are stored in the Wallet, and Ledger APIs can be called through the *Ledger Connection*, a default Connection that acts as access point to any ledger that the application supports. By default, the supported ledgers are Ethereum [12] and Cosmos [26], as well as any compatible ledger architectures. The framework allows for loading new types of Crypto and Ledger APIs types at runtime, through a global shared registry and plugin mechanism, hence achieving a high degree of extensibility and interoperability with other DLT systems.

3.5 Persistence

Certain parts of the agent's state, like for instance completed dialogues and their messages as well as other data accumulated at runtime, should be stored to avoid a continuous growing memory requirement at runtime and to be able to (automatically) recover the state from a crash. The current reference implementation provides an optionally configurable storage backend.

3.6 Dynamic Adaption and Security

AEAs are designed to dynamically add additional packages at runtime. To ensure integrity of the packages is maintained as they are shared and used in the AEA, the framework deploys a hashing strategy. All code is hashed using IPFS [9] multi-hashes. This ensures that an AEA can verify the integrity of a package at runtime.

3.7 Relationship to Other Agent Architectures

The AEA architecture attempts to combine deliberative and reactive components and can hence be seen as a hybrid agent: Handlers deal with reactive elements as representative of deductive reasoning agents. Behaviours and Tasks can deal with the deliberative elements of the belief-desire-intention (BDI) model and are more generally representative of features found in practical reasoning agents [49].

Furthermore, the AEA framework splits the deliberative and reactive elements into both vertical and horizontal layering. Skills are by default horizontally layered. Each Skill is connected to input (i.e. messages) so several Skills can act on the same input and produce suggestions (i.e. transactions) to the DecisionMaker. This means, Skills effectively compete as they consume the same messages but do not necessarily communicate. Within Skills, Handlers are vertically layered. Each type of input is dealt with at most one layer (one Handler).

The separation into Behaviours, Handlers and Tasks within Skills shows similarity to Turing Machines: Their planning layer is matched by our Behaviours. Their reactive layer is mirrored by our Handlers. Their modelling layer can be seen to relate to either our Behaviours or Tasks [27].

The Java-based JADE multi-agent framework [8] provides similar programming abstractions of ours regarding communication and execution model. The main differences specifically to JADE are: (*i*) each agent lives in its own Java thread, and must be associated to a JADE container (i.e. a Java process); our framework gives more flexibility by letting users run AEAs in different processes, in the same process but on different threads, or in the same process but using asynchronous programming; (*ii*) the proactive and reactive components are conflated into the single Behaviour abstraction, whereas we make a clear distinction by introducing the Handler abstraction; (*iii*) the scheduling of behaviours is cooperative, whereas ours is pre-emptive, either thread-based or asynchronous with configurable timeouts. Being a more mature framework, JADE provides features that the AEA framework does not currently support, e.g. ontology-based content, agent persistence, agent mobility services, and others.

SPADE [20] is a lightweight MAS library for agent development. Its major features are asynchronous execution based on Behaviours, a communication system built on the XMPP protocol [40], and a message dispatching mechanism based on message templates. The AEA framework almost completely covers the SPADE features in a modular and effective way: indeed, the AEA framework gives much more flexibility on the execution model to adopt and the transport layer to use (the XMPP protocol can be implemented as a custom Protocol-Connection pair of an AEA); and the same features of message templates can be achieved by relying on a Handler that based on certain attributes of the message spawns new Behaviours dynamically.

Jason [10] is a Java-based implementation of an extended version of the AgentSpeak programming language [37]. Jason is heavily based on the BDI agent architecture and logic programming, with reasoning cycles "sense-plan-act" that allows agents to evaluate which plans are triggered for execution each time an event occurs. Instead, the agent abstraction of our framework is closer to JADE's and SPADE's (agent loop that executes behaviours and handlers code), hence less declarative and succinct than Jason. This also reflects the different foci: where Jason has strong theoretical foundations and lends itself to implement BDI-type agents, our framework is general purpose (i.e. not tied to a specific agent-type), production-ready and with a focus on wide-spread adoption for DLT enabled consumer and industrial applications.

Unlike any other framework, the AEA framework provides a number of unique features: (*a*) native integration with DLTs for transacting and use of smart contracts, as well as economic control oriented design; (*b*) developers can package and re-use business-level functionality; (*c*) developers can distribute agents as finished products to end-users for deployment, for instance by using the AEA registry (https://aea-registry.fetch.ai) or IPFS [9]. Developers and researchers can leverage existing agent frameworks in the AEA framework by developing Connections and Protocols to bridge them.

4   Benchmark

We demonstrate a number of benchmark results of the Python implementation. These highlight that the framework is capable to serve a significant message load both in the single- and multi-agent per-process case.

All benchmarks use the same resource. A 2.2GHz Intel® Xeon® CPU with 15 GB of RAM and 4 cores is used. The benchmarks are run on a freshly provisioned machine. The scripts are available in the project codebase.[8]

4.1   Single-Agent: Reactiveness

We first measured the latency (milliseconds) and throughput (Envelopes processed per second) of an AEA, both in 'async' and 'threaded' runtime modes. The AEA has only one Connection and one Skill with a single Handler. The Connection continuously produces an Envelope containing a Message, deposits it in the InBox and waits for a response. The Handler simply echos received Messages back to the sender, the Connection itself. The experiment is run 100 times, and each run lasts for 10 s.

---

[8] Details on reproducability are provided in Appendix A.

Table 1. Benchmarks for both 'async' and 'threaded' runtime mode. The experiment is run 100 times, 10 s for each run. Latency and throughput are measured in milliseconds and envelopes per second, respectively.

Mode	Latency (ms)	Throughput (env/sec)
async	0.526 ± 0.521	1630.32 ± 16.211
threaded	0.800 ± 0.147	1106.762 ± 18.864

(a) Reactiveness

Mode	Throughput (env/sec)
async	6158.846 ± 516.349
threaded	4587.775 ± 820.525

(b) Proactiveness

The results shown in Table 1a demonstrate that the AEA is capable of processing in excess of 1630 envelopes per second in the async mode and 1106 in the threaded mode. Moreover, on average, the latency in the async mode is lower than the one in the threaded mode.

4.2 Single-Agent: Proactiveness

We next measured the latency and throughput of an AEA with a single Skill implementing a single Behaviour and a single Connection. The Behaviour continuously produces Messages. The Connection simply records receipt of a Message.

The results, reported in Table 1b, show that the AEA is capable to produce 34% more envelopes in async relative to threaded mode.

Given the architecture, it is to be expected that the async runtime mode dominates threaded in both reactive and proactive case. The tasks are well coordinated by the framework, hence cooperative multitasking should not pose a problem and the event loop implementation causes less context switching than threading.

4.3 Multi-agent, Single Process

We next measure the throughput when multiple agents are connected in a complete network and send each other envelopes. All agents are executed in the same process.[9] The individual agents are run in their own threads and each agent is run with the designated runtime mode. Each agent's OutBox is pre-populated with 100 envelopes which are then continuously circulated by the agents.

The round-trip times (RTT) are comparable for low numbers of AEAs in both runtime modes. For higher numbers of AEAs the async mode shows significantly lower RTT. A similar picture emerges for memory consumption. AEAs, irrespective of their runtime mode, are run in different threads and therefore multi-threading guarantees some form of non-starvation property and relatively equally distributed time slices across AEAs.

---

[9] The AEA framework is primarily targeting stand-alone AEA deployment matching its primary application as a multi-stakeholder MAS agent framework. This benchmark demonstrates that nevertheless multiple AEAs can be run in a single process.

Table 2. Multi-agent benchmark for both 'async' and 'threaded' runtime mode. The experiment is run 100 times, 10 s for each run. Initially 100 envelopes are deposited in each AEA's OutBox.

Agents	RTT (ms)		Memory (mb)	
	async	threaded	async	threaded
2	0.340 ± 0.006	0.339 ± 0.012	54.928 ± 0.236	54.89 ± 0.152
4	2.108 ± 0.033	1.998 ± 0.046	56.715 ± 0.676	56.672 ± 0.617
8	7.935 ± 0.538	8.170 ± 0.371	62.062 ± 0.846	62.447 ± 1.038
16	16.757 ± 1.824	25.966 ± 3.45	76.881 ± 1.868	80.422 ± 2.014

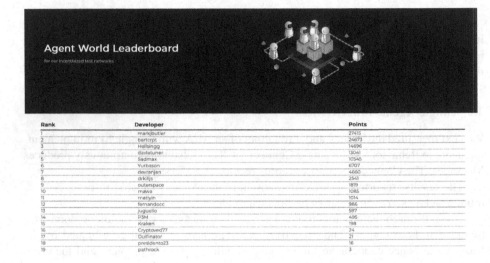

Fig. 3. Leaderboard of Agent World 4 (January and February 2021). Points equal transactions.

5 Use Cases

We ourselves and third parties have developed AEAs targeting a number of different use cases with the framework. We provide a short overview to demonstrate the breath in scope:

- **Trading Agent Competition:** [29, 30] demonstrate how a population of AEAs can replicate an exchange economy. Each AEA maintains a basket of digital assets and aims to increase its utility by executing bilateral trades autonomously. Agents negotiate using a FIPA-like [14] Protocol and settle trades atomically on a blockchain.
- **Decentralised Delivery Network (DDN)[10]:** AEAs represent drivers, passengers and packages in a delivery network. Humans interact with AEAs via user interfaces similar to those found in centralised solutions. The AEAs negotiate directly with each other to establish the fare terms and use escrow mechanisms deployed on

---

[10] Code not public at point of publication. Video: https://youtu.be/VAVZALKAVlA.

a distributed ledger to ensure a secure exchange. Similar to their centralised counterpart, the AEA-based solution addresses the problem of non-co-location of supply
and demand. It does so via a decentralised matching algorithm. This is implemented
on the protocol layer utilising the framework's Protocols.

- **Autonomous Supply Chain**: [50] demonstrate the feasibility of an autonomous supply chain using MAS—powered by the AEA framework—and Internet of Things.
  The scenario showcases a perishable food products supply chain mechanism. Five
  types of agents were implemented for this demonstration: retailer, wholesaler, sup-
  plier, logistics agent, and third-party logistics agent.
- **Agent Worlds 1 to 4:** We have demonstrated the production readiness of the framework and AEAs developed with it in the context of an online and public agent competition which took place in four stages from October 2020 until February 2021. Any
  participant could download a finished AEA from the registry (https://aea-registry.
  fetch.ai), connect it via configuration to a public weather or mobility API for various
  cities across the world, and then run it as a seller of public weather or mobility data.
  The AEA would register itself for the competition, provided the participant staked
  a small amount of crypto-currency on a smart contract deployed on the Ethereum
  blockchain.[11] An AEA created and run by the authors acted as a buyer of this data.
  At multiple time points throughout the day, it would search for one of the data types
  in one of the specified cities and then purchase the data from all sellers offering it
  which were registered for the competition. Figure 3 shows the results from Agent
  World 4. In excess of 2'000 agents competed over two months and performed a
  total of more than 110'000 transactions. Each transaction was settled on a Fetch.ai
  test-net blockchain and resulted in a micro-reward for the participants.
- **Autonomous Option Traders:** [1] use an AEA to maintain a portfolio of put and
  call options deployed on the Ethereum ledger. The AEA allows the user to manually
  submit option order requests via a graphical user interface. The AEA translates the
  HTTP requests into a sequence of actions which ultimately result in the order being
  executed on the ledger and being stored in local persistent storage. The AEA then
  monitors the option holdings of the user and exercises them when they are in-the-
  money (ITM) and due to expire within 5 min. This removes the possibility of ITM
  options expiring worthless and ensures users take profitable positions.
- **Rail-network Simulation**[12]: each station and train in the UK rail-network is represented by an AEA. Station AEAs maintain their arrival and departure boards. Trains
  display information about their journey, destination and origin. All information is
  live and obtained from third-party APIs. The project demonstrates how a large population of AEAs (several hundreds) can be run on a single machine as a simulation.

6 Discussion

6.1 Architecture Choices and Limitations

The reference implementation of the AEA framework in the Python programming language imposes an overhead at runtime relative to compiled programming languages.

---

[11] This acts as a spam protection and as an incentivisation mechanism.
[12] Code not public at point of publication. Video: https://youtu.be/TGZ6AX-KqCk.

This was a conscious choice at the start of the development cycle to enable rapid iteration and prototyping. It means that in practice running an AEA on devices with less resources than a Raspberry Pi is a challenge. However, as the benchmark demonstrates, environments with a Python interpreter and moderate networking, CPU and storage requirements can make full use of the framework. The listed use cases the framework supports are more than satisfiable with these minimal requirements. Furthermore, with increased adoption, a lightweight AEA library can be implemented in a compiled programming language like Golang.

Over time, we hope to provide, in the core of the framework, generic implementation(s) of the DecisionMaker component which permit increasingly powerful configuration or 'training' by the user. For simple use cases, where the utility of an agent can be easily represented and evaluated, this is already possible as we demonstrate in our use cases.

Further limitations are discussed in the framework's documentation.

6.2 Value Add

We identify five innovations which underpin our main contribution discussed in Sect. 1.

From a developer perspective the key benefit the framework provides are its modularity and composability. Unlike for other web and agent frameworks the componentisation and reusability extends to arbitrary application-specific business logic through the encapsulation in Skills. This flexibility does not necessarily lower the integrity of the system as the package hashing strategies deployed ensure that components are uniquely identified and tamper-proof.

From a software engineering perspective, all the software components are loosely coupled and an actor-like design approach maintained. Only a minimal amount of shared state exists and interactions between components is almost entirely via asynchronous message passing.

The generality of Skills presents another core contribution of the framework design. In particular, it means the agent framework does not prescribe the type of AI tools used, it is agnostic to whether the developer uses a deep learning model, reinforcement learning or traditional AI approaches.

The openness in the design approach is also maintained for Protocols. Unlike other agent framework we do not prescribe usage of a particular application or agent protocol (e.g. FIPA), instead developers have access to a generic protocol framework which can be adjusted to the relevant use case.

One of the biggest differentiators relative to existing agent and multi-agent frameworks is the native integration with distributed ledgers and the associated crypto-economic security concepts. This allows AEAs to be fully autonomous economic entities with an ability to transact and make commitments. It also allows arbitrary coordination mechanisms to be implemented.

The other big differentiator is offered on the user experience: agents can be distributed as finished products to end-users. This enables developers to share arbitrary agent-based solutions directly with their user base.

7   Conclusion

The AEA framework presented in this paper is the only production-ready framework we are aware of that unifies MAS and DLT. It is designed and built for production and in parallel to the development of real-world applications by ourselves and third parties. Arguably, several aspects of the framework, in particular the DecisionMaker, are underdeveloped. However, in the spirit of open-source development and to grow a community of AEA developers and researchers we believe it is crucial to start with an initial, useful implementation and iterate from there. We welcome contributions to the framework design and its implementation.

Acknowledgments. We thank Fetch.ai for supporting this research and the release of its implementation.

A   Experiments

In this section, we provide instructions to reproduce the experiments.

A.1   Requirements

The framework can be used on any major platform (GNU/Linux, macOS, Windows). However, to run the benchmark, we suggest using UNIX-like systems (e.g. GNU/Linux or macOS).

Make sure your platform has the following software installed and the associated binaries accessible from the system path of your operating system:

- Python 3.8. This can be downloaded from here: https://www.python.org/downloads/release/python-380/.
- Make sure you have Pip installed: https://pip.pypa.io/en/stable/installing/. Also, the script requires that the CLI tool `pip` should point to `pip3`. Note that on some platforms this is not the default configuration.
- Git. This can be downloaded from here: https://git-scm.com/downloads.

A.2   Steps to Reproduce the Experiments

- Download the following script in your working directory to reproduce results: https://raw.githubusercontent.com/fetchai/agents-aea/v0.10.1/benchmark/run_from_branch.sh. (Alternatively, for the latest version use: https://raw.githubusercontent.com/fetchai/agents-aea/main/benchmark/run_from_branch.sh.)
- Assign execution permissions to the script. For example, on UNIX systems:
    ```
    > chmod u+x run_from_benchmark.sh
    ```
- Run the script:
    ```
    > ./run_from_benchmark.sh
    ```

References

1. 8ball030: Autonomous hegician (2020). https://github.com/8ball030/AutonomousHegician
2. Adams, H., Zinsmeister, N., Salem, M., Keefer, R., Robinson, D.: Uniswap v3 core. Technical report, Uniswap (2021)
3. Agha, G.A.: Actors: a model of concurrent computation in distributed systems. Technical report, MIT (1985)
4. Arkko, J.: The influence of internet architecture on centralised versus distributed Internet services. J. Cyber Policy **5**, 30–45 (2020)
5. Baker, D.: The internet is broken (2017). https://www.wired.co.uk/article/is-the-internet-broken-how-to-fix-it
6. Basaure, A., Vesselkov, A., Töyli, J.: Internet of things (IoT) platform competition: consumer switching versus provider multihoming. Technovation (2020)
7. Beck, R., Müller-Bloch, C.: Blockchain as radical innovation: a framework for engaging with distributed ledgers as incumbent organization. In: HICSS (2017)
8. Bellifemine, F.L., Caire, G., Greenwood, D.: Developing Multi-agent Systems with JADE. Wiley, Hoboken (2007)
9. Benet, J.: IPFS - Content Addressed, Versioned, P2P File System. arXiv:1407.3561 (2014)
10. Bordini, R.H., Hübner, J.F., Wooldridge, M.: Programming Multi-agent Systems in AgentSpeak Using Jason. Wiley, Hoboken (2007)
11. Brown, D.R.: SEC 2: recommended elliptic curve domain parameters. SEC (2010)
12. Buterin, V.: Ethereum Whitepaper (2013). https://ethereum.org
13. Calvaresi, D., et al.: Multi-agent systems and blockchain: Results from a systematic literature review. In: PAAMS (2018)
14. Committee, I.F.S.: Communicative act library specification. Technical report, Foundation for Intelligent Physical Agents (2001)
15. Cullen, C.: Over 43% of the Internet is consumed by Netflix, Google, Amazon, Facebook, Microsoft, and Apple: Global Internet Phenomena Spotlight (2019). https://www.sandvine.com/blog/netflix-vs.-google-vs.-amazon-vs.-facebook-vs.-microsoft-vs.-apple-traffic-share-of-internet-brands-global-internet-phenomena-spotlight
16. DiNucci, D.: Fragmented future. Print 53 (1999)
17. Django Software Foundation: Django (2005). https://djangoproject.com
18. Finin, T., Fritzson, R., McKay, D., McEntire, R.: KQML as an agent communication language. In: CIKM (1994)
19. Goodfellow, I., Bengio, Y., Courville, A., Bengio, Y.: Deep Learning. MIT Press, Cambridge (2016)
20. Gregori, M., Palanca, J., Aranda, G.: A Jabber-based multi-agent system platform. In: ICAA (2006)
21. Haugeland, J.: Artificial Intelligence: The Very Idea. MIT Press (1989)
22. Hosseini, S.A., Minarsch, D., Favorito, M.: A practical framework for general dialogue-based bilateral interactions. In: Engineering Multi-Agent Systems (2021, to publish)
23. Karmani, R.K., Shali, A., Agha, G.: Actor frameworks for the JVM platform: a comparative analysis. In: PPPJ (2009)
24. Kashyap, V., Bussler, C., Moran, M.: The Semantic Web: Semantics for Data and Services on the Web. Springer, Heidelberg (2008). https://doi.org/10.1007/978-3-540-76452-6
25. Khoshafian, S.: Can the real web 3.0 please stand up? (2021). https://www.rtinsights.com/can-the-real-web-3-0-please-stand-up/
26. Kwon, J., Buchman, E.: Cosmos: a network of distributed ledgers (2016)
27. Lizán, F., Maestre, C.: Intelligent buildings: foundation for intelligent physical agents. IJERA (2017)

28. Minarsch, D., Hosseini, S.A., Favorito, M., Ward, J.: Autonomous economic agents as a second layer technology for blockchains: framework introduction and use-case demonstration. In: 2020 Crypto Valley Conference on Blockchain Technology (CVCBT), pp. 27–35 (2020)
29. Minarsch, D., Favorito, M., Hosseini, A., Ward, J.: Trading agent competition with autonomous economic agents. In: AAMAS, Auckland, New Zealand. IFAAMAS (2020)
30. Minarsch, D., Hosseini, S.A., Favorito, M., Ward, J.: Trading agent competition with autonomous economic agents. In: ICAART, vol. 13, pp. 574–582 (2021)
31. Nakamoto, S.: Bitcoin: a peer-to-peer electronic cash system. Technical report, Manubot (2019)
32. Poddey, A., Scharmann, N.: On the importance of system-view centric validation for the design and operation of a crypto-based digital economy. arXiv:1908.08675 (2019)
33. Poncibò, C., Di Matteo, L., Cannarsa, M., et al.: The Cambridge HB of Smart Contracts, Blockchain Technology and Digital Platforms. Cambridge University Press, Cambridge (2019)
34. Poslad, S.: Specifying protocols for MAS interaction. ACM Trans. Auton. Adapt. Syst. **2**, 15-es (2007)
35. Pschetz, L., Speed, C.: Autonomous economic agents. In: Living in the Internet of Things (IoT 2019) (2019)
36. Rahmani, L., Minarsch, D., Ward, J.: Peer-to-peer autonomous agent communication network. In: AAMAS, AAMAS 2021, Richland, SC, pp. 1037–1045. IFAAMAS (2021)
37. Rao, A.S.: AgentSpeak(L): BDI agents speak out in a logical computable language. In: Van de Velde, W., Perram, J.W. (eds.) MAAMAW 1996. LNCS, vol. 1038, pp. 42–55. Springer, Heidelberg (1996). https://doi.org/10.1007/BFb0031845
38. Ruby on Rails: Ruby on rails (2004). https://rubyonrails.org
39. Russell, S., Norvig, P.: Artificial Intelligence: A Modern Approach. Pearson (2020)
40. Saint-Andre, P., Smith, K., Tronçon, R., Troncon, R.: XMPP: The Definitive Guide. O'Reilly Media, Inc. (2009)
41. Sandbu, M.: The economics of big tech (2018). https://www.ft.com/economics-of-big-tech
42. Sandbu, M.: Fixing the Internet's broken markets (2018). https://www.ft.com/content/5fbc2848-17c2-11e8-9376-4a6390addb44
43. Silberschatz, A., Galvin, P., Gagne, G.: Operating System Concepts. Wiley (2018)
44. Sutton, R.S., Barto, A.G.: Reinforcement Learning: An Introduction. MIT Press (2018)
45. Torroni, P., et al.: Modelling interactions via commitments and expectations. In: Handbook of Research on Multi-agent Systems: Semantics and Dynamics of Organizational Models. IGI Global (2009)
46. Voshmgir, S.: Token Economy: How the Web3 Reinvents the Internet. BlockchainHub (2020)
47. Wang, S., et al.: Blockchain-enabled smart contracts: architecture, applications, and future trends. IEEE Trans. Syst. Man Cybern.: Syst. (2019)
48. Wattenhofer, R.: Distributed Ledger Technology: The Science of the Blockchain. CreateSpace Independent Publishing Platform (2017)
49. Wooldridge, M.: An Introduction to MultiAgent Systems. Wiley (2009)
50. Xu, L., Brintrup, A., Minaricova, M.: Autonomous supply chains (2020). https://vimeo.com/438586015/bf50c7bc9

Seamless Integration and Testing for MAS Engineering

Mostafa Mohajeri Parizi[(⊠)], Giovanni Sileno, and Tom van Engers

Informatics Institute, University of Amsterdam, Amsterdam, The Netherlands
{m.mohajeriparizi,g.sileno,t.m.vanengers}@uva.nl

Abstract. Testing undeniably plays a central role in the daily practice of software engineering, and this explains why better and more efficient libraries and services are continuously made available to developers and designers. Could the MAS developers community similarly benefit from utilizing state-of-the-art testing approaches? The paper investigates the possibility of bringing modern software testing tools as those used in mainstream software engineering into multi-agent systems engineering. Our contribution explores and illustrates, by means of a concrete example, the possible interactions between the agent-based programming framework ASC2 (AgentScript Cross-Compiler) and various testing approaches (unit/agent testing, integration/system testing, continuous integration) and elaborate on how the design choices of ASC2 enable these interactions.

Keywords: Multi-agent systems · Multi-agent systems engineering · Testing · Continues integration

1 Introduction

Software testing is attracting increased interest in industry [1] and it is one of the most used methods of software verification. One of the reasons of this success lies in the advancement and popularization in the software engineering community of methodologies commonly known as *DevOps*, in particular of techniques of automated testing in *continuous integration* (CI). Generally, CI refers to the facilitation provided by third-party tools for automating the build/test process of a software. In recent years, online DevOps services such as TravisCI[1] and CircleCI[2] have been increasingly used by software engineers to improve the efficiency of their testing process, a practice which plausibly resulted in increased quality of the developed software.

Very recently, Fisher et al. [18] have suggested that testing approaches would be an important complement to formal approaches to MAS verification, if they could be automated and integrated in a seamless way into MAS development.

---

[1] https://travis-ci.com/.
[2] https://circleci.com/.

© Springer Nature Switzerland AG 2022
N. Alechina et al. (Eds.): EMAS 2021, LNAI 13190, pp. 254–272, 2022.
https://doi.org/10.1007/978-3-030-97457-2_15

In our view, seamless integration does not mean only that agent programmers are able to use the vast amount of software testing tools available to mainstream languages like Java or Python, but, more importantly, that they are also able to use (almost) language- and framework- agnostic online services as those used for CI. This paper explores this idea, aiming to illustrate what the MAS community could gain by using industry standard testing tools and discussing what would be the theoretical and practical trade-offs for this choice. We investigate possible interactions of testing with agent-based programming, and its relation with other verification techniques. More concretely, we demonstrate various approaches to enhance the productivity of MAS development cycle in the AgentScript Cross-Compiler (ASC2) framework [27] via mainstream software testing and integration tools, and elaborate on the design choices of ASC2 that affect the testability of agent-programs with the mentioned tools. Then, we explore on how this approach can be generalized for other MAS frameworks.

The motivation for this work arises from research conducted on data-sharing infrastructures (e.g. data marketplaces). At functional level, a data-sharing application corresponds to a coordination of several computational actors distributed over multi-domain networks. Those actors generally include certifiers, auditors, and other actors having monitoring and enforcement roles, ensuring some level of security and trustworthiness on data processing [42]. Typically distributed across several jurisdictions, networks may be subjected to distinct norms and policies, to be added to various infrastructural policies provided at domain level and *ad-hoc* policies set up by the users. Some of these norms, as for instance the GDPR, bind processing to conditions and specific purposes, but, more in general, all compliance checking on social systems requires to know and to infer (in case of a failure on expectations) *why* an actor is performing certain operations. Agent-based programming, and particularly the Belief-Desire-Intention (BDI) model [35], by looking at computational agents as *intentional agents*, provides the "purpose" level of abstraction available by design, and for this reason it is a natural technological candidate for this application domain.

The BDI model been extensively investigated as basis to represent computational agents that exhibit rational behaviour [19] and multiple programming languages and frameworks have been introduced based on it, as AgentSpeak(L)/Jason [6,34], 3APL/2APL [11], and GOAL [22]. Recent works as e.g. [23,27] investigated various issues holding when mapping logic-oriented agent-based programs into an operational setting. In contrast, this paper focuses instead on the *development practice* aspect: as soon as we attempted to program data-sharing applications as agents, we experienced the lack of mature software engineering toolboxes, thus hindering a continuous integration with the infrastructural-level components developed in parallel by our colleagues.

The document proceeds as follows: Sect. 2 provides a background and related works on verification of MAS, in Sect. 3 we introduce our approach on MAS testing in ASC2 framework with mainstream tools. An illustrative example of this approach is presented in Sect. 4. Finally, Sect. 5 provides the discussion and comments on possible extensions and future developments.

2   Verification of (Multi-)Agent Systems

Verification is a crucial phase in any software (and system) development process, and as such it has been addressed also by the Multi-Agent Systems (MAS) community. The survey presented in [2] provides an empirical review of over 230 works related to verification of MAS.

At higher level, approaches for the verification of autonomous systems fall into five categories [18]: (a) *model checking*, (b) *theorem proving*, (c) *static analysis*, (d) *run-time verification*, and (e) *(systematic) testing*. While the first four approaches (a-d) are considered formal or at least semi-formal, testing (e) is deemed to be an informal approach to verification. Further, MAS verification can be targeted at different levels, varying from fine-grained verification of agents at a logical level [3] to verification of emergent properties in a system [12]. Ferber [16] identifies three levels: (i) *Agent level* considers internal mechanisms and reasoning of an agent (ii) *Group level* consists in testing coordination mechanisms and interaction protocols of agents, and (iii) *Society level* checks for emergent properties or if certain rules and/or norms are complied within the society. In general, the choice of a verification method depends on the required level of verification, as e.g. formal methods may not be applicable for the verification of a large MAS with non-deterministic characteristics at the society level.

Most of the works on MAS verification point out that testing agent programs is far harder than testing normal software, on the grounds that agents tend to have more complex behaviors, and deal with highly dynamic and often non-deterministic environments (including other agents), on which they have only partial control [30]. A series of recent empirical results [37,38] was used to conclude that, with respect to certain distinct test criteria, testing BDI agents can be practically infeasible. The *all-paths* criterion requires the test suite to cover all the paths of the agent's goal-plan graph; its application shows that the number of tests needed to run is intractable [38]. In subsequent work, the same authors study the minimal criterion of *all-edges*, requiring all edges of the goal-plan graph to be covered. While not *per se* infeasible, results show that even this criterion requires a (too) high number of tests [37].

These observations can explain why much of the work in verification of autonomous systems and specifically of BDI agents have been towards the *formal verification* of agent programs, a mathematical process for proving that the system under verification matches the specification given in formal logic [4]. One of the most successful formal methods for verification of software agents has been *model checking* [9]. Model checking of BDI agents can be done as e.g. in [5] by translating a simplified version of AgentSpeak(L) to Java programs and using the Java Path Finder (JPF) verification tool. Probably the most notable works that adopt a (semi-)formal model checking approach are those of the AJPF/MCAPL framework [13,17]; AJPF/MCAPL also relies on JPF to perform program model checking on agent programs developed in multiple JVM-based BDI frameworks by utilizing an implementation of the target language's interpreter. Nevertheless, although formal verification techniques as model-checking provide a high level of guarantee, they are typically both complex and slow to deploy [39].

A number of approaches to testing (that is, *informal verification*) have also been considered in the MAS literature. Some of those utilize model-based testing [33, 41] and rely on *design artifacts* such as Prometheus design diagrams [32] to generate tests and automate the testing process. Others consider a more fine-grained approach to verify intentional agents [15, 31], focusing on *white box* tests involving in the testing process the inner mechanisms of BDI agents (like plans and goals). This method of testing has however been criticized in [25] as being "too fine-grained", proposing instead to perform testing at a *module* level, that is, considering a set of goals, plans, and/or rules as a single unit. Still other works refer to *software testing* techniques applied on MAS development, focusing on testing agents and their interaction patterns as the main level of abstraction [10, 24]. At implementation level, such *unit testing* is performed in a *Jade* multi-agent system via the JUnit library. The distinct agent-roles that are present in the MAS are tested by means of *mock* agents that communicate with the implemented Jade agents to verify their behavior.

Levels of Testing. Software testing is generally categorized in four levels or activities: (a) *Unit testing* is done to verify different individual components of the software system in focus, (b) *Integration testing* verifies the combination of different components together, (c) *System testing* is done to test the system as a whole, and (d) *Acceptance testing* is done to check the compliance of the software with given end-users' and/or relevant stakeholders' requirements.

A categorization for MAS testing from a development-phase activity perspective has been proposed in [28], consisting of five levels: (i) *Unit testing* targets individual components of an agent, (ii) *Agent testing* aims at the combination of the components in an agent including capabilities like sensing its environment, (iii) *Integration or Group testing* includes the communications protocols and the interactions of the agent with its environment or other agents, (iv) *System or Society testing* considers the expected emergent properties of the system as a whole (v) *Acceptance testing* for a MAS stays the same as their counterpart in software testing.

All these categorizations can be seen as guidelines to draw a conceptual line between what should be tested for what purpose and when, in the different phases of software development. This means that for each project it is up to the designer to decide e.g. what counts as units, what interactions are considered group and what are the properties of the system/society. Indeed, testing libraries like JUnit or online continuous integration services like TravisCI or CircleCI stay relatively agnostic on what type of tests are being done. We will follow here the same principle by allowing the designer to create each test suite with different scenarios containing one or multiple agents with varying types and allowing for flexible success/failure criteria.

Coverage. An important measure giving insights on the quality of a certain test suite in a given system is *coverage*. Software engineering proposes different criteria for coverage [29], varying from simple *line coverage* (denoting the percentage of the code that is covered by the test cases), to more sophisticated metrics like cyclomatic complexity [26], more commonly known as *branch coverage*. Intuitively, the more a program is covered by a test suite the more confident the designer can be about the behavior of the software. In fact it is a common approach to set a minimum coverage boundary for software projects and if coverage is below this limit the build chain is considered a failure even if the code compiles correctly.

Several works have studied criteria for testing in Agent-Oriented Software Engineering, and particularly in BDI-based agent programming [31]. However, the abstract mechanisms underlying any BDI-based reasoning cycle concerning e.g. treatment of plan context conditions, plan selection and failure handling, alongside the procedural specifications given in one agent's script (e.g. the agent's plans), result in complicated branching in the agent's effective code, a fact that makes defining what is actually covered by a test suite difficult [37,38].

3   Approach

Instead of investigating dedicated tools for testing BDI agents, our motivation is to study under what conditions and how we can take advantage of existing software testing coverage tools, so as to enable an integration of BDI agent-based development with other types of development, occurring concurrently on a production-level system. This practical (and unavoidable) necessity motivated us to overlook or put aside the warnings and issues indicated in the literature.

Our study focuses in particular on the BDI framework AgentScriptCC (Cross-Compiler) [27], here denoted ASC2. A short overview of ASC2 is presented in Sect. 3.1, whereas Sect. 3.2 presents our approach to testing.

3.1   AgentScript Cross-Compiler (ASC2)

The ASC2 framework is a BDI agent programming framework centred around a *cross-compiler* performing a *source-to-source* translation of a high-level Domain Specific Language (DSL) inspired by AgentSpeak(L)/Jason [6,34] into executable JVM-based programs. Cross-compilation is not unique to ASC2 and has been used by other recent agent-oriented frameworks such as Astra [14] and Sarl [36]. ASC2 consists of: (1) a logic-based Agent-Oriented Programming DSL; (2) an abstract execution architecture; (3) a translator that generates executable models from models specified by the DSL; (4) tools that support the execution of models.

AgentScript DSL. The AgentScript DSL has a very close syntax to AgentSpeak(L)/Jason [6,34]. The main components of the DSL are (1) initial beliefs, (2) inferential rules, (3) initial goals, and (4) plan rules. The initial beliefs and goals express the mental state of the agent at the start of the execution. Initial beliefs are a set of Prolog-like facts, and the initial goals designate the first intentions to which the agent commits. Inferential rules are potentially non-grounded declarative rules (Prolog-like), used to infer beliefs from beliefs. Plan rules are potentially non-grounded reactive rules in the form of $e : c \Rightarrow f$ in which f is a sequence of executable steps called the *plan body* that the agent has to perform in response an internal (e.g. *goal adoption, belief-update*) or external (e.g. *message reception, perception*) event e, if a context condition c is believed to be true by the agent.

While the AgentScript DSL is very close to Jason, the translation-based nature of ASC2 produces some disparities with respect to execution. An important characteristic of this approach is how ASC2 agents access and perform primitive actions [27]. Typically, in interpreter-based BDI frameworks primitive actions need to be properly defined before they can be used by the agent. In ASC2 such redefinitions are not needed and the agent program can directly access any entity on the JVM's class path. An example of this would be the .print function in Jason, defined in the standard agent library and that underneath calls Java print. In contrast, in an ASC2 program there is no need to define the primitive action; the agent program can call Java/Scala's print function by simply using #print (where # is the prefix for calling any primitive action).

AgentScript Translator. The ASC2 translator generates concurrent programs in a lower-level executable language from agent scripts written in AgentScript DSL. The reasoning cycle of ASC2 follows the same principles of what is proposed for AgentSpeak(L) and further extended by Jason. This reasoning cycle generally includes steps to iterate over internal and external events, find relevant and applicable plans to react to these events, creating intentions to perform the plans and executing the intentions. But, while Jason and many other BDI frameworks implement an interpreter and a reasoning engine to drive the execution the of the agent programs as run time, in ASC2, all the mechanisms needed for execution with the exception of the externalized plan selection function are generated as part of the agent's executable code in form of control flow statements.

AgentScript Execution Architecture. The ASC2 implements an abstract execution architecture that is used as a template for the Translator to generate the concurrent agent programs. The architecture introduced in [27] defines each agent as a modular and extendable *actor-based* micro-system. The Actor model, introduced in [21], is a mathematical theory that treats *actors* as the primitives of computation [20]. Actors are essentially reactive concurrent entities, when an actor receives a message it can send messages to other actors; *spawn* new actors; modify its reactive behavior for the next message it receives. In the current implementation of ASC2, the underlying language is *Scala* and the agents utilize the actor model implementation of *Akka*[3]. The ASC2 architecture also

---

[3] https://akka.io.

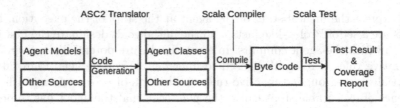

Fig. 1. Compile/Test process of an ASC2 program with sbt

defines multiple components of the agents like their belief base and communication layer as external dependencies, enabling modularity with respect e.g. automated reasoning or transportation functions.

3.2 Testing Approach

In a typical *unit* or *integration test* of a computational entity under test (e.g. a class, a web service), the designer sets up an initial setting (e.g. one or multiple object instances, web services, a client), and then, based on certain invocations (e.g. function calls, access/service requests), a set of *assertions* are checked to verify the internal state, or some observable behavior of the tested entity, or its effect on the environment (e.g. function results, service responses, modifications of other entities).

Internal attributes (of objects or services) are generally harder to access and therefore to verify. Best practices of Test-Driven Development (TDD) address this issue by means of *Dependency Injection* (DI): the dependencies of each entity should be instantiated from outside the entity and then passed to it e.g. as parameters (typically to the class constructor in object-oriented programming). This allows the tester to isolate and observe the internal mechanisms of the entity under test by using "mocked" dependencies. To enhance testability, multiple components of ASC2 agents, including their belief base and communications layer, are injected as external dependencies.

In any certain situation, we can look at a single agent or multiple agents (a MAS) as a computational entity under test, and this entity has also a set of internal attributes, observable behavior, and possible interactions with its environment. The single agent or multiple agents under test can be instantiated from one or more scripts. The setting could include any other types of entities e.g. other possibly mocked agents, external objects, etc. The initial state of the agent(s) and of the other related entities defines the initial setting of the test, the invocation/probing action of a test suite is typically a series of messages sent to the agents. The expected effect(s), behavior(s) or state(s) of an entity rely heavily on the entity under test. For a small system including one or only a few agents, each message or the beliefs of the agent(s) may be needed to be verified, whereas in a complex system, the designer may only need to verify emergent pattern in the interactions of the agents or major shifts in the state of the system.

```
1   +!init(W) : W > 1 =>
2       Nbr = "worker" + ((#name.replaceAll("worker","").toInt % W) + 1);
3       +neighbor(Nbr).
4
5   +!token(0) =>
6       #coms.achieve("master", done).
7
8   +!token(N) : neighbor(Nbr) =>
9       #coms.achieve(Nbr, token(N - 1)).
```

Listing 1: Token ring worker script in AgentScript DSL

In our approach, we aim to allow the designer to utilize any off-the-shelf testing tool (library, service, etc.) directly into their development chain, even more so to enable the designer to test their program via any standard build chain. In the case of the ASC2 framework, its current implementation is based on Scala, and we considered as target build tool *sbt*[4], which enables us to also use JVM/Scala testing libraries like *JUnit* or *ScalaTest*. We have then developed a sbt plugin[5] that —as part of the compile task—iterates over the scripts written in AgentScript DSL in the project sources and uses the AgentScript Translator to generate Scala implementations of the agents. Code generation is a standard part of build tools like sbt or maven, therefore, the generated sources are also managed by the build tool and are immediately available to rest of the project. The general overview of the *Compile/Test* cycle of an agent-based system developed via ASC2 and built by sbt is presented in Fig. 1. Note that this process is fully automated by sbt.

A MAS of this type can be started in two ways. After bootstrapping it as an empty instance of the MAS infrastructure, the designer can either use configuration files (e.g. JSON) to specify the agents of the system or alternatively, use lower-level code (e.g. Scala/Java) to manually spawn agents via their respective class in the generated code. In this work, we preferred the latter approach, as it provides better control over the test scenarios.

To complete our Compile/Test process, in addition to the *ScalaTest* library, we also used the *Akka Testing* library: at run-time, ASC2 agents are essentially Akka actor micro-systems and this library provides many convenient tools for testing actors. Both libraries are used out of the box and no modifications have been done to adapt them to the framework. With this configuration, each scenario to be verified can the written as a test suite in ScalaTest to test whether one or multiple agents behave as expected.

4   Illustrative Example

To illustrate an application of our testing approach we consider a MAS constructed around a Token Ring system, commonly used in both distributed sys-

---
[4] https://scala-sbt.org/.
[5] https://github.com/mostafamohajeri/sbt-scriptcc.

tems and MAS [8,27]. This system consists of one master agent and W worker agents; at the start of the program the master sends an $init(W)$ message to all worker agents to inform them of the total number of the workers in the ring, each worker upon receiving this message finds its neighbor, forming a closed ring. Then, T tokens are distributed among the workers, each token has to be passed N times in the ring formed by workers. When all T tokens have been passed N times and this was reported to the master, the program ends.

4.1   Unit/Agent Testing

We will focus in particular on the script of the worker agents shown in listing 1. We perform the tests taking the standpoint of a *whitebox* test engineer, meaning that we test the script of the agent knowing its internal workings; nevertheless, the tests are still performed externally, we do not modify the script in order to test it[6].

Testing Successful Scenarios. By viewing the script in listing 1, we can see that the agent has a total of 3 plans for 2 separate goals. Theoretically, we need at least 3 tests to cover the successful execution of all the plans. However, while the success criteria for plans is simple (completion of execution), achievements of goals can be more complicated and the testing framework needs to provide the flexibility to define them. The success criteria for the init(W) and token(N) goals are quite different. In the latter the expected behaviour in both plans is an observable event, i.e. a certain achieve message sent by the agent to another specific agent. In the former case there is no observable behavior and the success criterion is a specific update of the agent's belief base.

The test specification we used for the worker agent can be seen in listing 2. In line 3 an empty MAS object is created. The criterion of success for init(W) plan depends on the agent's beliefs, therefore we need to be able to verify the internal state of agent's belief base. First we create an instance of BeliefBase class (line 4) and when the agent under test (worker1) is being instantiated (line 10), this object is injected in the agent as its belief base; with this approach at any point in the tests we can simply access the agent's beliefs to query them for verification purposes or even modify the agent's belief base for setting up test scenario states.

Only one agent (worker1) is under test and the other agents present in the suite can be mocked. As ASC2 agents are actor micro-systems, an agent can be mocked by a single actor. In lines 5 and 6, two *probe* actors are created to be the stand-ins for the master agent and (worker1)'s neighbor in the tests and they are then registered to the system (lines 11 and 12). This type of mocking gives us the ability to verify all the interactions that the agent under test may have had with these probe actors.

The rest of the test suite contains 3 tests, in the first test in line 18 a goal event init(50) is sent to the worker1 agent and it is expected that after this

---

[6]   https://github.com/mostafamohajeri/agentscript-test.

```
1   class TokenRingWorkerSpec extends ... {
2
3     val mas = new MAS()
4     val verifiableBB  = new BeliefBase()
5     val mockedMaster = testKit.createTestProbe[IMessage]()
6     val mockedNeighbor = testKit.createTestProbe[IMessage]()
7     val worker
8
9     override def beforeAll(): Unit = {
10      mas.registerAgent(new worker(bb = verifiableBB), name = "worker1")
11      mas.registerAgent(mockedMaster, name = "master")
12      mas.registerAgent(mockedNeighbor, name = "worker2")
13      worker = mas.getAgent("worker1")
14    }
15
16    "A worker agent" should {
17      "have its neighbor in its belief base after '!init(N)'" in {
18        worker.event(achieve,"init(50)").send()
19        mockedMaster.expect(GoalAchievedMessage())
20        assert(verifiableBB.query("neighbor(worker2)") == true)
21      }
22
23      "send a '!done' to master on '!token(0)'" in {
24        worker.event(achieve,"token(0)").send()
25        mockedMaster.expect(event(achieve,"done").source(worker))
26      }
27
28      "send a '!token(N-1)' to its neighbor on '!token(N)'" in {
29        worker.event(achieve,"token(10)").send()
30        mockedNeighbor.expect(event(achieve,"token(9)").source(worker))
31      }
32    }
33  }
```

Listing 2: Test suite for the worker agent

goal is achieved (line 19), the belief base of the agent contains the belief defined by the term `neighbor(worker2)` which is verified in line 20. In the next test, a goal message `token(0)` is sent to the agent (line 24) and then it is verified that the agent sends a `done` message to the master (line 25). The final test follows the same pattern by sending a goal message `token(10)` (line 30) and the verification includes a `token(10--1)` message to its neighbor (line 30). Note that in all the tests, the messages sent to the `worker1` agent do not specify any source, this is because in the script in listing 1, the source of the messages is not checked meaning it is not necessary to specify the source. As these tests are written in a standard testing library, build tools such as *sbt* can execute them in their build chain. By running the tests in the sbt shell we are able to see the output presented in listing 3 that indicates our program has passed this test.

```
[info] A worker agent should
[info] - have its neighbor in its belief base after '!init(N)'
[info] - send a '!done' to master on '!token(0)'
[info] - send a '!token(N-1)' to its neighbor on '!token(N)'
...
[info] All tests passed.
```

Listing 3: Output of the worker agent test suite

```
1   "A worker agent" should {
2     "send a 'NoApplicablePlan()' on '!init(-1)'" in {
3       worker.event(achieve,"init(-1)").source(mockedMaster).send()
4       mockedMaster.expect(NoApplicablePlan())
5     }
6
7     "send a 'NoRelevantPlan()' on '!unknown'" in {
8       worker.event(achieve,"unknown").source(mockedMaster).send()
9       mockedMaster.expect(NoRelevantPlan())
10    }
11  }
```

Listing 4: Failure tests for worker agent

Testing Failure Scenarios. Successful executions are only a part of the full story. Indeed, in software testing it is acknowledged that covering *failures* is both more important and challenging, and thus requires more critical thinking by the test engineer [29]. Interestingly, failure tests are especially important in agent-based programming because failing under certain conditions may sometimes be the correct behavior for an agent.

Two failure tests are presented in listing 4. The first test sends a init(W) goal message to the agent with W=-1 (line 3) but the first plan is applicable only for W > 1 and the expected behavior of the agent in this situation is a failure which is verified by expecting a NoApplicablePlan message. In the second test, a goal message unknown is sent to the agent (line 8) for which the agent does not have any plans and it should reply with a NoRelevantPlan (line 9). Note that failure of a goal is not only reflected by the absence of an applicable plan or more generally failure in execution of a plan; similar to the success scenarios, the designer can define any other arbitrary criteria for a failure scenario.

Although we acknowledge that testing an agent program for every possible failure can easily become an infeasible task [37,38], certain failures may be particular important for the designer to test, therefore there is value in enabling this possibility.

4.2   Coverage

We explore at this point whether and how off-the-shelf coverage tools such as *scoverage*[7] can be used for code coverage analysis of agent programs written in ASC2, considering both statement and branch coverage aspect. To perform this we simply add the scoverage plugin to our project and generate a coverage report.

The coverage report produced for the worker agent by means of the previous tests is presented in Table 1. The `worker.Agent` row shows the coverage for the internal mechanisms of the agent, like e.g. *event handling*, while the other rows show the coverage report for each separate event, as an example, the `worker.token_1` refers to an event `token` in `worker` agent with 1 parameter. The branch coverage report mainly concerns conditional statements in the generated Scala code of the agent and should be regarded only as informal information about the coverage of the main script.

These results show that our tests indeed covered most of the behaviors that the agent might have. In fact, by exploring the coverage analysis we can see the reason for which the `worker.token_1` has less coverage: the missed branch can be explained by the fact that the tests did not include any scenario in which the `token(N)` plan fails. Also note that while the example script did not contain any sub-goals or conditional statements in the plans, ASC2 Translator generates sub-goal adoptions as function calls and translates conditional statements to their counterpart in the underlying language, therefore, coverage tools like *scoverage* are able to calculate the correct number of covered and total possible branches for deeper goal-plan trees.

Table 1. Coverage analysis of the `worker` agent

Component	Statement coverage %	Branch coverage (covered/total)
`worker.Agent`	93.5	6/6
`worker.init_1`	93.5	2/2
`worker.token_1`	80.2	3/4

4.3   Integration/System Testing

Even following the guidelines on categorizing different levels of testing in MAS [28], there is no definite technical distinction in place. Typically test libraries provide mechanisms such as annotations for the designer to label test suites with its (their) related level(s) to orchestrate their execution. As illustration, we consider an integration test to verify a token ring MAS system consisting of the previously mentioned `worker` agents and a `master` agent. The test suite is reported in listing 5.

---

[7] http://scoverage.org/.

```
1   class TokenRingIntegrationSpec extends ... {
2
3     //a communication layer that records a trace of the interactions
4     object recordedComs extends AgentCommunicationsLayer { ... }
5
6     val token_pattern = "token\\([0-9]+\\)".r
7     val done_pattern = "done".r
8
9     "A token ring MAS with W = 100, T = 50 and N = 4" should {
10       "have 250 'token(X)' and 50 'done' message" in {
11         // create the agents
12         mas.registerAgent(new worker(coms = recordedComs), num = 100)
13         mas.registerAgent(new master(coms = recordedComs), name = "master")
14         // invoke the system
15         mas.getAgent("master").event(achieve, "start(50,4)").send()
16         // verify the interactions
17         watchdog.expectTerminated( mas, 10.seconds )
18         assert(recordedComs.trace.count(token_pattern.matches) == 250)
19         assert(recordedComs.trace.count(done_pattern.matches) == 50)
20       }
21     }
22   }
```

Listing 5: Integration test suite for the token ring system

The test will be centered around the interactions between agents and the state of the system in a specific setting of our token ring. The token ring is defined with 100 worker agents and 1 master agent (lines 12–13), and, to be able to verify the exhibited interactions, we use dependency injection to initialize all the agents by means of an overridden instance of the communication layer (line 4), created to record every message passed in the system into a list.

To invoke the system, a start(T,N) is sent to the master agent (line 15). We are interacting with the master from a *black box* perspective: although the event start(T,N) is exposed, the internal mechanisms of this agent are assumed to be unknown.

Three criteria are verified for this system. Firstly, we consider a system level performance based criteria as we expect the system to be terminated under 10 s (line 17). Next, we use two known expectations from a token ring system to verify the correct execution of the system: at the end of execution, there should be (a) T number of done messages and (b) $T \times (N + 1)$ number of token(X) messages in the trace. The interaction verification statements are presented respectively in lines 18–19. Recalling the flexible definitions of testing levels, note that these integration/system test could be considered from the perspective of master agent as a unit/agent level test possibly with mocking the worker agents. Similar to previous tests, running this suite via sbt yields the output in listing 6.

```
[info] A token ring MAS with W = 100, T = 50 and N = 4 should
[info] - have 250 'token(X)' and 50 'done' message
...
[info] All tests passed.
```

Listing 6: Output of the token ring integration test suite

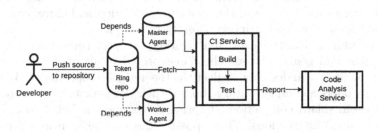

Fig. 2. Continuous integration applied on a Token ring program whose master and worker agent scripts are located on other repositories.

4.4 Continuous Integration

The proposed approach for testing can be easily combined with online CI services. This process generally includes utilizing source repositories like Github[8], CI services like TravisCI and code analysis services like Coveralls[9]. The only step needed to set the CI cycle for an ASC2 project is to configure the source repository of the project in a way that the automated CI cycle is triggered on every **push** to the repository. This can be done by adding a configuration file that provides information for the CI service how to compile and test the project via sbt.

Following this method, a MAS project does not need to be only located in a single source repository. For instance, different types of agents can be developed in different projects by separate teams and only be used as dependencies in the development of the system. We believe this is an interesting practical innovation, improving the scalability of MAS projects with respect to their development.

An overview of an example CI process for the token ring is presented in Fig. 2 in which the sources of **worker** and **master** agents are located in separate repositories, and a third token ring repository uses them as dependencies. When the system designer pushes the project to the repository, the CI service fetches the source and compiles and tests it via sbt and records the results[10]. Then, the code coverage report is committed to the code analysis service[11].

---

[8] https://github.com/.
[9] https://coveralls.io/.
[10] https://travis-ci.com/github/mostafamohajeri/agentscript-test.
[11] https://coveralls.io/github/mostafamohajeri/agentscript-test.

5   Discussion and Future Developments

Despite the critical points/observations concerning MAS testing raised in the literature, in this paper we provide several support arguments for using mainstream testing tools for MAS and agent-based programming, by means of a concrete use case. We implemented a multi-agent system reproducing a token ring benchmark with the framework ASC2, and then we run tests (success, failure, coverage) at unit/agent level as well as at integration/system level.

At the unit and agent level (unit testing) we performed tests concerning events, plans and goals. The somehow unexpected result of the experiment is that such an approach does not neglect the theoretical complexity of BDI agents but it truly offers a complementary tool for their development. We were able to test successful (plan) completions, internal states and the belief base, failures, and fine-grained interactions. These possibilities can be seen as offering constructs mapping e.g. to declarative and procedural goals in BDI agents [40]: the designer can define the achievement/failure of a goal not only in terms of completion/exception of a plan, but also as determined by any arbitrary indicator internal or external to the agent. This showed that testability of agent programs defined in a framework is closely related to the design choices of that framework.

At the integration/group and system/society level (integration testing) we performed tests with simple verification criteria, but these criteria can easily be extended to more sophisticated and realistic interaction analysis and verification methods developed by the MAS community [7]. Additionally, we illustrated how the proposed approach enables the MAS designer to take advantage of continuous integration (CI) services without extra effort. This is particularly important for MAS designers that require to integrate and test their work continuously with other projects.

There is an additional benefit of using mainstream test tools for BDI agents, and especially for frameworks that are based on higher-level logic-based DSLs. Those frameworks generally map primitive actions to constructs specified in a lower-level programming language like Java. By using a testing process compatible with both higher level models and lower level implementations, the testing process can be more efficient and seamless for the designer specially if the agent models are only a part of a project that includes other computational entities that are being developed alongside the agents.

An issue in using mainstream test libraries for a BDI framework with a logic-based DSL is the disparity between the high-level agent DSL and the lower-level language used for the tests. This can be addressed by either developing approaches to write tests in the high-level DSL or creating interfaces for the low-level language to enable the test engineer to implement tests at a proper level of abstraction. In this work we have taken the latter approach. The intuition behind this choice was that frameworks based on cross-compila-tion [14,36] produce source codes that can be directly integrated within standard build tools.

Can our results be generalized to other agent programming frameworks? Motivated by the success of works like AJPF/MCAPL [13] that provides model checking for multiple BDI frameworks, as a future study we intend to explore how to apply this approach to a wider range of MAS frameworks. Yet, we can already trace some higher-level considerations. The answer, at the unit/agent level, depends on compilation and the execution model of those frameworks. For frameworks like Jade and JS-son [23], that use mainstream programming languages to define agents, these tools should be compatible out of the box with minor effort [24]. For cross-compilation-based frameworks like Astra [14] and ASC2 [27] it is only the matter of tooling (e.g. build tool plugins) to allow them to use mainstream testing tools. For interpreter-based frameworks like Jason [6] and GOAL [22], because they require their own dedicated reasoning engines and execution environment, testing via such tools may prove to need more work and possibly modifications to the framework. This issue may be not so problematic, as there are already many works that propose dedicated testing and debugging approaches for interpreter-based frameworks [25].

At the integration and system level, and also with respect to compatibility with CI services, generally externalized to the execution of the tested entity, we believe it is possible to consolidate other frameworks regardless of their compile/interpret model. This could lead to seamless integration testing of systems defined in each framework with mainstream software testing tools or dedicated ones.

In perspective, our overarching research concerns socio-technical and complex multi-domain infrastructures; we believe that Agent-Oriented Software Engineering can be a powerful technical tool with robust theoretical foundations for designing, modelling, implementing and testing such systems. Enhancing their development cycle goes with a seamless integration of multi-agent systems into modern infrastructures. This is a critical requirement to utilize the full potential of MAS in a real production-level setting.

Acknowledgements. The work as presented in this paper has been done as part of the Dutch Research project 'Data Logistics for Logistics Data' (DL4LD), supported by the Dutch Organisation for Scientific Research (NWO), the Dutch Institute for Advanced Logistics 'TKI Dinalog' (http://www.dinalog.nl/) and the Dutch Commit-to-Data initiative (http://www.dutchdigitaldelta.nl/big-data/over-commit2data) (grant no: 628.009.001).

References

1. Software testing services market by product, end-users, and geography - global forecast and analysis 2019–2023 (2019). https://www.industryresearch.co/software-testing-services-market-14620379
2. Bakar, N.A., Selamat, A.: Agent systems verification?: systematic literature review and mapping. Appl. Intell. **48**(5), 1251–1274 (2018). https://doi.org/10.1007/s10489-017-1112-z

3. Behrens, T.M., Dix, J.: Model checking multi-agent systems with logic based Petri nets. Ann. Math. Artif. Intell. **51**(2–4), 81–121 (2007). https://doi.org/10.1007/s10472-008-9092-7
4. Bordini, R.H., Fisher, M., Visser, W., Wooldridge, M.: Verifiable multi-agent programs. In: Dastani, M.M., Dix, J., El Fallah-Seghrouchni, A. (eds.) ProMAS 2003. LNCS (LNAI), vol. 3067, pp. 72–89. Springer, Heidelberg (2004). https://doi.org/10.1007/978-3-540-25936-7_4
5. Bordini, R.H., Fisher, M., Visser, W., Wooldridge, M.: Verifying multi-agent programs by model checking. Auton. Agent. Multi-Agent Syst. **12**(2), 239–256 (2006). https://doi.org/10.1007/s10458-006-5955-7
6. Bordini, R.H., Hübner, J.F., Vieira, R.: Jason and the golden fleece of agent-oriented programming. In: Bordini, R.H., Dastani, M., Dix, J., El Fallah Seghrouchni, A. (eds.) Multi-Agent Programming. MSASSO, vol. 15, pp. 3–37. Springer, Boston, MA (2005). https://doi.org/10.1007/0-387-26350-0_1
7. Botía, J.A., Gómez-Sanz, J.J., Pavón, J.: Intelligent data analysis for the verification of multi-agent systems interactions. In: Corchado, E., Yin, H., Botti, V., Fyfe, C. (eds.) IDEAL 2006. LNCS, vol. 4224, pp. 1207–1214. Springer, Heidelberg (2006). https://doi.org/10.1007/11875581_143
8. Cardoso, R.C., Zatelli, M.R., Hübner, J.F., Bordini, R.H.: Towards benchmarking actor- and agent-based programming languages. In: Proceedings of the 2013 Workshop on Programming Based on Actors, Agents, and Decentralized Control, AGERE! 2013, pp. 115–126. Association for Computing Machinery, New York, NY, USA (2013)
9. Clarke, E.M., Grumberg, O., Peled, D.A.: Model Checking. MIT Press, Cambridge (2000)
10. Coelho, R., Kulesza, U., von Staa, A., Lucena, C.: Unit testing in multi-agent systems using mock agents and aspects. In: International Workshop on Software Engineering for Large-Scale Multi-Agent Systems, SELMAS 2006, pp. 83–90 (2006)
11. Dastani, M.: 2APL: a practical agent programming language. Auton. Agent. Multi-Agent Syst. **16**(3), 214–248 (2008). https://doi.org/10.1007/s10458-008-9036-y
12. David, N., Sichman, J.S., Coelho, H.: Towards an emergence-driven software process for agent-based simulation. In: Simão Sichman, J., Bousquet, F., Davidsson, P. (eds.) MABS 2002. LNCS (LNAI), vol. 2581, pp. 89–104. Springer, Heidelberg (2003). https://doi.org/10.1007/3-540-36483-8_7
13. Dennis, L.A., Fisher, M., Lincoln, N.K., Lisitsa, A., Veres, S.M.: Practical verification of decision-making in agent-based autonomous systems. Autom. Softw. Eng. **23**(3), 305–359 (2014). https://doi.org/10.1007/s10515-014-0168-9
14. Dhaon, A., Collier, R.W.: Multiple inheritance in AgentSpeak (L)-style programming languages. In: Proceedings of the 4th International Workshop on Programming Based on Actors Agents and Decentralized Control. Association for Computing Machinery (2014)
15. Ekinci, E.E., Tiryaki, A.M., Çetin, Ö., Dikenelli, O.: Goal-oriented agent testing revisited. In: Luck, M., Gomez-Sanz, J.J. (eds.) Agent-Oriented Software Engineering IX, AOSE 2008. Lecture Notes in Computer Science, vol. 5386, pp. 173–186. Springer, Berlin, Heidelberg (2009)
16. Ferber, J.: Multi-Agent Systems: An Introduction to Distributed Artificial Intelligence. USA, 1st edn. (1999)
17. Ferrando, A., Dennis, L.A., Ancona, D., Fisher, M., Mascardi, V.: Verifying and validating autonomous systems: towards an integrated approach. In: Colombo, C., Leucker, M. (eds.) RV 2018. LNCS, vol. 11237, pp. 263–281. Springer, Cham (2018). https://doi.org/10.1007/978-3-030-03769-7_15

18. Fisher, M., Mascardi, V., Rozier, K.Y., Schlingloff, B.-H., Winikoff, M., Yorke-Smith, N.: Towards a framework for certification of reliable autonomous systems. Auton. Agent. Multi-Agent Syst. **35**(1), 1–65 (2020). https://doi.org/10.1007/s10458-020-09487-2

19. Herzig, A., Lorini, E., Perrussel, L., Xiao, Z.: BDI logics for BDI architectures: old problems, new perspectives. KI - Künstliche Intelligenz **31**(1), 73–83 (2016). https://doi.org/10.1007/s13218-016-0457-5

20. Hewitt, C.: Actor model of computation: scalable robust information systems (2010)

21. Hewitt, C., Bishop, P., Steiger, R.: A universal modular actor formalism for artificial intelligence. In: Proceedings of the 3rd International Joint Conference on Artificial Intelligence, IJCAI 1973, pp. 235–245. Morgan Kaufmann Publishers Inc., San Francisco (1973)

22. Hindriks, K.V.: Programming rational agents in GOAL. In: El Fallah Seghrouchni, A., Dix, J., Dastani, M., Bordini, R.H. (eds.) Multi-Agent Programming, pp. 119–157. Springer, Boston, MA (2009). https://doi.org/10.1007/978-0-387-89299-3_4

23. Kampik, T., Nieves, J.C.: JS-son - a lean, extensible JavaScript agent programming library. In: Dennis, L.A., Bordini, R.H., Lespérance, Y. (eds.) EMAS 2019. LNCS (LNAI), vol. 12058, pp. 215–234. Springer, Cham (2020). https://doi.org/10.1007/978-3-030-51417-4_11

24. Khamis, M.A., Nagi, K.: Designing multi-agent unit tests using systematic test design patterns (extended version). Eng. Appl. Artif. Intell. **26**(9), 2128–2142 (2013)

25. Koeman, V.J., Hindriks, K.V., Jonker, C.M.: Automating failure detection in cognitive agent programs. In: Proceedings of the International Joint Conference on Autonomous Agents and Multiagent Systems, AAMAS pp. 1237–1246 (2016)

26. McCabe, T.J.: A complexity measure. IEEE Trans. Softw. Eng. SE-2(4), 308–320 (1976)

27. Mohajeri Parizi, M., Sileno, G., van Engers, T., Klous, S.: Run, agent, run! architecture and benchmarking of actor-based agents. In: proceedings of Programming based on Actors, Agents, and Decentralized Control (AGERE 2020), pp. 11–20 (2020)

28. Moreno, M., Pavón, J., Rosete, A.: Testing in agent oriented methodologies. In: Omatu, S., Rocha, Miguel P.., Bravo, José, Fernández, Florentino, Corchado, Emilio, Bustillo, Andrés, Corchado, Juan M.. (eds.) IWANN 2009. LNCS, vol. 5518, pp. 138–145. Springer, Heidelberg (2009). https://doi.org/10.1007/978-3-642-02481-8_20

29. Myers, G.J., Sandler, C.: The Art of Software Testing. Wiley, Hoboken (2012)

30. Nguyen, C.D., Perini, A., Bernon, C., Pavón, J., Thangarajah, J.: Testing in multi-agent systems. Lecture Notes in Computer Science 6038 LNCS, pp. 180–190 (2011)

31. Padgham, L., Zhang, Z., Thangarajah, J., Miller, T.: Model-based test oracle generation for automated unit testing of agent systems. IEEE Trans. Software Eng. **39**(9), 1230–1244 (2013)

32. Padgham, L., Winikoff, M.: Developing Intelligent Agent Systems: A Practical Guide, vol. 13. Wiley, Hoboken (2004)

33. Poutakidis, D., Winikoff, M., Padgham, L., Zhang, Z.: Debugging and testing of multi-agent systems using design artefacts. In: El Fallah Seghrouchni, A., Dix, J., Dastani, M., Bordini, R.H. (eds.) Multi-Agent Programming, pp. 215–258. Springer, Boston, MA (2009). https://doi.org/10.1007/978-0-387-89299-3_7

34. Rao, A.S.: AgentSpeak(L): BDI agents speak out in a logical computable language. In: Van de Velde, W., Perram, J.W. (eds.) MAAMAW 1996. LNCS, vol. 1038, pp. 42–55. Springer, Heidelberg (1996). https://doi.org/10.1007/BFb0031845

35. Rao, A.S., Georgeff, M.P.: BDI agents: from theory to practice. In: Proceedings of the First International Conference on Multi-Agent Systems (ICMAS1995), pp. 312–319 (1995)

36. Rodriguez, S., Gaud, N., Galland, S.: Sarl: a general-purpose agent-oriented programming language. In: International Joint Conferences on Web Intelligence (WI) and Intelligent Agent Technologies (IAT), vol. 3, pp. 103–110 (2014)

37. Winikoff, M.: BDI agent testability revisited. Auton. Agent. Multi-Agent Syst. **31**(5), 1094–1132 (2017). https://doi.org/10.1007/s10458-016-9356-2

38. Winikoff, M., Cranefield, S.: On the testability of BDI agent systems. IJCAI Int. Joint Conf. Artif. Intell. **51**, 4217–4221 (2015)

39. Winikoff, M., Dennis, L., Fisher, M.: Slicing agent programs for more efficient verification. In: Weyns, D., Mascardi, V., Ricci, A. (eds.) EMAS 2018. LNCS (LNAI), vol. 11375, pp. 139–157. Springer, Cham (2019). https://doi.org/10.1007/978-3-030-25693-7_8

40. Winikoff, M., Padgham, L., Harland, J., Thangarajah, J.: Declarative and procedural goals in intelligent agent systems. In: 8th International Conference on Principles of Knowledge Representation and Reasoning, KR 2002, pp. 470–481 (2002)

41. Zhang, Z., Thangarajah, J., Padgham, L.: Automated unit testing for agent systems, **7** 10–18 (2007)

42. Zhou, X., Cushing, R., Grosso, P., Engers, T.V.: Policy enforcement for secure and trustworthy data sharing in multi-domain infrastructures. In: Engineering Multi-Agent Systems, pp. 104–113 (2020)

Engineering Explainable Agents: An Argumentation-Based Approach

Alison R. Panisson[1]($\boxtimes$), Débora C. Engelmann[2], and Rafael H. Bordini[2]

[1] Federal University of Santa Catarina, Araranguá, SC, Brazil
`alison.panisson@ufsc.br`
[2] School of Technology, PUCRS, Porto Alegre, RS, Brazil
`debora.engelmann@edu.pucrs.br`, `rafael.bordini@pucrs.br`

Abstract. Explainability has become one of the most important concepts in Artificial Intelligence (AI), resulting in a complete area of study called Explainable AI (XAI). In this paper, we propose an approach for engineering explainable BDI agents based on the use of argumentation techniques. In particular, our approach is based on modelling argumentation schemes, which provide not only the reasoning patterns agents use to instantiate arguments but also templates for agents to translate arguments in an agent-oriented programming language to natural language. Thus, using our approach, agents are able to provide explanations about their mental attitudes and decision-making not only to other software agents but also to humans. This is particularly useful when agents and humans carry out tasks collaboratively.

1 Introduction

Explainability is pointed out as an essential characteristic in artificial intelligence applications so that users can effectively understand, trust, and manage such applications [18]. The need for explaining a decision/reasoning/actions was discussed as early as the 1970s, starting with the development of expert systems and the need for those systems to explain their decisions not only with traces but also with justifications [1]. These needs have become an essential characteristic in Multi-Agent Systems (MAS) [49], given that MAS are one of the most powerful paradigms to implement complex distributed systems powered by artificial intelligence techniques.

In this paper, we propose an approach for engineering explainable agents using argumentation-based techniques. In particular, we propose an approach in which a set of argumentation schemes (reasoning patterns for argumentation) provide means for agents to instantiate, reason, and communicate arguments as well as templates to translate those instantiated arguments into natural language arguments. Those arguments can be used to provide explanations, in computational and natural languages, about the agents' mental attitudes and the decision they make.

Argumentation schemes are patterns for arguments (or inferences) representing the structure of common types of arguments used both in everyday discourse

© Springer Nature Switzerland AG 2022
N. Alechina et al. (Eds.): EMAS 2021, LNAI 13190, pp. 273–291, 2022.
https://doi.org/10.1007/978-3-030-97457-2_16

as well as in special contexts such as legal and scientific argumentation [46]. Different social contexts enable the use of various different argumentation schemes, based on the state of the environment (e.g., a university, a court, a hospital), the roles played by the participating actors, and the relations between their roles (e.g., professors and students, judges and lawyers, doctors and patients, etc.). In this work, we propose the use of argumentation schemes as a tool for modelling explanation, using the already-known interpretability of computational arguments plus a natural language representation of arguments. Thus, an agent is able to explain itself to another agent using computational arguments as well as it is able to explain itself to a human user using natural language arguments. We argue that our work contributes towards the development of AI systems capable of sophisticated interactions between humans and software agents.

The main contributions of this work are: (i) we propose an approach for engineering explainable agents based on the modelling of argumentation schemes. Using our approach, agents are able to explain their mental attitudes and decision making not only to other agents, using a computational representation of arguments, but also to human users, using a natural language representation of such arguments; (ii) we demonstrate our approach through a hospital scenario in which agents explain their mental attitudes not only to other agents but also to humans; and (iii) we discuss the potential of our approach in the context of emerging research in areas such as Hybrid Intelligence [1] and Explainable Artificial Intelligence [17,18].

This work is organised as follow. In Sect. 2, we describe an overview of agent-oriented programming languages and argumentation schemes, which consist of the background of our work, including, in Sect. 2.3, an approach for argumentation-based reasoning and argumentation-based dialogues in multi-agent systems using argumentation schemes, based on our previous work published in [25,26,28,32]. In Sect. 3, we present our approach for engineering explainable agents using argumentation, introducing argumentation templates in natural languages and a set of argumentation schemes that allow agents to explain their beliefs. In Sect. 4, we present an example in the domain of healthcare, based on an application we are currently developing. In Section 5, we discuss the work we found related to our approach, and in Sect. 6, we conclude this work with some final remarks also pointing out future work.

2   Background

2.1   Agent Oriented Programming Languages

Among the many AOPLs and platforms, such as Jason, Jadex, Jack, AgentFactory, 2APL, GOAL, Golog, and MetateM, as discussed in [3], we chose the Jason platform [4] for our work. Jason extends the AgentSpeak language, an abstract logic-based AOPL introduced by Rao [37], which is one of the best-known languages inspired by the BDI architecture.

Besides specifying BDI agents with well-defined mental attitudes, the Jason platform [4] has some other features that are particularly interesting for our work, for example, strong negation, belief annotations, and (customisable) speech-act based communication. Strong negation helps the modelling of uncertainty, allowing the representation of things that the agent: (i) believes to be true, e.g., about(paper1, tom); (ii) believes to be false, e.g., ¬about(paper2, tom); (iii) is ignorant about, i.e., the agent has no information about whether a paper is about tom or not. Also, Jason automatically generates annotations for all the beliefs in the agents' belief base about the source from where the belief was obtained (which can be from sensing the environment, communication with other agents, or a mental note created by the agent itself). The annotation has the following format: about(paper1, tom)[source(reviewer1)], stating that the source of the belief that paper1 is about the topic tom (theory of mind) is reviewer1. The annotations in Jason can be easily extended to include other meta-information, for example, trust and time as used in [24, 30]. Another interesting feature of Jason is the communication between agents, which is done through a predefined (internal) action. There are a number of performatives that can be used in that internal (communicative) action, allowing rich communication between agents in Jason, as explained in detail in [4]. Furthermore, new performatives can be easily defined (or redefined) in order to give special meaning to them[1], which is an essential characteristic for this work.

2.2 Argumentation Schemes

Besides the familiar deductive and inductive forms of arguments, argumentation schemes represent forms of arguments that are *defeasible*[2]. This means that an argument may not be strong by itself (i.e., it is based on disputable inferences), but it may be strong enough to provide evidence that warrants rational acceptance of its conclusion [45]. Conclusions from argumentation schemes can be inferred in conditions of uncertainty and lack of knowledge. This means that we must remain open-minded to new pieces of evidence that can invalidate previous conclusions [46]. These circumstances of uncertainty and lack of knowledge are, inevitably, characteristics of multi-agent systems, which deal with dynamic environments and organisations [49].

The acceptance of a conclusion from an instantiation of an argumentation scheme is directly associated with the so-called *critical questions*. Critical questions may be asked before a conclusion from an argument (labelled by an argumentation scheme) is accepted, and they point out to the disputable information used in that argument. Together, the argumentation scheme and the matching set of critical questions are used to evaluate a given argument in a particular case, considering the context of the dialogue in which the argument occurred [46].

Arguments instantiated from argumentation schemes, and properly evaluated by means of their critical questions, can be used by agents in their reasoning and communication processes. In both situations, other arguments, probably instantiated from other argumentation schemes, are compared in order to arrive at an

---

[1] For example, new performatives for argumentation-based communication between Jason agents were introduced in [31,33].

[2] Sometimes called *presumptive*, or *abductive* as well.

acceptable conclusion. After an argument is instantiated from an argumentation scheme and evaluated by its set of critical questions, the process follows the same principle of any argumentation-based approach, where arguments for and against a point of view are compared until eventually arriving at a set of the acceptable arguments.

In regards to *conflict* between arguments, we can consider the existence of two types, according to [46]: (i) a strong kind of conflict, where one party has a thesis to be proved, and the other part has a thesis that is the opposite of the first one, and (ii) a weaker kind of conflict, where one party has a thesis to be proved, and the other part doubts that thesis, but has no opposite thesis of their own. In the strong kind of conflict, each party must try to refute the thesis of the other in order to win. In the weaker form, one side can refute the other, showing that their thesis is doubtful. This difference between conflicts are inherent from the structure of arguments, and can be found also in the work of others, e.g. [36].

To exemplify our approach, we adapted the argumentation schemes *Argument from Position to Know* from [47] to a multi-agent (organisational) platform, so that for example roles that agents play in the system can be referred to within the scheme. Consider the *Argument from role to know in multi-agent systems* (*role to know* for short) :

"Agent *ag* is currently playing a role *R* (its position) that implies knowing things in a certain subject domain *S* containing proposition *A* (**Major Premise**). *ag* asserts that *A* (in domain *S*) is true (or false) (**Minor Premise**). *A* is true (or false) (**Conclusion**)".

The associated critical questions are: **CQ1**: Does playing role *R* imply knowing whether *A* holds? **CQ2**: Is *ag* an honest (trustworthy, reliable) source? **CQ3**: Did *ag* assert that *A* is true (or false)? **CQ4**: Is *ag* playing role *R*?

The argumentation scheme introduced above can be represented in the Jason multi-agent platform as a defeasible inference as follows (based on [25,27]):

```
def_inf(Conclusion,[role(Agent,Role), role_to_know(Role,Domain),
    asserts(Agent,Conclusion),about(Conclusion,Domain)])
    [as(role_to_know)].
```

where the agents are able to instantiate such argumentation schemes with the information available to them in their belief bases and to evaluate the acceptability of the conclusion based on the interactions among such instantiated arguments [25].

Formally, in our framework, an argumentation scheme is a tuple $\langle sn, \mathcal{C}, \mathcal{P}, \mathcal{CQ} \rangle$ with $\mathcal{SN}$ the argumentation scheme name (which must be unique in the system), $\mathcal{C}$ the conclusion of the argumentation scheme, $\mathcal{P}$ the premises, and $\mathcal{CQ}$ the associated critical questions. Considering the example above, the corresponding components are $\mathcal{SN}$ = role_to_know, $\mathcal{C}$ = Conclusion, $\mathcal{P}$ = asserts(Agent,Conclusion), role(Agent,Role), role_to_know(Role, Domain) and about(Conclusion,Domain), $\mathcal{CQ}$ = $\langle$cq1,role_to_know(Role,

Conclusion)⟩,   ⟨cq2, reliable(Agent)⟩,   ⟨cq3, asserts(Agent, Conclusion)⟩
and ⟨cq4, role(Agent, Role)⟩.

2.3 Argumentation-Based Reasoning and Communication Using Argumentation Schemes

Formally, in our approach, an argument is a tuple $\langle S, c \rangle^{\theta}_{sn}$, where $\langle sn, C, P, CQ \rangle$ is the argumentation scheme used to instantiate that argument, θ is a most-general unifier for the premises in P and the agent's current beliefs, S is the set of premises and the inference rule of the scheme used to draw c (the conclusion of the argument). That is, S includes all instantiated premises from P—i.e., for all $p \in P, p\theta \in S$—and the inference rule corresponding to the scheme $(P \Rightarrow C)$; the conclusion c is the instantiation $C\theta$ such that $S \models c$ (c can be inferred from S).

For example, considering the argumentation scheme *role to know*, imagine that an agent ag knows that john (another agent in the system) is playing the role of doctor—role(john, doctor)—within the organisation of the multi-agent system. Further, ag knows that doctors know about cancer—knows(doctor, cancer). Therefore, if john asserts that *"smoking causes cancer"*—asserts(john, causes(smoking, cancer)), and given that causes of cancer are a subject matter related to cancer—about(causes(smoking, cancer), cancer), ag is able to instantiate the argumentation scheme *role to know*, which allows ag to conclude that smoking causes cancer— causes(smoking, cancer).

Arguments are evaluated both individually and collectively in order to determine which ones are acceptable arguments. Individually, the validity of an argument is evaluated through the critical questions pointed out in the argumentation scheme used to instantiate that argument [28]; in our example, an argument is individually acceptable by an agent if that agent is able to answer positively the critical questions $CQ1, CQ2, CQ3$, and $CQ4$. After evaluating arguments individually, conflicts/attacks between arguments are verified, and only those arguments that are not attacked by any other argument, or arguments that are defended by other arguments when attacked, remain; this leads to a set of acceptable arguments under some particular argumentation semantics (see [10]).

In reasoning, agents take the conclusions from the acceptable arguments as justified decisions, beliefs, actions, etc. In communication, agents use acceptable arguments to justify their position, reevaluating the set of acceptable arguments whenever they receive new information (possible new arguments) from other agents. Also, the critical questions from argumentation schemes provide a systematic way to evaluate disputable information used in arguments from other agents during dialogues [28].

3 Argumentation Scheme for Explainable Agents

We propose a general agent architecture in which agents use a computational and natural language representation of argumentation schemes. In our approach,

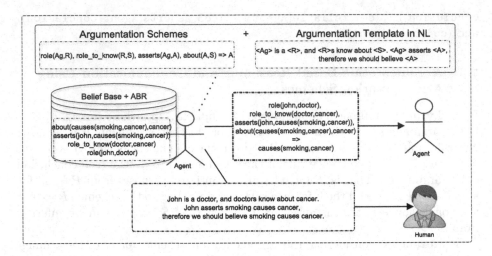

Fig. 1. Explainable agent architecture based on argumentation schemes.

agents instantiate arguments from the computational representation of argumentation schemes, using arguments for reasoning and communication (with other software agents). When communicating with human agents, they translate those arguments using the corresponding natural language representation of that reasoning pattern (argumentation scheme), as shown in Fig. 1.

3.1   Argumentation Templates in Natural Language

An essential part of our approach is modelling argumentation schemes in natural language, also considering the different instantiations for those reasoning patterns. We aim to model argumentation templates to translate arguments instantiated from argumentation schemes to their corresponding natural language representation.

Essentially, an argumentation template in natural language $\langle NLA \rangle_{\mathbf{sn}}$ for an argumentation scheme $\mathbf{sn}$ is a structure that concatenates natural language text and variables from $\mathbf{sn}$. An argument in natural language $\langle nla \rangle^{\theta}_{\mathbf{sn}}$ is an instance of an argumentation template in natural language $\langle NLA \rangle_{\mathbf{sn}}$ which uses the unification function from the corresponding computational argument (being translated) to instantiate the template. That is, an argumentation scheme $\mathbf{sn}$ is used by agents to instantiate arguments $\langle S, c \rangle_{\mathbf{sn}}$, being $\langle S, c \rangle^{\theta}_{\mathbf{sn}}$ a particular argument (in its computational representation) from the argumentation scheme $\mathbf{sn}$ according to the unification function given by θ. Also, being the argumentation template in natural language $\langle NLA \rangle_{\mathbf{sn}}$ a natural language template for $\mathbf{sn}$, then a natural language argument is obtained instantiating the corresponding argumentation template, in which $\forall \varphi \in NLA, \varphi \theta \in nla$, using the unification function from the computational representation of that particular argument being translated, given by θ.

For example, considering the argumentation scheme *role to know* introduced in the Sect. 2.2, we can create the following argumentation template to translate arguments instantiated from that argumentation scheme to natural language arguments:

⟨ "<Agent> is a <Role>, and <Role>s know about <Domain>. <Agent> asserts <Conclusion>, therefore we should believe that <Conclusion>".⟩[as(role_to_know)]

with its corresponding computational representation from [25,28] in Jason [4] agent-oriented programming language as follows:

```
def_inf(Conclusion,[role(Agent,Role), role_to_know(Role,Domain),
    asserts(Agent,Conclusion),about(Conclusion,Domain)])
    [as(role_to_know)].
```

Together, the computational representation of the argumentation scheme *role to know* and the template to translate arguments instantiated from it to natural language arguments, provide means for agents to communicate with both software and human agents.

For example, considering the scenario introduced in Sect. 2.3, an agent named *John* asserts that *smoking causes cancer. John is a doctor*, and *doctors are in a position to know whether smoking causes cancer or not.* Thus, any agent aware of John's assertion is able to construct an acceptable[3] argument concluding that *smoking causes cancer* based on the argumentation scheme *argument from role to know.*

When an agent needs to communicate that argument to another software agent, it is able to use the computational representation of that argument instantiated from the argumentation scheme *role to know*, as follows:

```
def_inf(causes(smoking,cancer),[role(john,doctor),
    role_to_know(doctor,cancer),
    asserts(john,causes(smoking,cancer)),
    about(causes(smoking,cancer),cancer)])
    [as(role_to_know)].
```

When an agent needs to communicate that argument to a human agent, it is able to use the natural language representation of that argument instantiated from the natural language template of that argumentation scheme, as follows:

⟨"john is a doctor, and doctors know about cancer. john asserts smoking causes cancer, therefore we should believe that smoking causes cancer".⟩[as(role_to_know)]

Note that the unification function $\theta = \{$Agent $\mapsto$ john, Role $\mapsto$ doctor, Domain $\mapsto$ cancer, Conclusion $\mapsto$ causes(smoking, cancer)$\}$ is used in both

---

[3] Here, we assume that the agent is able to answer the critical questions related to that argument instance.

instances, to instantiate a computational argument and its corresponding natural language argument, in which the predicate causes(smoking, cancer) is translated to *"smoking causes cancer"*.

3.2   Explaining Beliefs

Explaining beliefs relies on what kind of beliefs an agent is going to explain. According to [6], there exists some tension between the formation of some epistemic attitudes in agents and the way they access their available arguments. When analysing agent beliefs, two principles are mentioned in [6]:

(P1) Beliefs of an agent that should be partially determined by evaluating its available arguments. That means, given a predicate φ, an agent should first access its available arguments about φ and then form a belief based on the evaluation of those arguments, i.e., *belief formation by argument evaluation* [6].

(P2) The evaluation of arguments should take into account beliefs with respect to the premises of those arguments. That means, *argument evaluation is conditioned by belief formation* [6].

Clearly, using both principles together leads to infinite regress, in which arguments are used to form beliefs that are the basis to build and evaluate arguments that support beliefs, and so on. Thus, the authors in [6] propose to solve the tension between those two principles distinguishing *basic-explicit beliefs* (principle (P2)) and *argument-based beliefs* (principle (P1)).

Basic beliefs can be understood as agent beliefs whose justification is not inferential, i.e., it comes from other phenomena, such as observation or reliable communication. *Argument-based beliefs* can be understood as the conclusion of an acceptable argument according to a particular argumentation semantics (see [10]).

In order to explain an argument-based belief φ, agents simply communicate the argument supporting such belief, $\langle S, \varphi \rangle^{\theta}_{\text{sn}}$ to another software agent and $\langle nla \rangle^{\theta}_{\text{sn}}$ to a human agent, according to our approach presented early in this section. For example, when an agent believes that *"smoking causes cancer"* because it has an acceptable argument concluding that *"smoking causes cancer"*, then it will explain that particular belief using that argument. In our scenario, an agent will explain that *"smoking causes cancer"* using the argument that *"john is a doctor, and doctors know about cancer. john asserts smoking causes cancer, therefore we should believe that smoking causes cancer"*.

In order to explain a *basic belief*, we propose three argumentation schemes, as follows. The first argumentation scheme, the *argumentation scheme from perception* – as(perception) – basically states that if an agent has perceived something from the environment it also believes so:

"I have perceived **Info**, therefore I believe **Info**."

Its corresponding computational representation in the Jason platform is given by the following defeasible inference rule:

```
def_inf(believe(Me,Info),[perceived(Me,Info)])[as(perception)].
```

Also, in Jason, the predicate `perceived(Me, Info)` can be easily implemented through the following inference rule, using the source annotation `percept` and the internal action .my_name(Me) which unifies the variable Me with the agent's name:

```
perceived(Me,Info) :- .my_name(Me) & Info[source(percept)].
```

Further, the argumentation template in natural language for this argumentation scheme is represented as follows:

⟨"I have perceived <Info>, therefore I believe <Info>."⟩[as(perception)]

The second argumentation scheme, the *argumentation scheme from reliable source – as(rel_src) –* states that if an agent consult a source of information it trusts, it will believe the response to that queried information:

"I have consulted source **S** about **Info** and I trust source **S**,
therefore I believe **Info** is true."

Its corresponding computational representation in Jason is given by the following defeasible inference rule:

```
def_inf(believe(Me,Info),[source(S,Info),trust(Me,S)])[as(rel_src)].
```

Further, the argumentation template in natural language for this argumentation scheme is represented as follows:

⟨"I have consulted source <S> about <Info> and I trust source <S>, therefore I believe <Info> is true."⟩[as(rel_src)]

The third argumentation scheme, *argumentation scheme from reliable communication – as(rel_com) –* states that if an agent has received a piece of information from another agent it trusts, it will also believe that information:

"Agent **Ag** has told me **Info** and I trust agent **Ag** , therefore I believe **Info** is true."

Its corresponding computational representation in Jason is given by the following defeasible inference rule:

```
def_inf(believe(Me,Info),[asserts(Ag,Info)],trust(Me,Ag))[as(rel_com)].
```

Also, in the Jason platform, the predicate `asserts(Ag, Info)` can be easily inferred by agents through the following inference rule, using the source annotation on agents' beliefs:

```
asserts(Ag,Info) :- Info[source(Ag)].
```

Further, the argumentation template in natural language for this argumentation scheme is represented as follows:

⟨ "<Ag> has told me <Info> and I trust agent <Ag>, therefore I believe <Info> is true."⟩[as(rel_com)]

Note that there is a subtle difference between the *argumentation scheme from reliable communication* and the *argumentation scheme from reliable source*. Here, we are considering the agent's attitude on searching for a particular piece of information against the information to be given to it. While consulting an agent about a particular piece of information depends mostly on how credible/trustworthy that source is regarding that particular information, receiving such information from a source, without asking for it, relies on the intentions of the speaker besides the trust in it.

Feeding information to other agents, in the context of autonomous intelligent agents, relies on what are the intentions behind feeding that information, which might represent a deceptive attitude from those agents [34,41]. We believe that this aspect of communication (understand that a piece of information has been given instead of searched for) will play an important role in accountability in these systems, thus we believe it is important to consider that difference when an agent is providing an explanation about its beliefs.

Furthermore, note that we used the concept of trust, which has been applied to multi-agent systems in order to take into account different kinds of social relationship between agents [39]. Following [20,39], trust can arise from two views: (i) the first is a subjective property assessed particularly by each individual, in which an agent directly or indirectly undertakes interactions with other agents. This point of view describes the *trust* of an individual x from the point of view of an individual y; (ii) the second is a societal view of trust, which consists of observations by the society over past behaviour of agents (which is called *reputation*) that are made available to agents who have not interacted previously. This point of view can be seen as common-sense knowledge, in which the society agrees about the *reputation* of each individual in that society [39]. Here, both views fits into our approach, and they could be used without any discrimination.

4   Example

We present here an example in the domain of healthcare, inspired by a hospital scenario, which faces several challenges. One of the main challenges in this domain is related to maximising resource usage and avoiding hospital overcrowding. To address these challenges, it is necessary to improve the use of hospital resources and maintain high occupancy rates without creating chaos in the emergency room or long queues [16]. However, the current demands on hospitals and the growing financial constraints make planning and efficient allocation of hospital beds (and other resources) increasingly difficult [23].

Hospital beds are a scarce resource, and therefore allocating them optimally plays an important role in the overall planning of hospital resources [44]. Also, the staff responsible for bed allocation are concerned with several rules while carrying out bed allocations, such as the type of medical speciality, whether the patient is surgical or clinical, patient gender, age, etc. [35]. For allocating patients to hospital beds efficiently, it is necessary to consider many variables that make it difficult for a human to reach optimal solutions without any assistance. On the other hand, fully automated solutions are usually not acceptable, as the staff in charge would not trust an allocation if they did not participate in the decision-making process.

We are interested in applying multi-agent technologies in such domain in order to face those challenges, including resource allocation [12–14,29,42]. Our investigation moves towards the development of multi-agent systems, in which intelligent software agents are capable of assisting multiple tasks, and agents are able to interact with humans through sophisticated dialogues, where they eventually need to explain the recommendations they make.

Here, we will focus on a hospital scenario in which agents interact with other agents and humans, bringing to light the need for explanations. Our scenario starts with a nurse requesting a free bed to a multi-agent system that supports decision-making on bed allocation. However, at the moment of the request, there are no beds available, so the system commits itself to notify the nurse when a bed becomes available.

In our scenario, we consider an agent specialised in databases (*database_expert*) that has access to the hospital database and perceive changes in beds and patient status. We also consider an assistant agent (*assistant_ag*) who reasons and communicates with other agents. Moreover, there is an agent that specialises in communication (*communication_expert*), in particular it communicates through natural language with nurse users (*nurse_usr*) to assist in bed allocation.

Agent *database_expert* has access to the hospital database (*database*), which is a source of information for agents to check information about beds and patients. The *database_expert* agent believes that information in the database is correct and up to date, so it can trust the database. When the *database_expert* queries the database and finds that a specific bed is empty, it comes to believe that the specific bed in question is free based on the second argumentation scheme as(rel_src)

The corresponding computational representation in Jason of this argument is given below:

```
def_inf(believe(database_expert,bed(202b, free)),
[source(database,bed(202b, free)),
trust(database_expert,database)])[as(rel_src)].
```

Furthermore, the instance generated by the argumentation template in natural language is as follow:

⟨"I have consulted source database about bed 202b being free and I trust source database, therefore I believe bed 202b being free is true."⟩[as(rel_src)]

After finding a free bed, which is a current goal in the system, *database_expert* communicates this information to the *assistant_ag* using the computational representation of this argument to explain that it has acquired that information from the *database* – source(database, bed(202b, free)) – and it trusts that source of information – trust(database_expert, database) – therefore it believes that bed 202b is free – believe(database_expert, bed(202b, free)).

The *assistant_ag* is aware that the agent *database_expert* has access to the hospital's database, as well as it trusts *database_expert*. Therefore, when *database_expert* communicates to *assistant_ag* that a specific bed is free, based on the third argumentation scheme – as(rel_com) – *assistant_ag* also believes that bed 202b is free.

The corresponding computational representation in Jason of this argument is given below:

```
def_inf(believe(assistant_ag,bed(202b, free)),
[asserts(database_expert,bed(202b, free))],
trust(assistant_ag,database_expert))[as(rel_com)].
```

The instance of the predicate asserts(Ag, Info) is given below:

```
asserts(database_expert, bed(202b, free)):-
Info[source(database_expert)]
```

Furthermore, the instance generated by the argumentation template in natural language is as follow:

⟨"database_expert has told me bed 202b is free and I trust agent database_expert, therefore I believe bed 202b is free is true".⟩[as(rel_com)]

Note that the database_expert becomes the source of the information that bed 202b is free. That is, after being able to query a trustworthy source of information (i.e., the database), database_expert believes that information is true and asserts it to the *assistant_ag*, which takes database_expert as the source of that information. In case that the trace for the origin of that information was needed, it could be asked for *assistant_ag* why it believes on that information, and it would explain that database_expert asserted that, then it could be asked for database_expert why it believes on that information and it would assert that it has queried the database. Thus, for example, if there is any mistake on that information, it would be made by who introduced the information into the database.

Continuing our example, before communicating that bed 202b is free to the nurse, *assistant_ag* must check whether the nurse is online or not. The agent *assistant_ag* is aware that the agent that can perceive whether *nurse_ag* is online or not is the *communication_expert*, so it asks that agent whether the nurse is online.

The *communication_expert* can perceive when the nurse (*nurse_usr*) is online in the system to initiate a conversation with them or to inform another agent about this. Using its perception, based on the first argumentation scheme as(perception), the *communication_expert* agent believes that *nurse_usr* is online.

Its corresponding computational representation in Jason is given by the following defeasible inference rule:

```
def_inf(believe(communication_expert,online(nurse_usr)),
[perceived(communication_expert,online(nurse_usr))])[as(perception)]
```

Considering the information *communication_expert* has perceived – online (nurse_usr) [source(percept)] – it is able to infer believe(communication_expert,online(nurse_usr) using the inference rule perceived(Me,Info):-.my_name(Me) & Info[source(percept)] with the unification function {Me ↦ communication_expert, Info ↦ online(nurse_usr)}.

Furthermore, the instance generated by the argumentation template in natural language is given below:

⟨"I have perceived **nurse_usr is online**, therefore I believe **nurse_usr is online**".⟩[as(perception)]

The *communication_expert* informs the *assistant_ag* that the nurse is online, justifying that information using the computational representation of the argument supporting that belief. Now, being aware that the nurse is online, the *assistant_ag* informs *communication_expert* agent that bed 202b is free, becoming the source of that information for *communication_expert* agent, which as in the previous examples believes that bed 202b is free, according to the argument below:

```
def_inf(believe(communication_expert,bed(202b, free)),
[asserts(assistant_ag,bed(202b, free))],
trust(communication_expert,assistant_ag))[as(rel_com)].
```

After, it provides that information to the nurse, justifying it with the natural language representation of the argument supporting the belief believe(communication_expert, bed(202b, free)), i.e.:

*"assistant_ag has told me **bed 202b is free** and I trust agent assistant_ag, therefore I believe **bed 202b is free** is true".*

5   Related Work

In [40], the authors have reviewed the literature on explainable goal-driven agents and robots, and claim that most of the approaches to XAI have focused on data-driven XAI, and studies approaching goal-driven agents and robots are still missing.

In [19] and [5], the authors present a model for explainable BDI agents that enables agents to explain their behaviour in terms of underlying beliefs and goals in virtual training systems. Furthermore, considering that agent can generate different types of explanations, the authors proposed four different explanation algorithms, evaluating them with trainee users, and concluding which explanation types are more adequate for each condition. While [5,19] present an interesting approach to explainability in BDI agents, that work does not use argumentation.

In [22], the authors say that with the increasing use of robots in complex settings in which humans and robots work together, there is a growing need for effective methods of interacting with artificial agents. Among the needs, the authors are interested in querying agents about reasons for decision making, i.e., the capability of agents to explain their decision making. In [22], the authors are not concerned with having natural language explanation but in some format that could be easy for humans to understand.

In [11], the authors say that many of the challenges in designing and evaluating AI systems depends on *who* is the human in the loop. Thus, they present a case study with non-experts users to understand how they perceive different styles of generated rationales by an AI system in a simulated scenario of autonomous self-driving cars.

In [15], the authors introduce an argument-based system for enhancing human-computer dialogues in the medical domain, more specifically, in medical training. The proposed system uses ASPIC rules and argumentation schemes based on clinician argumentation. The user interacts with the chatbot using buttons.

In [2], the authors developed a coach agent to improve health and well-being using a multi-agent system and argumentation. They used argumentation schemes following the Argument Interchange Format (AIF) and a domain ontology to retrieve the topics of the dialogues. The user interacts with the chatbot using predefined buttons.

In [21], the authors developed a system called CONSULT, which is a collaborative decision-support tool to help patients suffering from chronic diseases self-manage their treatment plans. For this domain, a specific argumentation scheme was used. In a metalevel argumentation framework, the system uses an argumentation reasoning engine based on ASPIC$^+$. Using the predefined argumentation schemes and attack relations, it instantiates arguments from the received data. The system has a conversation interface with the user, in which the user can make utterances in natural language.

In [48], the authors use an argument mining approach to infer an argumentation structure from an annotated corpora of hotel reviews The annotated phrases serve as a model for Natural Language Generation (NLG). To determine the polarity of each review, they compare negative and positive annotated phrases. Using linear Euler-based restricted semantics, they are able to predict the user preferences based on bipolar weighted argument graphs (BWAGS). They present arguments to user via a multimodal output.

In [43], the authors used a Fuzzy Cognitive Map based on an argumentation model to construct an intelligent tutoring system, with an intelligent agent to conduct argumentative dialogues helping children learn ecosystems and adults to gain knowledge on diabetes risk factors. The user interacts with the chatbot using pre-defined buttons.

In [7], the authors created a recommendation system using pragmatic argumentation to check if this has the potential to affect the decision making of the elderly and help them pursue a healthier lifestyle. The system only makes recommendations; it does not support free conversation. The system was evaluated by 21 volunteers who interacted with the robot.

In [8], the authors discussed an approach to dialogue management using chatbots in combination with social practices and argumentation theory. Their future system will provide for the use of an avatar that expresses emotions and the user will be able to make utterances in natural language.

In [9], the authors described an XAI system that supports the monitoring of users' behavior and persuades them to follow healthy lifestyles, using logical reasoning. The user does not communicate with the chatbot in natural language. They evaluated the system in two steps. First with domain experts and then with 120 users that used a mobile application based on their platform. This application monitored the user and generated recommendations.

As it can be noted, most of that work focuses on a particular scenario, constructing an approach, tools, and interfaces to treat that particular problem. We propose an approach in which intelligent agents are able to explain themselves not only to humans but also to other agents, using a modular representation of argumentation schemes and argumentation templates in natural language. Our approach is more general than the work discussed above. When developing a new application, we only need to model the argumentation schemes, and argumentation templates in natural language, necessary for that particular application domain. We argue that by providing a representation of the argumentation schemes created by others, for example [15, 21], agents using our approach would be able to generate those same explanations.

6 Conclusion

The use of AI systems in our daily lives is becoming mature and ubiquitous, resulting in a growing emergence of systems where agents and humans work together [38], from which new concepts such as Hybrid Intelligence [1] also emerge. However, there are many challenges related to how humans and agents will interact in those systems, and how agents will explain their decisions and internal mental states so that they become more transparent and trustworthy [17, 18].

We believe that the use of argumentation in agent technologies can play an important role in facing these challenges, not only because it promotes explainability but also because it represents a sophisticated form of interaction commonly found in dialogues between humans. Thus, bringing such technologies to the context of Hybrid Intelligence [1] and Explainable AI [17,18] will allow us to develop AI systems that reflect natural interactions with which humans are already familiar.

In this paper, we contribute towards bringing argumentation technologies, such as argumentation schemes and natural language templates, to *explainable agents*. We showed how agents are able to explain themselves by communicating arguments. Further, our agents use computational arguments when communicating with other agents, and translate those arguments into natural language arguments when communicating with humans. That is possible given our approach for using both computational and natural language representation of reasoning patterns that agents can use to instantiate arguments.

In future work, we intend to apply such an approach in the scenario described in this paper, developing AI systems to support human expert tasks and decision making. Also, we intend to model argumentation schemes agents use to provide explanations about the domain rules, for example, constraints related to bed allocation, as well as goals, plans, actions, etc. that they have adopted. Thus, for example, agents would be able to explain to human users why a particular allocation violates a hospital norm that the user has failed to consider, or why a particular (re)allocation is needed.

Acknowledgements. The authors gratefully acknowledge partial funding from CNPq and CAPES.

References

1. Akata, Z., et al.: A research agenda for hybrid intelligence: augmenting human intellect with collaborative, adaptive, responsible, and explainable artificial intelligence. Computer **53**(8), 18–28 (2020)
2. Baskar, J., Janols, R., Guerrero, E., Nieves, J.C., Lindgren, H.: A multipurpose goal model for personalised digital coaching. In: Montagna, S., Abreu, P.H., Giroux, S., Schumacher, M.I. (eds.) A2HC/AHEALTH -2017. LNCS (LNAI), vol. 10685, pp. 94–116. Springer, Cham (2017). https://doi.org/10.1007/978-3-319-70887-4_6
3. Bordini, R.H., Dastani, M., Dix, J., Seghrouchni, A.E.F.: Multi-Agent Programming: Languages. Tools and Applications, 1st edn. Springer, Heidelberg (2009). https://doi.org/10.1007/978-0-387-89299-3
4. Bordini, R.H., Hübner, J.F., Wooldridge, M.: Programming Multi-Agent Systems in AgentSpeak using Jason. Wiley Series in Agent Technology. Wiley, Hoboken (2007)
5. Broekens, J., Harbers, M., Hindriks, K., Van Den Bosch, K., Jonker, C., Meyer, J.J.: Do you get it? User-evaluated explainable BDI agents. In: German Conference on Multiagent System Technologies, pp. 28–39. Springer (2010)
6. Burrieza, A., Yuste-Ginel, A.: Basic beliefs and argument-based beliefs in awareness epistemic logic with structured arguments. Front. Artif. Intell. Appl. **326**, 123–134 (2020)

7. Cheng, C.Y., Qian, X., Tseng, S.H., Fu, L.C.: Recommendation dialogue system through pragmatic argumentation. In: 2017 26th IEEE International Symposium on Robot and Human Interactive Communication (RO-MAN), pp. 335–340. IEEE (2017)
8. Dignum, F., Bex, F.: Creating dialogues using argumentation and social practices. In: Diplaris, S., Satsiou, A., Følstad, A., Vafopoulos, M., Vilarinho, T. (eds.) INSCI 2017. LNCS, vol. 10750, pp. 223–235. Springer, Cham (2018). https://doi.org/10.1007/978-3-319-77547-0_17
9. Donadello, I., Dragoni, M., Eccher, C.: Explaining reasoning algorithms with persuasiveness: a case study for a behavioural change system. In: Proceedings of the 35th Annual ACM Symposium on Applied Computing, pp. 646–653 (2020)
10. Dung, P.M.: On the acceptability of arguments and its fundamental role in non-monotonic reasoning, logic programming and n-person games. Artif. Intell. **77**, 321–357 (1995)
11. Ehsan, U., Riedl, M.: On design and evaluation of human-centered explainable AI systems. In: Glasgow 2019 (2019)
12. Engelmann, D., Couto, J., Gabriel, V., Vieira, R., Bordini, R.: Towards an ontology to support decision-making in hospital bed allocation. In: Proceedings of 31st International Conference on Software Engineering & Knowledge Engineering, pp. 71–74 (2019)
13. Engelmann, D.C.: Conversational agents based on argumentation theory and ontologies. In: Proceedings of the Fourth Summer School on Argumentation: Computational and Linguistic Perspectives (SSA 2020), pp. 10–12 (2020)
14. Engelmann, D.C.: An interactive agent to support hospital bed allocation based on plan validation. Dissertation, Pontifícia Universidade Católica do Rio Grande do Sul (2019)
15. Grando, A., Moss, L., Bel-Enguix, G., Jiménez-López, M.D., Kinsella, J.: Argumentation-based dialogue systems for medical training. In: Neustein, A., Markowitz, J. (eds.) Where Humans Meet Machines, pp. 213–232. Springer, New York (2013). https://doi.org/10.1007/978-1-4614-6934-6_10
16. Grübler, M.d.S., da Costa, C.A., Righi, R., Rigo, S., Chiwiacowsky, L.: A hospital bed allocation hybrid model based on situation awareness. Comput. Inform. Nurs. **36**, 249–255 (2018)
17. Gunning, D.: Explainable Artificial Intelligence (XAI) Defense Advanced Research Projects Agency (DARPA), and Web 2, 2 (2017)
18. Gunning, D., Stefik, M., Choi, J., Miller, T., Stumpf, S., Yang, G.Z.: XAI-explainable artificial intelligence. Sci. Robot. **4**(37), eaay7120 (2019)
19. Harbers, M., van den Bosch, K., Meyer, J.J.: Design and evaluation of explainable BDI agents. In: 2010 IEEE/WIC/ACM International Conference on Web Intelligence and Intelligent Agent Technology, vol. 2, pp. 125–132. IEEE (2010)
20. Huynh, T.D., Jennings, N.R., Shadbolt, N.R.: An integrated trust and reputation model for open multi-agent systems. Auton. Agents Multi-Agent Syst. **13**(2), 119–154 (2006)
21. Kökciyan, N., et al.: A collaborative decision support tool for managing chronic conditions. In: MedInfo, pp. 644–648 (2019)
22. Langley, P.: Explainable agency in human-robot interaction. In: AAAI Fall Symposium Series (2016)
23. Matos, J., Rodrigues, P.P.: Modeling decisions for hospital bed management - a review. In: 4th International Conference on Health Informatics, pp. 504–507 (2011)

24. Melo, V.S., Panisson, A.R., Bordini, R.H.: Argumentation-based reasoning using preferences over sources of information. In: Fifteenth International Conference on Autonomous Agents and Multiagent Systems (AAMAS) (2016)
25. Panisson, A.R., Bordini, R.H.: Knowledge representation for argumentation in agent-oriented programming languages. In: 2016 Brazilian Conference on Intelligent Systems, BRACIS (2016)
26. Panisson, A.R., Bordini, R.H.: Argumentation schemes in multi-agent systems: a social perspective. In: El Fallah-Seghrouchni, A., Ricci, A., Son, T.C. (eds.) EMAS 2017. LNCS (LNAI), vol. 10738, pp. 92–108. Springer, Cham (2018). https://doi.org/10.1007/978-3-319-91899-0_6
27. Panisson, A.R., Bordini, R.H.: Uttering only what is needed: enthymemes in multi-agent systems. In: Proceedings of the 16th Conference on Autonomous Agents and MultiAgent Systems, pp. 1670–1672. International Foundation for Autonomous Agents and Multiagent Systems (2017)
28. Panisson, A.R., Bordini, R.H.: Towards a computational model of argumentation schemes in agent-oriented programming languages. In: IEEE/WIC/ACM International Joint Conference on Web Intelligence and Intelligent Agent Technology (WI-IAT) (2020)
29. Panisson, A.R., et al.: Arguing about task reallocation using ontological information in multi-agent systems. In: 12th International Workshop on Argumentation in Multiagent Systems (2015)
30. Panisson, A.R., Melo, V.S., Bordini, R.H.: Using preferences over sources of information in argumentation-based reasoning. In: 2016 Brazilian Conference on Intelligent Systems, BRACIS (2016)
31. Panisson, A.R., Meneguzzi, F., Fagundes, M., Vieira, R., Bordini, R.H.: Formal semantics of speech acts for argumentative dialogues. In: Thirteenth International Conference on Autonomous Agents and Multiagent Systems, pp. 1437–1438 (2014)
32. Panisson, A.R., Meneguzzi, F., Vieira, R., Bordini, R.H.: An approach for argumentation-based reasoning using defeasible logic in multi-agent programming languages. In: 11th International Workshop on Argumentation in Multiagent Systems (2014)
33. Panisson, A.R., Meneguzzi, F., Vieira, R., Bordini, R.H.: Towards practical argumentation in multi-agent systems. In: 2015 Brazilian Conference on Intelligent Systems, BRACIS 2015 (2015)
34. Panisson, A.R., Sarkadi, S., McBurney, P., Parsons, S., Bordini, R.H.: Lies, bullshit, and deception in agent-oriented programming languages. In: Proceedings of the 20th International Trust Workshop co-located with AAMAS/IJCAI/ECAI/ICML 2018, Stockholm, Sweden, 14 July 2018. pp. 50–61 (2018)
35. Pinto, L.R., de Campos, F.C.C., Perpétuo, I.H.O., Ribeiro, Y.C.N.M.B.: Analisys of hospital bed capacity via queuing theory and simulation. In: Proceedings of the Winter Simulation Conference 2014, pp. 1281–1292. IEEE (2014)
36. Prakken, H.: An abstract framework for argumentation with structured arguments. Argument Comput. 1(2), 93–124 (2011)
37. Rao, A.S.: AgentSpeak(L): BDI agents speak out in a logical computable language. In: Van de Velde, W., Perram, J.W. (eds.) MAAMAW 1996. LNCS, vol. 1038, pp. 42–55. Springer, Heidelberg (1996). https://doi.org/10.1007/BFb0031845
38. Richardson, A., Rosenfeld, A.: A survey of interpretability and explainability in human-agent systems. In: XAI Workshop on Explainable Artificial Intelligence, pp. 137–143 (2018)
39. Sabater, J., Sierra, C.: Review on computational trust and reputation models. Artif. Intell. Rev. 24(1), 33–60 (2005)

40. Sado, F., Loo, C.K., Kerzel, M., Wermter, S.: Explainable goal-driven agents and robots-a comprehensive review and new framework. arXiv preprint arXiv:2004.09705 (2020)
41. Sarkadi, S., Panisson, A.R., Bordini, R.H., McBurney, P.J., Parsons, S.D., Chapman, M.D.: Modelling deception using theory of mind in multi-agent systems. AI Commun. **32**(4), 287–302 (2019)
42. Schmidt, D.: Ontologias para Representação de Tarefas Colaborativas em Sistemas Multi-Agentes. Master's thesis, Pontifical Catholic University of Rio Grande do Sul (2015)
43. Tao, X., Yelland, N., Zhang, Y.: Fuzzy cognitive modeling for argumentative agent. In: 2012 IEEE International Conference on Fuzzy Systems, pp. 1–8. IEEE (2012)
44. Teow, K.L., El-Darzi, E., Foo, C., Jin, X., Sim, J.: Intelligent analysis of acute bed overflow in a tertiary hospital in Singapore. J. Med. Syst. **36**, 1873–1882 (2012)
45. Toulmin, S.E.: The Uses of Argument. Cambridge University Press, Cambridge (1958)
46. Walton, D., Reed, C., Macagno, F.: Argumentation Schemes. Cambridge University Press, Cambridge (2008)
47. Walton, D.: Argumentation Schemes for Presumptive Reasoning. Routledge (1996)
48. Weber, K., Janowski, K., Rach, N., Weitz, K., Minker, W., Ultes, S., André, E.: Predicting persuasive effectiveness for multimodal behavior adaptation using bipolar weighted argument graphs. In: International Conference on Autonomous Agents and Multiagent Systems, AAMAS 2019, Auckland, New Zealand, May 2020, pp. 1476–1484 (2020)
49. Wooldridge, M.: An Introduction to Multiagent Systems. Wiley, Hoboken (2009)

TPO: A Type System for the Architecture of Agent Societies

Antônio Carlos da Rocha Costa(✉) (ID)

Programa de Pós-Graduação em Filosofia, Pontifícia Universidade Católica
do Rio Grande do Sul - PUCRS, 90.619-900 Porto Alegre, RS, Brazil
ac.rocha.costa@gmail.com

Abstract. We present *TPO*, a type system designed to support the
type-based modeling of the architectural structure of agent societies. The
basic concepts of *TPO* are presented. The *TPO*-typing of the multiagent system model supported by the multiagent programming framework
JaCaMo is presented to illustrate the scope of application of *TPO*.

Keywords: Agent societies · Typing systems for agent societies ·
Typing the *JaCaMo* Model

1 Introduction

1.1 Motivation

The concept of *type* is an optional feature in the definition of computational
languages, and may appear implicitly or explicitly in them. But its introduction
in the theory of programming languages represented a crucial step in the development and consolidation of methods and techniques of Software Engineering
because types are one of the formal bases upon which the essential computational
concepts of *object* and *module* are founded [1].

We think that the development of type systems for agents and agent systems
is a crucial step that is still generally lacking in the multiagent systems programming area, possibly being the main reason for the lack of a sound notion of
modularity in those systems.

In fact, the latter seems to be also the main reason for the conceptual difficulties that arise in attempts to integrate, on principled bases, *conventional* and
agent-based system models. In [2–4], we tried to tackle such issue by proposing
a notion of modularity for multiagent systems on the basis of which both multi-
agent *organizations* (more precisely, *organization units*) and full *agent societies*
may serve as *software components* for general multi-agent systems and conventional software systems.

© Springer Nature Switzerland AG 2022
N. Alechina et al. (Eds.): EMAS 2021, LNAI 13190, pp. 292–311, 2022.
https://doi.org/10.1007/978-3-030-97457-2_17

1.2 Objective

We present *TPO*, a societal type system, designed to support the type-based modelling of the *architectural components* of agent societies. *TPO* is a simple *set-based* type system. The types of *TPO* are *observational*, in the sense that they can type just the structural and operational features that *observers* of agent societies may grasp when they adopt an *externalist* point of view, i.e., when they refrain from examining the agents's minds. In this respect, *TPO* adheres to the classical modularity requirement of *information hiding* [5].

We consider only the principles and main concepts of *TPO*. Its full definition is given in [6], where SML, a *TPO*-based agent society modeling language, is also defined[1].

Notice that the issue of type checking (or type inference) algorithms for *TPO* are out of the scope of the paper.

1.3 Organization of the Paper

In Sect. 2, we informally indicate the basic architectural components of agent societies typed by *TPO*, as well as the main general type features of the system. In Sect. 3, the basic typing rules of *TPO* are formally presented.

In the case study given in Sect. 4, the *TPO*-typing of the basic elements of the *JaCaMo* multiagent system model [10], showing *TPO* as a *basic* type system for the modeling of agent societies, which can be *systematically extended* by building on the already defined types, whenever needed[2].

Section 5 is the Conclusion.

2 Basic Concepts

2.1 Agent Societies

Table 1 shows the main components of the architecture of agent societies that we take into account in the present work [9]: the *populational structure* (*Pop*), the *sociability structure* (*Soc*), the *organizational structure* (*Org*), the *material environment* (*MEnv*) and the *symbolic environment* (*SEnv*).

TPO provides a system of types to support the formal expression of the core features of such components: their structure, functioning and interaction.

---

[1] The acronym *TPO* is of a historical origin, meaning *Type System for the PopOrg model*, where *PopOrg* was the previous version [7,8] of our current *Agent Society model* [9].

[2] See [6] for other experiments in the *TPO*-typing of organizational models, regarding models like AGRE, Electronic Institutions, and OperA.

Table 1. The main elements of the architecture of agent societies.

Component		Main elements
Pop		Agents, agent networks
Soc	Soc_σ	Sociability roles
	Soc_Σ	Sociability networks
Org	Org_ω	Organizational roles
	Org_μ	Organization units
	Org_Ω	Social subsystems
$MEnv$		Material objects
$SEnv$		Symbolic objects

2.2   Material and Symbolic Environments

TPO distinguishes between *material* and *symbolic environments*. *Material environments* are usual in models of multiagent systems, to organize the set of *material objects* handled by the agents.

Symbolic environments, separate from material environments, are not so common. They are taken here to model the *cultural aspects* of agent societies [11–13]. In particular, they support the modeling of the *ideological notions* that regulate the way agents, organization units and societies behave and interact with each other [14].

Clearly, of the symbolic objects, *norms* are of particular importance, since they are the main means through which the *regulation of behaviors and interactions* is carried on.

2.3   Events, Processes and Exchange Processes

Processes are the fundamental *dynamic elements* in *TPO*. Any societal structure constructed according to *TPO* types may realize, internally or externally, one or more processes.

Processes are constituted by time-indexed sequences of *sets of events*. That is, we assume that *at each time instant*, the set of components of the society that can cause *processes* may perform a *set of events* at that time, in each of the processes that it realizes, not just *one* event.

Informally, an *exchange process* is a process realized by two societal components (agents, roles, organizational units, social subsystems) whose elements are *pairs of sets of events*, each set of events performed by one of the societal components participating in the exchange process.

But, notice that, formally in *TPO*, exchange processes are *not* a subtype of processes.

2.4 Animate and Inanimate Objects

TPO categorizes objects either as animate or as inanimate. *Animate* objects are objects (like *agents* and *organization units*) that are capable of driving their own behaviors. *Inanimate* objects (like most objects in the *material* and *symbolic* environments) are those that are unable of driving their own behaviors and are mostly handled by animate objects.

For each such kind of objects, *TPO* defines a set of *observational features* compatible with that kind:

- Animate objects may be typed with the following observational features:
  - *Properties*: the qualities that the animate objects may present;
  - *Behaviors*: the processes that they may cause;
  - *Interactions*: the composed processes that they may cause, together with other animate objects;
  - *Relations:* the non-interactive relationships they may have with other animate or inanimate objects;
- Inanimate objects may be typed with the following observational features:
  - *Properties*: the qualities that inanimate objects may present;
  - *Relations:* the non-interactive relationships they may have have with other inanimate objects.

Table 2 lists the main animate and inanimate types of *TPO* objects.

Table 2. Animate and inanimate *TPO* objects.

Animate objects	Inanimate objects
Material objects	Time instants
Agents	Properties
Sociability roles	Relations
Sociability role networks	Symbolic objects
Organizational roles	Processes
Organizational role networks	Exchange processes
Organization units	
Organization unit networks	
Agent societies	
Inter-societal agent systems	

2.5 Externalism and Internalism

It is usual to consider that the typing of the structure of *agents* requires an *internalist* point of view, where *mental concepts* play central roles (as components of the agents' *intentionality*), while in the typing of *organization units* and *agent societies* it is often enough to adopt an *externalist* point of view, focusing on their structure, functioning and interaction, and where *mental concepts* play only a complementary role, in the form of the objectified *cultural* features of those components[3].

TPO allows for the *combined* internalist and externalist approaches to the modeling of agents, organization units and agent societies.

2.6   Extensibility and Modularity

We take that the proper concept of *modularity of agent systems* is to be located, at two different levels, in *organization units* and in *agent societies* (see, e.g., [2]).

Organization units, structured as suggested by the *TPO* type system, together with an explicitly declared *interface* (e.g., *input* and *output ports*) to regulate their exchanges with the outside, may well operate as *organizational modules* for the internal constitution of agent societies.

Agent societies with appropriate interfaces (e.g., *import* and *export channels*), seem to be the appropriate level of modularity to be taken when integrating whole agent systems with conventional software systems.

TPO can easily accommodate such interfaces as extensions of its set of types (see [6]). Thus, using the type constructors provided by *TPO*, and others that can be systematically incorporated into it, *TPO* can be extended to account for *inter-societal agent systems*, which are systems of interacting agent societies (see e.g. [18])[4].

2.7   Internal and External Types

All types defined on the basis of the basic TPO types and operations are called *internal types*. Types imported from modules or systems that are externally connected to modules and systems defined on the basis of TPO are called *external types*.

That is, external types are *parameters* of *TPO* especifications. For instance, what is an *event* (i.e., an object of the type Event), in a given agent society, is to be defined externally to *TPO*.

3   The *TPO* Type System Formally Defined

The following is a revised and abridged formal definition of the type system *TPO* (see [6] for the full draft presentation). In particula:,

- we present only the *type construction* rules, not the *type destruction* ones;
- we omit the typing of the *sociability structure Soc* (see Table 1), which accounts for the variety of the agents' ways of *conviviality*, *amity*, etc., that are often developed through tradition.

---

[3] An *externalist* perspective, but set in much more strict terms, was proposed by Jacques Ferber and colleagues, in their seminal works [15–17].

[4] The technical report [6] does not contemplate *multisocietal agent systems*.

3.1   Type Constructors

TPO types are *sets*. The following are the main type constructors:

Sub-type: $T \subseteq T'$ means that type T is a *subtype* of type T';
Powerset: $\wp(T)$ is the *powerset* of the type T;
Function space: $T \to T'$ is the set of functions between types T and T';
External type: $[E...]_T$ where E is an *external object constructor*, compatible with type T, used to define objects of the external type T.

The *external object constructor* $[E...]_T$ builds on an expression E of an *external language*, which is expected to have been made interoperable with the programming language in which the agent society is programmed.

3.2   The Basic Types

Time: The objects of the type T are called *time instants*, or simply *times*. Type T is an *inanimate internal type*.

$$\frac{t \in \mathbb{N}}{t : \mathtt{Time}}\ R_{\mathtt{Time}}$$

Property: The objects of the type Prop are called *property expressions*. Type Prop is an *inanimate external type*.

$$\frac{[prop...]_{\mathtt{Prop}}}{prop : \mathtt{Prop}}\ R_{\mathtt{Prop}}$$

Event: The objects of the type Event are called *events*. The type Event is an *inanimate external type*.

$$\frac{[ev...]_{\mathtt{Event}}}{ev : \mathtt{Event}}\ R_{\mathtt{Event}}$$

Agent: The objects of the type Agent are called *agents*. The type Agent is an *animate external type*.

$$\frac{[ag...]_{\mathtt{Agent}}}{ag : \mathtt{Agent}}\ R_{\mathtt{Agent}}$$

Organizational role: The objects of the type OrgRo are called *organizational roles*. Type OrgRo is an *animate external type*.

$$\frac{[or...]_{\mathtt{OrgRo}}}{or : \mathtt{OrgRo}}\ R_{\mathtt{OrgRo}}$$

Symbolic object: The objects of the type *SymbObj* are called *symbolic objects*. The type *SymbObj* is an *inanimate external type*.

$$\frac{[so...]_{\texttt{SymbObj}}}{so : \texttt{SymbObj}} \; R_{\texttt{SymbObj}}$$

Material object: The objects of the type *MatObj* are called *material objects*. The type *MatObj* is an *animate external type*.

$$\frac{[mo...]_{\texttt{MatObj}}}{mo : \texttt{MatObj}} \; R_{\texttt{MatObj}}$$

For the sake of space, we omit here the presentation of the construction rules (of the form `TProp`, `TBeh`, `TInter`, and `TRel`, for the type `T`) that support the attachment of *properties*, *behaviors*, *interactions*, and *relations* to basic types (see [6] for their definitions). Also, we omit the indication of the *constraints* that certain types have to satisfy.

3.3   The Predefined Constructed Types

The set of predefined constructed types presented here were designed to fit our *Agent Society* model [9]. When the target is some other multiagent system organizational model, another set of constructed types may be required.

For the sake of space, we present here only the main predefined constructed types. The understanding of the *auxiliary types* that compose them should be straightforward. Also, we omit the set of *meta-level type constructors*, which allow for the creation of new types (see [6]).

Process: The objects of the type `Proc` are called *processes*. The type `Proc` is an *inanimate internal type*.

$$\frac{proc : T \to \wp(\texttt{Event})}{proc : \texttt{Proc}} \; R_{\texttt{Proc}}$$

Exchange process: The objects of the type `ExchProc` are called *exchange processes*. The type `ExchProc` is an *inanimate internal type*.

$$\frac{ep : T \to \wp(\texttt{Event}) \times \wp(\texttt{Event})}{ep : \texttt{ExchProc}} \; R_{\texttt{ExchProc}}$$

Populational structure: The objects of the type `Pop` are called *populational structures*. Type `Pop` is an *animate internal type*.

$$\frac{\begin{array}{c} AG : \wp(\texttt{Ag}) \\ AP : \wp(\texttt{AgProp}) \\ AB : \wp(\texttt{AgBeh}) \\ AI : \wp(\texttt{AgInter}) \\ AR : \wp(\texttt{AgRel}) \end{array}}{\langle AG, AP, AB, AI, AR \rangle : \texttt{Pop}} \; R_{\texttt{Pop}}$$

Organizational micro-level structure: The objects of the type `OrgMicro` are called *organizational micro-level structures*. Type `OrgMicro` is an *animate internal type*.

$$RO : \wp(\texttt{OrgRole})$$
$$ROProp : \wp(\texttt{OrgRoProp})$$
$$ROBeh : \wp(\texttt{OrgRoBeh})$$
$$ROInter : \wp(\texttt{OrgRoInter})$$
$$RORel : \wp(\texttt{OrgRoRel})$$
$$\frac{RONet : \wp(\texttt{OrgRoNet})}{\langle RO, ROProp, ROBeh, ROInter, RORel, RONet \rangle : \texttt{OrgMicro}} \; R_{\texttt{OrgMicro}}$$

where `OrgRoNet` is the *animate internal type* of the *organizational role networks*, given by:

$$OR : \wp(\texttt{OrgRole})$$
$$ORProp : \wp(\texttt{OrgRoProp})$$
$$ORBeh : \wp(\texttt{OrgRoBeh})$$
$$ORInter : \wp(\texttt{OrgRoInter})$$
$$\frac{ORRel : \wp(\texttt{OrgRoRel})}{\langle OR, ORProp, ORBeh, ORInter, ORRel \rangle : \texttt{OrgRoNet}} \; R_{\texttt{OrgRoNet}}$$

Organizational meso-level structure: The objects of the type `OrgMeso` are called *organizational meso-level structures*. Type `OrgMeso` is an *animate internal type*.

$$OU : \wp(\texttt{OrgUn})$$
$$OUProp : \wp(\texttt{UrgUnProp})$$
$$OUBeh : \wp(\texttt{OrgUnBeh})$$
$$OUInter : \wp(\texttt{OrgUnInter})$$
$$OURel : \wp(\texttt{OrgUnRel})$$
$$\frac{OUNet : \wp(\texttt{OrgUnNet})}{\langle OU, OUProp, OUBeh, OUInter, OURel, OUNet \rangle : \texttt{OrgMeso}} \; R_{\texttt{OrgMeso}}$$

where `OrgUn` is the *animate internal type* of the *organization units*, given by:

$$\langle OR, ORProp, ORBeh, ORInter, ORRel \rangle : \texttt{OrgRoNet}$$
$$Inp : \wp(\texttt{InpPort})$$
$$\frac{Out : \wp(\texttt{OutPort})}{\langle \langle OR, ORProp, ORBeh, ORInter, ORRel \rangle, Inp, Out \rangle : \texttt{OrgUnit}} \; R_{OrgUnit}$$

Organizational macro-level structure: The objects of the type `OrgMacro` are called *organizational macro-level structures*. Type `OrgMacro` is an *animate internal type*.

$$SSUB : \wp(\texttt{SSub})$$
$$SSUBProp : \wp(\texttt{SSubProp})$$
$$SSUBBeh : \wp(\texttt{SSubBeh})$$
$$SSUBInter : \wp(\texttt{SSubnInter})$$
$$SSUBRel : \wp(\texttt{SSubRel})$$
$$\frac{SSUBNet : \wp(\texttt{SSubNet})}{\langle SSUB, SSUBProp, SSUBBeh, SSUBInter, SSUBRel, SSUBNet \rangle : \texttt{OrgMacro}} \; R_{OrgMacro}$$

where `SSub` is the *animate internal type* of the *social subsystems*, given by:

$$OU : \wp(\texttt{OrgUn})$$
$$OUProp : \wp(\texttt{OrgUnProp})$$
$$OUBeh : \wp(\texttt{OrgUnBeh})$$
$$OUInter : \wp(\texttt{OrgUnInter})$$
$$\frac{OURel : \wp(\texttt{OrgUnRel})}{\langle OU, OUProp, OUBeh, OUInter, OURel \rangle : \texttt{SSub}} \; R_{SSub}$$

Organizational structure: The objects of the type `Org` are called *organizational structures*. Type `ORg` is an *animate internal type*.

$$OrgMicro : \texttt{OrgMicro}$$
$$OrgMeso : \texttt{OrgMeso}$$
$$\frac{OrgMacro : \texttt{OrgMacro}}{\langle OrgMicro, OrgMeso, OrgMacro \rangle : \texttt{Org}} \; R_{Org}$$

Symbolic environment: The objects of the type `SEnv` are called *symbolic environments*. Type `SEnv` is an *inanimate internal type*.

$$SO : \wp(\texttt{SymbObj})$$
$$SOProp : \wp(\texttt{SymbObjProp})$$
$$SORel : \wp(\texttt{SymbObjRel})$$
$$\frac{SONet : \wp(\texttt{SymbObjNet})}{\langle SO, SOProp, SORel, SONet \rangle : \texttt{SEnv}} \; R_{SEnv}$$

where *SymbObjNet* is the *inanimate internal type* of *symbolic object networks*, given by:

$$SO : \wp(\texttt{SymbObj})$$
$$SOProp : \wp(\texttt{SymbObjProp})$$
$$\frac{SORel : \wp(\texttt{SymbObjRel})}{\langle SO, SOProp, SORel \rangle : \texttt{SymbObjNet}} \; R_{SymbObjNet}$$

Material environment: The objects of the type MEnv are called *material environments*. Type MEnv is an *animate internal type*.

$$MO : \wp(\texttt{MatObj})$$
$$MOProp : \wp(\texttt{MatObjProp})$$
$$MOBeh : \wp(\texttt{MatObjBeh})$$
$$MOInter : \wp(\texttt{MatObjInter})$$
$$MORel : \wp(\texttt{MatObjRel})$$
$$\frac{MONet : \wp(\texttt{MatObjNet})}{\langle MO, MOProp, MOBeh, MOInter, MORel, MONet \rangle : \texttt{MEnv}} R_{MEnv}$$

where *MatObjNet* is the *animate internal type* of *material object networks*, given by:

$$MO : \wp(\texttt{MatObj})$$
$$MOProp : \wp(\texttt{MatObjProp})$$
$$MOBeh : \wp(\texttt{MatObjBeh})$$
$$MOInter : \wp(\texttt{MatObjInter})$$
$$\frac{MORel : \wp(\texttt{MatObjRel})}{\langle MO, MOProp, MOBeh, MOInter, MORel \rangle : \texttt{MatObjNet}} R_{MatObjNet}$$

Agent society: The objects of the type AgSoc are called *agent societies*. Type AgSoc is an *animate internal type*[5].

$$Pop : \texttt{Pop}$$
$$Org : \texttt{Org}$$
$$SEnv : \texttt{SEnv}$$
$$MEnv : \texttt{MEnv}$$
$$IMP : \texttt{ImpRel}$$
$$\frac{ACC : \texttt{AccRel}}{\langle Pop, Org, SEnv, MEnv, IMP, ACC \rangle : AgSoc} R_{AgSoc}$$

Figure 1 illustrates the structure of objects of the type *AgSoc* (cf. Table 1). The figure omits, however, the division of the *organizational structure* (of type Org) into its three organizational sub-levels (Org_ω, Org_μ, and Org_Ω, of types respective OrgMicro, OrgMeso and OrgMacro), and the sociability structure *Soc*, as mentioned before. The dashed arrows represent the *implementation relations* (*IMP*), the continuous arrows, the *access relations* (*ACC*)[6].

---

[5] For the sake of space, we omit here the typing of the *ports* and *channels* that constitute the *interfaces* of the meso-level or macro-level architectural components (see [6] for details).

[6] For the sake of space we omit here the definitions of the types ImpRel and AccRel (see [6]).

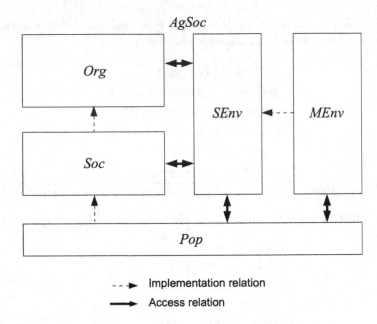

Fig. 1. The structure of the objects of type AgSoc.

4   An Example: *JaCaMo* Typed with *TPO* Types

This section presents the typing of some of the central elements of the *JaCaMo* model [10] with *TPO* types. The example illustrates the flexibility of *TPO* through the definition of several new types, defined specially for the typing of *JaCaMo*.

Recall that *JaCaMo* model articulates three component models:

- the *Jason* agent model [19];
- the *Moise+* organizational model [20];
- the *CArtAgO* environment model [21].

4.1   The *Jason* Model

Jason is an agent platform whose *agent model* evolved from the *BDI agent model*. The essential components of an agent, from the *JaCaMo* perspective, are [10](p. 751):

- Beliefs: the set of information that the agent assumes to be true about the state of its exterior, as well as about the state of its interior;
- Goals: the set of states (exterior as well as interior) that the agent intends to achieve;
- Plans: the set of structured sets of actions that the agent may put to work to achieve its goals;

- **Actions**: the set of either internal or external *primitive plans* that the agent may execute to achieve **basic goals**, that is, goals that do not decompose into simpler goals;
- **Events**: the set of possible *changes* either in the *current set of beliefs* or in the *current set of goals*, which trigger the execution of plans.

An *agent action* is a one-shot, concrete *behavior* that an agent may realize, at any time. *Events*, being changes in sets of beliefs or sets of goals, are *relations* between sets of beliefs, or relations between sets of goals. All the other elements are of a *symbolic character* and may be taken as properties that agents may have, at each time.

Taken as a whole, the set of agents running on a Jason platform constitutes the *population* of the agent system.

We type the *Jason agent model* with *TPO* types[7] as shown in Fig. 2.

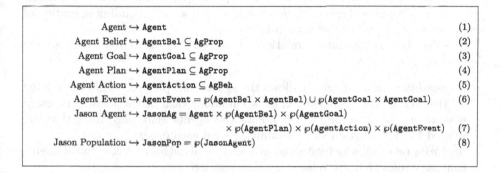

Fig. 2. The basic elements of the *Jason* component of the *JaCaMo* model, typed with *TPO* types.

4.2   The *MOISE+* Model

MOISE+ [22] is a MAS organization model, proposed by Jomi Fred Hübner and partners, that allows the separate specification of three aspects of a MAS organization:

- the *structural* aspect, corresponding to the so-called *structural dimension* of the organization, and captured by its *structural specification*;
- the *functional* aspect, corresponding to the so-called *functional dimension* of the organization, and captured by its *functional specification*;
- the link between those two aspects, corresponding to the so-called *deontic dimension* of the organization, and captured by its *deontic specification*.

---

[7] The symbol "$\hookrightarrow$" denotes the *typing operation*. Thus, $E \hookrightarrow T$ means that the element E gets the *TPO* type T. The names of the types and sub-types are supposed to be immediately readable, in an intuitive way.

The structural and functional dimensions are allowed to be specified independently of each other. The deontic dimension is to be specified on the bases of the latter two specifications.

The *Structural Dimension*. The *structural dimension* of *MOISE+* adopts the basic pattern first introduced by the AALAADIN model [15], namely, constituting the organizational structure of a MAS as a set of *roles* and *groups*.

As in the AALAADIN model, in the *MOISE+* model a role is just a *name* for one or more agents that undertake certain tasks and relations to other agents, in the organization.

However, while AALAADIN relates *roles* to each other by means of *interaction processes* (determined by *protocols*), *MOISE+* relates roles to each other by means of certain types of *role relations*, which do not necessarily involve interaction processes, but which may restrict the behaviors that the agents that play those roles may perform in the organization.

In addition, *MOISE+* defines a special type of role, called *abstract role*, whose purpose is to support a *specialization relation*, and a corresponding operation of *inheritance of properties*, between roles.

Besides that *specialization* relation, three other types of *role relations* are defined in *MOISE+* are:

- *acquaintance* relation, which allows the agents that play roles that are related by that relation to represent information about each other (identifiers, etc.);
- *communication* relation, which allows the agents that play roles that are related by that relation to communicate with each other;
- *authority* relation, which establishes a relation of authority between the agents that play roles that are related by that relation.

Clearly, although treated just as "links" between the agents that they relate, such relations also impose *norms* on the agents: for instance, norms of *permission* of communication and norms of *authorization*.

In addition, the *MOISE+* model defines a *compatibility relation* between roles, restricting the set of roles that an agent may play, simultaneously, in the organization.

Regarding groups: although a *group* is presented conceptually as capable of "operating *as* if it was a single entity" [22](p. 44), what happens is that, in their formal definition, *groups* are construed to be just *sets of roles*, without explicitly defined behaviors and interactions of their own.

Differently from the concept of group in AALAADIN, however, groups in *MOISE+* can be recursively structured in terms of other groups. But, accordingly, the sub-groups of a group do not constitute explicit operational units inside that group, due to their also being without explicitly defined behaviors and interactions of their own.

Formally, a group is a structure: $G = (R, SG, L_{intra}, L_{inter}, C_{intra}, C_{inter}, np, ng)$ where:

- R is the set of roles that constitute the group;
- SG is the set of sub-groups of the group;
- L_{intra} and L_{inter} are the sets of internal and external relations (links) of the group, respectively;
- C_{intra} and C_{inter} are the sets of internal and external relations of compatibility of roles, intra and inter groups, respectively (the latter called, here, simply *group compatibility*);
- np is a function determining the cardinality of the set of agents allowed to implement each role of the group;
- ng is a function determining the cardinality of sub-groups of each group.

Clearly, given the sets of external relations L_{inter} and C_{inter}, the set of *groups* constitutes a *network of groups*.

The typing of the *MOISE+* structural dimension with *TPO* types is shown in Fig. 3(a).

The *Functional Dimension*. The *functional dimension* of the *MOISE+* organizational model deals with the *aims* that a multiagent system has to attain. It specifies such aims by means of a set of so-called *social schemes*, each social scheme being a set of *goals*, structured as a *compound plan*. The goals of a social scheme are taken to be goals of the whole multiagent system.

Goals are assigned to roles through ordered sets of goals, called *missions*. The goals that constitute a mission assigned to a role may be present in any of the locations of the social scheme, so that the *assignment of missions to roles* amounts to a *distribution* of the compound plan of the social scheme among the roles that participate in its execution. Goals assigned to roles by means of missions become individual goals, that is, goals of the agents that play those roles. The agents that are assigned g_{soc} get the *right* to *start* the execution of the scheme.

Social schemes are structured in terms of *goal trees*, with a single goal as the root of the tree, said to be the *social goal of the scheme*, which we denote by g_{soc}. Sub-trees of the social schemes constitute *plans* for the realization of their particular top goals. Goals that occupy the leaves of a plan do not have indications, in the social scheme, of how to be achieved. It is up to the agents committed to such goals to find ways to satisfy them.

Three operators, which allow the composition of goals, and two properties constitute the structure of social schemes:

- *sequential* composition: $g_1 = g_2, g_3$;
- *choice*: $g_1 = g_2 \mid g_3$;
- *parallelism*: $g_1 = g_2 \parallel g_3$;
- *success probability*: the expected probability of success of the plan;
- *success rate*: the historical rate of success of the plan, updated each time the plan is executed.

Formally, a *social scheme* is a structure $Sch = (G, P, M, mo, nm)$ where:

- G: the set of all goals of the scheme, including a root goal (g_{soc});
- P: the set of plans that structure the scheme, one plan for each goal;
- M: the set of missions, spread over the set of goals, with a mission m_{soc}, corresponding to the achievement of the social goal g_{soc};
- mo: the function that assign sets of goals to missions;
- nm: the function that determines the minimum and maximum number of agents that may commit to a given mission.

A *preference order* $(\prec)$ may be imposed on missions that are committed to the same agent. That is, if an agent commits to two missions, and one of them is preferred, in comparison to the other, then the agent is supposed to give preference to the goals of the more preferred mission, whenever possible.

Formally, a *functional specification* is given, then, by a structure $FS = (Sch, \prec)$ where:

- Sch is a social scheme;
- $\prec$ is a preference order imposed on the missions of Sch.

The typing of the *functional dimension* of $MOISE+$ with TPO types proceed as follows:

- *social schemes* and *plans* are typed as *symbolic object nets*, related to each other by appropriate *symbolic object relations*;
- *goals* are typed as *symbolic objects*;
- *missions* are typed as sets of *symbolic objects*;
- *success probabilities* and *success rates* of goals, and *commitment cardinalities* of missions are typed as *symbolic object properties*;
- *preference orders* between missions are typed as *symbolic object relations*.

The typing of the $MOISE+$ functional dimension with TPO types is shown in Fig. 3(b).

The Deontic Dimension. The *deontic dimension* links the *structural dimension* with the *functional dimension* by specifying, for each role, which missions an agent that plays the role has to achieve, or is permitted to achieve.

Both *permissions* and *obligations* to achieve goals may be qualified by *temporal constraints*, in the form of time intervals in which those permissions are valid, or those obligations should be completed.

Formally, a *deontic specification* is a structure of the form $D = (P, O)$ where:

- $P \subseteq R \times M \times TI$ is a set of *permissions*, where R is the set of *roles* of the structural dimension, M is the set of *missions* of the functional dimension and TI is the set of possible time intervals;
- $O \subseteq R \times M \times TI$ is a set of *obligations*, defined on the same domain as P, containing at least one obligation, namely, $obl(R_{soc}, m_{soc})$.

The typing of the $MOISE+$ deontic dimension with TPO types as shown in Fig. 3(c).

4.3   The *CArtAgO* Model

CArtAgO supports the development of *environments* for agent systems, by means of the reification of environments' objects in terms of the so-called *artifacts*. From the perspective of the agents, artifacts are characterized by the following features [23]:

- *properties*, which agents can observe in them;
- *operations*, which agents can perform on them;
- *events*, which are messages they may send to agents, informing the realization of some operation on the artifact by some agent.

Artifacts may be used to model not only *material* and *symbolic objects*, thus implementing the *material* and the *symbolic environments* of agent societies, but they be used also to model *organizational objects*, thus implementing the *organizational structure* of agent societies, as is the case in the *JaCaMo* framework [24].

We type the main elements of *CArtAgO*, the *artifacts*, with *TPO* types as shown in Fig. 4. Notice that both *operations* and *events* typed as transformations of *properties* of artifacts.

4.4   The Articulation of the Three Models

A core of *JaCaMo* is the articulation of the three models, of agents (*Jason*), environments (*CArtAgO*) and organizations (*MOISE+*). This is done by mapping concepts from each model into concepts of the other models.

The main mappings are the following:

- *operations* that can be performed on *artifacts* are made available as *actions* that *agents* may perform (the so-called *external* actions);
- *observable events* that *artifacts* may generate are allowed to produce *events* in *agents*, concerning the activation of plans;
- *observable properties* that *artifacts* can expose are made available as beliefs in *agents* that deliberate to *focus* their attention on such artifacts through a specific *focus* operation;
- *organizational goals* that belong to the *social scheme* of the organization are mapped into *individual goals* that *agents* may attempt to achieve.

We type such conceptual mappings with *TPO* types by *subsuming types*, that is, by making a type, which is mapped into another, a *sub-type* of the latter. This shown in Fig. 5. where it should be noticed that the types *ArtBeh*, *ArtEv* and *ArtProp* subsume the corresponding types for every type of *artifact* and so subsume, in particular, the corresponding types for *organizational* artifacts [10].

(a) The Structural Dimension:

$$\text{Role} \hookrightarrow \text{Rol} \subseteq \text{SymbObj} \qquad (1)$$

$$\text{Role Norm} \hookrightarrow \text{RoleNrm} \subseteq \text{SymbObj} \qquad (2)$$

$$\text{Organizational Norm} \hookrightarrow \text{OrgNrm} \subseteq \text{SymbObj} \qquad (3)$$

$$\text{Group Norm} \hookrightarrow \text{GroupNrmSymbObj} \qquad (4)$$

$$\text{Intra Link} \hookrightarrow \text{IntraLink} = \text{Rol} \times \text{Rol} \times \text{OrgNrm} \qquad (5)$$

$$\text{Inter Link} \hookrightarrow \text{InterLink} = \text{Rol} \times \text{Rol} \times \text{OrgNrm} \qquad (6)$$

$$\text{Intra Compatibility Relation} \hookrightarrow \text{IntraCompatRel} = \text{Rol} \times \text{Rol} \times \text{RoNrm} \qquad (7)$$

$$\text{Inter Compatibility Relation} \hookrightarrow \text{InterCompRel} = \text{Rol} \times \text{Rol} \times \text{GroupNrm} \qquad (8)$$

$$\text{Role Cardinality} \hookrightarrow \text{RoleCard} \subseteq \text{SymbObjProp} \qquad (9)$$

$$\text{Group} \hookrightarrow \text{Group} = \wp(\text{Role}) \times \wp(\text{IntraLink}) \times \wp(\text{IntraCompatRel})$$
$$\times \wp(\text{RoleCard}) \qquad (10)$$

$$\text{SubGroup} \hookrightarrow \text{Group} \qquad (11)$$

$$\text{Group Population} \hookrightarrow \text{GroupPop} = \wp(\text{Group}) \qquad (12)$$

$$\text{Group Cardinality} \hookrightarrow \text{GroupCard} \subseteq \text{SymbObjProp} \qquad (13)$$

$$\text{Group Net} \hookrightarrow \text{GroupNet} = \text{GroupPop} \times \wp(\text{InterLink}) \times \wp(\text{InterCompatRel})$$
$$\times \wp(\text{GroupCard}) \qquad (14)$$

$$\text{Organization} \hookrightarrow \text{Organization} = \text{GroupNet} \qquad (15)$$

(b) The Functional Dimension:

$$\text{Goal} \hookrightarrow \text{Goal} \subseteq \text{SymbObj} \qquad (16)$$

$$\text{Sequential Operator} \hookrightarrow \text{SeqOp} \subseteq \text{SymbObjRel} \qquad (17)$$

$$\text{Choice Operator} \hookrightarrow \text{ChoiceOp} \subseteq \text{SymbObjRel} \qquad (18)$$

$$\text{Parallel Operator} \hookrightarrow \text{ParOp} \subseteq \text{SymbObjRel} \qquad (19)$$

$$\text{Plan} \hookrightarrow \text{Plan} \subseteq \text{SymbObjNet} \qquad (20)$$

$$\text{Mission} \hookrightarrow \text{Mission} \subseteq \wp(\text{Goal}) \qquad (21)$$

$$\text{Success Probability} \hookrightarrow \text{SuccProb} \subseteq \text{SymbObjProp} \qquad (22)$$

$$\text{Success Rate} \hookrightarrow \text{SuccRate} \subseteq \text{SymbObjProp} \qquad (23)$$

$$\text{Mission Cardinality} \hookrightarrow \text{MissionCard} = \text{Mission} \times \text{SymbObj} \qquad (24)$$

$$\text{Set of Goals} \hookrightarrow \text{SetGoals} = \wp(\text{Goal}) \qquad (25)$$

$$\text{Set of Plans} \hookrightarrow \text{SetPlans} = \wp(\text{Plan}) \qquad (26)$$

$$\text{Set of Missions} \hookrightarrow \text{SetMissions} = \wp(\text{Mission}) \qquad (27)$$

$$\text{Mission Preference Order} \hookrightarrow \text{MissionPrefOrd} = \text{Mission} \times \text{Mission} \qquad (28)$$

$$\text{Social Scheme} \hookrightarrow \text{SocScheme} = \wp(\text{Goal}) \times \wp(\text{Plan}) \times \wp(\text{Mission}) \times \text{MissionPrefOrd} \qquad (29)$$

(c) The Deontic Dimension:

$$\text{Time} \hookrightarrow \text{T} \qquad (30)$$

$$\text{Permission} \hookrightarrow \text{Permission} = \text{Rol} \times \text{Mission} \times \wp(T) \qquad (31)$$

$$\text{Obligation} \hookrightarrow \text{Obligation} = \text{Rol} \times \text{Mission} \times \wp(T) \qquad (32)$$

$$\text{Organizational Norm} \hookrightarrow \text{OrgNorm} = \text{Permission} \cup \text{Obligation} \qquad (33)$$

$$\text{Deontic Structure} \hookrightarrow \text{DeonStrct} = \wp(\text{OrgNrm}) \qquad (34)$$

Fig. 3. The basic elements of the *MOISE+* component of the *JaCaMo* model, typed with *TPO* types.

$$Artifact \hookrightarrow \texttt{Artifact} \subseteq \texttt{MatObj} \cup \texttt{SymbObj} \qquad (35)$$
$$Artifact\ Property \hookrightarrow \texttt{ArtProp} \subseteq \texttt{MatObjProp} \cup \texttt{SymbObjProp} \qquad (36)$$
$$Artifact\ Operation \hookrightarrow \texttt{ArtOp} \subseteq \texttt{ArtProp} \rightarrow \texttt{ArtProp} \qquad (37)$$
$$Artifact\ Event \hookrightarrow \texttt{ArtEv} \subseteq \texttt{SymbObj} \qquad (38)$$

Fig. 4. The *CArtAgO* artifacts, typed with *TPO* types.

(a) Mapping *artifact* elements into *agent* elements:

$$\texttt{ArtOp} \subseteq \texttt{AgBeh}$$
$$\texttt{ArtEv} \subseteq \texttt{AgEv}$$
$$\texttt{ArtProp} \subseteq \texttt{AgBel}$$

(b) Mapping *functional* elements into *agent* elements:

$$\texttt{Goal} \subseteq \texttt{AgentGoal}$$

Fig. 5. The conceptual mapping between *JaCaMo* components, typed with *TPO* types.

5 Conclusion

This paper presented the *TPO* type system, with its basic types, type constructors and constructed types for the *Agent Society* model.

TPO was applied to the typing of the main elements of the *JaCaMo* model, illustrating the possibility of *TPO* being applied to other organization models, besides *Agent Society*.

To the best of our knowledge, this the first work dealing with *organizational type systems* for agent societies and multiagent systems. The only two works that we know have made extensive use of the concept of *type* for multiagent systems are [25–27], but they are what we have called *first-order* type systems, that is, type systems concerned with typing basic societal elements (agents, organizational roles, environmental artifacts), not the higher-level *organizational components* of agent societies. The same consideration applies to works like [25, 28], for instance.

More specifically, the *external object constructor* mechanism makes of *TPO* a *parameterized* type system, i.e., a type system whose *basic types* (except for the type **Time**) are parameters that should be explicitly defined for each particular application. In other words, *TPO* is a *second-order type system* [1] for agent societies, whose main *first-order types* are the *external types* (of *agents*, *roles*, *interaction protocols* etc.), with respect to which *TPO* is neutral. That is precisely what accounts for *TPO*'s wide range of applicability, as exemplified in Sect. 4 and, more generally, in [6].

The flexibility and general applicability of *TPO* seems to indicate that the research on *typing systems* for languages dedicated to the specification and development of multiagent systems in general, and agent societies in particular, is an effort that can effectively add to the state-of-art of the engineering of those systems.

Acknowledgments. The author thanks the anonymous reviewers for their very helpful comments.

References

1. Cardelli, L.: Type systems. In: Tucker, A. (ed.) Computer Science Handbook. Chapman & Hall/CRC, Boca Raton (1996). Chap. 97
2. Costa, A.C.R.: Proposal for a notion of modularity in multiagent systems. In: van Riemskijk, M.B., Dalpiaz, F., Dix, J. (eds.) Informal Proceedings of EMAS 2014. AAMAS, Paris (2014)
3. Costa, A.C.R.: Agent organizations and agent societies as interoperable modules for agent and conventional software systems (2017). https://doi.org/10.13140/RG.2.2.35919.69284, https://www.researchgate.net/
4. Costa, A.C.R.: Two concepts of module, for agent societies and inter-societal agent systems. In: Informal Proceedings of the Workshop Engineering Multi-Agent Systems - EMAS@AAMAS2017, São Paulo, (2017)
5. Parnas, D.L.: On the criteria to be used in decomposing systems into modules. Communications of the ACM **15**, 1053–1058 (1972)
6. Costa, A.C.R.: TPO and SML - a societal type system and a society modeling language for agent societies. Technical report, Tutorial presented at WESAAC 2017, São Paulo (2017). http://wesaac.c3.furg.br, https://sites.google.com/site/foundationsofagentsocieties/Papers/2017
7. Demazeau, Y., Costa, A.C.R.: Populations and organizations in open multi-agent systems. In: 1st National Symposium on Parallel and Distributed Artificial Intelligence (PDAI 1996), Hyderabad, India (1996)
8. Costa, A.C.R., Demazeau, Y.: Toward a formal model of multi-agent systems with dynamic organizations. In: Proceedings of ICMAS 96–2nd International Conference on Mutiagent Systems, Kyoto, vol. 431. IEEE (1996)
9. Costa, A.C.R.: A Variational Basis for the Regulation and Structuration Mechanisms of Agent Societies. Springer, Cham (2019)
10. Boissier, O., Bordini, R.H., Hübner, J., Ricci, A.: Multi-Agent Oriented Programming: Programming Multi-Agent Systems Using JaCaMo. MIT Press, Cambridge (2020)
11. Costa, A.C.R.: Symbolic environments of agent societies. In: Alves, G.V., Lugo, G.G., Borges, A.P., Pantoja, C.E. (eds.) Anais do XIV Workshop-Escola de Sistemas de Agentes, seus Ambientes e apliCações - WESAAC 2020, UFPR, Ponta Grossa (2020). http://dainf.pg.utfpr.edu.br/wesaac2020
12. Costa, A.C.R.: Symbolic environments and the cultural aspects of augmented worlds (2016). https://www.researchgate.net/
13. Costa, A.C.R.: The cultural level of agent societies. In: WESAAC 2011–5o. Workshop-School of Agent Systems, their Environments, and Applications, Curitiba, Brazil (2011). (in Portuguese)

14. Costa, A.C.R.: Situated ideological systems: A core formal concept, some computational notation, some applications. Axiomathes **27**, 15–78 (2015)
15. Ferber, J., Gutknecht, O.: Aalaadin: a meta-model for the analysis and design of organizations in multi-agent systems. In: Demazeau, Y. (ed.) International Conference on Multi-Agent Systems - ICMAS 1998, pp. 128–135. IEEE Press, Paris (1998)
16. Ferber, J., Gutknecht, O., Michel, F.: From agents to organizations: an organizational view of multiagent systems. In: Giorgini, P., Müller, J., Odell, J. (eds.) Agent Oriented Software Engineering - AOSE IV, vol. 2935, pp. 214–230. Springer, Heidelberg (2004). https://doi.org/10.1007/978-3-540-24620-6_15
17. Ferber, J., Michel, F., Baez-Barranco, J.A.: Agre: integrating environments with organizations. In: Weyns, D., Parunak, H.V.D., Michel, F. (eds.) Environments for Multi-Agent Systems, vol. 3374, pp.48–56. Springer, Cham (2005)
18. Costa, A.C.R.: Ecosystems as agent societies, landscapes as multi-societal agent systems. In: Adamatti, D.F. (ed.) Multiagent Based Simulations Applied to Biological and Environmental Systems, pp. 25–43. IGI Global, Hershey (2017)
19. Bordini, R.H., Hübner, J.F., Wooldridge, M.: Programming Multi-Agent Systems in AgentSpeak using Jason. Wiley, London (2007)
20. Hübner, J.F., Sichman, J.S., Boissier, O.: Developing organised multi-agent systems using the MOISE+ model: programming issues at the system and agent levels. International Journal of Agent-Oriented Software Engineering **1**, 370–395 (2007)
21. Ricci, A., Viroli, M., Omicini, A.: CArtAgO: An infrastructure for engineering computational environments in MAS. In: Weyns, D., Parunak, H.V.D., Michel, F. (eds.) E4MAS2006 - 3rd International Workshop on Environments for Multi-Agent Systems, AAMAS, pp. 102–119 (2006)
22. Hübner, J.F.: Um Modelo de Reorganização de Sistemas Multiagentes. Ph.D. Thesis, Escola Politécnica - USP, São Paulo (2003)
23. Ricci, Alessandro, Viroli, Mirko, Omicini, Andrea: Programming MAS with Artifacts. In: Bordini, Rafael H.., Dastani, Mehdi M.., Dix, Jürgen., El Fallah Seghrouchni, Amal (eds.) ProMAS 2005. LNCS (LNAI), vol. 3862, pp. 206–221. Springer, Heidelberg (2006). https://doi.org/10.1007/11678823_13
24. Piunti, M., Ricci, A., Boissier, O., Hübner, J.F.: Embodied Organisations in MAS Environments. In: Braubach, L., van der Hoek, W., Petta, P., Pokahr, A. (eds.) MATES 2009. LNCS (LNAI), vol. 5774, pp. 115–127. Springer, Heidelberg (2009). https://doi.org/10.1007/978-3-642-04143-3_11
25. Ricci, A., Santi, A.: Designing a general-purpose programming language based on agent-oriented abstractions: the simpAL project. In: Videira, C., Fisher, K. (eds.) SPLASH Workshops, pp. 159–170. ACM (2011)
26. Baldoni, M., Baroglio, C., Capuzzima, F.: Typing multi-agent systems via commitments. In: Dalpiaz, F., DixM, J., van Riemsdijk, B. (eds.) Enginnering Multi-agent Systems - EMAS 2014, pp. 338–405. Springer, Chalm (2014)
27. Baldoni, M., Baroglio, C., Capuzzimati, F., Micalizio, R.: Type checking for protocol role enactments via commitments. Autonomous Agents and Multi-Agent Systems **32**(3), 349–386 (2018). https://doi.org/10.1007/s10458-018-9382-3
28. Saugar, S., Serrano, J.M.: Programming social middlewares through social interaction types. In: MALLOW 2009 - Multi-Agent Logics, Languages, and Organisations Federated Workshops (2009)

A Practical Framework for General Dialogue-Based Bilateral Interactions

Seyed Ali Hosseini[1(✉)], David Minarsch[1], and Marco Favorito[1,2]

[1] Fetch.ai, Cambridge, UK
{ali.hosseini,david.minarsch,marco.favorito}@fetch.ai
[2] Sapienza University of Rome, Rome, Italy

Abstract. For autonomous agents and services to cooperate and interact in multi-agent environments they require well-defined protocols. A multitude of protocol languages for multi-agent systems have been proposed in the past, but they have mostly remained theoretical or have limited prototypical implementations. This work proposes a practical realisation of a general framework for defining dialogue-based bilateral interaction protocols which supports arbitrary agent-based interactions. Crucially, this work is tightly integrated with a modern framework for the creation of autonomous agents and multi-agent systems, making it possible to go from protocols' specification to their implementation and usage by agents, and enables evaluation of protocols' effectiveness and applicability in real-world use cases.

Keywords: Interaction protocols · Dialogues · General protocols

1 Introduction

Motivation Multi-Agent System (MAS) is recognised as a promising paradigm for decentralised and ubiquitous computing that involves embedded and distributed devices interacting with each other [30]. The increasing complexity and scale of these systems necessitates the development of abstractions and tools that simplify their development and deployment. This demand gives rise to *interaction protocols* as a key mechanism that enables cooperation amongst agents while recognising their individuality in a decentralised environment and accommodating their competing interests [14].

Interaction protocols are a useful abstraction which not only help the process of agent design by limiting the space of all possible states and actions in specific interactions, but also enable analysis of agent-based systems to assess specific properties, for example checking whether a system could arrive at a deadlock [49].

There are a multitude of protocol languages in the MAS literature based on various formal abstractions and mathematical constructs, for example, based on UML [25], state machines [22,49], trace expressions [13,18], and session types [52]. However, to the best of our knowledge, they either remain theoretical (e.g. [13]), or have limited prototypical implementations (e.g. [6,49,52]). As a result, the applicability and effectiveness of interaction protocol systems, as part of agent-based solutions to real-world problems, are not fully explored.

© Springer Nature Switzerland AG 2022
N. Alechina et al. (Eds.): EMAS 2021, LNAI 13190, pp. 312–331, 2022.
https://doi.org/10.1007/978-3-030-97457-2_18

Requirements. There are two fundamental requirements that guide this work. Firstly, **(Req. 1)** we are interested in environments which are fully *decentralised*, a property often considered integral to MAS itself [14]. Decentralisation refers to the absence of central authorities that imperatively control aspects of the system (e.g. decision making, communication, authorisation, coordination, etc.). In decentralised environments, interactions are primarily peer-to-peer, without reliance on third-party facilitators. This assumption immediately distinguishes this work from proposals such as [6,21] in which interaction protocols are enforced via mediators and middleware.

Secondly, **(Req. 2)** the framework must be practically realised by an implementation that is accessible, enabling its application and evaluation in real-world use cases. We believe that not paying attention to implementation leads to unexplored aspects of the system design, or in some cases major oversights. For example, a number of protocols in the literature are defined with reference to private elements of an agent (e.g. mental state) [3] and it is not entirely clear how such protocols may be implemented and enforced in practice under standard MAS assumptions.

Contribution and Structure. This work resides in a larger body of work by the authors ([32–35,40]) to bring agent technologies to production by taking advantage of strategic integration with distributed ledger technologies (DLTs) [47].

In this paper, we propose a general framework for dialogue-based bilateral interactions that use protocols to govern the behaviour of interaction participants. The framework is formally defined and its implementation facilitates its application in real-world problems. The implementation is integrated into the *AEA framework*; a modern framework for the development and deployment of agents [34].[1] This allows interactions and protocols to be specified then implemented and used by agents.

After informally describing the setting and highlighting key design issues in Sect. 2, we formalise the framework in Sect. 3 and instantiate it to capture a specific interaction: bilateral negotiation. We then shift our attention in Sect. 4 to implementation, discussing the main components of the framework and the major implementation issues involved. Section 5 provides a discussion of related works. Finally, Sect. 6 concludes and outlines future work.

2 Dialogue-Based Bilateral Interactions

We define *Bilateral interactions* as well-defined high-level interactions between exactly two *players* that serve a clear purpose. In the kinds of environment we focus on, players could be agents, services or humans. Some example are, bilateral negotiations [4], state channels [31], information-seeking [27] and HTTP request/responses.

The decentralised nature of multi-agent systems, the autonomy of agents, and the heterogeneity of their designs have all contributed to the established practice of modelling events and interactions amongst agents as *messages* [9,12,15,20,50]. A *dialogue* then structures and encapsulates a series of messages exchanged as part of a single interaction [38]. There are many dialogue-based approaches [2,4,11,37,39] to various types of interactions (e.g. negotiation, persuasion, inquiry) [46].

---

[1] The AEA framework's repository can be found at https://github.com/fetchai/agents-aea.

The peer-to-peer nature of communication in fully decentralised environments (see **Req. 1**) motivates our focus on *bilateral* interactions. Of course, it also simplifies the system design and helps us focus our attention on achieving an end-to-end solution in line with **Req. 2**. The bilateral primitives can later be used as foundation for multilateral extensions of this proposal.

Any interaction serves a particular (set of) goal(s), called the *interaction's goal(s)*. This is what all participant's aim to achieve by taking part in the interaction. For instance, the goal of a negotiation is dividing scarce resources amongst multiple parties [46]. All players in an interaction also have *personal goals* which may not necessarily be the same as the interaction's goal. For instance, in negotiations, each player aims to maximise its share of the resources.

2.1 Protocols

Protocols specify the bounds within which players in an interaction may operate to ensure an interaction's goal(s) are fulfilled [19,28].

A key issue to consider, when designing a concrete implementation of agent interactions, is how players' adherence to protocols is verified. In particular, anyone who is observing an interaction must be able to confirm whether or not the players' actions conform to the protocol. This idea underpins proposals such as [6,21] which introduce middle-layer *moderator* agents that coordinate communications and enforce protocols on players. However, in decentralised environments, where the absence of such middleware is entailed, this responsibility may be reliably assigned only to the players participating in the interaction themselves.

A consequence of the above is that protocols are restricted, in design, to making reference only to public elements of an interaction [44]. For example, proposals (such as [3]) which make references, either in syntax or semantics of their protocols, to e.g. agents' mental states, private strategies, etc., are in our experience not straightforward to implement under standard MAS assumptions. Therefore, in this framework, protocols can only be defined with reference to public elements of an interaction and protocol adherence is verified by the players of the interaction themselves.

Another key design issue to consider is the assumption of (a)synchronicity in message delivery [23]. Many proposals for interaction protocols in the literature assume synchronous communication for simplicity [22,25]. However, we argue that the uncertainty associated with the communication infrastructure, coupled with agents' autonomy, and the possibility of agents engaging in parallel interactions make synchronous communication, which blocks some or all other agent processes, detrimental to the continuity and successful operation of a decentralised MAS. Therefore, in this framework, we do not take the synchronicity assumption on board and address the problems it causes on the framework level.

3 Framework

We now give a formal description of a general framework for bilateral dialogue-based interactions and then provide an instantiation that captures bilateral negotiations.

3.1 Bilateral Interactions

The environment is inhabited by players. In practice, a player might be an agent, service, human, or other entity.

Definition 1 (Player). *A finite set $\mathcal{A}$ is defined where each $a \in \mathcal{A}$ is a player.*

A role is a logical actor in the context of an interaction identified by a name (e.g. bidder, seller). Players participating in a dialogue are assigned roles (see Definition 11). This is how protocols apply to specific players in a dialogue instance.

Definition 2 (Role). *A set $\mathcal{R}$ is defined where any $r \in \mathcal{R}$ is a role and $|\mathcal{R}| \in \{1, 2\}$.*

$|\mathcal{R}| = 2$ means each player has a distinct role and $|\mathcal{R}| = 1$ indicates that both players have identical roles.

Dialogues progress by players exchanging messages. Before defining a message, we define the notions of speech-act (see [7]) and their reply structure:

Definition 3 (Speech-act). *A set $\mathcal{S}$ of speech-acts $\{s_1, \ldots, s_n\}$ is defined where each speech-act s_i is of the form $P(c_1, \ldots, c_n)$ where P is an element of a set $\mathcal{P}$ of performatives, and $c_1, \ldots, c_n$ is a sequence of contents.*

Example 1. Examples of speech-acts are *inform*(ϕ), *offer*(ψ), *commit*(ω), *request*$(\rho_1, \ldots, \rho_4)$ where *inform, offer, commit, request* are performatives and ϕ, ψ, ω (some information) and $\rho_1, \ldots, \rho_4$ (some resource descriptions) are contents.

Definition 4 (Reply). *A function* Reply $: \mathcal{S} \longrightarrow 2^{\mathcal{S}}$ *specifies the valid replies to each speech-act.*

Example 2 (Running Example). Consider a simple request and response dialogue. Let $\mathcal{S} = \{req(\phi), res(\psi)\}$ where the speech-acts respectively represent a request and response involving some information ϕ and ψ. We can define two alternative reply structure as follows:

$$\text{Reply}_1(req(\phi)) = \{res(\psi)\} \qquad \text{Reply}_2(req(\phi)) = \{res(\psi)\}$$
$$\text{Reply}_1(res(\psi)) = \emptyset \qquad\qquad \text{Reply}_2(res(\psi)) = \{req(\phi)\}$$

In both Reply_1 and Reply_2, a request is replied to by a respond. However, in Reply_1, a respond does not have a reply and effectively ends a request/respond dialogue, whereas in Reply_2 a respond may be replied to by a follow up request which in turn can be replied to by a follow up respond and so on.

Definition 5 (Message). *The set $\mathcal{M}$ of messages is defined as $\{\langle id, pl, sa, ta \rangle \mid id \in \mathbb{N}, pl \in \mathcal{A}, sa \in \mathcal{S}, ta \in \mathbb{N}\}$ such that the four elements of a message m are respectively denoted by:*

- id(m): *the* identifier *of the message*
- player(m): *the* player *sending the message*
- speech-act(m): *the* speech-act *in the message*
- target(m): *the* target *of the message (i.e. the id of the message it replies to)*

Note how each message targets another in a dialogue. This is how protocols (defined later) use the notion of reply.

Definition 6 (Dialogue). *The set of dialogues, denoted $\mathcal{D}$, is the set of all finite sequences $m_1, \ldots, m_n$ from $\mathcal{M}$ such that each ith message in the sequence has identifier i. Given a dialogue d, the set of players participating in d is denoted by $\mathcal{A}^d$, and for every message $m_i \in d$, $\texttt{player}(m_i) \in \mathcal{A}^d$.*

A dialogue is thus a sequence of messages exchanged between a set of participating players, as viewed by any player. A dialogue is bilateral if messages are exchanged between exactly two players:

Definition 7 (Bilateral Dialogue). *A dialogue d is bilateral iff $\mathcal{A}^d = \{a, b\}$ for some players $a, b \in \mathcal{A}$ where $a \neq b$.*

Remark 1. The above definitions for dialogues specify the structure that each dialogue participant maintains and not a construct globally shared between them. Due to the asynchronous message exchange, the order of messages in dialogues on either side may be different. This is discussed more in Sect. 4.1.

Notation 8. *Let $d = m_1, \ldots, m_i, \ldots, m_n$ be some arbitrary dialogue. Then:*

- d_0 *represents an empty dialogue.*
- d_i *represents $m_1, \ldots, m_i$.*
- d, m *represents the continuation of dialogue d with message m.*
- $d_{n'}$ *is a sub-dialogue of d_n iff $n' \leq n$ and the first n' messages in d_n is the same as those in $d_{n'}$.*

An interaction must specify how a dialogue commences by describing the speech-act(s) which can be used to start a dialogue:

Definition 9 (Commencement). *A non-empty subset $\mathcal{C} \subseteq \mathcal{S}$ of speech-acts $\mathcal{S}$ is defined as* initial. *Any dialogue d_n is* commenced *at 1 and $\texttt{speech-act}(m_1) \in \mathcal{C}$.*

In some cases, it is useful for an interaction to define dialogue termination criteria so the participating agents have prior agreement as to when their dialogue is terminated. These criteria are defined in our framework via speech-acts.

Definition 10 (Termination). *A subset $\mathcal{T} \subseteq \mathcal{S}$ of speech-acts $\mathcal{S}$ is defined as* terminal. *A dialogue d_n is* terminated *at n, iff $\texttt{speech-act}(m_n) \in \mathcal{T}$ and it is not the case that d is terminated at an earlier point $n' < n$.*

Note that if $\mathcal{T} = \emptyset$, an interaction does not impose dialogue termination, and it is up to the participants to decide the criteria for recognising when a dialogue is terminated (e.g. after a period of inactivity).

Example 3 (Example 2 continued). We define one set $\mathcal{C}$ of initial and two alternative sets $\mathcal{T}_1$ and $\mathcal{T}_2$ of terminal speech-acts where they correspond with the two reply functions $\texttt{Reply}_1$ and $\texttt{Reply}_2$ in Example 2 (although any combination is possible).

$$\mathcal{C} = \{req(\phi)\}$$
$$\mathcal{T}_1 = \{res(\psi)\}$$
$$\mathcal{T}_2 = \{\}$$

The role of a player in a dialogue is decided based on the initial message of the dialogue. For example, a player a who sends a *request* message in a simple negotiation dialogue is the buyer, and the player who receives the *request* message is the seller.

Definition 11 (Role Assignment). *A partial function* $\mathrm{R} : \mathcal{A} \times \mathcal{M} \longmapsto \mathcal{R}$ *assigns a role to a player* a *given a message* m *iff:*

1. $\texttt{speech-act}(m) \in \mathcal{C}$
2. $\texttt{player}(m) \in \{a, a'\}$ *and* $\{a, a'\} \in \mathcal{A}^d$ *for some dialogue* d *and where* $a' \neq a$ *is some player.*

If any of the above conditions are not met, i.e. m *is not an initial message (condition 1) or player* a *is not a participant in a dialogue with the initial message* m *(condition 2), then* $\mathrm{R}(a, m) = \texttt{undefined}.$

Example 4 (Example 3 continued). Let $\mathcal{R} = \{inquirer, respondent\}$, speech-acts from Example 2, and initial speech-acts from Example 3. We define roles of players in request/response dialogues as follows:

$$\mathrm{R}(a, m) = \begin{cases} inquirer & \text{iff } \texttt{player}(m) = a \\ respondent & \text{otherwise} \end{cases}$$

A turn-taking function defines how turns shift in a dialogue:

Definition 12 (Turn-Taking). *A turn-taking function is* $\texttt{Turn} : \mathcal{D} \longrightarrow 2^{\mathcal{A}}$ *where* $\texttt{Turn}(d) \in \mathcal{A}^d$, *specifying the player(s) who have the right to send the next message in a dialogue.*

Example 5 (Example 4 continued). We define two alternative turn-taking functions for our simple request/response dialogues. $\texttt{Turn}_1$ imposes a more rigid structure where players alternate to send a message, and $\texttt{Turn}_2$ being a more liberal definition, effectively allows any participant to send a message at any point in a dialogue. Let $x, x' \in \mathcal{A}$ such that $x \neq x'$:

$$\texttt{Turn}_1(d_i) = \begin{cases} \{x\} & \text{iff } i \text{ is even} \\ \{x'\} & \text{otherwise} \end{cases} \qquad \texttt{Turn}_2(d_i) = \{x, x'\}$$

We now define the notion of well-formed dialogues:

Definition 13 (Well-Formed Dialogue). *A subset of dialogues* $\mathcal{D}^w \subseteq \mathcal{D}$ *are well-formed with the condition that a)* d_0 *is always in* $\mathcal{D}^w$, *and b) iff* $d_n \in \mathcal{D}^w$ *so are all of* d_n's *sub-dialogues* $d_{n'}$ *where* $n' < n$.

Any terminated well-formed dialogue has an outcome that determines the state in which the dialogue is terminated. A partial function $\texttt{Outcome}$ assigns an outcome to any such dialogue. This function can be utilised by dialogue participants as part of their particular strategies. For example, a learning-based agent aiming to optimise its negotiation strategy can use this function to keep track of the outcomes of its negotiations and update its model accordingly.

Definition 14 (Outcome). *A non-empty finite set $\mathcal{O}$ is defined where each $o \in \mathcal{O}$ is a dialogue* outcome. *A partial function* Outcome $: \mathcal{D}^w \longrightarrow \mathcal{O}$ *maps any terminated dialogue d to an outcome and* Outcome$(d) =$ undefined *if d is not terminated.*

Protocols define the legality of a message with reference to a dialogue:

Definition 15 (Protocol). *A protocol is a labelling function* Legal $: \mathcal{D}^w \times \mathcal{M} \longrightarrow$ {True, False} *which satisfies protocol rules* $R_1 - R_6$ *below:*
   For any $d_n \in \mathcal{D}^w$ and $m \in d_n$, Legal$(d_n, m) =$ True *iff:*

- R_1: player$(m) \in$ Turn(d_n)
- R_2: speech-act$(m) \in \mathcal{S}$.
- R_3: id$(m) = n + 1$
- R_4: target$(m) = 0$ *iff* id$(m) = 1$, *otherwise* $1 \leq$ target$(m) <$ id(m).
- R_5: *if m replies to $m' \in d_n$, then* speech-act$(m) \in$ Reply(speech-act(m')).
- R_6: d_n *is not terminated at n.*

Protocol rules R_1 and R_2 respectively ensure that messages are sent by the 'right' players in a dialogue, as specified by the turn-taking function, and that they have the correct speech-acts (per Definition 3). Protocol rule R_3 ensures that each message is correctly placed right after the last message in the dialogue. R_4 and R_5 regulate replies by stating that only the first message replies to no other message (target$(m_1) = 0$), and any other message targets another one in the dialogue while respecting the reply structure of speech-acts (Definition 4). Finally, R_6 states that once a dialogue is terminated, no other message can be legally added.

Together, the above rules define a lower bound on message legality. Of course, additional rules may be defined in specific interactions, for example, in the protocol that will be described in the next section.

Definition 16 (Well-Formed Dialogues Against Protocols). *A dialogue d_n is well-formed against a protocol* Legal, *iff* Legal$(d_{n-1}, m_n) =$ True.

Remark 2. Note that dialogues, well-formed under any protocol, are recursively well-formed on their sub-dialogues due to Definition 13.

Proposition 1. *Let $\mathcal{I}$ be an interaction dialogue system where $s \notin C$ and $\nexists s' \in \mathcal{S}$ such that $s \in$ Reply(s'). There is no well-formed dialogue d in $\mathcal{I}$ that contains a message m where speech-act$(m) = s$.*

Proof. Let us assume any well-formed dialogue d.

- *speech-act*$(m_1) \neq s$ from $s \notin C$ and Definition 9.
- For any $i > 1$, m_i targets some earlier message m_j due to R_4 and speech-act$(m_i) \in$ Reply(speech-act(m_j)) due to R_5. However, because s does not reply to any speech-act, *speech-act*$(m_i) \neq s$.

An interaction dialogue system can now be defined:

Definition 17 (Interaction Dialogue System). *An Interaction Dialogue System is a tuple $\langle \mathcal{R}, \mathcal{S},$ Reply, $C, \mathcal{I},$ R, Turn, Outcome, Legal$\rangle$ where $\mathcal{R}$ is a set of roles, $\mathcal{S}$ is a set of speech-acts,* Reply *is a reply function, C is the initial speech-acts, $\mathcal{I}$ is the terminal speech-acts,* R *is a role assignment function,* Turn *is a turn-taking function,* Outcome *is an outcome function, and* Legal *is a protocol.*

3.2   Framework Instantiated: Bilateral Negotiation

The framework presented above is abstract and needs to be instantiated to capture specific interactions. In this section, we present a simple two-party negotiation as an instance of the framework. A bilateral negotiation [3,4,43] is an interaction between two agents that negotiate over a set of resources.

Definition 18 (Negotiation Dialogue System). *An* interaction dialogue system for bilateral negotiation *is an interaction dialogue system* $\langle \mathcal{R}_n, \mathcal{S}_n, \text{Reply}_n, \mathcal{C}_n, \mathcal{T}_n, \text{R}_n, \text{Turn}_n, \text{Outcome}_n, \text{Legal}_n \rangle$ *where:*

- *(Negotiation Roles)* $\mathcal{R}_n = \{b, s\}$ *where b stands for* buyer *and s* seller
- *(Negotiation Speech-acts)* $\mathcal{S}_n = \{cfp(e), propose(e, p), accept(), decline()\}$ *where e is a non-empty set of resources and* $p \in \mathbb{R}_{\geq 0}$ *denotes a price*
- *(Negotiation Reply)*

$$\text{Reply}_n(cfp(e)) = \{propose(e, p), decline()\}$$
$$\text{Reply}_n(propose(e, p)) = \{propose(e, p'), accept()\}$$
$$\text{Reply}_n(accept()) = \text{Reply}(decline()) = \emptyset$$

- *(Negotiation Commencement)* $\mathcal{C}_n = \{cfp(e)\}$
- *(Negotiation Termination)* $\mathcal{T}_n = \{accept(), decline()\}$
- *(Negotiation Role Assignment) Let m be an initial message and* $x \in \mathcal{A}$:

$$\text{R}(x, m) = \begin{cases} b & \textit{iff}\, \text{player}(m) = x \\ s & \textit{otherwise} \end{cases}$$

- *(Negotiation Turn-Taking) Let* $x, x' \in \mathcal{A}$ *such that* $x \neq x'$:

$$\text{Turn}_n(d_i) = \begin{cases} \{x\} & \textit{iff}\, i \textit{ is even} \\ \{x'\} & \textit{otherwise} \end{cases}$$

- *(Negotiation Outcome)* $\mathcal{O}_n = \{\text{a-r}, \text{a-u}\}$ *where* a-r *stands for* agreement-reached *and* a-u *for* agreement-unreached:

$$\text{Outcome}_n(d_i) = \begin{cases} \text{a-r} & \textit{iff}\, \text{speech-act}(m_i) = accept() \\ \text{a-u} & \textit{otherwise} \end{cases}$$

- *(Negotiation Protocol)* $\text{Legal}_n : \mathcal{D}^w \times \mathcal{M} \longrightarrow \{\text{True}, \text{False}\}$ *is a protocol, that in addition to* R_1, R_6, *satisfies the negotiation rule* N_1 *below: For any* $d_i \in \mathcal{D}^w$ *and* $m \in d_i$, $\text{Legal}_n(d_i, m) = \text{True}$ *iff:*
  - N_1: *if* $\text{speech-act}(m) = propose(e, p)$ *or* $\text{speech-act}(m) = accept()$, *and m replies to* m' *then* $\text{player}(m) \neq \text{player}(m')$.

4 Implementation

In line with **Req. 2** in the introduction, we developed a technical implementation of the formalism we proposed in Sect. 3. In what follows, we describe its major components and highlight important implementation issues.

4.1 Practical Considerations

Asynchronisation. Recall from Sect. 2 that in this work, we do not assume communication between agents to be synchronous. The asynchronisation means that the two dialogue structures (see Definition 6), held by each participant in a dialogue, may not necessarily be identical. Consider an example interaction with the following turn taking function:

$$\text{Turn}(d) = \{a, b\} \text{ for any } d, \text{ where } a, b \in \mathcal{A}^d$$

Let us assume a dialogue d_n between a and b. At point n, agent a sends message m while simultaneously b sends m' (note the turn-taking function essentially allows any participant to send a message at any point in the dialogue). After these moves, a's dialogue is d, m, m' and b's is d, m', m.

This discrepancy entails that in addition to the explicit dialogue structures held by each participant in a dialogue, there exists an *implicit* structure, which crucially no participant has access to, that could represent the global state of the dialogue. This structure, unlike local dialogues, is not a sequence, rather a poset (i.e. partially ordered set) where only some of the messages are ordered and some are incomparable.

Definition 19 (Global Dialogues). *A global dialogue is a tuple $\langle M, \prec \rangle$ where $M \subset \mathfrak{m}$ is a set of messages and $\prec$ is a partial order.*

Note that $m_i \prec m_j$ means m_i precedes m_j in both participants' dialogues, and having $m_i \not\prec m_j$ and $m_j \not\prec m_i$ means m_i and m_j are incomparable and thus ordered differently in the two dialogues.

In the implementation, this means that messages are not uniquely identified only by their *id* (e.g. when identifying which message is being replied to). Instead, *id* and *player* combined are used to uniquely identify each message. This is achieved in the implementation by splitting the set of non-zero integers into $\mathbb{Z}^+$ and $\mathbb{Z}^-$, assigning the former to the player starting the dialogue (let us call it a) and the latter to the other player (let us call it b). As a result, a continuously increments and b decrements the *id* of the messages they send (replacing R_3 in Definition 15). The second part of R_4 then is replaced with the condition that $\text{target}(m)$ is between the smallest negative and largest positive *id* excluding 0.

The incomparability of certain messages in an implicit global dialogue, and hence the discrepancy of orders between local dialogues is not, in and of itself, a problem. In some use cases, this incomparability does not matter, especially when taking into account that the reply mechanism, strictly enforced in protocols, can cover causal ordering (e.g. a speech-act s which is strictly required to be after s' can be defined as its reply). It is however an issue that must be considered when designing specific interactions.

Moreover, there are interaction designs with specific reply structures and turn-taking functions that guarantee total ordering over messages in the global dialogue. These results are beyond the scope of this work and will be presented in future work on the properties of interaction designs.

Parallel Dialogues. In practice, agents may be engaged in multiple interactions and dialogues at the same time. Therefore, an agent x who is having two simultaneous negotiations with an agent y, should be able to recognise the correct dialogues y's messages belong to. To address this, each dialogue in the implementation is assigned a reference by its two players. Thus, in addition to the four elements in Definition 5, each message includes a reference to the dialogue to which it belongs.

4.2 Protocol Specification

The decentralised nature of multi-agent systems means agents may be designed and developed independently. Any implementation of interaction protocols must therefore support agents with heterogeneous technical requirements (e.g. hardware, platform, or programming language) and diverse implementations.

For this reason, we have created a format for describing interactions and protocols according to the formalism in Sect. 3.1, while being independent of specific programming languages in which agents may be implemented. The format is based on YAML [10], itself a language for structured data that is both machine and human-readable (and as such, easy to edit with any standard text editor).

An example protocol specification corresponding with the bilateral negotiation example of Sect. 3.2, as well as technical description of specification's format can be found in Sect. A in the appendix.

4.3 From Specification to Code

A protocol specification is only a high-level description of an interaction protocol and is designed to be independent of agents' implementations. For agents to engage in an interaction however, they need to have access to the protocol's definitions in the language they use. For instance, an agent developed in Python who wants to negotiate using the protocol in Sect. 3.2 with another agent developed in Go, each require an interpretation of the same specification in their own language.

The framework thus includes a *protocol generator*, which for any agent, given a protocol specification, produces the protocol package in the language this particular agent uses. Currently, the generator only takes into account the programming language that agents use. This architecture however allows for other agent constraints to be added later for consideration by the generator (e.g. an agent with limited resources may receive a more resource-bounded interpretation of a protocol's data structures).

Any generated protocol package consists of a) the technical definitions of the underlying concepts, e.g. a message, speech-acts and the reply structure, b) verification checks on messages according to the protocol, and c) description of how messages may be serialised and deserialised. Instructions on how to generate a protocol package from a specification is given in Sect. C in the appendix.

4.4   Serialisation

The messages agents exchange in dialogues may contain arbitrary contents with local representations (i.e. objects). However, in order to send these messages over a network, their local representations must be serialised by the sender and deserialised by the receiver. The framework uses Protocol Buffers [29] as the serialisation mechanism for cross-platform support.

Upon generating a protocol, the generator produces a protocol buffer schema, describing serialised models, as well as encoding and decoding logic corresponding with the protocol's specification. The protocol buffer schema generated for bilateral negotiations specification can be found in Sect. B of the appendix.

4.5   Protocol Adherence Verification

A protocol package, generated to meet the needs of an agent, provides all the definitions needed for this agent to know *"what can be done in these interactions?"*. The question, *"what to do in an interaction?"*, naturally arising, must be addressed for agents to partake in and benefit from interactions.

The framework places a separation of concerns with a clear distinction between the roles of a protocol designer and an agent developer. The former designs an interaction protocol whose constructs are publicly accessible (e.g. what is a valid reply to any speech-act). The latter designs the agent, most likely independent of the protocol designer, and has access to constructs privately owned by its agent (e.g. the agent's utility function). The second question is addressed by agent developers, who create strategies for their agents to engage in specific interactions.

The peer-to-peer nature of communication between agents, a direct consequence of the environment's decentralised nature, also means that in any interaction, the participating players' adherence to the protocol is verified only by the players themselves. Any message m is thus verified by its sender before being sent and by its receiver right after it is received. The dialogue-based design of interaction protocols enables the resolution of errors and failures of compliance via dialogues themselves [24].

5   Related Work

One of the most widely used notations for designing interaction protocols is Agent UML (AUML) [26]. AUML is an extension of UML 2.0 [42] with additional agent-specific features. AUML is a graphical notation and for relatively simple interactions is intuitive. However, it is one of the most complex notations [36] with 17 distinct graphical constructs compared with 11 for Statechart [22], and 5 or fewer for other graphical notations [1,41,49].

AUML assumes message delivery is synchronous, therefore protocols suffer from the *enactability problem* [18] which has to be addressed externally. The reliance on UML also presents a major issue for AUML in that it is a semi-formal language. There are no formal semantics for Interaction Diagrams and some of its elements make use of unstructured text (e.g. guards). This means ambiguities and misunderstandings are possible, which in turn makes the realisation of tools and implementations of AUML Interaction Diagrams difficult. Therefore, AUML is not considered a precise language.

Statechart is another popular and highly influential notation for agent interaction protocols [22]. Similar to AUML, Statechart is a graphical notation, but unlike AUML, it supports variables and parallel protocols, allowing them to model information-driven interactions. Also similar to AUML, interaction protocols in statecharts are designed with the synchronicity assumption, which means Statechart protocols are prone to the same enactability problem.

Compared to FSMs and Petri nets, Statechart's notation is fairly complex, both graphically (with 11 distinct graphical elements) and due to unstructured text in certain elements (e.g. guards and effects). Furthermore, there are more than twenty semantics, of differing types proposed for Statecharts. This means the same statechart can be interpreted completely differently under different semantics [17,45].

Statecharts were designed from the outset for reactive event-driven distributed systems, and not multi-agent systems. Therefore, they do not support the notion of roles, and transitions represent events rather than messages. This means that message attributes such as sender/receiver are not specified.

Hierarchical Agent Protocol Notation (HAPN) is a relatively more recent proposal [49]. HAPN focuses on addressing the problems its authors found in prior proposals, namely, a) flexible data-driven protocols, b) role representation and mapping to agents, and c) hierarchical modularity.

HAPN is a graphical notation, with some structured textual elements, and uses Hierarchical Finite State Machines [1] as its underlying conceptual model. It allows modelling parallelism and exceptions, supports information-driven interactions by adding flexibility on order of messages, and has some support for protocols with multiple role instances.

Similar to the other two notations above, HAPN assumes synchronous message delivery and the authors acknowledge the problems with this assumption, but argue that this is a standard and long-standing assumption in protocol design notations and suggest external processes for addressing them, e.g. [18].

Other research strands less closely related to our proposal include, commitment-based [8,48,51] and norm-based [5,16] interaction protocols, and BSPL [44]. They are all promising proposals, though some have fundamentally different assumptions than ours (e.g. norm-based methods are usually applied in organisational settings which are not entirely decentralised). However, none of these proposals has yet matured into a widespread practical methodology.

6 Conclusion

In this work, we propose a general framework for dialogue-based bilateral interactions that use protocols to govern their participants' behaviours. There are many proposals in the literature that focus on one or some aspects of the above problem. What sets this work apart is its end-to-end approach, from formalisation and specification of interactions to implementation and deployment as part of agent solutions.

The multi-agent and strictly decentralised nature of the environments we focus on (see **Req. 1**) requires that protocols are verifiable by interaction participants and support asynchronous message delivery. The practicality requirement (see **Req. 2**) means the framework has to be formal and precise to be computational, and easy to use to be practical. Although it is straightforward to verify the former via practical use, the latter is harder to measure.

Our end-to-end approach means that we focused on a minimal complete proposal. It can be further improved and extended in various directions:

- The replying nature of messages in dialogues lends itself nicely to a graph-theoretical interpretation. This, in turn, enables studying the properties of interactions under graph-theoretical assumptions and facilitates the creation of tools for visualising protocols during design-time and easily analysing dialogues during run-time. A graph-based characterisation further provides a natural way of defining protocol modularity (i.e. sub-protocols) via sub-graphs.
- A logical extension of this work is supporting multi-lateral interactions. A key problem we expect to encounter is staying within the true decentralisation assumption where communication continues to be peer-to-peer and asynchronous. To overcome this problem, exploring the use of specific cryptographic methods such as digital signatures in messages could prove useful.
- Although the framework is fully formalised and practically accessible, the properties of its interaction instances are left unspecified. It would be useful to present these properties and highlight the effects of different interaction designs, including best practices, on the characteristics of the resulting interactions.
- Drawing in-depth comparisons between our proposed formalism and others in the literature, identifying conditions under which protocols expressed under each are equivalent, and creating translations is another potential line of research. Once formal connections are made, existing formalisms enjoy access to a practical framework allowing them to be applied in and evaluated against real-world use cases.
- Another line of work could focus on increasing the expressiveness of the protocol specification language and the cross-platform support of the protocol generator, covering more programming languages and platforms, and meeting other technical requirements by agents, thus increasing support for more heterogeneous agents.

Acknowledgments. We thank Fetch.ai for supporting this research and the release of its implementation.

A   Protocol Specification

Listing 1 shows the protocol specification corresponding with bilateral negotiation in Sect. 3.2. Protocol specifications are formatted in YAML.[2] and consist of three YAML documents (enclosed between − − − and ...):

---

[2] See https://yaml.org.

```
---
name: negotiation
author: EMAS_authors
version: 0.1.0
description: 'A protocol for bilateral negotiations.'
license: Apache-2.0
aea_version: '>=1.0.0, <2.0.0'
protocol_specification_id: EMAS_authors/negotiation:1.0.0
speech_acts:
  cfp:
    e: ct:Resources
  propose:
    e: ct:Resources
    p: pt:float
  accept: {}
  decline: {}
...
---
ct:Resources: |
  bytes resources_bytes = 1;
...
---
initiation: [cfp]
reply:
  cfp: [propose, decline]
  propose: [propose, accept, decline]
  accept: []
  decline: []
termination: [accept, decline]
roles: {b, s}
end_states: [agreement_reached, agreement_unreached]
keep_terminal_state_dialogues: true
...
```

Listing 1: Protocol Specification for Bilateral Negotiation

- The first document contains basic information about the protocol as well as its speech-acts. Speech-acts are each listed as key-values, where the key is the performative and the value is a dictionary of its contents specifying their name and type. For example, *cfp* has one content, named e whose type is ct : Resource. The specification also comes with a language-independent type system. A summary of the types are in Table 1.
- The second document contains protocol buffer schema snippet of any custom types defined for speech-act contents.
- The third document contains the dialogue definitions where the fields are self-explanatory and correspond with definitions in Sect. 3.1.

Table 1. Protocol specification content types

Code	Type	Format	Example	In Python
⟨CT⟩	Custom types	ct:RegExp(^[A−Z][a−zA−Z0−9]*$)	ct:DataModel	Custom Class
⟨PT⟩	Primitive types	pt:bytes	pt:bytes	bytes
		pt:int	pt:int	int
		pt:float	pt:float	float
		pt:bool	pt:bool	bool
		pt:str	pt:str	str
⟨PCT⟩	Primitive collection types	pt:set[⟨PT⟩]	pt:set[pt:str]	FrozenSet[str]
		pt:list[⟨PT⟩]	pt:list[pt:int]	Tuple[int,...]
⟨PMT⟩	Primitive mapping types	pt:dict[⟨PT⟩, ⟨PT⟩]	pt:dict[pt:str,pt:bool]	Dict[str,bool]
⟨MT⟩	Multi types	pt:union[⟨PT⟩/⟨CT⟩/⟨PCT⟩/⟨PMT⟩,..., ⟨PT⟩/⟨CT⟩/⟨PCT⟩/⟨PMT⟩]	pt:union[ct:Model,pt:set[pt:str]]	Union[Model,FrozenSet[str]]
⟨O⟩	Optional	pt:optional[⟨MT⟩/⟨PT⟩/⟨CT⟩/⟨PCT⟩/⟨PMT⟩]	pt:optional[pt:bool]	Optional[bool]

```
syntax = "proto3";

package aea.EMAS_authors.negotiation;

message NegotiationMessage{

    // Custom Types
    message Resources{
        bytes resources_bytes = 1;
    }


    // Performatives and contents
    message Cfp_Performative{
        Resources e = 1;
    }

    message Propose_Performative{
        Resources e = 1;
        float p = 2;
    }

    message Accept_Performative{}

    message Decline_Performative{}


    oneof performative{
        Accept_Performative accept = 5;
        Cfp_Performative cfp = 6;
        Decline_Performative decline = 7;
        Propose_Performative propose = 8;
    }
}
```

Listing 2: Protocol Specification for Bilateral Negotiation

B Protocol Buffer Schema

An example of the protocol buffer schema that the protocol generator produces from the specification in Listing 1 is given in Listing 2.

C Instructions on Using the Framework

Note that detailed and up-to-date instructions can be found at https://github.com/fetchai/agents-aea.

- Ensure you have Python 3.7 installed on your machine.
- Install the AEA framework using pip (python package installer):
    ```
    > pip install aea[all]
    ```
- You many need to create a registry account (this is so you can publish your agent's packages on a registry):
    ```
    > aea init
    ```
  Then follow the on-screen instructions.
- Create an agent:
    ```
    > aea create agent
    ```
- Enter the newly created agent directory:
    ```
    > cd agent
    ```
- Generate the protocol:
    ```
    > aea generate protocol <path>
    ```
  where ⟨path⟩ is the path to the protocol specification file.
- The protocol package can now be found under .../agent/protocols/ negotiation.

References

1. Alur, R., Kannan, S., Yannakakis, M.: Communicating hierarchical state machines. In: Wiedermann, J., van Emde Boas, P., Nielsen, M. (eds.) ICALP 1999. LNCS, vol. 1644, pp. 169–178. Springer, Heidelberg (1999). https://doi.org/10.1007/3-540-48523-6_14
2. Amgoud, L., Dimopoulos, Y., Moraitis, P.: A unified and general framework for argumentation-based negotiation. In: Proceedings of the 6th International Joint Conference on Autonomous Agents and Multiagent Systems, AAMAS 2007, pp. 158:1–158:8. ACM, New York (2007)
3. Amgoud, L., Parsons, S., Maudet, N.: Arguments, dialogue, and negotiation. In: ECAI 2000, Proceedings of the 14th European Conference on Artificial Intelligence, Berlin, Germany, 20–25 August 2000, pp. 338–342 (2000)
4. Amgoud, L., Vesic, S.: A formal analysis of the role of argumentation in negotiation dialogues. J. Log. Comput. 22(5), 957–978 (2012)
5. Andrighetto, G., Governatori, G., Noriega, P., van der Torre, L.: Normative multi-agent systems. Schloss Dagstuhl-Leibniz-Zentrum fuer Informatik (2013)
6. Arcos, J.L., Esteva, M., Noriega, P., Rodríguez-Aguilar, J.A., Sierra, C.: Engineering open environments with electronic institutions. Eng. Appl. Artif. Intell. 18(2), 191–204 (2005). Agent-oriented Software Development
7. Austin, J., Austin, J., Urmson, J., Urmson, J., Sbisà, M.: How to Do Things with Words. Harvard University Press, A Harvard paperback (1975)
8. Baldoni, M., Baroglio, C., Marengo, E., Patti, V.: Constitutive and regulative specifications of commitment protocols: a decoupled approach. ACM Trans. Intell. Syst. Technol. 4(2), 1–25 (2013)
9. Bellifemine, F.L., Caire, G., Greenwood, D.: Developing Multi-Agent Systems with JADE (Wiley Series in Agent Technology). Wiley, Hoboken (2007)
10. Ben-Kiki, O., Evans, C., Ingerson, B.: Yaml ain't markup language (YAML™) version 1.2. Tech. rep., YAML (2009)
11. Black, E., Hunter, A.: An inquiry dialogue system. Auton. Agent. Multi-Agent Syst. 19(2), 173–209 (2009). https://doi.org/10.1007/s10458-008-9074-5

12. Boissier, O., Bordini, R.H., Hübner, J.F., Ricci, A., Santi, A.: Multi-agent oriented programming with JaCaMo. Sci. Comput. Program. **78**(6), 747–761 (2013)
13. Castagna, G., Dezani-Ciancaglini, M., Padovani, L.: On global types and multi-party sessions. In: Bruni, R., Dingel, J. (eds.) Formal Techniques for Distributed Systems, pp. 1–28. Springer, Berlin Heidelberg, Berlin, Heidelberg (2011)
14. Chopra, A.V.S., Singh, M.: An evaluation of communication protocol languages for engineering multiagent systems. J. Artif. Intell. Res. **69**, 351–1393 (2020). https://doi.org/10.1613/jair.1.12212
15. Collier, R.W., Russell, S., Lillis, D.: Exploring AOP from an OOP perspective. In: Proceedings of the 5th International Workshop on Programming Based on Actors, Agents, and Decentralized Control, pp. 25–36. AGERE! 2015, Association for Computing Machinery, New York (2015)
16. Dastani, M., van der Torre, L., Yorke-Smith, N.: Commitments and interaction norms in organisations. Auton. Agent. Multi-Agent Syst. **31**(2), 207–249 (2015). https://doi.org/10.1007/s10458-015-9321-5
17. Eshuis, R.: Reconciling statechart semantics. Sci. Comput. Program. **74**(3), 65–99 (2009)
18. Ferrando, A., Winikoff, M., Cranefield, S., Dignum, F., Mascardi, V.: On enactability of agent interaction protocols: towards a unified approach. In: Dennis, L.A., Bordini, R.H., Lespérance, Y. (eds.) EMAS 2019. LNCS (LNAI), vol. 12058, pp. 43–64. Springer, Cham (2020). https://doi.org/10.1007/978-3-030-51417-4_3
19. Freire, J., Botelho, L.: Executing explicitly represented protocols. In: In Workshop on Challenges in Open Systems at AAMAS 2002 (2002)
20. Gregori, M., Palanca, J., Aranda, G.: A jabber-based multi-agent system platform. In: Proceedings of the International Conference on Autonomous Agents, vol. 2006, pp. 1282–1284 (2006)
21. Hanachi, C., Sibertin-Blanc, C.: Protocol moderators as active middle-agents in multi-agent systems. Auton. Agent. Multi-Agent Syst. **8**, 131–164 (2004). https://doi.org/10.1023/B:AGNT.0000011159.53397.ea
22. Harel, D.: Statecharts: a visual formalism for complex systems. Sci. Comput. Program. **8**(3), 231–274 (1987)
23. Herlihy, M., Rajsbaum, S., Tuttle, M.R.: Unifying synchronous and asynchronous message-passing models. In: Proceedings of the Seventeenth Annual ACM Symposium on Principles of Distributed Computing, PODC 1998, pp. 133–142. Association for Computing Machinery, New York (1998)
24. Hosseini, S.A.: Dialogues incorporating enthymemes and modelling of other agents' beliefs. Ph.D. thesis, King's College London (2017)
25. Huget, M.-P., Odell, J.: Representing agent interaction protocols with agent UML. In: Odell, J., Giorgini, P., Müller, J.P. (eds.) AOSE 2004. LNCS, vol. 3382, pp. 16–30. Springer, Heidelberg (2005). https://doi.org/10.1007/978-3-540-30578-1_2
26. Huget, M.P., Odell, J., Bauer, B.: The AUML approach. In: Bergenti, F., Gleizes, M.P., Zambonelli, F. (eds.) Methodologies and Software Engineering for Agent Systems. Multiagent Systems, Artificial Societies, and Simulated Organizations (International Book Series), Springer, Boston (2004). https://doi.org/10.1007/1-4020-8058-1_15
27. Hulstijn, J.: Dialogue models for inquiry and transaction. Ph.D. thesis, Universiteit Twente, Proefschrift Universiteit Twente, The Netherlands (2000)
28. Kakas, A., Maudet, N., Pavlos, M.: Modular representation of agent interaction rules through argumentation. Auton. Agent. Multi-Agent. Syst. **11**, 189–206 (2005). https://doi.org/10.1007/s10458-005-2176-4
29. Kaur, G., Fuad, M.M.: An evaluation of protocol buffer. In: Proceedings of the IEEE SoutheastCon 2010 (SoutheastCon), pp. 459–462 (2010)

30. Leppänen, T., Álvarez Lacasia, J., Tobe, Y., Sezaki, K., Riekki, J.: Mobile crowdsensing with mobile agents. Auton. Agent. Multi-Agent Syst. **31**(1), 1–35 (2015). https://doi.org/10.1007/s10458-015-9311-7

31. McCorry, P., Buckland, C., Bakshi, S., Wüst, K., Miller, A.: You sank my battleship! a case study to evaluate state channels as a scaling solution for cryptocurrencies. In: Bracciali, A., Clark, J., Pintore, F., Rønne, P.B., Sala, M. (eds.) Financial Cryptography and Data Security, pp. 35–49. Springer International Publishing, Cham (2020)

32. Minarsch, D., Hosseini, S.A., Favorito, M., Ward, J.: Autonomous economic agents as a second layer technology for blockchains: framework introduction and use-case demonstration. In: 2020 Crypto Valley Conference on Blockchain Technology (CVCBT), pp. 27–35 (2020)

33. Minarsch, D., Favorito, M., Hosseini, A., Ward, J.: Trading agent competition with autonomous economic agents. In: Proceedings of the 19th International Conference on Autonomous Agents and MultiAgent Systems, AAMAS 2020, International Foundation for Autonomous Agents and Multiagent Systems, pp. 2107–2110. Richland, SC (2020)

34. Minarsch, D., Favorito, M., Hosseini, S.A., Turchenkov, Y., Ward, J.: Autonomous economic agent framework. In: Engineering Multi-Agent Systems (to publish) (2021)

35. Minarsch, D., Hosseini, S.A., Favorito, M., Ward, J.: Trading agent competition with autonomous economic agents. In: Proceedings of the 13th International Conference on Agents and Artificial Intelligence - Volume 1: SDMIS, pp. 574–582. INSTICC, SciTePress (2021). https://doi.org/10.5220/0010431805740582

36. Moody, D., van Hillegersberg, J.: Evaluating the visual syntax of UML: an analysis of the cognitive effectiveness of the UML family of diagrams. In: Gašević, D., Lämmel, R., Van Wyk, E. (eds.) SLE 2008. LNCS, vol. 5452, pp. 16–34. Springer, Heidelberg (2009). https://doi.org/10.1007/978-3-642-00434-6_3

37. Parsons, S., Wooldridge, M., Amgoud, L.: Properties and complexity of some formal inter-agent dialogues. J. Log. Comput. **13**(3), 347–376 (2003)

38. Prakken, H.: Coherence and flexibility in dialogue games for argumentation. J. Log. Comput. **15**(6), 1009–1040 (2005)

39. Prakken, H.: Formal systems for persuasion dialogue. Knowl. Eng. Rev. **21**, 163–188 (2006)

40. Rahmani, L., Minarsch, D., Ward, J.: Peer-to-peer autonomous agent communication network. In: Proceedings of the 20th International Conference on Autonomous Agents and Multi-Agent Systems, AAMAS '21, International Foundation for Autonomous Agents and Multiagent Systems, p. [to appear] (2021)

41. Reisig, W.: Petri Nets: An Introduction. Springer-Verlag, Berlin, Heidelberg (1985). https://doi.org/10.1007/978-3-642-69968-9

42. Rumbaugh, J., Jacobson, I., Booch, G.: Unified Modeling Language Reference Manual, The (2nd Edition). Pearson Higher Education (2004)

43. Sadri, F., Toni, F., Torroni, P.: Logic agents, dialogues and negotiation: an abductive approach. In: In Proceedings of AISB 2001 Convention, The Society for the Study of Artificial Intelligence and the Simulation of Behaviour, pp. 71–78 (2001)

44. Singh, M.P.: Information-driven interaction-oriented programming: BSPL, the blindingly simple protocol language. In: The 10th International Conference on Autonomous Agents and Multiagent Systems - Volume 2, AAMAS 2011, International Foundation for Autonomous Agents and Multiagent Systems, pp. 491–498. Richland, SC (2011)

45. Taleghani, A., Atlee, J.M.: Semantic variations among UML state machines. In: Nierstrasz, O., Whittle, J., Harel, D., Reggio, G. (eds.) MODELS 2006. LNCS, vol. 4199, pp. 245–259. Springer, Heidelberg (2006). https://doi.org/10.1007/11880240_18

46. Walton, D.N., Krabbe, E.C.: Commitment in Dialogue: Basic Concepts of Interpersonal Reasoning. State University of New York, Albany (1995)

47. Wattenhofer, R.: Distributed Ledger Technology: The Science of the Blockchain, 2nd edn. CreateSpace Independent Publishing Platform, North Charleston (2017)

48. Winikoff, M., Liu, W., Harland, J.: Enhancing commitment machines. In: Leite, J., Omicini, A., Torroni, P., Yolum, P. (eds.) DALT 2004. LNCS (LNAI), vol. 3476, pp. 198–220. Springer, Heidelberg (2005). https://doi.org/10.1007/11493402_12
49. Winikoff, M., Yadav, N., Padgham, L.: A new hierarchical agent protocol notation. Auton. Agent. Multi-Agent Syst. **32**(1), 59–133 (2017). https://doi.org/10.1007/s10458-017-9373-9
50. Wooldridge, M.: An Introduction to MultiAgent Systems, 2nd edn. Wiley, Hoboken (2009)
51. Yolum, P., Singh, M.P.: Commitment machines. In: Meyer, J.-J.C., Tambe, M. (eds.) ATAL 2001. LNCS (LNAI), vol. 2333, pp. 235–247. Springer, Heidelberg (2002). https://doi.org/10.1007/3-540-45448-9_17
52. Yoshida, N., Hu, R., Neykova, R., Ng, N.: The scribble protocol language. In: Abadi, M., Lluch Lafuente, A. (eds.) Trustworthy Global Computing, pp. 22–41. Springer International Publishing, Cham (2014). https://doi.org/10.1007/978-3-319-05119-2

Implementing Durative Actions with Failure Detection in GWENDOLEN

Peter Stringer$^{(\boxtimes)}$ ⓘ, Rafael C. Cardoso ⓘ, Clare Dixon ⓘ,
and Louise A. Dennis ⓘ

Department of Computer Science, The University of Manchester, Manchester, UK
peter.stringer@postgrad.manchester.ac.uk,
{rafael.cardoso,clare.dixon,louise.dennis}@manchester.ac.uk

Abstract. We present an extension of the semantics for action execution in the GWENDOLEN BDI programming language. This extension firstly explicitly assumes that actions have durations and, moreover, that the reasoning cycle of the agent can not be stopped while such an action is executing but needs to continue in order to monitor for important external events. Secondly, the extension assumes that actions may often fail and this needs to be detected. This forms part of a larger project to develop a framework plan/action adaptation within BDI agents in order to enable long-term autonomy. We have implemented the extension and demonstrate its operation in a simple case study.

Keywords: Engineering MAS · Action failure · Knowledge representation

1 Introduction

We are interested in the use of Belief-Desire-Intention (BDI) agent programming languages [23, 26] for the high-level control of autonomous robotic systems and particularly in support at the agent level for *long-term autonomy*. Agents are frequently considered a suitable paradigm for decision-making in autonomous systems because of their encapsulation of the Sense-Reason-Act cycle. BDI agents, with their high-level and declarative representation of concepts such as beliefs and goals, are an attractive paradigm where such control needs to be amenable to analysis (e.g., for assurance purposes). BDI agents have been deployed to control an array of cyber-physical autonomous systems such as autonomous vehicles, spacecraft and robot arms (e.g., Mars Rover [7], Earth-orbiting satellites [12] and robotic arms for nuclear waste-processing [1]).

Most BDI languages typically operate within a *reasoning cycle* that captures the agent Sense-Reason-Act cycle. Within this cycle, the agent selects programmer supplied plans for execution based on the agent's current beliefs and goals.

This work has been supported by The University of Manchester's Department of Computer Science and the EPSRC "Robotics and AI for Nuclear" (EP/R026084/1) and "Future AI and Robotics for Space" (EP/R026092/1) Hubs.

© Springer Nature Switzerland AG 2022
N. Alechina et al. (Eds.): EMAS 2021, LNAI 13190, pp. 332–351, 2022.
https://doi.org/10.1007/978-3-030-97457-2_19

These plans may change the agent's mental state, but often also contain actions (or capabilities) that are executed by the agent and have some effect on the outside world (with these effects being perceived by the agent in the Sense phase of its reasoning cycle).

In [15], Dennis and Fisher highlight two problems with the way BDI languages typically handle actions: Firstly, it is claimed that in some languages, that "execution of the BDI program waits for the action to complete before processing other intentions, goals and plans"—in robotic systems, where an action such as moving between two waypoints in a map, may take some time to complete preventing the agent from monitoring the environment for other events (for instance the need to avoid obstacles during movement). It should be noted that this is only true for some BDI languages and there are notable exceptions to this assumption [2,27]. Secondly, many languages lack principled mechanisms within their semantics for detecting whether an action has succeeded and reacting appropriately to failure if it has not. Dennis and Fisher propose a generic BDI semantics based on the concept of *goal lifecycles* to allow for actions with durations and failure but provide no implementation of this semantics.

We are particularly interested in the latter, with the matter of *failure detection*. Robotic autonomous systems operating in real-world environments may encounter intermittent failures of actions. Sometimes these failures will be transitory and can be ignored in terms of the long term operation of the system, in other situations failures may be persistent indicating some change in the robot or its environment which must be compensated for. Stringer et al. [33] propose an *action lifecycle* in which actions are paired with descriptions of their operation that may be deprecated in the event of repeated action failure and integrated with mechanisms for repairing the descriptions and/or plans that involve those actions (e.g., as proposed in [6]). This paper adapts the semantics from [15] to integrate with this concept of action lifecycles and implements it in the GWENDOLEN agent programming language with a view to ultimately implementing the full action lifecycle and reconfigurability process from [33].

The rest of this paper is structured as follows. Section 2 contains a brief description of BDI agents, how actions are normally treated in BDI-based languages, and the basics of the action theory in the GWENDOLEN agent programming language. Next, in Sect. 3 we present how we have extended the aforementioned GWENDOLEN's action theory to support durative actions with failure detection and share an illustrative example. The implementation of such adaptation is discussed in Sect. 4 and evaluated through the use of a practical case study. To conclude the paper we discuss related work and its similarities and differences with our proposed approach (Sect. 5) and present our concluding remarks along with a summary of future work (Sect. 6).

2   Background

An 'agent' is an abstraction developed to capture autonomous behaviour within complex, dynamic systems [35]. It is defined in [29] as something that "can be viewed as **perceiving** its environment through **sensors** and **acting** upon that environment through **effectors**".

Cognitive agents [5,26,36] have explicit reasons for the choices they make. These are often described in terms of the agent's *beliefs* and *goals*, which in turn determine the agent's *intentions*. This view of cognitive agents is encapsulated within the BDI model [25,26]. *Beliefs* represent the agent's (possibly incomplete, possibly incorrect) information about itself, other agents, and its environment, *desires* represent the agent's long-term goals while *intentions* represent the goals that the agent is actively pursuing (the representation of intentions often includes partially instantiated and/or executed plans and so combines the goal with its intended means).

There are *many* different agent programming languages and agent platforms based, at least in part, on the BDI approach [4,8,22]. Agents programmed in these languages commonly contain a set of *beliefs*, a set of *goals*, and a set of *plans*. Plans determine how an agent acts based on its beliefs and goals and form the basis for *practical reasoning* (i.e., reasoning about actions) in such agents. As a result of executing a plan, the beliefs and goals of an agent may change and actions may be executed.

2.1   Actions in BDI Programs

Many BDI languages represent environmental interaction as an atomic *action*. When an action is invoked it executes some low-level code invisible at the BDI level or interacts directly with the external world. Such an action is often a ground atomic command, and its effect is judged via agent perception, though it may have an explicit return value (typically, 'success' or 'failure'). Languages that treat interaction in this way include *Jason* [4] and GWENDOLEN [13].

Interaction may also be modelled as *capabilities*. These have explicit *pre-* and *post*-conditions such that the interaction is executed only if the pre-conditions are true and, after the interaction has concluded, the post-conditions are asserted explicitly by the language. Other effects may be subsequently observed via perception mechanisms. It is possible that a capability executes no low-level code, particularly when an agent is executing in some simulated setting where it is considered sufficient to use just the post-conditions to represent the result of the interaction. Languages that treat interaction in this way include GOAL [20] and 3APL [11].

While some of these action representations contain mechanisms for the detection of action failure, this is generally not reflected in the language semantics where little attention has been paid to how these failures should be handled. Moreover, when we consider robotic systems, we also need to account for actions that have durations while typical BDI language semantics generally assume a near-instantaneous return after an action command is executed.

In [15], Dennis and Fisher propose a generic framework for integrating durative actions with failure modes into BDI programming languages. This proposal builds on work on Goal life-cycles for BDI languages [18] that have *active, suspend* and *abort* stages. They propose that actions be associated with *success*, *failure* and *abort* conditions; the abort condition is intended to handle situations where the action execution is deemed to have continued for "too long" without either success or failure being detected. When an action is executed as part of a plan, the goal the plan was to achieve is suspended pending completion of the action. This suspended state allows the processing of other goals to occur. If the action's success condition is met then the goal is returned to the active state and the plan continues processing, otherwise the goal is returned to a pending state for re-planning.

Stringer et. al [33] consider what happens when the performance of actions in a BDI program change over time – for instance as hardware performance degrades. They introduce the concept of an *action lifecycle* in which an action is introduced into the system as *Functional*, may move into a *Suspect* state if it is failing and finally becomes *Deprecated* following repeated failures. Cardoso et al. [6] assumes a framework along these lines and builds upon it to outline a mechanism that allows reconfiguration of a BDI agent's plans in order to continue functioning as intended if some action has become *Deprecated*. Our work here is intended to integrate with such a framework by implementing a process by which action degradation can be detected prior to designating an action as either *Suspect* or *Deprecated*.

2.2   The GWENDOLEN Programming Language

We use the GWENDOLEN language for our implementation in part because of its use to provide a high-level agent reasoner in a number of autonomous robotic applications [1] and because of its link to the Agent Java Pathfinder (AJPF) model-checker [14] since we have an interest in the assurance of autonomous robotics.

A full operational semantics for GWENDOLEN is presented in [13], but its key components are, for each agent, a set, B, of beliefs that are ground first-order formulae and a set, I, of intentions that are stacks of *deeds* associated with some event. Deeds can be the addition or deletion of beliefs, the adoption of new goals, and the execution of primitive actions. A GWENDOLEN agent may have several concurrent intentions and will, by default, execute the first deed on each intention stack in turn. GWENDOLEN is event-driven and events include the acquisition of new beliefs (typically via perception), messages and goals. A programmer supplies plans that describe how an agent should react to events by extending the deed stack of the relevant intention. These plans contain actions for execution.

Action Theory in GWENDOLEN
The actions in GWENDOLEN exist as atomic actions. When an action appears in a plan and is placed on an intention then, when processing of the intention reaches the action, it is executed and all other processing ceases until execution has completed. As a result of the issues with this style of action execution (particularly that no further perception takes place and so new events can not be reacted to), it has become typical in GWENDOLEN programs to treat the

execution of actions as the *initiation* of the action. A specialised "wait for" construction is then used to *suspend* the intention containing the action until some success criterion is perceived. This is analogous to the "suspend" state in the Goal-lifecycle literature [15,18] since intentions are often created by the acquisition of a goal. Thus, GWENDOLEN loosely supports the concept of actions with durations by making use of this "wait for" command.

In the GWENDOLEN operational semantics [13], action execution is represented by Eq. (1). The equation has been simplified by removing all reference to unifiers, edge cases and some specialised action types. The state of the system is represented by an environment, ξ, coupled with a large tuple containing the components required by the agent to function of which we are primarily interested in the current intention, i. As noted above intentions represent a stack of deeds to be executed in order to handle some event (e.g., to achieve a goal). We use $\mathtt{hd}(i)$ to represent the top (head) deed on this stack and $\mathtt{tl}(i)$ to represent the tail of the stack after the top deed is removed[1].

$$\frac{\mathtt{hd}(i) = a \quad \xi \xrightarrow{\mathtt{do}(a)} \xi'}{\langle \xi, \langle \ldots i \ldots \rangle \rangle \rightarrow_{\mathtt{action}} \langle \xi', \langle \ldots \mathtt{tl}(i) \ldots \rangle \rangle} \tag{1}$$

Thus (1) states that when the top deed on the intention is flagged as action, $\mathtt{hd}(i) = a$, and the outcome of that action is to change the environment, ξ, to become ξ', represented by $\xi \xrightarrow{\mathtt{do}(a)} \xi'$, then performing the action transforms the pair of the environment and the tuple of agent components by changing the environment and removing the top of the current intention, i, (i becomes $\mathtt{tl}(i)$). The other items in the agent's tuple remain unchanged (represented by $\ldots$).

The "wait for" command is governed by Eqs. (2) and (3) (again these have been simplified to remove unifiers, edge cases and references to Prolog-style *reasoning rules*). Here $* \ldots b$ represents the instruction "wait for b to become true", $B \models b$, expresses that the formula b is a logical consequence of the agent's belief base, B. While $\mathtt{suspend}(i)$ suspends intention i.

$$\frac{\mathtt{hd}(i) = * \ldots b \quad B \models b}{\langle \xi, \langle \ldots i \ldots B \ldots \rangle \rangle \rightarrow_{\mathtt{wait\_for}} \langle \xi, \langle \ldots \mathtt{tl}(i) \ldots B \ldots \rangle \rangle} \tag{2}$$

$$\frac{\mathtt{hd}(i) = * \ldots b \quad B \not\models b}{\langle \xi, \langle \ldots i, \ldots, B \ldots \rangle \rangle \rightarrow_{\mathtt{wait\_for}} \langle \xi, \langle \ldots \mathtt{suspend}(i), \ldots, B \ldots \rangle \rangle} \tag{3}$$

So if the top deed on an intention is the instruction to wait for b to become true ($* \ldots b$) and that belief is believed to have become true, $B \models b$, then the intention continues processing (2). If not, the intention is suspended (3).

Lastly, existing intentions are unsuspended when new beliefs are added. This can happen either as a result of perception or as deeds that appear in plans, in both cases the new beliefs appear on the top of some intention:

---

[1] For simplicity of presentation, we here treat the intention as a stack of deeds but it should be noted that more information, such as the goal to be achieved, is also included in the full semantics.

$$\frac{\mathtt{hd}(i) = +b}{\langle \xi, \langle \ldots i, I, B \ldots \rangle \rangle \rightarrow_{\mathtt{add\_belief}}} \tag{4}$$
$$\langle \xi, \langle \ldots \mathtt{tl}(i), \mathbf{unsuspend}(I, b) \cup \mathbf{new}(+b, \epsilon), B \cup \{b\}, \ldots \rangle \rangle$$

Here **unsuspend**(I, b) unsuspends all suspended intentions in I (the agent's intention set) that are waiting for b to become true. Whilst $\mathbf{new}(e, d)$ creates a new intention from an event and a deed[2]. Therefore this rule adds a new belief, $+b$, to the belief base, B, and a new intention noting the appearance of the new belief. At the same time, all intentions that are waiting for b to be achieved as part of their suspend condition are unsuspended.

3 Adapting GWENDOLEN's Action Theory

Following [15] we associate actions with three terminating conditions: *Success*, *Failure*, and *Abort*. These conditions are represented in an extended action notation as $a : (\phi_s, \phi_f, t_o)$ where ϕ_s is the success condition, ϕ_f is the failure condition and t_o is a *time out* period after which the action should be aborted. Whilst a time period has been used as an abort condition in this example, it must be noted that this condition is not limited to solely time-based criteria. We assume that the agent can perceive from the environment the length of time an action, a, has been executing as a percept, $time(a, t)$. We also extend our agent to maintain two *action logs* that track action failures and aborts. In future work, we intend to use these logs to determine when an action is *Suspect* or *Deprecated* [33].

When an action is executed either it is an instantaneous action (in which case one of its termination conditions is either instantly or trivially true), or it has a duration and the current intention is suspended. This follows [15] where the goal is suspended since, as already noted, GWENDOLEN's intention life-cycles map onto the goal-lifecycles of [18] and [15].

We consider first the case in which one of the termination conditions is true when the action executes—i.e., it is instantaneous. Equation (5) shows the case where the success condition is true. This behaves as (1) since this situation is analogous to action execution in the existing GWENDOLEN semantics.

$$\frac{\mathtt{hd}(i) = a : (\phi_s, \phi_f, t_o) \quad \xi \xrightarrow{\mathtt{do}(a)} \xi' \quad B \models \phi_s}{\langle \xi, \langle \ldots i, B, \ldots \rangle \rangle \rightarrow_{\mathtt{action}} \langle \xi', \langle \ldots \mathtt{tl}(i), B, \ldots \rangle \rangle} \tag{5}$$

Where the failure condition is encountered this is logged and the action is retried (6). We represent our two action logs as a mapping, $L_i : A \rightarrow \mathbb{N}$ (where $i \in \{failure, abort\}$) from the set of actions, A, to the number of times the action is failed/aborted. We use the notation $L_i(a) \leftarrow n$ to indicate that the value of $L_i(a)$ has been changed to the number n. We include this rule for completeness, though it is difficult to think of a situation where an action is presumed to be a

---

[2] This process of creating a new intention is not of relevance to this paper, but allows a GWENDOLEN agent to react to changes in its beliefs – e.g., to avoid an obstacle.

failure at the point of execution[3]. The current intention, i, is unchanged. Next time the intention is selected the action will be attempted again.

$$\frac{\texttt{hd}(i) = a : (\phi_s, \phi_f, t_o) \quad \xi \xrightarrow{\texttt{do}(a)} \xi' \quad B \models \phi_f}{\langle \xi, \langle \ldots i, B \ldots, L_{failure} \rangle \rangle \rightarrow_{\texttt{action}} \langle \xi', \langle \ldots i, B \ldots, L_{failure}(a) \leftarrow L_{failure}(a) + 1 \rangle \rangle} \tag{6}$$

Note that we do not have a case here for the abort conditions. Since we are treating aborts explicitly as time outs in this notation and this makes no sense in the case of instantaneous action completion.

We now consider the case where none of the termination conditions hold when the action is executed. In this case intention is suspended with the action marked as **executing** (7). We use : to indicate the concatenation of a deed to the top of an intention stack.

$$\frac{\texttt{hd}(i) = a : (\phi_s, \phi_f, t_o) \quad \xi \xrightarrow{\texttt{do}(a)} \xi' \quad B \not\models \phi_s \quad B \not\models \phi_f}{\langle \xi, \langle \ldots i, B \ldots \rangle \rangle \rightarrow_{\texttt{action}} \langle \xi', \langle \ldots \texttt{suspend}(\texttt{executing}(a) : \texttt{tl}(i)), B \ldots \rangle \rangle} \tag{7}$$

The transition rule (4) is left unchanged. It unsuspends the intention if any of the termination conditions are perceived. We then use (8), (9) and (10) to either process the rest of the intention (if the action has terminated with success) or to update the log and attempt the action again (if we have terminated with failure) and, in the case of an abort to explicitly abort the action execution in the environment.

$$\frac{\texttt{hd}(i) = \textbf{executing}(a : (\phi_s, \phi_f, t_o)) \quad B \models \phi_s}{\langle \xi, \langle \ldots i, B \ldots \rangle \rangle \rightarrow_{\texttt{action}} \langle \xi, \langle \ldots \texttt{tl}(i), B \ldots \rangle \rangle} \tag{8}$$

$$\frac{\texttt{hd}(i) = \textbf{executing}(a : (\phi_s, \phi_f, t_o)) \quad B \models \phi_f}{\langle \xi, \langle \ldots i, B \ldots L_{failure} \rangle \rangle \rightarrow_{\texttt{action}}}$$
$$\langle \xi, \langle \ldots a : (\phi_s, \phi_f, t_o) : \texttt{tl}(i), B \ldots, L_{failure}(a) \leftarrow L_{failure}(a) + 1 \rangle \rangle \tag{9}$$

$$\texttt{hd}(i) = \textbf{executing}(a : (\phi_s, \phi_f, t_o)) \quad B \models time(a, t) \wedge t_o \leq t$$
$$\frac{\xi \xrightarrow{\texttt{do}(\texttt{abort}(a))} \xi'}{\langle \xi, \langle \ldots i, B \ldots L_{abort} \rangle \rangle \rightarrow_{\texttt{action}}}$$
$$\langle \xi', \langle \ldots a : (\phi_s, \phi_f, t_o) : \texttt{tl}(i), B \ldots, L_{abort}(a) \leftarrow L_{abort}(a) + 1 \rangle \rangle \tag{10}$$

We also need a rule to resuspend an intention if it transpired that none of the termination conditions had been met. This was because the process for detecting when an intention should unsuspend was based on identifying individual ground predicates and, in particular, did not identify abort time outs well and so we adapted it to unsuspend the intention whenever a new stamp was perceived.

---

[3] It is possible the failure conditions could be used here a bit like pre-conditions in capabilities, but that would really be an abuse of the notation.

This is shown in (11).

$$\frac{\mathrm{hd}(i) = \mathbf{executing}(a : (\phi_s, \phi_f, t_o))}{B \not\models \phi_s \quad B \not\models \phi_f \quad \neg(B \models \mathit{time}(a, t) \wedge t_o \leq t)}{\langle \xi, \langle \ldots i, B \ldots \rangle \rangle \rightarrow_{\mathrm{action}} \langle \xi, \langle \ldots \mathbf{suspend}(\mathbf{executing}(a) : \mathrm{tl}(i)), B \ldots \rangle \rangle} \tag{11}$$

3.1   Example

To illustrate the operation of this semantics we consider a simple example of a wheeled inspection robot tasked to navigate around a space represented as a topological map and take images at specific locations in that map. We consider a specific example where the robot is moving through a hallway to the fire exit, where it is supposed to log an image of the fire exit (for later human inspection to verify that the fire exit is clear). However, the hallway is constructed in such a way that, particularly at times when many people are moving through it, the obstacle avoidance behaviour of the robot means it sometimes ends up at the wrong location—the entrance door and sometimes the movement takes far longer than the expected duration (5 min) of the move.[4]

We are therefore considering two actions one with a duration (*move_to_fire_exit*) and one without (*take_image*):

$$move\_to\_fire\_exit : (at(fire\_exit), at(entrance), 5) \tag{12}$$

$$take\_image : (\top, \bot, 0) \tag{13}$$

We represent the agent's intention stack as a stack of deeds, ignoring some of the other information GWENDOLEN stores in intentions which is irrelevant here. At the point where it starts traversing the hallway, it has two deeds on the stack – the action to move to the fire exit, followed by the action to take an image.

deed
move_to_fire_exit
take_image

The agent attempts to execute `move_to_fire_exit`. At this point the agent is neither at the fire exit nor at the entrance so the intention is suspended and `move_to_fire_exit` is marked as executing (according to (7)). The intention becomes:

	deed
Suspended:	executing(move_to_fire_exit)
	take_image

Three things may now happen.

---

[4] Many robot path planning algorithms will reach their target events but when integrated with high level decision-making it is often announced that the robot has reached another waypoint.

1. Firstly, the robot may reach the fire exit. The agent perceives $at(fire\_exit)$ and the intention is unsuspended. At this point the agent makes a transition in accordance with (8) and the intention becomes:

$$\frac{\overline{\text{deed}}}{\texttt{take\_image}}$$

   The agent may then execute `take_image`. This is an instantaneous action with a trivial success condition. A transition occurs according to (5) and the intention becomes:

$$\frac{\overline{\overline{\text{deed}}}}{\rule{1.5cm}{0.4pt}}$$

   This intention is now complete and will be cleared away as part of the rest of the reasoning process.

2. Secondly, the robot may reach the entrance. The agent perceives $at(entrance)$ and the intention is unsuspended. At this point the agent makes a transition in accordance with (9) and the intention becomes:

$$\frac{\overline{\text{deed}}}{\begin{array}{c}\texttt{move\_to\_fire\_exit}\\\texttt{take\_image}\end{array}}$$

   At the same time the failure log is updated to note the failure of `move_to_fire_exit`. We are now back in our original state and the action will be re-attempted.

3. Thirdly, after five minutes the robot may have reached neither the fire exit nor the entrance and may still be attempting to move through the hallway. The agent perceives $time(\texttt{move\_to\_fire\_exit}, n)$ where $n \geq 5$ and the intention is unsuspended. At this point the agent makes a transition in accordance with (10). The agent performs the action, $abort(\texttt{move\_to\_fire\_exit})$ and the intention becomes:

$$\frac{\overline{\overline{\text{deed}}}}{\begin{array}{c}\texttt{move\_to\_fire\_exit}\\\texttt{take\_image}\end{array}}$$

   At the same time, the abort log is updated to note the abort of `move_to_fire_exit`. We are now back in our original state and the action will be re-attempted.

It should be noted that, particularly in the case of an abort, we might not want to simply re-attempt the action. For instance, we might want to wait until the hallway was less crowded before attempting to move again. Providing a richer set of tools for reacting to failures and aborts, ideally involving analysis of the logs, is future work (see Sect. 6).

4   Implementation

We implemented the extended semantics for GWENDOLEN[5]. GWENDOLEN is implemented using the Agent Infrastructure Layer (AIL), a Java framework that contains support for implementing interpreters for agent programming languages by representing the operational semantics directly. The key tasks, therefore, were to extend the class representing GWENDOLEN actions to contain the termination conditions and time outs and then integrate our new rules into the existing GWENDOLEN interpreter which we did by extending the existing action execution rule (1) with additional cases. The tuple representing the agent state also had to be extended to include the abort and failure logs.

The new rules that have been integrated in top the existing GWENDOLEN interpreter are represented by a set of algorithms (Algorithms 1, 2, 3 and 4). They are separated for clarity: Algorithm 1 represents the operational rule that handles durative actions, making use of the other three algorithms within that handle the terminating conditions (Algorithms 2, 3 and 4). The original rule for handling actions also appears in Algorithm 1 to account for actions without durations.

Algorithm 1: Handle Durative Action

1	**Function** handleDurativeAction(*Agent*)
2	*Environment* ⟵ get_environment(*Agent*);
3	*Intention* ⟵ get_intention(*Agent*);
4	*Action* ⟵ get_topdeed(*Intention*);
5	**if** *Action* **instanceof** *DurativeAction* **then**
6	**if** *Action is not executing* **then**
7	execute_action(*Action*);
8	*ActionStatus* = executing;
9	check_success(*Agent*);
10	check_failure(*Agent*);
11	check_abort(*Agent*);
12	**else**
13	handle_action(*Agent*);

As previously stated, Algorithm 1 represents the new operational rule for handling durative actions. The agent is required as a parameter for the rule in order to initialise the environment and intention variables from which the appropriate action is identified (lines 1–4). After establishing that the following action is a durative action and should have terminating conditions and a duration, the agent executes the action (if the action is not already being executed) and the status of that action is changed to *executing* (lines 5–8). As any duration

---

[5] The implementation can be found in https://github.com/peterstringer/mcapl/tree/dev.

of action is accepted, the checks for terminating conditions begin immediately (lines 9–11) and continue to be checked every time this rule is called for that action. If the action is not considered to be a durative action, the regular action handling rule is called (lines 12–13).

Algorithm 2: Handle Action Success

1 **Function checkSuccess(***Agent***)**
2   *Action* ⟵ get_action(*Agent*);
3   *SuccessCondition* ⟵ get_success_conditions(*Action*);
4   **if** *agent_believes*(*SuccessCondition*) **then**
5   drop_top_deed;
6   get_next_deed;
7   *ActionStatus* = notExecuting;

The Handle Action Success rule is described in Algorithm 2. The action in question is retrieved from the agent, and in turn the success conditions for that action are also retrieved (lines 1–3). The agent now considers whether the expected success conditions have been reached or not, by attempting to find those conditions in the belief base. If the conditions are believed then the top deed is dropped and the next deed on the stack is set as the new top deed, whilst the status of the action is set to *notExecuting*.

Algorithm 3: Handle Action Failure

1 **Function checkFailure(***Agent***)**
2   *Action* ⟵ get_action(*Agent*);
3   *FailureCondition* ⟵ get_failure_conditions;
4   **if** *agent_believes*(*FailureCondition*) **then**
5   *ActionStatus* = notExecuting;
6   log_fail(*Action*);
7   drop_top_deed;
8   get_next_deed;
9   print_failure_message;

Algorithm 3 represents the Handle Action Failure rule. Similarly to the Handle Action Success Rule, the action is retrieved from the agent before getting the failure conditions for that action. If the agent then believes the failure conditions have been met, the action status is changed to *notExecuting* and the action is marked on the log as failed. Next, the top deed is dropped and replaced by the next deed on the stack before printing a failure message.

Algorithm 4: Handle Action Abort

```
1  Function checkAbort(Agent)
2  │   Action ⟵ get_action(Agent);
3  │   AbortCondition ⟵ get_abort_conditions(Action);
4  │   if agent_believes(AbortCondition) then
5  │   │   if Action = Executing then
6  │   │   │   execute_action(abort(Action));
7  │   │   ActionStatus = notExecuting;
8  │   │   log_abort(Action);
9  │   │   drop_top_deed;
10 │   │   get_next_deed;
11 │   │   print_abort_message;
```

Lastly, in Algorithm 4, we describe the operational rule for Handle Action Abort. The action is retrieved from the agent and the action's abort conditions are also retrieved, before checking if the agent believes that these conditions have been met. If so, an abort action is created using the action as an argument, and immediately executed. Next, the status of the action is changed to *notExecuting*, and the action abort is logged in the abort log. The top deed is then dropped and the next deed on the stack is set as the new top deed, before printing a message to note the abort.

Case Study

To show our extended action theory in practice, we have deployed an agent into an environment containing four waypoints represented in a topological map at the agent level (this could be easily integrated into a robotic system using the approach described in [9]). The goal for the agent is to navigate through four waypoints within an expected time allowance between each point. Whilst an agent struggling to achieve this simple goal consistently is not likely to be deployed in a remote environment, for the following examples our agent is assumed to be functional and capable of achieving this goal routinely with any failures and aborts having been constructed to show the operation of our extended action theory. To simulate the dynamic nature of a real-world environment, the action outcomes were occasionally randomised.

```
:name: Rover                                                    1
                                                                2
:Initial Beliefs:                                               3
at(0)                                                           4
                                                                5
:Initial Goals:                                                 6
gotowaypoint                                                    7
                                                                8
:Plans:                                                         9
+!gotowaypoint:                                                 10
    { ⊤ }                                                        11
    ←                                                           12
    +!goto01,                                                   13
    +!goto02,                                                   14
    +!goto03,                                                   15
    +!goto04;                                                   16
                                                                17
+!goto01 : {B at(0)} ←  move_to1;                               18
+!goto02 : {B at(1)} ←  move_to2;                               19
+!goto03 : {B at(2)} ←  move_to3;                               20
+!goto04 : {B at(3)} ←  move_to4,                               21
                        +at_waypoint;                           22
                                                                23
+at(4) : {B at_waypoint} ←  print(arrived_at_waypoint);        24
```

Listing 1. Gwendolen Agent: Rover

4.1 The GWENDOLEN Agent

This case study makes use of a GWENDOLEN agent, called Rover, with the initial belief that it is at(0), the starting position, and has an initial goal of performing the gotowaypoint goal. The body of this goal is detailed in the *Plans* section of the GWENDOLEN agent. We use a standard BDI syntax to describe this: where !*g* indicates a goal, and +!*g* indicates the commitment to perform that goal.

The plan for the addition of the gotowaypoint goal contains a list of sub-goals denoting a route through three waypoints, appropriately named 1, 2, and 3, before reaching the final waypoint, 4. Each sub-goal contains a guard (e.g., {B at(0)}) containing a belief to ensure the agent believes it is at the required location before attempting the subsequent action. The subgoal +!goto04 differs only by the addition of a belief (+at_waypoint) that the agent has reached the final waypoint. Finally, once the agent believes it has arrived at waypoint 4, a print action is executed to mark the end of the journey.

4.2 Durative Actions and Their Terminating Conditions

To allow the agent to recognise the expected outcomes of each action, a record is kept containing the action with a *success* and *fail* condition. The record of actions required for this case study are shown in Listing 2, in the format: {success-condition} action-name {failure-condition}.

```
{at(1)}  move_to1  {at(0),  at(2),  at(3),  at(4)}        1
{at(2)}  move_to2  {at(0),  at(1),  at(3),  at(4)}        2
{at(3)}  move_to3  {at(0),  at(1),  at(2),  at(4)}        3
{at(4)}  move_to4  {at(0),  at(1),  at(2),  at(3)}        4
```

Listing 2. Durative Actions

Action Success. The *success* condition for each action in this case study is a single belief that the agent is at the expected waypoint. If the agent believes this condition, the action has succeeded. The expected output for an action success is shown in Listing 3.

```
INFO:  Executing  action:  move_to(1)                     1
INFO:  Rover  done  move_to(1)                            2
```

Listing 3. Action Success Log Output

Action Failed. Similarly to the success condition, the *fail* condition for an action in this case study is the belief that the agent is at a waypoint that isn't listed as the expected waypoint. The expected output for an action failure is shown in Listing 4.

```
INFO:  Executing  action:  move_to(1)                     1
INFO:  Rover  done  move_to(1)                            2
ACTION  FAILED  −  RETRYING                               3
```

Listing 4. Action Failure Log Output

After which the failed action will be executed again until successful or aborted.

Action Abort. Whilst the abort condition for actions has not yet been explicitly stated, for this example the action aborts as a result of a "time out". An action is considered to "time out" if the time passed in the environment during execution exceeds the expected duration of the action. The expected output for an action abort is shown in Listing 5.

```
INFO:  Executing  action:  move_to(2)                     1
INFO:  Rover  done  move_to(2)                            2
ABORTING  ACTION  −  TIMED  OUT                           3
INFO:  Rover  done  abort({at(2)}  move_to2  {at(0),  at(1),    4
       at(3),  at(4)}  )
```

Listing 5. Action Abort Log Output

4.3   Results

If the rover executed each move_to action and managed to achieve their success conditions, the output in the log would be as shown in Listing 6.

```
INFO: Executing action: move_to(1)                                    1
INFO: Rover done move_to(1)                                           2
INFO: Executing action: move_to(2)                                    3
INFO: Rover done move_to(2)                                           4
INFO: Executing action: move_to(3)                                    5
INFO: Rover done move_to(3)                                           6
INFO: Executing action: move_to(4)                                    7
INFO: Rover done move_to(4)                                           8
INFO: Executing action: print(arrived_at_waypoint)                    9
INFO: Executing action: printlogs                                    10
INFO: Rover done printlogs                                           11
arrived_at_waypoint                                                  12
Process finished with exit code 0                                    13
```

Listing 6. Success Log Output

Whilst deploying the rover into an environment with occasional randomisation of action outcomes returns a log similar to Listing 7.

```
INFO: Executing action: move_to(1)                                    1
INFO: Rover done move_to(1)                                           2
ACTION FAILED — RETRYING                                              3
INFO: Executing action: move_to(1)                                    4
INFO: Rover done move_to(1)                                           5
INFO: Executing action: move_to(2)                                    6
INFO: Rover done move_to(2)                                           7
ABORTING ACTION — TIMED OUT                                           8
INFO: Rover done abort({at(2)} move_to2 {at(0), at(1),                9
    at(3), at(4)})
INFO: Executing action: move_to(2)                                   10
INFO: Rover done move_to(2)                                          11
INFO: Executing action: move_to(2)                                   12
INFO: Rover done move_to(2)                                          13
INFO: Executing action: move_to(3)                                   14
INFO: Rover done move_to(3)                                          15
INFO: Executing action: move_to(4)                                   16
INFO: Rover done move_to(4)                                          17
INFO: Executing action: print(arrived_at_waypoint)                  18
INFO: Executing action: printlogs                                   19
INFO: Rover done printlogs                                          20
arrived_at_waypoint                                                 21
Failures: :{at(1)} move_to(1) {at(3)} — 1                           22
Aborts::{at(2)} move_to(2) {at(4)} — 1                              23
Process finished with exit code 0                                   24
```

Listing 7. Log Output with Randomness

In this instance, the rover experienced one action abort and one action failure. The rover has aborted the move_to(2) action after it had timed out, which was the action's current abort condition. After aborting the action, the agent notes the completion of the abort in the log, stating the capability that has timed out before attempting to execute the action again. Once the rover completes the task, the log of aborts and failures is printed with a tally of how many times each has occurred. Failures are logged similarly to aborts but only occur once an action has completed rather than terminating during execution. In this case, the move_to(1) action does not achieve the expected post-condition and instead satisfies the failure condition of the action, the agent subsequently logs this failure and retries the action. At this stage of implementation, if an agent encounters a failure or abort condition it is logged then the action is retried until successful. Further analysis of this log could determine the optimal solution for an action that is not performing as expected, as mentioned previously this will be considered in future work.

5 Related Work

In general BDI languages do not explicitly treat actions as having durations. A notable exception is the *Brahms* language [31] in which actions, called *activities*, explicitly involve durations. *Brahms* was originally developed as a simulation language and its focus was upon answering questions about whether human-agent teams could complete tasks within particular times. In its original presentation, *Brahms* had no formal semantics. However, one was later provided [32] though this focuses primarily on the effect of duration on simulation without any formal framework for activity failure or monitoring.

The field of AI Planning has invested considerable effort in the modelling of actions and capabilities with durations and stochastic outcomes, both theoretically as variants on Markov Decision Procedures [24,37] and practically capturing such concepts in planners (e.g. [10]) and domain description languages such as the PDDL 2.1 extension of PDDL [17]. In planning the effect of the action duration is of most importance during the generation of the plan, rather than its execution. Executable plans are represented as sequences of actions and lack the manipulation of mental states that is the defining feature of BDI approaches.

The modelling of actions with durations has been considered in logics for agency. Troquard et. al [34] represent these using continuations within STIT logic. The logic does not explicitly link the issue of durations with aborts, nor does it adequately account for the need to suspend working on a goal while waiting for an action to complete. As such this work was less attractive as a starting point for our GWENDOLEN implementation than that in [15].

The modelling of actions with durations has also been considered in recent versions of the GOAL programming language [21], although there is no support for failures and dealing with failures.

The task of defining and deploying durative actions for use beyond a simplistic atomic perspective has also been well explored in the research area [16,19,28].

A formalism for modelling dynamic environments is proposed in [19] with specific consideration for actions that might not be achieving expected outcomes. Whilst the research considers many of the issues encountered whilst deploying an agent into a dynamic environment, it focuses specifically on defining a formalism for multi-agent simulation (as intended by the authors) rather than implementation. Work in [28] critiques the modelling of actions in BDI languages, outlining not only the inadequacy of current action theory for use in a dynamic environment but also the additional facets of feedback for actions that can be exploited whilst using a dynamic environment. Specifically the ability to consider an action's success or failure from environment perceptions. The focus of [28] is to provide an improved action and perception model for complex endogenous environments, and takes a different research direction to that which is considered in our work (see 6).

In [16], poor domain specification is highlighted as an issue and an extension of action theory is considered to account for a more dynamic environment. However, BDI languages were deemed inappropriate for the endeavour, although for reasons that have since been rectified.

There has been a great deal of work on plan failure in BDI programming languages (e.g., [3,30]). This has not distinguished goal failure from action/capability failure. This is understandable, when an action fails its most important effect is on the goal which may need to be dropped or re-planned. As a result, work has focused on goal dropping and re-planning mechanisms which are captured in the work on BDI goal life-cycles in [18] upon which much of our work is also based. Clearly, integration of our action failure logs with mechanisms for goal dropping and re-planning is an important future step and we anticipate drawing upon this research then.

6   Conclusions and Future Work

In this paper, we have adapted the abstract semantics from [15] to the question of failure detection and logging. In [15], when an action fails or is aborted, the goal/intention moves back to a pending state for re-planning and it is clearly anticipated that mechanisms such as those outlined in [3] would be employed at that point to drop or re-plan the goal. However, since we are working in an application area where sometimes actions fail without the need to replan, we have replaced this concept with the idea of *failure logs* and action re-attempts which will, in future, need to be integrated into a process for goal re-planning.

We also needed to implement an explicit abort call from the agent to the action executing in the environment, where [15] implicitly assumes this has happened externally and the agent just detects an abort has taken place. This would appear to be an oversight in the abstract semantics—while an action can be expected to complete execution itself (either in a successful or failure state), it is less reasonable to assume that responsibility for decisions to abort an action should be external to the high-level agent.

Finally, we have implemented this adaptation to GWENDOLEN and demonstrated its functioning on a simple inspection example.

This work is a step towards realising the process for BDI agent reconfigurability outlined in [33]. Their action behaviour is monitored and actions are marked first *suspect* and then *deprecated* if a judgment is made that their behaviour has changed as a result of either hardware degradation or changing environmental conditions. Once an action is deprecated techniques outlined in [6] could be used to replace the appearance of the action in an agent's plans with suitable alternatives. Ultimately we also want to investigate the learning of "new" actions that can replace deprecated ones by updating some description of the action's behaviour that appears in an internal self-model for the agent. The integration of failure detection and logging in a principled way into an agent programming language was an important first step towards this goal but there is clearly more work to be done.

References

1. Aitken, J.M., Veres, S.M., Shaukat, A., Gao, Y., Cucco, E., Dennis, L.A., Fisher, M., Kuo, J.A., Robinson, T., Mort, P.E.: Autonomous nuclear waste management. IEEE Intell. Syst. **33**(6), 47–55 (2018)
2. Boissier, O., Bordini, R.H., Hubner, J., Ricci, A.: Multi-agent Oriented Programming: Programming Multi-agent Systems Using JaCaMo. MIT Press, Cambridge (2020)
3. Bordini, R.H., Hübner, J.F.: Semantics for the Jason variant of AgentSpeak (Plan failure and some internal actions). In: ECAI, pp. 635–640 (2010). https://doi.org/10.3233/978-1-60750-606-5-635
4. Bordini, R.H., El Fallah Seghrouchni, A., Hindriks, K., Logan, B., Ricci, A.: Agent programming in the cognitive era. Auton. Agents Multi-Agent Syst. **34**(2), 1–31 (2020). https://doi.org/10.1007/s10458-020-09453-y
5. Bratman, M.E.: Intentions, Plans, and Practical Reason. Harvard University Press, Cambridge (1987)
6. Cardoso, R.C., Dennis, L.A., Fisher, M.: Plan library reconfigurability in BDI agents. In: Dennis, L.A., Bordini, R.H., Lespérance, Y. (eds.) EMAS 2019. LNCS (LNAI), vol. 12058, pp. 195–212. Springer, Cham (2020). https://doi.org/10.1007/978-3-030-51417-4_10
7. Cardoso, R.C., Farrell, M., Luckcuck, M., Ferrando, A., Fisher, M.: Heterogeneous verification of an autonomous curiosity rover. In: Lee, R., Jha, S., Mavridou, A., Giannakopoulou, D. (eds.) NFM 2020. LNCS, vol. 12229, pp. 353–360. Springer, Cham (2020). https://doi.org/10.1007/978-3-030-55754-6_20
8. Cardoso, R.C., Ferrando, A.: A review of agent-based programming for multi-agent systems. Computers **10**(2), 16 (2021). https://doi.org/10.3390/computers10020016
9. Cardoso, R.C., Ferrando, A., Dennis, L.A., Fisher, M.: An interface for programming verifiable autonomous agents in ROS. In: Bassiliades, N., Chalkiadakis, G., de Jonge, D. (eds.) Multi-Agent Systems and Agreement Technologies, pp. 191–205. Springer, Cham (2020). https://doi.org/10.1007/978-3-030-66412-1_13
10. Cirillo, M., Karlsson, L., Saffiotti, A.: Human-aware task-planning: an application to mobile robots. ACM Trans. Intell. Syst. Technol. **1**(2), 15 (2010)
11. Dastani, M., van Birna Riemsdijk, M., Meyer, J.-J.C.: Programming multi-agent systems in 3APL. In: Bordini, R.H., Dastani, M., Dix, J., El Fallah Seghrouchni, A. (eds.) Multi-Agent Programming. MSASSO, vol. 15, pp. 39–67. Springer, Boston, MA (2005). https://doi.org/10.1007/0-387-26350-0_2

12. Dennis, L., Fisher, M., Lisitsa, A., Lincoln, N., Veres, S.: Satellite control using rational agent programming. IEEE Intell. Syst. **25**(3), 92–97 (2010). https://doi.org/10.1109/mis.2010.88

13. Dennis, L.A.: Gwendolen semantics: 2017. Technical Report ULCS-17-001, University of Liverpool, Department of Computer Science (2017)

14. Dennis, L.A.: The MCAPL framework including the agent infrastructure layer and agent Java pathfinder. J. Open Source Softw. **3**(24), 617 (2018). https://doi.org/10.21105/joss.00617. The Open Journal

15. Dennis, L.A., Fisher, M.: Actions with durations and failures in BDI languages. In: ECAI. pp. 995–996 (2014). https://doi.org/10.3233/978-1-61499-419-0-995

16. Ferber, J., Müller, J.P.: Influences and reaction: a model of situated multiagent systems. In: Proceedings of Second International Conference on Multi-Agent Systems (ICMAS-1996), pp. 72–79 (1996)

17. Fox, M., Long, D.: PDDL2.1: an extension to PDDL for expressing temporal planning domains. JAIR **20**, 61–124 (2003)

18. Harland, J., Morley, D.N., Thangarajah, J., Yorke-Smith, N.: An operational semantics for the goal life-cycle in BDI agents. Auton. Agents Multi-Agent Syst. **28**(4), 682–719 (2013). https://doi.org/10.1007/s10458-013-9238-9

19. Helleboogh, A., Vizzari, G., Uhrmacher, A., Michel, F.: Modeling dynamic environments in multi-agent simulation. Auton. Agents Multi-Agent Syst. **14**(1), 87–116 (2007). https://doi.org/10.1007/s10458-006-0014-y

20. Hindriks, K.V.: Programming rational agents in GOAL. In: El Fallah Seghrouchni, A., Dix, J., Dastani, M., Bordini, R.H. (eds.) Multi-Agent Programming, pp. 119–157. Springer, Boston, MA (2009). https://doi.org/10.1007/978-0-387-89299-3_4

21. Hindriks, K.V.: Programming cognitive agents in goal (2021)

22. Logan, B.: An agent programming manifesto. Int. J. Agent-Oriented Softw. Eng. **6**(2), 187–210 (2018)

23. Mascardi, V., Demergasso, D., Ancona, D.: Languages for programming BDI-style agents: an overview. In: WOA, vol. 2005, pp. 9–15 (2005)

24. Weld, D.S.: Planning with durative actions in stochastic domains. JAIR **31**, 33–82 (2008)

25. Rao, A.S., Georgeff, M.P.: Modeling agents within a BDI-Architecture. In: Proceedings of 2nd International Conference on Principles of Knowledge Representation and Reasoning (KR&R), pp. 473–484. Morgan Kaufmann (1991)

26. Rao, A.S., Georgeff, M.P.: An abstract architecture for rational agents. In: Proceedings of 3rd International Conference on Principles of Knowledge Representation and Reasoning (KR&R), pp. 439–449. Morgan Kaufmann (1992)

27. Ricci, A., Piunti, M., Viroli, M.: Environment programming in multi-agent systems: an artifact-based perspective. Auton. Agents Multi-Agent Syst. **23**(2), 158–192 (2011). https://doi.org/10.1007/s10458-010-9140-7

28. Ricci, A., Santi, A., Piunti, M.: Action and perception in agent programming languages: from exogenous to endogenous environments. In: Collier, R., Dix, J., Novák, P. (eds.) ProMAS 2010. LNCS (LNAI), vol. 6599, pp. 119–138. Springer, Heidelberg (2012). https://doi.org/10.1007/978-3-642-28939-2_7

29. Russell, S., Norvig, P.: Artificial Intelligence, A Modern Approach, 2nd edn. Prentice Hall, Hoboken (2003)

30. Sardina, S., Padgham, L.: A BDI agent programming language with failure handling, declarative goals, and planning. Auton. Agents Multi-Agent Syst. **23**(1), 18–70 (2011)

31. Sierhuis, M.: Modeling and Simulating Work Practice. BRAHMS: a multiagent modeling and simulation language for work system analysis and design. Ph.D. Thesis, SWI, University of Amsterdam, SIKS Dissertation Series No. 2001-10 (2001)
32. Stocker, R., Sierhuis, M., Dennis, L., Dixon, C., Fisher, M.: A formal semantics for Brahms. In: Leite, J., Torroni, P., Ågotnes, T., Boella, G., van der Torre, L. (eds.) CLIMA 2011. LNCS (LNAI), vol. 6814, pp. 259–274. Springer, Heidelberg (2011). https://doi.org/10.1007/978-3-642-22359-4_18
33. Stringer, P., Cardoso, R.C., Huang, X., Dennis, L.A.: Adaptable and verifiable BDI reasoning. In: Cardoso, R.C., Ferrando, A., Briola, D., Menghi, C., Ahlbrecht, T. (eds.) Proceedings of the First Workshop on Agents and Robots for reliable Engineered Autonomy, Virtual event, 4th September 2020. Electronic Proceedings in Theoretical Computer Science, vol. 319, pp. 117–125. Open Publishing Association (2020). https://doi.org/10.4204/EPTCS.319.9
34. Troquard, N., Vieu, L.: Towards a logic of agency and actions with duration. Front. Artif. Intell. Appl. **141**, 775 (2006)
35. Wooldridge, M.: An Introduction to Multiagent Systems. Wiley, New York (2002)
36. Wooldridge, M., Rao, A. (eds.): Foundations of Rational Agency. Applied Logic Series. Kluwer Academic Publishers (1999)
37. Younes, H.L.A., Simmons, R.G.: Solving generalized semi-Markov decision processes using continuous phase-type distributions. In: Proceedings of AAAI, p. 742 (2004)

Concept Description and Definition Extraction for the ANEMONE System

David Toluhi[✉][iD], Renate Schmidt[iD], and Bijan Parsia[iD]

The University of Manchester, Manchester M13 9PL, UK
{david.toluhi,renate.schmidt,bijan.parsia}@manchester.ac.uk

Abstract. We present algorithms for computing *definitions* and *concept descriptions* that agents can use to restrict and adapt their knowledge with respect to signature shared with other agents. This ensures that knowledge shared is understood by the communication partners. We focus on agents that make use of description logic ontologies to represent their expertise. We have implemented and evaluated the performance of the algorithms in the form of a case study and on a freely accessible ontology. Our evaluation suggests that definition extraction can reduce the amount of messages exchanged by agents, thus optimising the communication time and effort of the agents.

Keywords: Agent · Ontologies · Approximation · Definitions

1 Introduction

One of the appealing characteristics of agents and multi-agent systems MAS(s) is that each agent can provide distinct services and likewise have a distinct set of facts about the world. This avoids the need for massive upfront coordination and various sorts of integration but introduces fundamental communication challenges including the determination of common knowledge and potential increasing amount of knowledge shared between any set of agents.

Establishing common knowledge for communicating agents is non trivial, and has been studied in the literature as part of the topics of *agent negotiation* and *ontology alignment* [7]. Ontology alignment rises from the need to find correspondences between related entities of different ontologies and has several applications including agent communication, ontology engineering, and ontology versioning. The correspondences may be one of several semantic relations including *equivalence, consequence, subsumption*, or *disjointness*, between ontology entities [7]. Beyond the establishment of common ground, agents require the ability to communicate and convey knowledge in their ontologies in terms of common knowledge or established correspondences. Humans have the ability to approximate knowledge naturally, for example, doctors approximate diagnoses into terms patients can understand without using any complex medical terms. Often, either the agent knowledge representations or the messages exchanged

© Springer Nature Switzerland AG 2022
N. Alechina et al. (Eds.): EMAS 2021, LNAI 13190, pp. 352–372, 2022.
https://doi.org/10.1007/978-3-030-97457-2_20

are expressed entirely in a language restricted to *atomic* predicates (especially monadic predicates a.k.a "classes" or "concepts"). That is, the correspondences are between *terms* and not more complex *expressions* and this can limit the efficiency and efficacy of communication.

We focus on agents that use description logics DL(s) to model the expertise in their domain of specialisation in the context of the ANEMONE framework [21]. A framework comprising of dynamic communication protocols that agents may use to convey concepts to each other depending on varying levels of their common vocabulary. ANEMONE's application to free and accessible ontologies (such as those found on the BioPortal [22] and typically modelled using the OWL [2] language) is limited because it is designed using a less [1] expressive lan-gauge. The methods we investigate are designed for use on OWL ontologies and intended to be compatible with ANEMONE thus make its application to OWL ontologies more suitable. The implicit hypothesis is that expressive languages such as those found in naturally occuring languages enable rich descriptions of unshared concepts and thus reduce the amount of messages exchanged between the agents.

We study *definitions* in the context of ANEMONE and DL(s) and how they may be extracted and used for conveying meaning and concepts. Definitions in the DL sense (DL-definitions) do not always exist, as such, we introduce and study *concept descriptions* an alternative to conventional definitions in DL that can be used to characterise concepts based on restricted vocabularies. We com-pare DL-definitions, concept descriptions, and definitions in the ANEMONE sense (ANEMONE-definitions) and evaluate their performance on a case study adopted from [21]. We show that DL-definitions are optimal in terms of size and interpretation compared to concept descriptions and ANEMONE-definitions thus making DL-definitions the more suitable candidates for efficient communi-cation. Concept descriptions tend to be bulky in size, and thus suboptimal, as a result, we introduce *minimal concept descriptions* as an alternative to concept descriptions and demonstrate that they are smaller in terms of size compared to concept descriptions and ANEMONE-definitions, but larger than DL-definitions (when they exist).

Our contributions are as follows:

1. A method for extracting definitions in $\mathcal{ALC}$ ontologies ($\mathcal{ALC}$ is formally described in Sect. 1.1).
2. A method for extracting *concept descriptions*.
3. A case study of how definition extraction and concept descriptions can enhance ANEMONE for use with expressive DL(s).
4. An experimental evaluation of ANEMONE-definitions and DL-definitions on an $\mathcal{ALC}$ ontology.

The rest of this paper is organised as follows: Preliminaries are described in Sect. 1.1, Sect. 2 discusses the ANEMONE system in detail, Sect. 3 discusses conventional definitions in DL and our method for extracting definitions in $\mathcal{ALC}$

---

[1] Relative to free and accessible occuring ontologies.

ontologies, Sect. 4 discusses concept descriptions, an overview on related work is provided in Sect. 5, and finally, Sect. 6 provides a case study and experimental evaluation of how the methods presented can be applied to the ANEMONE system.

1.1   Preliminaries

We refer to monadic predicates as *concepts*, and binary predicates as *roles* (sometimes also referred to as *properties*) in the usual logical sense. Let N_C be a set of atomic concepts, N_R a set of atomic roles, and N_I a set of individuals (or instances). $\mathcal{ALC}$-concepts have one of these forms: $\top \mid a \mid A \mid \neg C \mid C \sqcup D \mid C \sqcap D \mid \forall r.C \mid \exists r.D$, where $a \in N_I$, $A \in N_C$, $r \in N_R$, C and D are arbitrary $\mathcal{ALC}$ concepts. An $\mathcal{ALC}$ ontology consists of axioms which either belong to the TBox or ABox. TBox axioms are of the form $C \sqsubseteq D$ or $C \equiv D$ which can be expressed by two general inclusion axioms $C \sqsubseteq D$ and $D \sqsubseteq C$. ABox axioms are of the form $C(a)$ called *concept assertions* or $r(a, b)$ called *role assertions*.

The language $\mathcal{AL}$ is a restricted form of $\mathcal{ALC}$ that only allows for atomic negation ($\neg A$), concept intersection ($C \sqcap D$), universal restrictions ($\forall r.C$) and limited exisential quantification ($\exists r.D$).

The function $sig()$ returns the set of concepts, roles, and individuals occurring in a given ontology, concept or axiom.

For $\mathcal{ALC}$, an interpretation $\mathcal{I}$ over N_C, N_R, and N_I is a pair $\langle \Delta^{\mathcal{I}}, \cdot^{\mathcal{I}} \rangle$, where $\Delta^{\mathcal{I}}$ is a non-empty set representing an interpretation domain, and $\cdot^{\mathcal{I}}$ is an interpretation function that maps every $A \in N_C$ to a subset $A^{\mathcal{I}}$ of $\Delta^{\mathcal{I}}$; every $r \in N_R$ to a binary relation $r^{\mathcal{I}}$ over $\Delta^{\mathcal{I}}$, to every individual a in N_I to element $a^{\mathcal{I}} \in \Delta^{\mathcal{I}}$. The interpretation function $\cdot^{\mathcal{I}}$ is extended to concepts as follows:

$$\bot^{\mathcal{I}} = \emptyset \quad (\neg C)^{\mathcal{I}}) = \Delta^{\mathcal{I}} \setminus C^{\mathcal{I}} \quad (C \sqcup D)^{\mathcal{I}} = C^{\mathcal{I}} \cup D^{\mathcal{I}} \quad (C \sqcap D)^{\mathcal{I}} = C^{\mathcal{I}} \cap D^{\mathcal{I}}$$
$$(\forall r.C)^{\mathcal{I}} = \{x \in \Delta^{\mathcal{I}} \mid \forall y.(x, y) \in r^{\mathcal{I}} \rightarrow y \in C^{\mathcal{I}}\}$$
$$(\exists r.C)^{\mathcal{I}} = \{x \in \Delta^{\mathcal{I}} \mid \exists y.(x, y) \in r^{\mathcal{I}} \land y \in C^{\mathcal{I}}\}$$

A concept name A is called cyclic if $O \models A \sqsubseteq C$ such that $A \neq C$, and $A \in sig(C)$.[2] An ontology O is said to be acyclic if it contains no cyclic concept names.

2   The ANEMONE System

The purpose of communication in the ANEMONE system is mainly to share assertional knowledge. Intuitively speaking, an agent A_1 conveys a concept C to an agent A_2 so that A_2 can share instances of C under its knowledge.

The ontology semantics in ANEMONE differs from those in OWL ontologies which makes its application to such ontologies limited. We find that the

---

[2] It is worth noting that this definition of cyclicity is simplified here for brevity. For a more comprehensive description, refer to [10].

closest adaptation of the ontology semantics in ANEMONE to OWL semantics
[2] is $\mathcal{AL}$ without concept intersection, negation, universal restrictions, and limited existential quantification. In addition, a non-standard *overlap* operator $\oplus$
is introduced which is interpreted as follows:

$$C \oplus D \quad \text{iff} \quad C^{\mathcal{I}} \not\subseteq D^{\mathcal{I}}, D^{\mathcal{I}} \not\subseteq C^{\mathcal{I}}, \quad \text{and} \quad C^{\mathcal{I}} \cap D^{\mathcal{I}} \neq \emptyset$$

Note, that by this definition, equivalent classes do not overlap. It is also worth
noting that the $\oplus$ operator is inconsequential to retrieving and sharing instances,
for example, adding $C \oplus D$ to the ontology $\{C(a), C(c), D(b), D(a)\}$ does not
affect the query for instances of C.

ANEMONE has three design objectives: (i) Minimal and effective communication, (ii) Laziness, (iii) Decentralised communication. The minimal and
effective objective ensures communicated knowledge is not superfluous and can
be processed optimally. The laziness objective ensures knowledge sharing only
occurs on a *as-need* basis, i.e., knowledge should only be exchanged when strictly
necessary. The decentralised objective ensures there is no central control or location of the knowledge.

The laziness objective of ANEMONE is realised through the use of communication layers. There are three layers of communication: (i) normal communication protocol (ii) concept definition protocol (iii) concept explication protocol.
All conversations start by assuming that there are no misunderstandings and
occur in the normal communication protocol which is the uppermost layer. If
any misunderstanding occurs, the agents switch to the concept definition protocol where they may attempt to resolve the misunderstandings by exchanging
definitions of concepts that may have caused the misunderstanding (ideally in
terms of concepts that are shared by both agents.). If misunderstandings persist
in the concept definition protocol, the agents switch to the concept explication
protocol where agents convey the meaning of a concept by exchanging positive
and negative examples of the misunderstood concept. The communication protocols help realise the *as-need* requirement of the laziness objective: agents only
resort to using complex communication mechanisms only when needed.

ANEMONE specifies two performatives to be used in communication, the
Inform and *ExactInform* performatives. Let X be a concept an agent is
attempting to convey, if X or an equivalent concept C is communicated to the
other agent, the *ExactInform* performative is used, however, if some other
concept that is not equivalent to X is conveyed to the hearer agent, then the
Inform performative is used. The use of these performatives dictates whether
the conversation should switch from the normal communication protocol to the
concept definition protocol: the use of the *Inform* performative hints at some
loss in communication and often suggests that the agents have to switch to the
concept definition protocol. When the agents are communicating in the concept
definition protocol (attempting to resolve the meaning for some concept X),
they switch to the concept explication protocol if the definition extracted for X
is perceived as inadequate by the hearer agent. A definition is deemed inadequate if the hearer agent can not infer the relation of the definition with every

other concept in the hearer agents ontology. Intuitively speaking, the notion of adequacy in ANEMONE is motivated by expecting the hearer agent to be able to place an unshared concept in an exact point in the hierarchy of its ontology, however, as we demonstrate, OWL ontologies may have multiple hierarchies on concepts which results in this notion of adequacy being moot.

The concept explication protocol is underpinned by ensuring the ontologies of the communicating agents are *grounded*, meaning that the domain of discourse contains all the objects the agent may wish to speak about, e.g. the set of URLs on the internet. The use of grounded ontologies enables agents to realise the intended interpretation of concepts that are used in communication. Grounded knowledge bases, contain *classifiers* (intended to be realised using machine learning techniques) in addition to symbolic descriptions to ensure the agents can classify objects in the domain of discourse. In a more traditional sense, these classifiers can be considered as the sensors of the agent.

Terminological negotiation [18] and related approaches to concept explication can be adopted to realise the concept explication protocol, as such we focus our efforts on the Normal Communication and concept definition protocols which can benefit from known knowledge approximation techniques in DL, this is where our primary contribution lies. ANEMONE provides a specification of how ANEMONE-definitions should be extracted.

Computing Definitions in the ANEMONE System. ANEMONE specifies that an ANEMONE-definition for a concept X w.r.t a signature Σ should be constructed by extracting all the relations X has with the concepts in Σ under O. Let X be concept-name, Σ a signature and O an ontology that conforms to the semantics of those in [21] such that $\Sigma \subseteq sig(O)$, a definition for X following [21] is defined as $\{X \sqsubseteq A \mid O \models X \sqsubseteq A \wedge A \in \Sigma\} \cup \{A \sqsubseteq X \mid O \models A \sqsubseteq X \wedge A \in \Sigma\} \cup \{A \equiv X \mid O \models A \equiv X \wedge A \in \Sigma\} \cup \{A \sqcap X \sqsubseteq \bot \mid O \models A \sqcap X \sqsubseteq \bot \wedge A \in \Sigma\}$.

Example 1. The example is adapted from [21]. In it, we have two agents A_1 and A_2 which are both personal news agents that classify news articles according to the ontologies provided in Table 1.

Table 1. Ontologies of agents A_1 and A_2 used throughout the paper.

Ontology O_1 of agent A_1	Ontology O_2 of agent A_2
LawnTennis $\sqsubseteq$ BallAndRacquetGames,	LawnTennis $\equiv$ Tennis
Wimbledon $\sqsubseteq$ LawnTennis,	Tennis $\sqsubseteq$ RacquetGames,
UKNews $\sqsubseteq$ RegionalNews,	RacquetGames $\sqsubseteq$ BallAndRacquetGames,
SoftwareAgents $\sqsubseteq$ ComputerScience,	BallAndRacquetGames $\sqsubseteq$ Sports,
ComputerScience $\sqsubseteq$ ScienceNews,	EuropeNews $\sqsubseteq$ RegionalNews,
BallAndRacquetGames $\sqcap$ RegionalNews $\sqsubseteq \bot$,	SoftwareAgents $\sqsubseteq$ ScienceNews,
BallAndRacquetGames $\sqcap$ ScienceNews $\sqsubseteq \bot$,	Sports $\sqcap$ RegionalNews $\sqsubseteq \bot$,
RegionalNews $\sqcap$ ScienceNews $\sqsubseteq \bot$	Sports $\sqcap$ ScienceNews $\sqsubseteq \bot$,
	RegionalNews $\sqcap$ ScienceNews $\sqcap \sqsubseteq \bot$

Let $\Sigma = sig(O_1) \cap sig(O_2) = \{$LawnTennis, RegionalNews, SoftwareAgents, ScienceNews, BallAndRacquetGames$\}$. A definition for $Wimbledon$ w.r.t. Σ under O_1 would be: $\{$Wimbledon $\sqsubseteq$ BallAndRacquetGames, Wimbledon $\sqsubseteq$ LawnTennis, Wimbledon $\sqcap$ RegionalNews $\sqsubseteq \perp$, Wimbledon $\sqcap$ SoftwareAgents $\sqsubseteq \perp$, Wimbledon $\sqcap$ ScienceSubjects $\sqsubseteq \perp \}$.

In OWL ontologies, concepts may be defined using *rich* concept descriptions that allow the usage of OWL constructs and therefore may include constructs such role restrictions and disjunctions (which the semantics ANEMONE currently does not allow). The increased expressivity of OWL ontologies suggests that there may be equivalent concepts that can not be expressed using the semantics of ANEMONE. When communicating in the normal communication protocol, agents must only use concepts in the common vocabulary or concepts equivalent to concepts not in the common vocabulary provided such equivalent concepts are expressed in the common vocabulary. The requirements of communication in the normal communication protocol suggests that an ANEMONE system with agents that have ontologies modelled using OWL may unnecessarily switch to the concept definition or explication protocols, thus potentially increasing the cost of communication and possible errors in communication. This problem also extends into concept definition protocol and to concepts without any equivalent concepts because the higher expressivity[3] of ontologies modelled using OWL implies that rich concept descriptions can exist in such ontologies, thus ANEMONE definitions for concepts in such ontologies may result in some information loss.

OWL allows the modelling of ontologies that have the DL $\mathcal{ALC}$ which allows for role restrictions ($\forall r, \exists r$), negation ($\neg$), and disjunctions ($\sqcup$) making it have semantics more expressive than the semantics of ANEMONE ontologies. The methods we present in this paper aim to curtail this issue by adopting a knowledge summarisation technique called *uniform interpolation* that can help agents extract equivalent concepts w.r.t. restricted vocabularies in $\mathcal{ALC}$ ontologies.

The next section provides background on DL-definitions which are used characterise equivalent concepts in $\mathcal{ALC}$ ontologies.

3 Explicit and Implicit Definitions

In DL, concepts are defined using *equivalance* class axioms of the form $C \equiv D$. Following the DL Handbook [3], a TBox O defines a concept A if O entails some axiom of the form $A \equiv C$ where the A is the defined concept name [3]. Thus, a DL-definition C for a concept-name A may only exist in one of two forms: (i) *Explicitly* via a syntactic TBox axiom of the form $A \equiv C$ such that $A \notin sig(C)$, or (ii) *Implicitly* via a set of general inclusion axioms in O such that for any model of O, the interpretation of A is uniquely determined by the interpretation of the symbols in $sig(C)$. In this paper explicit and implicit definitions are to be considered forms of DL-definitions. Intuitively, if a concept is explicitly defined

---

[3] *Higher* relative to ANEMONE ontologies.

in an ontology, its equivalent concept is obvious and easy to extract, however, if it is implicitly defined, its equivalent concept is not so obvious. It is worth noting that a concept that is explicitly defined may become implicitly when considered under a subset signature of the ontology.

A logical language is said to be definitorially complete if a concept that is defined implicitly can also be defined explicitly (formal definitions can be found in [19]). Intuitively speaking, this means an obvious definition can be extracted for every implicitly defined concept. Languages that are definitorially complete are said to have the *Beth Definability* property, and ensure that the interpretation of a defined concept is equivalent to the interpretation of its DL-definition thus are suitable for instance-sharing applications (such as that of ANEMONE). The DL $\mathcal{ALC}$ is shown to have the Beth Definability property in [19] Finding concepts that are defined over a given signature is paramount for agents conversing in the normal communication protocol of ANEMONE as this dictates whether they may have to switch to lower protocols.

A result of [19] is a test for determining implicit definability for a concept over a given signature and ontology. Let X be a concept, O an ontology, O' a copy of O, and Σ a subset signature of O such that $X \in sig(O)$, $X \notin \Sigma$, $\Sigma \subseteq sig(O)$, and O' is O with every concept-name and role symbol $A \notin \Sigma$ replaced by a copy A', X is implicitly definable using symbols from Σ under O iff $O \cup O' \models X \equiv X'$. This can be easily performed using a reasoner such as Hermit [8].

3.1   Extracting DL-Definitions for Implicitly and Explicitly Defined Concepts

After detecting an implicitly definable concept, agents also need to be able to extract a DL-definition or concept that is equivalent. Strongest necessary conditions SNCs can be used to compute DL-definitions for concepts that are implicitly or explicitly defined in an ontology [6]. The primary contribution of this paper is a practical method to compute Strongest Necessary Conditions using uniform interpolation in DL.

Definition 1 ((Strongest) Necessary Conditions). *Let Σ be a set of concept names and role symbols, X a concept, and O an ontology, such that $\Sigma \subseteq sig(O)$, we define a necessary condition of X over Σ relative to O to be any concept α such that $sig(\alpha) \subseteq \Sigma$ and $O \models X \sqsubseteq \alpha$. It is a strongest necessary condition denoted $SNC(X; O; \Sigma)$, if for any other necessary condition α' of X over Σ relative to O we have that $O \models \alpha \sqsubseteq \alpha'$.*

Definition 2 (Forgetting and Uniform Interpolation). *Given an ontology O, a set of symbols Σ such that $\Sigma \subset sig(O)$, a uniform interpolant for O over Σ is an ontology $\mathcal{V}$ such that $O \models \mathcal{V}$ and $\mathcal{V}$ is a strongest such entailment for Σ, i.e., for any other entailment $\mathcal{V}'$ of O (i.e., $O \models \mathcal{V}'$) and $sig(\mathcal{V}') \subseteq \Sigma$, then $\mathcal{V} \models \mathcal{V}'$. The ontology $\mathcal{V}$ is called a uniform interpolant of O for signature Σ. We refer to Σ as the uniform interpolation signature. We also call $\mathcal{V}$ the result of forgetting $\bar{\Sigma}$ from O, where $\bar{\Sigma}$ denotes $sig(O) \setminus \Sigma$.*

A consequence of Definition 2 is that for every axiom ψ with $sig(\psi) \subseteq \Sigma$ such that $O \models \psi$, $\mathcal{V} \models \psi$.

Algorithms for computing strongest necessary conditions exist in the propositional logic [6,13] and first order logic (FOL) [6]. Since DL is a fragment of FOL, we have adapted the SNC algorithm presented in by Doherty et al. [6]: for any first-order formula X, set of relation symbols Σ, and closed theory O, the SNC is the uniform interpolant (Definition 2) computed for $O \wedge X$ over Σ. As such, in DL we can compute the SNC for a concept name X over a signature Σ and ontology O by computing the uniform interpolant for O, X^4 over Σ and there are known practical implementations of the uniform interpolation methods provided in [11]. This method does compute an SNC for X, however, it is not suitable for our purposes as the result may contain axioms unrelated to X, we call such axioms *redundant*. Consider the ontology U_1 as discussed in Example 1, to compute the SNC for $Wimbledon$ w.r.t. O_1 and Σ we compute the uniform interpolant over $O_1, Wimbledon$ w.r.t. Σ which is {LawnTennis $\sqsubseteq$ BallAndRacquetGames, BallAndRacquetGames $\sqsubseteq \neg$ RegionalNews, BallAndRacquetGames $\sqsubseteq \neg$ ScienceSubjects, RegionalNews $\sqsubseteq \neg$ ScienceSubjects, SoftwareAgents $\sqsubseteq$ ScienceSubjects, LawnTennis}. Observe that the result still satisfies Definition 1, however, as can be seen, there are axioms in the result not related to $Wimbledon$, the TBox axiom $SoftwareAgents \sqsubseteq ScienceSubjects$ for example, is not related to $Wimbledon$.

Proposition 1 lets us deal with such redundant axioms. Let O be an ontology, Σ a subset signature of O, a a fresh individual such that $a \notin O$ and X a concept name for which we wish to compute an SNC for w.r.t. O and Σ, we compute a uniform interpolant $\mathcal{V}$ over Σ for $O, X(a)$ and solve the issue of redundancies in the result by returning a conjunction of concepts of the form $C(a)$ in the uniform interpolant: it follows from Proposition 1 that all such concepts C are necessary conditions of X, and thus their conjunction satisfy Definition 1. This approach used in Algorithm 1.

Proposition 1. *Let O be an acyclic ontology, X a concept, $\Sigma \subseteq sig(O)$, and a a fresh individual, such that $a \notin sig(O)$, $sig(X) \nsubseteq \Sigma$. Suppose $O \not\models X(a)$. Let $\mathcal{V}$ be a uniform interpolant for Σ relative to $O, X(a)$, we have that $\mathcal{V} \models C(a)$ iff $O \models X \sqsubseteq C$, where C is an arbitrary $\mathcal{ALC}$-concept such that $sig(C) \subseteq \Sigma$.*

Proof. If $\mathcal{V} \models C(a)$, then $O \models X \sqsubseteq C$: Since $\mathcal{V}$ is a uniform interpolant for Σ of $O, X(a)$, $O, X(a) \models \mathcal{V}$. Given that $\mathcal{V} \models C(a)$, we have that $O, X(a) \models C(a)$. This implies $O, X(a), \neg C(a)$ is unsatisfiable and hence $O \models X \sqsubseteq C$, since $O \models X \sqsubseteq C$ iff $O, X(a'), \neg C(a') \models \bot$ for some fresh individual a'.

If $O \models X \sqsubseteq C$, then $\mathcal{V} \models C(a)$: Because $O \models X \sqsubseteq C$, for every interpretation $\mathcal{I}$ such that $\mathcal{I} \models O$, we have that: $x \in X^{\mathcal{I}}$ implies $x \in C^{\mathcal{I}}$ for any individual $x \in \Delta^{\mathcal{I}}$. Therefore, given a fresh individual a not occuring in $sig(O)$, $O, X(a) \models C(a)$. Since $\mathcal{V}$ is a uniform interpolant for $\Sigma \cup \{a\}$ of $O, X(a)$, $\mathcal{V}$ is a strongest entailment for $\Sigma \cup \{a\}$ of O. Since $sig(C(a)) \subseteq \Sigma$, it follows from Definition 2 that $\mathcal{V} \models C(a)$.

---

[4] We use the notation O, α as a shorthand to denote $O \cup \{\alpha\}$.

A consequence of Proposition 1 and Definition 2 is that $\bigsqcap_{C(a) \in \mathcal{V}} C$ is a strongest necessary condition of X.

Algorithm 1: SNC Extraction

Input: An ontology O, a definiendum X, a signature Σ, an individual a where $\Sigma \subseteq sig(O)$, $X \in sig(O)$, $X \notin \Sigma$, $a \notin sig(O)$.
Output: An $\mathcal{ALC}$ concept C which is a SNC of X.

Step 1: Add $X(a)$ to O to get O'.

Step 2: Add a to Σ to get Σ' and compute a uniform interpolant denoted $\mathcal{V}$ over O' w.r.t. Σ'. I.e. forget $\overline{\Sigma'}$ from O'.

Step 3: Return $\bigsqcap_{C(a) \in \mathcal{V}} C$ as $SNC(X; O; \Sigma)$.

Proposition 2. *Let O be an acyclic ontology, Σ a subset of $sig(O)$, C a concept such that $sig(C) \not\subseteq \Sigma$. If there exists a concept D such that $O \models C \equiv D$, and $sig(D) \subseteq \Sigma$, then (i) $O \models C \equiv SNC(C; O; \Sigma)$, and therefore, (ii) $C \equiv SNC(C; O; \Sigma)$ is an explicit DL-definition of C in O.*

Proof. If $O \models C \equiv D$, then it follows that $O \models C \sqsubseteq D$. Since $sig(D) \subseteq \Sigma$, it follows from Definition 1 that $O \models SNC(C; O; \Sigma) \sqsubseteq D$. If $O \models C \equiv D$, then it also follows that $O \models D \sqsubseteq C$, and since $O \models SNC(C; O; \Sigma) \sqsubseteq D$, it follows that $O \models SNC(C; O; \Sigma) \sqsubseteq C$. Thus, $O \models SNC(C; O; \Sigma) \sqsubseteq C, C \sqsubseteq SNC(C; O; \Sigma)$ which means that $O \models C \equiv SNC(C; O; \Sigma)$ and (i) holds. If there exists a concept D such that $O \models C \equiv D$ and $sig(D) \subseteq \Sigma$ then C is explicitly defined, thus (ii) holds.

It follows from Proposition 2 that computing strongest necessary conditions can be used to extract DL-definitions from an ontology.

ANEMONE does not provide any specification for testing whether a concept is implicitly definable, presumably, it is intended to be used with explicit definitions only. This means that not only does a concept have to be explicitly defined, but the signature of the definition must be expressed in the common signature of the agents. ANEMONE can be enhanced using Algorithm 1 when applied to agents with OWL ontologies. If agent A_1 wants to convey a concept X that is not explicitly defined under the common signature of the agents, it may simply perform an implicit definability check and compute a definition for X using Algorithm 1. It is worth stressing that if a DL-definition exists for a concept, then communication remains in the normal communication protocol. Given a concept X that is implicitly or explicitly defined under an ontology O_1, extracting an explicit or implicit definition ϕ will enable an agent A_1 use the $ExactInform$ performative to convey ϕ in place of X and thus ensure that conversation stays in the normal communication protocol. If X is neither implicitly or explicitly defined, the agents may attempt to use concept descriptions as an alternative to definitions, which we discuss next.

4 Concept Descriptions

We propose Concept Descriptions (CDs) are an alternative to standard definitions in DL that address the ANEMONE objective of stating the relation of a
defined concept with other concepts in an ontology under a given subset signature. Let X be a concept name, for the agent communication context of this
paper, we say X is described w.r.t. an ontology O if either there is a concept D
such that $O \models D \sqsubseteq X$ or a concept C such that $O \models X \sqsubseteq C$ or a concept S
such that $O \models X \equiv S$ where C, D, S are concepts and X is an atomic concept.

Given a concept name X, a signature Σ and an ontology O, such that $X \notin \Sigma$
and $\Sigma \subseteq sig(O)$, a mechanism for extracting concept descriptions should satisfy
the following requirements.

1. *Comprehensiveness*: Let ϕ be a description for X w.r.t. O and Σ, we say
   ϕ is *comprehensive* for X if for any concept C such that $O \models X \sqsubseteq C$ and
   $sig(C) \subseteq \Sigma$, we have that $\phi \models X \sqsubseteq C$ and for any concept D such that
   $O \models D \sqsubseteq X$ and $sig(D) \subseteq \Sigma$, we have that $\phi \models D \sqsubseteq X$ and for any concept
   E such that $O \models X \equiv E$ and $sig(E) \subseteq \Sigma$, we have that $\phi \models X \equiv E$.
2. *Description-specificity*: Let ϕ be a description for X w.r.t. O and Σ, we say
   ϕ is *description-specific* for X if for every axiom ψ in ϕ, we have that either
   $\psi = X \sqsubseteq C$ or $\psi = C \sqsubseteq X$ or $\psi = X \equiv C$ where C is a concept such that
   $sig(C) \in \Sigma$.

Concept descriptions may be extracted using the notions of *compiled superconcept* and *compiled subconcept* formally defined in Definitions 3 and 4.

Definition 3 (Compiled Superconcept). *Let O be an ontology, A a concept
name and C a concept. We call C an compiled superconcept of A if $O \models A \sqsubseteq C$
and for any other concept C' such that $O \models A \sqsubseteq C'$ and $O \not\models \top \sqsubseteq C'$, we
have that $\models C \sqsubseteq C'$. We denote the compiled superconcept by $CSP(A; O)$ and
$CSP(A; O; \Sigma)$ if it is restricted to a signature Σ.*

Definition 4 (Compiled Subconcept). *Let O be an ontology, A a concept
name and C a concept. We call C an compiled subconcept of A if $O \models C \sqsubseteq A$
and for any other concept C' such that $O \models C' \sqsubseteq A$ and $O \not\models C' \sqsubseteq \bot$, we
have that $\models C' \sqsubseteq C$. We denote the compiled subconcept by $CSB(A; O)$ and
$CSB(A; O; \Sigma)$ if it is restricted to a signature Σ.*

Algorithm 2: Concept Description Extraction

Input: An ontology O, a definiendum X, a signature Σ, where
$\Sigma \subseteq sig(O_B)$, $X \in sig(O_B)$, $X \notin \Sigma$.
Output: An ontology ϕ which is a concept description for X

Step 1: Compute $CSP(X; O; \Sigma)$.
Step 2: Compute $CSB(X; O; \Sigma)$.
Step 3: Return $\{X \sqsubseteq CSP(X; O; \Sigma), CSB(X; O; \Sigma) \sqsubseteq X\}$ as a concept
description for X.

Our approach to extracting concept descriptions is presented in Algorithm 2. Algorithm 2 satisfies the requirements for *comprehensiveness* and *description-specificity*: any superconcept C of X such that $O \models X \sqsubseteq C$ and $sig(C) \subseteq \Sigma$ would be a superconcept of $CSP(X;O;\Sigma)$, as such, the axiom $X \sqsubseteq CSP(X;O;\Sigma)$ would entail axioms of the form $X \sqsubseteq C$ that follow from O, similarly, $CSB(X;O;\Sigma)$ is a subconcept of any subconcept D of X where $O \models D \sqsubseteq X$ and $sig(D) \subseteq \Sigma$, as such, the axiom $X \sqsubseteq CSB(X;O;\Sigma)$ would entail axioms of the form $D \sqsubseteq X$ that follow from O.

4.1   Minimal Concept Descriptions

Concept descriptions may end up being too large and violate the minimal objective of ANEMONE. To curtail this, we introduce *minimal concept descriptions* (MCDs). Given a concept C, an ontology O and a signature Σ such that $\Sigma \subseteq sig(O)$ and $sig(C) \not\subseteq \Sigma$ a minimal concept description for C should capture the closest summarisation of C in terms of Σ. Let ϕ be a concept description for X w.r.t. O and Σ, we say ϕ is *minimal* if the following conditions hold:

1. $\phi \models X \sqsubseteq C$ such that $sig(C) \subseteq \Sigma$ and for any other concept C' such that $O \models X \sqsubseteq C'$ and $sig(C') \subseteq \Sigma$, we have that $O \models C \sqsubseteq C'$.
2. $\phi \models D \sqsubseteq X$ such that $sig(D) \subseteq \Sigma$ and for any other concept D' such that $O \models D' \sqsubseteq X$ and $sig(D') \subseteq \Sigma$, we have that $O \models D' \sqsubseteq D$.
3. If it *description-specific* as discussed above.

Definition 5 ((Weakest) Sufficient Conditions). *Let Σ be a set of concept names and role symbols, X a concept, and O an ontology, such that $\Sigma \subseteq sig(O)$, we define a sufficient condition of X over Σ relative to O to be any concept β such that $sig(\beta) \subseteq \Sigma$ and $O \models \beta \sqsubseteq X$. It is a weakest sufficient condition denoted $WSC(X;O;\Sigma)$, if for any other sufficient condition β' of X over Σ relative to O we have that $O \models \beta' \sqsubseteq \beta$.*

Minimal concept descriptions can be computed using strongest necessary conditions and weakest sufficient conditions. An algorithm to compute a minimal concept description is provided in Algorithm 3.

Algorithm 3: Minimal Concept Description Extraction

Input: An ontology O, a definiendum X, a signature Σ, where $\Sigma \subseteq sig(O_B)$, $X \in sig(O_B)$, $X \notin \Sigma$.
Output: An ontology ϕ which is a minimal concept description for X

Step 1: Compute $SNC(X;O;\Sigma)$.
Step 2: Compute $WSC(X;O;\Sigma)$.
Step 3: Return $\{X \sqsubseteq SNC(X;O;\Sigma), WSC(X;O;\Sigma) \sqsubseteq X\}$ as a minimal concept description for X.

Weakest sufficient conditions are an inverse of strongest necessary conditions, as such an algorithm for computing strongest necessary conditions can be tweaked to compute weakest sufficient conditions. Let O be an ontology, X be a concept name, for any concept C such that $O \models C \sqsubseteq X$, we have that $O \models \neg X \sqsubseteq \neg C$, hence, if we compute the strongest necessary condition for $\neg X$ the result obtained is a negation of the weakest sufficient conditions for X: in order to compute an weakest sufficient conditions for X, we compute the strongest necessary condition of $\neg X$ and negate the result.

5 Related Work

Terminological negotiation [18] implements the *ontology negotiation* framework specified in [20]. It aims to solve the problem of communication amongst agents with overlapping signatures by generating translations and mappings between symbols in the different ontologies. Our approach differs in the sense that it aims to solve the problem by extracting DL-definitions or descriptions for concept names as opposed to direct one-to-one mappings between concepts. It is possible for both systems to coexist: concepts with mappings can be considered as part of the common signature when extracting DL-definitions or descriptions.

In [5] a framework is provided for agents to learn new concepts based on the assumption that the agents share some minimal common ground. Learning concepts in ontologies is investigated in [1] from a corporation perspective and uses a similar approach to [20]: both methods utilize positive and negative examples of concepts to find mappings between concepts.

Ontology alignment is employed in reducing misunderstanding between communicating agents. One approach to constructing alignments is learning mappings through examples. This approach assumes a closed world of agents and relies on the agents exchanging positive and negative examples of concepts they wish to align. This is employed in efforts such as [1,20]. Similar applications to agent communication include [12,16,17].

6 Evaluation of Concept Descriptions and Definitions

6.1 Case Study

The data used is that of the agents and ontologies in Table 1. We evaluate ANEMONE-definitions, DL-definitions, concept descriptions, and minimal concept descriptions for the unshared concepts, *Wimbledon*, *RacquetGames*, and *UKNews*. All forms of definitions and concept descriptions are extracted using the methods discussed in the previous sections. The hypotheses we evaluate are as follows: $\mathcal{H}_1$: DL-definitions are the most optimal in terms of axiom size and still convey the same amount of information as ANEMONE-definitions, concept descriptions, and minimal concept descriptions. $\mathcal{H}_2$: (Minimal) Concept descriptions are as effective as ANEMONE-definitions in conveying information about a concept. $\mathcal{H}_3$: Minimal Concept Descriptions are smaller (in terms of axioms) than ANEMONE-definitions and Concept Descriptions. $\mathcal{H}_4$: Expressive languages allow for richer descriptions which help avoid the descent into lower communication protocols. Recall from Sect. 2 that if a DL-definition (or equivalent concept) exists for an unshared concept, communication may remain in the normal communication protocol. For each unshared concept, we list the possible inferences regarding the unshared concept that can be derived from all methods combined and highlight the specific axioms in the corresponding tables (Tables 2, 3 and 4).

Case Wimbledon A_1 attempts to convey *Wimbledon* to A_2.

1. Wimbledon $\sqsubseteq$ BallAndRacquetGames
2. Wimbledon $\sqcap$ SoftwareAgents$\sqsubseteq \perp$
3. Wimbledon $\sqcap$ ScienceNews $\sqsubseteq \perp$
4. Wimbledon $\sqcap$ RegionalNews $\sqsubseteq \perp$
5. Wimbledon $\sqcap$ EuropeNews $\sqsubseteq \perp$
6. Wimbledon $\sqsubseteq$ Sport
7. Wimbledon $\sqsubseteq$ RacquetGames
8. Wimbledon $\sqsubseteq$ Tennis
9. Wimbledon $\sqsubseteq$ LawnTennis

Table 2. Case *Wimbledon*: axioms and inferences of definitions and descriptions as computed w.r.t O_1 and O_2. ANEMONE-D stands for 'ANEMONE-definition'. The row labelled 'axioms' displays the axioms that are in the definition or description from O_1 w.r.t Σ the common vocabulary for the corresponding description or definition method in each column. The row labelled 'inferences' displays the inferences that are derived from the O_2 w.r.t the description or definition of the corresponding axioms in each column.

	ANEMONE-D	CD	MCD	DL-definition
Axioms	1, 2, 3, 4, 9	1, 2, 3, 4, 9	9	–
Inferences	5,6,7,8	5,6,7,8	1,2,3,4,5,6,7,8	–

Case Racquet Games A_1 attempts to convey *RacquetGames* to A_2.

1. RacquetGames $\sqsubseteq$ BallAndRacquetGames
2. RacquetGames $\sqcap$ UKNews $\sqsubseteq \perp$
3. RacquetGames $\sqcap$ ComputerScience $\sqsubseteq \perp$
4. RacquetGames $\sqcap$ ScienceNews $\sqsubseteq \perp$
5. RacquetGames $\sqcap$ SoftwareAgents $\sqsubseteq \perp$
6. RacquetGames $\sqcap$ RegionalNews $\sqsubseteq \perp$
7. LawnTennis $\sqsubseteq$ RacquetGames

Table 3. Case *RacquetGames*

	ANEMONE-D	CD	MCD	DL-definition
Axioms	1, 4, 5, 6, 7	1, 4, 5, 6, 7	1, 7	–
Inferences	2, 3	2, 3	2, 3, 4, 5, 6	–

Case UKNews A_1 attempts to convey *UKNews* to A_2.

1. UKNews $\sqsubseteq$ RegionalNews
2. UKNews $\sqcap$ Sport $\sqsubseteq \bot$
3. UKNews $\sqcap$ Tennis $\sqsubseteq \bot$
4. UKNews $\sqcap$ RacquetGames $\sqsubseteq \bot$
5. UKNews $\sqcap$ ScienceNews $\sqsubseteq \bot$

6. UKNews $\sqcap$ SoftwareAgents $\sqsubseteq \bot$
7. UKNews $\sqcap$ BallAndRacquetGames $\sqsubseteq \bot$
8. UKNews $\sqcap$ LawnTennis $\sqsubseteq \bot$

Table 4. Case *UKNews*

	ANEMONE-D	CD	MCD	DL-definition
Axioms	1, 5, 6, 7, 8	1, 5, 6, 7, 8	1	–
Inferences	2, 3, 4	2, 3, 4	2, 3, 4, 5, 6, 7, 8	–

Size evaluation: In all cases, we can see that the minimal concept description is also the smallest in terms of size, which supports $\mathcal{H}_3$ and all inferences follow from the axioms extracted by all methods, thus supporting $\mathcal{H}_2$. We also observe that DL-definitions do not exist in those cases, further highlighting the importance of concept descriptions.

Descent evaluation: None of the cases involve a defined concept, thus the descent evaluation here is focused on switching from the concept definition protocol to the concept explication protocol which is guided by the adequacy of the extracted definition or description. Observe that in the cases for *Wimbledon* and *RacquetGames* all definitions and descriptions are adequate in the sense that the hearer agent can relate the unshared concept to all terms in its ontology. However, in the case of *UKNews*, none of the extracted definitions or descriptions are adequate. *Tennis* is the only unshared defined concept in O_1 and O_2, futhermore, its case is trivial and does not let us test $\mathcal{H}_4$ as a result, we have extended the ontologies with axioms in Table 5.

Table 5. Extensions to the ontologies in Table 1. The first column contains the axioms added to O_1 for agent A_1, and the second column contains the axioms added to O_2 for agent A_2

Extensions to O_1	Extensions to O_2
Tournament $\equiv$ KnockoutTournament $\sqcup$ LeagueTournament, Wimbledon $\sqsubseteq$ KnockoutTournament, KnockoutTournament $\sqsubseteq$ EliminationCompetition, LeagueTournament $\sqsubseteq$ GroupCompetition, EliminationCompetition $\sqsubseteq \neg$ GroupCompetition	USOpen $\sqsubseteq$ Tournament, PremierLeague $\sqsubseteq$ GroupCompetition

Now $\Sigma = sig(O_1) \cap sig(O_2) = \{LawnTennis, RegionalNews, Software-Agents, ScienceNews, BallAndRacquetGames, KnockoutTournament, GroupCompetition\}$. O_1 now has the disjunctive axiom Tournament $\equiv$ KnockoutTournament $\sqcup$ LeagueTournament thus making it an $\mathcal{ALC}$ ontology. The defined concepts in O_1 are now $\{Tournament, KnockoutTournament, LeagueTournament\}$. $KnockoutTournament$ and $LeagueTournament$ are the only defined unshared concepts and we evaluate the definition and description methods on both concepts (Tables 6 and 7).

Case League Tournament A_1 attempts to convey *LeagueTournament* to A_2.

1. LeagueTournament $\equiv$ Tournament $\sqcap$ GroupCompetition

2. LeagueTournament $\sqsubseteq$ Tournament $\sqcap$ GroupCompetition

3. Tournament $\sqcap$ GroupCompetition $\sqsubseteq$ LeagueTournament

4. LeagueTournament $\sqsubseteq$ GroupCompetition

5. LeagueTournament $\sqsubseteq$ Tournament

Table 6. Case *LeagueTournament*

	ANEMONE-D	CD	MCD	DL-defintion
Axioms	4, 5	2, 3	2, 3	1
Inferences	2	1, 4, 5	1, 4, 5	2, 3, 4, 5

Case KnockoutTournament Possible Inferences of *KnockoutTournament* w.r.t O_2

1. KnockoutTournament $\equiv$ Tournament $\sqcap$ ¬GroupCompetition

2. Tournament $\sqcap$ ¬GroupCompetition $\sqsubseteq$ KnockoutTournament

3. KnockoutTournament $\sqsubseteq$ Tournament $\sqcap$ ¬GroupCompetition

4. KnockoutTournament $\sqsubseteq$ Tournament

5. KnockoutTournament $\sqsubseteq$ ¬GroupCompetition

Table 7. Case *KnockoutTournament*

	ANEMONE-D	CD	MCD	DL-defintion
Axioms	4, 5	2, 3	2, 3	1
Inferences	3	1, 4, 5	1, 4, 5	2, 3, 4, 5

In both cases, observe that without Algorithm 1, equivalent concepts (DL-definitions) for *KnockoutTournament* and *LeagueTournament* can not be extracted and thus conversation will switch to the concept description protocol, which supports $\mathcal{H}_4$. Futhermore observe that $\mathcal{H}_1$ is further supported as the DL-definition (extracted using Algorithm 1) has only one axiom. These cases also highlight a weakness of ANEMONE-definitions: the information conveyed by the ANEMONE-definition is incomplete, however, the information captured by concept descriptions and minimal concept descriptions is complete.

6.2   Experimental Evaluation

Agents may convey concepts using ANEMONE definitions or MCDs, and what is conveyed depends on whether the concept is definable or not. Our evaluation assumes the perspective of an agent attempting to convey a concept that is not included in the common signature using only terms in the common signature. A clear limitation of this evaluation thus follows: the interpretation of the conveyed concept is not evaluated, this is due to a lack of data but will be addressed in future work. The experiments were performed on the Cancer Care Treatment Outcome Ontology [14] (CCTOO). CCTOO is an $\mathcal{ALC}$ ontology consisting of 4,494 axioms, 1,133 concept-names, and six roles. We compare the ability of ANEMONE-definitions and MCDs methods in their ability to convey concepts, however, using the frameworks as is would conflate and confound several measures of evaluation. To simplify things, we use the following measures: (1) Ability to extract a definition for a concept. (2) Ability to extract a superconcept or a subconcept for a concept. Measure (1) applies to the case where the concept to be conveyed is defined, measure (2) applies to the case where the concept to be conveyed is not defined. Using these measures, we evaluate the ANEMONE-definitions and MCDs over varying common signature sizes ranging from 10% to 70% of the ontology's signature (using an interval of 10%), these signature sizes determine the portion of the ontology's signature that are randomly selected to serve as the common signature. For example, if the ontology's signature had a size of 70, for the 50% sample, thirty-five symbols are randomly chosen to serve as the common signature. We repeated this process three times, resulting in three samples for each subset signature.

Intuitively speaking, the ANEMONE-definition specification requires testing whether a concept is equivalent, disjoint, a subsumer of, or subsumed by concept-names in the common signature of the agents. We implemented this specification using the Hermit reasoner [8] which we henceforth refer to as *ANEMONE-prototype*. We also implemented the DL-definition extraction algorithm (Algorithm 1) using LETHE [11] and extended it to implement Algorithm 1 and 3. All experiments were run on a mac-mini (late 2014) with operating system MacOS Catalina, Dual-Core Intel Core i5 2.6 GHz processor, and eight gigabytes of RAM (1600 MHz DDR3).

Evaluation of Ability to Extract Definitions. For each sample signature we iterated over each concept-name that was not in the sample signature which we call the *unshared concept*. For every concept-name not within the common signature, we determine if it is defined (in the DL sense) using the implicit definability test discussed in Sect. 3 (implemented using Hermit and the OWL-api [9]), if it is, we evaluate ANEMONE-definition ability to extract a DL-definition. Definition extraction is deemed successful if the signature is a subset of the sample signature and if and the ontology entails that the unshared concept is equivalent to the definition. For the ANEMONE-prototype, we iterate over the concept names in the sample signature and use Hermit to check if it is equivalent to the unshared concept. We use Algorithm 3 to extract an MCD, if either the strongest necessary condition or weakest sufficient condition is equivalent to the unshared concept, and either of the conditions is a subset of the sample signature, we deem the MCD successful in extracting a DL-definition. Given the outcome of the case-study and the fact that SNCs and WSCs are not restricted to atomic concepts and can extract more expressive concepts, we expect MCDs to be more successful on average than the ANEMONE-definition. The results are in Table 8. These show that Algorithm 1 failed in some cases, this may be due to the signature of the extracted definition not being a subset of the sample signature. This hints at the unshared concept being cyclic as defined in Sect. 1.1; LETHE introduces *definer symbols*[5] to represent cyclic concept-names that need to be eliminated. An interesting observation from Table 8 is that minimal concept descriptions are more succesful than strongest necessary conditions in extracting DL-definitions, this is probably due to the weakest sufficient condition satisfying the requirements as opposed to the strongest necessary condition. Observe that for all samples, minimal concept descriptions and strongest necessary conditions extract more definitions than the ANEMONE prototype, which matches our expectations and supports hypothesis $\mathcal{H}_2$ from Sect. 6.1.

Evaluation of Ability to Extract Superconcepts and Subconcepts. Similar to the previous evaluation we only focus on sharing concept-names not in the common signature, the main difference being we restrict this evaluation to concept without any DL-definitions (determined using the implicit definability test). For such concepts we only extract an ANEMONE-definition and a minimal concept description. The extraction is deemed successful if it extracts a description or ANEMONE-definition that is non trivial (i.e., not $\top$ or $\bot$) and whose signature is a subset of the sample signature. The results are in Table 9 and we observe that in overall, the minimal concept description is more successful than the ANEMONE-prototype, but not by a large magnitude (for cases outside the 10% signature).

6.3 Discussion of ANEMONE Framework

Reliance on Assertional Knowledge. Given agent A_1 requesting for instances of B, a shared concept-name, from agent A_2, all that is expected is that A_2 returns instances of B w.r.t O_2. This is problematic because O_1 may interpret B differently than O_2 w.r.t. the TBox, it is not difficult to imagine a case where B is interpreted differently. This implies that the queries results returned

---

[5] Symbols not in the signature of the ontology.

Table 8. Successful definitions and descriptions extracted for signature samples of CCTOO. Each column (apart from the first) displays the percentage of the CCTOO signature that forms the simulated common vocabulary. The 'ANEMONE' row displays the definitions successfully extracted using the ANEMONE-prototype. The 'MCD' row displays the definitions successfully extracted using Algorithm 3. The 'SNC' row displays the definitions successfully extracted using Algorithm 1.

	10 %	20 %	30 %	40 %	50 %	60 %	70 %
Sample 1							
Defined concepts	0	1	4	8	6	4	5
ANEMONE	0	0	1	1	2	1	0
Algorithm 3(MCD)	0	0	1	2	4	2	2
Algorithm 1(SNC)	0	0	0	2	0	2	2
Sample 2							
Defined concepts	0	0	3	6	2	2	2
ANEMONE	0	0	2	2	0	1	0
Algorithm 3(MCD)	0	0	3	6	2	2	2
Algorithm 1(SNC)	0	0	3	0	2	0	2
Sample 3							
Defined concepts	0	0	1	2	1	2	3
ANEMONE	0	0	1	0	0	1	1
Algorithm 3(MCD)	0	0	1	2	1	2	3
Algorithm 1(SNC)	0	0	0	2	1	2	3

Table 9. Successful definitions and descriptions extracted for signature samples of CCTOO. Each column (apart from the first) displays the percentage of the CCTOO signature that forms the simulated common vocabulary. The 'ANEMONE' row displays the concept-descriptions successfully extracted using the ANEMONE-prototype. The 'MCD' row displays the concept-descriptions successfully extracted using Algorithm 3.

	10 %	20 %	30 %	40 %	50 %	60 %	70 %
Sample 1							
Undefined concepts	1133	1132	1129	1125	1127	1129	1128
ANEMONE	106	891	760	678	541	455	342
Algorithm 3(MCD)	987	896	768	678	546	449	342
Sample 2							
Undefined concepts	1133	1133	1130	1127	1131	1131	1131
ANEMONE	1020	891	790	573	554	443	342
Algorithm 3(MCD)	1020	900	790	668	564	445	342
Sample 3							
Undefined concepts	1133	1133	1132	1131	1132	1131	1130
ANEMONE	102	797	760	671	565	456	341
Algorithm 3(MCD)	997	893	772	677	565	456	341

by the agents can be potentially irrelevant and faulty making some interactions of the agents ineffective and useless. Let O_2 be $\{A \sqsubseteq B, A(a), B(c), B(d)\}$ and O_1 be $\{B \sqsubseteq \neg D, D(a)\}$, then A_2 would return a as an instance of B to A_1, and this information clearly contradicts A_1's knowledge. In the current framework, this condraction can not be handled and is not discussed. Observe that this can be mitigated by imposing a constraint stating that all shared concepts must be query inseparable [4] over all common instances, or at the very least that one of the agents ontology should be a conservative extension [15] of the other over the common signature.

Adequacy for ANEMONE-Definitions. ANEMONE specifies a description as adequate if every symbol in the hearers ontology has a relation to the description. This is not practical in DL ontologies as not all concepts in DL have relations to one another. Furthermore, given that the speaker agent will utilise the information returned to the hearer agent, the speaker agent has to also evaluate the adequacy of a description it generates for an unshared concept. Adequacy should be measured relative to the communication objective which is to exchange assertional knowledge, however, stating the relation of an unknown concept to other concepts has little to no effect on the assertional knowledge that may be associated with the unknown concept. Consider agent A_1 with ontology $\{A \sqsubseteq D, F \sqsubseteq \neg A, F(a), A(d)\}$ and agent A_2 with ontology $\{E \sqsubseteq B, B \sqsubseteq F, F(b), E(c)\}$. Consider the description $\{F \sqsubseteq \neg A\}$ which relates A to every concept in A_2's ontology, this description although deemed *adequate* gives A_2 no information on how find assertions of A in its ontology thus making it irrelevant for communication.

7 Conclusion

We have demonstrated methods for extracting DL-definitions and concept descriptions in the context of the ANEMONE framework. Our results suggest that the definition extraction methods presented can potentially reduce the amount of descent into lower communication protocols, thus reducing the amount of messages exchanged between agents. We have also proposed concept descriptions and minimal concept descriptions as alternatives to describe concepts that are not defined. Experiment results suggest that minimal concept descriptions are more portable than ANEMONE-definitions but yet just as effective for communication. Computing concept descriptions relies on computing compiled superconcepts and compiled subconcepts as discussed in Sect. 4. Future work will focus on developing ways of using uniform interpolation to compute compiled superconcepts and compiled subconcepts.

References

1. Afsharchi, M., Didandeh, A., Mirbakhsh, N., Far, B.H.: Common understanding in a multi-agent system using ontology-guided learning. Knowl. Inf. Syst. **36**(1), 83–120 (2013). https://doi.org/10.1007/s10115-012-0524-7

2. Antoniou, G., van Harmelen, F.: Web ontology language: OWL. In: Staab, S., Studer, R. (eds.) Handbook on Ontologies. International Handbooks on Information Systems. Springer, Berlin, Heidelberg (2004). https://doi.org/10.1007/978-3-540-24750-0_4

3. Baader, F., Calvanese, D., McGuinness, D., Patel-Schneider, P., Nardi, D.: The Description Logic Handbook: Theory, Implementation and Applications. Cambridge University Press, Cambridge (2003)

4. Botoeva, E., Lutz, C., Ryzhikov, V., Wolter, F., Zakharyaschev, M.: Query inseparability for $\mathcal{ALC}$ ontologies. Artif. Intell. **272**, 1–51 (2019)

5. van Diggelen, J., Beun, R.J., Dignum, F., van Eijk, R.M., Meyer, J.J.: Optimal communication vocabularies and heterogeneous ontologies. In: van Eijk, R.M., Huget, M.P., Dignum, F. (eds.) Agent Communication, pp. 76–90. Springer, Berlin, Heidelberg (2005). https://doi.org/10.1007/978-3-540-32258-0_6

6. Doherty, P., Lukaszewicz, W., Szalas, A.: Computing strongest necessary and weakest sufficient conditions of first-order formulas. In: Proceedings of the IJCAI, pp. 145–154 (2001)

7. Euzenat, J., Shvaiko, P., et al.: Ontology Matching, vol. 18. Springer, Cham (2007). https://doi.org/10.1007/978-3-642-38721-0

8. Glimm, B., Horrocks, I., Motik, B., Stoilos, G., Wang, Z.: HermiT: an OWL 2 reasoner. J. Autom. Reason. **53**(3), 245–269 (2014). https://doi.org/10.1007/s10817-014-9305-1

9. Horridge, M., Bechhofer, S.: The OWL API: a Java API for OWL ontologies. Semant. Web **2**(1), 11–21 (2011)

10. Koopmann, P., Schmidt, R.A.: LETHE: a saturation-based tool for non-classical reasoning. In: Dumontier, M., et al. (eds.) Proceedings of ORE-2015. CEUR Workshop Proceedings, vol. 1387. CEUR-WS.org (2015)

11. Koopmann, P., Schmidt, R.A.: Uniform interpolation and forgetting for $\mathcal{ALC}$ ontologies with aboxes. In: Bonet, B., Koenig, S. (eds.) Proceedings of AAAI-2015, pp. 175–181. AAAI Press (2015)

12. Laera, L., Blacoe, I., Tamma, V., Payne, T., Euzenat, J., Bench-Capon, T.: Argumentation over ontology correspondences in mas. In: AAMAS, pp. 1–8 (2007)

13. Lin, F.: On strongest necessary and weakest sufficient conditions. Artif. Intell. **128**(1–2), 143–159 (2001)

14. Lin, F.P.Y., Groza, T., Kocbek, S., Antezana, E., Epstein, R.J.: The cancer care treatment outcomes ontology (CCTO): a computable ontology for profiling treatment outcomes of patients with solid tumors (2017)

15. Lutz, C., Walther, D., Wolter, F.: Conservative extensions in expressive description logics. In: IJCAI, pp. 453–458 (2007)

16. Mascardi, V., Ancona, D., Bordini, R.H., Ricci, A.: CooL-AgentSpeak: enhancing AgentSpeak-DL agents with plan exchange and ontology services. In: 2011 IEEE/WIC/ACM International Conferences on Web Intelligence and Intelligent Agent Technology, vol. 2, pp. 109–116. IEEE (2011)

17. Payne, T.R., Tamma, V.: Negotiating over ontological correspondences with asymmetric and incomplete knowledge. In: AAMAS, pp. 517–524 (2014)

18. Souza, M., Moreira, A., Vieira, R., Meyer, J.-J.C.: Integrating ontology negotiation and agent communication. In: Tamma, V., Dragoni, M., Gonçalves, R., Ławrynowicz, A. (eds.) OWLED 2015. LNCS, vol. 9557, pp. 56–68. Springer, Cham (2016). https://doi.org/10.1007/978-3-319-33245-1_6

19. Ten Cate, B., Franconi, E., Seylan, I.: Beth definability in expressive description logics. JAIR **48**, 347–414 (2013)

20. Van Diggelen, J., Beun, R.J., Dignum, F., Van Eijk, R.M., Meyer, J.J.: Ontology negotiation: goals, requirements and implementation. IJAOSE **1**(1), 63–90 (2007)
21. Van Diggelen, J., Beun, R.J., Dignum, F., Van Eijk, R.M., Meyer, J.J.: ANEMONE: an effective minimal ontology negotiation environment. In: AAMAS, pp. 899–906. ACM (2006)
22. Whetzel, P.L., et al.: Bioportal: enhanced functionality via new web services from the national center for biomedical ontology to access and use ontologies in software applications. Nucleic Acids Res. **39**(suppl-22), W541–W545 (2011)

GenGPT: A Systematic Way to Generate Synthetic Goal-Plan Trees

Yuan Yao[1,2]([envelope])[iD] and Di Wu[1]([envelope])[iD]

[1] College of Computer Science and Technology, Zhejiang University of Technology,
Hangzhou, China
{yaoyuan,2112012103}@zjut.edu.cn
[2] Department of Computer Science, University of Nottingham Ningbo China,
Ningbo, China

Abstract. Deciding "what to do next" is a key problem for BDI agents with multiple goals, which is termed the intention progression problem (IPP). A number of approaches to solving the IPP have been proposed in the literature, however, their evaluations are all taken in different forms. The lack of standard benchmarks and testbeds for evaluating the IPP makes it difficult for researchers to contribute to this topic. To foster research around the IPP and BDI agents, this paper proposes a way to generate test cases in the form of goal-plan trees which can be used to represent the agent's intentions in various agent languages and platforms.

Keywords: BDI Agents · Intention progression problem · Goal-plan tree generator

1 Introduction

The Belief-Desire-Intention (BDI)[5] agents select plans to achieve the goals based on their mental states (beliefs, goals and intentions) is one of the most popular approaches to developing intelligent systems. Beliefs are the agent's information about the environment and itself, goals are the state of affairs the agent is aiming to bring about, and the lists of execution steps the agent has committed to achieving its goals form its intentions. BDI model is popular for building inteligent agent in complex environment where the agents are usually required to pursue multiple goals in parallel. A key problem for BDI agents is to decide "what to do next". That is, at each deliberation cycle a BDI agent needs to decide which of its intentions should be executed, and if the next step of the selected intention is a goal, which plan should be used to achieve it. This problem is termed the *intention progression problem* (IPP) [4].

The problem of intention progression is critical for BDI agents, as poor choices can give rise to conflicts which may result in a failure to achieve the goals.

Supported by Zhejiang Provincial Natural Science Foundation of China (LQ19F030009) and National Natural Science Foundation of China (61906169).

N. Alechina et al. (Eds.): EMAS 2021, LNAI 13190, pp. 373–380, 2022.
https://doi.org/10.1007/978-3-030-97457-2_21

A number of approaches to solving the IPP have been proposed in the literature [6–10,12–16], all of which have shown that they outperform the basic Round-Robin (RR) and First-In-First-Out (FIFO) strategies. However, the evaluations of these techniques are all taken in different forms and none of the programs to generate the test cases is available online.[1] The lack of the standard benchmark and testbed for evaluating IPP makes it difficult for researchers to contribute to this topic, especially it is very difficult for researchers to fairly evaluate their own approaches. To foster research around the IPP and BDI agents, this paper proposes a way to randomly generate synthetic goal-plan trees (GPTs) of different shapes and difficulties. These GPTs can be used to represent the agent's intentions in different languages and platforms and hence to provide general test cases for evaluating IPP approaches.

2   Synthetic Goal-Plan Trees

In the BDI model, each agent has a library of pre-defined plans to achieve its goals. Each plan consists of a sequence of execution steps which are either primitive actions that can directly change the state of the environment or subgoals that are in turn achieved by subplans. This relationship naturally forms a tree structure termed a goal-plan tree (GPT) [6–8,17]. The root of a GPT is a top-level goal, and its children are the plans to achieve it. As the agent only need to select one plan to achieve its goal, the plan-nodes are viewed as "OR" nodes. The children of the plans are a sequence of actions and subgoals, all of which must be performed if the plan is selected for execution. Hence, these nodes are viewed as "AND" nodes. Subgoals are in turn have the subplans to achieve them as their child nodes, giving rise to a tree structure representing all the ways an agent can achieve its top-level goals.

We represent an agent's intentions as a tuple $I = (T, S)$, where $T = \{t_1, \ldots, t_n\}$ are GPTs for each top-level goal g_i, and $S = \{s_1, \ldots, s_n\}$ are a set of current step pointers for each GPT. All the successor steps of s_i together form the agent's intention to achieve g_i. Representing intentions using the GPT structure has the advantage that it is totally language-independent. Intentions in most of the popular agent languages and platforms like Jason [1] and JACK [11] can be easily translated into GPTs. Hence, developers no longer need to worry about which agent language and platform they should use to test their approaches. Moreover, the GPT structure has already been widely used in solving IPP in the literature and in the Intention Progression Competition [4].

We therefore focus on the problem: "How we generate GPTs to evaluate approaches to the IPP?". Real-world examples like the elevator domain [3] can be a well-suited case study for IPP approaches, but it may suffer from the limitations of the problem itself, i.e., some approaches may work well for specific problem domains but fail to apply to the others. Thus, in the interests of generality, we propose to use randomly-generated GPTs as the basis for evaluating the IPP approaches. To generate random GPTs we need to decide not only the

---

[1] There is a very brief discussion on generating synthetic goal-plan trees in [2].

shape of the tree but also a set of conditions in the GPTs including the pre- and postcondition of each action, the precondition of each plan and the goal-condition of each goal. The action's pre and postconditions are respectively a set of literals that must be true for the action to begin execution and another set of literals that are made true by executing the action. The plans' precondition (or context condition) specifies the situation when the plan is applicable, and the goal-condition specifies a set of literals that need to be satisfied to achieve the goal. These conditions decide the executability of each plan, hence define the rationality and correctness of each GPT. Ideally, the random GPTs should satisfy the following properties:

1. Each plan is well-formed. That is, if the precondition of a plan is satisfied then it must be executed successfully in some environment.[2] Otherwise, the plan itself is faulty.
2. Taken individually, there is at least one way to achieve the top-level goal of each GPT in some environment.
3. The shape of GPTs can be precisely controlled and are not always balanced, i.e., plans to achieve the same goal may require a different number of steps.

3   GenGPT

Here, we present GenGPT, a package to generate synthetic GPTs. GenGPT can be used in a standalone fashion using the bundled Java application to generate sets of GPTs (in XML format) as input to another program. Alternatively, the source code provided can be integrated directly into another program. In the following, we briefly describe how GenGPT works and shows it can solve all the challenges mentioned in Sect. 2.[3]

First of all, the shape and properties of the randomly-generated GPTs are controlled by a set of input parameters. These parameters are: the random seed s, the maximum depth of the tree d, the number of subgoals in each plan g, the number of plans to achieve each goal p, the number of actions in each plan a, the probability that a plan being a leaf plan l, the total number of environment variables v, the number of variables selected for each intention e, the number of trees we are going to generate t, and finally the output file path f.[4] The parameters d, g, p, a and l decide the shape of the trees, i.e., how many goals and actions in each plan and how many plans to achieve a goal. We assume the achievement of a single top-level goal can only affect a subset of the variables in the environment.[5] Thus, the parameters v and e together can be seen as the likelihood of conflicts between intentions.

---

[2] Here, we ignore the changes caused by the execution of other intentions.
[3] The source code and a detailed instruction manual can be found at the following url: "https://github.com/yvy714/GenGPT.git".
[4] We omit all these static parameters in the input of the algorithm for legibility.
[5] This assumption is reasonable, as there is very few real world plans will affect all the environment variables.

Before start generating GPTs, a set of v variables Vs representing the current state of the environment are generated with random initial values, i.e. true or false. For each GPT, e variables are randomly selected from Vs, which forms a set Es, and we use Rs to represent the set of all remaining variables such that $Vs = Es \cup Rs$. That is, the execution of each GPT can only affect the values of the variables in its corresponding set of Es. For legibility, we omit the appearance of Es and Rs in the input of all the algorithms below, as they will be used all the time during the generation of GPT. The generation process starts from the root node all the way down to the leaf action nodes. We use two algorithms to generate goal nodes and plan nodes in each GPT.

Algorithm 1. Generate a goal with specified goal-conditions

1: **procedure** $GenGoal(dp, Pc, Gc)$
2:    $n \leftarrow$ *a goal node with goal-condition Gc*
3:    **for** $i \leftarrow 1, p$ **do**
4:        $Prec \leftarrow Pc \cup \{a\ variable\ randomly\ selected\ from\ Rs\}$
5:        $pl \leftarrow \mathtt{GenPlan}(dp, Prec, Gc)$
6:        $n.\mathtt{Add}(pl)$
      return n

Algorithm 1 is used to generate a single goal node in the GPT which requires three parameters as its input: the depth of the goal in the GPT, dp, the set of conditions that are required by all plans to achieve the goal, Pc, and the goal-condition Gc. The algorithm first generates a goal node n with the given goal-condition Gc (line 2), and then generates p plan nodes to achieve this goal and adds them as the children of node n (lines 3–6). Finally, the goal node n is returned as the output of this algorithm. For each plan to achieve the goal-node n, their preconditions $Prec$ consist of two parts (line 4). The first part Pc represents the preconditions that are common to all the plans, which are usually set up by previous steps of this plan. While the second part is a variable randomly selected from Rs, which could be seen as purely environmental conditions representing different applicable situations for the plans. For example, the plans for an agent to move from the office room to the library all require that the agent is currently in the office room (which is the Pc part). Depending on the weather condition and the amount of money the agent has, the agent could choose to walk to the library or take a taxi to the library.

The plan nodes are generated by Algorithm 2 which also requires three parameters as its input: the depth of the plan in the tree, dp, the precondition of the plan, Pc, and the goal condition this plan is going to achieve Gc. In Algorithm 2, we first decide if the plan we are going to generate is a leaf plan (i.e., plans that only contain actions). A plan is a leaf plan if it reaches the maximum depth of the tree or a randomly generated number is less than the threshold l (line 2).[6] The algorithm then randomly generates a list of execution steps (line 3). If the plan is a leaf plan, then a list of a actions is generated,

---
[6] l is one of the input parameters.

Algorithm 2. Generate plans to achieve a goal

1: **procedure** $GenPlan(dp, Pc, Gc)$
2:     $isLeaf \leftarrow dp == d \parallel random() < l$
3:     $pb \leftarrow \textbf{GenPB}(isLeaf)$
4:     $Cs \leftarrow Pc$
5:     **for each** $step$ **in** pb **do**
6:         $prec \leftarrow random(Cs)$
7:         $post \leftarrow \neg random(Es)$
8:         **if** $step$ is the first step in pb **then**
9:             $prec \leftarrow Pc$
10:        **else if** $step$ is the last step in pb **then**
11:            $post \leftarrow Gc$
12:        $Es \leftarrow Es \cup \{post\} \setminus \{\neg post\}$
13:        $Cs \leftarrow Cc \cup \{post\} \setminus \{\neg post\}$
14:        **if** $step$ is an $Action$ **then**
15:            $step \leftarrow$ an action with precondition $prec$ and postcondition $post$
16:        **else**
17:            $step \leftarrow \textbf{genGoal}(depth + 1, prec, post)$
        return a plan node with precondition Pc and plan body pb

---

otherwise, the plan body will contain a actions and g subgoals. We assume the first and the last steps in a plan are actions, the former has the plan's precondition Pc as its own precondition and the later has the goal-condition Gc as its postcondition (lines 8–11). This ensures that if the precondition of a plan is satisfied, then the first step in the plan must be executable, and if the last step of the plan has been executed successfully, then the goal must be achieved. The postcondition of each step in the plan (apart from the last step) is randomly selected from the set Es, and the value of the postcondition is the negation of the selected variable (line 7), e.g., if the selected variable is currently true, then the postcondition of this step is to make it false. We then use the postcondition of this step to update the set Es and a set Cs which stores candidate preconditions for each step (lines 12–13). The precondition of each step in a plan is a variable randomly selected from the set Cs. Cs is initially the precondition of the plan (line 4) and is updated as the postcondition of each step is generated. This ensures the precondition of each step is either the precondition of the plan, or it is a condition established by one of its preceding steps that has not been undone by any intermedia steps. We then check each step in the plan body. If it is an action, then an action node with corresponding pre- and post-conditions will be generated (lines 14–15). Otherwise, a subgoal will be generated by calling Algorithm 1 (line 17). Finally, a plan node with preconditions Pc and a plan body pb is returned.

The application of GenGPT could be easily invoked from the command-line and generate an output XML using the following command:

```
java -jar GenGPT.jar <args>
```

Once the generation starts, Algorithm 1 is called to generate the top-level goal of each GPT. To generate a top-level goal, the value of dp is set to 1, the Pc is set to an empty set, and Gc is a unique goal-conditions that cannot be established by any other GPTs. Algorithm 1 then generates preconditions for the plans to achieve the top-level goal and calls Algorithm 2 to generate the plan nodes. After that, Algorithm 2 iteratively calls Algorithms 1 and itself to generate its subgoals and all the hierarchies below until all the leaf plans are generated. Finally, the GPT structure is translated into XML file by the Java package *jdom2*.

During the generation of the GPTs, the parameter d determines the maximum depth a plan can be placed, i.e., all plans at depth d are leaf plans. For all other plans, they have l chance to be a leaf plan at any depth which potentially make the GPT unbalanced. Parameters p, a and g determines the number of plans, actions and subgoals in each GPT.[7] As a result, GenGPT is able to precisely control the shape of GPT and the trees are not always balanced if l is set to nonzero. Thus, the third property mentioned in Sect. 2 is satisfied. Given a plan in the random GPT, if its precondition holds in the current environment, then we could easily know that the first step in this plan is also executable as its precondition is the same as the plan's precondition. In GenGPT, the precondition of the second step is either the postcondition of the first step in the plan or the precondition of the plan, so the second step in this plan is executable after the first action finishes its execution. By induction, we could conclude that any of the steps in a plan is executable if all its previous steps have been successful executed, which implies the plan is well-formed and thus the first property mentioned in Sect. 2 is satisfied. Moreover, as all the plans in the GPT are well-formed, we could know that the plans to achieve the top-level goal are also well-formed. In an environment where there is an applicable plan to achieve the top-level goal, it should be straightforward to know the corresponding GPT is executable, thus, the second property is also satisfied. Overall, GenGPT is able to generate GPTs to satisfy all three properties mentioned in Sect. 2 which makes it a potential tool to generate benchmarks to IPP.

4   Conclusion and Future Work

This paper presents a goal-plan tree generator, which is used to generate synthetic GPTs for evaluating approaches to IPP. We have shown the necessity of using GPT to represent intentions from the different agent programming language and the challenges in generating random GPTs. We also provided the basic idea of how GenGPT works and how the mentioned problems are solved. In future work, we plan to add parallel constructs and other types of goals.

Acknowledge. We would like to thank Brian Logan and John Thangarajah for many helpful discussions relating to the work presented here.

---

[7] In this paper, we choose to use fixed number of goals, plans and actions for simplicity. However, it is straight forward to change it to a more flexible version with minimal and maximum number of goals, plans and actions.

References

1. Bordini, R.H., Hübner, J.F., Wooldridge, M.: Programming Multi-agent Systems in AgentSpeak Using Jason. Wiley, Hoboken (2007)
2. Castle-Green, S., Dewfall, A., Logan, B.: The intention progression competition. In: Baroglio, C., Hubner, J.F., Winikoff, M. (eds.) EMAS 2020. LNCS (LNAI), vol. 12589, pp. 144–151. Springer, Cham (2020). https://doi.org/10.1007/978-3-030-66534-0_10
3. Koehler, J., Schuster, K.: Elevator control as a planning problem. In: Proceedings of the Fifth International Conference on Artificial Intelligence Planning Systems, Breckenridge, CO, USA, 14–17 April 2000, pp. 331–338. AAAI (2000)
4. Logan, B., Thangarajah, J., Yorke-Smith, N.: Progressing intention progression: a call for a goal-plan tree contest. In: 16th Conference on Autonomous Agents and MultiAgent Systems, pp. 768–772. IFAAMAS (2017)
5. Rao, A.S., Georgeff, M.P.: An abstract architecture for rational agents. In: 3rd International Conference on Principles of Knowledge Representation and Reasoning, pp. 439–449. Morgan Kaufmann (1992)
6. Thangarajah, J., Padgham, L.: Computationally effective reasoning about goal interactions. J. Autom. Reasoning **47**(1), 17–56 (2011). https://doi.org/10.1007/s10817-010-9175-0
7. Thangarajah, J., Padgham, L., Winikoff, M.: Detecting and avoiding interference between goals in intelligent agents. In: Proceedings of the Eighteenth International Joint Conference on Artificial Intelligence (IJCAI-2003), pp. 721–726. Morgan Kaufmann, Acapulco, August 2003
8. Thangarajah, J., Winikoff, M., Padgham, L., Fischer, K.: Avoiding resource conflicts in intelligent agents. In: Proceedings of the 15th Eureopean Conference on Artificial Intelligence, pp. 18–22. IOS Press, Lyon, July 2002
9. Waters, M., Padgham, L., Sardina, S.: Evaluating coverage based intention selection. In: Proceedings of the 13th International Conference on Autonomous Agents and Multi-agent Systems (AAMAS 2014), pp. 957–964. IFAAMAS (2014)
10. Waters, M., Padgham, L., Sardina, S.: Improving domain-independent intention selection in BDI systems. Auton. Agents Multi-Agent Syst. **29**(4), 683–717 (2015). https://doi.org/10.1007/s10458-015-9293-5
11. Winikoff, M.: Jack™ intelligent agents: an industrial strength platform. In: Bordini, R.H., Dastani, M., Dix, J., El Fallah Seghrouchni, A. (eds.) Multi-Agent Programming. MSASSO, vol. 15, pp. 175–193. Springer, Boston, MA (2005). https://doi.org/10.1007/0-387-26350-0_7
12. Yao, Y., Alechina, N., Logan, B., Thangarajah, J.: Intention progression under uncertainty. In: Proceedings of the Twenty-Ninth International Joint Conference on Artificial Intelligence, IJCAI 2020, pp. 10–16 (2020). https://ijcai.org/
13. Yao, Y., Logan, B.: Action-level intention selection for BDI agents. In: 15th International Conference on Autonomous Agents and Multiagent Systems, pp. 1227–1236. IFAAMAS (2016)
14. Yao, Y., Logan, B., Thangarajah, J.: SP-MCTS-based intention scheduling for BDI agents. In: Proceedings of the 21st European Conference on Artificial Intelligence, ECCAI. IOS Press, Prague, August 2014
15. Yao, Y., Logan, B., Thangarajah, J.: Intention selection with deadlines. In: ECAI 2016–22nd European Conference on Artificial Intelligence, vol. 285, pp. 1700–1701. IOS Press (2016)

16. Yao, Y., Logan, B., Thangarajah, J.: Robust execution of BDI agent programs by exploiting synergies between intentions. In: 30th AAAI Conference on Artificial Intelligence, pp. 2558–2565. AAAI Press (2016)
17. Yao, Y., de Silva, L., Logan, B.: Reasoning about the executability of goal-plan trees. In: Baldoni, M., Müller, J.P., Nunes, I., Zalila-Wenkstern, R. (eds.) EMAS 2016. LNCS (LNAI), vol. 10093, pp. 181–196. Springer, Cham (2016). https://doi.org/10.1007/978-3-319-50983-9_10

Author Index

Printed in the United States
by Baker & Taylor Publisher Services

Printed in the United States
by Baker & Taylor Publisher Services